HARLAXTON MEDIEVAL STUDIES

VOLUME TWO

ENGLAND IN THE ELEVENTH CENTURY

PAUL WATKINS

MEDIEVAL STUDIES
General Editor: Shaun Tyas
Consultant Editor: David Roffe

1. ANDERSON, Alan Orr, *Early Sources of Scottish History AD 500-1286*; a new edition with corrections, in 2 vols. (1990).

2. HARMER, Florence, *Anglo-Saxon Writs*; a new edition comprising the original work together with her later essay 'A Bromfield and Coventry Writ of King Edward the Confessor' (1989).

3. STENTON, Sir Frank Merry, *The Early History of the Abbey of Abingdon*; reprinted for the first time since 1913. (1989).

4. SPITTAL, Jeffrey and FIELD, John, *A Reader's Guide to the Place-names of the United Kingdom* (1990).

5. HILL, Sir Francis, *Medieval Lincoln*; reprinted with an introductory essay by Dorothy Owen (1990).

6. PARSONS, David (ed.), *Eleanor of Castile 1290-1990, Essays to Commemorate the 700th Anniversary of her death: 28 November 1290* (1991).

7. COATES, Richard, *The Ancient and Modern Names of the Channel Islands, a Linguistic History* (1991).

8. FOULDS, Trevor (ed.), *The Thurgarton Cartulary* (forthcoming).

9. ORMROD, W. M. (ed.), *England in the Thirteenth Century*, Harlaxton Medieval Studies I (1991).

10. ANDERSON, Alan Orr, *Scottish Annals from English Chroniclers, 500-1286 AD*; a new edition with corrections (1991).

11. LINDLEY, Phillip, *Gothic to Renaissance: Essays on Sculpture in England* (forthcoming).

12. HICKS, Carola (ed.), *England in the Eleventh Century*, Harlaxton Medieval Studies II (1992).

HARLAXTON MEDIEVAL STUDIES, II

ENGLAND
IN THE
ELEVENTH CENTURY

Proceedings of the 1990
Harlaxton Symposium

Edited by
Carola Hicks

PAUL WATKINS
STAMFORD
1992

Published in 1992 by
Paul Watkins
18, Adelaide Street,
Stamford,
Lincolnshire, PE9 2EN

ISBN
1 871615 50 X

Photoset from the discs and essays of the authors in Garamond
by Paul Watkins (Publishing)

Printed on long-life paper

Printed and bound by Woolnoughs of Irthlingborough

CONTENTS

THE ENGLISH LANGUAGE

LIST OF CONTRIBUTORS

David Bates	University of Wales, College of Cardiff
Cecily Clark	Cambridge
Jan Gerchow	Max-Planck-Institut für Geschichte, Göttingen
George Henderson	Downing College, Cambridge
Carola Hicks	Newnham College, Cambridge
Joyce Hill	University of Leeds
Peter Jackson	Emmanuel College, Cambridge
Henry Loyn	St Albans
Jane Martindale	University of East Anglia
Elisabeth Okasha	University College, Cork
Richard W. Pfaff	University of North Carolina
Cassandra Potts	Middlebury College, Vermont
Barbara Raw	University of Keele
Nicholas Rogers	Sidney Sussex College, Cambridge
David Rollason	University of Durham
D. G. Scragg	University of Manchester
Matthew Strickland	University of Glasgow
E. C. Teviotdale	Davidson College, North Carolina
Jonathan Wilcox	University of Iowa
Patrick Wormald	Christ Church, Oxford

LIST OF ILLUSTRATIONS

vii

FIGURES

PREFACE

The 1990 Harlaxton Symposium studied England in the eleventh century, the earliest period so far to receive the attention of the Symposium's inter-disciplinary approach to the Middle Ages. Although the papers published in these proceedings are grouped thematically for ease of immediate reference, the essence of the Symposium lies in its role as a forum for specialists in different disciplines not only to present their own research but also to become more aware of each other's work in areas perhaps less familiar.

Eleventh-century England encompasses a series of dramatic changes both in its connections with the Continent and in the processes of church and state. Yet one of the recurrent themes here is that of continuity, emphasised in topics such as the survival of Cnut's secular code, the pre-Conquest manifestations of Romanesque style, the strength of the vernacular up to and even after Domesday, and the charters which show the earlier links between England and Normandy as well as the survival of English practice following the Conquest. Propaganda is another theme, with art and orthography, monastic chronicles and even relic-lists being used to make political statements. We learn to read a picture by separating the underlying message of the selected image from the detailed analysis of sources and workshop practice. A different form of statistical analysis shows that it is necessary to read between the lines of Domesday Book.

These Proceedings are published as the second volume of the new Harlaxton Medieval Studies series, which it is intended will carry on the standards of excellence and variety set by the earlier series. All contributors, participants and readers must remain indebted to the organisers of this annual Symposium at Harlaxton Manor.

One sad note was the death of Cecily Clark as this book was nearing its first proof stage. Overleaf is a tribute to her life and work.

Carola Hicks
May 1992

CECILY CLARK

Cecily was a warm, generous and spontaneous person whose enthusiasm for life, and horses in particular, was known to all who are active in Anglo-Saxon and Anglo-Norman studies.

Her career can be divided more or less into two sections. She herself always asserted that her best work belonged to the second half. The first period resulted in her splendid edition of the Peterborough Chronicle, the version of the Anglo-Saxon Chronicle which continued after the Norman Conquest until 1154. Her philological skills and her historical interest in name studies is already noticeable here. However, not until the second half of her career (after a period of some self-doubt?) did she take off with what is generally regarded as an innovative, thought-provoking and original study, 'Women's names in post-Conquest England' (*Speculum* 53, 1978). This was followed by an impressive series of publications mostly concerned with the historical significance of the change and development of name-giving in England after 1066. Amongst the most notable are her studies of the lists of patronyms from Battle Abbey and Thorney Abbey. Central to her arguments were the role played by women in the tradition of name-giving, and the persistence with which the Anglo-Saxon language survived long after the Conquest. She was also an active editor of the journal *Nomina*.

It is hoped that all this work can be put together and published in one volume. There is no way in which we can honour the life of work of Cecily Clark more suitably.

Lisbeth van Houts
Newnham College
May 1992.

The Conqueror's Charters
DAVID BATES

> If we could dispose of his time, we would set him to edit the charters (and,
> by way of beginning, the royal charters) of the Norman time. This work
> ought to be done, and it ought to be done as a national enterprise, and no
> one, at least no Englishman, would do it better than Mr. Round.[1]

These words of F. W. Maitland embody a frequently expressed
late-nineteenth-century aspiration for an edition of the charters of the
Norman kings. The culmination, the first volume of the *Regesta Regum
Anglo-Normannorum*,[2] an incomplete calendar of the charters of William I,
William II and Robert Curthose, fell far short of the grand ideals which
Round had set out in 1892; he wanted 'a real cartulary – printing everything
in full'.[3] The *Regesta*'s Preface tells a sad story of collaborators who had fallen
by the wayside and of the necessary incompleteness of the volume.[4] It was
critically reviewed by Round in the *English Historical Review* and by Haskins
in the *American Historical Review*.[5] Round's ten-page review consisted mostly
of a catalogue of errors. Haskins, in a courteously restrained, and notably
short, review criticised the treatment of Norman documents and the poor
quality of the Introduction. He considered the work to be unsatisfactory in
comparison with contemporary continental scholarship and noted that
English scholars seemed only to be at ease with PRO calendars where the
material was already organised for them.

It is easy to belabour the first volume of the *Regesta*. There are mistakes
in the description of almost every document, the judgements concerning

[1] F. W. Maitland, review of J. H. Round, *Feudal England* (London, 1895) in *The
Athenaeum*, no. 3533 (13 July 1895), p. 62. This paper has benefitted from
discussions with the late Professor R. H. C. Davis, who was also a most generous
and consistent supporter of my project to edit the Conqueror's charters.
Extensive travelling in pursuit of manuscripts has been funded by several awards
from the British Academy.

[2] The outlines of the story have been told by E. King, 'John Horace Round and the
"Calendar of Documents preserved in France"', *Anglo-Norman Studies*, 4 (1981),
93-103.

[3] Round to Maitland, Cambridge, University Library, Add. MS 7006, no. 40; cited
by King, p. 93.

[4] 'It is to be feared that the work, to which so many scholars have contributed,
may disappoint their legitimate expectations', *Regesta Regum Anglo-
Normannorum, I, 1066-1100*, ed. H. W. C. Davis (Oxford, 1913), p. vii.

[5] J. H. Round, in *EHR*, 29 (1914), 347-56; C. H. Haskins, in *American Hist. Rev.*,
19 (1913-14), 594-96.

authenticity and diplomatic are poor, and there are numerous omissions. For Normandy and France, no archival research was undertaken and condemnatory judgements were made on entirely authentic Norman and French charters according to the Insular canons of English diplomatic scholarship; so little sensitivity was shown to the other side of the Channel that documents were said to reside in an institution known as the Bibliothèque Royale.[6] All this has been said before and it is futile to dwell on it. The one genuine regret we ought to have about volume 1 of the *Regesta* arises from a letter which Haskins wrote to G. B. Adams on 13 January 1914 referring to the fact that he 'felt hurt by his (i.e., H. W. C. Davis's) inclusion of Norman documents' and to 'the division of territory' which he and Davis had made several years before, an arrangement which Davis acknowledged in his Preface.[7] The prospect that Haskins might have edited the Norman charters of William the Conqueror and Robert Curthose is one to savour, but with the reservation that his chapter in *Norman Institutions* on Normandy under William the Conqueror does not demonstrate either a full or a profound acquaintance with the number or the diplomatic of William's Norman and French charters.[8]

It is doubtful whether those who aimed so high at the turn of the century actually grasped the scale of the task they were proposing. Davis worked during what Professor Edmund King has called 'a quarter-century in which British charter scholarship had stood still'.[9] For England, many documents had emerged via the Rolls Series and the endeavours of the Historical Manuscripts Commission, and there was even a PRO calendar of chancery enrolments of William I's charters.[10] But for Normandy and France, the spade-work was only starting to be done. It is, I would strongly suggest, only on the secure foundation of the great technical advances made during the twentieth century that anyone could set out with any confidence to edit the Conqueror's charters. In particular, we should note Pierre Chaplais's magisterial work on seals and original writs, and his dramatic demonstration that many of the documents which were once confidently dated to the Conqueror's time were in fact twelfth-century productions.[11] There is also

---

[6]   See, for example, *Regesta*, I, no. 142.

[7]   Yale University Library, G. B. Adams Papers 6/28. I owe this reference to the kindness of Professor Edmund King. For Davis' acknowledgement, *Regesta*, I, p. v.

[8]   C. H. Haskins, *Norman Institutions* (Cambridge (Mass.), 1918), pp. 3-61.

[9]   King, 'John Horace Round', p. 102.

[10] *Appendix to the Twenty-Ninth Report of the Deputy Keeper of the Public Records* (London, 1868), pp. 32-43.

[11] T. A. M. Bishop and P. Chaplais, *Facsimiles of English Royal Writs to A.D. 1100* (Oxford, 1957), pp. xiii-xxiv; P. Chaplais, 'Une charte originale de Guillaume le

Lucien Musset's superb study of the many-layered diplomatic structure of the *pancartes* from the two Caen abbeys, providing the means to free ourselves from the Anglocentric judgements on authenticity made by Davis,[12] together with Marie Fauroux's splendid edition of the pre-1066 acta of the Norman rulers.[13] To these we can add, *inter alia*, Florence Harmer's fundamental work on Anglo-Saxon writs and Simon Keynes' 'Regenbald', which has set the diplomas and writs of the Conqueror's first years in England into their Old English context; the excellent work on Norman *pancartes* of Jean-Michel Bouvris and Véronique Gazeau; and studies such as Eleanor Searle's on the Battle abbey forgeries.[14] *En passant*, it is worth noting how few among these scholars are British.

The final edition of the Conqueror's charters will contain at least 350,000 words. The mass of the Norman material in particular is daunting. There are numerous technical difficulties to face, which make William I's charters much more difficult to deal with than, say, Henry I's; there are forgeries, or at least likely forgeries, around every corner; it is also necessary to deal with the continuation of distinct English, Norman, Manceau and Angevin diplomatic traditions, so the editor needs to feel some confidence in his footing on both sides of the Channel.

The first benefit from an edition of the Conqueror's charters will be to have new facts. There are sixty or so documents not in the William I section of the *Regesta*, and there are many texts for which the calendaring was so inadequate that we can have no serious idea of what is in them. The discovery of a *pancarte* from the abbey of Grestain provides us with notable material on the early history of a Norman abbey, our only eleventh-century

---

Conquérant pour l'abbaye de Fécamp: la donation de Steyning et de Bury' and 'The Original Charters of Herbert and Gervase, Abbots of Westminster (1121-1157)' in *Essays in Medieval Diplomacy and Administration* (London, 1981), chapters XVI and XVIII.

[12] L. Musset, *Les actes de Guillaume le Conquérant et de la reine Mathilde pour les abbayes caennaises* (Caen, 1967), pp. 25-41.

[13] M. Fauroux, *Recueil des actes des ducs de Normandie de 911 à 1066* (Caen, 1961).

[14] F. E. Harmer, *Anglo-Saxon Writs* (Manchester, 1952; reprint Stamford, 1989); S. Keynes, 'Regenbald the Chancellor (*sic*)', *Anglo-Norman Studies*, 10 (1987), 185-222; V. Gazeau, 'L'aristocratie autour du Bec au tournant de l'année 1077', *Anglo-Norman Studies*, 7 (1984), 90-103; *idem*, 'Le domaine continental de l'abbaye de Notre-Dame et Saint-Léger de Préaux au XIe siècle', in L. Musset et al., *Aspects de la Société et de l'Economie dans la Normandie médiévale (Xe-XIIIe siècles)* (Caen, 1988), 165-83; J. -M. Bouvris, 'La renaissance de l'abbaye de Montivilliers et son développement jusqu' à la fin du XIe siècle' in *L'Abbaye de Montivilliers à travers les âges. Actes du colloque organisé à Montivilliers, le 8 mars 1986: Recueil de l'Association des Amis du Vieux Havre*, 48 (1988), 67-84; E. Searle, 'Battle Abbey and exemption: the forged charters', *EHR*, 83 (1968), 449-80.

reference to Herleva, and compelling reason to reinterpret the career of Herluin de Conteville and aspects of the history of the Conqueror's family.[15] The relocation of a writ for the abbey of Ramsey into William II's reign suggests that some of the judicial work associated with the Domesday survey continued after the Conqueror's death.[16] A charter from Saint-Benoît-sur-Loire, which should probably be dated to 9 January 1084, suggests that the date of Robert Curthose's second exile ought to be placed after Mathilda's death, confirmation of what has long been thought psychologically likely.[17] More complex conclusions follow from the grant of Piddle Hinton (Dorset) to the church of Notre-Dame of Mortain, which Davis, following Round, dated to 1082 x 1084. This text is interesting because it contains information about hidage (*Et hoc non solvent nisi quatuor hide; relique sex sunt in dominio et quiete*) which is closer to the *Inquisitio Gheldi* than to Domesday Book.[18] Since the document, which exists in two eighteenth-century copies and which has actually never been published, either began or was given the introduction *Regnante beate memorie primo ex Normannis Anglorum rege Willelmo* by a later copyist, it should be dated to 1087 x 1094. As the sentence which describes the hidage is in the present tense, it too dates from after the Conqueror's death. On logical grounds, the redating strengthens Galbraith's case for assigning the *Inquisitio Gheldi* to 1086.[19] Domesday Book and its making are illustrated in another way by the record of the inquest into the

---

[15] D. Bates and V. Gazeau, 'L'abbaye de Grestain et la famille d'Herluin de Conteville', *Annales de Normandie*, 30 (1990), 5-30.

[16] D. Bates, 'Two Ramsey Abbey Writs and the Domesday Survey', *Historical Research*, 63 (1990), 337-39.

[17] *Hec .... gesta sunt anno MLXXXIII Dominice Incarnationis, anno XVIII regni ipsius, Recueil des chartes de l'abbaye de Saint-Benoît-sur-Loire*, ed. M. Prou and A. Vidier, 2 vols (Paris, 1908-12), I, no. 92. The eighteenth year of William's reign began on 25 December 1083, so this looks like an instance where the year was dated from the Annunciation. For the suggestion that Robert went into exile after Mathilda's death, see, for example, *The Ecclesiastical History of Orderic Vitalis*, ed. and trans. M. Chibnall, 6 vols, Oxford Medieval Texts (Oxford, 1969-80), III, p. 102.

[18] There are two 18th-century copies of this document: Paris, Bibliothèque Nationale, MS latin 12878, f. 285r, a copy by Dom. Martène; Bibliothèque Nationale, MS latin 5441, II, p. 406, a copy by Noel Mars. For the references, see J. H. Round, *Calendar of Documents preserved in France illustrative of the History of Great Britain and Ireland* (London, 1899), no. 1206; *Regesta*, I, no. 204. Domesday Book states that there were 5 hides in demesne and *Inquisitio Gheldi* gives 5 hides and 3 virgates. See further A. Williams, *VCH Dorset*, III, p. 130. The document can be dated between the deaths of the Conqueror and Roger de Montgomery.

[19] V. H. Galbraith, 'The Date of the Geld Rolls', *EHR*, 65 (1950), 7-15; reprinted with corrections in V. H. Galbraith, *The Making of Domesday Book* (Oxford, 1961), pp. 223-30.

holdings of the abbey of Fontenay, which dates from 1070 x 1079.[20] The document records that William ordered the barons of the Taisson fee to assemble in Caen before Richard, *vicomte* of Avranches and William, abbot of Saint-Etienne of Caen, in order to record on oath what Ralph I and Ralph II Taisson had given to the abbey. In Caen, four lawful men were chosen from among them to testify to the record's accuracy. The four, whom the document names, include the reeve (*prepositus*) of Ralphs I and II Taisson. The information was then recorded in a *carta*, which may well have been written by a scribe supplied by the abbey of Saint-Etienne of Caen, and read out before William and his barons. The texts of the earliest Fontenay charters show that pre-existing documentary material was used to compile the record.[21] The document, which is usually cited in the context of the debate about the origins of the English jury, is describing something which appears to me to be akin to the procedure of the Domesday survey.[22]

On broader questions of the interpretation of the Conqueror's reign and of the Norman Conquest, the charters will provide a gold-mine of precious information. I want to suggest some possibilities. But final judgements must wait until the complete edition is available, since so much rests on how individual documents are read. It is necessary, for example, to establish what can, or cannot, be used from Westminster documents or from the Battle 'forgeries'.[23]

William's itinerary after 1066 has never been accurately established.[24] It is well known that he left England in February 1067 and remained in Normandy until December of the same year.[25] An unpublished charter

---

20 *Gallia Christiana*, 16 vols (Paris, 1715-1877), XI, instr. cols 62-65, apparently from the lost 14th-century cartulary of the abbey.

21 L. Musset, 'Actes inédits du onzième siècle: V. Autour des origines de Saint-Etienne de Fontenay', *Bull. Soc. Ant. Normandie*, 56 (1961-62), 13-15, 33-40. For the suggestion, based on style, that the document was written by a scribe from the abbey of Saint-Etienne of Caen, Musset, *Actes pour les abbayes caennaises*, p. 36.

22 See, for example, D. M. Stenton, *English Justice between the Norman Conquest and the Great Charter* (London, 1965), p. 15.

23 On the former, see for now E. Mason, assisted by the late Jennifer Bray, *Westminster Abbey Charters 1066-c.1214*, London Record Society (London, 1988), pp. 25-40; on the latter, Searle, 'Battle Abbey', *passim*.

24 For an attempt to establish William's itinerary, *Regesta*, I, pp. xxi-xxii. An interesting demonstration of the distortions which result from following Davis has recently been provided by M. Biddle, 'Seasonal Festivals and Residence: Winchester, Westminster and Gloucester in the Tenth and Eleventh Centuries', *Anglo-Norman Studies*, 8 (1985), 64-65.

25 *Regesta*, I, p. xxi.

allows us to extend his known itinerary to Lyons-la-Forêt.[26] David Douglas rightly suggested that there was a visit to Normandy in late 1068 and early 1069.[27] There was certainly also a visit in late 1070 and early 1071. An impeccable notice from the abbey of St-Amand of Rouen has William in Normandy at a date between Christmas 1070 and William fitz Osbern's death on 22 February 1071;[28] the dating-clause in a Rochester writ which supposedly has him in England at this time occurs only in thirteenth-century and later copies, and not in the two earliest manuscripts.[29]

There was a visit to England in 1073 after William had restored Norman power in Maine and, according to the Anglo-Saxon Chronicle, he did not leave the kingdom until 1074.[30] A charter shows that he was in Normandy by May 1074,[31] and Lanfranc's letters demonstrate that it was only late in the year 1075 that the threat of a Danish invasion brought him back to England.[32] It is possible, although not certain, that William remained in England until after the execution of earl Waltheof on 31 May 1076, before leaving to pursue the rebel earl Ralph to Dol, where the king sustained the first significant military defeat of his life.[33] From then until the middle of the year 1080, as is well known, William was continuously occupied in France. The exact date of William's return to England in 1080 is unknown; he was still at Caen on 14 July, but, before the year was out, he had already sent his son Robert north to confront the king of Scots, and at Christmas, he was at

---

[26] Paris, BN, MS latin 12878, ff. 230r-31r, an 18th-century copy of a charter for Marmoutier by Dom. Martène.

[27] D. C. Douglas, *William the Conqueror* (London, 1964), pp. 217-18. Douglas's hesitancy regarding the charters' authenticity is groundless.

[28] M. -J. Le Cacheux, 'Histoire de l'abbaye de Saint-Amand de Rouen', *Bull. Soc. Ant. Normandie*, 44 (1936), p. 250, from a late 11th-century *pancarte*, Rouen, Archives Départementales de la Seine-Maritime, 55H, fonds de Saint-Amand de Rouen, non classé, carton 1; cf, *Regesta*, I, p. xxii.

[29] The reasoning is given in D. Bates, 'The Origins of the Justiciarship', *Anglo-Norman Studies*, 4 (1981), at p. 168, n. 25.

[30] *The Anglo-Saxon Chronicle: A Revised Translation*, ed. D. C. Douglas, D. Whitelock and S. I. Tucker (London, 1961), 'D' and 'E', *sub anno* 1074.

[31] F. Lot, *Etudes critiques sur l'abbaye de Saint-Wandrille* (Paris, 1913), recueil des chartes, no. 38.

[32] *The Letters of Lanfranc, Archbishop of Canterbury*, ed. H. M. Clover and M. T. Gibson, Oxford Medieval Texts (Oxford, 1979), no. 36.

[33] The sequence of events in *Anglo-Saxon Chronicle*, 'D' and 'E', *sub anno* 1076 implies that William remained until after the execution. *Orderic*, II, p. 320 appears to suggest that William was no longer present when Waltheof was condemned and executed.

Gloucester.[34] The years 1080 and 1081 were a time when William showed off his power throughout as much of Britain as was within his reach after his long absence; there was not only the expedition to Scotland, but also his one known visit to Wales.[35] Although deductions drawn from the counting of attestations to charters should be regarded with some suspicion,[36] and conclusions drawn from the small number of the Conqueror's English diplomas should be regarded with even greater suspicion, the undeniable conclusion from diplomas and chronicles is that in 1080-81 William had his family around him in England, perhaps for the first time.[37]

By late 1081, William had recrossed the Channel and was in Maine around Christmas.[38] We should disregard a Westminster writ which apparently has him in England at Christmas 1081; it is a product of the Westminster 'factory' of the twelfth century, and, whichever of its contents may derive from an authentic base, its witnesses are a group which appears on several other similar Westminster documents and can, in this case, be shown to be physically impossible.[39] William remained in France until the autumn of 1082,[40] then crossed to England to arrest his brother, bishop Odo, returning to Fécamp for Easter 1083. There were acts of government during

[34] *Regesta*, I, no. 125 for the visit to Caen. The visit to Gloucester is implied by *Regesta*, I, no. 128 and by Simeon of Durham, *Opera Omnia*, ed. T. Arnold, 2 vols, RS (London, 1882-85), I, p. 119; II, p. 211.

[35] *Anglo-Saxon Chronicle*, 'E', 1081.

[36] D. Bates, reviewing C. W. Hollister, *Monarchy, Magnates and Institutions in the Anglo-Norman World* (London, 1986), in *Albion*, 19 (1987), 592-93.

[37] *Regesta*, I, nos 135, 137, 140. Davis regarded no. 137 for Bury St Edmunds as spurious, an opinion shared by A. Gransden, 'Baldwin, Abbot of Bury St. Edmunds, 1065-1097', *Anglo-Norman Studies*, 4 (1981), 65-76 at 71-72. I would disagree, as too did the late Professor R. Allen Brown, who was editing the Bury charters, in a private communication. For now, see Keynes, 'Regenbald', p. 220, n. 217.

[38] Douglas, *William the Conqueror*, pp. 404-05; see also *Cartulaire du chapitre royal de Saint-Pierre-de-la-Cour*, ed. M. le vicomte S. Menjot d'Elbenne and L.-J. Denis (Le Mans, 1903-07), no. VIII, which is taken from an 18th-century copy of a lost 13th-century cartulary, Le Mans, Archives Départementales de la Sarthe, G 479, p.5.

[39] *Regesta*, I, no. 143, from Westminster Abbey Muniments, no. xxiii, and written by the same scribe who wrote an original charter of abbot Herbert of Westminster (1121-36). Count Robert of Meulan attested a charter of king Philip I on 6 January 1082 and is therefore unlikely to have been at Westminster at Christmas, *Recueil des Actes de Philippe Ier, roi de France (1059-1108)*, ed. M. Prou (Paris, 1908), no. CVI. For a commentary, *Westminster Abbey Charters 1066-c.1214*, no. 34.

[40] Bates and Gazeau, 'L'Abbaye de Grestain', pp. 9-10.

this visit – I suspect that a new round in the Ely land pleas was set on foot then – but one can, I think, only conclude that this crossing was an unplanned one, provoked by a serious crisis.[41]

The period from 1083 to 1085 is obscure. There is no evidence whatsoever to support the suggestion that William was in England at Whitsun and Christmas 1083 and at Easter and Christmas 1084.[42] The view that he was at Westminster for Whitsun 1084 is based on Matthew Paris, who had incorrectly placed Henry of Huntingdon's paraphrase of the entry in the 'E' version of the *Anglo-Saxon Chronicle* for 1086 in that year.[43] The charters in fact show William in Normandy on 18 July 1083 and somewhere in France on 9 January 1084.[44] Since Mathilda died in the intervening period on 2 November, we can reasonably presume that he did not leave the duchy. For 1084, there are two charters which record a visit to Rouen,[45] and for 1085 there is additional material which looks to be Norman.[46] At some stage in this period, William was involved in Maine with the siege of Sainte-Suzanne, an operation whose length impressed contemporaries, but whose conduct William eventually left to his military household.[47] The rebel, Hubert de Sainte-Suzanne, *vicomte* of Le Mans, finally crossed to England to make his peace with William. The actual evidence for William's presence in England during these years is slim; even the celebrated entry in the *Anglo-Saxon Chronicle* referring to the six-shilling geld does not actually state that William visited the kingdom, although we ought probably, although cautiously, to conclude that there was a brief visit in the spring.[48] It was at this time, also, that William's youngest son Henry is recorded as being in England while his father and brothers (*sic*) were in Normandy, which suggests that he may have been left there as some sort of representative.[49] Light only dawns when

---

41 For William at Fécamp, Rouen, Bibliothèque Municipale, MS 1193 (Y.44), 30v-31r; *Regesta*, I, p. xxii.

42 Biddle, 'Seasonal Festivals and Residence', p. 64.

43 *Regesta*, I, p. xxii.

44 Musset, *Actes pour les abbayes caennaises*, no. 17; *Recueil des chartes de l'abbaye de Saint-Benoît-sur-Loire*, no. 92, on which see above, note 17.

45 Rouen, Archives Départementales de la Seine-Maritime, 14 H.344; *Chartes de l'abbaye de Jumièges (v.825-1204) conservées aux archives de la Seine-Inférieure*, 2 vols, ed. J.-J. Vernier (Rouen and Paris, 1916), I, no. 33.

46 *Regesta*, I, nos. 206, 207.

47 *Orderic*, IV, pp. 46-52.

48 *Anglo-Saxon Chronicle*, 'E', *sub anno* 1083: 'And in this same year, after Christmas (i.e., early in 1084), the king had a great and heavy tax ordered all over England – it was 72*d*. for every hide.'

49 *Chronicon Monasterii de Abingdon*, ed. J. Stevenson, 2 vols, RS (London, 1858) II, p. 12.

William appears in England to set on foot the Domesday survey at Gloucester at Christmas 1085. From here on everything is much clearer. The king left England for the last time in the autumn of 1086, campaigned in the Vexin, and died outside Rouen on 9 September 1087.

I recently used this outline to suggest that, after 1072, William spent about 130 months out of a possible 170 in France.[50] The reasons for the imbalance are speculative, as are their significance, since the relationship of itinerary and the practical exercise of power needs exploration. It is possible, for example, that the demands of war in France and the insecurity which followed from Robert Curthose's revolts explain William's long stays in France, rather than personal preference. The symbolic reflection of the lengthy absences is surely titles like *Anglis imperante supradicto Guillelmo Normannorum strenuissimo duce*, in an original charter of 1084, which are far from indicative of the kind of integrated Anglo-Norman realm in which the late Professor Le Patourel believed.[51] William's visits to England should be seen as dramatic displays of power, whose *raison d'être* was often crisis, and whose length was apparently usually no more than was strictly necessary. The geographical range of his itinerary can be shown to have been limited almost exclusively to the kingdom of Wessex, in a pattern which follows broadly that of Edward the Confessor.[52] For this, and many other reasons, some of which are touched on below, we might ultimately believe that William's prime purpose was to present himself as an Old English king.

William's limited itinerary has fundamental consequences for the way in which Norman government evolved in England. Absence implied delegation; and not just delegation of a kind which made bishop Odo of Bayeux a regent in England between 1077/78 and 1080 and archbishop Lanfranc the recipient and executor of royal orders over a longer period.[53] Delegation absorbed other members of William's family, most notably Mathilda and Robert

---

[50] D. Bates, *William the Conqueror* (London, 1989), p. 110. It is possible that I have here under-estimated the length of time spent in England in 1073-74, but this has little or no effect on the final conclusions.

[51] Rouen, Archives Départementales de la Seine-Maritime, 14 H. 344; see further D. Bates, 'Normandy and England after 1066', *EHR*, 104 (1989), 851-80 at p. 863, n. 3.

[52] See the convenient map in D. Hill, *An Atlas of Anglo-Saxon England* (Oxford, 1981), p. 94.

[53] The arguments for the distinction implied by this sentence are set out in Bates, 'Origins of the Justiciarship', pp. 2-6. It is additionally worth noting that Odo's seal is alone treated as the equivalent of the royal seal in Domesday Book, T. A. Heslop, 'English Seals from the mid-ninth century to 1100', *JBAA*, 133 (1980), 1-17, at p. 11.

Curthose.[54] In England it also required that many sheriffs became great powers in their shires in a manner which made them officials of a very different type from their Anglo-Saxon predecessors, while William's absences permitted some among them to abuse their position.[55] Absence was surely associated with the creation of territorial earldoms, in which earls exercised powers which are sometimes called 'palatine', and with the creation in the Midlands and the North of territorial castellanries. The establishment of these new units of power is nowadays enmeshed in debates about the nature of Anglo-Saxon society and whether the Conquest represented a 'tenurial revolution'. It is nonetheless interesting that one of the participants in these controversies notes that 'Great Norman lords unlike their Anglo-Saxon counterparts had the seats of their power and a substantial portion of their land on the outskirts of the kingdom and not in the Midlands...'.[56] This redistribution of territorial, and therefore of political, power is a phenomenon whose consequences must be fully worked out by historians of the twelfth and thirteenth centuries. For me, it means that the England and the Britain which evolved after 1066 were bound to be profoundly different from those which would have evolved if Harold Godwinesson had won on the field of Hastings. It also means that William I had a genuine scheme for Anglo-Norman government, although rather a different one from that proposed by Douglas and Le Patourel.[57] He governed a cross-Channel realm from a central unit of land, primarily from Normandy, intervening outside it when crisis required, and in England doing all he could to look like an Old English king.

It has been established by Dr Simon Keynes that, in diplomatic terms, William's English charters conform to a pattern which is demonstrably a continuation of English practice from before 1066.[58] It has likewise been shown that William's post-1066 Norman charters maintain Norman

---

54   Bates, 'Origins of the Justiciarship', pp. 6-8; note also ...*Robertoque, Willelmi regis Anglorum filio, Cenomannicam urbem gubernante, Cartulaire de l'abbaye de Saint-Vincent du Mans*, ed. R. Charles and M. le Vicomte Menjot d'Elbenne (Mamers and Le Mans, 1886-1913), no. 589.

55   In general, see J. Green, 'The Sheriffs of William the Conqueror', *Anglo-Norman Studies*, 5 (1982), 129-45.

56   R. Fleming, 'Domesday Book and the Tenurial Revolution', *Anglo-Norman Studies*, 9 (1986), 87-102, at p. 96.

57   See the suggestive remarks in R. Frame, *The Political Development of the British Isles 1100-1400* (Oxford, 1990), pp. 16-19, 25.

58   Keynes, 'Regenbald', pp. 217-21; for a contrary opinion, R. Allen Brown, 'Some Observations on Norman and Anglo-Norman Charters', in D. Greenway, C. Holdsworth, J. Sayers (eds), *Tradition and Change: Essays in honour of Marjorie Chibnall presented by her friends on the occasion of her seventieth birthday* (Cambridge, 1985), pp. 145-63, with the specific point at p. 162.

traditions.[59] Less well known, but equally important for the way we view the Conqueror's government of his far-flung lands, is the fact that his charters for Maine continue Manceau traditions. The charters from Maine are few in number and often are nothing more than confirmations of grants already confirmed by previous counts. No originals survive, but we have a superb description of one by Roger de Gaignières in an eighteenth-century copy now in the Bibliothèque Nationale: the diploma concerned was a charter of Hugh III, count of Maine (died 1014), for the abbey of Saint-Pierre de la Couture at Le Mans, written on a large piece of parchment with the witnesses arranged in columns, on which the politically astute monks had obtained the confirmations in turn of William and of counts Geoffrey the Bearded and Fulk Rechin of Anjou.[60] This story of broad continuity and distinctive traditions of documentary production is one which will have to be qualified with all kinds of subtleties once the final edition is complete; Norman charters do, for example, occasionally reflect English traditions and we now have to take account of a writ issued in the name of that supposed administrative incompetent, duke Robert Curthose;[61] in England, a new Norman foundation, Saint Pancras of Lewes, had its grants confirmed in a document whose form is pure Norman;[62] a writ directed to William's representatives in Maine survives.[63] But it is a conclusion which will, I am sure, hold. Fusion of Anglo-Norman documentary traditions, mostly into the style of English writ-form, occurred in the twelfth century, not the eleventh. The enduring distinctions represent significant differences in governmental practice. The introduction of writ-form into Normandy was eventually done in a way which was conditioned by Norman custom.[64]

[59] See the general remarks in Musset, *Actes pour les abbayes caennaises*, p. 25. Also, J. Le Patourel, *The Norman Empire* (Oxford, 1976), pp. 244-45; D. Bates, 'The Earliest Norman Writs', *EHR*, 100 (1985), 267-70.

[60] Paris, BN, MS latin 17123, pp. 187-90, for the abbey of Saint-Pierre de la Couture at Le Mans. The currently available printed text is from a 15th-century *vidimus*, *Cartulaire des abbayes de Saint-Pierre de la Couture et de Saint-Pierre de Solesmes*, ed. Les Bénédictins de Solesmes (Le Mans, 1881), no. IX.

[61] J.-M. Bouvris, 'Un bref inédit de Robert Courte-Heuse, duc de Normandie, relatif à l'abbaye de Montebourg, au diocèse de Coutances', *Actes du cent cinquième congrès national des sociétés savantes, Caen (1980): Section de Philologie* (Paris, 1984), pp. 125-50.

[62] See the facsimile in *Early Yorkshire Charters, VIII, The Honour of Warenne*, ed. C.T. Clay (Wakefield, 1949), pl. 1; from Paris, BN, coll. Bourgogne, vol. LXXVIII, no. 121.

[63] *Chartularium Insignis Ecclesie Cenomanensis quod dicitur Liber Albus Capitulis*, ed. abbé Lottin (Le Mans, 1869), no. 1. I am grateful to M. Jean-Michel Bouvris for identifying the editor of this cartulary.

[64] Bates, 'Earliest Norman Writs', pp. 266-84.

The conservatism of William's Manceau charters is paralleled by the conservatism of his English charters. Given that we are dealing with the drama of a conquest, I am surprised that there are not more of them, and that they do not do more. I hope that this impressionistic judgement can be forgiven, at least in so far as it is useful to convey a point. Some new documents can be added to the *corpus* of English writs and charters, but there are others, out-and-out forgeries, which should be deleted. When we clear away the unacceptable texts, we are left with about 140.[65] There are famous texts, such as the sequence of Ely writs, about which new things can be said when we rely on the earliest manuscripts rather than on *Liber Eliensis*, the writ ordering the collection of Peter's Pence, the reports of the great land pleas, and so on, some of which reflect the circumstances of the Conquest. Many, when placed in context, clearly have hidden meanings and are in fact associated with pleading.[66] But a great number are simple confirmations of the grant of a single manor or of less than that; the confirmation of the grant of Winsham to the bishopric of Wells or of Coton-in-the-Elms to Burton abbey, for example.[67] The quantity of documents as well as the usage are in fact not greatly dissimilar from the survivals from Edward the Confessor's reign.[68] They also survive in disproportionately large numbers from certain religious houses, such as Westminster and Bury St Edmunds, in the same way that Edward the Confessor's do.[69] Furthermore, the number is small if we think in terms of what we are led to expect by Freeman's statement that 'The necessity of the king's grant for the lawful possession of any property is the principle on which all the doctrines of Domesday are founded. And the great advantage of having the king's writ and seal as the surest witness of grant is

---

[65] There is no space to survey the forged charters here. For additional documents not in *Regesta*, see Lambeth Palace, MS. 1212, pp. 15, 187, 332-3. See also the writs printed in Harmer, *Anglo-Saxon Writs*, BL, MS Cotton Faustina (for Westminster) [pp. 493-4, 507].

[66] See, for example, *Chronicon Monasterii de Abingdon*, II, p. 1 (*Regesta*, I, no. 49), and the two writs concerning Newington (*Regesta*, I, no. xxii and *Historia Monasterii Sancti Augustini Cantuariensis*, ed. C. Hardwick, RS (London, 1858), p. 349).

[67] *Regesta*, I, nos. 160, 223.

[68] S. Keynes, *The Diplomas of King Æthelred 'The Unready'* (Cambridge, 1980), p. 47, appears to suggest a total in excess of 120, if the 99 writs usually attributed to Edward are added in; M. T. Clanchy, *From Memory to Written Record: England, 1066-1307* (London, 1979), 249, suggests the lower figure of 100 once non-authentic texts have been removed. Harmer, *Anglo-Saxon Writs*, p. 19, observed that the great majority of Old English writs refer to 'the tenure of land, and/or rights of jurisdiction'.

[69] See Keynes, *Diplomas*, pp. 142-44.

shown by a great number of cases',[70] views which raise the possibility of a great explosion in the use of written documents after the Conquest, an explosion of which all documentary trace has apparently vanished.

Obviously many documents which once existed have been lost. However, the serious question is whether proportionately more documents from William the Conqueror's reign have been lost than from, say, Edward the Confessor's, William II's or Henry I's. Why should they have been? I cannot myself see why an ecclesiastical archive should keep a writ of William Rufus, but destroy one of his father. The evidence of Domesday Book suggests not so much that lots of writs have been lost, as that contemporaries expected that land would be conveyed either by writ or by oral means. As Welldon Finn pointed out, we hear most often of cases where the holder of a manor could not produce a writ,[71] and, by implication, therefore, of cases where a writ might have been expected, but where one did not in fact exist. In Surrey, for example, there are eleven mentions of the king's writ and seal, but in only one instance was either actually produced or recorded as in existence.[72] In Berkshire, where the survey appears to have been following different conventions, there are no references to the expectation that a William writ could be produced and only one to an actual writ.[73] In Essex and Suffolk the picture is similar. It is also interesting that, in the majority of cases where a writ was either produced or expected, variations in the initial Norman settlement are at issue rather than the original grants to the French newcomers.[74]

There is such broad comparability in both the content and use of Edward the Confessor's and William I's writs and charters that there must have been a basic continuity of usage over 1066. If William's English writs and charters are taken alongside the Domesday evidence in the context of modern concerns about the literate or non-literate character of eleventh-century English government, then they support James Campbell's observation that there was an 'extensive use of writs', because of the expectation that royal writs would be received by hundred courts, and for other reasons which

---

[70] E. A. Freeman, *The History of the Norman Conquest of England, Its Causes and Its Results*, 6 vols (Oxford, 1867-79), V, p. 787.

[71] R. W. Finn, *An Introduction to Domesday Book* (London, 1963), p. 31.

[72] *Azor tenuit donec obiit et dedit ecclesie pro anima sua tempore regis Willelmi, ut dicunt monachi, et inde habent brevem regis*, Domesday Book, I, f. 34r, recording a gift to the abbey of Chertsey. For the other Surrey references to either *sigillum regis* or *breve regis*, Domesday Book, I, ff. 32r (four instances), 35r, 36r (four instances), 36v.

[73] *Domesday Book*, I, f. 62r.

[74] Note, for example, the cases mentioned in the Lincolnshire text and *clamores*, *Domesday Book*, I, ff. 342r, 375r.

Campbell detailed.[75] Since no writ relating to the original settlement has survived, and since few among the mentions of writs in Domesday Book appear to refer to it, they may also support Galbraith's view that the original grants to the tenants-in-chief seem to have been made *sine carta*. Alternatively – and more probably – they favour Professor R. H. C. Davis's suggestion that special writs were drawn up for the original settlement and returned in 1086.[76] It is the making of Domesday Book, and not the Norman Conquest, which seems therefore to mark a significant stage in the routine usage of the writ in English administration. Because we ought to lower the line for William I on the graph in Dr Clanchy's *From Memory to Written Record*, there must have been a more significant growth under William II than is currently believed. Then – and this requires explanation – the numbers explode from the very first year of Henry I's reign.[77] Also, from 1100 onwards, there is for the first time a dramatic disparity between the quantity of Norman and English documents.[78] If the conservatism of William's English writs and charters points again to a king seeking to stress continuity – in a grand manner, perhaps – they also suggest that a serious study of William II's and Henry I's writs and charters will produce important results. There seems to have been a growth in the use of written documentation after the making of Domesday Book which greatly exceeds the average growth elsewhere in the medieval West.

We have recently heard much about the great wealth and power of the Anglo-Saxon state.[79] In the context of 1066 and all that, William's English, Norman, Manceau and French charters raise anxieties about this view only to the extent that some theories are being advanced which neglect entirely the evidence of charters and which do not examine what we might find in Normandy before and after 1066.[80] One advantage which will accrue from an edition of the Conqueror's charters is that all the Continental and English evidence will be brought together in a single volume. We will be able to look at the documents side-by-side. The edition will kill that hoary old myth,

---

[75] J. Campbell, 'Some Agents and Agencies of the Late Anglo-Saxon State', in *Domesday Studies*, ed. J. C. Holt (Woodbridge, 1987), pp. 214-15.

[76] Galbraith, *The Making of Domesday Book*, pp. 46-47; R. H. C. Davis, 'The Norman Conquest', *History*, 51 (1966), 279-286, at pp. 282-83; *idem*, 'Domesday Book: Continental Parallels', in *Domesday Studies*, ed. Holt, pp. 28-9.

[77] Clanchy, *From Memory to Written Record*, p. 44.

[78] See the figures in Bates, 'Earliest Norman Writs', p. 267.

[79] Most recently, J. Campbell, 'The Sale of Land and the Economics of Power in Early England: Problems and Possibilities', *Haskins Soc. Jnl*, I, ed. R.B. Patterson (London and Ronceverte, 1989), 23-37.

[80] W. L. Warren, 'The Myth of Norman Administrative Efficiency', *Trans. R. Hist. Soc.*, 34 (1984), 113-32.

against which the late Professor R. Allen Brown protested so vigorously, that English documentation is superior in quantity and quality to the Norman.[81] The Norman documents are more numerous, more explicit, and longer. Brevity may well be indicative of the power of the state and of there being no need to explain details which could be handled by officers and courts. But on the other hand, Emily Zack Tabuteau has recently given massive testimony to the complexity and sophistication of Norman society in a remarkable book based on a thorough knowledge of the charters.[82] If a procedure similar to the Domesday inquest was employed in Normandy before 1086, does not it at the least indicate why the great survey was politically possible and solve some of the problems with which Professor Holt grappled so in 1986?[83] Should we consider *Domesday Book* as a kind of giant Norman *pancarte?* Technically, probably no, but spiritually, perhaps, yes. The terminology used to describe both was the same: *carta.* And the great *pancartes* were concerned, in a settled society, with some of the same phenomena; how property had been acquired, how and by whom it was held.[84] On both sides of the Channel, William the Conqueror's reign was a great time for the production of written records. With these brought into focus by an edition of the Conqueror's post-1066 charters, we should be better placed to understand their significance. We may even overcome that silly competitiveness of Norman *versus* English which has done much to hold back the study of the Norman Conquest.

---

[81] Brown, 'Norman and Anglo-Norman Charters', pp. 145-63.

[82] Emily Z. Tabuteau, *Transfers of Property in Eleventh-Century Norman Law* (Chapel Hill, 1988), *passim.*

[83] J. C. Holt, '1086', in *Domesday Studies*, ed. Holt, 55-62.

[84] Note the discussion recorded in P. R. Hyams, '"No Register of Title": The Domesday Inquest and Land Adjudication', *Anglo-Norman Studies*, 9 (1986) 127-142, at p. 139.

De Iure Domini Regis: A Comment on
Royal authority in eleventh-century england
HENRY LOYN

Although it may seem eccentric to offer a title so firmly in the old fashioned mould of legal and constitutional history in a collection avowedly interested in art, texts and the totality of experience, there is method in the apparent madness. For increasingly we become aware of the physical manifestations of lordship in this formative phase of Western European growth when royal power supplied so much of the motor power that led to social change. In that sense the Norman Conquest, that great traumatic event, represented not only a symbolic turning-point in English affairs but a critical moment in the formulation of ideas and practice of Christian kingship in the West. William's conquest stands out as a formidable example, perhaps unique, of the taking over by force of arms of a crown (and all that is implied in Christian lordship) of a Christian people by an already Christian ruler of a different people of non-royal status. Charles the Great's assumption of the Lombard crown bears some parallels but more contrasts. The see-saw relationship of late Carolingians and Capetians hints at situations capable of resolution in similar ways; but they were not. The ultimate coronation of Roger of Hauteville in Sicily in 1130 may have owed something to the precedent of 1066, but again there are more contrasts than parallels.

What then was happening to kingship in eleventh-century England? Let me start with a look at a block of evidence that is a slight cheat, the *Leges Henrici Primi*, the so-called Laws of Henry I.[1] This is a private compilation, probably put together about A.D. 1118 by someone practised in the exercise of law in public courts in or near the city of Winchester. It is a considerable rag-bag. Long extracts are taken from Anglo-Saxon law and from Continental codes and strung together not always with an eye to consistency or accuracy. One section is worth careful thought as we approach the problem of royal authority and that is the tenth clause, rubricated in the main manuscripts *de iure regis*, concerning the *jus*, the jurisdiction or legal right of the King. The matter of the *jus* is sub-divided further into three parts. A great omnibus clause (Clause 10.1) is inserted first which attempts to list all the *iura* which the king has *solus et super omnes homines* retained through a proper ordering of peace and security. This consists of no fewer than thirty-six separate headings, ranging from traditional rights concerning a breach of the king's peace given by his hand or his writ to elements reflecting conditions in the new feudal world, such as regulations concerning fortifications of the depth

1   *Leges Henrici Primi*, ed. L. J. Downer (Oxford, 1972), Clause 10, *De iure regis*, pp. 108-09.

of three walls (*castellatio trium scannorum*). Then (Clause 10.2), qualifying for separate and special treatment, comes a statement that all highways (*herestrete*) are completely the concern of the king and all places of execution (*qualstowa*) are wholly within his soke or jurisdiction. The third relatively simple statement (Clause 10.3) brings out the royal pastoral and residual authority in its insistence that the king must act as kinsman and advocate (*cognatio et advocatus*) to all persons in Holy Orders, strangers, poor people, and those who have been cast out if they have no one else to look after them. In summary (Clause 10.4) our writer declares that all these constitute the pleas of the king as lord (*dominica placita regis*) and belong to the sheriff or his officials or bailiffs only if specific arrangements have been made beforehand. We shall come back later to the substance of the thirty-six special pleas. For the moment it is enough to note that an experienced lawyer of the early twelfth century took it as axiomatic that the king in law should have cognizance of a multiplicity of pleas with a massive residual potential over highways, the gallows, and all who for one reason or another lay outside the normal web of lordship. The man or woman with no obvious lord or kin belonged to the king in a firm legal sense.

An experienced lawyer of 1118 must have received his training in the late eleventh century. Was he merely repeating the commonplaces of late Anglo-Saxon law? We have firm measure of comparison if we turn back to the laws of Cnut, an authoritative source for much practical law in the eleventh century.[2] These were drawn together largely by Wulfstan, bishop of Worcester and archbishop of York (1002-23), to define the legal situation in conquered England. The homiletic note is strong, but so also is the sense of business. Emphasis is placed on the strengthening of a general peace but this is interwoven with attempts to improve the coinage. Concern is expressed that all should be done to the advantage of the ordinary householder (the Scandinavian term *bonda* is used): defence against theft is much in the legislator's mind. Reiteration from earlier codes of the maintenance of good standards for weights and measures and insistence on the *trinoda necessitas* (repair of boroughs and bridges and fyrd-service) is followed by a concise statement of royal rights in Wessex and Mercia with mention of additional rights in the Danelaw.[3] The theocratic notion of peace guaranteed by the king and buttressed by the church may well be overriding but great interest is also shown in the specific and practical formulation of royal rights that will give the lawyers headings under which could be grouped all the huge variety

[2] F. Liebermann, *Die Gesetze der Angelsachsen*, I (Halle, 1903) (hereafter Lieb.I), I Cnut (ecclesiastical), pp. 278-307 and II Cnut (the very important secular code), pp. 308-71; a reliable and conveniently accessible translation of most of the laws appears in EHD, I, ed. D. Whitelock (2nd edn London, 1979), no. 49, pp. 454-67.

[3] II Cnut, 12-15.

of offences likely to be met in ordinary litigation, and treatment of offences in public courts. Five rights were mentioned, all of which needed explanation when transposed to the Latin law-books of the twelfth century: *mundbryce*, *hamsocn*, *forsteal*, *flymena fyrmðe*, and *fyrdwite*.[4] Together they give the king and his officers a comprehensive brief : special penalties for breach of the king's protection, for those guilty of house-breaking, of obstructing justice, of harbouring fugitives, of failing to perform army service. Outlawry was a royal preserve, and only the king could grant peace to a man punished by sentence of outlawry. Similar rights in the Danelaw included a fine for fighting and rights over the breaking of peace in a more general sense (*grithbryce*).[5] Of vital importance was the close association of royal authority and the preservation of peace. Once this was firmly established in men's minds the capacity for growth in royal institutions calculated to preserve the peace was virtually unlimited, and the king's positive functions in the art of government could be extended and deepened in response to more sophisticated ideas of what truly constituted social peace. Domesday Book spells it out for us, as it does so often if properly addressed. The Worcester customs are particularly informative when they tell us that if anyone has broken the peace which the king has given with his own hand he shall be judged an outlaw. If there is infringement of the king's peace given by the sheriff the penalty is harsh – a fine of 100 shillings, but far short of outlawry.[6] The Chester customs go further, though with anomalies. For we are told there that breach of the peace given by the king's hand or by his writ or by his legates shall incur the penalty of 100 shillings, though the ominous rider is added that no one could restore peace to an outlaw *nisi per regem*.[7] The difference in land-holding structures between Worcestershire and Cheshire in 1086 may account for the difference in emphasis. The king held no land in Cheshire but in Worcestershire royal interests and the interests of the comparatively recently endowed church of Westminster in the shire may have resulted in a stronger affirmation of the current commonplace that preservation of peace, effective exercise of the law, and royal authority marched together.

We are now in a position to look back to the detailed provisions of the *Leges Henrici Primi*. We remember that no fewer than thirty-six rights were mentioned as falling within the *jus* of the king. A handful refer to conditions after the Conquest, the *murdrum* fine, forests, fortifications of three walls,

---

[4] Lieb. I, p. 317: Quadripartitus and *Instituta Cnuti*.

[5] II Cnut, 15.

[6] Domesday Book, I, 172: easily accessible in the Phillimore edition, *Worcestershire*, ed. F. and C. Thorn (Chichester, 1982).

[7] Domesday Book, I, 262v.: in the Phillimore edition, *Cheshire*, ed. P. Morgan (Chichester, 1978).

reliefs of barons, and possibly the greater legal precision relating to treasure trove, wreck of the sea and things cast up by the sea. The bulk of the contents comes from Anglo-Saxon law, principally the laws of Cnut. The concept of peace, a general peace for the whole community, is intimately linked to the king's peace, and associated with possible written orders, a peace given by hand or by writ. Breach of the king's *mund* had been recognized by the lawyers as far back as the reign of Æthelred as a serious offence, capable of no compensation if given by the king's own hand, but the precise reference now to the king's writ is further evidence of the increased importance of written instruments of government, a product of the litigious turbulent eleventh century.[8] Contempt of the royal writ or command is treated as a specially severe category of offence, and there are further elaborations of the basic notion of *mundbryce* in reference to any contemptuous remark made or slander of the king.[9] Royal servants had to be protected so that any death or injury was to be answered for, and the thought leads the compiler of this list of rights to include breach of fealty and treason. He then in direct sequence from his initial elaboration of *mundbryce* brings in what we would term a heavy criminal element, giving royal jurisdiction theoretical rights of oversight in virtually all matters connected with serious offences against person or property: theft punishable by death, counterfeiting coinage, arson, unlawful appropriation of the king's land or money, rape, abduction. The familiar rights of Clause 12 of Cnut's secular code appear in slightly different order: *hamsocn, forestal, fyrding, flymenfyrm*. Premeditated assault, robbery (II Cnut,63) and *stretbreche* – obstruction to the highway – fill out this section of the long clause. For the last section of his list, after some mention of the obvious post-Conquest rights, the author again draws heavily on Cnut, assembling statements that deal with failures in personal service (connected with *borhbryce* (*borchbrege*) or breach of pledged security or protection) such as fighting in the king's dwelling or household or breach of peace in the king's troop. In proper lawyer's style the list closes with mention of false judgement, failure of justice, and violation (*prevaricatio*) of the king's law.[10]

Too much has been lost to enable us to reconstruct in detail the manuscript sources from which the author of the *Leges Henrici Primi* drew his material, but it is easy to see the drift of his mind and possible to gather from internal evidence the method by which he set about his task. His main source was a version of Cnut's secular code which he was able to supplement from other manuscripts and from his own court experience. His main line of

---

8 *Leges Henrici*, cl. 10.1: *infractio pacis regie per manum vel breve date.*

9 *despectus vel maliloquium de eo.*

10 L. J. Downer in his introduction to the *Leges Henrici*, p. 32, gives examples of the biblical use of *prevaricatio* and draws attention to cl. 34.8 in the *Leges*, based on II Cnut, 83, *qui prevaricator vel eversor conscripte legis extiterit.*

analysis was firm, giving hints of some training in the new methods of revived Roman law with its insistence on clear terms of reference supported by commentary and expansion. *Mundbryce*, that is infringement of the king's peace, *hamsocn*, that is breaking into a freeman's dwelling with its associated crimes, ambush, failing to perform army duty, harbouring outlaws, *borhbryce* with its implications for violence, and finally – an indication that general rules applied now to a large number of people involved in administering the law – the evils attendant upon failure to see that proper legal rules were observed. Weaving in and out of this framework were emphatic statements by implication on crime and elements proper to the new feudal world. But the fabric was the simple insistence on peace, order, and the personal protection due to the king and his officers.

This is all well and good as far as it goes, but what has it to do with our principal concern, society and culture in eleventh-century England? We can all see that the notion of the king's peace, rooted in Carolingian precedent, blossomed and burgeoned in the eleventh century, dramatically so under new direction, first by Cnut and then under William the Conqueror. Eleventh-century England proved something of an ideal school for the evolution of so-called feudal monarchy, and even more so Christian monarchy, since we should be careful about using the term 'feudal' at all before 1066. We can see, too, how the reality of government demanded an increase in the use of written instruments, and the survival of 150 or so writs from pre-Conquest days serves as a vigorous reminder of one aspect and manifestation of this process.[11] Domesday Book, the satellite and incidental productions connected with its construction and the wealth of documentation that is now known to lie behind it provide massive evidence of the existence of written record.[12] We are also beginning to appreciate more fully the consequences of the royal concern for suppressing criminal acts. In every way the differential between royal peace and the peace that every lord, especially an ecclesiastical lord, was expected to exercise over his dependants was sharpening and becoming more precise. We touch here delicately on the old problem of private jurisdiction and sake and soke. It seems increasingly certain, the more the legal evidence is carefully examined, that in late Anglo-Saxon England all effective jurisdiction over serious cases stemmed ultimately and for the most part immediately from the king.

---

[11] F. E. Harmer, *Anglo-Saxon Writs* (Manchester, 1952; reprinted Stamford, 1989).

[12] H. R. Loyn, 'General Introduction to Domesday Book', *Domesday Studies*, ed. A. Williams and R. W. Erskine, pp. 5-7. The work of Sally Harvey, starting with a seminal article on 'Domesday Book and its predecessors', *EHR*, 86 (1971), 753-73, has contributed greatly to our understanding of the volume of written evidence that lay behind the Domesday Book inquiry.

The implications of this finer awareness of royal legal superiority are great in the political and artistic worlds. Royal subordinates, earls, ealdormen, tenants-in-chief, could employ builders, artists, architects, and craftsmen, but in this they shadowed the activities of the king and the royal court. At the top political level power-struggles concerned control of the royal court more than the setting up of a strong local base. Take Eadric Streona for example, increasingly cast in the role of wicked influence on King Æthelred II.[13] When the new man took over his days were numbered and he was executed by the order of Cnut. The Godwin family found itself in a curious position in mid-century: having exceeded their power in 1051, they were temporarily removed but came back in 1052, and in the end Harold had to aim at the kingship itself. Under King William and his successors the great tenants-in-chief were subordinate in law if not by nature. And the solvent running through the whole century was the church and the leading ecclesiastical princes, often formidable men, bishops and abbots. Again we sense the reality that lay behind theocratic ideals: if government and control of resources were to be permanent then church support was essential.

In all manner of ways the symptoms of growth in and consolidation of peace-giving authority in eleventh-century England made themselves manifest. The legal position was clear-cut, ripe for refinements brought in by Norman bishops but secure on an Anglo-Saxon base. A steady growth in business at the shire courts and indeed at the hundred courts (even when financially in private hands) was connected with the maintenance of a general peace in the royal name.[14] The coinage was regalian and so too for the most part were the boroughs. We understand now better the significance of the new post-Conquest tax of *monetagium* which marked a potentially important milestone in the status-building of towns under the sheriff's guidance.[15] The shire itself was a manageable administrative unit. Domesday Book was a survey of shired England which explains the fuzziness in the North-West where there was as yet no Lancashire, and in the North. At base agrarian level there was a tightening of manorial control, associated with the imposition of gelds, long before the Conquest and it is not surprising that the manor was used as the fundamental element in land-holding in the Domesday survey.

---

[13] S. Keynes, 'A Tale of Two Kings: Alfred the Great and Æthelred the Unready', *Trans. R.Hist. Soc.*, 5th Ser.36 (1986), 195-217, esp. pp. 213-17.

[14] H. R. Loyn, 'The Hundred in England in the Tenth and Eleventh Centuries', *British Government and Administration*, ed. H. Hearder and H. R. Loyn (Cardiff, 1974), pp. 1-15.

[15] P. Grierson, 'Domesday Book, the *Geld De Moneta* and *Monetagium*: a forgotten Minting Reform', *British Numismatic Jnl*, 55 (1985), 84-94.

Two contemporary observations, one from the beginning of the eleventh and the second from the *Leges Henrici* in the early twelfth century, will help to point the differences and to illustrate the development in active kingship. Wulfstan, bishop of Worcester and archbishop of York (1002-23) spent much time and effort on describing the workings of society. He gives us our best insight into the detailed routine of a bishop's life, while on the king and the royal office he adopts a positively puritanical tone. A Christian king among a Christian people was to be a comfort to the folk and a righteous shepherd to the Christian flock, to further the cause of Christendom, to protect the church, to make peace and composition among all Christian folk with righteous laws, and to punish severely with secular punishments all those that do evil – to hate and harry thieves and robbers and bandits.[16] The king was to hold booklearning in great honour.[17] The disciplinary side of things is brilliantly summed up in a fine rhetorical clause (Clause 14). 'If there is anyone among the people too headstrong (*stræc*) that he will not hold to the right as he should and spurn God's law or break the folk law (*folclage myrre*) then it is to be reported to the king if needs must and he straightway shall advise about remedy and pursue the wrongdoer energetically against his will (*huru unpances*) if there is no other course.'[18]

God's law, the folk law, the king as executive agent: the homiletic note is powerful. The good Christian king makes for good Christian government. He has to cleanse his people in spiritual and secular matters if he himself is to earn God's mercy. He is often to think about what is to be done and what is to be avoided according to God's law – and then fame and honour will come to him both in this life and the next. Wulfstan spells out the full high theocratic theory, a rhetorical elaboration of the coronation oath. And, teacher as well as statesman, he plays the number game, reducing some of his basic ideas to numbered subheadings that can be learned easily by heart. The seven essential attributes of a king are that he should fear God, love righteousness, be humble to the good, resolute against evil, help the poor, support the church, and deliver rightful judgements to kinsfolk and foreigners alike.[19] The three orders that support the throne are those that pray, those that work, and those that fight : let one slip and the throne slides.[20] All this is high theory indeed, and one wonders what Harold Harefoot or Harthacnut or William Rufus might have thought. There is not much doubt what Cnut and William I and Henry I made of it – and out of it!

[16] *Die 'Institutes of Polity, Civil and Ecclesiastical'*, ed. K. Jost (Bern, 1959), pp. 40-43.
[17] *Ibid.*, p.48.
[18] *Ibid.*, p.49 : clause 14 in BL Cotton Nero A.i but clause 17 in BL Cotton Junius 121.
[19] *Ibid.*, p.53.
[20] *Ibid.*, pp.55-58: *awacige heora ænig, sona se stol scilfð.*

Such theory if backed by physical power offered hope for permanence of rule and dynasty. In a sense that is what is at the heart of so much of the eleventh-century political scene. Firm national groupings are brought into being in the eleventh-century West ready for the creation in the twelfth century of national myths.

It is in connection with this that I should like to conclude with a reminder again of a key reflective passage from the *Leges Henrici Primi*:

> 9.10 The kingdom of England is divided into three parts: Wessex, Mercia and the Danelaw.

> 9.10a English law is also divided into three parts, distinguished in the same way: over and above everything stand the pleas of the royal court, which preserves the use and custom of its law at all times and in all places with constant uniformity.[21]

And this is truly reflective because the author has already stated before tormenting himself with detail the main proposition of his scheme of analysis. The kingdom is divided into three. The law is divided into three. There are two archbishoprics, fifteen bishoprics, thirty-two shires, many subdivisions. But above it all looms (Clause 6.2) *tremendum regie maiestatis..... imperium quod preesse iugiter legibus ac salubriter frequentamus advertendum.*

---

21 L. J. Downer ed., pp.106-09.

The Early Norman Charters:
A New Perspective on an Old Debate
CASSANDRA POTTS

In 1898 at the University of Cambridge, William Henry Stevenson opened his series of lectures on the Anglo-Saxon chancery by describing 'an erroneous view that is not yet extinct – the view that almost everything we call civilization was introduced into this country by the Normans'.[1] Stevenson was speaking specifically of the tendency of Continental scholars to underestimate the contribution of Anglo-Saxon traditions in the production and transmission of royal documents in England after 1066. His objections were addressed in particular to Arthur Giry, who had asserted four years earlier that the documents of the Anglo-Saxon period 'did not serve as models for those of the following epoch' in England. Instead, Giry argued, 'the diplomatic succession of the English royal acts, like the history of England itself, is divided into two great periods by the Norman Conquest'.[2] Following Stevenson, many scholars on the English side of the Channel have challenged Giry's statements, affirming the existence of several post-Conquest chancery practices in England before 1066, including the centralized production of charters, the use of seals and the development of writs.[3] While the dispute over the continuity or discontinuity of secretarial arrangements from Anglo-Saxon to Norman times remains lively a century after Stevenson, relatively few historians have considered the question of

[1] W. H. Stevenson, 'The Anglo-Saxon Chancery', ed. S. Keynes and H. Kleinschmidt, in *The Anglo-Saxon Chancery and Other Studies*, forthcoming. I am very grateful to the editors of this important study for providing me with a copy before its publication. I would like to thank the Fulbright Commission, the Social Science Research Council, the Institut Français de Washington and the University of California, Santa Barbara for generous support from 1987 to 1988 which permitted me to spend fourteen months in the archives and libraries in France engaged on the research on which this article is largely based. I would like to extend special thanks to the archivists at the Archives départementales, Seine-Maritime (hereafter ADSM) for providing me with approximately one hundred photographs and photocopies of 11th-century Norman charters. I would like to express my gratitude to Lauren Helm Jared and Todd Hannahs for their comments and suggestions on earlier drafts of this paper.

[2] A. Giry, *Manuel de diplomatique* (Paris, 1894), p. 795 (hereafter Giry). Stevenson also cited H. Brunner, *Zur Rechtsgeschichte der römischen und germanischen Urkunde* (Berlin, 1880), pp.161-62, as an advocate of this mistaken opinion.

[3] This is not the place to provide a bibliography of the last century of research on Anglo-Saxon diplomatic. For a survey of recent studies, see N. Brooks, 'Anglo-Saxon Charters: the work of the last twenty years', *ASE*, 3 (1974), 211-31.

what the Norman traditions were.[4] To what extent did Norman charters before 1066 conform to Frankish models? And how did Norman charters evolve in the course of the eleventh century? These questions not only address a curiously neglected aspect of the debate, but offer a better understanding of the impact of the Norman Conquest on English diplomatic.

In contrast to the study of Anglo-Saxon charters, Norman diplomatic has attracted only a handful of scholars.[5] In 1964, David Douglas described the charter evidence of Normandy before 1066 as 'the least worked source of Anglo-Norman history in this age', and he urged scholars to address this evidence.[6] His call has remained largely unheeded. The lack of diplomatic studies of the eleventh-century Norman charters continues to elicit comments over twenty years later.[7] This gap in Anglo-Norman scholarship is due in part to the difficulty in accessing early Norman charters. Until Marie Fauroux's edition of pre-Conquest Norman ducal *acta* appeared in 1961, even the charters of the dukes were scattered haphazardly through obscure and outdated volumes, if they were edited at all. As for the post-Conquest Norman ducal *acta*, the first volume of *Regesta Regum Anglo-Normannorum* merely calendared those Norman charters which were known through English manuscripts.[8] It is therefore of quite limited use to the field of

4   The most recent contribution to the debate over the continuity or discontinuity of Anglo-Saxon secretarial arrangements in post-Conquest England is: S. Keynes, 'Regenbald the Chancellor (*sic*)', *Anglo-Norman Studies*, 10 (1987), 185-222.

5   At this date the two most thorough studies of Norman diplomatic are Marie Fauroux's introduction to her edition of ducal charters before 1066, *Recueil des actes des ducs de Normandie de 911 à 1066* (Caen, 1961) (hereafter Fauroux), and Lucien Musset's introduction to his edition of William the Conqueror's and his wife's charters for St Etienne and la Trinité, Caen, *Les actes de Guillaume le Conquérant et de la reine Mathilde pour les abbayes caennaises* (Caen, 1967). Both scholars tend to focus specifically on the documents at hand; neither express much interest in considering Norman charters in the broader context of the political changes within the duchy or in comparison to the charters of their neighbours. Previous work on Norman diplomatic is limited to two 19th-century theses from the Ecole des Chartes submitted by L. Duhamel and A. Bénet. Duhamel's 1865 thesis is lost, known only from his brief description in *Positions des Thèses*, according to Fauroux p. 40, whereas Bénet's 1881 thesis today lies mouldering in the municipal library of Evreux. I am grateful to the librarians at Evreux for granting me access to Bénet's work, which consists primarily of transcriptions of the ducal acts without collation or analysis.

6   D. C. Douglas, *William the Conqueror* (Berkeley, 1964), p. 12.

7   For example, see E. Z. Tabuteau, *Transfers of Property in Eleventh-Century Norman Law* (Chapel Hill, 1988), p. 273, n. 36 (hereafter Tabuteau).

8   *Regesta Regum Anglo-Normannorum*, 1066-1154, ed. H. W. C. Davis, I (Oxford, 1913). Some thirty-two of William the Conqueror's previously published *acta*

diplomatic, and we must await David Bates' revision of *Regesta I* for full transcriptions of William the Conqueror's acts. Outside the corpus of ducal charters, the number of private charters pertaining to eleventh-century Normandy is daunting.[9] Although many have been published, hundreds remain unedited in the archives, libraries, and private collections in France.[10] Furthermore, over a hundred Norman charters before 1100 survive as originals or contemporary copies, a rich resource for the study of how charters were produced and under what conditions. Some of these have appeared as facsimiles in various works on Norman and Anglo-Norman history, but the great majority remain accessible only in the archives themselves.[11]

Giry himself was in part responsible for deflecting attention away from the Norman charters by writing that they were 'like all the acts of the great lords of this epoch, imitations of the royal Capetian diploma'.[12] Speaking diplomatically, Giry's description implied that the Conquest of England was a Capetian achievement through Norman intermediaries. And this implication has been strengthened by the tendency of subsequent students of diplomatic to concentrate on the distinctive features of the French charters: their seals, their lack of attestors, their distinctive script, the monetary fines with which they threaten potential violators, and their authentication by the

---

were overlooked by the editors of *Regesta*, and another fifteen unmentioned in *Regesta* have never appeared in print at all. I am indebted to D. Bates for this information.

9   The term 'private charter' is limited in this study to charters in which no reference to ducal or royal confirmation or participation is made.

10   The charters of Jumièges are published in J. Vernier, *Chartes de l'abbaye de Jumièges (v.825 à 1204)*, 2 vols (Rouen, 1916). Most but not all of St Wandrille's charters have been edited by F. Lot, *Etudes critiques sur l'abbaye de Saint-Wandrille* (Paris, 1913). More 11th-century Norman charters can be found in *Neustria Pia*, ed. A. Du Monstier (Rouen, 1663) and *Gallia Christiana* vol. 11 (Paris, 1759, reprt 1874). These works are especially valuable because they were compiled before the French Revolution during which many documents were lost. Various other *acta* are scattered in local histories, journals, and antiquarian studies on specific noble families.

11   V. H. Galbraith and P. Chaplais had planned to publish *Facsimiles of Norman and Anglo-Norman Charters* in Oxford, 1962, but this edition has never materialised. Several charters appear in P. Chevreux and J. Vernier, *Les archives de Normandie et de la Seine-Inférieure* (Rouen, 1911). J. Vernier's *Recueil de facsimilés de chartes normandes* (Rouen, 1919) contains only two charters dating before the 12th century. Other works which include facsimiles of 11th-century Norman charters include C. H. Haskins, *Norman Institutions* (Cambridge, 1918), and Musset, 'Les actes de Guillaume le Conquérant'.

12   Giry, p. 795.

royal chancellor. All these aspects of royal charters in Carolingian and Capetian France have been seen to contrast with their counterparts in Anglo-Saxon England. According to Maitland, Stevenson and others, these differences resulted from the fact that English royal diplomas derived from the late Roman private deed, whereas royal documents in France were drawn up on the model of formal imperial decrees, the public acts of the late Roman empire.[13]

Following Giry's argument that Norman charters were derived from the royal diploma, R. Allen Brown applied the distinction between descent from private acts in England versus descent from public acts in France to the Norman charters as well:

> In their differences from the Old English royal diplomas the Norman ducal charters are descended from the Carolingian diploma and thus also from the late Roman public deed. It could scarcely be otherwise, for wherever one stands in the debate about continuity or discontinuity at and over 911, the nascent Normandy has ultimately to be seen as one of the Carolingian successor states.[14]

Reaffirming Giry's view that the Norman charters were modelled on the chancery products of the French kings, Brown therefore concluded that they also derived ultimately from the public acts of the late Roman empire.

The problem with this interpretation is that it rests on assumptions that were no longer valid by the time of the Conquest of England. The eleventh century is known to students of diplomatic in France as a period of anarchy during which rules regarding the redaction of royal charters broke down and documents came to be written more and more by their beneficiaries rather than by the royal chancery. Georges Tessier speaks with some disapproval of the 'contamination private acts exercised on the presentation of royal diplomas', while Giry complains of the 'poor taste of the times and peculiarities of expression' which characterised charters of the early Capetians.[15] The distinction between royal and non-royal charters and

[13] F. W. Maitland, *Domesday Book and Beyond* (Cambridge, 1897, reprt 1907), pp.230-31; Stevenson 'Anglo-Saxon Chancery', pp. 7-13; F. M. Stenton, *The Latin Charters of the Anglo-Saxon Period* (Oxford, 1955), p. 33; P. Chaplais, 'Some Early Anglo-Saxon Diplomas on Single Sheets: Originals or Copies?', in *Prisca Munimenta: Studies in Archival and Administrative History Presented to Dr. A. E. J. Hollaender*, ed. F. Ranger (London, 1973), 63-87 at pp. 71-72; S. Keynes, *The Diplomas of King Æthelred 'the Unready'* (Cambridge, 1980), pp. 29-30.

[14] R. Allen Brown, 'Some observations on Norman and Anglo-Norman Charters', in *Tradition and Change: Essays in Honour of Marjorie Chibnall Presented by her friends on the occasion of her seventieth birthday*, ed. D. Greenway, C. Holdsworth, J. Sayers (Cambridge, 1985), 145-63 at p. 149 (hereafter Brown).

[15] G. Tessier, *Diplomatique royale française* (Paris, 1962), p. 208 (hereafter Tessier); Giry, p. 735.

therefore between public and private acts was breaking down in eleventh-century France. Private charters were receiving royal sanction, and royal charters were assuming the characteristics of private acts.[16] To say that Norman charters were drafted in imitation of Capetian charters therefore says little beyond implying their heterogeneity. And to assert that the Norman charters were therefore descended from public rather than private documents makes little sense in a period which witnessed the 'contamination' of public acts by private. More importantly, Norman charters were evolving over the course of the eleventh century in response to political and social changes within the duchy. To trace that evolution, it is necessary to take a closer look at the internal and external characteristics of the Norman documents themselves and to consider the context in which they were written.

In contrast to eleventh-century Anglo-Saxon charters, early Norman charters were extremely diverse in form and content. It is difficult to make any generalisations that apply to the entire corpus surviving from the eleventh century. One overall rule, however, is that the Norman charters were essentially ecclesiastical in nature. With only three exceptions, they concerned the rights and privileges of ecclesiastical institutions, the majority recording agreements involving gifts, sales, mortgages and precarial grants between laymen and clerics.[17] A second general rule is that the documents were almost always drafted by the beneficiaries of these agreements, the monks or secular clergy involved in the transaction. This is apparent from the repeated use of certain formulas by specific houses, and also from the evidence of the same scribe writing documents exclusively for one *scriptorium*. Only a few of Richard II's charters in favour of different monasteries show enough unity of style to suggest a common origin.[18] Decentralisation of charter production helps account for the great diversity among early Norman documents.

In size eleventh-century Norman charters ranged from quite small – one document describing a sale to the abbey of Troarn measures only 15 x 26 cm[19] – to quite large, such as the pancarte of Saint Amand, measuring 75 x 50

---

[16] J. F. Lemarignier, *Le Gouvernement royal aux premiers temps capétiens* (Paris, 1965), pp. 42-46, 107-11.

[17] Those exceptions all concerned dowers: Fauroux nos 11, 58, and an unedited charter located at Archives départementales de l'Orne, 'Livre blanc' of St Martin de Sées, f. 35v-36r, cited in Tabuteau, pp. 138, 346-47, n. 172.

[18] See below, pp. 30ff.

[19] Archives départementales du Calvados H7843, ed. R. N. Sauvage, *L'Abbaye de Saint-Martin de Troarn au diocèse de Bayeux des origines au seizième siècle* (Caen, 1911), pp. 303-04.

cm with writing spilling over to the verso.[20] The script also varied greatly in these documents, from an elaborate diplomatic minuscule with high, curling ascenders and dramatic ligatures, to a simple bookish minuscule. Most charters were ruled on the back with dry point, but some were unruled. Validation was usually provided by a cross or a series of crosses placed below the text of the charter whereby participants in the act and witnesses expressed their consent. Their crosses were sometimes drawn by the witnesses themselves, sometimes added by scribes. The names of signatories were usually placed above or beside their crosses in the genitive form. There was, however, much variation in this practice. Sometimes the subscription lists appeared simply as *Signum* or *S* with the names of the witnesses written in the genitive; other times the names of the witnesses were simply listed below the text in the nominative case. And all these forms might even appear on the same charter.

The internal characteristics of these charters also show great diversity. Although they follow the general steps of protocol, text and eschatocol common to French and English charters, much variety exists within these parameters. For more than a century scholars have noted the absence of conformity and of consistent formulas in Norman charters. In his 1881 unpublished thesis, Armand Bénet noted a 'lack of fixed rules, divergences of dispositive sections, of formulas and above all of titles'.[21] And in 1988 Emily Zack Tabuteau likewise described the 'inconsistency of the charters', 'the absence of formulas', 'great fluidity of language concerning even the simplest transactions and virtual anarchy when complex ones are involved'.[22] Written on behalf of different ecclesiastical institutions by scribes who had come from many regions to restore the *opus dei* to this corner of north-western France, the early Norman charters not surprisingly assumed a great variety of forms.

Despite this diversity, certain patterns emerge when the charters are compared broadly over the reigns of Richard II, Robert the Magnificent and William the Conqueror. Under Duke Richard II, acts issued in his name and bearing his confirmation appear more often to conform to the model of royal diplomas before the 'decadence' deplored by French *diplomatistes*. The script frequently employed was like that of the royal chancery, a diplomatic minuscule with the first line written in elongated, highly stylized letters. As was often the case with traditional royal *acta*, this elongated script was

---

20 ADSM, 55H, *carton* 1, ed. M. J. Le Cacheux, *Histoire de l'abbaye de Saint Amand de Rouen des origines à la fin du XVIe siècle* in *Bull. Soc. Ant. Normandie*, 44 (1936), pièces justificatives, no. 2, 243-253.

21 A. Bénet, 'Etude sur la diplomatique des ducs de Normandie (912-1189)', *Positions des thèses*, École des Chartes (Paris, 1881), p. 3. On Bénet's thesis, see above note 5.

22 Tabuteau, p.12.

occasionally repeated in the final line of the charter.[23] One example of this format is the Saint Ouen charter of which the first and last lines were written by Dudo of Saint Quentin (Pl.1).[24] The script of this document, the presentation of the witnesses, and the chancery formula at the bottom were all reminiscent of traditional royal Carolingian diplomas surviving in the abbey's archives.[25] The ducal monogram appeared on four of Richard II's charters, in at least one case clearly modelled on the monogram of Robert the Pious,[26] and the only evidence of a *ruche* on a Norman charter also occurred under Richard II.[27] These features all reflect the influence of royal chancery practices on Richard II's *acta*.

More significant, however, was the frequent authentication of Richard II's charters by a single cross. Out of seventeen extant original charters of Richard II which bear crosses, eight were confirmed by the duke's cross alone. A charter for Marmoutier dated 1013-20 provides a borderline case since only two crosses appear at the bottom – one for Richard II and one for Richard III, who by that date was associated on the throne with his father.[28] Even in certain cases when the duke merely confirmed a charter written on behalf of someone else, it was his cross alone which authenticated the charter.[29] Although several documents during Richard II's reign were attested by many witnesses in the tradition of the Frankish private act, the sanction of ducal power, signified by Richard II's single cross, appeared sufficient corroboration for slightly over half his extant original charters which employ crosses. Thus, although Richard II did not routinely authenticate his charters with a seal in the royal manner, the authority of his cross in Normandy bears resemblance to the use of the royal seal in

[23] Giry, p. 513; Tessier, p. 76.

[24] Fauroux, no. 13. On this charter, see M. Fauroux, 'Deux autographes de Dudon de Saint-Quentin (1011, 1015)', *Bibliothèque de l'École des Chartes*, 11 (1953), 229-234.

[25] Two original charters from Charles the Bald dating 863 and 876 survive today in the fonds of St Ouen, ADSM 14H 143, edited by G. Tessier, *Recueil des actes de Charles II le Chauve*, 2 (Paris, 1952), nos 259, 407. These charters, although in poor condition, bear a striking resemblance to Fauroux no. 13.

[26] Fauroux, nos 15, 17, 34, 47; Fauroux, pp. 95-96, note 0.

[27] Fauroux, no. 34. This ruche was pointed out by Brown, p. 153, but it appears on a charter which survives only as a pseudo-original.

[28] Extant original charters with single crosses: Fauroux, nos 9, 15, 19, 21, 32, 37, 41, 44. The Marmoutier charter is edited, Fauroux, no. 23. I am very grateful to Simon Keynes for locating a facsimile of this charter for me.

[29] Fauroux, nos 19, 21, 37.

Carolingian documents.[30]

Internally, Richard II's charters also shared many characteristics with traditional Carolingian diplomas. The use of the monogrammatic and verbal invocations, and the pretentious, convoluted language of the preambles in many of Richard II's charters were reminiscent of royal charters of the ninth and tenth centuries.[31] Certain formulas also reflected Carolingian influence, in particular the *incipit 'Divina propitiante clementia'*.[32] The infrequency of the address, the frequency of devotion formulas, and the wordiness of the final clauses were all shared by the royal diplomas.[33] Also, the inclusion of fines in the sanctions of five of Richard II's charters recalled the monetary penalties for contravening Carolingian royal charters.[34]

An examination of the documents surviving in original form suggests that most of Richard II's charters were produced in two or three stages. Generally, the document appears to have been written ahead of time and presented to the duke for his confirmation during or shortly after the ceremony of conveyance. The duke's cross would be placed after the text, and subscriptions of other witnesses who were present at the ceremony would then be added and identified. An illustration of this procedure is provided by Plate 2. This charter described the donation which an individual named Hugh made to the abbey of Saint Ouen between 996 and 1026. The text of the charter was written first, the ducal cross was placed below the text, while the subscriptions of Richard II, Robert archbishop of Rouen and Hugh *qui hanc dedit* were written after the text in a different hand.[35]

---

[30] No actual seals appear on any of the surviving pre-Conquest Norman documents, but indirect evidence has led Fauroux, pp. 45-47, and Brown, pp. 153-55, to argue that Richard II occasionally used a seal to authenticate his charters. Although lost today, the authors of the 18th-century *Nouveau traité de diplomatique* IV (Paris, 1759),. Doms Grenier, Tassin and Toustain, described and provided a sketch of a pendant seal attached to Richard II's charter in favour of Saint Quentin, bearing the motto *Richardus nutu dei comes*. The characteristics of this seal, as it was reproduced in the *Nouveau traité*, are consistent with those of other seals from the late Carolingian period and therefore argue in favour of it representing an original ducal seal. I am very grateful to Dr Sandy Heslop for his comments regarding this evidence. The only pre-Conquest extant Norman charter with physical evidence of sealing is Richard II's *Propitia* charter for Fécamp, but this testimony is also indirect since internal evidence reveals that the charter as it survives is a pseudo-original.

[31] Fauroux, pp. 44-51; Giry, pp. 446-48; Tessier, pp. 84-85; A. de Boüard, *Manuel de diplomatique française et pontificale*, 1 (Paris, 1929), pp. 261-62.

[32] Fauroux, nos 34, 35, 36. This expression first appears in Normandy in a royal charter of Robert the Pious dated 1006. See below, note 51.

[33] Fauroux, pp. 48-49, 52; Tessier, pp. 85-88.

[34] Fauroux, nos 18, 34, 35, 36, 53.

Although this was not a ducal gift *per se*, and although it was confirmed by three men, the ducal cross alone corroborated the act.

A handful of charters from Richard II's reign provide exceptions to the general rule of decentralised charter production. As Fauroux has shown, four confirmations of the estates of the abbeys of Fécamp, Bernay, Jumièges and Saint Ouen reveal a unity of style and composition that indicate their common origin.[36] Since the Fécamp charter includes the subscription of *Hugo, cancellaris, scripsit et subscripsit*, Fauroux suggests that the abbey of Fécamp provided the outline of a ducal chancery under Richard II. Notarial subscriptions in imitation of the royal chancery appear on five other charters from Richard II's reign, two of them written by Dudo.[37] Fauroux also points out similarities between two charters for Saint Ouen and Saint Wandrille.[38] Both of these date from Richard II's reign, but nothing associates them directly to the four confirmation charters from Fécamp. Nevertheless, they support the argument against all charters during Richard II's reign being drawn up by their beneficiaries. Brown placed special emphasis on this evidence of central production of charters in the duchy, concluding that it 'strongly suggests that the duchy was ahead of the [Anglo-Saxon] kingdom' regarding secretarial arrangements.[39] The evidence for his case, however, was limited with few exceptions to these examples from Richard II's reign.

Giry's statement that the Norman *acta* imitated Capetian charters is to a certain extent supported by the charters from Richard II's reign, in that they shared many characteristics with the formal royal diploma. The occasional use of a monogram and frequent use of a single cross as authentication in Richard II's *acta* fit the pattern of the royal diploma, insofar as royal charters were traditionally confirmed by the king's seal alone, without the subscription of other attestors. The same is true of the archaic script of many charters, the long preambles, replete with passages from scripture, the extended final clauses with monetary fines supplementing spiritual penalties, and the chancery formulas. The possibility of chancery production also fits the royal pattern. After Richard II's reign, however, many of these features disappeared. In terms of their external form, both ducal and nonducal charters under Robert the Magnificent and William the Conqueror tended to be written in a minuscule more rounded and clear than the formal diplomatic script. The ducal monogram appeared on only one of Robert the

---

[35] Fauroux, no. 37.

[36] Fauroux, pp. 42-43.

[37] Fauroux, nos 13, 15, 18, 34, 42.

[38] Fauroux, p. 42, nos 24, 30.

[39] Brown, p. 161.

Magnificent's extant charters,[40] and on none of the Conqueror's.

More significant, however, is the disappearance of the single ducal cross as validation.[41] Of the twenty-eight extant original ducal charters from the reigns of Robert the Magnificent and William the Conqueror before 1066, none were authenticated by the ducal cross alone. Charters under Dukes Robert and William instead tended to have several crosses drawn beneath their texts for confirmation, thus conforming more closely to the model of private Frankish charters. A charter from Jumièges (Pl. 3) illustrates this shift in subscription styles.[42] In this case it is clear that various lords confirmed the charter by drawing their own crosses and a scribe wrote the name of each lord beside or above his cross. Only Archbishop Mauger attempted to sign his name himself. While charters with multiple crosses were not unknown during Richard II's reign, they were in the minority. During the reigns of Richard II's successors, on the other hand, multiple cross charters represented the great majority of acts, whereas the single cross act disappeared after Richard II's death.

Related to this change was the tendency after Richard II to have important charters which had been written years earlier presented again to the duke and other dignitaries for additional confirmation, with the result that even more crosses were added to the parchment. For example, Plate 4 shows the bottom part of a charter in favour of Saint Wandrille originally subscribed by Richard II and Richard III, then later presented to Robert the Magnificent, and later again to William the Conqueror.[43] Odo abbot of Cluny must have signed it during his visit to northern France in 1027, and Henry king of France in 1033. *Signum Heltonis* and the names of additional witnesses were added at yet a later time. This practice of collecting additional confirmations not only cluttered the bottom of the document, but led to some apparent chronological inconsistencies among subscriptions, which pose especially thorny problems to us today if the charter was later recopied in a single hand. Nor were later addenda necessarily restricted to the bottom part of the charter. On two separate occasions William the Conqueror confirmed and then modified a charter pertaining to Mont Saint Michel which his father had issued.[44] Both times the autograph cross of the Conqueror and the associated text were inserted in the middle of Robert the

---

40 Fauroux, no. 90.

41 The only charter after Richard II's reign that I have found bearing a single cross is that of Yves count of Beaumont on behalf of Fécamp, dated 1027-59, located at the Musée de Bénédictine, Fécamp, no. 12.

42 Fauroux, no. 100.

43 Fauroux, no. 55.

44 Fauroux, nos 73, 111. On this charter, see S. Keynes, 'The Æthelings in Normandy', *Anglo-Norman Studies*, 13 (1990), 173-205, at pp. 196-200.

Magnificent's charter, after the final clauses and before the subscriptions of Duke Robert's witnesses. The witnesses of William's confirmation, however, followed those of his father's grant. In the following century this arrangement posed a challenge to the author of the cartulary of Mont Saint Michel, who attempted to untangle Robert's charter from his son's later acts.[45]

In addition to including a greater number of people in the confirmation process, affixing more *signa* and reconfirming charters previously confirmed, it became more common for charters after Richard II's reign to show different witnesses participating in various stages of an agreement. Plate 5 illustrates this trend.[46] In 1088 Ralph son of Ansered made a donation to the monks of Jumièges with the consent of his lord Ralph of Mortemer to whom the property pertained. In exchange for his consent Ralph of Mortemer was to receive the *societatem* of the monks as well as fifteen pounds of Rouen money. These facts were stated in the main text of the charter and a row of autograph crosses followed, as the two Ralphs, their wives, children, assorted laymen and one ecclesiastical witness confirmed the agreement. Below the subscriptions a smaller, fainter hand recorded that Ralph of Mortemer's servant then placed the monks in possession of this property and his toll collector received fifteen pounds of Rouen money to deliver to Ralph of Mortemer. Three autograph crosses of Robert Curthose, his brother Henry and William count of Evreux then followed beside the left margin, and the names of the witnesses on behalf of Ralph son of Ansered and on behalf of the monks were listed beside them. Below that, the previous fainter script from above continued that Roger 'prior of this place', with two other men received possession of the land, and a final row of subscriptions followed, including those of three archdeacons, a chaplain, a chamber servant and several laymen.

What to make of this rather messy document? It seems the main text was written after the terms of the grant had been settled between Ralph son of Ansered, his lord Ralph of Mortemer and the monks of Jumièges. Witnesses present at the formal ratification of this agreement then signed their crosses. Because of the way the smaller, fainter script accommodated the crosses of Robert Curthose, Henry and William of Evreux, as well as the list of witnesses, it appears that these three crosses and the witness list were written before the fainter script, perhaps at the same time as the subscriptions above or shortly afterwards. Then the fainter hand recorded later that Ralph of Mortemer's toll collector received on his lord's behalf the fifteen pounds of money he had been promised, and Prior Roger gained formal possession of the property on behalf of Jumièges. And those who witnessed the final stage

45   Bibliothèque d'Avranches, MS 210, ff.26r, 29v.
46   Vernier, no. 37.

of this agreement added their crosses on the unruled portion of the parchment. The generous use of the autograph cross at different stages in these proceedings demonstrated the final move away from the single cross of Richard II's reign. It was more important that many people remembered participating in this act than that it was corroborated by the duke of Normandy.

As the single cross of Richard II's charters disappears, evidence of a chancery also fades. Fauroux's analysis of the ducal charters led her to conclude that the reign of Richard II offers the only indication of the possible existence of a centralised chancery.[47] An examination of the nonducal charters supports this statement, at least before 1066. Charters in favour of different ecclesiastical institutions might share certain features and formulas, but these similarities were too infrequent to argue in favour of central production, whereas charters in favour of the same houses often reveal closer affinity. Internal changes in Norman charters after Richard II's reign generally reflect an increased simplification and shortening of the text.[48] The lengthy preamble of Richard II's charters was reduced and in many cases omitted altogether. The notification, which appeared less frequently in Richard II's charters, came into regular use under Robert the Magnificent and William the Conqueror. Several charters simply began with the notification *Notum sit omnibus hominibus*, thereby skipping the invocation and preamble. And the final clauses, prominent during the reign of Richard II, gradually disappeared from the charters of his successors. In the later acts, moreover, the formula of corroboration which introduced the witnesses often separated them into two groups, witnesses on behalf of one party versus witnesses on behalf of the other. This development, which was not at all a characteristic of Richard II's charters, underlines the increased emphasis on the presence of witnesses and their part in the proceedings.

The evolution of Norman charters from Richard II's reign to William the Conqueror's reflects several developments in eleventh-century Norman history. One has to do with the perception of ducal authority, another with the rise of benefactions by nobles and lesser lords to ecclesiastical institutions, and a third with the increased participation of the laity in written records. The reign of Richard II was in several respects a high point of Norman history which was not regained until after 1066. In David Bates' words, Richard II was a ruler 'universally respected as someone who kept the peace at home and who was, in the broader context of northern French political life, a dedicated supporter of order and ecclesiastical reform'.[49] His

[47] Fauroux, p. 42.
[48] Fauroux, pp. 47-52.

reign also witnessed the creation of a literary school, centred around the duke's brother Robert archbishop of Rouen, which may well have had connections with Æthelwold's school at Winchester.[50] Certainly, the predilection for convoluted and exotic language was common to both.

Richard II was a loyal supporter of his king, Robert the Pious, who travelled to Normandy in 1006 and confirmed through a separate charter the duke's concessions to Fécamp.[51] On this occasion we see two scribes, one royal, the other Norman, drafting charters side by side.[52] Given the importance of the occasion, it is not surprising that the Norman scribe should endeavour to make his document as impressive as possible. This charter, the oldest original Norman charter in existence, appears to have set the standard for Richard II's subsequent formal acts with its diplomatic minuscule, its elongated first and last lines, and its single ducal cross. It may even have been a deliberate model for later acts, since the reform of the Norman monasteries emanated from Fécamp, with William of Dijon setting up schools to train both clerics and laymen.[53] Royal Carolingian diplomas with similar characteristics had also survived the Viking invasions at the monasteries of Jumièges, Saint Ouen and Saint Wandrille, as well as at the cathedral of Rouen, providing guidelines for the early ducal charters.[54] And the literary circle of Archbishop Robert no doubt also influenced the composition of Richard II's charters, as attested by the flowery language and

[49] D. Bates, *Normandy before 1066* (London, 1982), pp. 67-68. Also see H. Prentout, 'Le règne de Richard II, duc de Normandie, 996-1027: Son importance dans l'histoire', *Academie nationale des sciences, arts et belles lettres de Caen*, 5 (1929), 57-104.

[50] L. Musset, 'Le satiriste Garnier de Rouen et son milieu', *Revue du moyen âge latin*, 10 (1954), 237-66; M. Lapidge, 'Three Latin poems from Æthelwold's school at Winchester', *ASE*, 1 (1972), 85-137, at pp. 101-02; J. Campbell, 'England, France, Flanders and Germany: Some Comparisons and Connections', *Æthelred the Unready: Papers from the Millenary Conference*, ed. D. Hill, BAR, British Series, 59 (1978), pp. 255-70.

[51] Musée de la Bénédictine at Fécamp, no. 1, ed. *Recueil des historiens des Gaules et de la France*, 10 (Paris, 1874, reprt 1968), pp. 587-88. Richard II's charter is Fauroux no. 9. A facsimile of this document is published at the back of Haskins, *Norman Institutions*, pl. 1.

[52] These two charters were written on the same day and they share several passages. A comment in the royal charter that Richard II had already made his donation to Fécamp *et per cartae testamentum firmavit* indicates that the duke's charter was written first. *Ego Wido notarius* explained that he wrote Richard II's charter on the command of the duke.

[53] Bates, *Normandy before 1066*, pp. 193-94.

[54] Tabuteau, 273, n. 36. On the survival of royal Carolingian charters for the monastery of St Ouen, see above, note 25.

the spattering of Greek in some of his acts.[55] These diplomatic pretensions of grandeur fade, however, after Richard II's reign, in response to the breakdown of public control during the hard times of Robert the Magnificent's reign and the minority of William the Conqueror. As the perception of ducal authority declined, redactors of charters turned from models which emphasised the authority of the duke to those which focussed on the testimony of the witnesses. This explains the shift from single to multiple crosses as validation, the need to have old charters reconfirmed whenever the opportunities arose, as well as the impetus behind recording the participation of more witnesses in different stages of transactions and benefactions.

These changes were reinforced by two related developments: the increase in benefactions to ecclesiastical institutions by nobles and lesser lords, and the increased participation of these people in the literate form of the written charter. Although difficulties in dating charters render a precise number impossible, it is evident that relatively few Norman charters survive from Richard II's reign which technically deserve to be called private, that is, lacking any reference to the public, i.e. ducal or royal, authority. After Richard II's reign, however, and especially during the second half of the century, private Norman *acta* which survive as originals, contemporary copies or later cartulary copies number in the hundreds. The sharp increase of charters recording agreements and transactions between monasteries and lesser lords during the second and third quarters of the eleventh century on one hand reflect wider use of the written records.[56] Ecclesiastical institutions were more often securing their agreements with written as well as oral testimony. The same period also witnessed much greater participation on the part of lay people in the restoration of ecclesiastical life in the duchy. It was not simply a matter of better record-keeping which makes their participation visible today; new monasteries were founded and former ones revived by these lords after the first quarter of the eleventh century.[57] The increased involvement of secular men and women in the revival of monasticism in

---

[55] L. Musset, 'Sur la connaissance du grec et de l'écriture runique en Normandie sous Richard II: une erreur d'attribution', *Annales de Normandie*, 3 (1953), 84-87.

[56] On this subject in general, see M. Clanchy, *From Memory to Written Record, 1066-1307* (London, 1979); B. Stock, *The Implications of Literacy: Written Language and Models of Interpretation in the Eleventh and Twelfth Centuries* (Princeton, 1983).

[57] For a brief survey of this aristocratic contribution to the revival of monasticism in Normandy, see C. Potts. 'Les ducs normands et leurs nobles: le patronage monastique avant la conquête de l'Angleterre', *Etudes Normandes*, 3 (1986), 29-37.

Normandy and the growing use of charters to record transactions were two separate but interrelated trends.

The new private charters of early Normandy tended to be simple and short, moving from a brief invocation, if any, to notification and dispositive section. Final clauses were kept to a minimum and the witnesses either appeared with their crosses in the subjective form of the subscription or they were simply listed in the nominative. This stream-lined document had made a tentative debut during Richard II's reign, but then it had been more the exception than the rule. In the decades that followed, it came to be used more and more consistently for private acts, and it also influenced the form of ducal charters. Nor was it unique to Normandy. As Fauroux has already noted, outside influences, especially from the monasteries in the Loire valley, encouraged the Norman scribes to simplify their documents.[58] The origin of the short, non-solemn Norman acts, especially the row of autograph crosses which followed the text, lay with early Frankish private acts, themselves derived from late Roman private deeds.[59]

In conclusion, Giry's contention that the Normans brought to England in 1066 a diplomatic style imitating that of their king in France is misleading. In response to political and social conditions within the duchy, Norman charters by 1066 had evolved into something quite different from the traditional royal style. And although charters of the French kings in the eleventh century also assumed certain characteristics of private acts, similar development does not signify mimicry. As we have seen, the increase in the number of attestors became most striking in Normandy after Richard II's death in 1027. But the rise in royal charters with multiple subscriptions did not become significant until the reign of King Philip I, 1060-1108.[60] The statement that Norman charters at the time of the Conquest were modelled on Capetian charters cannot be sustained, and the corollary, that they originated from the public acts of the late Roman empire, has no basis. The distinction between descent from public acts in pre-Conquest Normandy versus descent from private acts in Anglo-Saxon England should therefore be abandoned. Once this misconception is dismissed, it becomes evident that although Norman and Anglo-Saxon charters at the time of the Conquest differed in many respects, in particular in the Norman use of the autograph

---

[58] Fauroux, pp. 47-48.

[59] For examples outside Normandy of charters with autograph crosses and successive stages of confirmations, see P. Colmant, 'Les actes de l'abbaye de Marmoutier jusque vers le milieu du XIIe siècle', *Positions des thèses*, École des Chartes (Paris, 1907), 51-56; P. Gasnault, 'Les actes privés de l'abbaye de Saint-Martin de Tours du VIIIe au XIIe siècle', *Bibliothèque de l'École des Chartes*, 112 (1954), 24-66.

[60] Lemarignier, *Le Gouvernement royal*, pp. 107-11.

crosses, multiple layers of attestors, and in diversity of form, they nevertheless shared certain characteristics which they both owed to early private acts. By 1066, Norman charters, like their counterparts in Anglo-Saxon England, generally appeared as unsealed acts written in a clear minuscule, bearing no notarial subscription, attested by many witnesses, threatening spiritual penalties for those who infringed upon their stated terms. These similarities suggest that it is not so much a question of which side of the Channel was ahead of the other regarding secretarial arrangements in 1066, but that the Conquest of England brought together diplomatic traditions in England and Normandy which were not incompatible.

Slaughter, Slavery or Ransom:
the Impact of the Conquest on Conduct in Warfare.
MATTHEW STRICKLAND

That the Conquest saw an aristocratic revolution, the near total replacement of the existing Anglo-Scandinavian nobility by one drawn from Normandy and North-West France is one of the most fundamental and incontrovertible consequences of the Norman invasion. But to what extent did the two aristocracies share conventions concerning conduct in war? Were the concepts of knighthood and the behavioural usages in war adopted and developed by the Norman nobility and recognisable from the early eleventh century essentially similar to those in operation among the late Saxon aristocracy, or did the Conquest bring a profound change not only in military institutions but also in perceptions of warfare? To address the totality of such a broad question is naturally beyond the scope of a single paper, so I have chosen to concentrate on one fundamental aspect of behaviour in war that reflects many of the broader issues, namely the question of ransom and the treatment of enemy warriors in battle. Constraints of space and time here preclude an exhaustive study of so central a theme; what follows therefore must only be some preliminary thoughts on the 'prehistory of ransom'.

How and when the heirs of Rollo and his Vikings abandoned the infantry tactics common to both the Scandinavians and Anglo-Saxons, and took to fighting from the saddle in the manner of the Franks is uncertain.[1] Equally obscure is the process by which the Norman settlers assimilated existing Frankish conventions concerning conduct in war, those behavioural customs operating in siege and battle that become clear and familiar from the late eleventh century, but which can be perceived, though only as through a

[1] Uncertain too is the date by which the charge with the couched lance became the predominant method of such cavalry warfare. See D. J. A. Ross, 'L'originalité de "Turoldus": le maniement de la lance', *Cahiers de civilisation médiévale*, 6 (1963), 127-38, and J. Flori, 'Encore l'usage de la lance... La technique du combat chevaleresque vers l'an 1100', *ibid*, 31 (1988), 213-40. It can only be noted here that the *Psalterium Aureum* of St Gall, c.884, shows a Carolingian horseman apparently with a couched lance (F. Mütherich and J. E. Gaehde, *Carolingian Painting* (London, 1977), p. 46), while the evidence of the Bayeux Tapestry strongly supports R. Allen Brown's translation of William of Poitiers which has Duke William using this method of attack in a skirmish in the early 1050s (R. Allen Brown, *The Norman Conquest* (London, 1984), p. 19 n.7). I would like here to record my considerable debt to Dr Simon Coupland for his generous assistance and advice on matters Carolingian.

glass darkly, in later Carolingian and early Capetian France.[2] Yet by frequent warfare, the Normans must have been exposed not only to such conventions, but also to the developing notions of Frankish knighthood, notions which, as Janet Nelson's penetrating study of Nithard has shown, were gaining a degree of coherence as early as the mid-ninth century.[3] Gleanings from William of Jumièges and the brief but vivid glimpse of the knightly *familia* of Gilbert of Brionne supplied by Gilbert Crispin's *Vita Herluini*[4] suggest that at least by the 1030s, significant elements of such conventions were in operation among the Norman aristocracy. With William of Poitiers' *Gesta Guillelmi*, we are unequivocally in a world where Norman lords perceived themselves as knights – as *milites*, heavily-armed, professional cavalrymen, belonging collectively to a warrior elite, a *militia*.

Though clouded by the language and style of classical imitation, the operation of conventions in war equally emerges from the *Gesta*: William, for example, pays compensation to the men of Dover when, despite their efforts to surrender, indisciplined Norman troops fire the burgh, while similarly the city of Exeter is guarded from sack once the citizens have capitulated.[5] Given the high incidence of siege warfare in and on the frontiers of the pre-Conquest duchy, the development of conventions concerned with siege is far from surprising, though their application in an Anglo-Saxon context suggested by these two examples is of the utmost interest. Equally significant, the *Gesta* clearly reveals the process of ransom at work in certain theatres of combat in which knights consciously sought to take enemy warriors prisoner rather than to slay them. Thus William of Poitiers recounts how while serving with the feudal host of the French king around 1050, Duke William slipped away from his main contingent and attacked a group of enemy knights. He unhorsed his first opponent, taking care, Poitiers specifically

2   See A. Levy, *Beiträge zum Kriegsrecht im Mittelalter insbesondere in den Kämpfen, an welchen Deutschland beteiligt war (8, 9, 10 Jahrhundert – Anfang des 11. Jahrhunderts)* (Untersuchen zur Deutschen Staats– und Rechtsgeschichte) 29, Breslau, 1889).

3   J. L. Nelson, 'Ninth-century Knighthood: the Evidence of Nithard', *Studies in Medieval History Presented to R. Allen Brown*, ed. C. Harper-Bill, C. J. Holdsworth, J. L. Nelson (Woodbridge, 1989), pp. 255-66.

4   Guillaume de Jumièges, *Gesta Normannorum ducum*, ed. J. Marx (Rouen, 1914); *Vita domni Herluini abbatis Beccensis*, ed. J. A. Robinson in his *Gilbert Crispin, Abbot of Westminster: A Study of the Abbey under Norman Rule* (Cambridge, 1911), p. 88 ff.

5   *Guillaume de Poitiers, Histoire de Guillaume le Conquérant*, ed. R. Foreville (Paris, 1952) (hereafter William of Poitiers), pp. 210-13. For the siege of Exeter in 1068, see *The Ecclesiastical History of Orderic Vitalis*, ed. M. Chibnall, 6 vols (Oxford, 1969-80) (hereafter Orderic), II, pp. 210-15, esp. pp. 214-15, an account based on the lost portion of William of Poitiers' *Gesta Guillelmi*.

notes, not to run him through. By the time the duke's retinue found their lord, he was leading seven other knights captive.[6] This emphasis on capture, as opposed to slaying, stands, I shall suggest, in stark contrast to Saxon and Viking conduct in regard to enemy warriors.

Nevertheless, it should be stressed from the outset that the application of ransom by the Norman knighthood was anything but universal or mandatory. The decision to capture rather than kill knightly opponents was dependent on a variety of factors. Of these, the most fundamental was the nature of the enemy. In warfare against the knights of the Capetian king, killing might be deliberately avoided. Hence Orderic notes that at the siege of Chaumont in 1098, the French defenders took care merely to slay the costly chargers of Rufus's knights, leaving the warriors themselves unharmed.[7] The pitched battle between the forces of Henry I and Louis VI at Brémule was similarly conspicuous for its lack of noble fatalities, with only three knights being slain,[8] while in 'civil' warfare within the Anglo-Norman *regnum*, such as the battles of Tinchebrai, 1106, or Bourgthéroulde, 1124, considerations of kinship, friendship or political empathy frequently ensured casualties remained at a minimum.[9]

The converse might be true, however, in the localized but bitter feuding between elements of the Norman aristocracy in the duchy both in the 1030s and 1040s and under the ineffectual rule of Robert Curthose. The taking of prisoners for ransom always remained a question of personal volition, and frequently the dictates of animosity and vendetta outweighed the financial advantages of ransom. Thus warfare between such families as Tosny, Clères and Beaumont could be singularly sanguinary.[10] Orderic recalled of Robert of Grandmesnil that it had been the death of his father Robert, and of Roger de Tosny and his two sons in battle against Roger de Beaumont that led him

6   William of Poitiers, pp. 24-27. The incident took place during the king's expedition against Geoffrey Martel and the siege of his castle of Mouliherne in Anjou, either in 1048 or 1051.

7   Orderic, V, pp. 218-19.

8   Orderic, VI, pp. 240-41. For a discussion of the veracity of these statements by Orderic see M. J. Strickland, *The Conduct and Perception of War under the Anglo-Norman and Angevin Kings, 1075-1217* (Unpublished PhD thesis, Cambridge University, 1989), pp. 88-94.

9   *Ibid.*, pp. 97-98.

10   D. C. Douglas, *William the Conqueror* (London, 1964), p. 42. Examples of knights being slain in localized feuds during Robert Curthose's troubled rule of the duchy are numerous. Thus, for example, Theobald, son of Waleran of Breteuil, and Guy 'the Red' were killed in the war between Robert of Bellême and Hugh of Grandmesnil (Orderic, IV, pp. 232-33), while during the war of the Breteuil succession in 1103, Reginald de Grancy personally slaughtered the vanquished defenders of a castle (*ibid.*, VI, pp. 44-45).

to abandon the world.[11]

Other constraints on the taking of prisoners for ransom concerned the practicalities of combat itself. If knights were hard pressed, or the opposing odds seemed too great, it was neither possible nor expedient to take prisoners in any number. The principal opportunity for capturing opponents lay less in the thick of the fray than in the pursuit, when the enemy were routed or retreating in disorder, and when assurance of victory gave freer rein to considerations of clemency and profit. Some notorious figures, such as Robert of Bellême, might spurn the notion of ransom altogether, preferring to let their captives die by torture or starvation. Such men, however, were the exception, and despite significant limitations, the convention of ransom was widespread enough among the Norman knighthood to offer a degree of security from immediate butchery on capture.[12]

The financial gains from ransom, moreover, ensured its frequent application, even if the exigencies of war meant that there would always be some fatalities in combat between knights. Indeed, the ransoming of important knightly captives was becoming such an integral part of aristocratic warfare that the acquisition of ransom was now a principal motive in warriors' participation in hostilities. This phenomenon is neatly encapsulated by Orderic Vitalis' account of William I's prolonged and unsuccessful siege of the impregnable hill-top fortress of Sainte-Suzanne in Maine from c. 1083-85 against Hubert, vicomte of Maine. The Normans, unable to take the site by storm, established a siege-castle in the nearby valley of Beugy, but their efforts were frustrated by the stout defence of the garrison, which was daily swelled by mercenary knights from all over France, seeking fame and spoils. Many leading Normans were slain, and eventually the toll of lives forced William to come to a negotiated settlement. But though there had been significant casualties, it was the wealth gained from ransoms that had attracted the soldiers of fortune and which had enabled Hubert to prolong his resistance indefinitely. As Orderic explains:

> Wealthy Norman and English lords were frequently captured, and Hubert the vicomte and Robert the Burgundian... and their other supporters made an honourable fortune out of the ransoms of these men. In this way, Hubert kept the Normans at bay for three years, growing rich at the expense of his enemies and remaining unvanquished.[13]

The convention of ransom was thus paradoxically a means of limiting the extent of killing and yet concomitantly an incentive for the prolongation and escalation of war. With similar ambivalence, an incident that occurred at the battle of Brémule in 1119 demonstrates both the limitations on the

11 Orderic, II, pp. 40-41.
12 Strickland, *Conduct and Perception*, pp. 111 ff.
13 Orderic, IV, pp. 48-49.

concept of sparing a noble opponent, and yet equally the extent to which the convention of ransom had become an accepted part of knightly conduct. A leading Norman rebel, William Crispin, fighting with the French, succeeded in breaking through the Anglo-Norman ranks and in striking Henry I a blow on his helmet. The knights surrounding the king struck down William and would have killed him in order to avenge the king had not Roger FitzRichard thrown himself bodily upon the prostrate knight, thereby risking his own life to take him captive.[14] In this instance, Henry's knights were ready to kill, not capture, whereas FitzRichard felt able to disregard the dictates of vengeance, even where the king was concerned, in order to gain a valuable ransom and spare William Crispin's life.

What then of Anglo-Saxon and Viking conduct in war? Mechanisms to restrict and contain the extent of fighting were clearly in operation. Particularly when armies were on an equal footing such as in the Alfredian wars or during the 'Reconquest', hostilities might be frequently punctuated by truces or more lasting treaties, often ratified by the exchange of hostages.[15] Repeated and unilateral extraction of tribute in return for the cessation of hostilities was more characteristic of the second phase of Viking assaults, sharply revealing the predominantly economic motive behind Viking aggression.

But if financial considerations dominated the inception, continuation and strategy of such warfare, conduct in battle itself appears to have been far less mitigated by a profit motive than among the Frankish and Norman aristocracy. It may be, of course, that the nature of the sources is misleading, creating a distinction more apparent than real, but even the most cursory reading of the *Anglo-Saxon Chronicle* conveys a strong impression of the frequency with which considerable numbers of high ranking men were slain in battle. Ealdorman Brythnoth and his men who perished at Maldon in 991 gained 'undying word-fame' by virtue of a skilful *scop's* verse, but many shared a similar fate. To take only Æthelred's wars, we read that in 1001, the Viking army joined battle with the men of Hampshire near Dean, 'and there Æthelweard the king's high-reeve was killed, and Leofric of Whitchurch and Leofwine the king's high-reeve, and Wulfhere the bishop's thegn, and

---

[14] *Ibid.*, VI, pp. 238-39.

[15] To give but a few examples, the *Anglo-Saxon Chronicle* records the giving of hostages and the swearing of oaths in 874, 876, 877, 878, and 893, while earlier it records merely that 'peace' was made with the Vikings, presumably for a price, in 865, 866, 867, 868, 871, 872, 873, and 874. All subsequent references to the *Anglo-Saxon Chronicle* (hereafter *ASC*) are to the translation by D. Whitelock, *English Historical Documents*, I (2nd edn, London, 1979) (hereafter *EHD*, I) for annals up to 1041, and for annals from 1042-1144 to the translation of S. I. Tucker in *English Historical Documents*, II, ed. D. C. Douglas (2nd edn, London and New York, 1981).

Godwine of Worthy, Bishop Ælfsige's son, and 81 men killed in all'.[16] Both the *Chronicle* and the skalds refer to heavy Saxon losses in the two battles fought by Ulfcetel against the Vikings, the first near Thetford in 1004, where 'the flower of the East Anglian people were killed', the second at Ringmere in 1010: 'the king's son in-law Æthelstan was killed there, and Oswig and his son, and Wulfric, Leofwine's son, and Eadwig, Ælfric's brother, and many other good thegns and a countless number of people'.[17] Ulfcetel himself perished, along with Ealdorman Ælfric of Hampshire and Ealdorman Godwine of Lindsey, during the great battle of Ashingdon in 1016, when, lamented the chronicler, 'all the nobility of England was there destroyed'.[18] Hyperbole perhaps, but the flood of obits of Saxon notables in such annals is as unequivocal as it is striking.

Such bloodletting, moreover, was by no means only the prerogative of victorious Viking armies: the Anglo-Saxons equally displayed a propensity to kill rather than capture enemy warriors. One Viking king and five jarls perished in the battle of Ashdown in 871, while several more jarls were killed in engagements that same year.[19] In 878, Ubba, the brother of Ivar, was defeated and killed in Devon along with 840 of his men, while in 893, the Saxon forces besieging Chester slew all those Vikings emerging from the beleaguered town.[20] The *Chronicle* records how in 1016, as Edmund Ironside pushed Cnut's army into Sheppey, 'the king killed as many of them as he could overtake', while Harold Godwineson's victory at Stamford Bridge resulted not only in the deaths of his brother Tostig and Harald Hardraada, but also in the virtual annihilation of the Norwegian force.[21]

16 *ASC* 'A', *s.a.* 1001.
17 *ASC* 'C' ('D','E'), *s.a.* 1004, and 1010. Though naturally their verse is heavily formulaic, the skalds convey a similar impression of Ringmere being a hard-fought battle. See Sighvald's *Ólafsdrápa*, Ottar the Black's *Head-Ransom* and Thord Kolbeinsson's *Eiríksdrápa* (*EHD* 1, pp. 333, 334).
18 *ASC* 'C' ('D', 'E'), *s.a.* 1016. Cf. Ottar the Black's *Knútsdrápa*, c. 8 (*EHD* 1, p. 336).
19 *ASC* 'C' ('A', 'B', 'D', 'E', 'F'), *s.a.* 871.
20 *Ibid.*, *s.a.* 878, 893.
21 *ASC* 'C' ('D', 'E'), *s.a.* 1016, 1066. The 'D' version of the *Chronicle s.a* 1066 says that after a heavy slaughter, Harold 'gave quarter to Olaf, son of the Norse king, and their bishop and the earl of Orkney and all those who survived on the ships'. Although one should not place overmuch reliance on the *Chronicle's* numerical precision, the extent of the Norwegian losses is suggested by the fact that whereas Hardraada's force that joined Tostig in the Humber in 1066 was estimated at 300 ships ('C'), the survivors filled only 24 ships ('D'). The statement by Snorri Sturluson in his *King Harald's Saga*, that Harold Godwineson offered quarter to Tostig and the Norwegians after the death of Harald Hardraada, but that they refused and fought to the death, is wholly unreliable (*King Harald's Saga*, trans.

The conclusion seems inescapable that the convention of taking prisoners for ransom *in battle*, clearly visible among Normans and Franks as a mechanism for controlling the extent of killing and for offering both fiscal gain and mutual protection to aristocratic opponents, was not an integral feature of Anglo-Scandinavian conduct. Killing in battle thus stands in marked contrast to raiding, where the Vikings in particular were anxious to seize as many captives as possible. So predominant an objective was this that the Vikings in Francia co-ordinated attacks on major religious centres to coincide with feast days, when they would be swollen with pilgrims, or they might take care not to destroy a monastery completely, but rather milk it regularly for slaves.[22] But the crucial point is that the majority of captives thus seized were not ransomed to kin, friends or lords, but enslaved and sold abroad, as one of the staple commodities – if not *the* staple commodity – of trade in the Viking world.[23]

The Saxons too might enslave captives. Some of the Ætheling Alfred's men seized by Godwine in 1036 were sold into slavery, while in 1052, when Harold Godwineson ravaged the coast near Porlock he seized 'what came his way in cattle, men and property'.[24] These latter men may have been redeemed, but this is certainly not the implication of the *Chronicle's* statement that in 1065, the Northumbrians who had marched on Northampton following their expulsion of Tostig not only ravaged the area but 'captured many hundreds of people and took them north with them, so that that shire and other neighbouring shires were the worst for it for many years'.[25] It seems, indeed, that the Saxons, Welsh, Strathclyde Britons, Irish and Vikings shared the same general attitude to the enslavement of prisoners of war. Males stood a greater chance of being slain outright, while women and children were destined for the slave markets of northern Europe or the

---

M. Magnusson and H. Pálsson (Harmondsworth, 1966), p. 153), for Snorri's account of Stamford Bridge is little more than a garbled conflation of a description of Hastings. He has the men from the ships run to the battle, take up Hardraada's standard and under Eystein Orri fight till the death, whereas it is clear from the *Chronicle* that it was precisely these men who had been guarding the longships and who had not taken part in the main engagement that were spared by King Harold.

[22] J. M. Wallace-Hadrill, 'The Vikings in Francia', *Early Medieval History* (Oxford, 1975), p.232 ; A. P. Smyth, *Scandinavian York and Dublin*, 2 vols (Dublin, 1975, 1979), II, pp. 130-31.

[23] See, for example, A. P. Smyth, *Scandinavian Kings in the British Isles, 850-880* (Oxford, 1977), esp. pp. 154-68, and *idem, Scandinavian York and Dublin*, II, pp. 24, 26, 30-33, 64, 72, 130-34, 240-42.

[24] *ASC* 'C' ('D'), *s.a.* 1036; *ibid.* 'E', *s.a.* 1052.

[25] *ASC* 'D' ('E'), *s.a.* 1065.

East.[26]

As Dr Chibnall has remarked, the Conquest was the first major invasion of England that did not result in the increase of the servile population.[27] Norman churchmen were firmly against the practice, and Orderic Vitalis, for example, roundly condemned the Norman marcher lord Robert of Rhuddlan for enslaving his Welsh captives.[28] In such actions, Robert was very much the exception among the Anglo-Norman knighthood, the majority of whom ransomed prisoners, sometimes even those of lowly rank.[29] It may be that Robert felt behavioural restrictions did not apply to the Welsh, regarded by the Normans as sub-human savages, but as one of the Normans operating in England prior to the Conquest, it is equally tempting to see his conduct as an assimilation of native Anglo-Saxon or indeed Welsh behaviour towards prisoners.

None of this is to suggest, of course, that the practice of ransom was wholly unknown before the Conquest. One might well argue that the extortion of *geld* from localities or kingdoms was a form of ransom on a grand scale, but in truth this was closer to the traditional practice prevalent between the barbarian kingdoms of the payment of tribute by a subject people to one exercising overlordship by virtue of military superiority.[30] On an individual basis, sporadic references occur to the ransoming of leading ecclesiastics by the Vikings. Thus in 858, the Franks bought back the royal chancellor, Abbot Louis of St Denis, and his brother Gauzlin for such a vast sum that a levy on the churches had to be supplemented with contributions from the king and the nobility in order to meet the required ransom.[31] In

---

26   Smyth, *Scandinavian Kings*, pp. 156, 158, and *Scandinavian York and Dublin*, II, p. 171 for a possible Norse-Scottish slaving raid against England. For slaving by Anglo-Saxons see D. A. E. Pelteret, 'Slave Raiding and Slave Trading in Early England', *ASE*, 9 (1981), 99-114, while for Wales see E. I. Bromburg , 'Wales and the Medieval Slave Trade', *Speculum*, 17 (1942), 263-69. Slaving by the Scots and Galwegians is discussed in Strickland, *Conduct and Perception*, pp. 305-311.

27   M. Chibnall, *Anglo-Norman England, 1066-1166* (Oxford, 1986), pp. 187-88. See also J. S. Moore, 'Domesday Slavery', *Anglo-Norman Studies*, 11 (1988), 191-220.

28   Pelteret, 'Slave Raiding and Slave Trading', pp. 111-114; Orderic, VI, pp. 138-39.

29   Thus, for example, following the suppression of the revolt by the citizens of Rouen in 1091, Robert of Bellême, William of Breteuil and other of Duke Robert's magnates took many of the wealthy burghers captive and forced them to ransom themselves (Orderic, IV, pp. 226-27). Similarly, Orderic mentions with approval how Richer de L'Aigle spared about a hundred peasants from Gacé who had sought sanctuary by a wayside cross, 'from whom he might have extorted a great price if he had been so irreverent as to capture them' (VI, pp. 250-51).

30   For an excellent discussion of tribute see T. Reuter, 'Plunder and Tribute in the Carolingian Empire', *Trans. R. Hist. Soc.*, 35 (1985), 75-94.

914, Edward the Elder had ransomed Bishop Cyfeliog of Archenfield for a far more modest 40 pounds, while it was Archbishop Ælfheah's refusal to allow money to be paid for his release that led to his death in 1012 at the hands of the men of Thorkel the Tall.[32]

Seculars could also be ransomed, though the majority of instances involve those only of the highest rank. In 923, the Limerick Vikings seized the retired king of Munster, Flaithbertach mac Inmainén who had entered the monastery of Loch Cré, while three years later the Dublin Vikings took prisoner and ransomed Fáelán, king of Leinster, and his son, Lorcán.[33] In 939, the Norse leader Óláfr Gothfrithsson gained two prisoners from whom he could expect great ransoms, Muirchertach, king of the Northern Uí Néill, and the Mercian noblewoman Wulfrun, the latter seized following an attack on Tamworth.[34]

Similar instances are furnished by the Frankish material. Thus the *Chronicle of Fontanelle* records that as early as 841, the Vikings ransomed 68 prisoners for 26 *lbs* of silver, Regino of Prüm that in 881 Eberhard the Saxon, son of Count Meginhard, was ransomed by his mother Evesa for a great price, while the Edict of Pitres, 864, forbade anyone to ransom themselves by giving the Vikings arms, armour or horses.[35] The edict's repeated prohibition of this practice suggests it was regarded as widespread.

But though such instances reveal the process of ransom at work, two qualifications need to be made. First, the majority of those thus ransomed had been taken not in battle, but during Viking raids or following the capture of cities or fortifications. Examples of warriors being spared in pitched battle expressly for ransom are rare, and I can find no examples of this phenomenon being recorded in the Anglo-Saxon sources. Second, the ransoming of captives by Viking forces – even their enslavement – was by no

---

[31] *Annales de St Bertin* (hereafter Annals of St Bertin), ed. F. Grat *et al.* (Paris, 1964), p. 77.

[32] ASC 'B', *s.a.* 914, ('A', *s.a.* 917, 'C, D', *s.a.* 915) : *ibid.* 'C' ('D', 'E'), *s.a.* 1012. The inflated account by Theitmar of Merseburg in his *Chronicle* has Ælfheah (mistakenly referred to as Dunstan) first offer to pay his captors a ransom to escape torture, but following the expiry of the time set for payment, instead bravely facing martyrdom (*EHD* I, pp. 349-350).

[33] Smyth, *Scandinavian York and Dublin*, II, pp. 21 and nn.19, 22.

[34] *Ibid.*, pp. 90, 91. Wulfrun was the mother of the great Mercian noble Wulfric Spott, who refounded Burton Abbey and of Ælfhelm, ealdorman of Northumbria (*cf. EHD*, I, no. 119 and 125).

[35] *Fragmentum chronici Fontanellensis, MGH, Scriptores* (hereafter *SS*), II, p. 307 ; *Reginonis abbatis Prumensis chronicon* (hereafter *Regino*), ed. F. Kurze; *Monumenta Germaniae Historica* (hereafter *MGH*), *Scriptores in usum scholarum* (Hannover, 1890), p. 117 ; *MGH, Leges*, I, p. 494.

means habitual. Even the greatest lords might be deliberately put to death on capture: thus the Frankish duke Seguin was executed in 845, and likewise King Edmund of East Anglia in 870, while in the same campaign, the *Chronicle* records that the Vikings slew the abbot and monks of Peterborough.[36] Between 858-59, a Danish force on the Seine had slain Baltfrid, bishop of Bayeux, Ermenfrid, bishop of Beauvais, and Immo, bishop of Noyon, while in 910 Archbishop Madalbert of Bourges met the same fate.[37] If some ecclesiastics taken on raids might be ransomed, there are as many if not more instances of high ranking clergy being slain in battle. Egbert's defeat at the hands of Viking raiders at Carhampton in 836 had cost the lives of bishops Herefrith and Wigthegn of Winchester, while in 871 Bishop Heahmund of Sherborne perished in the battle of *Meretun*.[38] The heavy Saxon losses at the battle of Ashingdon in 1016 included Bishop Eadnoth of Dorchester and Abbot Wulfsige of Ramsey.[39] While the integral role of bishoprics and abbeys to Anglo-Saxon military organization has long been recognized, the extent of such casualties raises important questions concerning the role of leading ecclesiastics in battle itself. The death rate would strongly suggest that rather than being present merely in a spiritual role, such churchmen were in arms and participating fully in the fighting. This was certainly true of Bishop Leofgar of Hereford, killed in action against the Welsh in 1056, while the presence of several abbots with Harold at Hastings may represent the Anglo-Saxon counterparts to militant Norman ecclesiastics such as Odo of Bayeux and Geoffrey of Coutances.[40]

If important lay and ecclesiastical figures were slain, other ranks and the *inerme vulgus* were still more vulnerable. The populations of Quentovic and Nantes, to cite but a few examples, were put to the sword, as were the citizens of Rouen who were not carried off; in 890, the garrison of St Lô was massacred.[41] The *Translation of St Germain* records how, following a raid, the Vikings retired with their captives but then hanged 111 of them.[42] Similarly, the *Annals of St Bertin* record how in 859, the Vikings entered Noyon, captured many leading clergy and laity, but having taken them away,

---

36   Ademar of Chabannes, *Historia*, ed. J. Lair, *Etudes critiques sur divers textes des xe et xie siècles*, II (Paris, 1899), III, p 17; *ASC* 'E', s.a. 870.

37   *Annals of St Bertin*, p. 81; *Annales Masciacenses*, MGH, SS, III, p. 170 ; J. M. Wallace-Hadrill, 'The Vikings in Francia', p. 224.

38   *ASC* 'C' ('A', 'B', 'D', 'E', 'F'), s.a. 836, 871.

39   *Ibid.* 'C', s.a. 1016.

40   *Ibid.* 'C', s.a. 1056 ; F. Barlow, *The English Church, 1000-1066* (London, 1963), pp. 170-71. For a general discussion of clerics in arms up to the 10th century see F. Prinz, *Klerus und Krieg im früheren Mittelalter* (Stuttgart, 1971).

41   Wallace-Hadrill, 'The Vikings in Francia', p. 229 ; *Regino*, p. 135.

42   *Miraculi sancti Germani*, MGH, SS, XV, pt. I, p. 12.

killed them.[43] The Annals of St Vaast record how in 880, the Vikings slew the captives they had taken in the Tournai region, while Regino of Prüm states explicitly that in 891 the Vikings put to the sword all those they captured after their victory on the river Geule. Likewise, Abbo of St Germain's account of the siege of Paris in 886-87 contains several instances of the slaughter of Frankish captives.[44]

One of Abbo's episodes is particularly revealing. At one point in the siege, a group of twelve Franks were surrounded by Northmen and called upon to lay down their arms. This they did, fully expecting that they could buy themselves back from captivity, but instead, they were treacherously cut down where they stood.[45] The Franks clearly anticipated the provision for ransom, only to be rudely disabused. Similarly in 881, during a pitched battle against the Vikings, Hugh, son of King Louis the Younger was wounded then slain. His father, however, believing that he had been captured, and hoping to buy him back, ordered his men to disengage.[46] It may be, of course, that such expectation for ransoms was a product of Frankish interactions with the Vikings, but these two instances at least suggest that notions of ransom were more developed among the Frankish aristocracy, and that in this area the Norman knights of the early duchy drew upon Frankish rather than Viking tradition.

How, then, does one account for such seemingly unrestrained killing in battle? In the earlier wars of the Anglo-Saxon heptarchy, the blood-feud certainly played a significant role,[47] although feuds might occasionally be bought off.[48]

---

[43] *Annals of St Bertin*, p. 81.

[44] *Annales Vedastini, MGH, SS*, I, p. 518 ; *Regino*, p. 137, and p. 138, where he notes that the following year, the Vikings slew all the inhabitants of a fortification in the Ardennes which they had stormed ; *Abbon: Le siège de Paris par les Normands*, (hereafter Abbo), ed. H. Waquet (Paris, 1942), pp. 38-40, 55-57.

[45] Abbo, pp. 56-7.

[46] *Annales Vedastini, MGH, SS*, I, p. 518.

[47] See, for example, Bede's story of the Northumbrian thegn Imma, captured following a bloody battle between Ecgfrith and Æthelred of Mercia in 679. His captor, a Mercian gesith, informed him that he deserved to die because several of the gesith's kin had perished in the engagement. It is significant both that Imma had first tried to pass himself off as a mere ceorl bringing food to the army (with the implication that as a warrior his life would have been at far greater risk), and that when spared, he was not ransomed back to his own people, but sold into slavery to a Frisian merchant. (*The Ecclesiastical History of the English People* (hereafter Bede's *Ecclesiastical History*), ed. B. Colgrave and R. A. B. Mynors (Oxford, 1969), pp. 400-05; J. M. Wallace-Hadrill, *Bede's Ecclesiastical History of the English People: A Historical Commentary* (Oxford, 1988), pp. xxv-xxvi, 161-62).

51

How much the concept of vengeance and feud played in subsequent wars, particularly the Anglo-Scandinavian conflicts of the ninth to the eleventh centuries, is far less clear. That a bitter and destructive feud could operate on a national scale in an earlier period is clearly seen in *Beowulf* in relation to the Geats' wars with the Frisians and the Swedes, but little or no weight can be placed on the revenge motives attached by late and unreliable sources to the invasions of the sons of Ragnarr Lothbrok, avenging their father's death in the snake-pit of Ælle of Northumbria, or to that of Svein Forkbeard, avenging his kin slain in the massacre of St Brice's day, 1002.[49]

Nevertheless, the concept of avenging one's lord, kin, and brothers in arms remained a highly potent source of motivation in war and battle. In her study of the poem *The Battle of Maldon*, Rosemary Woolfe argued against any strong historical or literary link between the poem and the old Germanic obligation recorded by Tacitus of dying for one's lord, suggesting instead that the Maldon poet might have been inspired by motifs drawn from the Old Norse *Bjarkamal*.[50] It is the concept of vengeance rather than self-sacrifice *per se* which is to the fore in the Maldon poem and in its Anglo-Saxon literary analogues. In *Beowulf* too, the hero tells Hrothgar on the death of his beloved thegn Æschere, 'Do not be sorrowful, wise man. It is better for anyone that he should avenge his friend than mourn greatly'.[51] Though one must be extremely cautious of saga material, it is worth noting that vengeance for a fallen comrade was specifically enjoined on the members of the Vikings of Jom, and it would seem unlikely if the military brotherhoods of Anglo-Scandinavian housecarls such as those of Cnut or Harold did not share a similar sentiment.[52]

48   Æthelred of Mercia. for example, paid the wergild of Ecgfrith's slain brother, Bede's *Ecclesiastical History*, pp. 400-01; *ASC* 'C' ('A', 'B', 'D', 'E', 'F'), s.a. 694, when the men of Kent paid Ine 30,000 pence for having burnt Mul, brother to Caedwalla of Wessex, seven years earlier.

49   The legend of Ragnarr's death at the hands of Ælle is fully discussed by Smyth, *Scandinavian Kings*, pp. 38-53. The story, from the *Speculum Historiale* of Richard of Cirencester (d. 1401), that Svein's aggression was to avenge the death of his sister Gunnhild and her husband, ealdorman Pallig, is cited uncritically by L. M. Larson, *Canute the Great* (New York and London, 1912), pp. 39-40. For details of the St Brice's day incident see S. D. Keynes, *The Diplomas of Æthelred 'The Unready', 978-1016* (Cambridge, 1980) (hereafter *Æthelred 'The Unready'*), pp. 202, 203-205.

50   R. Woolf, 'The Ideal of Men Dying with Their Lord in the *Germania* and the *Battle of Maldon*', *England before the Conquest*, ed. P. Clemoes and K. Hughes (Cambridge, 1971), pp. 63-81, 78 ff.

51   *Beowulf*, ed. and trans. M. Swanton (Manchester, 1978), pp. 100-01.

52   L. M. Larson, *The King's Household in England before the Norman Conquest* (Madison, 1904), pp. 154-56 ; C. W. Hollister, *Anglo-Saxon Military Institutions on*

Two further considerations may account for the sanguinary nature of pitched battle: the religious dimension of Christian against pagan, and in the case of the Anglo-Saxons, the desire to defend the homeland. The majority of warfare fought against the Vikings by Anglo-Saxons or Franks took place when the former were pagan, and their opponents were acutely conscious that they fought in defence of their faith. 'The heathen shall fall in battle' says Brythnoth, while Æthelweard, describing the battle of Tettenhall in 910, noted that in addition to the other leaders slain, 'Ivar lost his sovereignty and hastened to the court of hell'.[53] Wallace-Hadrill has remarked on the developed sense of Alfred as a champion not only of Anglo-Saxon independence but also of Christianity, visible both in Asser's *Life* and Alfred's own literary endeavours.[54] The same was equally true of Æthelred's wars, though here repeated defeat lent the struggle a far more pronounced penitential aspect, reflected for example in Æthelred's 'seventh' law code, the *agnus Dei* coinage, and Wulfstan's *Sermo Lupi*.[55] The baptism of Guthrum in 878 and that of Olaf Trygvasson in 994, to cite but two prominent examples, clearly illustrates the importance placed on conversion as a method of combating Viking aggression.[56]

The wars of both Alfred and Æthelred, moreover, were not merely wars against the heathen, but were unequivocally wars of defence, and as such received the unambiguous moral approbation of the Church. Ecclesiastical thinking had been set by Augustine who, drawing in turn on Cicero, had regarded a war of defence, fought as it was not for vainglory or a lust for conquest but to secure safety, freedom and the well being of the *patria*, as the most readily justifiable of all wars. As J. E. Cross has shown in a fine paper, the Anglo-Saxons were clearly conscious of this tradition, and applied it to their own circumstances.[57] Ælfric, for example, commented on Isidore's definition of a just war: '*Iustum bellum* is just war against the cruel seamen or against other nations who wish to destroy our homeland'.[58] Even when the

---

the *Eve of the Conquest* (Oxford, 1962), pp. 13-15. In this respect it is significant that II Cnut 77-78 stipulates that while a man who deserted his lord or comrades in battle was to lose his life and his lands, the heirs of a man who distinguished himself in battle by falling at the side of his lord were exempt from his heriot and could accede to his landed estate (*EHD*, I, p. 466).

53   *The Battle of Maldon*, ed. D. G. Scragg (Manchester, 1981), ll. 54-55; *EHD* I, p. 210 n.5. Cf. *The Chronicle of Æthelweard*, ed. A. Campbell (London, 1962), pp. 52-53.

54   J. M. Wallace-Hadrill, 'War and Peace in the Early Middle Ages', *Early Medieval History* (Oxford, 1975), 30.

55   Keynes, *Æthelred 'The Unready'*, pp. 217-19 ; *EHD* I, no. 240.

56   *ASC* 'C' ('A', 'B', 'D', 'E', 'F'), *s.a.* 878 ; *ibid.*, 'C', *s.a.* 994.

57   J. E. Cross, 'The Ethic of War in Old English', *England before the Conquest*, (hereafter 'Ethic of War'), pp. 269-82.

invading armies of 1066 were no longer pagan – Hardraada was nominally a Christian and a bishop was with him at Stamford Bridge[59] – Anglo-Saxon contemporaries would have viewed Harold's campaigns as an entirely justified war of defence.[60]

When the enemy was heathen, the armies of the Anglo-Saxons were fighting a *rihtlic gefeoht*, a just war on the double grounds of defence of the realm and a war against unbelievers. This attitude was clearly reflected in the penitentials. Homicide in a public war, or at the command of a legitimate ruler generally required abstention from church going and penance of forty days, whereas 'if an invasion of pagans overruns the country, lays churches waste, ravages the land and arouses Christian people to war, whoever slays someone shall be without grave fault, but let him merely keep away from entering the church for seven, or fourteen or forty days and when purified in this way let him come to church'.[61] Killing the heathen, moreover, might win eternal reward.[62] Rather than mitigating the extent of slaughter in battle, the Christian dimension may well have intensified it.

We must be careful, however, in transferring any equivalent concepts to the pagan Scandinavians. The idea that the Viking raids or settlements were motivated by militant paganism, fuelled by the cult of Odin, sits somewhat uneasily with the stress by current scholarship on the diversity and individuality of Viking worship and eschatological beliefs in this pantheistic culture.[63] Individual warriors doubtless worshipped Odin – Egil Skallagrimson or the Jarl Erik celebrated in the *Eriksmal* are cases in point[64] – but many men in large, composite armies such as the 'micel here' of 865, or

---

58   *Ibid.*, p. 272.

59   ASC 'D', *s.a.* 1066, 'the king [Harold] gave quarter to Olaf, son of the Norse King, and their bishop, and the earl of Orkney...'.

60   On his way to Stamford Bridge, Harold was met by Ælfwine, abbot of Ramsey, who told him that King Edward had appeared in a vision, promising that God would grant him victory in battle (Osbert de Clare, *Vita beati ac gloriosi regis Anglorum Eadwardi*, M. Bloc, 'La vie de S. Édouard le Confesseur par Osbert de Clare', *Analecta Bollandiana*, 41 (1923), 5-131, at p. 114).

61   Cross, 'Ethic of War', p. 281

62   For such ideas in a Carolingian context see S. Coupland, 'The Rod of God's Wrath or the People of God's Wrath? The Carolingians' Theology of the Viking Invasions', *Jnl of Ecclesiastical History*, 42 (1991), 535-54. I am grateful to Dr Coupland for allowing me to see this paper before publication.

63   A good summary is given by H. R. Ellis Davidson, *Gods and Myths of Northern Europe* (London, 1964).

64   For Egil's adherence to Odin, repeatedly stressed in his skaldic verse, see *Egil's Saga*, trans. H. Pálsson and P. Edwards (Harmondsworth, 1976) ; the *Eiríksmál* is translated in N. Kershaw, *Anglo-Saxon and Norse Poems* (Cambridge 1922).

those of Svein Forkbeard, may have honoured Thor or other deities. In short, while equally one must not underplay the extent of destruction suffered by the Church and lay society at the hands of the Vikings, it is dangerous to apply monotheistic, Christian, notions of corporate religious sentiment, still less carefully developed theories of the justification of killing, to Viking armies.

One need perhaps look no further than the simple dictates of military and political pragmatism to explain the habitual slaying of opponents, particularly those of high rank. The deliberate massacre of captives or anyone offering resistance might be a highly effective psychological weapon against the enemy, sapping the will to resist by studied terrorism; such a policy was to be employed to great effect by, among others, the Mongols and the Swiss. Enemy commanders or military elites, moreover, have always been a prime target in warfare. 'As the saying goes', noted the *Chronicle* when describing Ealdorman Ælfric's treachery in 1003, '"When the leader gives way, the whole army will be hindered".'[65] Resistance would crumble all the more if enemy leaders were slain. Thus the killing by the Vikings of the two rival kings of Northumbria in 867, or of King Edmund of East Anglia in 870, removed powerful figureheads around which resistance might concentrate, and facilitated the suppression and occupation of an area for settlement.[66] Likewise, there could be no more certain way of crippling the military potential of a kingdom or of an invading force than by physically slaying as high a proportion of its warrior aristocracy as possible. Cnut's seemingly untroubled rule in England must owe a good deal to the fact that many leading Saxon nobles had perished in the past twenty or so years of warfare before the bloody coup of 1017, while the carnage at Hastings, which was to be unequalled on English soil till the battle of Evesham in 1265, strongly suggests that similar considerations were to the fore of Duke William's mind in 1066. Papal sanction, the claim that Harold was a perjurer and the Saxon rebels in arms against his rightful authority gave him a legitimate reason to extirpate the house of Godwine and many of their leading supporters on the field of battle to an extent that would have been scarcely conceivable in contemporary warfare between Norman and Norman, or Norman and Frank. It seems no coincidence that to find a precursor of the penitential drawn up by the Norman episcopate and endorsed by Ermenfrid of Sion by 1070, one has to go as far back as the general penance issued by the Council of Soissons in 924, following the bloody engagement between Robert, count of Paris and Charles the Simple.[67] The issue of such a penitential strongly

---

65 *ASC 'C'*, s.a. 1003.

66 *Ibid.*, 'C' ('A', 'B', 'D', 'E', 'F'), s.a. 867, 870.

67 The penitential of Ermenfrid and its context, including the penitentials issued after the battles of Fontenoy, 842, and Soissons, 924, are fully discussed by H. E. J.

suggests that to European ecclesiastics at least, Hastings involved quite unusual carnage.

If the distinction I have suggested between Norman and Anglo-Scandinavian behaviour towards their opponents is a valid one, how is one to explain this divergence of conduct? The answer seems to lie in the nature and context of the warfare itself. Late Saxon military institutions – the burghal system, the fyrd and the fleet – were designed essentially for defence, to ward off the constant threat of raiding and invasion by external enemies, and were deployed by a strong 'centralized' monarchy. Though the society was geared for war, periods of actual hostilities were restricted largely to the latter years of Æthelred's reign, the incursions of Gruffyd ap Llywelyn in the 1050s, and the year of battles in 1066. When war was fought, it was against foreigners – Danes, Norse, Welsh and in 1066, Normans – as an act of expulsion or destruction culminating in bloody pitched battles such as Ashingdon, Fulford, Stamford Bridge and Hastings. Though men like the ætheling Æthelwold in 903 or Tostig who served with a foreign invader might be cut down,[68] the events of 1051 and 1052 reveal a deep seated reluctance on the part of many of the Anglo-Scandinavian nobility to fight against either their kinsmen and countrymen when internal conflicts came to a head. As the *Chronicle* noted, war was avoided following Godwine's return to England in 1052 because 'it was hateful to almost all of them to fight against men of their own race, for there was little else that was worth anything apart from Englishmen on either side'.[69]

In eleventh-century Normandy, the context of war was radically different. Private war was endemic both before Duke William's consolidation of power and later under the ineffectual rule of Robert Curthose. And though the military forces of the duchy might be frequently directed against any or all of Normandy's neighbouring principalities, the castles, military households and enfeoffed vassals of the Norman nobility were designed as much for defence and aggression against each other and to resist ducal authority as to counter Angevin, Capetian, Manceaux or Breton attack. The religious dimension so prominent in Æthelred's wars was largely if not wholly absent, since opponents were all Christian.[70] Instead of urging the

---

Cowdrey, 'Bishop Ermenfrid of Sion and the Penitential Ordinance following the Battle of Hastings', *Jnl. Ecclesiastical Hist.*, 20 (1969), 225-42; *cf.* Cross, 'Ethic of War', pp. 280-81.

[68] *ASC* 'A', 'B', 'C', 'D', *s.a.* 903 : *ibid.* 'C', 'D','E', *s.a.* 1066.

[69] *ASC* 'C', 'D', *s.a.* 1052 ; *cf. ibid.* 'D', *s.a.* 1051, and 'Florence of Worcester', *s.a.* 1051 (*EHD* II, pp. 219).

[70] A notable exception was Count Helias of Maine's decision to treat his defence of Maine against William Rufus as fulfilment of his crusading vow (Orderic, V, pp. 228-31).

extirpation of the heathen, here the role of the Church, through the Peace and Truce of God, was to attempt to regulate and confine hostilities between the knighthood of northern France.[71]

Still more important, in assimilating the Frankish institutions of the castle, heavy cavalry and the accompanying tenurial structures, the descendants of Rollo had inevitably come to abandon their highly mobile tactics of raiding in favour of a more static, land-based form of warfare, in which they fought on horseback as knights, displaying their prowess with lance and sword. The warhorse had replaced the longship as the principal vehicle for offence.[72]

The consequences of this change were profound. First, the constant training needed to fight from the saddle created a heightened sense of a profession of arms and a milieu in which the aristocracy came increasingly to identify itself with its military function. Thus, as George Duby has shown, first castellans, then greater nobles and finally counts and dukes came to style themselves *miles* in charter attestations; not every knight was a great lord, but every great lord was a knight.[73] If William of Jumièges' portrait of Duke Robert I still has a late Carolingian flavour to it, Duke William I emerges from Poitiers' *Gesta Guillelmi* predominantly as a knight, not simply a just prince but the flower of the *militia* of northern France.

Secondly, the Norman aristocracy had become a settled, landowning nobility, closely interconnected by ties of kinship, marriage and vassalage. Thus for all the incessant dynastic feuding between Norman families, opponents in such engagements were well known quantities, permanent if aggressive neighbours, not sporadic alien invaders. Raiding and slaving on an occasional basis from a distant kingdom was one thing, but such actions against fellow countrymen, who were not only knights but actual or potential kinsmen, was quite another. Not only were the slave markets less accessible once Normandy had turned from the Scandinavian world toward France, but from Carolingian times, the Church had not tolerated the enslavement of Christian captives. Besides, there were only so many times that one could ravage a neighbour's lands with profit, and to depopulate

---

71   See H. E. J. Cowdrey, 'The Peace and Truce of God in the Eleventh Century', *Past and Present*, 46 (1970), 42-67.

72   For the use of warhorses and development of studs by the Normans see R. H. C. Davis, 'The Warhorses of the Normans', *Anglo-Norman Studies*, 10 (1987), 67-82, and *idem*, *The Medieval Warhorse* (London, 1989), p. 55ff.

73   G. Duby, 'The Origins of Knighthood', *The Chivalrous Society*, trans. C. Postan (London, 1977), pp. 158-170. *Cf.* R. Allen Brown, 'The Status of the Anglo-Norman Knight', in *War and Government in the Middle Ages*, ed. J. Gillingham and J. C. Holt (Woodbridge, 1984), pp.18-32.

totally his estates made little long-term sense, as well as creating a dangerous precedent.

Something of the resulting attitudes of neighbouring knightly families in the early duchy is suggested by the later *conventio* of the 1140s between the earls of Chester and Leicester, which demonstrates the mentality of two powerful lords, confronting each other territorially but equally enough matched to regulate in writing the nature of future hostilities between them.[74] No such document survives for the eleventh-century duchy, if indeed any were written, but it amply conveys the need, equally vital in Normandy, for regulation and restraint in conduct between lords who had no option but to co-exist, even where future hostilities were presupposed.

Private war, moreover, was on a very modest scale, consisting of skirmishes, raids and ravaging over a restricted area launched from castles in the locality. The interminable nature of these petty quarrels suggests that the forces of warring aristocratic families were as a rule equally balanced; unless ducal intervention tipped the scales, there could be no swift victories achieved by overwhelming odds, no permanent settlement by force of arms. Such considerations were equally valid for war between the territorial principalities themselves. The protracted nature of this warfare, moreover, was only exacerbated by the dominance of the castle and the prevalence of siege in an age when the art of defence still considerably outstripped that of attack.

This combination of the localized, familiar nature of the enemy and the changed methods of warfare itself provided a context in which behavioural conventions were bound to develop. If war was to be an integral part of a warrior's existence – and there is nothing to suggest the Normans would have had it any other way – then it was in the best interests of the *militia*, of the knighthood as a class, to develop and adhere to conventions of conduct which afforded mutual advantage and a degree of protection. The change from ship-borne raiding to land-based cavalry warfare must have severely restricted the opportunities for pillage and enrichment from booty formerly enjoyed by the Vikings. Certain expeditions beyond the duchy's frontiers might well be profitable – the invasion of England stands, of course, *sui generis* in this context – but there was no more *geld*. Ransom offered an effective alternative: it made war pay handsomely, offered some guarantee of eventual release and security from killing and enabled a man, if he was wealthy enough, to survive defeat on more than one occasion.

By 1066, killing on the scale habitually seen in Anglo-Scandinavian warfare was a remote phenomenon for the Norman knighthood. The Conquest was to see not simply the introduction of knight-service, but also

---

74 For the text and translation of this famous *conventio* see F. M. Stenton, *The First Century of English Feudalism* (Oxford, 1961), pp. 250-53, 286-88.

that of differing conceptions and conventions of warfare. There is thus a certain irony that the battle of Hastings, which made such a transformation possible, was for many Normans to be the largest and most bloody engagement they would ever experience, fought as it was in a desperate war of conquest against men felt to be beyond the behavioural restraints in operation between members of the Norman knighthood itself.

Domesday Lawsuits:
a Provisional List and Preliminary Comment
PATRICK WORMALD

Of all the myriad questions raised by the wonder that is Domesday Book, the most insistent seems almost ungrateful: what in fact was it *for*? Whatever else it says, it does not tell us this. Nearly a century ago, Maitland gave a characteristically lapidary answer: 'Domesday Book is no register of title, no register of all those rights and facts which constitute the system of landholdership. One great purpose seems to mould both its form and its substance; it is a geld-book.' The 'geld-book' view as such was of course thoroughly demolished by Galbraith. That 'Domesday Book is no register of title' has also been questioned. Another trend, inaugurated in 1933 by David Douglas, has upheld what might be called the 'loose ends' proposition: twenty years after Hastings, as death approached, the Conqueror felt a need to resolve the many disputes of the 'Conquest Settlement', to cut the knots and smoothe the creases left by 1066. Christmas 1085, when William still faced the greatest international crisis of his life, may seem an odd time to be tidy-minded; nor could he have foreseen the accident that killed him at a robust sixty. These objections, however, have now been magisterially met by Sir James Holt's own contribution to his valuable collection of novocentenary essays. Holt has no doubt that the survey's main concern was to make manorial lordship yield fiscal dividends. But this asked a lot of baronial landowners. Domesday Book was also, therefore, their *quid pro quo*. It gave them formal title of endowment; it was the charter of the new regime. The urgency was that because William planned to attack the French king, he had to be sure of his men's exclusive support. The Domesday 'charter' was thus exchanged for the 'Oath of Salisbury', when the landowners of England 'swore... loyalty to him against all other men'. Holt's case was simultaneously reinforced by Hyams, whose 1986 paper in effect challenges the view encapsulated by the phrase, 'No register of title'.[1]

[1]   F. W. Maitland, *Domesday Book and Beyond*, reissue with introduction by E. Miller (London, 1960), p. 25; V. H. Galbraith, *Domesday Book. Its Place in Administrative History* (Oxford, 1973), pp. 161-73 – the last of many statements of his case; D. C. Douglas, 'Odo, Lanfranc and the Domesday Survey', in *Historical Essays in Honour of James Tait*, ed. J. G. Edwards, V. H. Galbraith, E. F. Jacob (Manchester, 1933), pp. 47-57 – followed up in his 'The Domesday Survey', *History*, 21 (1936), 249-57, esp. at pp. 256-57, and in his *The Domesday Monachorum of Christ Church Canterbury* (London, 1944), pp. 26-33, as well as in his *William the Conqueror* (London, 1964), pp. 346-54 esp. at pp. 352-53; E. Miller, 'The Ely land pleas in the reign of William I', *EHR*, 62 (1947), 438-56 – perhaps the most effective of arguments along the Douglas lines; J. C. Holt,

This line of argument might have been expected to inspire some study of the disputes actually recorded in the Book itself, but this is not the case, as Hyams noted. The first thing to stress about the list which I have here attempted to compile is its limitations. I see this as a first step on a long road, where I neither expect nor hope to travel alone if I travel further at all. There may well be gaps, and there must surely be inconsistencies (the original text is by no means wholly consistent itself). My cross-references depend heavily on the indices of the Morris/Phillimore series, whose shortcomings thus become my own. I have not used any Domesday data-base (though I have received welcome help from Robyn Fleming, the human agent for one of them). But we now have a ground-base of sorts for further advance. This paper also essays a new (if necessarily brief) glance at the 'loose ends' theory in the light of it.[2]

I begin with the criteria set out at the head of my catalogue of Domesday lawsuits (p. 77, below), which determine what gets into the main list and what is relegated to appendices (the latter intended, among other things, as some sort of recompense to those satisfied by looser criteria). The first is obvious enough. Domesday Book also refers to twenty-nine suits of the previous twenty years (only five otherwise recorded), along with thirty-seven forfeitures or amercements for what passed as crime. Interesting and important as these are, the main list consists of suits heard or generated by the 1086 enquiry itself. The others appear in Appendices A and B. The second point is rather more difficult. Throughout Domesday Book, there are

'1086', in *Domesday Studies. Papers read at the Novocentenary Conference, Winchester 1986*, ed. J. C. Holt (Woodbridge, 1987), 41-64; P. R. Hyams, '"No Register of Title": the Domesday Inquest and Land Adjudication', *Anglo-Norman Studies*, 9 (1986), 127-41. This paper is so far as possible what was read at the Harlaxton 1990 proceedings. But I have modified some of the arguments, and corrected a number of errors, with the help of those who first heard it, and several other Domesday *doyens* who kindly read it since: I am especially grateful to the late Ralph Davis, and to David Bates, Judith Green, Sir James Holt, John Hudson, Simon Keynes, Henry Loyn, David Postles, David Roffe, Peter Sawyer, Tessa Webber, Ann Williams and (alphabetically last but never least) Jenny Wormald.

2 Sir Henry Ellis set a trend when devoting just one page to the 'clamores', *A General Introduction to Domesday Book*, 2 vols (London, 1833) I, pp. 32-33. Short too, if incisive, was V. H. Galbraith, *The Making of Domesday Book* (Oxford, 1961), pp. 70-74. R. Welldon Finn, *The Domesday Inquest and the Making of Domesday Book* (London, 1961), pp. 92-111, is the most extensive discussion; and his *An Introduction to Domesday Book* (London, 1963), pp. 61-67, 89-92, anticipates some of the arguments set out below (see note 14). The selection of Domesday suits in R. C. van Caenegem's important *English Lawsuits from William I to Richard I* (Selden Society, 106-7, 1990-91) uses stricter criteria than mine, so arriving at 111 cases (counting some I classify as 'king's pleas').

a very large number of instances where a claim is recorded, sometimes with a foretaste of formal legal process, but where no explicit verdict is offered. We may suspect, we may even know (e.g. Appendix D nos 5, 49), that a judgement was in fact given. The difference between cases included or excluded can be as slight as that between the words *'testatur'* and *'gaurant'* used of Roger Bigot's shrieval support respectively in no. 295, and Appendix D no. 58. But one has to draw lines in such exercises, and it is best to do so where the survey seems, however fortuitously, to draw them itself. Appendix D contains a selection of cases excluded by my second criterion. The most problematic criterion is the third: main-list lawsuits are those where *both* parties were king's subjects. Some of the most colourful and absorbing 1086 disputes have the king, so to speak, as a litigant. At issue is endorsement of a party's title as such, without reference to any specific rival. That title did apparently have to be endorsed by royal authority is of course hugely important. But title to which the king takes exception in his own right is not the same thing as title contested by two sets of claimants. Further, had I included the 114 pleas of that type tentatively listed in Appendix C, I should logically have included too the *'invasiones'* added to the survey of the three eastern shires in Domesday Vol. II, together with the *'Terrae Occupatae'* incorporated by *Liber Exoniensis*. These annexations or usurpations are explicitly or implicitly *'super regem* (against the king)'; but in what sense, and for what reasons, are awkward questions.[3] And, besides raising a number of special difficulties which I prefer at present to avoid, their inclusion would expand my list well beyond the bounds of manageability.

To show how the criteria operate, the following example is roughly half way through the list (no. 177):

> In Willoughby Hundred [Lincs], the bishop of Durham claims *(clamat)* against *(super)* Gilbert de Ghent the land of Alnoth the priest. And the men of the Riding say *(dicunt)* that they never saw that the bishop's predecessor *(antecessorem)* was put in possession *(saisitum)* either by writ *(brevem)* or by official *(legatum)*. And they attest it to the use *(testantur ad opus)* of Gilbert.

This dispute belongs to the largest single category of Domesday lawsuits: those *'clamores'* included as supplements to the records for the three counties of Huntingdonshire, Yorkshire and Lincolnshire. It evidently meets the operative criteria; it was heard before the 1086 commissioners; local opinion is given its say; invocations of a 'writ' or 'official' are often encountered in 'king's pleas'; but they relate here to the Bishop of Durham's right (or lack of

---

3   *Domesday Book* (hereafter *DB*), II 99a, 273b, 447b; *Essex* 90, *Norfolk* 66, *Suffolk* 76; *Exon.* ff. 495-525. Cf. (e.g.) Appendix C nos 22, 35, 47, 84-86. Galbraith, *Making of Domesday Book*, p. 176, rightly protested against tendencies to lump *'invasiones'* together with the *'clamores'* (lawsuits proper) found as appendices to counties in 'Circuit VI' (see below).

it) as against a competitor. The suit is also a good illustration of the issues usually involved in Domesday disputes. Quite a high proportion are straightforward contests over parcels of property (frequently tiny, as in this instance, where what is at stake can no longer be located). Reference is often made to pre-Conquest tenants, named or otherwise, and the connection, if any, between them as *antecessores* and present incumbents. There are 339 such lawsuits in Domesday Book. Whatever regrets may be felt about the many more confined to my appendices or excluded even there, this should be quite enough for preliminary comment.

The first point to note from the list and subjoined statistics is that the incidence and description of dispute settlement in Domesday Book varies so much between 'circuits'. A simple illustration is the nature of the testifying body, revealed in the penultimate column.[4] On the so-called 'first', 'third' and 'seventh' circuits (i.e. those of the south-east, Home Counties and East Anglia) the hundred has a virtual monopoly of the evidence, though shire and even sheriff get in on the act occasionally in the first, and still more occasionally in the third and seventh. The county, on the other hand, is always cited on the fifth (north-western) circuit, while on the second (south-western), Wiltshire cases quote the 'thegns' of the shire, and Devon 'the Frenchmen'. The sixth circuit (north, plus Huntingdonshire on the way up the Great North Road) contains all but two of the references to *sworn* evidence, though we do of course know that all evidence submitted to the Commissioners had to be on oath.[5] In fact, both Huntingdonshire and Yorkshire lose interest in 'jurors' as such after a few entries, while the title of the South Riding *'clamores'* is one of very few references to oaths in the huge

---

4   For the 'Circuits': C. Stevenson, 'Notes on the Composition and Interpretation of Domesday Book', *Speculum*, 22 (1947), 1-15; with Galbraith, *Making of Domesday Book*, p. 8; and *Domesday Book*, pp. 37-39; see too note 6. Neither Galbraith and Stevenson, nor the earlier scholars they criticized, seem to have been much influenced by adjudicatory variation; but my table strongly supports Galbraith's apparently impressionistic survey, *Making of Domesday Book*, pp. 70-74.

5   Sworn evidence furth of Circuit VI: no. 62, and Appendix C no. 3; evidence for the general use of sworn inquest procedures: Galbraith, *Making of Domesday Book*, pp. 35-39, 60-63; and *Domesday Book*, pp. 33-36. It should be noted that the adjudicatory pattern of 'king's pleas' is essentially the same as that of the main list; but the shire features in Appendix C nos 3, 10, 14, 18, 20, 22, 25-27, 32-36, the hundred in nos 29, 69, 'thegns' in 30, 'English' in 28, and 'French and English' in 31 (the *'francigenae'* of *Exon.* in main list no. 26 may perhaps be identifiable with the *'baronibus regis'* said by Domesday Book itself to have given a seemingly earlier judgement for Bishop Osbern, but cf. the *'barones'* of Appendix C no. 28). Appendix C nos 46 and 48-49 give the county as the adjudicating body (such as it was) of 'Circuit IV'.

corpus of Lincolnshire pleas. The pattern on this circuit can be broken down further. When not citing jurors, Yorkshire's East Riding uses the county in all but the last instance, whereas the West always cites wapentakes before a final reference to a Riding. In Lincolnshire, the dominant wapentake makes way for Riding or Shire in some of the Lindsey suits, but not in those of Kesteven, where only the last few feature the 'men of Holland'. The conclusion to be drawn from this may merely be that the collection of evidence was differently organized from place to place, which is interesting but not surprising. But variations in the actual distribution of cases have more disturbing implications.

Among the notorious deficiencies of 'Circuit IV' is that it gives no 1086 disputes at all. 'Circuits' II and V are not very much more informative. By contrast, Lincolnshire's 126 inter-subject conflicts make up over 37% of the total. Yorkshire and Huntingdonshire add forty-one and sixteen respectively, meaning that 'Circuit VI' accounts for nearly 55%. This is of course because only these three shires add supplements of *clamores* to their lists of fiefs and manors. But another 20% are from the three eastern shires of putative 'Circuit VII', without counting their appended *Invasiones*. The East Anglian circuit also supplies about 60% of 1066-86 forfeitures, and almost half the pre-Domesday suits too (Appendices A nos 16-29, B nos 17-37). Yorkshire, Lincolnshire, Norfolk, Suffolk and Essex were large or populous counties. But that hardly goes for Bedfordshire, Huntingdonshire, Cambridgeshire or Hertfordshire, with fifty-eight pleas between them. How else may the patchiness of Domesday litigation be explained?

There are perhaps three possible solutions. The first appeals to the survey's extremely tight timetable. One might suppose that each circuit was supposed to iron out its disputes before making its final returns. The silence of 'Circuit IV' would then be testimony to its greater efficiency. On the other hand, 'Circuit VII' is extant on its own as Vol. II, 'Little Domesday'. The usual explanation for the failure to incorporate its report into 'Great Domesday', the fair copy or 'Exchequer text' that constitutes Vol. I, is that its work was held up by the manifest complexity of East Anglian arrangements. So the seventy-two surviving suits from the eastern counties may be a corollary of the fact that its results remain undigested. Similarly, it has recently been argued that 'Circuit VI' may have been the first part of 'Great Domesday' to be drafted, and this work was already in progress as new commissioners went back to resolve disputes left over by the original report. The northern circuit is distinct in using a marginal annotation 'K' (for *'Clamor'* or *'Calumpnia'*, presumably). These may be thought to have marked cases reserved for special attention from jurors. But the difficulty of integrating the resulting adjudications into a pre-existing main text meant that detached packages of *clamores* had to be appended.[6] An older view ascribes Circuit VI's idiosyncrasies to the delays caused by mere geography. One way or another, the commissioners responsible for northern and eastern circuits were exceptionally pressurized.

Yet 'Circuit IV' does record occasional claims without verdict (Appendix D nos 20-22), as well as an unattributed verdict on Isham (no. 19). Further, the Warwickshire survey contains a graphic account (Appendix A no. 11) of how, at some point between the Conquest and the Survey, Bishop Wulfstan had proved his claim to the manor of Alveston, 'before Queen Mathilda, in the presence of four sheriffdoms, for which he has a writ of King William, and the testimony of the county of Warwickshire'. What is significant about this plea is that it is *added*, squeezed in at the foot of a column, as if it had been tacked on to the 'Original Return', and only come to the master-scribe's attention at the last moment. There is no very obvious reason why this *previous* plea should be inserted if this circuit had already pruned out its litigation. But it might well have been added if the original aim was to ignore all controversial issues. Again, *Liber Exoniensis* is justly reckoned to have roughly the status for the south-west circuit that unincorporated Vol. II has for East Anglia. But its lawsuits are as few as 'Little Domesday's' are many. The one case covered by *Exon.* to the extent that it can be overlooked by 'Great Domesday' is a 'king's plea' (Appendix C no. 28). The other two Devon king's pleas, together with its one entry in the main list (no. 26), appear more or less identically in Exeter and Exchequer texts alike.[7] Thus, the reason why the south-western counties have few lawsuits is not that Domesday HQ had digested the 'Circuit II' report. Its very thin report was barely digested at all. South-western cases were either resolved at an earlier stage than *Exon.*, or else received much less attention than those of eastern England from the relevant commissioners. As for 'Circuit VI', closer examination of the 'K' marks has unexpected results. *Clamores* in the supplements are not always foreshadowed by a corresponding 'K' in the main text, nor is a judgement always recorded for those disputes elsewhere marked 'K'.[8] Neither Nottinghamshire's one dispute, nor Yorkshire's forty-one, have

6 D. Roffe, 'Domesday Book and Northern Society: a Reassessment', *EHR*, 105 (1990), 310-36, esp. at pp. 325-26. The evidence for a second perambulation is of course the famous contemporary report by Robert of Hereford, most conveniently in *Select Charters of English Constitutional History*, ed. W. Stubbs, 9th edn revised by H. W. C. Davis (Oxford, 1921), p. 95; see further below, p. 71.

7 It should be noted that the *Exon.* entry for Appendix C no. 30 is a marginal (so somewhat later) addition; for all this, see the notes to the Morris/Phillimore *Devon* volume by C. & F. Thorn, esp. on 2:2, *Exon.* 3:32, and cross-references. See further below, note 18, on the 'double-listing' of some south-western entries.

8 Huntingdonshire's 'K'-marked suits are nos 85, Appendix C no. 54, Appendix D nos 31-34 (the last actually 'D' – for *'disracionari'*, as suggested by the Morris/Phillimore note?); Lincolnshire's are nos 144, 149-56, 158, 228, Appendix

'K' marks. Derbyshire's three unresolved cases (Appendix D nos 35-37) are marked 'K'; not so, its sole specimen on the main list (no. 99).

The reticence of Nottinghamshire and Derbyshire on the otherwise garrulous northern circuit introduces the much more telling point that it is just as much from shire to shire as from circuit to circuit that the distribution of lawsuits varies. In the south-east, Hampshire has more than half the total pleas against Sussex's one. Buckinghamshire, on 'Circuit III', is as taciturn as Bedfordshire and Cambridgeshire are voluble. The importance of this is that, while variations between circuits may well reflect differences in efficiency or initiative at an organizing (i.e. governmental) level, those between shires are more likely to say something about local conditions. Theoretically, some shires may have met the circuit deadline while others did not. But, however intractable the problems of massive Yorkshire or Lincolnshire, those of tiny Huntingdonshire cannot have been too daunting. Variation is more probably a function of differentials in local demand. This would in turn suggest that dispute settlement was less something that the 1086 commissioners set out to perform than an experience that confronted them on their travels.

It also brings us to a second possible solution, that some areas have more lawsuits than others because they had more trouble. Historians have been brought up to see the west and south-west, areas with a low 'suit count', as those of consolidated manors, whereas the east and north, with their profusion of pleas, are lands of fragmented or dispersed lordship. On an instant impression, the disputes of Yorkshire and Lincolnshire, and those of Norfolk and Suffolk to a lesser extent, do indeed relate in significant numbers to the 'soke' which, to the evident bewilderment of some of England's new rulers, was by no means always co-terminous with pre-Conquest units of tenure. Yet, even if it were true that the north-east/south-west contrast in tenurial complexity was a fact of social geography, and not (as now suggested) another by-product of Domesday machinery, we should then expect more than one plea apiece from Nottinghamshire and Derbyshire. There would be no warrant for the discrepancy between Northamptonshire on the one hand, Cambridgeshire and Bedfordshire on the other; nor for the fact that Leicestershire is apparently as free of dispute as Warwickshire on 'Circuit IV'. Essex should not have more lawsuits than Norfolk, nor Hampshire than Kent.[9] More immediately political troubles may also be relevant. It seems

---

D nos 45-46 (and cf. no. 47).

[9] Compare P. H. Sawyer, '1066-1086: A Tenurial Revolution?', in *Domesday Book. A Reassessment*, ed. P. H. Sawyer (London, 1985), 71-85, esp. at pp. 81-83; D. Roffe, 'From Thegnage to Barony: Sake and Soke, Title and Tenants-in-Chief', *Anglo-Norman Studies*, 12 (1989), 157-176, esp. at pp. 163-66; and his 'Domesday Book and Northern Society' 328-33 (if simplified procedures might account for few pleas in Nottinghamshire and Derbyshire, they should also mean few in Huntingdonshire). Classification of lawsuits is beyond the scope of this paper, but

very likely that Ely's twenty-nine disputes have some connection with the confusing events of 1070-71. A good many Yorkshire suits evidently arose from whatever happened to the Malet fief at much the same time. What can hardly be explained along these lines is that all but eight out of sixty-nine listed Lincolnshire tenants-in-chief (those eight with little more than £60 worth of land between them) are found to be at loggerheads, when few of their properties elsewhere are recorded as controversial.[10]

Further attention to actual disputants prompts a rather different consideration. The incidence of 'king's pleas' corresponds by and large to that of subjects' suits. But their spread is less uneven overall: otherwise prolific Lincolnshire's fourteen compares to Norfolk's thirteen and Essex's eleven; loquacious Yorkshire has ten, the same as Hampshire. That a king should pursue his interests across his realm in a fairly uniform way is no surprise. Also predictable is a more regular pattern of ecclesiastical litigation across England. Abbeys other than Ely suffered from the experience of their new guests. So it is that 'Circuit V' would be as blank as 'IV' without church pleas, in only one of which (no. 75) is a bishop not ostensibly representing a mother-church. If, in Yorkshire's and Lincolnshire's *clamores*, we concentrate on disputes of ecclesiastical corporations, and give the archbishop of York and the bishops of Durham and Lincoln the baronial *persona* normally accorded to Odo of Bayeux or Geoffrey de Coutances, the total of church pleas in Lincolnshire falls to twenty, and in Yorkshire to five. The 'Circuit VI' pattern thus comes into line with that of 'VII'.[11] What then stands out all the more starkly is the variable record of secular tenants-in-chief. Kings or churches were always ready to bring grievances to court. Lay lords seem to have needed encouragement such as they only received in some shires.

---

crude analysis suggests that suits where 'soke' is explicitly an issue are barely half in Lincolnshire, well under half in Yorkshire, and quarter in Huntingdonshire; while to exclude suits apparently arising from other types of 'dispersal' (leasehold apart) leaves about half the total in Essex, Suffolk, Norfolk, Cambridgeshire and Hampshire, and means a significant reduction only in Bedfordshire.

10 Exceptions (excluding major churches and 'greater tenants-in-chief', and omitting the rest of 'Circuit VI'): Ralph de Mortemer (11, 13, 19), Hugh fitz Baldric (15), Guy de Raimbeaucourt (43), Alfred of Lincoln (69-70), Drogo de la Beuvrière (296), Ivo Tallboys (307), Roger de Poitou (321), Ralph Pagnell (333), Eudo fitz Spirewic (335).

11 This is to count as episcopal/baronial pleas, nos 108-09, 115, 117, 134, 144-45, 147, 151, 154, 158-59, 173, 177, 183-84, 198, 203, 210, 212, 225-27, 230, 247; and as abbatial/collegial, nos 104, 113-14, 140 (St John's Beverley), 102 (St Peter's York), 166 (St Mary's Lincoln), and 201 (St Mary's Stow). 'Circuit VII's' only church plea of episcopal/baronial type is no. 272 (and even this may in fact relate to the community of Holy Cross Waltham).

All of this pushes us towards a third way of understanding the singular discrepancies of the Domesday lawsuit record. Its major determinant was the extent to which different 1086 commissioners were interested in dispute settlement. Obliged, as even the most fiscally-minded surveyors must have been, to adjudicate those competing claims that were actually pressed upon them, some interpreted their mission as demanding more thorough investigation of contested title than did others. It is, for example, interesting and perhaps revealing that 'Circuits III' and 'VII', with most lawsuits in the main body of their text (rather than as supplementary *clamores*), are also those which pay most attention to details of pre-Conquest tenure in general.[12] Some who began with an enthusiastic approach to claims, as on 'Circuit VI', may have thought better of it before they finished: hence, unresolved 'K'-marked cases, and notably thin tallies from Nottinghamshire and Derbyshire. Exhaustion or impatience may account as well as anything else for contrasts between Buckinghamshire and Bedfordshire, or Sussex and Hampshire. Disputed title in 1086 was a can of worms. What crept into the record depended on how far the lid was opened and how soon it was slammed shut again. This solution does not of course wholly preclude the others. Demand, fed by tenurial confusion or unusually bitter experience, will have been one of the pressures affecting the behaviour of various circuits. The rigours of the 1086 timetable must have been a factor in a circuit's decision to cut its deliberations short. But only if the first two solutions are governed by the third do they begin to cover all the eccentricities of the evidence. And if that is so, it must cast doubt on the proposition that registration of title was *a main purpose* of the survey.

We can now move to a yet more arresting point. The final column of my list contains an indication of a dispute's outcome and treatment in the survey. For these purposes, I have adapted the system of the football pools. '1' ('home-win') denotes that the defending party to the suit is upheld by the evidence of local opinion. '1½' ('away-win') means that it has endorsed the plaintiff, and this is duly reflected by listing of the property at issue in his Domesday fiefs. '2' ('goalless draw') indicates that the plaintiff has not made his attested superiority tell: the property to which he is declared entitled is nevertheless listed among the holdings of his defeated opponent. '3' ('scoring draw'), by contrast, is to say that an item in dispute is listed under *both* parties. Lastly, 'X' ('void match') amounts to the fact that a dispute's

---

12 See Roffe, 'Thegnage to Barony', pp. 160-63, with P. A. Clarke, 'The Aristocracy of England in the Reign of Edward the Confessor', unpublished D. Phil. thesis (Oxford, 1987), pp. 4, 70-73. (Note too that 'Circuit IV' is the least helpful on pre-1066 circumstances.) The famous 'terms of reference' recorded in the *Inquisitio Eliensis* (1816 *Additamenta*, p. 497) are unfortunately unhelpful, inasmuch as dispute-settlement, like pre-1066 sub-tenures, might or might not be seen by commissioners as integral to the brief set out therein.

outcome is too obscure to allow further comment.[13] The table of statistics gives the position that emerges. The total of 339 reduces to 273 by excluding void results. Of these, 60 see 'home sides' comfortably ensconced. However, of the apparent 213 plaintiff gains, just 42 have their results properly reflected in the way the survey is set out. Another 15 produce ostensible 'wins' for both sides. But no fewer than 156 'wins' for plaintiffs are entirely ignored by the Book's actual construction. Regardless of what shire, riding, hundred or wapentake has said, the property at stake appears only among the fiefs of the discredited party. Thus, take (again more or less at random) the list's no. 61: 'William Speke was seised of half a hide and half a virgate through the king and his deliverer, but William de Warenne disseised him without a writ of the king, and took away two horses from his men and has not yet returned them. This the men of the Hundred attest.' This entry is in William de Warenne's fief, and there is no trace of the half-hide, the half-virgate or indeed the horses in that of William Speke. Over 80% (including 'double-listed' items) of seemingly successful plaintiffs are frustrated in so far as their vindicated lands are still ascribed to their opponents. In 46% of cases (wholly denied plaintiff 'victors' as a proportion of the overall total), local panels could have saved their breath. To retain the pools analogy, there are far too many 'draws' for any worthwhile dividend. More soberly, this is odd behaviour for any 'register of title'.[14]

There can certainly be no escape, this time, by recourse to the trundling apparatus of the Domesday survey. 'Circuit VI's' statistics should admittedly be set aside: the Huntingdonshire and Lincolnshire *clamores* were clearly drawn up after, and nearly always without effect upon, their lists of fiefs. Thus, the main body of the Lincolnshire text records (no. 147) that, 'in the same Drayton, Bishop Wulfwig had a carucate... It was St Benedict's of Ramsey by witness of men of the Hundred who say that they do not know through whom the bishop held it.' There is no 'K' in the margin, but among the Kesteven *clamores*, we find this: 'In Drayton hundred, Count Alan has one carucate of land from St Benedict of Ramsey. Bishop Remigius claims it, and the Wapentake bears witness for him that his *antecessor* Wulfwig held it

13 In a few cases, land seems to be listed with defeated *plaintiffs*: e.g. nos 6, 109, 172. It seems reasonable to regard these as instances of loose terminology, and to take apparent plaintiffs as defendants in fact. Cf. nos 113-14, where the Bishop of Durham is surely defendant in both cases, albeit the local view upholds him in one but not the other. In nos 92-93, cross-references show that William de Warenne was unsuccessful plaintiff to the first, and discredited defendant to the second. Cf. nos 158-59, 219-20, 318-19.

14 Finn alone registered this point: *Introduction*, p. 91; but it presumably underlies Stephenson's view, 'Notes', p. 14: 'As legal reports, such entries are distinctly bad'; and see now D. Roffe (ed.), *The Huntingdonshire Domesday* (London, 1989), p. 4.

of St Benedict *TRE*.' The truth of the matter is now known, but the main text is unchanged (cf. no. 91 and Appendix C no. 72). There was evidently no inclination to incorporate the report of the second commissioners' visit (if that is what the *clamores* amount to) into the first; and the special circumstances of the northern circuit mean that it can be no basis for generalization. The fact remains that the proportion of suits numbered '2' for the 'first', 'third' and 'fifth' circuits is about as high as for the 'sixth' or 'seventh' (omitting their more numerous imponderables). Over half the duly registered plaintiff 'wins' come from the three shires of Wiltshire, Bedfordshire and Essex. These show what might have happened. By that token, they bring out what usually did not. Nearer the norm are two registered gains out of a possible nine in Hertfordshire.[15]

Another way out would be the argument that the verdicts of local juries were not conclusive but merely evidence upon which the king's judges might be expected to proceed, without necessarily being bound by it.[16] Local opinions are not often couched in judgemental terms; the usual words, as in the above examples, are 'say', 'saw', 'attest', 'bear witness', the language of evidence. The following are among possible rebuttals of that argument: inquest procedure, such as the Survey used, did of course give sworn evidence much of the force of judgement. Not infrequently, the words 'justly', 'unjustly', or 'ought' appear; to 'attest to the use' already begins to elide the categories of evidence and judgement. References to the 'king's barons' or the king himself occur, but they are rare (the nine marked **, plus Appendix C no. 24); if this was normal procedure, why are these cases singled out? To deny judgemental effect to local verdicts leaves the problem that they seem to have worked a lot more like judgements in some shires than others; it is, to repeat, the apparent implementation of some decisions that highlights the non-implementation of so many more. Above all, local evidence is almost always the nearest Domesday ever gets to judgement. If sworn evidence on tenurial rights and wrongs 'in King Edward's time' and 'now' were not the decisive consideration that the 'terms of reference' imply, then Domesday Book does even less to endorse legitimate possession than is indicated by my 'football pools' symbols. It is a strange 'register' whose sole contribution to disputed title is local comment of questionable relevance.[17]

---

15 Nor is the picture strikingly different as regards the 'king's pleas' of Appendix C: pleas that might be numbered '2' or at best '3' at the king's own expense include nos 5-10, 14-19, 22, 26 [14/26 on 'Circuit I'], 35-38, 40-45 [10/14 on 'Circuit III'].

16 Cf. Hyams, '"No Register of Title"', p. 138.

17 Dr Hudson has suggested to me that we should bear in mind the way that so many major disputes of this era in legal history end with the sort of 'compromise' that was often the only means of giving judgement any effect. This consideration may well be relevant to cases marked '3' (cf. e.g. no. 235, but also next note); it is

The argument does, however, lead on to more promising lines of thought. Granted that Domesday Book itself did not act on the results of the investigations into title that it had set in motion, these were nonetheless grounds for future action. There is just enough evidence in the survey itself to suggest the possibilities. An annotation in the margin of the Hampshire section attests one requisite restoration, for Nunnaminster (no. 15). The fact that all six Wiltshire decisions were implemented one way or the other is extremely interesting in the light of Holt's arguments about Salisbury, and the good case recently made by Dr Tessa Webber that *Liber Exoniensis* was penned in the Salisbury *scriptorium*.[18] Venturing further into a Serbonian bog of speculation, we might likewise connect Essex's ten registered wins with the possible role of St Paul's, another house of secular canons with a recent 'Chancellor' as presiding bishop, in drafting the 'Circuit VII' returns that became 'Little Domesday'. Ely's success in getting its victories at least double-listed in Cambridgeshire and Essex might perhaps be linked with the fact that Abbot Symeon was the brother of Bishop Walkelin, whose see at Winchester has a well-established later role in Domesday history. The same explanation could underlie other evidence of extra activity in Hampshire (nos 9-11).[19] Dr Chaplais' plausible assignment of responsibility for compilation of the 'fair copy' to Bishop William of St Calais and his Durham scribe may derive faint support, similarly, from presentation of some of the bishop's suits (e.g. nos 145, 272). Having said all that, however, we must once again observe that what *is* done along such lines in Domesday Book merely sets off much more that was *not*.

None of this would matter so much if it were demonstrable that Domesday judgements were consistently put into effect in the survey's aftermath.[20] To investigate that possibility would be far beyond the scope of any preliminary comment. But it can hesitantly be said here that initial impressions do not suggest a rush to realize Domesday justice. Much attention has been given in recent years to writs and related documents which cite or otherwise tie up with survey evidence. Their number is still not large. Of the 156 cases where the Book's presentation overlooked a decision

---

not so helpful for those according vindicated plaintiffs no recognition at all.

18   T. Webber, 'Salisbury and the Exon Domesday: Some Observations concerning the Origin of Exeter Cathedral MS 3500', *English Manuscript Studies*, I (1989), 1-18. 'Double-listing' of *Exon.* circuit's no. 26, with Appendix C no. 29, may be pertinent; but cf. Appendix D no. 5.

19   Cf. also *DB*, I 48b, *Hampshire* 44:3; note too the action taken on main list no. 8 and Appendix C 13 (below, note 21).

20   This was evidently the answer that Finn had in mind: see note 14. See also D. Bates, 'Two Ramsey Writs and the Domesday Survey', *Historical Research*, 63 (1990), 337-39 (but see next note below).

for a plaintiff, just one (a Hampshire case, as it happens) was covered in this way.[21] The most explicit of all writ references to the survey is perhaps also the most significant. It demands service in general terms from all those holding lands claimed by Ely 'which my Winchester *carta* shows to have been sworn to its fief'. The writ's terms leave no doubt that 'swearing to a fief' in 1086 was meant to have results. They also make it pretty clear that Ely's dues had not been forthcoming; and the writ dates at least forty years after Domesday Book.[22] A search of the *VCH* for counties where it has reached the stage of publishing manorial histories is revealing. In shires with significant numbers of pleas, there are thirty-one marked '2' where *VCH* details are available. Four and a half such cases were eventually put right, seven seem unclear and nineteen and a half remain unchanged.[23] Similarly, thirty-one of Lincolnshire's unimplemented judgements could be checked in the *Lindsey Survey* of Henry I's reign. The evidence for most remains obscure or ambiguous. But there are three possible instances of restitution, as against up to a dozen where the 1086 *status quo* survives.[24] Once more, there are

21 *Regesta Regum Anglo-Normannorum*, I, ed. H. W. C. Davis (Oxford, 1913), II, ed. C. Johnson & H. A. Cronne (Oxford, 1956) no. 483a [main list no. 8]. Writs relating to Domesday cases not marked '2' are *Regesta* nos 322 [main list no. 86], 447 [main list no. 91, the writ clearly referring to *DB* I 204d, *Huntingdonshire* 6:17, rather than I 207b, 27:1], 1860b [main list no. 85]; and see next note. Other writs relate to Appendix cases: *Regesta* nos 284 [Appendix C 13], 288b [Appendix D no. 19], 378 [Appendix C 28], 385/385bc [Appendix C 95]. The remaining writs usually invoked in this context have no bearing on listed cases: *Regesta* nos 236, 373, 386a, 468, 976, 1000, 1488, 1515.

22 *Regesta* no. 1500; *Liber Eliensis*, III 11, ed. E. O. Blake, Camden Soc. 3rd series 92 (1962), p. 253.

23 (Main list numbers in brackets, with eventual restorations marked *, and unclear cases +). *VCH Bedfordshire*, II (1908), p. 300 [65]; vol. III (1912), p. 129 [63]; p.134 [61]; p. 171 [62]. *VCH Cambridgeshire*, V (1973), pp. 70, 89 [49]; pp. 148-49 [46]; VI (1978), pp. 5-6 [51]; p. 183 [45]; VIII (1982), p. 251 [45]; IX, p. 142 [55*]; p. 148 [40]. *VCH Essex*, IV (1956), p. 190 [285*]. *VCH Hampshire*, II (1903), pp. 492, 508-9 [12+]; III (1908), p. 131 [8*]; IV (1911), p. 191 [15*], pp. 256, 296 [13]; p. 475 [16+]; pp. 561-2 [14+]. *VCH Hertfordshire*, II (1908), pp. 201-02 [33]; III (1912), p. 78 [29+]; p. 132 [35]; p. 161 [31]; p. 417 [34+]; IV (1914), p. 21 [36]; p. 75 [32+]. *VCH Huntingdonshire*, II (1932), p. 303 [88]; pp. 310, 379-80 [90]; p. 351 [88*]; III (1936), p. 22 [97]; pp. 29-30 [93]; pp. 50, 120 [87]; p. 146 [98]. See also E. Miller, *The Abbey and Bishopric of Ely* (Cambridge, 1951), pp. 66-70, for further Ely experiences that are evidently not wholly exceptional.

24 (Numerical system above, but omitting obscurities). 'The Lindsey Survey', ed. C. W. Foster & T. Longley, *The Lincolnshire Domesday and the Lindsey Survey*, Lincoln Record Society 19 (1924) 1:9, [218]; 3:19 [210]; 7:14 [195]; 8:8 [155*]; 8:10 [159]; 9:5 [192]; 10:1 [203]; 10:3 [201]; 11:12 [190]; 11:26 [156*]; 15:13 [172]; 18:2 [164]; 18:4 [167]; 18:7 [169*] 18:14 [163]. Kesteven is not covered by the Lindsey

enough cases where something is done to argue that this should have been done very much more often. The most economical, if not the only, explanation for such a state of affairs is that rectification of title was never a pressing concern. It would of course be extraordinary if the judicial activity of 1086 had not developed some momentum. But the evidence does not – anyway as yet – support the proposition that Domesday Book was part of a sustained campaign to clarify the tenurial confusion left by the Norman Conquest.

Whatever happened after the Domesday scribes laid down their pens makes no difference, in any case, to the limitations as a 'Register of Title' of what they actually wrote. Each of the various resolutions of the Domesday lawsuits conundrum must confront the insuperable fact that the Book is itself an inefficient guide to the outcome of the lawsuits it incorporates. Just as its coverage of dispute is patchy, so is its treatment of results inconsistent. With the one riddle, as with the other, we are thrown back on the answer that settlement of disputes was not a prime 1086 objective. Holt's own principle is that 'what we have in Great Domesday is what was intended'.[25] What we have in Great Domesday is that (depending on how one frames the equation) from nearly half to more than three-quarters of the evidence as to contested tenure proffered by local opinion on peril of its soul was ignored. Unless local opinion was silently quashed more often than not, registration of results in the main text depended, like the form that judgements took, on what had been done at shire-level. For most shires, this was evidently a relatively low priority. Unquestionably too, it was low among the priorities of Domesday's 'master-mind'. On the unchallengeable evidence of 'Great Domesday', he was capable of an extraordinary feat of administrative and intellectual organization. To incorporate judicial decisions where the logic of their outcome indicated, he had to do no more than was usually managed by his deputies in Bedfordshire and Essex. That he did not contrive, using his own admirable contents tables, to transfer items from the fief of a defeated party to that of the victor can only mean that he was not much bothered with such matters. If, then, barons were induced to co-operate with the survey by a promise that it would enshrine their rights, they were deceived.

Before concluding, I should perhaps offer a more positive, if even more tentative, reaction to the peculiarities of the Domesday lawsuit pattern. Kings had been heavily amercing defeated claimants in property suits since at least the days of Edgar. One thing we are told by the *Chronicle* about the events of 1086, as Holt observes, is that William took 'a very great amount of money

---

Survey, but for continuing denial of Westminster [162] and Crowland [254], see E. King, 'The Origins of the Wake Family', *Northamptonshire Past and Present*, 5 (1973-77), 163-76, at 167-68, 170.

25   Holt '1086', p. 47.

from his men where he had any pretext for it, either justly or otherwise'. If one of William's objectives was simply to exact cash for false title, then listing properties in losers' fiefs made excellent sense.[26] Further, the 'terms of reference' bring out a close connection between title and value. Any system of property assessment is logically interested in the precise identity of the assessee. But there was in England an especially strong link, forged well before 1066, between security of tenure and payment of geld. Dr Lawson has drawn attention to an electrifying passage in Heming's cartulary, describing the mechanism whereby those with eyes on church property simply paid the geld due on it and secured their title, regardless of whether the church was able or willing to pay itself. In another famous text, the Chronicler describes how William 'sold land on very hard terms: then came someone else, and offered more than the other, and the king let it go to him, then came a third and offered still more, and the king gave it into his hands, and did not care how sinfully the reeves had got it from poor men'. One can well see how the geld mechanism, thus operated, could give incoming loot-laden aristocrats the veneer of legitimacy that was undeniably important to what historians persist in calling 'the Norman settlement'.[27] It is just possible, then, that judgements reached by hundreds and others were beside the point – or relevant only to the extent that they put an obligation on unjustified tenants to make a proffer that outbid an allegedly just claimant. The actual injustice of his title could then be overlooked – at least until more was proffered by the originally vindicated tenant. If that is right, the 'loose ends' proposition would tie up in a nicely ironical way with the essentially fiscal targets of this *'Descriptio'*.

It would be as well to end by stressing what this paper does *not* contend. I do not deny that Domesday Book came to be seen by some later property holders as a *'carta'* of unchallengeable authority. I am not arguing that validated title was of no real moment to the incoming ruling class. Domesday lawsuits are of a piece with much other 1066-86 evidence that the conquerors were strikingly pre-occupied with 'right' in a context where they might well have been satisfied with their own 'might'. It is no part of my case that Domesday Book is anything less than a most precious source for early

---

26   *Two of the Saxon Chronicles Parallel* '1085', ed. J. Earle and C. Plummer, 2 vols (Oxford, 1892-99) I, p. 217; cf. Robert of Hereford (see note 6), *'ex congregatione regalis pecuniae'*; Holt, pp. 44, 46. For pre-1066 amercements in property suits, see chapter 9 of P. Wormald, *The Making of English Law. King Alfred to the Norman Conquest* (Oxford, forthcoming).

27   *Saxon Chronicles* '1086', p. 218; for Domesday lawsuits that do seem to arise from the operation of this mechanism, see (e.g.) main list no. 35 (with Appendix B no. 6), Appendix B 9, and perhaps main list nos. 48, 158. M. K. Lawson, 'The Collection of Danegeld and Heregeld in the reigns of Æthelred II and Cnut', *EHR*, 99 (1984), 721-38, e.g. at 735; cf. Hyams, '"No Register of Title"', pp. 128-29.

English law and litigation. It is the one record before the Plea Rolls begin over a century later that offers evidence even approaching Plea Rolls in range and quality of information. We are left with the strong impression that it is through the jagged edges of the disputes arising from the 'Norman Settlement' that we glimpse the answer to one of the huge questions of English history: what actually happened in the twenty years after 1066? But neither a charter for historians, nor even a *carta* for post-Domesday generations, is the same thing as a deliberately designed title-deed for the new regime. I once observed that 'wise historians think at least twice before dissenting from Maitland' — advice which I unwisely went on to ignore. So I shall finish by saying it again, and meaning it this time.

> [The King] may learn, as it were by the way, whether any of his barons or other men have presumed to occupy, to 'invade', lands which he has reserved for himself. Again, if several persons are in dispute about a tract of ground, the contest may be appeased by the testimony of shire and hundred, or may be reserved for the king's audience; at any rate, the existence of an outstanding claim may be recorded by the royal commissioners... But all this is done sporadically and unsystematically. Our record is no register of title...[28]

So far as disputed title is concerned, this is as near the essence of the matter as any Domesday scholar has come in more than ninety years.

[28] F. W. Maitland, *Domesday Book and Beyond*, p. 27. That Maitland went on to repeat that 'it is a geld-book' does not devalue his other comments: abandonment of the 'geld fallacy' need not, and increasingly does not, entail denial of Domesday's wider fiscal preoccupations.

Domesday Lawsuits

This is a list (hopefully rather than necessarily comprehensive!) of all Domesday Book cases, which:

1) Were apparently heard before the commissioners in the course of the survey (omitting cases recorded in Domesday Book but certainly or probably heard before 1086, cf. Appendices A, B);

2) Reached the point of formally recorded testimony/adjudication by shire, hundred, wapentake etc., or else were deferred to higher courts (ignoring stated claims with no recorded verdict, cf. Appendix D);

3) Were disputes *between subjects* (excluding not only disputes about tolls etc., but also those 'king's cases' that centred on the right to title as such, with no specified competitor, cf. Appendix C).

References to Domesday folios are followed by the section designated in the Morris/Phillimore series. The first party listed is the apparent plaintiff (including one or two cases where the context shows that an apparent defendant is an actual plaintiff); references to *Liber Exoniensis* (*Exon.*) are to folio numbers as reported in the 1816 *Additamenta* edition. Names of parties are followed by the form of testifying body. Suits between the same parties within one county are counted together as a single plea when they have the same result.

1 designates a plea 'won' by ostensible defendant and listed under defendant; 1½ is for a plea 'won' by apparent plaintiff and listed under plaintiff; 2 is for a plea 'won' by plaintiff but listed under defendant; 3 is for disputed lands listed under both parties; X marks pleas whose uncertainties preclude such assessment. Further, ** before a case's numerical outcome records its reservation for later judgement in a 'higher' court.

ENGLAND IN THE ELEVENTH CENTURY

'Circuit I'

No.	Reference	Names	Descriptor	Value
1.	i 10b + 12d, *Kent* 5:149 + 7:30.	St Augustine's, (Odo of Bayeux).	Hundred, Shire.	3
2.	i 13a, *Kent* 9:9.	St Martin's Dover, Hugh de Montfort.	Hundred, burgesses, lathe.	X
3.	i 23b, *Sussex* 11:8.	New Minster, Roger of Mongomery.	Hundred.	2
4.	i 31c, *Surrey* 5:3.	Lufa (kg's reeve), (Odo of Bayeux).	Hundred.	2
5.	i 34a, *Surrey* 8:29.	Chertsey, (Odo of Bayeux).	Hundred.	1½
6.	i 35c, *Surrey* 19:35.	Chertsey, Richard fitz Gilbert.	Hundred.	2
7.	i 36c, *Surrey* 28:1	Robert Malet, Durand.	*Homines* (?of Hundred).	1½
8.	i 43c, *Hampshire* 10:1.	Old Minster, Jumièges.	Hundred (+ Abt Ramsey).2	
9.	i 44d, *Hampshire* 23:3.	William de Chernet, Picot.	Shire, Hundred *(meliores / antiqui /villani /vilis plebs / prepositi).*	**1½
10.	i 45b, *Hampshire* 23:16.	Hugh de Port, Thurstan *camerarius* (cf. i 48a, 40:1)	Hundred.	1½
11.	i 45d + 47a, *Hampshire* 23:44 + 29:15.	Hugh de Port, Ralph de Mortemer.	Hundred.	3
12.	i 46c, *Hampshire* 27:1.	William Mauduit, Edward of Salisbury (cf. i 47c, 35:2).	Shire, Hundred.	2
13.	i 47a, *Hampshire* 29:9.	Old Minster, Ralph de Mortemer.	Hundred.	2
14.	i 48a, *Hampshire* 43:6.	Hugh de Port, Gilbert de Breteuil.	Hundred.	2
15.	i 48b, *Hampshire* 44:1.	Nunnaminster, Hugh fitz Baldric.	Sheriffdom, Hundred.	2
16.	i 48d, *Hampshire* 53:2.	Aldred brother of Odo, William the Archer.	Sheriff, Hundred.	2
17.	i 48d, *Hampshire* 54:2.	William d'Eu, Herbert son of Remigius.	Hundred.	1
18.	i 62b, *Berkshire* 41:6.	Azor *dispensator* R.E., Robert d'Oilly.	Hundred.	2
19.	i 62d, *Berkshire* 46:4.	? Old Minster, Ralph de Mortemer.	Shire.	2

DOMESDAY LAWSUITS: A PROVISIONAL LIST

'Circuit II'

20.	i 66d, *Wiltshire 7:15*.	Glastonbury, Waleran.	Thegns.	1½
21.	i 69a + 68c, *Wiltshire 23:7 + 16:3*.	Amesbury, 'Earl' Aubrey.	Thegns of shire.	3
22.	i 69c + 74d, *Wiltshire 24:19 + 68:23*.	Edward of Salisbury, William fitz Ansculf.	*'Angli'*, Thegns.	3
23.	i 70c *Wiltshire 26:19*.	Edward (Alfred of Marlborough), Durand of Gloucester.	Thegns of shire.	1½
24.	i 71b, *Wiltshire 28:10*.	Siward (Milo Crispin), Durand of Gloucester.	Thegns of shire.	1½
25.	i 74d + 71b, *Wiltshire 68:23 + 29:5*.	Gilbert de Breteuil, William fitz Ansculf.	Thegns.	3
26.	i 101d +118b, *Devon 2:2 + 52:34 (Exon. 117a2)*.	Bp of Exeter, Dunn.	*'Francigenae'?*	3

'Circuit III'

27.	i 130b, *Middlesex 15:1*.	St Paul's, Robert Fafiton.	Hundred.	2
28.	i 130d, *Middlesex 25:2*.	Geoffrey de Mandeville, Ælfgifu wife of Hwætmann of London.	Hundred.	2
29.	i 133b, *Hertfordshire 2:1*.	Westminster, Abp of Canterbury.	Hundred.	2
30.	i 135d, *Hertfordshire 10:6*.	St Alban's, Robert of Mortain.	Hundred.	1½
31.	i 136d-137a, *Hertfordshire 16:1*.	Westminster, Count Alan.	Hundred.	2
32.	i 138c, *Hertfordshire 24:2*.	Count Eustace, Ralph Baynard.	Hundred.	2
33.	i 139b, *Hertfordshire 32:1*.	St Alban's, Edward of Salisbury.	Hundred.	2
34.	i 140b-c, *Hertfordshire 34:13*.	Ralph de Limésy, Geoffrey de Bec.	Shire.	2
35.	i 141a, *Hertfordshire 36:9*.	King's sokeman, Peter de Valognes.	Shire, Hundred.	2
36.	i 141d-142a, *Hertfordshire 37:19*.	Count Alan, Hardwin de Scales.	Hundred.	2
37.	i 142c, *Hertfordshire 42:11*.	A priest, William Black (Odo of Bayeux).	Hundred.	1½

38.	i 148d, *Buckinghamshire* 17:20.	William of Cholsey, William fitz Ansculf.	Hundred.	2
39.	i 151c, *Buckinghamshire* 38:1.	Bertram de Verdun, Geoffrey de Mandeville.	Hundred.	1½
40.	i 190c, *Cambridgeshire* 3:5.	Ely, Bp of Lincoln.	Hundred.	2
41.	i 190c, *Cambridgeshire* 5:2.	Ely, St Wandrille.	Hundred.	1½
42.	i 191ab + 199b, *Cambridgeshire* 5:22 + 26:57.	Ely, Hardwin de Scales.	Hundred.	3

42. (cont.)
191b + 198b, *Cambs.* 5:26 + 26:18.
191bc + 198c, 5:32 + 26:30
191c + 198c, 5:35 + 26:33
[cf. i 190c + 199b, 5:2 + 26:50, 3; 190d + 199b, 5:5 + 26:51, 3; 190d + 199b, 5:7 + 26:52, 3;
190d + 199b, 5:10 + 26:53, 3; 191a + 199b, 5:17 + 26:54, 3; 191a + 199b, 5:19 + 26:55, 3;
191a + 199b, 5:21 + 26:56, 3; 191b + 198c, 5:29 + 26:27, 3; 191b + 198c, 5:30 + 26:29, 3; 199a, 26:48-9, 2].

43.	i 191c + 200a, *Cambs.* 5:33 + 31:1	Ely, Guy de Raimbeaucourt.	Hundred.	3
44.	193b, *Cambridgeshire* 13:2.	Roger of Montgomery, Hardwin de Scales.	Hundred.	1½
45.	i 196c, *Cambridgeshire* 18:3 (cf.18:7).	Ely, William de Warenne.	Hundred.	2
46.	i 197a, *Cambridgeshire* 21:5.	St Mary's Chatteris, Robert Gernon.	Hundred.	2
47.	i 197a, *Cambridgeshire* 22:5.	Geoffrey de Mandeville, Robert Gernon.	Hundred.	1½
48.	i 197b, *Cambridgeshire* 22:6.	?Picot/Hugh de Port? (Ordgar), Geoffrey de Mandeville.	Hundred.	2
49.	i 197d, *Cambridgeshire* 25:9	Ely, Eudo *dapifer*.	Hundred.	2
50.	i 199c, *Cambridgeshire* 28:2.	Ely, Hugh de Port.	Hundred.	2
51.	i 199d, *Cambridgeshire* 29:10.	Count Alan, Aubrey de Vere.	Hundred.	2
52.	i 201d, *Cambridgeshire* 35:1.	Count Alan, John fitz Waleran.	Hundred.	2
53.	i 201d, *Cambridgeshire* 35:2.	Ely, John fitz Waleran.	Hundred.	2
54.	i 202a, *Cambridgeshire* 39:2.	David D'Argentan, Eustace of Huntingdon.	Hundred.	1½
55.	i 202a, *Cambridgeshire* 40:1.	Ely, 2 king's carpenters.	Hundred.	2

DOMESDAY LAWSUITS: A PROVISIONAL LIST

		Homines (?of Hundred, borough?).	X
56.	i 209a, *Bedfordshire* B.	St Paul's Bedford, Bp of Lincoln.		
57.	i 210a, *Bedfordshire* 3:6.	Geoffrey de Coutances, Sigar de Choques	Hundred.	1½
58.	i 210b, *Bedfordshire* 4:2.	William de Cairon, Hugh de Beauchamp.	Hundred.	1½
59.	i 210d, *Bedfordshire* 8:2.	Ramsey, Nigel d'Aubigny & Walter of Flanders.	Hundred.	1½
60.	i 211c, *Bedfordshire* 16:3.	Herfast (Nigel d'Aubigny), Walter Giffard.	Hundred.	2
61.	i 211d, *Bedfordshire* 17:1.	William Speke, William de Warenne.	Hundred.	2
62.	i 211d, *Bedfordshire* 17:2+4	Hugh de Beauchamp, William de Warenne.	Hundred, 'sworn of sheriffdom'	2
63.	i 212a, *Bedfordshire* 19:1.	Ramsey, Milo Crispin.	Hundred.	2
64.	i 212b, *Bedfordshire* 21:6.	Eudo *dapifer*, Hugh de Beauchamp.	Hundred.	1½
65.	i 213a, *Bedfordshire* 23:12.	St Alban's, Hugh de Beauchamp.	Hundred.	2
66.	i 215a, *Bedfordshire* 25:7.	William Speke, Eudo *dapifer*.	Hundred.	1½
67.	i 215b, *Bedfordshire* 29:1.	Ranulf bro. Ilger, Gilbert son of Solomon.	Half-hundred.	1½
68.		Ranulf bro. Ilger, Hugh de Grandmesnil.	(Half-hundred).	1½
69.	i 215c + 215d, *Bedfordshire* 31:1 + 32:7	Alfred of Lincoln, Walter of Flanders.	Hundred.	3
70.	215c, *Bedfordshire* 31:1	Alfred of Lincoln, Geoffrey de Coutances.	Hundred.	1½
71.	i 216b, *Bedfordshire* 40:3.	William *camerarius*, (Odo of Bayeux).	Hundred.	1½
72.	i 217d, *Bedfordshire* 54:2.	Adelaide wife of Hugh de Grandmesnil, Hugh de Beauchamp.	Hundred.	1½

'Circuit V'

73.	i 169a, *Gloucestershire* 56:2.	Abingdon, Walter fitz Roger.	County.	1
74.	i 175c, *Worcestershire* 9:5c.	Pershore, Evesham.	County.	1½
75.	i 177a, *Worcestershire* 23:1.	Bp of Chester, William fitz Ansculf.	County (*meliores*).	2

No.	Reference	Parties	Court	
76.	i 177d *Worcestershire* 26:15-17.	Evesham, Urse d'Abetot.	County.	2
77.	i 185c, *Herefordshire* 15:1.	Gloucester, William fitz Baderon.	County.	2
78.	i 259b, *Shropshire* 4,26:3.	St Chad's Shrewsbury, Roger the Huntsman.	County.	2
79.	i 263a + 264b, *Cheshire* B:13 + 2:1.	Bp of Chester, Robert son of Earl Hugh.	County.	3
80.	264b, 2:5.		County.	1
81.	i 264a, *Cheshire* 1:35.	St Werburh's Chester, Earl Hugh.	County.	2
82.	i 268a, *Cheshire* 27:3.	St Chad's Chester, Men of Earl Hugh.	County.	2

'Circuit VI'

No.	Reference	Parties	Court	
83.	i ?203a + 208a, *Huntingdonshire* ?B:10 + D:2.	Leofgifu (?wife of Sheriff Ælfric + son), Sheriff Eustace.	(Jurors).	X
84.	i ?203a + 208a, *Hunts.* ?B:12 + D:1.	Priests of Huntingdon (?Burgred & Thorkell), Sheriff Eustace.	Jurors.	X
85.	i 204b + 208a, *Hunts.* 6:3 + D:4.	Sheriff Eustace, Ramsey.	Jurors.	1
86.	?208c, ?D:27.	? same parties (cf. i 206a, 19:1).	Jurors.	X
87.	i 206b + 208b, *Hunts.* 19:15+17 + D:21.	Ælfwold & brothers, Sheriff Eustace.	Hundred, County.	2
88.	i 206c + 208b, *Hunts.* 19:27 + D:11.	Countess Judith, Sheriff Eustace.	County.	2
	?206c + 208b, ?19:31 + D:12.	?same parties.	(County).	
89.	i 208a, *Huntingdonshire* D:3.	Burgesses (Gos & Hunef), Countess Judith (cf. i 203a, B:14).	Jurors.	X
90.	i 208a, *Huntingdonshire* D:7.	Ramsey, Aubrey de Vere (cf. i 207a, 22:1-2).	County.	2
91.	i 208a, *Huntingdonshire* D:8.	Ramsey, Ralph fitz Osmund (cf. i 204d + ?207b, 6:17 + ?27:1).	County.	X
92.	i 208a, *Huntingdonshire* D:10.	William de Warenne, Robert Fafiton (cf. i 207b, 25:1).	County.	1
93.	208b, D:17.	Robert Fafiton, William de Warenne (cf. i 205cd, 13:4).	County.	2

DOMESDAY LAWSUITS: A PROVISIONAL LIST

#	Reference	Parties	Forum	No.
94.	i 208b, *Huntingdonshire* D:13.	Robert Fafiton, Sheriff Eustace (cf. i 206c, 19:28; 207b, 25:1).	County.	1
95.	i 208b, *Huntingdonshire* D:18.	Countess Judith, William de Warenne (cf. i 205d, 13:5).	(County).	X
96.	i 208b, *Huntingdonshire* D:19.	Ely, Sheriff Eustace.	County.	X
97.	i 208b, *Huntingdonshire* D:23.	?Countess Judith, ?William d'Eu (cf. i 205c, 10:1, 207a, 20:8).	County.	2
98.	i 208c, *Huntingdonshire* D:26.	Thorney, Countess Judith (cf. i 206d, 20:1).	County.	2
99.	i 276a, *Derbyshire* 6:99.	Ralph fitz Hubert, Henry de Ferrers.	Wapentake.	2
100.	i 291b, *Nottinghamshire* 20:7.	Ilbert de Lacy, (Roger de Poitou).	Wapentake.	**1½
101.	i 373a, *Yorkshire* CN:1.	Earl Hugh, William de Percy.	?	X
102.	i 373a, *Yorkshire* CN:2.	Ralph Pagnell, St Peter's York (cf. i 303b, 2N:15).	Jurors.	1
103.	i 373a, *Yorkshire* CN:4.	Malet, Hugh fitz Baldric (cf. i 327d, 23N:30).	Jurors.	2
104.	i 373a, *Yorkshire* CE:11.	Nigel Fossard (Robert of Mortain), St John's Beverley (cf. i 307a, 5E:37).	(Jurors).	2
105.	i 373ab, *Yorkshire* CE:13+19-21.	Malet, Nigel Fossard (Robert of Mortain) (cf. i 306bc, 5E:1+9+11+13-15).	Jurors.	2
106.	373c, CW:2-3 i 373a, *Yorkshire* CE:14.	?same parties (cf. i 307cd, 5W:7).	Jurors. Wapentake.	2
107.	i 373ab, *Yorkshire* CE:15. 373b, CE:26. 373c, CE:29. CE:30. CW:2. CW:3. 374a, CW:25. CW:31.	Ralph de Mortemer, Gilbert Tison (cf. i 326c, 21E:5). Malet, William de Percy (cf. i 322c, 13E:11 etc.). (cf. i 322c, 13E:5-7). (cf. i 322d, 13E:14). (cf. 13E:13). (cf. i 321c, 13W:3). (cf. i 321c, 13W:1-2, 4). (cf. i 321d, 13W:16). (cf. 13W:17).	Jurors. Jurors. County. County. Jurors. Wapentakes. Wapentakes. Wapentake. Wapentake.	2

No.	Reference	Entry	Category	
108.	i 373b, *Yorkshire* CE:16.	Gilbert Tison, Bp of Durham.	Jurors.	X
109.	i 373b, *Yorkshire* CE:17.	Robert Malet, Bp of Durham (cf. i 304c, 3Y:5).	Jurors.	2
110.	i 373b, *Yorkshire* CE:18.	Earnwine the priest, Nigel Fossard (Robert of Mortain) (cf. i 306c, 5E:7).		
111.	i 373b, *Yorkshire* CE 22.	Malet, Gilbert Tison (cf. i 326d, 21E:10).	Jurors.	2
112.	i 373b, *Yorkshire* CE:23.	Malet, ?King's thegns (cf. i 331a, 29E:11,13,25). (if not Fossard, Percy, Tison).	Jurors.	2
113.	i 373b-c, *Yorkshire* CE:24.	St John's Beverley, Bp of Durham (cf. i 304c, 3Y:7).	County.	2
114.	373c, CE:33.	(cf. i 304a + 304c, 2E:4, 3Y:1).	County.	1
115.	i 373b, *Yorkshire* CE:25.	Abp of York, William de Percy (cf. i 322c, 13E:6).	Wapentake.	2
116.	i 373b, *Yorkshire* CE:27.	Earnwine the priest, William de Percy, Nigel Fossard (cf. i 307a, 5E:38).	County.	2
117.	i 373c, *Yorkshire* CE:28.	Abp of York, Gilbert Tison (cf. i 326d, 21E:12).	County.	X
118.	i 373c, *Yorkshire* CE:31.	Richard de Sourdeval, (Gamal) (cf. i 331a, 29E:13).	County.	1
119.	i 373c, *Yorkshire* CW:1.	Osbern de Arches, Ilbert de Lacy (cf. i 315b, 9W:12).	Jurors.	1
120.	i 374a, *Yorkshire* CW:36.	Osbern de Arches, ?	Wapentakes.	2
121.	i 373c, *Yorkshire* CW:2.	Malet, Osbern de Arches	(Wapentake).	X
	CW:3.	(cf. i 329c, 25W:29, but also no. 105 above).	Wapentakes.	2
	373d-374a CW:24,27,29	(cf. i 329c, 25W:29-30).	Wapentakes.	
	374a, CW:26	(cf. i 329a, 25W:1,3,6).	Wapentake.	
	CW:28.	(cf. i 329c, 25W:21,26).	Wapentake.	
	CW:32.	(cf. i 329b, 25W:15?).	Wapentake.	
		(Earnwine the priest) (cf. i 329b, 25W:13-14,16).	Wapentakes.	
122.	i 373c, *Yorkshire* CW:3.	Malet, Ilbert de Lacy (cf. i 315b-d, 9W:19,24,31,33).	Wapentakes.	2
123.	i 373c, *Yorkshire* CW:4.	Gilbert of Ghent, ?Ilbert de Lacy (cf. i 315c, 9W:26?).	Wapentakes.	X
124.	i 373d, *Yorkshire* CW:5.	?Ilbert de Lacy, William de Percy (cf. i 321c, 13W:1, 314a, 9W:3 etc).	Wapentakes.	1
125.	i 373d, *Yorkshire* CW:6.	Cospatric, Richard de Sourdeval (Robert of Mortain) (cf. i 330b + 330d, 28W:30 + 29W:24, 308a + 308c, 5W:18+36).	Wapentakes.	X

DOMESDAY LAWSUITS: A PROVISIONAL LIST

No.	Reference	Parties	Court	
126.	i 373d, *Yorkshire* CW:7.	Roger de Busli, William de Warenne (cf. i 321b, 12W:1,3).	Wapentake.	1
127.	i 373d, *Yorkshire* CW:11-13.	Nigel Fossard, William de Warenne? (cf. i 321ba, 12W:12,21-3,25?).	Wapentake.	X
128.	i 373d, *Yorkshire* CW:14.	Fulk de Lisors, ?Nigel Fossard (Robert de Mortain) & ?William de Warenne, (cf. i 307d, 5W:8, 321ba, 12W:1,27)	(Wapentake).	X
129.	i 373d, *Yorkshire* CW:15.	Roger de Busli, Geoffrey Aselin (cf. i 326a, 18W:2).	(Wapentake).	2
130.	CW:19.	Geoffrey Aselin, Roger de Busli (cf. i 319a, 10W:2).	(Wapentake).	2
131.	CW:16	Geoffrey Aselin, ?Nigel Fossard (Robert of Mortain) (cf. i 307d, 5W:8),	(Wapentake).	2
132.	i 373d, *Yorkshire* CW:18.	Nigel Fossard, ?Roger de Busli (cf. i 319a, 10W:2?).	(Wapentake).	X
133.	CW:21.	? same parties (cf. i 319cd, 10W:27?).	(Wapentake).	X
134.	i 373d, *Yorkshire* CW:22.	Abp of York, Roger de Busli (cf. i 320a, 10W:39.).	Wapentake.	X
135.	i 373d, *Yorkshire* CW:30	Malet, Landric. (??cf. i 331c, 29W:27)	Wapentake.	2
136.	i 374ab, *Yorkshire* CW:33+40. CW:35	William de Percy, Geoffrey Aselin (cf. i 321d, 13W:12) ? same parties	(Wapentake).	X
137.	i 374ab, *Yorkshire* CW:34+41.	Osbern de Arches, Geoffrey Aselin (cf. i 329a, 25W:9).	(Wapentake).	X
138.	i 374a, *Yorkshire* CW:37.	?Osbern de Arches, Nigel Fossard (Robert de Mortain) (cf. i 308c, 5W35 + ?329a, 25W:1,3-5,7).	(Wapentake).	
139.	i 374a, *Yorkshire* CW:38.	Ralph Pagnell, Osbern de Arches (cf. i 329b, 25W:20).	(Wapentake).	X
140.	i 374a, *Yorkshire* CW:39.	St John's Beverley, Drogo de la Beuvrière.	Wapentake.	2
141.	i 374b, *Yorkshire* CE:34-52.	Malet, Drogo de la Beuvrière (cf. i 324a-325a, 14E:12,17-19,52 etc.).	Riding. Holderness jurors.	X 2
142.	i 336a, *Lincolnshire* C:10.	Ivo Tallboys, Countess Judith.	Burgesses.	X
143.	i 336b, *Lincolnshire* C:16.	Earnwine the priest, Peterborough.	Burgesses.	X
144.	i 340d + 359d-360a + 376a, *Lincolnshire* 3:21-2,25, 29:10-11,30-1, CN:30. CS:21-2.	Eudo fitz Spirewic., Bp of Durham. (cf. i 340c, 3:10).	Wapentake, County. Wapentakes.	1 X
145.	375b, [cf. i 340cd + 359d, 3:11-12 + 29:6-7, 3; i 340d + 359d, 3:15 + 29:8, 3.]			

ENGLAND IN THE ELEVENTH CENTURY

No.	Reference	Description	Category	
146.	i 341a + 377c, *Lincs.* 3:32 + CK:52.	Bp of Durham, Wulfgeat.	Wapentake.	1
147.	i 348b + 377d, *Lincs.* 12:59 + CK:65.	Bp of Lincoln, Count Alan.	Wapentake.	2
	377d	(cf. i 348d, 12:89).	Men of Holland.	
148.	375a	CS:4.	Wapentake.	X
149.	i 348d + 377a, *Lincs.* 12:92 + CK:29.	Svartbrandr, Siward (Count Alan).	Wapentake.	1
150.	i 352a + 353d, *Lincs.* 16:6 + 22:5.	William de Percy (Roger de Poitou).	Wapentake.	3
151.	i 352a + ?376a, *Lincs.* 16:8 + ?CN:15.	?(Odo of Bayeux) & Bp of Lincoln, (Roger de Poitou).	(Riding).	2
152.	i 352b + ?376c, *Lincs.* 16:28 + ?CW:15.	?Guy de Craon, (Roger de Poitou).	Wapentake.	2
153.	i 354a + 375c, *Lincs.* 22:17 + 19 + CS:30-1.			
154.	i 354a + 375c, *Lincs.* 22:20 + CS:32.	Gilbert de Ghent & Norman d'Arcy, William de Percy.	Wapentake, County.	2
155.	i 356b + 376a, *Lincs.* 25:10 + CN:24.	Bp of Durham, William de Percy.	Wapentake.	2
156.	i 358d + 375d, *Lincs.* 27:64 + CN:8.	William de Percy, Hugh fitz Baldric.	Wapentake.	2
157.	i 360d + 376d, *Lincs.* 30:32 + CK:6.	Hugh fitz Baldric, Alfred of Lincoln (cf. i 361c, 32:2).	Riding.	2
158.	i 364a + 375c, *Lincs.* 40:8 + CS:29.	Peterborough, Drogo de la Beuvrière.	Wapentake.	2
159.	375d, *Lincolnshire* CN:9	Abp of York, Rainer de Brimeux.	County.	2
	CN:10	Rainer de Brimeux, Abp of York (cf. i 339c, 2:6).	Wapentake.	
	CN:11	(cf. i 340a, 2:25).	(Wapentake).	
	CN:23	(cf. i 339c, 2:8).	(Wapentake).	
	376a	(cf. 2:9).	Wapentake.	
160.	i 367c, *Lincolnshire* 57:18.	Waldin the Breton, Guy de Craon (cf. i365b, 46:1).	Wapentake.	X
161.	i 364b + 375a, *Lincs.* 40:26 + CS:11.	Rainer de Brimeux, ?	Riding.	X
162.	i 370a + 377a, *Lincs.* 65:1-5 + CK:27.	Westminster, Baldwin the Fleming.	Wapentake, County.	2
163.	i 375a, *Lincolnshire* CS:1.	(Odo of Bayeux), Robert *dispensator* (cf. i 363cd, 38:12).	Wapentake.	2
164.	i 375a, *Lincolnshire* CS:2.	(Odo of Bayeux), Earl Hugh (?cf. i 349c, 13:28).	Wapentake.	2
165.	i 375a, *Lincolnshire* CS:3.	Robert *dispensator*, Jocelyn son of Lambert.	Wapentake.	X
166.	i 375a, *Lincolnshire* CS:5.	Bp of Lincoln, ?William de Percy (cf. i 344a, 7:13?).	Wapentake.	1½
167.	i 375a, *Lincolnshire* CS:7.	William de Percy, Kolsveinn of Lincoln (cf. i 357a, 26:20?).	Wapentake.	2

168.	i 375a, *Lincolnshire* CS:9.	Siward Buss, Alfred of Lincoln.	Riding.	X
169.	i 375a, *Lincolnshire* CS:10.	Alfred of Lincoln, Ilbert (Odo of Bayeux) (cf. i 343b, 4:73).	Riding.	2
170.	i 375a, *Lincolnshire* CS:12.	Robert *dispensator*, Earl Hugh (cf. i 349a, 13:3).	Riding.	1
171.	i 375a, *Lincolnshire* CS:13.	Losoard, Gilbert de Ghent (cf. i 355c, 24:68).	Riding.	1
172.	i 375a, *Lincolnshire* CS:14.	Earl Hugh, Rainer de Brimeux (cf. i 364b, 40:22).	Riding.	2
173.	i 375ab, *Lincolnshire* CS:15.	Bp of Durham, Earl Hugh (cf. i 349a, 13:7).	Riding.	1
174.	i 375b, *Lincolnshire* CS:16.	Alfred of Lincoln, Earl Hugh (cf. i 358d, 27:60-1).	Riding.	1½
175.	i 375b, *Lincolnshire* CS:17.	Alfred of Lincoln, Ketilbjorn (cf. i 370d, 68:14).	Riding.	2
176.	i 375b, *Lincolnshire* CS:18.	Count Alan, Gilbert de Ghent (cf. i 355b, 24:55).	Riding.	1
177.	i 375b, *Lincolnshire* CS:19.	Bp of Durham, Gilbert de Ghent.	Riding.	X
178.	i 375b, *Lincolnshire* CS:20.	Ketilbjorn, ?Ivo Tallboys.	Riding.	X
179.	i 375b, *Lincolnshire* CS:23. 375c, CS:33. CS:36.	Robert *dispensator*, Gilbert de Ghent (cf. i 354d, 24:16). (cf. i 354d, 24:20+22). (cf. i 355b, 24:47).	Wapentake. Wapentake. Wapentake.	1
180.	i 375b, *Lincolnshire* CS:24.	Robert *dispensator*, Erneis de Buron & Earl Hugh & (Odo of Bayeux). (cf. i 362b, 34:12).	Wapentake, Riding.	X
181.	i 375b, *Lincolnshire* CS:25.	Rainer de Brimeux, Alfred of Lincoln (cf. i 358a, 27:21).	Wapentake, Riding.	1
182.	i 375bc, *Lincolnshire* CS:26.	Erneis de Buron, William de Percy (cf. i 354b, 22:37).	Wapentake.	2
183.	i 375c, *Lincolnshire* CS:27.	Abp of York, Ivo Tallboys (cf. i 351a, 14:59 + 339d, 2:16).	Wapentake, Riding.	1
184.	i 375c, *Lincolnshire* CS:28.	Abp of York, (Odo of Bayeux) (cf. i 343a, 4:53).	County.	2
185.	i 375c, *Lincolnshire* CS:34.	Robert *dispensator*, Ketilbjorn (cf. i 370d, 68:6)	(Wapentake).	2
186.	i 375c, *Lincolnshire* CS:35.	Ivo Tallboys, Earl Hugh (cf. i 349a, 13:6?).	Wapentake.	X
187.	i 375c, *Lincolnshire* CS:37.	Ketilbjorn, Gilbert de Ghent (cf. i 355b, 24:47).	Wapentake.	1
188.	i 375d, *Lincolnshire* CN:4.	'Alfred', ?'Hugh' (cf. i 371b, 68:39?).	(County).	X
189.	i 375d, *Lincolnshire* CN:5.	Drogo de la Beuvrière & 'Alfred', 'Hugh' (cf. i 371b, 68:40).	Wapentake.	1
190.	i 375d, *Lincolnshire* CN:7.	'Jocelyn', Count Alan (cf. i 347a, 12:10)	County.	2
191.	i 375d, *Lincolnshire* CN:12.	Alfred of Lincoln, Durand Malet (cf. i 357d + 365a, 27:3 + 44:8).	(Wapentake).	X

192. i 375d-376a, *Lincolnshire* CN:13. Rainer de Brimeux, (Odo of Bayeux) (cf. i 342c + 343b, 4:27+69 & no. 195). (Wapentake). — 2

(Odo of Bayeux), ?Siward the priest (cf. i 371b, 68:42).

193. i 376a, *Lincolnshire* CN:16. Jocelyn son of Lambert, ?Siward the priest (?cf. i 371b, 68:43/46). (Wapentake). — 2

194. i 376a, *Lincolnshire* CN:17. Rainer de Brimeux, Jocelyn son of Lambert (cf. i 359b, 28:20). (Wapentake). — X

195. i 376a, *Lincolnshire* CN:18. Jocelyn son of Lambert, 'Geoffrey' (Ivo Tallboys) (cf. i 350a, 14:11). Riding. — 2

196. i 376a, *Lincolnshire* CN:19. William Blunt, Ivo Tallboys (cf. i 350b, 14:15). (Riding). — X

197. i 376a, *Lincolnshire* CN:20. Bp of Durham, Count Alan (cf. i 340c + 347bc, 3:6-7 + 12:19+30). (Riding). — X

198. i 376a, *Lincolnshire* CN:21 + 25. Count Alan & Drogo de la Beuvrière, Wapentake. — X

199. i 376a, *Lincolnshire* CN:22. Robert *dispensator*. (cf. i 363d, 38:14). Wapentake. — 2

200. i 376a, *Lincolnshire* CN:26. Kolsveinn, Count Alan (cf. i 347c, 12:29/31). Wapentake. — 1

201. i 376a, *Lincolnshire* CN:27. Bp of Lincoln, Drogo de la Beuvrière (cf. i 360c, 30:20). (Wapentake). — 2

202. i 376a, *Lincolnshire* CN:28. Drogo de la Beuvrière, Ivo Tallboys. Riding, County. — X

203. i 376a, *Lincolnshire* CN:29. Bp of Durham, Berengar de Tosny (cf. i 353a, 18:9). Wapentake. — 2

204. i 376b, *Lincolnshire* CW:1. ?Gilbert de Ghent, Svartbrandr (cf. i 370d, 68:1 + 354c, 24:3?). (Wapentake). — 1

205. i 376b, *Lincolnshire* CW:2. Peterborough, Kolsveinn (cf. i 345d, 8:13). Wapentake. — 1½

206. i 376b, *Lincolnshire* CW:3. Jocelyn son of Lambert, Norman *crassus* (cf. i 362a, 33:1). Wapentake. — 2

207. i 376b, *Lincolnshire* CW:4. Norman *crassus*, ?Gilbert de Ghent (cf. i 354c, 24:1). (Wapentake). — X

208. i 376b, *Lincolnshire* CW:5. Norman *crassus*, Kolsveinn (cf. i 356d, 26:5). (Wapentake). — 2

209. i 376b, *Lincolnshire* CW:6. Gilbert de Ghent, Peterborough (cf. i 345c, 8:2). (Wapentake). — 1

210. i 376b, *Lincolnshire* CW:7. Bp of Lincoln, Gilbert of Ghent (cf. i 354c, 24:8). Wapentake. — 2

211. i 376b, *Lincolnshire* CW:8. Ranulf de St Valéry & Kolsveinn, Wapentake. — X

Peterborough (cf. i 345c + ?364d, 8:3 + ?43:5).

212. i 376b, *Lincolnshire* CW:13. ?Bp of Lincoln, Jocelyn son Lambert & Ivo Tallboys (cf. i 350b + 359a, 14:21 + 28:4). (Shire). — 1

213. i 376c, *Lincolnshire* CW:16. ?, Peterborough (cf. i 345d-346a, 8:15,17,20,23). Shire. — X

214. i 376c, *Lincolnshire* CW:17 a). Norman *crassus*, Geoffrey de la Guerche (cf. i 369b, 63:7). Riding. — 2

DOMESDAY LAWSUITS: A PROVISIONAL LIST

No.	Reference	Parties	Court	
215.	i 376c, *Lincolnshire* CW:17 b,d).	Gilbert de Ghent, Geoffrey de la Guerche (cf. 369bc, 63:12,25).	Riding.	2
216.	i 376c, *Lincolnshire* CW:17 c).	Henry de Ferrers, Geoffrey de la Guerche (cf. i 369c, 63:17).	Riding.	2
217.	i 376c, *Lincolnshire* CW:18.	?Gilbert de Ghent, Erneis de Buron (cf. i 362c, 34:25).	Wapentake.	X
218.	i 376c, *Lincolnshire* CW:20.	Norman d'Arcy, Drogo de la Beuvrière (cf i 360b, 30:3).	Wapentake.	2
219.	i 376d, *Lincolnshire* CK:1	Robert de Tosny, Alfred of Lincoln (cf. i 353a + 358b, 18:11-12 + 27:34,37-9). (cf. i 358a + 358c, 18:16 + 27:55).	Wapentake, Riding.	1
220.	377b, CK:47 376d, CK:9	Alfred of Lincoln, Robert de Tosny (cf. i 353b, 358b, 18:19 etc., 27:34,41).	Wapentake.	
221.	i 376d, *Lincolnshire* CK:2.	?Peterborough/Alfred of Lincoln, Countess Judith (cf. i 366d, 56:4).	Wapentake.	1
222.	i 376d, *Lincolnshire* CK:3.	Gunfrid de Choques, Atsurr (?Gilbert de Ghent) (cf. i 354d/355a, 24:29/35?).	Wapentake.	2
223.	i 376d, *Lincolnshire* CK:4.	??Odger the Breton, Peterborough (cf. i 346b, 8:34-5,37, & no. 254 below).	Wapentake.	2
224.	i 376d, *Lincolnshire* CK:7.	Ratbod, ?Peterborough (?cf. i 345c, 8:7).	Wapentake.	1
225.	i 376d, *Lincolnshire* CK:8.	Bp of Lincoln, Abp of York (cf. i 340b, 2:37).	(Wapentake).	X
226.	i 376d, *Lincolnshire* CK:12.	Bp of Lincoln, Robert of Stafford (cf. i 368d + 345a, 59:20 + 7:53).	Wapentake.	1
227.	i 376d, *Lincolnshire* CK:13.	Bp of Lincoln, Bp of Durham. (cf. i 341b, 3:37, 345a, 7:53).	Wapentake.	2
228.	i 376d, *Lincolnshire* CK:14.	Walter d'Aincourt, ?Heppo *ballistarius* (?cf. i 369a, 61:5, 361b, 31:11).	Wapentake.	1
229.	i 376d, *Lincolnshire* CK:15.	?Walter d'Aincourt, ?Durand Malet (cf. i 361b, 31:14-15, 365b, 44:16).	Wapentake.	X
230.	i 376d, *Lincolnshire* CK:16.	Robert of Stafford, Abp of York (cf. i 339d, 2:17, 368d, 59:19).	(Wapentake).	X
231.	i 376d, *Lincolnshire* CK:17.	Earl Hugh, ?(Roger de Poitou) (cf. i 352a + ?352c, 16:12 + ?50).	Wapentake.	1
232.	i 377a, *Lincolnshire* CK:18.	Svarbrandr, Geoffrey de Coutances (cf. i 343d, 6:1).	Wapentake.	1
233.	i 377a, *Lincolnshire* CK:19.	Robert de Tosny, Countess Judith (cf. i 366d, 56:6-7).	Wapentake.	2
234.	i 377a, *Lincolnshire* CK:20.	Robert de Tosny, Robert Malet (cf. i 368b, 58:4).	Wapentake.	2

No.	Reference	Entry		
235.	i 377a, *Lincolnshire* CK:20.	Robert of Stafford, Robert Malet (cf. i 368b + 353b, 58:4 + 18:27-8).	Wapentake.	2
236.	i 377a, *Lincolnshire* CK:22.	Ivo Tallboys, Robert de Tosny.	Wapentake.	X
237.	i 377a + 377c, *Lincolnshire* CK:23 + 51	Robert of Stafford, Karli (Count Alan) (cf. i 348a + 348d, 12:55+91).	Wapentake.	1
238.	i 377a, *Lincolnshire* CK:25.	Osbern *legatus regis*, Countess Judith (cf. i 367a, 56:15).	Wapentake.	2
239.	i 377a, *Lincolnshire* CK:26.	Drogo de la Beuvrière, Osbern de Arches.	Wapentake.	X
240.	i 377a, *Lincolnshire* CK:28.	Kofsi (Ralph de Mortemer), Westminster (cf. i 346b, 9:2, 363a, 36:3-4).	Wapentake.	2
241.	i 377a, *Lincolnshire* CK:30.	?Gilbert de Ghent, 'Martin' (cf. i 365b, 45:4, ?355a, 24:38).	Wapentake.	X
242.	i 377ab, *Lincolnshire* CK:31.	Ralph Pagnell, Kolsveinn (cf. i 357a, 26:27).	Wapentake.	1
243.	i 377b, *Lincolnshire* CK:32.	Waldin the Breton, Ramsey (cf. i 346c, 10:1).	Wapentake.	1
244.	i 377b, *Lincolnshire* CK:35.	Robert Malet, Gilbert de Ghent (cf. i 356a + 355d, 24:99+83).	Wapentake.	2
245.	i 377b, *Lincolnshire* CK:36.	Gilbert de Ghent, Robert de Vesci (cf. i 363b, 37:2).	Wapentake.	1
246.	i 377b, *Lincolnshire* CK:37-8.	Count Alan, William de Warenne (cf. i 351d, 15:1-2).	Wapentake.	1
247.	i 377b, *Lincolnshire* CK:39.	Bp of Durham, ?Osbern priest & Ralph (cf. i 366c, 54:1).	Wapentake.	X
248.	i 377b, *Lincolnshire* CK:40.	Drogo de la Beuvrière, Odger the Breton (cf. i 364c, 42:1-2).	Wapentake.	1
249.	i 377b, *Lincolnshire* CK:41-2.	Heppo *ballistarius*, Odger the Breton (cf. i 364cd, 42:6 + 17-18).	Wapentake.	2
250.	i 377b, *Lincolnshire* CK:43.	Ramsey, Odger the Breton (cf. i 364d, 42:19).	Wapentake.	2
251	i 377b, *Lincolnshire* CK:44.	Gilbert de Ghent, Odger the Breton (cf. i 364c, 42:14).	Wapentake.	2
252.	i 377b, *Lincolnshire* CK:45.	Peterborough, Bp of Lincoln (cf. i 344c, 7:30).	Wapentake.	2
253.	i 377b, *Lincolnshire* CK:46.	Robert de Tosny, Odger the Breton (cf. i 364c, 42:11).	Wapentake.	1
254.	i 377b-c, *Lincolnshire* CK:48.	St Guthlac's Crowland, Odger the Breton (cf. i 364c, 42:13).	Wapentake.	2
255.	i 377c, *Lincolnshire* CK:49.	St Guthlac's Crowland, Guy de Craon (cf. i 367b, 57:12).	Wapentake.	2
256.	i 377c, *Lincolnshire* CK:53.	Ralph Pagnell, Guy de Craon (cf. i 367c, 57:15).	Wapentake.	2
257.	i 377c, *Lincolnshire* CK:56.	Peterborough, Robert de Tosny (cf. i 353b, 18:24).	Wapentake.	2
258.	i 377c, *Lincolnshire* CK:57.	Walter d'Aincourt, Guy de Raimbeaucourt (cf. i 363d, 39:3).	Wapentake.	1

DOMESDAY LAWSUITS: A PROVISIONAL LIST

No.	Reference	Parties	Court	Value
259.	i 377c, *Lincolnshire* CK:58.	Drogo de la Beuvrière, Guy de Craon (cf. i 367c, 57:22).	Wapentake.	1
260.	i 377c, *Lincolnshire* CK:60.	Kolgrimr, Guy de Craon (cf. i 367c, 57:25).	Wapentake.	2
261.	i 377c, *Lincolnshire* CK:61.	Kolgrimr, Guy de Raimbeaucourt (cf. i 363d, 39:4).	Wapentake.	1
262.	i 377c, *Lincolnshire* CK:62.	Bishop Osmund, ?Walter d'Aincourt (cf. i 361a, 31:5?).	Wapentake.	X
263.	i 377c, *Lincolnshire* CK:63.	Gilbert de Ghent, Ivo Tallboys (cf. i 351c, 14:89).	Wapentake.	1
264.	i 377c, *Lincolnshire* CK:64.	Robert of Stafford & Kolsveinn, ?Osbern priest & Ralph (?cf. i 366c, 54:2).	Wapentake.	X
265.	i 377d, *Lincolnshire* CK:66.	Count Alan, Guy de Craon (cf. i 368ab, 57:44+56).	'King's barons'.	**2
266.	CK:69.	Guy de Craon, Count Alan (cf. i 348c, 12:76).	?	1
267.	i 377d, *Lincolnshire* CK:68.	Alfred of Lincoln, Count Alan (cf. i 348d, 12:90).	Men of Holland.	2

'Circuit VII'

No.	Reference	Parties	Court	Value
268.	ii 2a, *Essex* 1:2.	Ely, Jocelyn Lorimer.	Hundred.	X
269.	ii 13b, *Essex* 5:10.	St Paul's, Ralph Baynard.	Hundred.	1½
270.	ii 14a, *Essex* 6:1.	Westminster, St Martin's London.	County.	1½
271.	ii 14b + 100a, *Essex* 6:8 + 90:17.	Westminster, Mauger (Hugh de Montfort).	Hundred.	1½
272.	ii 15b + 80b, *Essex* 7:1 + 37:9.	Bp of Durham, Ranulf brother of Ilger.	Hundred.	3
273.	ii 18b, *Essex* 9:14.	Barking, Odo (Sveinn).	Hundred.	1½
274.	ii 19a + ?36b, *Essex* 10:2 + ?22:8.	Ely, William de Warenne.	Hundred.	3
275.	ii 19a + 75a, *Essex* 10:3 + 34:30.	Ely, Ranulf Peverel.	Hundred.	3
276.	74a, 34:19.		Hundred.	2
277.	ii 19a + 51a, *Essex* 10:3 + 25:20.	Ely, Eudo *dapifer*. (Geoffrey de Mandeville).	Hundred.	3
278.	49a + 62a, 25:3 + 30:41. [cf. 18b + 50a, 10:1 + 25:12, 3.]	(Geoffrey de Mandeville).	Hundred.	2
279.	ii 19b, *Essex* 10:5.	Ely, William Cardon (Geoffrey de Mandeville).	Hundred.	1½
280.	ii 23a, *Essex* 18:6-7.	?, (Odo of Bayeux).	'English'.	2

ENGLAND IN THE ELEVENTH CENTURY

281.	ii 25a, *Essex* 18:36.	Ely, Thorold of Rochester (Odo of Bayeux).	Hundred.	X
282.	ii 31b-32a, *Essex* 20:56.	Ranulf Peverel, Count Eustace.	Hundred.	2
283.	ii 50b, *Essex* 25:16.	Geoffrey de Mandeville, Eudo *dapifer*.	Hundred.	2
284.	ii 54a, *Essex* 27:14.	Ely, Hugh de Montfort.	Hundred.	2
285.	ii 57b, *Essex* 30:3.	Barking, Geoffrey de Mandeville.	Hundred.	2
286.	ii 60a, *Essex* 30:23.	Geoffrey de Mandeville, Richard fitz Gilbert.	Hundred.	1½
287.	ii 60ab, *Essex* 30:27.	Ely, Geoffrey de Mandeville.	Hundred.	2
288.	ii 71a + 99b, *Essex* 33:21 + 90:8.	Ralph Baynard, Theodoric Pointel.	?	**1½
289.	ii 89b, *Essex* 47:3.	Hugh de Gournai, (Roger de Poitou).	Hundred.	1½
290.	ii 93a + 99a *Essex* 60:1 + 90:1.	Godwin Woodhen, Hugh de St Quentin.	?	1½
291.	ii 94b, *Essex* 66:1.	William the deacon, Hamo *dapifer*.	Hundred.	**1½
292.	ii 97b, *Essex* 79:1.	Ely, Reginald *ballistarius*.	Hundred.	2
293.	ii 100b, *Essex* 90:34.	Geoffrey de Mandeville, William Cardon.	?	X
294.	ii 102b, *Essex* 90:64.	Engelric (?Count Eustace), Richard fitz Gilbert.	Hundred.	X
295.	ii 148b, *Norfolk* 4:39.	Robert Malet, Count Alan.	Roger Bigot (Sheriff).	2
296.	ii 158b + 172ab, *Norfolk* 8:8 + 137.	Drogo de la Beuvrière, William de Warenne.	Hundred.	2
297.	ii 159b, *Norfolk* 8:17.	St Benet Holme, William de Warenne.	Hundred.	2
298.	ii 161b, *Norfolk* 8:29.	Reginald fitz Ivo, William de Warenne.	Hundred.	2
299.	ii 174ab, *Norfolk* 9:13.	St Benet Holme, Roger Bigot.	Hundred.	2
300.	ii 176b-177a, *Norfolk* 9:49.	Count Alan, Roger Bigot.	Hundred.	1
301.	ii 181b, *Norfolk* 9:104.	(Ailwin of Thetford), Roger Bigot.	Hundred.	1
302.	ii 186a, *Norfolk* 9:167.	Roger Bigot, ?under-reeve of Earsham.	Hundred.	1½
303.	ii 190a, *Norfolk* 9:227.	Hermer de Ferrers, Roger Bigot.	Hundred.	1
304.	ii 208a, *Norfolk* 13:19.	Ely, Hermer de Ferrers.	Hundred.	2
305.	213a, 15:2.	Hermer de Ferrers, Ely.	Hundred.	1
306.	ii 224a, *Norfolk* 19:24.	St Benet Holme, William d'Écouis.	Hundred.	2

DOMESDAY LAWSUITS: A PROVISIONAL LIST

No.	Reference	Parties	Court	
307.	ii 245a, *Norfolk* 27:2.	Ivo Tallboys, Roger fitz Reynard.	Hundred.	1½
308.	ii 245a, *Norfolk* 28:1.	Ralph de Tosny, Ralph de Limésy.	Hundred.	2
309.	ii 249b + 253b, *Norfolk* 31:11 + 44.	Robert fitz Corbucion, Ralph Baynard.	Hundred.	1
310.	ii 250b + 275a, *Norfolk* 31:20 + 66:35.	Ely, Ralph Baynard.	Hundred.	2
311.	ii 259b, *Norfolk* 35:11.	St Benet Holme, Robert fitz Corbucion.	Hundred.	2
312.	ii 264b, *Norfolk* 47:7.	'A poor nun', Isaac.	Hundred.	2
313.	ii 276b, *Norfolk* 66:59.	Bury St Edmund's, Drogo (Robert Malet).	?	X
314.	ii 278ab, *Norfolk* 66:86.	Count Eustace, Herbert *camerarius* of Roger Bigot.	?	**X
315.	ii 291a, *Suffolk* 2:6.	Hugh de Montfort, Robert of Mortain.	Hundred.	1
316.	ii 409a, *Suffolk* 31:48.	Robert of Mortain, Hugh de Montfort (?possibly same plea).	Hundred.	2
317.	ii 299b, *Suffolk* 4:13.	Count Alan, Earl Hugh.	Hundred.	2
318.	ii 313a, *Suffolk* 6:92.	Roger Bigot, Robert Malet.	Hundred.	2
319.	332a, 7:13.	Robert Malet, Roger Bigot.	Hundred.	1
320.	ii 337b + 338ab, *Suffolk* 7:64+68.	Roger de Rames, Roger Bigot.	Hundred.	1
321.	ii 352a, *Suffolk* 8:63.	Roger de Rames, (Roger of Poitou).	Hundred.	2
322.	ii 373a, *Suffolk* 16:3.	Ely, Roger Bigot (Odo of Bayeux).	Hundred.	2
323.	ii 377a, *Suffolk* 16:34.	Earl Hugh, Roger Bigot (Odo of Bayeux).	Hundred, County, King's Barons.	**1
324.	ii 379a, *Suffolk* 18:4.	Bury St Edmunds, Bp of Thetford.	Hundred.	2
325.	ii 393a, *Suffolk* 25:53.	Ely, Richard fitz Gilbert.	Hundred.	2
326.	ii 397b, *Suffolk* 25:105.	?, Richard fitz Gilbert.	Hundred.	1
327.	ii 399b-400a, *Suffolk* 26:12d.	Count Alan, William de Warenne.	Hundred.	2
328.	ii 400a, *Suffolk* 26:13-14.	Robert Malet, William de Warenne.	Hundred.	2
329.	ii 405b + 448b, *Suffolk* 30:3 + 76:14.	William d'Auberville, Hugh de Houdain.	Hundred.	**1½
330.	ii 406b, *Suffolk* 31:13a.	Ely, Hugh de Montfort.	Hundred.	2
331.	ii 407b, *Suffolk* 31:34.	?Earl Hugh, Hugh de Montfort (cf. ii 302a, 4:40?).	Hundred.	2

ENGLAND IN THE ELEVENTH CENTURY

332.	ii 421b, *Suffolk* 38:3.	Ely, Roger de Rames.	Hundred.	2
333.	ii 424a, *Suffolk* 39:3.	Ralph Pagnell, Ranulf brother of Ilger.	Hundred.	1
334.	ii 433a, *Suffolk* 52:1.	Robert Malet, Humphrey *camerarius*.	Hundred.	2
335.	ii 434b-435a, *Suffolk* 53:6.	Robert Malet, Eudo fitz Spirewic.	Hundred.	2
336.	ii 443b, *Suffolk* 67:30.	Ely, Hervey de Bourges.	Hundred.	X
337.	ii 448b, *Suffolk* 76:8-12.	Bury St Edmund's, William de Parthenay.	?	X
338.	ii 449a, *Suffolk* 76:18.	William de Warenne, Robert de Courson.	?	X
339.	ii 450a, *Suffolk* 77:1-4.	Mother of Robert Malet, (Odo of Bayeux) (see Appendix A 29).	Hundred.	**X

Statistics

Circuit	County	Count	1:	1½:	2:	3:	X:
Circuit I: 19:	Hants.	10 (3 church)	1: 1,	1½: 2,	2: 6,	3:1,	X: 0
	Surrey	4 (2 church)	1: 0,	1½: 2,	2: 2,	3: 0,	X: 0
	Kent	2 (2 church)	1: 0,	1½: 0,	2: 0,	3: 1,	X: 1
	Berks.	2 (1 church)	1: 0,	1½: 0,	2: 2,	3: 0,	X: 0
	Sussex	1 (1 church)	1: 0,	1½: 0,	2: 1,	3: 0,	X: 0
	Total:	9 church	1: 0,	1½: 4,	2: 11,	3: 2,	X: 1
Circuit II: 7:	Wiltshire	6 (2 church)	1: 0,	1½: 3,	2: 0,	3: 3,	X: 0
	Devon	1 (1 church)	1: 0,	1½: 0,	2: 0,	3: 1,	X: 0
	Total:	3 church	1: 0,	1½: 3,	2: 0,	3: 4,	X: 0
Circuit III: 46:	Bedford.	17 (4 church)	1: 0,	1½: 10,	2: 5,	3: 1,	X: 1
	Cambs.	16 (10 church)	1: 0,	1½: 4,	2: 10,	3: 2,	X: 0
	Herts.	9 (4 church)	1: 0,	1½: 2,	2:7,	3: 0,	X: 0
	Bucks.	2 (0 church)	1: 0,	1½: 1,	2: 1,	3: 0,	X: 0
	Middlesex	2 (1 church)	1: 0,	1½: 0,	2: 2,	3: 0,	X: 0
	Total:	19 church	1: 0,	1½: 17,	2: 25,	3: 3,	X: 1
Circuit V: 10:	Cheshire	4 (4 church)	1: 1,	1½: 0,	2: 2,	3: 1,	X: 0
	Worcs.	3 (3 church)	1: 0,	1½: 1,	2: 2,	3: 0,	X: 0
	Glos.	1 (1 church)	1: 1,	1½: 0,	2: 0,	3: 0,	X: 0
	Hereford.	1 (1 church)	1: 0,	1½: 0,	2: 1,	3: 0,	X: 0
	Shrops.	1 (1 church)	1: 0,	1½: 0,	2: 1,	3: 0,	X: 0
	Total:	10 church	1: 2,	1½: 1,	2: 6,	3: 1,	X: 0
Circuit VI: 185:	Lincs.	126 (40 church)	1: 36,	1½: 3,	2: 54,	3: 1,	X: 32
	Yorks.	41 (10 church)	1: 7,	1½: 0,	2: 18,	3: 0,	X: 16
	Hunts.	16 (7 church)	1: 3,	1½: 0,	2: 6,	3: 0,	X: 7
	Derby.	1 (0 church)	1: 0,	1½: 0,	2: 1,	3: 0,	X: 0
	Notts.	1 (0 church)	1: 0,	1½: 1,	2: 0,	3: 0,	X: 0
	Total:	57 church	1: 46,	1½: 4,	2: 79,	3: 1,	X: 55
Circuit VII: 72:	Essex	27 (17 church)	1: 0,	1½: 10,	2: 9,	3: 4,	X: 4
	Suffolk	25 (7 church)	1: 6,	1½: 1,	2: 15,	3: 0,	X: 3
	Norfolk	20 (8 church)	1: 5,	1½: 2,	2: 11,	3: 0,	X: 2
	Total:	32 church	1: 11,	1½: 13,	2: 35,	3: 4,	X: 9
TOTALS: 339		130 church	1: 60	1½: 42	2: 156	3: 15	X: 66

Appendices

A. *Pre Domesday (and post-Conquest) Suits*
  [* = otherwise recorded; restorations without reference to formal process are omitted]

*1. i 2a, *Kent* C:8.   Christ Church & St Augustine's
                                                Canterbury, Brumann the reeve.

*2. i 5b, *Kent* 4:16.   Rochester, Odo of Bayeux [Penenden Heath].

3. i 32a, *Surrey* 5:28.   Odo of Bayeux, Rannulf the Sheriff.
4. i 32a, *Surrey* 5:28.   Men of Southwark, ?Count Eustace.
5. i 35b, *Surrey* 19:25.   Richard fitz Gilbert, ?.
6. i 36d, *Surrey* 36:1.   Oswald brother of Abbot of Chertsey,
                                                Geoffrey the Small.

7. i 48d, *Hampshire* 53:2.   Aldred brother of Odo, ?William the Archer.

8. i 101d *Devon* 2:2 (*Exon.* 117a2).   Bp of Exeter, Dunn.

9. i 121a, *Cornwall* 4:21.   St Petroc's, (Earl Harold).

10. i 190a + 199d,
      Cambs. 1:16 + 29:12.   Sheriff Picot, Aubrey de Vere.

11 i 238c, *Warwickshire* 3:4.   Bp of Worcester, Beorhtnoth and Æthelwig.
12. i 244c, *Warwickshire* 44:12.   Leofwin, Bp of Worcester.

13. i 173a + 173d, *Worcs.* 2:24 + 63.   Abp Aldred, Brictric son of Doda.
*14. i 175d, *Worcestershire* 10:12.   Evesham, Urse D'Abtetot etc. *[Ildberga].*

15. i 376d, *Lincolnshire* CK:10.   Abp Aldred, Ilbold.

16. ii 10a, *Essex* 3:7.   St Paul's, ?.
17. ii 61a, *Essex* 30:30.   Geoffrey de Mandeville, ?.

*18. ii 213b + 214ab, *Norfolk* 15:10 +
      13 + 22 + ii 383a + 385a-b + 388a
      + 403a + 404b, *Suffolk* 21:17 + 19 +
      45-6 + 49-50 + 52 + 95 + 28:2 + 29:9.   Ely, sundry parties ['Kentford'].
19. ii 221a, *Norfolk* 17:63.   Bury St Edmunds, Godric (King?)
20. ii 221b, *Norfolk* 19:2.   Earl Ralph, ?
21. ii 242a, *Norfolk* 25:15.   Earl Ralph, ?
*22. ii 381a, *Suffolk* 20:1.   Rochester, (Picot) [Freckenham suit, also at
                                                Penenden Heath?].
23. ii 394ab, *Suffolk* 25:60.   Richard fitz Gilbert, Bp of Thetford.
24. ii 412a, *Suffolk* 32:16.   King, ?
25. ii 418b, *Suffolk* 35:3.   King, Ralph Tallboys & Finn.

26. ii 421b, *Suffolk* 38:3.   Ely, ?
27. ii 424a, *Suffolk* 39:3.   Ralph Pagnell, Ranulf brother of Ilger.
28. ii 446b, *Suffolk* 74:11.   Sheriff, Flint.
29. ii 447b, *Suffolk* 75:5.   Mother of Robert Malet, Odo of Bayeux
                                                  (see main table, no. 339).

B. Forfeitures 1066-86

1. i 1a, *Kent* D:9.   Two forfeitures, ? same offender.
2. i 30a, *Surrey* 1:1c.   Pre-1066 tenant.
3. i 32b, *Surrey* 6:1.   Forfeiture '*propter inimicitiam*'?.
4. i 62d, *Berkshire* 46:4.   Abt Ælfsige of Ramsey.

5. i 137a, *Hertfordshire* 16:2.   Earl Ralph (uncounted subsequent
                                                  references, esp. in Norfolk, Suffolk).
6. i 141a, *Hertfordshire* 36:9.   Sokeman forfeited for not paying king's geld.
7. i 153b, *Buckinghamshire* 57:18.   Alric Bolest.
8. i 210c, *Bedfordshire* 6:1.   Wulfmær, priest of King Edward.
9. i 216c, *Bedfordshire* 46:1.   Forfeiture for refusal to pay '*gablum*'.

10. i 162d, *Gloucestershire* 1:6.   Wulfweard.
11. i 175b, *Worcestershire* 9:1b.   Atsurr.

12. i 298a, *Yorkshire* C:10.   Forfeiture to Earl Hugh as Sheriff.
13. i 336b, *Lincolnshire* C:14.   Siward the priest forfeiture of 40 shillings.
14. i 375a + 375c, *Lincs.* CS:12+36.   Vigleikr forfeited '*contra*' Gilbert de Ghent.
15. i 375c, *Lincolnshire* CS:37.   ?Godric.
16. i 376b, *Lincolnshire* CW:10.   Gunnhvatr.

17. ii 24a, *Essex* 18:23.   A 'free man'.
18. ii 48a, *Essex* 24:65.   Brihtsige.
19. ii 49b, *Essex* 25:5.   A '*francus homo*'.
20. ii 59a, *Essex* 30:16.   Scalpi ('died in outlawry in Yorkshire').
21. ii 66b, *Essex* 32:28.   A 'free man' forfeited for theft.
22. ii 98a, *Essex* 83:1.   'Men' (with 1 hide).
23. ii 98a, *Essex* 83:2.   Godman ('unable to emend').
24. ii 158b, *Norfolk* 8:8.   Humphrey.
25. ii 176b, *Norfolk* 9:49.   Ælfric outlawed.
26. ii 199a, *Norfolk* 10:67.   Forfeiture of woman for premature marriage.
27. ii 200a, *Norfolk* 10:76-7.   Outlawry of Eadric the helmsman.
28. ii 214a, *Norfolk* 15:12.   Wulfric forfeiture of £8.
29. ii 217b, *Norfolk* 17:22.   Forfeiture of 30 acres.
30. ii 274a, *Norfolk* 66:5.   Godwin outlawed.
31. ii 277b, *Norfolk* 66:78.   A 'free man' outlawed.
32. ii 278a, *Norfolk* 66:82.   Alfred forfeited (later '*quietus*').
33. ii 299b, *Suffolk* 4:15.   Walter of Dol (several subsequent references).
34. ii 383a, *Suffolk* 21:16.   Harduin.
35. ii 405b + 448b, *Suffolk* 30:3
        + 76:14.   Arrest of Hugh de Houdain.

36. ii 443b, *Suffolk* 67:30. Three 'free men' forfeited to Abt of Bury
St Edmund's.
37. ii 448a, *Suffolk* 76:5. Wihtgar.

C *'King's Pleas'*
[Understood for these purposes as adjudications (other than *'Terrae Occupatae'* in *Liber Exoniensis*, and *'Invasiones'* appended to the three shires in Vol. II), where the king is one of the parties and there is no third; fiscal pleas, relating merely to geld, appurtenances to manors, tolls etc., are also omitted.]

1. i 2c, *Kent* 1:1. Helto *dapifer* & nephew.
2. i 2c, *Kent* 1:1. Hugh de Port.
3. i 30a + 32a, *Surrey* 1:1c-e + 5:28. (Odo of Bayeux).
4. i 30b, *Surrey* 1:5. Bp of Lisieux.
5. i 32a, *Surrey* 5:25. Hugh de Port (Odo).
6. i 32a, *Surrey* 5:26. Herfrid (Odo).
7. i 35b, *Surrey* 19:27. Richard fitz Gilbert.
8. i 35d-36a, *Surrey* 21:3. William fitz Ansculf.
9. i 36a, *Surrey* 23:1. Walter de Douai.
10. i 36b, *Surrey* 25:1-2. Geoffrey de Mandeville.
11. i 39b, *Hampshire* 1:42. Geoffrey *camerarius*.
12. i 39c, *Hampshire* 1:47. Robert of Mortain.
13. i 42ab, *Hampshire* 4:1. Abp of York.
14. i 43a, *Hampshire* 6:1. New Minster.
15. i 44b, *Hampshire* 18:2. Count Alan.
16. i 44d, *Hampshire* 21:7. Roger of Montgomery.
17. i 46c, *Hampshire* 28:1. Robert fitz Gerald.
18. i 49d, *Hampshire* 69:4. Edwin.
19. i 50a, *Hampshire* 69:16. Alwin 'Rat'.
20. i 50b, *Hampshire* 69:33. Sæwin.
21. i 56b, *Berkshire* B:1. Nigel (? plus son of Ælfsige of Faringdon,
& Humphrey Visdeloup).

22. i 57d + 60cd, *Berkshire* 1:37-8
+ i 21:13 + 17 + 20 + 22. Henry de Ferrers.
23. i 58a, *Berkshire* 1:43. Ælfwold *camerarius*.
24. i 58c, *Berkshire* 5:1. Bp of Exeter.
25. i 59b, *Berkshire* 7:38. Abingdon.
26. i 63b, *Berkshire* 58:2. Hugolin the helmsman.

27. i 64d, *Wiltshire* 1:1. Alfred 'of Spain'.
28. *Exon.* 178b2, cf. *DB* i 101b,
Devon 1:50. Tavistock Abbey.
29. i 100b + 107a, *Devon* 1:5 + 16:74. Robert de Pont-Chardon.
30. i 102c, *Devon* 3:32. Geoffrey de Coutances.
31. i 114a, *Devon* 34:5. Ralph de Pomeroy.

32. i 132b, *Hertfordshire* 1:1. St Mary's Chatteris.
33. i 132d + 133a, *Hertfordshire*

	1:9 + 12-13.	Geoffrey de Bec.
34.	i 133a, *Hertfordshire* 1:17.	King's sokeman.
35.	i 133c, *Hertfordshire* 4:1.	Bp of London.
36.	i 141b, *Hertfordshire* 36:13.	Peter de Valognes.
37.	i 142a, *Hertfordshire* 38:2.	Edgar Ætheling.
38.	i 149b, *Buckinghamshire* 18:3.	William de Bosc-le-hard & brother Roger.
39.	i 189d, *Cambridgeshire* 1:11.	Ely.
40.	i 190a + 199d + 199c, *Cambs.* 1:16 + 29:12 + 29:4+6.	Aubrey de Vere.
41.	i 201d, *Cambridgeshire* 37:1.	William de Keynes.
42.	i 202a, *Cambridgeshire* 38:2.	Robert Fafiton.
43.	i 210c + ?218b, *Bedfordshire* 6:1 + ?56:3.	Ordwig (Bury St Edmund's).
44.	i 211a, *Bedfordshire* 14:1.	Earnwine the priest.
45.	i 215d, *Bedfordshire* 32:15.	Walter of Flanders, Sighere.
46.	i 154c, *Oxfordshire* 1:6.	Ilbert de Lacy & Walter fitz Poyntz & Henry de Ferrers.
47.	i 158d, *Oxfordshire* 29:13.	Reginald (Roger D'Ivry).
48.	i 238c, *Warwickshire* 3:4.	Bp of Worcester.
49.	i 248a, *Staffordshire* 8:5.	Roger of Montgomery.
50.	i 164b, *Gloucestershire* 1:60.	(William fitz Osbern).
51.	i 164b, *Gloucestershire* 1:63.	Edward of Salisbury.
52.	i 168c, *Gloucestershire* 50:4.	Osbern Giffard.
53.	i 172a, *Worcestershire* C:3 (cf. i 172c + 175c, 2:1 + 9:7).	Worcester, Pershore, Evesham.
54.	i 203d + 208c, 203d + 208d *Hunts.* 2:6 + D:29, 2:9 + D:16.	Bp of Lincoln.
55.	i 208ab, *Huntingdonshire* D:9+15 + 25 (cf. i 206c + 206a, 19:26+11).	Sheriff Eustace.
56.	i 208b, *Huntingdonshire* D:14.	William de Warenne.
57.	i 208c, *Huntingdonshire* D:28.	Peterborough.
58.	i 277d, *Derbyshire* 13:2.	Gilbert de Ghent.
59.	i 298a, *Yorkshire* C:2.	Bp of Durham.
60.	i 298a, *Yorkshire* C:10.	William de Percy (Earl Hugh).
61.	i 373a, *Yorkshire* CN:3+9	Malet.
62.	i 373ab + 373d, *Yorkshire* CN:5 + CE:1-4+8+10+20 + CW:20.	Nigel Fossard (Robert of Mortain).
63.	i 373a, *Yorkshire* CE:5.	Hamelin.
64.	i 373a, *Yorkshire* CE:6-7.	Richard de Sourdeval (Robert of Mortain).
65.	i 373c, *Yorkshire* CE:32.	Odo *ballistarius*.
66.	i 373d, *Yorkshire* CW:8-10.	William de Warenne.
67.	i 373d, *Yorkshire* CW:23.	Ilbert de Lacy.
68.	i 374b, *Yorkshire* CW:42.	Count Alan.
69.	i 337d + 377a, *Lincolnshire*	

1:9-10 + CK:21.	Bishop of Durham.
70. i 337d-338a + 361a + 377c, *Lincs.*	
1:15-16 + 31:3 + CK:55, CK:59.	Walter d'Aincourt.
71. i 338c + 375d + 376b + 377b, *Lincs.*	
1:65 + CN:6, CW:9-11, CK:33.	Bp of Lincoln.
72. i 348c + 377d, *Lincolnshire*	
12:83-4 + CK:71.	Count Alan.
73. i 375a, *Lincolnshire* CS:6.	Earl Hugh.
74. i 375a, *Lincolnshire* CS:8.	Alfred of Lincoln.
75. i 375b, *Lincolnshire* CS:24.	Robert *dispensator*.
76. i 375d, *Lincolnshire* CN:3.	Ivo Tallboys.
77. i 376c, *Lincolnshire* CW:14.	Ralph de Nevill (Peterborough).
78. i 376cd, *Lincolnshire*	
CW:19 + CK:5+11.	Ralph Pagnell.
79. i 377a, *Lincolnshire* CK:24.	Bp of Salisbury.
80. i 377b, *Lincolnshire* CK:34.	Kolsveinn.
81. i 377c, *Lincolnshire* CK:50.	Drogo de la Beuvrière.
82. i 377d, *Lincolnshire* CK:70.	Ketill of Sutton.
83. ii 7a, *Essex* 1:28.	Robert Gernon.
84. ii 66b, *Essex* 32:28.	Robert 'the lascivious' (Robert Gernon).
85. ii 7a, *Essex* 1:28.	Clerk of Count Eustace.
86. ii 13ab, *Essex* 5:8.	St Paul's.
87. ii14b-15a, *Essex* 6:9.	Westminster.
88. ii 25b, *Essex* 18:44.	Thorold of Rochester (Odo of Bayeux).
89. ii 54b, *Essex* 27:17.	Hugh son of Mauger (Hugh de Montfort).
90. ii 61b + 62b, *Essex* 30:39+47.	Geoffrey de Mandeville.
91. ii 75a, *Essex* 34:28.	Ranulf Peverel.
92. ii 87b, *Essex* 43:1.	Roger de Rasmes & Roger Bigot.
93. ii 91a, *Essex* 52:2	Walter de Douai.
94. ii 123b-124a, 124b, 173a, 176ab +	
277b-278a, 182b, 185b, *Norfolk*	
1:106, 120-1, 9:1, 9:42 + 66:81,	
9:111, 9:160	Roger Bigot.
[cf. ii 124a, 1:111]	
95. ii 125b, 194a + 195a, Norfolk 1:128	
+ 10:21+28+30.	Bp of Thetford.
96. ii 130a, *Norfolk* 1:172.	Bury St Edmund's.
97. ii 132b, *Norfolk* 1:192.	Humphrey, nephew of Ranulf brother of Ilger.
98. ii 133a, *Norfolk* 1:195.	Thorald (William de Warenne).
99. ii 133b, *Norfolk* 1:197.	Robert Malet.
100. ii 145a + 146a, 146b, *Norfolk*	
4:10+20, 4:25.	Count Alan.
101. ii 166a + 172b, *Norfolk* 8:71+138	
[cf. ii 162a, 8:37].	William de Warenne
102. ii 208a, *Norfolk* 13:21.	Hermer de Ferrers.

103. ii 214b, *Norfolk* 15:18.	Ely.
104. ii 239b, *Norfolk* 24:1.	Eudo *dapifer*.
105. ii 242a, *Norfolk* 25:15.	Walter Giffard.
106. ii 258a, *Norfolk* 34:17.	Peter de Valognes.
107. ii 285b, *Suffolk* 1:77.	Burgheard of Mendlesham.
108. ii 318a, *Suffolk* 6:169.	Robert Malet.
109. ii 336a, *Suffolk* 7:55.	Roger Bigot.
110. ii 360b + 371a, *Suffolk* 14:37 + 146.	Bury St Edmund's.
111. ii 393a, *Suffolk* 25:52.	Richard fitz Gilbert.
112. ii 407b + 409b, *Suffolk* 31:34 + 53.	Hugh de Montfort.
113. ii 418b, *Suffolk* 35:3.	Aubrey de Vere.
114. ii 427a, *Suffolk* 41:11.	Walter the deacon.

D. Sample pleas not explicitly assessed
[Criteria include (i) cases just failing to meet main list criteria, (ii) cases in counties with few if any otherwise attested pleas, (iii) cases, whether or not marked 'K' etc., which occur in the body of the survey for counties with '*clamores*' sections, 'ut which appear to have no corresponding '*clamor*'.]

1. i 6a, *Kent* 5:4.	? Alnoth cild, Ralph son of Thorold (Odo of Bayeux).
2. i 38c, *Hampshire* 1:21.	King, Bishop of Winchester.
3. i 49b, *Hampshire* 67:1.	Odo of Winchester, Geoffrey *camerarius*.
4. i 71c, *Wiltshire* 30:5.	*Miles* of Milo Crispin, Durand of Gloucester.
5. i 81cd (*Exon.* 49a1), *Dorset* 36:8.	Son of Odo *camerarius*, William de Mohun.
6. i 83c, *Dorset* 55:3.	Men of Hugh son of Grip, Abt of Abbotsbury.
7. i 111d, *Devon* 23:6.	Walter de Douai, ?.
8. i 121c, *Cornwall* 3:7.	Tavistock Abbey, Robert of Mortain.
9. i 137d, *Hertfordshire* 20:2.	William man of Robert Gernon, ?
10. i 141c, *Hertfordshire* 36:19.	Haldane, Peter de Valognes.
11. i 193c, *Cambridgeshire* 13:8.	Sheriff Picot, Roger of Montgomery.
12. i 196c, *Cambridgeshire* 19:1.	Ely, Richard fitz Gilbert.
13. i 216c, *Bedfordshire* 46:1.	Osbern the Fisherman, ?King.
14. i 218b, *Bedfordshire* 56:2.	William Speke, Godwin.
15. i 218c, *Bedfordshire* 57:6.	Ketelbert, King.
16. i 159c, *Oxfordshire* 35:25.	Ordgar, Milo Crispin.
17. i 160d, *Oxfordshire* 58:27.	Manasseh, King.
18. i 225d, *Northamptonshire* 35:1e.	King, William Peverel.
19. i 228a, *Northamptonshire* 55:1.	Ramsey, Eustace of Huntingdon.
20. i 229b, *Northamptonshire* 56:65.	Winemar (Geoffrey de Coutances), Countess Judith.
21. i 232b, *Leicestershire* 13:21.	Hugh de Grandmesnil, ?Alwin Buxton.
22. i 233b, *Leicestershire* 14:16.	Countess Judith, Henry de Ferrers.
23. i 241a, *Warwickshire* 17:16.	William, King?.

24. i 241c, *Warwickshire* 17:56.   Ermenfrid (King), Thorkell of Warwick.

25. i 164cd, *Gloucestershire* 2:8-10.   Abp of York, St Peter's Gloucester etc.
26. i 166d, *Gloucestershire* 31:2.   Henry de Ferrers, William d'Eu.
27. i 175c, *Worcestershire* 9:4.   Urse d'Abetot, Pershore.
28. i 176a, *Worcestershire* 11:2.   Evesham, Urse d'Abetot (Odo of Bayeux).
29. i 186b, *Herefordshire* 19:8.   St Guthlac's Hereford, Alfred of Marlborough.
30. i 259b, *Shropshire* 4:26:2.   Roger the Huntsman *et al.*, Albert.

31. i 203d, *Huntingdonshire* 2:2.   Ramsey, Bp of Lincoln.
32. i 204c, *Huntingdonshire* 6:7 + 8.   Sheriff Eustace, Ramsey.
33. i 206b, *Huntingdonshire* 19:13.   Tovi, Sheriff Eustace.
34. i 206d, *Huntingdonshire* 20:3.   Sheriff Eustace, Countess Judith.
35. i 274c, *Derbyshire* 6:27.   Geoffrey Alselin, Henry de Ferrers.
36. i 278b, *Derbyshire* 16:2.   Earnwine, Fulk (Roger de Busli).
37. i 278c, *Derbyshire* 17:9.   Dolfin, Steinulf & Dunning (King).
38. i 291b, *Nottinghamshire* 20:4.   Ilbert de Lacy, Bp of Lincoln.
39. i 293c, *Rutland* 2(7).   Alfred of Lincoln, Countess Judith.
40. i 301c, *Yorkshire* 1W:53.   King, William de Percy.
41. i 373a, *Yorkshire* CE:12.   ?   ?
42. i 373d, *Yorkshire* CW:17.   ?   ?
43. i 336ab, *Lincolnshire* C:21.   Norman *crassus* (King), Peterborough.
44. i 342a, *Lincolnshire* 4:1.   King, Ralph *dapifer* & Gilbert de Ghent (Odo of Bayeux).
45. i 352a, *Lincolnshire* 16:3.   ?, (Roger de Poitou) (but cf. i 359b, 28:19).
46. i 358a, *Lincolnshire* 27:25.   ?, Alfred of Lincoln.
47. i 360b, *Lincolnshire* 30:14.   (Odo of Bayeux) & Ralph de Mortemer, Drogo de la Beuvrière.

48. ii 12b, *Essex* 5:2.   St Paul's, Peter de Valognes.
49. ii 13a, *Essex* 5:6.   St Paul's, ?
50. ii 14a, *Essex* 6:4.   King, Westminster.
51. ii 39a, *Essex* 23:3.   Vitalis, Richard fitz Gilbert.
52. ii 110b + 137a, *Norfolk* 1:10 + 213.   King, ?Siward.
53. ii 193a, *Norfolk* 10:19.   Count Alan, Bp of Thetford.
54. ii 217b, *Norfolk* 17:22.   King, Ailwy of Colchester.
55. ii 221b, *Norfolk* 19:2.   Wulfwig, man of Radfrid (William d'Écouis).
56. ii 232a, *Norfolk* 21:14.   Rainald fitz Ivo.
57. ii 236a, *Norfolk* 22:13.   Roger Bigot, Ralph de Tosny.
58. ii 290b, *Suffolk* 1:122f.   Count Alan, Thorkell & Eadric.
59. ii 372b, *Suffolk* 15:3.   John nephew of Waleran, Christ Church Canterbury.
60. ii 388a, *Suffolk* 21:95.   William de Bouville, Ely.
61. ii 389b, *Suffolk* 25:1.   St John's Clare, Richard fitz Gilbert.
62. ii 393b, *Suffolk* 25:56.   Roger de Rames & Ranulf Peverel, Richard fitz Gilbert.

Monastic Reform and the Secular Church: Ælfric's Pastoral Letters in Context
JOYCE HILL

Sometime between 992 and 1002 Ælfric, then monk and masspriest at the newly founded Benedictine Reform monastery of Cerne Abbas, wrote a pastoral letter in Old English for his diocesan bishop, Wulfsige of Sherborne.[1] Ælfric attached to it a Latin prefatory letter addressed to Wulfsige, in which he identifies himself as the actual author, but it is Wulfsige that we seem to hear throughout the Old English text because, as Ælfric explains, the pastoral letter 'quasi ex tuo ore dictata sit'. It begins 'Ic secge eow preostum...' and this rhetorical stance is continued throughout, varying as appropriate only to the extent of using 'we' as an alternative, 'we biscepas', or authoritative plural imperatives which imply the episcopal voice.

In 1005 Ælfric wote two more pastoral letters, this time in Latin, for Wulfstan, then Bishop of Worcester and Archbishop of York. Again the voice is that of the bishop, but there is no doubt that Ælfric was the actual author of each because in 1006, by now abbot of the newly-founded Benedictine house at Eynsham, he produced English versions of both at Wulfstan's request and sent them to Wulfstan together, prefaced by a Latin letter which explains his authorship and which alludes to the relevant correspondence between the two men.[2] Neither Old English letter is a

---

[1] The letter is in *Die Hirtenbriefe Ælfrics*, ed. B. Fehr, Bibliothek der angelsächsischen Prosa, IX (Hamburg, 1914), reprinted with a supplementary introduction by P. A. M. Clemoes (Darmstadt, 1964), and is translated in *Councils and Synods with other Documents relating to the English Church, I, A.D. 871-1204: Part I: 871-1066*, ed. D. Whitelock, M. Brett, C. N. L. Brooke (Oxford, 1981), pp. 191-226 (Whitelock was responsible for *Part I: 871-1066*). Reference will be made by page and § number (as appropriate) to Wulfsige's letter as edited by Fehr. For the dating of Ælfric's work throughout I follow P. A. M. Clemoes, 'The Chronology of Ælfric's Works', in *The Anglo-Saxons: Studies in Some Aspects of their History and Culture presented to Bruce Dickins*, ed. P. A. M. Clemoes (London, 1959), pp. 212-47. In dating the Wulfsige letter as written between 992 and 1002 Clemoes was accepting what were thought to be the dates of Wulfsige's episcopacy, but it is possible that he became bishop in 993 and that the date of his death is earlier than 1002. For comments on these problems and for information about Wulfsige's career, see *Councils and Synods*, p. 189 n. 1, p. 193, and F. Barlow, *The English Church 1000-1066*, 2nd edn (London, 1979), pp. 222-24.

[2] The Wulfstan letters, to which reference is made by page and § number as appropriate, are edited in *Die Hirtenbriefe Ælfrics:* first Latin letter, pp. 35-57; second Latin letter, pp. 58-67; first OE letter, pp. 68-145; second OE letter, pp.

verbatim translation of its original Latin one of a year earlier and Ælfric in his prefatory letter signals this by the standard formula when he says that the English versions are '[n]on tamen semper ordinem sequentes, nec uerbum ex uerbo, sed sensum ex sensu proferentes' (p. 68). There are in fact passages where the Latin and Old English are very close, but the differences are significant and pervasive: Ælfric took the opportunity to omit, add, expand, explain and rearrange, obviously recognising that, in changing languages, he was encompassing a different intellectual milieu, priestly still, but addressing now, in the vernacular, those who, as the first Old English letter states in the opening sentence, 'ne cunnon þæt leden under-standan' (p. 68).

In commissioning Ælfric to write their pastoral letters, Wulfsige and Wulfstan were drawing upon the resources of the monastic reform and in particular were choosing to use the services of a man who was a determined advocate of it. From his committed reform base Ælfric was prepared to reach out to the secular church in providing model homilies or by responding — albeit reluctantly at times — to demands from influential laity for various materials in the vernacular such as a translation of Genesis or an English version of the monastic legendary. But his position was always clearly that of the monk making available to laity and secular priests the intellectual riches, the orthodoxy and the accuracy which he saw as the hallmarks of the reform and which he found sadly lacking in the secular church. The pastoral letters fit well into this context and it is impossible to believe that Wulfsige and Wulfstan, influenced as they also were by the reform, were discounting Ælfric's monastic and reformist outlook when they called upon him to write in their names for their secular clergy.

Wulfsige was appointed abbot of Westminster, a refoundation associated with Glastonbury and thus with Dunstan, in the reign of Edgar.[3] In or about 993 Æthelred appointed him to the diocese of Sherborne, which he held in plurality with his abbacy at Westminster until he resigned the abbacy in 997. At some point, probably in 998, he established monks in his cathedral. He

---

146-221. The first OE letter is translated in *Councils and Synods*, pp. 255-302. Ælfric identifies himself as 'humilis frater' in the prefatory letter to Wulfsige (Fehr, p. 1) but as 'Aelfricus abbas' by the time he writes to Wulfstan in 1006 (Fehr, p. 68). The supposition that his abbey was Eynsham is circumstantial and is reflected by C. E. Hohler, 'Some Service-Books of the Later Anglo-Saxon Church', in *Tenth-Century Studies: Essays in Commemoration of the Millennium of the Council of Winchester and 'Regularis Concordia'*, ed. D. Parsons (London, 1975), pp. 60-83 (p. 73). Against Hohler, see M. McC. Gatch, 'The Office in late Anglo-Saxon Monasticism', in *Learning and Literature in Anglo-Saxon England: Studies Presented to Peter Clemoes*, ed. M. Lapidge and H. Gneuss (Cambridge, 1985), pp. 341-62 (p. 348, n. 28).

3   For Wulfsige's career, see note 1 above, and C. H. Talbot, 'The Life of Saint Wulsin of Sherborne by Goscelin', *Revue Bénédictine*, 69 (1959), 68-85.

died in 1002 and he was revered as a saint by the monastic community, which was maintained at Sherborne until the see was moved as a result of reorganisation in 1078. Wulfsige was thus a man whose career ended with activity in the secular church, who had held office as abbot since the early days of the Reform, and who changed the ecclesiastical life of his own cathedral in making it monastic. The pattern of his career suggests that he was as likely as Ælfric to look for ways of transmitting to the secular church some of the standards and ideals that he found in the reformed monastic life.[4]

There is much more evidence for Wulfstan's career and ecclesiastical interests. As Dorothy Whitelock summarises it: 'Wulfstan was evidently active in religious reform by his own studies, by encouragement of manuscript compilation, by the issue of a rule of life for canons and a code for the priesthood in general, by the circulation of pastoral letters for the clergy of his diocese and by the preaching of homilies to the laity'.[5] In all this, although it was directed at the secular church, the impetus given to him by the monastic reform must not be underestimated. William of Malmesbury thought that Wulfstan was not a monk, but the *Historia Eliensis* and Florence of Worcester both claim that he was;[6] in 1002, when he became Archbishop of York, he simultaneously became Bishop of Worcester, a monastic see which had previously been held by Oswald, one of the three leading monastic reformers (bishop 961-992), and Ealdwulf (bishop 992-1002), formerly abbot of Peterborough, a house reformed in the tradition of Æthelwold's monastery at Abingdon. Wulfstan drew heavily upon source texts which entered England with the reform, he had an interest in the *Regularis Concordia* as a source text for practices in the secular church,[7] he corresponded with Ælfric and made use of him for more than just the pastoral letters, and he shared the reformers' desire for regulation, although in his case this was necessarily directed outwards towards the secular church by means of his homilies and codes. Thus, as with Wulfsige, the apparent voice of the pastoral letters, actually written by Abbot Ælfric, is that of a bishop whose attitudes were shaped by the reform and who, in his own career, bridged what in his eyes as well as Ælfric's was a significant gap between the standards of the monastic and the secular churches.

We can therefore assume a genuine identity of purpose between Ælfric and the two bishops whose voices he adopted; the pastoral letters need to be

---

4   Sisam, however, suggests that Ælfric was the more rigorous reformer; *Studies in the History of Old English Literature* (Oxford, 1953), p. 169.

5   D. Whitelock 'Archbishop Wulfstan, Homilist and Statesman', *Trans. R. Hist. Soc.*, 4th Series, 24 (1942), 25-45 (p.35).

6   Whitelock, *ibid.*, p. 39, reviews the conflicting statements from the middle ages and concludes that he was a Benedictine.

7   See below, pp. 106-108.

considered not simply for what they appear to tell us about the secular church at which they were directed, but also for what they tell us about the ideals and aspirations of men whose attitudes were shaped by the monastic reform and who wished in some way to extend that reform into other areas of ecclesiastical life. How far they succeeded in influencing the early-eleventh-century church, even on a local scale, is another matter. Utilitarian material in general circulation – if indeed the letters did circulate as widely as was presumably intended – does not have much chance of survival. What stand a much higher chance are copies written into large reference collections, as is in fact the case with these pastoral letters, but the route by which the copies enter these collections and the circulation and use of the collections themselves may be symptomatic of a specialised aspect of the texts' history which could well differ from common contemporary use. The form and context in which the letters survive nevertheless need to be considered if these texts are to be assessed as documents which may or may not have had an effect on the eleventh-century church, and I shall comment on this evidence below (pp. 111-15). To begin with, however, I wish to focus on the evidence within the letters for the nature and extent of their Benedictine Reform inspiration.

The most obvious sign of Benedictine Reform influence is the exploitation in the second Old English letter for Wulfstan of the *Regularis Concordia*, that landmark of the reform in England. It is drawn upon here for the liturgical practices of Holy Week (Fehr §§23-63).[8] This extensive passage has no counterpart in the letter as it has come down to us in its Latin form. I have noted above that neither of Wulfstan's Old English letters translates its Latin original verbatim, but the differences between them are nowhere else as extensive as this. All extant copies of the Old English letter include this Holy Week material, and all extant copies of the corresponding Latin letter do not. Unless the Latin letter was abbreviated by the excision of this material at a very early date, it appears to be an addition to the letter, presumably at the request of Wulfstan, at the time of its vernacular rewriting.[9]

Only one year earlier Ælfric had adapted the *Regularis Concordia* in drawing up the Eynsham consuetudinary.[10] Now, in adapting its Holy Week

---

[8] The passage corresponds to p. 108 line 1 to p. 123 line 4 'Regularis Concordia Anglicae Nationis', ed. T. Symons, S. Spath, M. Wegener, K. Hallinger, in *Consuetudinum saeculi X/XI/XII monumenta non-Cluniacensia*, ed. K. Hallinger, Corpus Consuetudinum Monasticarum, *VII. 3* (Siegburg, 1984).

[9] The Latin letter does not survive in its original form (see below. pp. 112-13), but insofar as we can trace the modifications, they do not point to large-scale omission. Whitelock, *Councils and Synods*, p. 258, suggests that better educated clergy, who could read the Latin letter, would not have needed the information because they could be expected to possess a sacramentary.

material for secular clergy, the adjustments are even greater. The basic of the special rituals are retained, however, as are the specifications of liturgical texts, and throughout there is the assumption that the practices are carried out by a group, in this case identified as priests, who not only perform the distinctive rituals of Maundy Thursday, Good Friday and Holy Saturday, but who also, as a matter of course, sustain a regular round of Hours ('tydsangas', Fehr § 26, and referred to individually by name at various points).

From their monastic viewpoint both Wulfstan and Ælfric would have been keenly aware of – and no doubt, responsive to – the effects of the rituals of this most solemn period of the church's year, and would have seen the spiritual value of bringing the secular church more in line with the monastic. But we can develop a fuller understanding of Wulfstan's responses to the *Regularis Concordia* as a liturgical resource for the secular church – which is how it is used in the pastoral letter – by turning to two of the manuscripts which reflect his commonplace book.[11] One of these, Cambridge, Corpus Christi College, MS 265, a Worcester manuscript of the mid-eleventh century, includes the sole surviving copy of Ælfric's Eynsham consuetudinary. Presumably Wulfstan obtained a copy directly from Ælfric, perhaps because, as a customary based upon but moving somewhat away from the elaborate procedures of the *Regularis Concordia*, he was interested in it as a model and reference text; it possibly gave him the idea for further modification for seculars. The other relevant commonplace book manuscript is Corpus Christi College, MS 190 which, in its present form, is made up of

---

10 'Aelfrici abbatis epistula ad monachos Egneshamnenses directa', ed. H. Nocent, in *Consuetudinum X/XI/XII monumenta non-Cluniacensia*, pp. 149-85. For discussion, see M. Bateson, 'Rules for Monks and Secular Canons after the Revival under King Edgar', *EHR*, 9 (1894), 690-708 (pp. 702-07); J. R. Hall, 'Some Liturgical Notes on Aelfric's Letter to the Monks at Eynsham', *Downside Review*, 93 (1975), 297-303; M. McC. Gatch, 'The Office in late Anglo-Saxon Monasticism', pp. 348-62. Whitelock, *Councils and Synods*, p. 259, repeats Fehr's supposition, *Die Hirtenbriefe Ælfrics*, p. lxiv, that §§ 23-63 of the pastoral letter draws upon the Eynsham consuetudinary, rather than the *Regularis Concordia* direct. But one was a simplification for monks, the other for priests, and both reveal Ælfric's intimate familiarity with the *Regularis Concordia*. It seems to me more reasonable to suppose that Ælfric exploited his familiarity to produce two modifications in succession, rather than working in a more laboured fashion from one modification to the next.

11 On the 'commonplace book', see D. Whitelock, 'Archbishop Wulfstan'; D. Bethurum, 'Archbishop Wulfstan's Commonplace Book', *PMLA*, 57 (1942), 916-29; R. G. Fowler, '"Archbishop Wulfstan's Commonplace-Book" and the Canons of Edgar', *Medium Ævum*, 32 (1963), 1-10. For details about CCC 190 and 265, see Fehr's introduction to *Die Hirtenbriefe Ælfrics*, pp. xiv-xix, and the supplementary introduction by Clemoes, pp. cxxviii, cxxx-cxxxi.

two manuscripts, one Latin and one Old English. The 'first' (Latin) manuscript includes a body of material entitled 'Item de ecclesiastica consuetudine' which, between pp. 213 and 225, makes judiciously selective verbatim extracts from the *Regularis Concordia*. This text, which continues as far as p. 264, is not a finished document but is a body of preparatory or reference materials assembled either at Wulfstan's direction or by Wulfstan himself. The use made of the *Regularis Concordia* is symptomatic of Wulfstan's relationship to the Benedictine Reform, but the principles of selection and the firmly episcopal material with which it is associated in the manuscript indicates that Wulfstan saw it as a resource on which the secular church could usefully draw, as his second Old English pastoral letter confirms.[12] CCC 190 also has, in the English part, two vernacular translations of short extracts from the *Regularis Concordia*, giving information respectively about the Vigil readings for Holy Saturday and for Pentecost and apparently intended for parish priests who knew little Latin.[13] There is no reason to suppose that Wulfstan was responsible for making them, but they are in one of his commonplace books and are immediately followed by a typically Wulfstanian miscellany: ecclesiastical laws, codes and customs, mainly concerned with penance. Like the other adaptations of the *Regularis Concordia* associated in some way with Wulfstan, they reach out towards the secular church, regulating and elaborating its liturgical observances.

No other single source text for the Pastoral Letters points as forcefully as the *Regularis Concordia* does to the shaping influence of the Benedictine Reform, but cumulatively the major source materials have the effect of defining the reforming position that the bishops allowed Ælfric to map out.[14] Although some of these items, such as Rufinus's *Historia Ecclesiastica*, Isidore's *Etymologiae* and *De ecclesiasticis officiis* and certain homiletic materials, had long been available, many of the important sources were much newer, for example a number of the penitentials used, the Capitulary of

---

12 For more detailed discussion of this and the other derivatives of the *Regularis Concordia* referred to in this paper, see my article, 'The *Regularis Concordia* and its Latin and Old English Reflexes', *Revue Bénédictine*, 101 (1991), 299-315. The 'Item de ecclesiastica consuetudine' is partially printed by Fehr as Appendix III to *Die Hirtenbriefe Ælfrics*, pp. 234-49, but his attribution to Ælfric is erroneous: see P. A. M. Clemoes, 'The Old English Benedictine Office, Corpus Christi College, Cambridge, MS 190, and the Relations between Ælfric and Wulfstan: A Reconsideration', *Anglia*, 78 (1960), 265-83 (pp. 275-77).

13 Hall, 'Aelfric's Letter', pp. 301-02. They are printed by Fehr as Appendixes I and II to *Die Hirtenbriefe Ælfrics*, pp. 228 and 230, and p. 232.

14 Sources, which are more extensive than those mentioned here, are identified by Fehr in his edition and by Whitelock for the two letters printed in *Councils and Synods*.

Aachen, the pseudo-Alcuin *De divinis officiis*, and works by Theodulf of Orléans and Amalarius of Metz. These all have a number of features in common: they are continentally-derived materials which entered England with the Benedictine Reform, as did so much else from ninth-century Francia; they are texts which regulate and define, again as is characteristic of the continental texts on which the English reform drew so heavily; and they are precisely the materials that come down to us copied, extracted and adapted in the great commonplace book manuscripts of the eleventh century. Individually they are not necessarily monastic works; indeed some are specifically aimed at secular clergy. But it was the reform which was the channel of transmission from the Continent and which provided the impetus for their use, since they advocated the standard of ecclesiastical conduct which the reform held dear: a regulated life and a sophisticated sacramental and liturgical observance.

Whether these standards were achieved, or were even likely to be achievable, in the secular church is something that we cannot easily deduce from Ælfric's five pastoral letters. If we wish to take an optimistic view, we can point to their liturgical elements, for these assume that priests can exercise a considerable degree of liturgical competence, both on special occasions and on a daily basis,[15] that they have access to liturgical texts, and an ability to identify and employ readings, antiphons and the like, which are often referred to in familiar and thus rather cryptic ways. Such expectations seem to apply in these letters to all priests, whether regular canons in a minster or the single masspriest in his own church,[16] and there is an assumption also, made explicit in the Wulfsige letter (Fehr § 102), that priests, apparently without exception, live according to an agreed rule.[17] It is

---

[15] The letters assume, for example, that all priests will say daily Hours: see p. 107 above and Fehr pp. 12 (letter for Wulfsige §§ 49-50), 42 (first Latin letter for Wulfstan §§ 62-4), 98, 100 (first OE letter for Wulfstan §§ 69-73).

[16] The letters reflect this distinction within the secular church: see, for example, §157 in the Wulfsige letter, and §§ 86 and 82 in the Latin and OE versions respectively of the first letter for Wulfstan, where 'mynster-preost' equates with 'regularis canonicus' and 'mæsse-preost' with 'presbyter'. For modern scholarship on minsters and parish churches, communities of regular canons and the singular priest, see J. Blair, 'Local Churches in Domesday Book and Before', in *Domesday Studies*, ed. C. J. Holt (Woodbridge, 1987), pp. 265-78; *Minsters and Parish Churches: The Local Church in Transition 950-1200*, ed. J. Blair, Oxford University Committee for Archaeology Monograph 17 (Oxford, 1988); R. Morris, *Churches in the Landscape* (London, 1989), pp. 128-39.

[17] The rule is not named, but the most likely are the enlarged Rule of Chrodegang, translated into English at about this time, Amalarius' *De regula canonicorum*, or possibly, as Whitelock suggests in *Councils and Synods*, pp. 216 and 195, the Capitulary of Aachen. It is indicative of Wulfsige's and Ælfric's positions that in

worth noting that, in setting down these regulated practices, the letters do not adopt a rhetorical stance which suggests the introduction of something new; the tone is rather that of reminder, reinforcement and improved regulation building upon recognised foundations.

Against this, however, one has to set the somewhat hectoring comments on the practical behaviour of priests and the poor level of knowledge and understanding that the letters imply. If the clergy needed to be told extremely basic information about function, if they needed to be told not to get drunk, not to let the reserved host go mouldy, not to cavort in church instead of keeping vigil, not to celebrate mass with a wooden or horn chalice, not to poach dead bodies from other parishes, and not to let mouse-droppings or dung lie on the altar, one wonders whether they were capable of living well according to a rule, diligently and reverently reciting their Hours, and competently executing the rituals of the mass and special feasts. The letters present us with something of a contradictory picture: on the one hand a regular life is assumed with some competence in liturgy and Latin; on the other these assumptions are belied by the habits described and by the equally clear suppositions that the clergy are not competent, not well educated and, as Wulfstan says directly in the opening sentence of his first Old English letter, cannot understand Latin. It was this fundamental inability which prompted the vernacular redraftings of his two Latin letters. Even then, Wulfstan had misgivings, for he rewrote the first Old English letter himself to make it more accessible.[18] Yet both he and Wulfsige prescribe impressive lists of books that every masspriest should own. Wulfsige's list consists of: *saltere, pistolboc, godspellboc, mæsseboc, sangboc* (pl. *sangbec* in two MSS), *handboc, gerim* (i.e. computus), *passionalem* (for which *pastoralem* in CCC 190 is presumably an error), *penitentialem*, and *rædingboc* (Fehr, p. 13). Wulfstan's list is almost the same, but not quite, and there are slight variations, which may be more apparent than real, between the first Latin letter (which presumably reflects what Ælfric thought was necessary) and its Old English counterpart, and between this Old English list and the one in Wulfstan's own rewriting of the letter. The Latin list runs as follows: 'missalem, lectionarium, quod quidam uocant epistolarium, psalterium, nocturnalem, gradalem, manualem, passionalem, penitentialem, compotum, et librum cum lectionibus ad nocturnas' (Fehr, p.51). The list in Ælfric's translation is shorter: *mæsseboc, pistelboc, sangboc, rædingboc, saltere, handboc, penitentialem* and *gerim* (Fehr, p. 126). *Godspellboc* and *passionalem* are not specified (although they could be caught up under *rædingboc*) and *sangboc* is singular. Wulfstan's own list, in the rewritten letter, is *mæsseboc, sangbec* (plural),

---

the preceding sentence (§ 101) the monks' obedience to the Benedictine Rule is presented as a model of the regulated life.

18   Edited by Fehr as MS D, *Die Hirtenbriefe Ælfrics*, pp. 68-140.

rædingbec (this also plural, perhaps subsuming a number of items that Ælfric had originally named separately), *saltere, handboc, penitentialem* and *gerim* (Fehr, p. 126).[19] All versions of this letter and the letter for Wulfsige state that the texts are to be well corrected, an admirable ideal, but one which I think we should see primarily as reflecting Ælfric's frequently expressed anxieties about textual accuracy rather than being a statement about a responsibility that most secular priests would be willing or able to carry out.[20] Looking at the booklists in context one must, after all, ask not whether secular priests were likely to have corrected copies of all these things, but whether they were likely to have such a collection at all and whether, given the limitations of knowledge that the pastoral letters otherwise imply, they would have been able to use them intelligently even if they had owned them.

Of course one must not dismiss all secular clergy as ignorant and incompetent. But the internal contradictions in the pastoral letters tell us, I think, as much about Ælfric and the bishops as they do about the secular church. I do not know how often Wulfsige met drunken priests, how often he came upon priests cavorting in church instead of keeping vigil, or how many times Wulfstan found mouse-droppings on the altars of his diocese. But statements about such lax or inappropriate behaviour need not always derive from direct observation, since they point to a written tradition of ecclesiastical reform with which Wulfsige and Wulfstan wished to ally themselves. That such details are deployed in the letters is generally indicative of a secular church which they were convinced was below par, but their use has a rhetorical importance also in defining the bishops' position as authority figures who wished to establish standards and who saw the secular church contrastively, as a world far removed from the regulated and reformed life which they themselves knew.

In practical terms, what impact did they have? If we could show that the letters circulated widely, or that they were excerpted, adapted and modified,

[19] The lists are interpreted by Fehr, *Die Hirtenbriefe Ælfrics*, pp. lxxxvi-xcii, and are further discussed by M. McC. Gatch, *Preaching and Theology in Anglo-Saxon England: Ælfric and Wulfstan* (Toronto, 1977), pp. 42-44, although his description (p. 44) of the variations of requirement between the versions is inaccurate. See also H. Gneuss, 'Liturgical books in Anglo-Saxon England and their Old English Terminology', in *Learning and Literature in Anglo-Saxon England: Studies Presented to Peter Clemoes*, ed. M. Lapidge and H. Gneuss (Cambridge, 1985), pp.91-141.

[20] Hohler, 'Service-books', draws attention to the degree of error in service-books. Ælfric's injunctions to the scribe to transmit his work as written and to check his copy against the exemplar covers the major part of his output: the *Catholic Homilies* (OE prefaces), the *Lives of Saints* (OE preface), the *Grammar* (OE preface), the preface to *Genesis*, and the *Libellus de ueteri testamento et nouo*.

we could make some reasonable deductions but, for reasons noted above (p.106), the manuscript evidence is ambiguous. Some circulation takes place in the eleventh century, as the table (p.117) indicates, but the surviving copies, with few exceptions, do not take us far from the originators.[21] Cambridge, University Library MS Gg.3.28, which includes the Wulfsige letter, is a copy not far removed from an Ælfrician original; it is a manuscript very close to the date of composition and, as Malcolm Godden has argued, it is 'either a product of Ælfric's own scriptorium or a remarkably faithful copy of such a manuscript'.[22] The letter, which has lost its ending because of the loss of leaves from the manuscript, was not part of the original manuscript compilation, but was added on spare leaves at the end, presumably at Ælfric's direction. It must therefore be seen as a file copy, and not as a circulating copy. The manuscripts which I have grouped together for various reasons under Wulfstan's name are a little harder to interpret, but the first four listed, CCC 190, Copenhagen, Kongelike Bibliotek, MS Gl. Kgl. Sam. 1595, CCC 265, and Oxford, Bodleian Library MS Junius 121, are all Wulfstan commonplace book manuscripts and of these the Copenhagen manuscript and CCC 265 as well as Oxford, Bodleian Library MS Bodley 343 seem to transmit the letters in the way in which they must have been written out as file copies. As is evident from Ælfric's prefatory letter to Wulfstan (Fehr, pp. 68-69), he sent the letters to Wulfstan in twos: the pair of Latin ones and, later, the pair of Old English ones. Since they are nevertheless separate letters, manuscript evidence for general circulation is likely to break the pairing and disturb the order. But in the Copenhagen MS, CCC 265 and Bodley 343 (despite its twelfth-century date) the letters continue to be copied as pairs: two Latin or two Old English, always in the right order and always consecutive in the manuscript as a pair. The same pattern of consecutive pair in the right order is found also in the Old English part of CCC 190 (Part B, mid-eleventh century), and textual relationships seem to confirm that the Old English pair in this manuscript and in Bodley 343 ultimately derive from the manuscript which Ælfric sent to Wulfstan. The Latin part of CCC 190 (Part A, first half of the eleventh century) is less clear, however, because the two Latin letters appear in reverse order separated by other material. There

21 For descriptions of the component parts of the manuscripts, the place of the letters within them, their date and provenance, see Fehr's introduction to *Die Hirtenbriefe Ælfrics*, pp. x-xxii, and the supplementary introduction by Clemoes, pp. cxxvii-cxxxiii. Those manuscripts which preserve the OE letters are also described by N. R. Ker, *Catalogue of Manuscripts containing Anglo-Saxon* (Oxford, 1957). In what follows I acknowledge my debt to Clemoes' deductions about textual relationships: *Die Hirtenbriefe Ælfrics*, pp. cxxxiii-cxlv.

22 *Ælfric's Catholic Homilies: The Second Series. Text*, ed. M. Godden, EETS SS 5 (London, 1979), p. xliii.

are some problems too in the textual evidence for these letters, if one examines the three sets of copies in CCC 190, the Copenhagen manuscript and CCC 265, since it is evident that they have been modified. In certain circumstances such textual disturbance could indicate circulation and use, but not, I think, in this case, since the modifications are found in all three manuscripts, including the authoritative Copenhagen manuscript in which Wulfstan's hand is apparent, and in the second Latin letter almost all the modification is taken from a private Latin letter that Ælfric wrote to Wulfstan.[23] All of this, along with the incidence of scribal error, makes it seem likely that the two Latin letters in all three manuscripts share a common source, which may have been the manuscript which Ælfric himself sent to Wulfstan, and that the modifications took place whilst the letters were in Wulfstan's possession. The Copenhagen manuscript is from Worcester or York; CCC 265 is probably a Worcester manuscript, and Bodley 343 is commonly attributed to the west Midlands.[24] CCC 190 received additions at Exeter in the second half of the eleventh century. Thus the most that we can deduce from these manuscripts is that there was some limited circulation in episcopal reference materials derived from Wulfstan's commonplace book, although, in this group of manuscripts which transmit file copies of the Wulfstan letters, CCC 190, with its Exeter connections, is the only evidence of this. The horizon is not extended by Junius 121, a commonplace book as already noted, and from Worcester. Its copy of the second Old English letter for Wulfstan has close textual relationships with those in CCC 190 and Bodley 343 and seems, like them, to be derived from the manuscript which Ælfric sent to Wulfstan.

What remain to be considered are the Wulfsige letter in CCC 190 and Junius 121, Wulfstan's rewritten version of the first Old English letter in CCC 201, and the partial survivals and extracts in British Library Cotton MSS, Tiberius A.iii and Vespasian D.xiv. Here we come across some evidence for circulation and use, although it is striking how inadequately they reflect the Wulfstan letters as written by Ælfric, and that neither of the Latin letters is represented.

As already noted (p. 110, above) Wulfstan rewrote the first Old English letter, and one copy of this version survives, in CCC 201. There is evidence that this manuscript was at Winchester in the mid-eleventh century, which tells us something about circulation, but the places suggested for its writing out include Worcester (commonly), Canterbury, a London scribe working in York, the regions of Mercia and the south-east or, more cautiously, the south

---

[23] The private letter, written between 1002 and 1005, is edited by Fehr (as Brief 2a) in *Die Hirtenbriefe Ælfrics*, pp. 222-27, and in *Councils and Synods*, pp. 242-55. For Wulfstan's hand in the Copenhagen manuscript, see Ker, *Catalogue*, p. 140.

[24] Godden, *Ælfric's Catholic Homilies*, p. xl, suggests a possible Worcester origin.

of England generally.[25] If a non-Worcester location is correct, as seems likely, that would itself be evidence of circulation, although it is of one text only out of the four Wulfstan had Ælfric write, and it is in the version that he modified in order to make more concessions to the audience than Ælfric did in his already audience-aware vernacular rewriting of the original Latin.

Cotton Tiberius A. iii is a Canterbury manuscript and contains part of the second Old English letter (see table), but it breaks off in mid-sentence. There is strong punctuation, however, and the rest of the folio is taken up by a Latin text. It would appear that the Canterbury scribe had access only to an incomplete exemplar. The manuscript into which it was copied seems to be a reference collection and in its earlier part is strongly monastic, both visually and textually.[26]

The other south-eastern manuscript, Vespasian D. xiv, counts for little in considering the circulation and possible impact of Wulfstan's letters as written because the extracts found in it are so partial and unrepresentative. Fehr §§ 30-34 from the first Old English letter stands, with appropriate modification of the lead-in, as a self-contained passage on chastity; Fehr §§ 120-45 from the second Old English letter is presented as a tract on the ten commandments, with the scribal title 'Decalogum Moysi'.

Evidence for the circulation of Wulfsige's letter is a little more positive, however. I have commented already on Ælfric's file copy in CUL Gg.3.28. That in Junius 121 is copied into a Wulfstan commonplace book and we might suppose that a copy of this letter was available in Worcester because Ælfric sent it to Wulfstan. If so, this would not tell us anything about circulation within the secular church, despite the geographical movement. But the copy in CCC 190 does. Here the Wulfsige letter is not part of the original nucleus of the second or Old English part of the manuscript, but is on pages in the three quires, mainly in one hand of Exeter type, which were added in the second half of the eleventh century and this points to transmission between neighbouring dioceses. Furthermore, CCC 190 does not include a revision made by Ælfric (Fehr §§ 105-10) and which is found in his own file copy in CUL Gg.3.28 (although incomplete through loss of

25 For a review of the unusually wide range of opinions about this manuscript, see Hill, 'The *Regularis Concordia* and its Latin and Old English Reflexes', p. 311.

26 The leaves of this manuscript are now out of order, but it originally began with a full-page miniature of St Benedict preceding the text of the Benedictine Rule and Supplements, followed by another full-page miniature of a monk holding a scroll kneeling before figures, also holding a scroll, who are interpreted as King Edgar, seated between Archbishop Dunstan and Bishop Æthelwold. The scene refers to the creation of the *Regularis Concordia*, the text of which follows immediately. Whitelock, *Councils and Synods*, p. 256, wrongly reports the letter in this manuscript as 'ending at § 27'. It in fact ends at line 27 on f.107v, but this is § 62 in Fehr's edition.

leaves) and in Junius 121, whose exemplar Ælfric presumably sent to Wulfstan, but it *does* include apparently unauthorised additional material, not found in Junius 121. The addition is Fehr §§ 150-161, of which §§ 150-58 read like a synodical decision on fasts and feasts.[27] The CCC 190 version, then, testifies not only to circulation at diocesan level, but also to use, through its modification. We may deduce further, through the lack of Ælfric revisions and also of the personal prefatory letter to Wulfsige, which would not have been distributed, that the ultimate source for the Corpus 190 copy is the letter as originally sent to Wulfsige and circulated by him. In itself this is good evidence for circulation at diocesan level but, taken all in all, it has to be admitted that the nature of the surviving manuscripts is such that they do not generally allow us to see the pastoral letters being used in the circles for which they were intended.[28]

In her recent book on the political and social history of England in the tenth and eleventh centuries, Pauline Stafford commented on the monastic bias of our sources and noted that for most writers of the time 'the state of monasticism is the index of the state of the church'.[29] Stafford was referring to the almost exclusive concern with monastic life. Wulfsige, Wulfstan and Ælfric did not share this exclusivity, but their letters, which intend to reach out, in fact define the gap between secular and monastic. For these men too then, although in a different way from the one Stafford meant when she used the phrase, the state of monasticism was an index of the state of the church. Measured against that index, the secular church fared badly and something

---

[27] The end of CUL Gg.3.28 is lost, as already noted, and so this manuscript is no help here. Fehr, *Die Hirtenbriefe Ælfrics*, p. xxii, thought that the letter in Junius 121 contained §§ 150-161 but that these leaves had been lost. Clemoes, *Die Hirtenbriefe Ælfrics*, p. cxxxi, shows that there are no leaves missing from Junius 121 at this point, so that the letter must always have ended at Fehr § 149, as it now does. However, Whitelock in *Councils and Synods*, pp. 193-95, argues that § 149 could not have been the original conclusion, and she suggests that Fehr §§ 159-161, now only in CCC 190, was Ælfric's original ending, moved to come after the unauthorised insertion. If so, and if Clemoes' deduction about Junius 121 is correct, then the Junius copy cannot ever have had the original ending.

[28] As noted above, p. 106, this is because the nature of the manuscripts in which the letters survive differ from the nature of the manuscripts in which they presumably circulated. We have evidence of a circulating copy of the Wulfsige letter because it happened to be copied, apparently as a matter of record, into quires added to a large reference manuscript (CCC 190) of the type which, in the event, stood a reasonable chance of survival. If we had more circulating texts, we would perhaps find more evidence of subsequent modification than our predominantly 'reference' survivals indicate.

[29] P. Stafford, *Unification and Conquest: A Political and Social History of England in the Tenth and Eleventh Centuries* (London, 1989), p. 181.

needed to be done about it. All that we can safely say of the pastoral letters, however, is that they give insights into the minds of three men who, with monastic standards as their touchstone, attempted to take action. What we cannot do with confidence is assess the degree of bias in the picture they present or judge what effect they, and perhaps others like them, actually had on the eleventh-century secular church.

ÆLFRIC'S PASTORAL LETTERS: THE MANUSCRIPTS

	OE (Wulfsige) Fehr I c.992-1002	1st.Lat. (Wulfstan) Fehr 2 c.1005	2nd.Lat. (Wulfstan) Fehr 3 c.1005	1st,O.E. (Wulfstan) Fehr II c.1006	2nd.OE (Wulfstan) Fehr III c.1006
(1) MANUSCRIPTS ASSOCIATED WITH ÆLFRIC					
C.U.L. Gg.3.28 [Fehr MS Gg] s.x/xi	ff.264r-266v				
(2) MANUSCRIPTS ASSOCIATED WITH WULFSTAN					
CCC190 [Fehr MS 0] *Part A* s.xi med. +3 quires s.xi2 *Part B* s.xi med.	pp.295-308	pp.188-201	pp.151-159	pp.320-336	pp.336-349
Cop.Gl.kgl.S.1595 [Not known to Fehr] s.xi1		ff.67r-74r	ff.74r-77v		
CCC 265 [Fehr MS C] s.xi med.		pp.160-173	pp.174-180		
Junius 121 [Fehr MS X] s.xi 3rd. quarter	ff.101v-110v				ff.111r-124r
Bodley 343 [Fehr MS Oz] s.xii2				ff.133r-137r	ff.137r-140v
(3) OTHER MANUSCRIPTS					
CCC 201 [Fehr MS D] *Part B* s.xi med.				pp.31-40 [Wulfstan's rewriting]	
Cot.Tib.A.iii [Fehr MS N] s.xi.med.					ff.106r-107v [Fehr, §§ 1-62]
Cot.Vesp.D.xiv [Fehr MS V]				ff.74r-75v [Fehr, §§ 30-34]	.13v-15r [Fehr, §§ 120-45]

The Vitas Patrum *in Eleventh-Century Worcester*
PETER JACKSON

It has long been recognized that the century after the Norman Conquest was a crucial one in the history of English book-production. Texts were copied and recopied; there was a regular traffic of scribes and manuscripts among scriptoria; the entire scope and content of English monastic libraries, which just before the Conquest had often been out-dated and parochial, were altered almost out of recognition to reflect a more cosmopolitan and scholarly taste.[1] Yet this perception, true though it is, has sometimes distracted attention from the achievements of English scribes and librarians in the generations immediately before the Conquest – achievements made all the more remarkable when one remembers that the Danish invasions had destroyed centres of learning and book-production. It may well be that a fresh examination of the evidence provided by surviving manuscripts and booklists would reveal that, in this area as in others, the break between the old and new orders was not so sharp as has sometimes been thought. It is not my purpose to make such an examination here; but perhaps the major principle that one is needed can best be shown by a minor example such as that I hope to address – the study of the *Vitas Patrum* in eleventh-century Worcester.

I must begin with a problem of definition, for in the Middle Ages the term *Vitas Patrum* was often used in vague or contradictory senses, to denote almost any text that described the lives and sayings of the first monks, the 'desert fathers' of Egypt and the Near East.[2] Yet throughout the Middle Ages these books demonstrably circulated under this title either on their own, or together, or in various combinations, and the term would thus have had a distinct meaning to every audience that encountered it – to an Anglo-Saxon audience as much as to any other.

However, the evidence as to the meaning of the term to the audience I am concerned with here – that in eleventh-century Worcester – is at least reasonably clear. As J. E. Cross has noted, in the four instances where Ælfric

---

1   N. R. Ker, *English Manuscripts in the Century after the Norman Conquest* (Oxford, 1960), pp. 7-8; R. M. Thomson, 'The Norman Conquest and English Libraries', in *The Role of the Book in Medieval Culture*, ed. P. Ganz, 2 vols., Bibliologia 3-4 (Turnhout, 1986), II, pp 27-40.

2   This point is well made by C. M. Batlle, *Die "Adhortationes Sanctorum Patrum" ("Verba Seniorum") im lateinischen Mittelalter*, Beiträge zur Geschichte des alten Mönchtums und des Benediktinerordens, 31 (Münster, Westfalen, 1972), pp. 1-4. Batlle also notes (pp. 7-9) that in the title, the irregular nominative plural form, 'Vitas', is found more often in the early medieval period than either 'Vitae' or 'Vita'. See also W. Berschin, *Greek Letters and the Latin Middle Ages from Jerome to Nicholas of Cusa* (Washington, DC, 1988), pp. 57-59.

(whose homilies were undoubtedly being read and studied at Worcester) names the work and extracts an anecdote, the material comes from only one source – the *Verba Seniorum* of Pelagius and John.[3] The only evidence I know that the term could have meant anything other at Worcester is an inscription in the Worcester manuscript to be discussed at some length below (pp. 117-21). This inscription reads: 'In nomine Dei summi incipit Vita *(sic)* Patrum' (f. 49r). The reference this time is to the *Historia Monachorum in Aegypto*, by Rufinus of Aquileia.

In this paper, then, I shall assume that these two books, and these only, were regarded as *Vitas Patrum* in eleventh-century Worcester. For this reason I cannot discuss here at any length the longer biographies of the desert fathers, such as Evagrius of Antioch's translation of Athanasius' *Life of Antony*,[4] or the *Life of Malchus* by Jerome,[5] or more sophisticated ascetic writings such as the *Collations* of John Cassian,[6] beyond mentioning the fact that there is clear evidence that these books too were certainly being read and studied at Worcester.[7] I will now describe briefly the two texts on which I will concentrate.

The *Verba Seniorum*[8] is a collection of over 700 sayings, aphorisms and anecdotes about the first Egyptian monks, ranging from one-line apophthegms to extended narratives, and divided into twenty-two chapters, each devoted to a particular topic – discretion, chastity, patience, and the like. The origins of the collection are deeply obscure, and in any case it is beyond the scope of this paper to discuss them,[9] but the sayings and

---

3   J. E. Cross, 'On the Library of the Old English Martyrologist', in *Learning and Literature in Anglo-Saxon England: Studies presented to Peter Clemoes*, ed. M. Lapidge and H. Gneuss (Cambridge, 1985) pp. 227-49, at p. 244 n. 84.

4   Ptd PL 73: 125-70.

5   'Sancti Eusebii Hieronymi Vita Malchi Monachi Captivi', ed. C. C. Mierow, in *Classical Essays presented to James A. Kleist, S.J.*, ed. R. E. Arnold (Saint Louis, 1946), pp. 31-60, 117.

6   *Iohannis Cassiani Conlationes XXIIII*, ed. M. Petschenig, CSEL 13 (Vienna, 1886).

7   For the *Life of Antony* and the *Life of Malchus*, see pp. 119 and 124, below. Cassian's *Collations* are preserved in a mid-11th century copy from Worcester, now Oxford, Bodleian Library, Hatton MS 23, ff. 1v-135r.

8   The most recent edition is still that by H. Rosweyde, *Vitæ Patrum*, second edition (Antwerp, 1628), reptd PL 73:855-1022. A few sayings have been edited separately by C. M. Batlle, '"Vetera Nova". Vorläufige kritische Ausgabe bei Rosweyde fehlender Vätersprüche', in *Festschrift Bernhard Bischoff*, ed. J. Autenrieth and F. Brunhölzl (Stuttgart, 1971), pp. 32-42. There is an invaluable (if still provisional) list of surviving manuscripts in Batlle, *"Adhortationes Sanctorum Patrum"*.

9   The surest guide to this immensely complex topic is J.-C. Guy, *Recherches sur la tradition grecque des* Apophthegmata Patrum, 2nd edn, Subsidia Hagiographica, 36 (Brussels, 1984); see also J. G. Freire, 'Traductions latines des *Apophthegmata*

anecdotes that constitute it are thought to have circulated orally at first, been written down in Greek in the fourth century, and been translated into Latin by Pelagius the deacon (later Pope Pelagius I) and John the sub-deacon (later Pope John III) sometime in the 530s. Such a text had an obvious appeal to a monastic audience, for it offered paradigms of religious conduct in a way that was both striking and easily memorable. Its widespread popularity is attested by the survival of over one hundred manuscripts of the entire collection dating from the seventh century to the fifteenth; manuscripts of selections or of isolated sayings from it are more numerous still.[10]

Almost equally popular was the *Historia Monachorum*,[11] which represents a slightly later strand of ascetic writing than the *Verba Seniorum*. Here the various sayings and narratives are embodied in an account of a visit to the Egyptian monasteries and hermitages made by seven Palestinian monks in the winter of 394-95, and told by one of the travellers shortly after his return; each chapter describes the way of life and teaching of a monk, or group of monks, whom the visitors met on their journey.[12] The work was translated into Latin shortly after its composition by Rufinus of Aquileia, who had himself spent time in Egypt, and who incorporated some of his own experiences in his translation.[13] I hope to show what manuscript evidence and literary evidence there is that these two books were being read and appreciated at Worcester in the eleventh century, and then to consider the reasons for their popularity there at such a time.

Patrum', in *Mélanges Christine Mohrmann*, nouveau recueil (Utrecht and Antwerp, 1973), 164-71.

[10] See Batlle, *"Adhortationes Sanctorum Patrum"*, *passim*. G. Philippart lists five additional manuscripts, including Worcester, Cathedral Library F.48 ('*Vitae Patrum*. Trois travaux récents sur d'anciennes traductions latines', *Analecta Bollandiana*, 92 (1974), 353-65 at p. 356), and others certainly remain to be listed and described.

[11] Tyrannius Rufinus, *Historia Monachorum sive De Vita Sanctorum Patrum*, ed. E. Schulz-Flügel, Patristische Texte und Studien, 34 (Berlin and New York, 1990; hereafter Schulz-Flügel).

[12] The *Historia Monachorum* is usually thought to be the record of an actual journey: *The Lausiac History of Palladius*, ed. C. Butler, 2 vols., Texts and Stud., OS 6 (Cambridge, 1898-1904), I, pp. 198-203; B. Ward, 'Introduction', *The Lives of the Desert Fathers*, trans. N. Russell, Cistercian Stud. Series, 34 (Oxford, 1981), pp. 3-46 (at pp. 4-6). However, a different view is expressed by Schulz-Flügel, who regards the work as a kind of travel novel, based on a variety of oral and written sources (pp. 5-17).

[13] On Rufinus as the translator of the work see Butler, *Lausiac History*, I, pp. 11 and 264-66, and G. Trettel, 'Rufino e la Historia Monachorum (paternità dell'opera: tentativo di soluzione)', in *Rufino di Concordia e il suo tempo*, Antichità Altoadriatiche, 31, 2 vols (Udine, 1987), I, pp. 215-26; Schulz-Flügel, pp. 37-48.

To begin with the manuscript. Worcester Cathedral F.48.[14] at present is a single parchment manuscript of 164 leaves,[15] preserving the work of five scribes, as follows: (1) ff. 1r-48v, s.xi/xii; (2) ff. 49r-104v, s.xi 1/2(?); (3) ff. 105r-123v 1.5 and ff. 123v 1.22-164r, s.xi med.(?); (4) ff. 123v 1.6-1.21, s.xii (written over an erasure); (5) f. 164v, s.xii med.[16] Though now bound as a single manuscript, F.48 originally consisted of three separate books, with the breaks occurring after ff. 48 and 104. It will be seen that the second and third manuscripts were at Worcester c.1100; the second (the *Historia Monachorum*) is most likely of continental origin, but there is no reason to think that the first and third were not written at Worcester.[17]

The first section (ff. 1r-48v) preserves copies of Jerome's *Lives* of St Hilarion, the founder of Palestinian monasticism, of St Paul of Thebes, traditionally the first Christian hermit,[18] and of Evagrius of Antioch's translation of Athanasius' *Life* of Antony,[19] who initiated the monastic

---

14 Described by Schulz-Flügel, pp. 135-36 (her MS W), and by J. K. Floyer, *Catalogue of Manuscripts preserved in the Chapter Library of Worcester Cathedral*, ed. S.G. Hamilton (Oxford (pr.) 1906), pp. 22-23. Though, as will be seen, I disagree with some of Schulz-Flügel's conclusions about the date and origins of the manuscript, her description is nonetheless a considerable improvement on Floyer and Hamilton's, which contains numerous errors.

15 Following the modern foliation, Floyer/Hamilton and Schulz-Flügel each give the number of leaves (excluding flyleaves) as 166. In fact the foliation skips from 66 to 68 and from 98 to 100, making 164 leaves in all. Hence the numbering given in this paper will differ at several points from that given in earlier sources. At least one leaf is missing from the end of the manuscript.

16 I am indebted to Dr Julia Crick and Dr David Dumville for help in dating the various hands. The third hand, which Bishop (see below) rightly describes as 'degenerate', is particularly difficult to date: I hope to study it further on another occasion. I. Atkins and N. R. Ker (ed.), *Catalogus Librorum Manuscriptorum Bibliothecae Wigorniensis, made in 1622-1623 by Patrick Young* (Cambridge, 1944), p. 51, date the entire manuscript s.xi med. T. A. M. Bishop considers ff. 105-64 to be 'of unknown date (probably s.xi)' (*English Caroline Minuscule* Oxford, 1971), p. 17). We will be in a position to reach more positive conclusions when Dr Dumville has completed an important study of the Worcester scriptorium in the 10th and 11th centuries.

17 Schulz-Flügel (p. 135) claims that ff. 49r-164v are written by a single 10th-century hand without Insular features, but this is certainly wrong. Dr Crick and Dr Dumville advise me that while a foreign scribe may well have been responsible for ff. 49r-104v (the *Historia Monachorum*), there are numerous indications (e.g. the use of the Insular r and the et ligature) that the extracts from the *Verba Seniorum* on ff. 105r-164r were undoubtedly copied in England. Dr Crick, Dr Dumville and I also date ff. 49r-164r considerably later than Schulz-Flügel does. I hope to discuss these matters in greater detail on another occasion.

18 Ptd PL 23:29-54 and 17-30 respectively.

movement in Egypt. The second original manuscript – now ff. 49r-104v – is a copy of Rufinus' *Historia Monachorum*, extensively corrected in a late-eleventh-century hand. The final item, on f. 164v, is an incomplete copy of the *Life* of Thais, a courtesan who was reclaimed from a life of sin by the Egyptian monk Paphnutius.[20]

But I wish to pay particular attention here to the last substantial item in the manuscript, a copy of the *Verba Seniorum* on ff. 105r-64r. The *Verba Seniorum* was not an unusual book to find in an English monastic library. A late seventh- or early eighth-century copy of Books I-XV:39, now Brussels, Bibliothèque Royale, lat. 9850-52, written originally at the monastery of St Médard in Soissons, was among the books given *c*.1070 to the monastery of Saint-Vaast in Arras by Sæwold, the last Saxon abbot of Bath. Sæwold had fled to the Continent after the Conquest and had presumably taken this manuscript with him into his exile.[21] Four incomplete leaves of a manuscript of the work written *c*.700 survive as part of the binding of a twelfth-century cartulary from Winchester (British Library, Add. MS 15350, ff. 1 and 121).[22] A single story from Book XVIII (No. 9) found its way into a tenth-century manuscript miscellany from Kent, now BL Cotton MS, Vespasian D.vi, ff. 67r-68v.[23] And there are explicit borrowings from and references to the book in the writings of Bede and Alcuin, in the *Old English Martyrology*, and in the homilies of Ælfric.[24]

---

19   See note 4, above.

20   Ptd PL 73:661-62. V. I. J. Flint suggests that this copy of the *Life* was known to Honorius Augustodunensis, but if my dating is correct, it was written some fifty years too late to have been used by him ('The Career of Honorius Augustodunensis. Some Fresh Evidence', reptd from *Revue Bénédictine*, 82 (1972), 63-86, at p. 80 in *Ideas in the Medieval West: Texts and their Contexts*, Variorum Reprints, Collected Studies Series 268 (London, 1988), no. V; see also M. O. Garrigues, 'Utrum Honorius ubique sit totus?', *Abhandlungen der Braunschweigischen Wissenschaftlichen Gesellschaft*, 35 (1983), 31-64, at pp. 33 and 35).

21   Described by L. Delisle, 'Notice d'un manuscrit Mérovingien de la Bibliothèque Royale de Belgique, no 9850-9852', *Notices et extraits des manuscrits de la Bibliothèque Nationale*, 31 (1884), 33-47. See also Batlle, "*Adhortationes Sanctorum Patrum*", p. 17; M. Lapidge, 'Surviving Booklists from Anglo-Saxon England', in *Learning and Literature*, pp. 33-89, at pp. 59 and 61; P. Grierson, 'Les livres de l'abbé Seiwold de Bath', *Revue Bénédictine*, 52 (1940), 96-116 (at pp. 107-08); *CLA* 1547a.

22   *CLA* 164.

23   Described by N. R. Ker, *Catalogue of Manuscripts containing Anglo-Saxon* (Oxford, 1957, reptd 1990), pp. 268-69 (no. 207).

24   The evidence for this knowledge is too detailed to set out here but is discussed in my article, 'Vitae Patrum: Verba Seniorum', in *Sources of Anglo-Saxon Literary*

What is surprising, however, is that there is no early manuscript of the work that is of demonstrably English origin. The two larger manuscripts mentioned above (Brussels, BR 9850-52 and BL Add. 15350) are both of continental, not English, manufacture, and the existence of the single story that does survive in an English manuscript (in BL Cotton Vespasian D.vi) hardly counts as evidence the other way. To find a copy made in England of any substantial part of the *Verba Seniorum* we have to turn to the copy preserved in Worcester V.48.

This copy is unusual in one important respect. The *Verba Seniorum* is a long work – 742 sayings and stories in all – and incomplete and imperfect manuscripts of it are far from uncommon. But the copy in Worcester F.48 consists of two sets of carefully judged selections from the complete work, a fact uncommon enough to merit attention here.[25]

The first set of selections (nos 1-42) is taken from Books I-XIX of the *Verba Seniorum*. Not every book has been drawn on, and those from which sayings have been taken have been used very unevenly – there are no extracts at all from some books, and others are represented by only a single item. Judging by the distribution of the sayings and stories that he chose to extract, this selector's particular concerns would appear to have been the associated virtues of obedience and humility (seven and eight sayings respectively from Books XIV and XV) and the contrastingly connected subjects of chastity and fornication (five and six sayings respectively from Books IV and V).

The second collection of extracts (nos 43-171) is longer and less uneven than the first. There are fewer anomalies here than in the first collection, and only two books are entirely unrepresented. The most popular books this time were Books X, on discretion, with sixteen sayings, and, once more, Book IV, on chastity, with thirteen; and there seems to have been a deliberate attempt to rectify the imbalances of the earlier collection – for example, Books VIII and XXI, which contributed no sayings at all to the first collection, are represented by twelve each in the second.

It is apparent, then, that the selector had access to a complete copy of the *Verba Seniorum*, and that he went through the entire collection, systematically, twice – a procedure that is without parallel in the other surviving manuscripts of the book. Moreover, late in the eleventh century the text (like the *Historia Monachorum*) was extensively supplemented with readings from another manuscript now lost.

The F.48 text aroused the interest of another later Worcester monk as well. N. R. Ker has shown that it was among the manuscripts annotated by a monk who elsewhere signs his name as 'Coleman'.[26] (I accept Ker's

---

Culture, ed. F.M. Biggs, T. D. Hill and P. E. Szarmach (forthcoming).

25 Unfortunately, a list of these extracts would be too long to print in full here.

26 N. R. Ker, 'Old English notes signed "Coleman"', rptd from *Medium Ævum*, 18

suggestion that this is the Coleman who was chancellor to Bishop Wulfstan of Worcester in 1089 and who wrote the lost vernacular Life of the bishop.) Four Latin marginalia by Coleman survive in F.48, and three of these have been noticed and printed by Ker. All are found in either the *Historia Monachorum* or the *Verba Seniorum*. At f. 148v, opposite a copy of *VS* XVIII:3, the account of a Eucharistic miracle, he has written: 'De quodam sene simplice. qui errabat in fide de corpore et sanguine domini' ('Concerning a simple old man who erred in his belief concerning the body and blood of the Lord'). Six pages later, on f. 151v, another passage drew his attention, the story of a nun, who, as an act of humility, pretended to be an imbecile and as a result was treated as a domestic drudge by the other sisters (*VS* XVIII:19). Coleman has written: 'De sanctimoniali que se stulta simulauit. a sancto piterione cognita.' ('Concerning a nun who pretended to be an imbecile and was discerned by St Pityrion'). The next item in the manuscript (*VS* XVIII:20) was the last in the *Verba Seniorum* to be annotated by him. This story derives from Paul the Simple, one of the disciples of St Anthony, and in the margin opposite the beginning of the passage (on f.152v) Coleman has written the three words 'De paulo simplice'.[27]

In addition to these passages from the *Verba Seniorum*, however, Coleman annotated one further passage in the manuscript, this time from the *Historia Monachorum*, and this note has not been printed or discussed before. It is found on f. 86r, opposite the beginning of c. XVI of the *Historia Monachorum*, which tells the story of a search made by the monk Paphnutius to find 'which of the saints who had lived a virtuous life he most resembled.'[28] This time Coleman has written: 'Quomodo papnutius orauit dominum ut sibi ostenderet similem sui' ('How Paphnutius prayed to the Lord that he would show him one whom he resembled').

But this interest in the *Vitas Patrum* – both in the Worcester scriptorium in general and by Coleman in particular – was not confined to the Latin originals. Translations of parts of it into the vernacular were being read and studied at Worcester too.

(1949), 29-31, in *Books, Collectors and Libraries: Studies in the Medieval Heritage*, ed. A. G. Watson (London and Ronceverte, [1985]), 27-30. Further Old English and Latin notes by Coleman are edited and discussed by E. A. McIntyre, 'Early 12th century Worcester Cathedral Priory, with Special Reference to the Manuscripts copied there' (unpublished DPhil dissertation, Oxford University, 1978), pp. 40-45 and 77-80; J. Hill, 'Ælfric's "Silent Days"', *Leeds Studies in English*, NS 16 (1985), 118-31, at p. 121; and W. P. Stoneman, 'Another Old English Note signed "Coleman"', *Medium Ævum*, 56 (1987), 78-82. Various of these notes are also discussed by M. McC. Gatch, *Preaching and Theology in Anglo-Saxon England: Ælfric and Wulfstan* (Toronto and Buffalo, 1977), pp. 56-57 and 210 n. 105.

27 These three stories are ptd PL 73:978-80, 984-85 and 985-88 respectively.

28 'cui sanctorum similis haberetur' (XVI:1.2; Schulz-Flügel, p. 340).

Readers of Ælfric's *Lives of Saints* will be familiar with the Sermon on the Life of St Swithun (no. XXI in Skeat's edition).[29] At the end of the sermon Skeat adds a thirty-five line 'continuation', describing a miracle that was worked by the Egyptian monk Macarius, and borrowed by Ælfric from c.XXVIII of the *Historia Monachorum*.[30] The passage was printed by Skeat from the only manuscript in which he knew it – BL Cotton Julius E. vii, f. 103r-v, in which, as J.C. Pope says, it does indeed follow 'immediately after ... the account of St Swithun's miracles'.

But this story occurs in another context too, one that was not known to Skeat. It is found in two manuscripts as part of a longer enlargement of *Lives of Saints* no. XVII, the homily 'De Auguriis'. (The rest of the enlargement was a careful exposition, also written by Ælfric, of the story of Saul and the witch of Endor). Pope has given convincing reasons for believing that the setting accorded to the story in Skeat – at the end of the homily on St Swithun – is both earlier than the other and authoritative. It was only added at the end of 'De Auguriis' by an anonymous compiler who smoothed the transition from the preceding homily by adding three lines of his own composition to bridge the gap.[31]

No doubt the compiler added this new material because, like *De Auguriis*, it concerned superstition and witchcraft. But it may also be significant that both the manuscripts in which the addition is found at this point are of Worcester origin – Cambridge, Corpus Christi College 178, pp. 97-98,[32] which was written there a little before the middle of the eleventh century, and Oxford, Bodleian Library, Hatton 116, pp. 360-61, written in the first half of the twelfth[33] and I would argue that the compiler of CCC 178 was interested enough by a story that he recognized from the *Historia Monachorum* to transfer it and the story of Saul and the witch of Endor from their original settings to the one at the end of 'De Auguriis'. Perhaps half a century later, the passage still provoked enough interest to be annotated on p.97 by Coleman, this time in Old English: 'Bysne be drymannum 7 be anum godan men macharius gehatæn' ('An *exemplum* about magicians and about a

---

29 *Ælfric's Lives of Saints*, ed. W. W. Skeat, 4 vols. in 2, EETS OS 76, 82, 94 and 114 (London, 1881-1900; reptd in 2 vols., London, 1966), I, XXI, II. 464-98 (pp. 470-72).

30 XXVIII:3; Schulz-Flügel, pp. 366-67.

31 *Homilies of Ælfric: A Supplementary Collection*, ed. J. C. Pope, 2 vols., EETS OS 259, 260 (London, 1967-68), II, 786-89 (introduction), 790-98 (text and notes). See also J. Hill, 'The Dissemination of Ælfric's Lives of Saints: A Preliminary Survey', in *A Collection of New Essays by Various Hands on Old English Prose Saints' Lives*, ed. P. E. Szarmach (Albany, forthcoming).

32 Ker, *Catalogue of Manuscripts*, pp. 60-64 (no. 41).

33 *Ibid.*, pp. 403-06 (no. 333).

good man called Macarius') – and it is worth noting that it was the story about Macarius, not the longer and more elaborate exposition of the story of Saul and the witch of Endor, that drew his attention. Coleman, like the compiler who copied the story, would have recognized its sources in the *Historia Monachorum*, a work that we have already seen he had read and annotated.

Another fruit of the interest in the *Vitas Patrum* in the Worcester scriptorium was the Old English translation of two stories from the *Verba Seniorum*, found on ff. 137v-139v of BL Cotton MS Otho C.i, vol. 2.[34] This manuscript was certainly at Worcester in the thirteenth century (when it was glossed in the well known 'tremulous' hand), and almost certainly there in the second half of the eleventh, when running titles were added that closely resemble those found in Bodleian, Hatton 113/14, which is undoubtedly a Worcester manuscript. The presumption must be that Cotton Otho C.i, vol.2, was written at Worcester too. Both stories were written in a single hand, and palaeographically and linguistically the translation can be dated to the middle of the eleventh century.[35] The stories are followed by another piece about the desert fathers, an Old English translation of Jerome's *Life of Malchus*. (It has been shown, however, that this piece was written by another and slightly later scribe, and that it differs linguistically from the two other stories.)[36]

The two stories that were translated from the *Verba Seniorum* were Book V, nos 37 and 38 – stories that invariably follow one another in complete copies of the Latin original. They were also among the extracts copied in Worcester F.48, but they are found in quite different parts of the manuscript: V:37 was among the stories copied in the second selection and V:38 in the first.[37] Obviously, then, the translator of the stories in Cotton Otho C.i cannot have taken them directly from F.48. What is more likely is that several monks at Worcester had access to a common exemplar there that is now lost. It is possible that the same manuscript was used by the compilers of

---

[34] Ibid., pp. 236-38 (no. 182); ptd B. Assmann, *Angelsächsische Homilien und Heiligenleben*, Bibliothek der angelsächsischen Prosa, 3 (Kassel, 1889), reptd with a supplementary introduction by P. Clemoes (Darmstadt, 1964), pp. 195-98 (no.XVIII: 1 and 2).

[35] Assmann characterizes the language as 'rein Spätwestsächsisch' (p. 267). In a private communication, Paul Bibire confirms Assmann's opinion of the date.

[36] Ed. Assmann, *Homilien*, pp. 199-207 (no. XVIII:3). On the date of this piece, see K. Sisam, 'An Old English Translation of a Letter from Wynfrith to Eadburga (A.D. 716-17) in Cotton MS Otho C.1', reptd from *Modern Language Review*, 18 (1923), 253-72 (at p. 256), in *Studies in the History of Old English Literature* (Oxford, 1953), pp. 199-231 (at p. 204).

[37] On f. 126r-v and ff. 108r-109r respectively.

Worcester F.48 and the translator of the stories in Cotton Otho C.i; it is likely, after all, that both were working about the same time, c.1050. Another possibility is that this lost common exemplar was the one used to correct Worcester F.48 later in the century.

I hope that by now it will have become apparent that the lives of the desert fathers were studied with close attention in the Worcester community. Copies of their biographies and sayings were made and annotated; selections from their sayings were translated into English; vernacular homilies that dealt with their lives were translated and studied. It is hardly possible that such interest could have been merely haphazard or fortuitous. There must have been some compelling reason for it, either institutional – the existence of a noticeably more austere tradition of monasticism there than elsewhere – or personal – the presence of a strong directing personality who encouraged the production of such books in the Worcester scriptorium. In practice, of course, it is impossible to distinguish these factors; and to discover the reason for this interest in the *Vitas Patrum*, I believe it is necessary to look a little more closely at the life and activities of the best known member of the Worcester community in the mid-eleventh century – Bishop Wulfstan II.[38]

Wulfstan was born in Itchington, Warwickshire, about 1008, the son of moderately prosperous and devout parents who both entered monasteries in their old age. He was ordained a priest after study at Evesham and Peterborough. But his natural inclinations were towards a monastic way of life, and at his own request he was made a monk in the cathedral priory,

[38] The primary source for the life of Wulfstan is William of Malmesbury's Latin version of the lost OE biography by Coleman, edited (together with other early sources) by R. R. Darlington, *The Vita Wulfstani of William of Malmesbury*, Camden Soc., 3rd series, 40 (London, 1928). In quoting translations of William's Life I use the translation by J. H. F. Peile, *William of Malmesbury's Life of St Wulstan [sic], Bishop of Worcester* (Oxford, 1934). There is a more recent translation by M. Swanton, in *Three Lives of the Last Englishmen*, Garland Library of Medieval Literature, 10, series B (New York and London, 1984), pp. 91-148. However, Swanton omits several important passages in which William describes his methods of translation and the differences of his own work from Coleman's – the entire 'Epistola Willelmi' (Darlington, pp. 1-2 l.23), also Darlington p. 11, lines 25-27 (I:5); p. 23, line 27 - p. 24, line 2 (I:16) and p. 58, lines 4-9 (III:18). There is an important recent biography of the saint by E. Mason, *St Wulfstan of Worcester, c.1008-1095* (Oxford, 1990). A study of the intellectual and spiritual life of 11th century Worcester is still to be written. A Worcester booklist from c.1050 has been ptd and discussed by M. Lapidge, 'Booklists', 62-64; the list makes no mention of the *Vitas Patrum*, but as it includes only eleven books (three of them duplicates), it can hardly be exhaustive. It is worth adding, however, that among these books (one of '.ii. englissce dialogas') may be BL Cotton MS Otho C.i, vol.2. A late 11th-century booklist, possibly from Worcester, is also ptd by Lapidge ('Booklists', pp. 69-73).

which at the time had scarcely a dozen inmates. Of this community he was successively schoolmaster, precentor, sacristan and eventually (from the mid-1050s) prior, and in 1062 he was elected Bishop of Worcester. He held the see until his death in 1095, the last survivor of the pre-Conquest episcopate and an outstandingly successful mediator of the old order to the new.

Wulfstan combined a career of vigorous secular and religious reform with more obviously intellectual pursuits. He abolished the slave trade between Bristol and Ireland, rebuilt his cathedral at Worcester, pursued an active programme of church expansion within his diocese, and agitated successfully for the return of various church lands. But Wulfstan was also a patron of scholarship and learning: he ordered the monk John to undertake a universal chronicle, made the collection of material that was later to form the basis of Hemming's *Cartulary*, and inspired the collection and copying of books in his cathedral library. What is especially of interest for my present purpose is that his early biographers uniformly draw attention to the austere ascetic discipline that he imposed on himself and expected in others.

Here the best witness is the Latin *Life of Wulfstan* by William of Malmesbury.[39] William used as the basis of his life a vernacular biography of the saint by Coleman, who had been Wulfstan's chaplain and chancellor towards the end of his life, and whose own interest in the *Vitas Patrum* has already been noticed and discussed. This vernacular life is now lost, but William claims to have followed it closely in making his translation. According to the *Life*, Wulfstan

> passed his days in fasting, and whole nights in watching. ... Every day he genuflected at each verse of the seven [penitential] psalms: and the same at night in the cxix psalm. ... Feather bed or other bed he had none. He did not yield himself to sleep, but snatched it. He would lie with his head on the step before the altar, and his body on the bare ground. Or again he would put a book under his head and take a little sleep on bare boards. Before each of the eighteen altars that were in the Old Church he prostrated himself seven times a day.[40]

---

39 For an edn and translation of the *Life*, see note 38, above. Recent studies include A. Gransden, *Historical Writing in England*, c. 550 to c. 1307 (London, 1974), pp. 87-89 and E. Mason, *St Wulfstan*, pp. 286-94.

40 'dies ieiuniis, et uigiliis totas continuabat noctes ... Diebus omnibus ad unumquemque uersum vii psalmorum genua flectere; idem noctibus in psalmo centesimo octauo x^o facere. ... Plumam et ullum omnino lectum non habere; sopori non indulgere, sed surripere. Super gradus ante altare capite posito se humo exponere; uel etiam codice aliquo uertici summisso, super lignum tenuem inuitare soporem. Ante unumquodque decem et viii^{to} altarium que in ueteri ecclesia erant septies in die prosterni' (I:3; Darlington p. 9, trans. Peile pp. 12-13).

It is also reported that 'thrice in the week he abstained altogether from food, and continued his fast through the night until dawn. ... On the other three days of the week his food was leeks and boiled cabbage with a crust of bread'.[41] He continued these austerities even after he became a bishop.

All these practices – the limited diet, the prolonged vigils, the extended prayers – are found everywhere in the *Vitas Patrum*. For example, in the *Historia Monachorum* Rufinus repeats stories that the monk Apollonius would pray one hundred times each day, and as often at night, while some of the monks who lived with him would spend the entire night reciting the scriptures or in hymn-singing.[42] As regards diet, in the *Verba Seniorum* it is recorded that the monk Pastor would fast two and three days at a time, if not longer;[43] while according to the *Historia Monachorum*, Theon's diet consisted entirely of uncooked vegetables, while Pityrion went even further and ate only a little soup made with corn-meal, and that only twice a week.[44]

Such stories could be multiplied almost indefinitely. No doubt it would be unfair to put too much reliance on them. It could be argued that at least some of the details I have mentioned were Coleman's invention. It has already been seen that he had read and annotated the *Vitas Patrum* with some care. What would have been more natural than that he would have imported some incidents or emphases from it (or from other saints' lives) to his own work? William himself admits that in making his translation 'I have left out some fine words and phrases which Coleman borrowed from the Acts of other saints, and in his blind devotion inserted'.[45] But in this passage William is apparently referring only to Coleman's language – not to the events and incidents he describes. The whole purpose of Coleman's work would have been spoiled if he had filled his account with obviously exaggerated and fictitious stories, – not least as his account was written not long after Wulfstan's death, at a time when the community at Worcester must have included other monks who had known the saint. I do not believe that Coleman's reading in the *Vitas Patrum* led him to invent stories of ascetic excess in his *Life of Wulfstan*. Rather, I believe that it was Wulfstan's own interest in the desert fathers that led him to adopt the practices he did, and that it was Coleman's knowledge of these details of Wulfstan's life that

---

41 'Tri'us in ebdomada diebus, omnis cibi abstemius; noctem perinde ac lucem continuabat ieiunio. ... Tribus reliquis porros caulesue coctos uel elixos, panis cibaria aditiens; et uictum transigebat' (I:10; Darlington p. 17, trans. Peile p. 25).

42 VII:2.5 and 14.2, Schulz-Flügel pp. 288 and 303.

43 X:44; PL 73:920.

44 VI:8 and XIII:5; Schulz-Flügel pp. 285 and 334.

45 'Nec minus alta uerba declamantiunculas quasdam; quas ille ab aliorum sanctorum gestis assumptas, prona deuotione inseruit' (I:16; Darlington, p. 23, trans. Peile p.35).

both sharpened his own interest in the *Vitas Patrum*, and led him to make his annotations in Worcester F.48.

More than this, it is possible to bring the two stories translated at Worcester from the *Verba Seniorum* into a particularly close connection with Wulfstan, for each of them can be shown to have had a theme that would have been congenial to him.[46] The first story (V:37) describes the unsuccessful attempt made by a prostitute to seduce a monk. The woman arrived one evening at the monk's cell and demanded entry, claiming that she was being threatened by wild beasts that were prowling outside. When, despite his misgivings, the monk let her in, he at once demonstrated his iron self-control in the face of temptation by holding his hand in the flame of his candle until the fingers had burned away. In the morning the woman was found to be lying dead on the floor of the cell. The monk, not wishing to return evil for evil, raised her to life again, and the woman spent the rest of her life in chastity.

The theme of this story is obviously the need for utter self-discipline by a monk when tempted by sexual desire, and the Latin *Life* makes it clear that such self-control was a quality that Wulfstan especially valued: 'The sin of incontinence he abhorred, and approved continence in all men, and especially in clerks in holy orders'.[47] Even in his private reading, we are told, he would 'give heed especially to those [books of the Bible] which commend chastity, a virtue which he followed earnestly in himself, and sharply rebuked the lack of in others'.[48] It has already been seen that stories about chastity were popular with the compilers of extracts from the *Verba Seniorum* in Worcester F.48, and it may be that Wulfstan's influence was at work there too, just as it is possible to see in the translation of this story from the *Verba Seniorum* evidence of his characteristic concern for this virtue, not least among the clergy.

Similar and more specific evidence is provided by the next story to be translated (V:38). This anecdote concerns a monk who wished to marry the daughter of a pagan priest. The girl's father would agree only on condition that the young man denied his God and renounced his monastic vows. The monk did so, but the pagan priest still withheld his consent, as he had been warned by a demon that God had not yet abandoned the monk. On being told of this, the monk recovered his senses and returned to the desert, where

---

[46] PL 73:883-84 (V:37); 884-85 (V:38).

[47] 'Labem impudicicie oderat, integritati fauebat in omnibus; et maxime sacrati ordinis hominibus' (III:12; Darlington p. 53, trans. Peile p. 81).

[48] 'tum in his diligentes pretendebat excubias, qui sibi castimoniam commendarent; eius integritatem in se alacriter exsequi corruptionem in aliis acriter insequi' (I:5; Darlington p. 11, trans. Peile p. 16).

he was reconciled to the Holy Spirit through the intercession of an older brother.

Obviously, this story, like the earlier one, is intended as a warning against sexual temptation. But there is a more specific point of interest here too, for, as has already been suggested, among the most striking features of Wulfstan's episcopate were the strenuous efforts he made – in line with eleventh-century continental reforms – to prevent his clergy from marrying, and to persuade those priests who had married before he became bishop to renounce their wives.[49] Coleman, in William of Malmesbury's version, is once more the main authority. He says:

> Wedded priests he brought under one edict, commanding them to renounce their fleshly desires or their churches. If they loved chastity, they might remain and be welcome: if they were the servants of bodily pleasures, they must go forth in disgrace. Some there were who chose rather to go without their churches than their women: and of these some wandered about till they starved: others sought and at last found some other provision. A few, taking the wiser way, honourably grew old in their benefices. The Bishop, to avoid future scandal, would not thereafter ordain to the priesthood any who was not sworn to celibacy.[50]

Seen in the light of passages such as this, the two extracts from the *Verba Seniorum* take on a different complexion. It was no mere coincidence that these two stories, out of all the hundreds in the *Verba Seniorum*, were alone chosen to be put into English. The translation had a definite ideological intention, as part of Wulfstan's endeavour to encourage chastity as a virtue, especially among the clergy; and the second story was particularly well adapted for his purposes, for in it not only is the intended marriage of a Christian monk explicitly condemned, but the villain of the piece is actually a married (pagan) priest.

According to the *Life*, it was Wulfstan's practice to 'have edifying books read at his table, and silence was kept that all might hearken and when men had well eaten he would expound what had been read in the vulgar tongue, that he might impart heavenly food to them for whose bodily sustenance he

---

[49] Ironically enough, Wulfstan was himself the son of a married priest (Mason, *St Wulfstan*, pp. 30-31).

[50] 'Uxoratos presbiteros omnes uno conuenit edicto; aut libidini aut ecclesiis renuntiandum pronuntians. Si castimoniam amarent, manerent cum gratia; si uoluptati seruirent, exirent cum iniuria. Fueruntque non nulli, qui ecclesiis quam mulierculis carere mallent. Quorum aliquos uagabundos fames absumpsit; aliquos res familiaris aliunde quesita, in extremum tutata, non destituit. Pauci quos sanior regebat ratio, abdicatis illicitis, preclaro in ecclesiis suis consenuere otio. Quare antistes cauens in posterum, nullum ulterius promouit ad presbiterum, qui non de castitate seruanda daret sacramentum' (III:12, Darlington pp. 53-54, trans. Peile p. 81). See also Mason, *St Wulfstan*, pp. 162-64.

had already made provision'.[51] It is possible to imagine the translation of the *Verba Seniorum* arising from a milieu such as this. The *Vitas Patrum* was among the books recommended for reading in the Benedictine Rule,[52] and there is evidence from the twelfth century (when manuscripts of it were far more numerous) that it was being read at collation at Durham.[53] Doubtless it was read in a similar context at Worcester also, and with his interest in the vernacular transmission of such 'edifying books' Wulfstan would have been the obvious person to inspire the translation of stories from it.[54]

The dissemination of the *Vitas Patrum*, no less than that of other books, benefited from the programme of expansion and improvement in monastic libraries in the century after the Conquest. By the end of the twelfth century several English monasteries could claim to have copies of the *Verba Seniorum* and the *Historia Monachorum* in their libraries;[55] another book with close affinities to the *Historia Monachorum*, the *Paradisus Heraclidis* of Palladius of Helenopolis, had been introduced (or re-introduced) to England from the

---

51   This passage is missing from the unique manuscript of the *Life* (BL Cotton MS Claudius A.v, ff. 160v-198r), the folio that contained it having been lost. However, its contents may be learned from an early 13th-century abridgement of the *Life*: 'Legebantur ad mensam eius libri edificationi accommodi; cunctis interim summum pre mentibus silentium. Iam uero quiete data epulis; exponebat lectionem patria lingua, ut celestem impertiret alimoniam; quibus corporalem ministrauerat' (Darlington p. 94; trans. Peile p. 70).

52   *Benedicti Regula*, ed. R. Hanslik, CSEL 75, 2nd edn (Vienna, 1977), XLII:3 (p.114).

53   *Catalogues of the Library of Durham Cathedral*, [ed. B. Botfield], Surtees Society Publications, [7] (London, 1838), p. 9.

54   One matter which deserves further attention is the precise relation between the monastic audience for whom the translation was presumably made and the secular clergy whom Wulfstan was trying to persuade to be celibate. Wulfstan himself had regularly preached and baptized while still a monk (*Life* I:7 and 8), and Worcester monks may have been carrying out pastoral work with secular colleagues. The topic is too large to broach here; but see M. Chibnall, 'Monks and Pastoral Work: A Problem in Anglo-Norman History', *Jnl. Ecclesiastical History*, 18 (1967), 165-72, and G. Constable, 'Monasteries, Rural Churches and the *cura animarum* in the Early Middle Ages' reptd from *Settimane di Studio del Centro Italiano di Studi sull'alto Medioevo*, 28 (1982 for 1980), 1, 349-95, esp. p. 377, in *Monks, Hermits and Crusaders in Medieval Europe*, Variorum Reprints, Collected Studies Series, 273 (London, 1988), no. II.

55   *Verba Seniorum*: Cambridge, University Library, Mm.4.28, ff. 65r-140v (s.xii); Oxford, Bodleian Library Bodley MS 386, ff. 58r-163r (s.xii ex.); Winchester, College Library, 18, vol. 1, ff. 143v-243v (s.xii ex.). *Historia Monachorum*: Cambridge, Gonville and Caius College MS 301 (515), ff. 166r-184v (s.xii); Cambridge, Sidney Sussex College MS 47, ff. 40v-67r (s.xii 3/4). These lists are selective.

continent;[56] and Reginald of Canterbury had turned Jerome's *Life of Malchus* into over 3300 lines of Anglo-Latin verse.[57]

Yet much of this activity had been anticipated at an English monastery even before the Conquest. It was at Worcester that the texts in the *Vitas Patrum* were first systematically collected and copied; it was at Worcester that the first translations of them into the vernacular were made; and there can be little doubt that it was Wulfstan, first as schoolmaster, later as prior and eventually as bishop, who directed and encouraged this work. Antonia Gransden and Emma Mason have reminded us that Wulfstan's long episcopate, spanning the reigns of Edward the Confessor and William Rufus, was a period of evolution or transition rather than revolution,[58] and doubtless this is as true of the intellectual activity at Worcester as of any other. The survival of these copies and translations from the mid-eleventh century is an important testimony to the fact that the great revival of learning that took place after the Conquest had English as well as continental roots; and the fact that they were made at all is a witness to the pastoral care of one who was reckoned by his contemporaries as the greatest English churchman of his age.

56   Hereford, Cathedral Library MS P.ii.5, ff. 1v-92r (s.xi ex.); Cambridge, University Library MS ff.5.27 (s.xi/xii, Durham); Edinburgh, National Library of Scotland, Adv. 18.4.3, ff. 1r-52v (s.xii, Durham). This list is not exhaustive. I discuss the possibility that the *Paradisus Heraclidis* was known in Anglo-Saxon England in 'Vitae Patrum: Paradisus Heraclidis', in *Sources of Anglo-Saxon Literary Culture: A Trial Version*, ed. F. M. Biggs, T. D. Hill and P. E. Szarmach, Medieval and Renaissance Texts and Studies, 74 (Binghamton, 1990), pp. 163-65.

57   *The Vita Sancti Malchi of Reginald of Canterbury*, ed. L. R. Lind, Illinois Studies in Language and Literature, 27, nos 3 - 4 (Urbana, 1942).

58   A. Gransden, 'Cultural Transition at Worcester in the Anglo-Norman Period', in *Medieval Art and Architecture at Worcester Cathedral*, BAA Conference Transactions, 1 (1978 for 1975), 1-14; cf. 'Traditionalism and Continuity during the Last Century of Anglo-Saxon Monasticism', *Jnl. Ecclesiastical History*, 40 (1989), 159-207 (at pp. 199-200); Mason, *St Wulfstan*, pp. 196-232.

Monasteries and Castles: the Priories of St-Florent de Saumur in England after 1066
JANE MARTINDALE

What prompted a secular benefactor to endow or found a religious community? The archives of monastic houses preserve numerous documents of the eleventh century invoking the donor's wish to entrust a body of men or women vowed to the religious life with services designed to secure 'the remission of my sins','the souls of my father and mother... and of my relatives'. Sometimes, as in a charter drawn up in the name of the Norman lord William de Briouze for the Angevin abbey of St-Florent de Saumur, a donor will also ask for spiritual benefits for a wider circle of men and women – like the family of his lord, 'William King of the English, and Mathilda his wife,... the souls of their fathers and mothers, and also... their sons and daughters'.[1]

Desire for intercession and commemoration after death provided powerful motives for acting generously towards monastic communities: the fear of retribution after death for sins committed during life was the motive force underlying many secular benefactions to monastic houses during the course of the eleventh century. It has even been argued that the eleventh century was a time when the organisation of commemorative practices became more elaborate than ever before, and that such practices were 'orchestrated' by monks so as to attract the generosity of laymen and women who frequently did not have education, time – or perhaps inclination – to fulfil the requirements of a religious life withdrawn from the world.[2]

---

[1] *Ego Willelmus de Braiosa pro Radulfi Waldi filii, Radulfi filii sui atque Ga(u)ffridi anima, et pro meorum remissione peccatorum et pro genitoris genitricisque mea anima, et pro hpilippo* (thus) *filio unigenito voluntate concedente, atque pro parentum meorum animabus, necnon pro Willelmo Anglorum rege, ac pro Mahilde regina uxore sua, et patrum eorumque atque matrum animabus, ac eciam pro filiis filiabusque eorum...* quotation taken from a *pancarta* recording the English and Norman possessions given to St-Florent by William de Briouze, Angers, Archives Départementales de Maine-et-Loire: H.3653 a), no.1 (capitals and punctuation, but not spelling, modernised); cf. below, n. 38. My warmest thanks are due to the Archivists and all staff at Angers for their help during a visit in September 1990 which had to be shorter than I could have wished. My return to Angers after presenting a draft of this paper at Harlaxton in July 1990 necessitated substantial revision of the text, but also (for lack of space) the omission of a number of topics then considered. I should like especially to thank Dr Marjorie Chibnall and Dr David Bates for modifications which they suggested at Harlaxton, but errors which remain are my own responsibility.

[2] Discussion of this topic has been renewed by J. Le Goff, *La naissance du*

A general expression by benefactors or founders of their need for intercessory prayers and for commemoration after death does not necessarily answer the question why members of the laity decided to endow one religious house rather than another. In post-Conquest England, in particular, it is not always easy to see why the newcomers' choice should fall on the abbot and monks of one distant establishment across the Channel, rather than another. But these new monastic enclaves had an important role to play in the transformation of the English kingdom during the years following the Battle of Hastings, whether the newcomers' creations are viewed essentially as 'outposts' of foreign religious communities, or as part of a more complicated process through which the indigenous aristocracy of pre-Conquest England was supplanted by a foreign élite.[3] The purpose of this paper is to look at one of these new enclaves, a little group of priories founded for the abbey of St-Florent de Saumur in Anjou by followers of the

---

purgatoire (Paris, 1981), esp. 166-73; but see R. Southern's review, 'Between Heaven and Hell', Times Literary Supplement, 19 June 1982. For comprehensive accounts of the development of commemorative practices within the liturgy, O. Oexle, 'Memoria und memorialüberlieferung im Mittelalter', Frühmittelalterliche Studien, 10 (1976), 70-96; A. Anengenendt, 'Missa specialis, Zugleich ein Betrag zur Entstehung der Privatmessen', ibid., 17 (1983), 152-221; and for an interesting recent survey of the extensive bibliography on the subject, J. Gerchow, 'Societas et fraternitas: A report on a research-based project based at the Universities of Freiburg and Münster', Nomina, 12 (1988-89), 153-71.

3 'Forty foreign monasteries and cathedral chapters' are stated as being established in England before the Conqueror's death by D. Matthew, The Norman Monasteries and their English Possessions (Oxford, 1962), pp.13-14. F. Barlow, The English Church, 1066-1154 (London, 1979), pp.184-85, cites thirty priories or cells founded for Norman monasteries, and fourteen for 'abbeys neighbouring the duchy', during the years between 1066 and 1100; cf. J. Le Patourel, The Norman Empire (Oxford, 1976), pp. 39,66, 315-18; M. Chibnall, Anglo-Norman England 1066-1166 (Oxford, 1986), pp. 81, 100-01, 148. For studies devoted specifically to lay benefactors in Anglo-Norman and Angevin England, R. Mortimer, 'Religious and secular motives for some English monastic foundations' in Religious Motivation: Biographical and Sociological Problems of the Church Historian, Studies in Church History, 15 (1978), 77-85; E. Mason, 'Timeo barones et donas ferentes', ibid., 61-75; C. Harper-Bill, 'The piety of the Anglo-Norman knightly class', Anglo-Norman Studies, 2 (1979), 63-79, 173-6; B. Golding, 'The coming of the Cluniacs', ibid., 3 (1980), 65-77, 208-12; idem, 'Anglo-Norman knightly burials', in The Ideals and Practice of Medieval Knighthood, 1, ed. C. Harper-Bill and R. Harvey (Woodbridge, 1986), 35-48; J. Ward, 'Fashions in monastic endowment: the foundations of the Clare family (1066-1314)', Jnl Ecclesiastical Hist., 32 (1981), 427-51; K. Cooke, 'Donors and daughters: Shaftesbury Abbey's benefactors, endowments and nuns', Anglo-Norman Studies, 12 (1989), 29-45. Cf. also C. H. Lawrence, Medieval Monasticism, Forms of Religious Life in Western Europe in the Middle Ages, 2nd edn (London, 1989), pp. 133-41.

Norman duke; but its chief aim is to enquire why the men who founded those priories should have chosen to endow that distant abbey with lands in England.

The motives of benefactors endowing a distant monastic house like St-Florent de Saumur during the mid-eleventh century clearly cannot be explained without some understanding of the religious reputation of that community, as well as of the abbey's position in Anjou.[4] First of all, however, it has to be remembered how much the monastic landscape of England must have changed after Duke William of Normandy's military victory. The native English would now rarely have had the resources to make grants to the old-established religious houses: while among King William's followers prospective benefactors would naturally be drawn to the Norman abbeys which they or their immediate ancestors had already endowed or founded in their native land. After all, the dozens of 'alien priories' planted by William's men in his new kingdom show that for them England was a foreign country. It is surely also probable that monks from Normandy or further afield would have been more willing or sympathetic recipients of grants made to expiate sins committed on the field of Hastings and in the engagements and skirmishes which followed that victory.[5] Historians have

---

4   St-Florent attracted many donations, although unfortunately its documents are not easy to use. Paul Marchegay, archivist at Angers, planned to print over 930 of its charters which dated from before the year 1200; but these were to be scattered throughout a dozen regional and learned periodicals, *Cartulaire général de St-Florent près Saumur* (Les Roches-Baritaud, 1879), pp. 1-4. Editions by Marchegay principally cited in this paper are: (i) 'Chartes normandes de l'abbaye de Saint-Florent près Saumur de 710 à 1200 environ', *Mém. Soc. Ant. Normandie*, 3rd series, 10 (1880), 633-711 (a virtually identical edition was separately printed, Les Roches-Baritaud, 1879); (ii) 'Les prieurés anglais de St-Florent près Saumur, Notices et documents inédits tirés des archives de Maine-et-Loire', *Bibliothèque de l'Ecole des Chartes*, 40 (1879), 154-94; (iii) *Chartes anciennes du prieuré de Monmouth en Angleterre* (Les Roches-Baritaud, 1879), (extracted from no. (ii), with considerable alterations). The most important of these documents for English historians were calendared by J. H. Round, *Calendar of Documents Preserved in France illustrative of the History of Great Britain and Ireland: AD918-1216* (London, 1899), pp. 395-415, nos. 1109-51; but Round's entries were not always made independently of Marchegay's, and can be misleading at a number of critical points (below, notes 19, 45. Extensive revision is desirable). A far better guide to, and calendar of, the archives of this abbey and its dependencies is provided by *Inventaire sommaire des Archives Départementales antérieures à 1790: Maine-et-Loire, Série H, II, Abbaye de Saint-Florent de Saumur*, ed. M. Saché (Angers, 1926): where necessary reference will be made to the MSS or to Saché's calendar.

5   H. E. J. Cowdrey, 'Ermenfried of Sion and the penitential ordinance following the Battle of Hastings', *Jnl Ecclesiastical Hist.*, 20 (1969), 225-42, esp. 241. It is

often stressed the intrinsic merits of the ecclesiastical changes introduced into the English kingdom after 1066, but at the time these frequently involved a serious disruption of the religious life, so that 'reform' could sometimes only be imposed by violence.[6]

The extension to England of links already forged between secular benefactors and Norman monastic houses would strengthen existing religious ties, but the foundation of dependent communities in England could also act as an expression of social and political solidarity on the part of individuals who wished to emphasize their coherence as a group. The family of Gilbert of Brionne, who protected Bec in its early days before it became a 'spiritual and intellectual centre', offered that Norman monastery lands across the Channel with the opportunity to found new priories there; and Bec's expansion in England was also promoted by the vassals and tenants of the honour of Clare, held by the descendants of Count Gilbert.[7] Many other abbeys, of course, benefited materially from the greatly increased resources acquired by their Norman and French patrons once these men were granted land across the Channel: it would be natural enough to recreate a network of secular and ecclesiastical ties when Norman political domination was imposed in England.[8] Geographical proximity, or personal and family associations, might reinforce motives of a religious character, or determine the choice of religious house already endowed by an individual and his kin in the duchy of Normandy or elsewhere within the Capetian kingdom.

---

especially noteworthy that there was provision for the 'making' or 'enlarging' of a church by those who did not know whom they had killed *in magno proelio*; but contrast E. Hallam, 'Monasteries as "War Memorials": Battle Abbey and La Victoire', in *The Church and War: Studies in Church History*, 20 (1983), 50-54, 57.

[6] The most dramatic cases are well-known to all historians of the Anglo-Norman period, but there is perhaps now greater scepticism about the superior religious merits of Norman 'innovations', Barlow, *English Church*, p. 179; D. Bates, *Normandy before 1066* (London, 1982), p. 207: 'It should not be overlooked that his [i.e. William's] first instinct in England after 1066 was to rob the Church'; cf. e.g. D. C. Douglas, *The Norman Achievement* (London, 1969), pp. 118-20; R. Allen Brown, *The Normans and the Norman Conquest* (London, 1969), pp. 252-3, 258-62. However, there can be no doubts about 'the great and rapid growth' of the Old English monasteries in the long term, D. Knowles, *The Monastic Order in England*, 2nd edn (Cambridge, 1963), pp. 113-27, and esp. at 126-27.

[7] M. Morgan (M. Chibnall), *The English Lands of the Abbey of Bec*, 2nd edn (Oxford, 1968), pp. 10-13; Ward, 'Fashions in Monastic Endowment', pp. 427-36; Harper-Bill, 'Piety', p. 74; Golding, 'Burials', pp. 47-48. For this family's wealth in England, R. Mortimer, 'The beginnings of the honour of Clare', *Anglo-Norman Studies*, 3 (1980), 119-40.

[8] See below, pp. 146-50.

Nevertheless, the inspiration which led the Norman Conqueror's followers to call on monks from distant parts to settle in England remains difficult to explain. Although the Loire region – or even Burgundy or the Bordelais – were not *ultra mare* to a family living in Normandy, they were still remote from the duchy; and yet offshoots from monasteries in those regions were soon established in England, sometimes within a decade of the Battle of Hastings. King William's well-known failure to prevail upon Abbot Hugh of Cluny to send monks from Burgundy to guide the foundation of his 'Battle' abbey suggests that his contemporaries were sometimes aware of the disadvantages of making religious plantations in distant lands.[9] On the other hand, the visit by William de Warenne and his wife to Cluny, together with their subsequent grant of land at Lewes to the Burgundian monastery, is among the best-known episodes of the history of the 'Monastic Order' in late-eleventh-century England. To some extent it might even be regarded as cancelling out Abbot Hugh's refusal to accept an invitation from the king. Perhaps St Hugh revised his opinions about the inconvenience of sending monastic colonists to the English kingdom; but the continuing satisfaction of the Warennes with their original arrangements can be judged, both from their decision to establish a second Cluniac house at Acre in Norfolk, and from the choice of Lewes as their burial-site for many generations to come.[10] Historians of monasticism may deplore that in religious terms the 'Cluny of St Hugh gave nothing permanent to England'; even so Cluny's renown as an exponent of reformed monastic observance accounts for the transmission of much newly acquired wealth to a religious house far beyond the frontiers of the Anglo-Norman kingdom. The establishment of Cluniacs at Lewes and Acre – as elsewhere in England – could certainly not have taken place without the 'redistribution' of land resulting from Norman conquest and colonisation ; but the Warennes were originally inspired to make their grant to the Burgundian abbey by a visit which they paid to the great church at Cluny, and by the spiritual advantages which they would obtain from association with the monks of that community.[11]

[9] In many respects this episode remains mysterious, Knowles, *Monastic Order*, pp. 151-58; Cowdrey, *The Cluniacs and the Gregorian Reform* (Oxford, 1970), p. 190; N. Hunt, *Cluny under St Hugh* (London, 1967), pp. 130, 152; Barlow, *The English Church*, pp. 184-85; cf. next note.

[10] Knowles, *ibid.*; Hunt, *ibid.*, pp. 130, 161, 170-75; Golding, 'Coming of the Cluniacs', pp. 64-67; *idem*, 'Burials', p. 42.

[11] For the quotation, Knowles, *Monastic Order*, p. 153; and see works cited in note 2 above. The scale of the commemorative arrangements organised by dependencies of this abbey may be imagined from the 10,000 names in the necrology discussed by J. Wollasch, 'A Cluniac necrology from the time of Abbot Hugh' in *Cluniac Monasticism in the Central Middle Ages*, ed. and trans. N. Hunt (London, 1971), pp. 143-90; cf. H. E. J. Cowdrey, 'Unions and confraternity with Cluny', *Jnl*

This may be the most famous but is not the only case of the lasting impression left by pilgrimage on the minds of the laity; while a number of other monastic communities in England also owed their origin to the determination of secular benefactors to create tangible and lasting memorials of journeys to a distant religious house. Such pilgrimages were often a common denominator in the grants made by such founders to monasteries situated outside the territories where they themselves held land and revenues. It has recently been shown, for instance, that the refoundation of the abbey of Bardney in Lincolnshire (c.1079-84) was prompted by a pilgrimage made by Gilbert of Ghent to the abbey of Charroux in the county of Poitou; it would certainly otherwise be difficult to account for Gilbert's grant of that once flourishing pre-Conquest English monastery to a religious house far removed from both Flanders and Normandy.[12] Similarly at nearby Burwell in Lincolnshire, a priory founded for monks established at La Sauve-Majeure in the county of Bordeaux was the outcome of a pilgrimage to Compostela. Burwell was not founded until the early twelfth century; but it was preceded by the rather earlier grant of Quatford in Shropshire to the same monastery of La Sauve by the sons of Roger Montgomery. The cartulary of La Sauve contains no reference to the occasion on which Quatford was offered to this southern house; but because of the distances involved it seems likely that pilgrimage and the hospitality of the monks of the 'great forest' also account for the generosity shown by the Montgomery family to La Sauve. Subsequently Gual, the seneschal (*dapifer*) of Hugh Montgomery, followed his lord's example with the grant of further land in Shropshire.[13] Ste-Foi de

---

Ecclesiastical Hist., 16 (1965), 152-61.

12 My thanks are due to Professor Beech for sending me his stimulating article before publication, G. Beech, 'Aquitanians and Flemings in the refoundation of Bardney Abbey (Lincolnshire) in the later eleventh century', *Haskins Soc. Jnl*, 1, (1989), 75-90. The abbey of Charroux was celebrated for its possession of a relic of the True Cross, acquired under the Carolingians.

13 J-P. Trabut-Cussac, 'Les possessions anglaises de l'abbaye de la Sauve-Majeure, le prieuré de Burwell (Lincolnshire)', *Bulletins philologiques et historiques du comité des travaux historiques* (1957), 138-83 (Quatford is noted, together with Gual's grant of Worfield, pp. 138-39). La Sauve-Majeure was an abbey established in the Entre-Deux-Mers region c.1075 (not in 1080 as Trabut-Cussac thought) by Guy-Geoffrey, Count of Poitou and Duke of Aquitaine, so that gives a *terminus a quo* for both these foundations. The possession of Quatford did not survive Roger de Bellême's forfeiture in 1102, J. F. A. Mason and P. Barker, 'The Norman castle at Quatford', *Trans. Shropshire Archaeol. Soc.*, 57 (1961-64), 39-62, esp. 39-41; idem, 'Roger de Montgomery and his sons', *Trans. R. Hist. Soc.*, 13 (1963), 1-28 and esp. 18-19; and idem, 'The officers and clerks of the Norman Earls of Shropshire', *Trans. Shropshire Archaeol. Soc.*, 56 (1957-60), 244-57, esp. at p. 249. Cf. also D. W. Lomax, 'The first English pilgrims to Santiago de Compostela' in *Studies in Medieval History presented to R. H. C. Davis*, ed. H. Mayr-Harting and

Conques – geographically an even remoter monastery in the Rouergue – received the gift of the church of Horsham in Norfolk for the foundation of a priory: that grant, too, was the result of pilgrimage.[14] At first it seemed that one at least of the grants of English land and resources to St-Florent might also have been prompted by a pilgrimage to this monastery on the Loire; but it soon became apparent that any explanation of these particular benefactions would have to take into account an elaborate web of relationships between clergy and laity. Political and territorial interests seem to have played a large part too in the foundation of the English priories of St-Florent de Saumur.[15]

Between Duke William's accession as king of the English and the early years of the twelfth century, St-Florent de Saumur was granted land and resources which enabled the abbot of this monastery to found four priories in the Anglo-Norman kingdom. Geographically these were widely dispersed, being situated in Sussex, Hampshire, Norfolk and – on the western frontier between England and Wales – in Herefordshire. All the priories were founded by laymen: the two most important were centred (at least in their early years) on the donors' castles. The earliest grant was made by William de Briouze, the next by 'Wihenoc of Monmouth'; and both were confirmed by the Conqueror. The Briouze foundation in the county of Sussex was given to St-Florent between the year of the King's military expedition to Maine (in 1073) and the time when a comprehensive royal confirmation was enacted at St-Georges de Boscherville (almost certainly in the year 1080); the royal confirmation, on the other hand, consisted of lands and churches in both Normandy and England (*in terra Anglica sicut in Normannia*), including 'the church of St Nicholas of my castle at Bramber' (*eclesiam* [thus] *Sancti Nicholai de castello meo de Brembre*), together with revenues *ultra mare* (in particular 'half' of 'tithe' owed to the donor), other churches and ploughlands. Thus this English priory of St-Florent was closely linked to a castle designed to secure the defence of the Conqueror's new realm.[16]

R. I. Moore (London, 1985), esp. pp. 167-69.

[14] *Cartulaire de l'abbaye de Conques en Rouergue*, ed. G. Desjardins (Paris, 1879), nos 497, 516, 519-21. As in the case of La Sauve-Majeure, the documents can only be dated on internal evidence: the majority of grants are post-1100, but the earliest may go back to the last decades of the 11th century. (I hope to return to the topic of the English priories of Ste-Foi.)

[15] The cult of St-Florent – unlike that of, say, St Faith – does not seem to have been either popular or especially widespread; although a charter of rather strange form attributes the cure of a *principis filie* to this saint, 'Chartes normandes', no.2 (dated *c*.1055-66). For Philip de Briouze's journey to St-Florent, see below, note 34.

[16] The grants and royal confirmation are recorded in the *pancarta* noted above, note 1, ed. Marchegay, 'Chartes normandes', no.14 = *CDF*, nos. 1112-13; cf. *Regesta regum Anglo-Normannorum (1066-1154)*, 4 vols, I, ed. H. W. C. Davis (Oxford,

A castle recently constructed on the frontier of the English kingdom was the site of the second of these priories. It consisted originally of 'all tithes and lands at Monmouth' which *Wethenocus de Monemud* had already given to St-Florent. This same benefactor also gave land at Cirencester to these monks, but the priory's chief resources were almost all situated in the border region, and most of these grants were confirmed *gratissima* by King William 'at the castle called Salisbury' [plate 6].[17] Then Alan FitzFlaald – the subject of one of J. H. Round's most dazzling genealogical *tours de force* – also gave the monks of St-Florent land to found a priory at Sporle in Norfolk; but little otherwise appears to be known or published about those possessions of St-Florent.[18] Lastly, King William II gave them the important church of

---

1913), no. 121; Matthew, *Norman Monasteries*, pp. 38-40 (chiefly concerned with the dispute between St-Florent and Fécamp, below, note 21). Bramber, sited '*in rapo Willelmi de Braiose*', was certainly of later creation than the other territorial units designed specifically for coastal defence; but it still had great political importance, Mason, 'The rapes of Sussex and the Norman Conquest', *Sussex Archaeol. Collections*, 102 (1964), 68-93; S. Harvey, 'Taxation and the economy' in *Domesday Studies*, ed. J. C. Holt (Woodbridge, 1987), p. 259. Cf. T. P. Hudson, 'The origins of Steyning and Bramber, Sussex', *Southern History*, 2 (1990), 16-29 (in the topographical development of these sites no reference is made to the establishment of this important 'alien priory'). D. Bates, *A Bibliography of Domesday Book* (London, 1986) has been invaluable on all items relating to English regional history. As Duke, William had already given Flottemanville in the diocese of Coutances to St-Florent before 1066, *Recueil des actes des ducs de Normandie (911-1066)*, ed. M. Fauroux, *Mém. Soc. Ant. Normandie*, 36 (1961), no. 199.

17   Angers, Arch. Dép., H.3170, no.1 (this is a notice of the King's confirmation which continues on the verso of a single sheet of parchment), ed. Marchegay, (i) 'Les prieurés anglais', no. 11 ; (ii) *Chartes anciennes*, no. II - *CDF* no. 1135; *Regesta*, I, no. 227 [see Pl. 6]; but it has been considered that Monmouth was founded by William de Briouze, Matthew, *Norman Monasteries*, 57. An account of Monmouth priory, together with other monastic communities of this border region, is given by R. Graham, 'Four alien priories in Monmouthshire', *JBAA*, 35 (1929), 102-21 (this relies almost entirely on Round's *CDF* for the period immediately post-Conquest). Discrepancies contained in the documents relating to St-Florent de Saumur which survived in English archives have unfortunately never been resolved: see W. Dugdale, *Monasticon Anglicanum* (rev. edn London, 1823) IV, 595-97. The two first charters there printed in the *Monasticon* are highly suspect, since they appear to contain a number of anachronistic features, but unfortunately the topic cannot be pursued here.

18   Earlier authorities considered that this was founded in the mid-12th century or even later, Dugdale, *Monasticon Anglicanum*, VI 2, 1051; F. Blomefield, *An Essay towards a Topographical History of the County of Norfolk* (London, 1807), VI, pp. 121-22 (allegedly founded by Henry 'Earl of Anjou'). No original or contemporary document relating to this priory has apparently survived in the

Andover 'just as it was in the time of King Edward'. The monks were to hold this with its subject churches, and to establish a priory there; and, although this grant has been condemned as at least highly suspect, it does not seem that the criticism was well founded.[19]

The castle-priories founded for St-Florent in Sussex and on the Welsh border appear to provide the most interesting glimpses of their founders' intentions, as well as throwing interesting light on conditions in England during the decades after the Conquest. The apprehensions aroused by war originally prompted William de Briouze to make an important endowment of land and spiritualities for canons established at the church of St Nicholas on his Sussex lands, for his first recorded grant was made 'when he crossed the sea and travelled with King William of the English in the army to Maine' (*quod tunc habebat quando mare transfretavit & cum Willelmo Anglorum rege in Cenomannem in exercitu perrexit*). The arrangements made at that time (almost certainly in the year 1073) cannot have lasted long, since within a few

St-Florent archives at Angers, although the original grant of Sporle was transcribed onto the last folio of the cartulary, H.3713 (*livre blanc*), f.130v, ed. Marchegay, 'Les prieurés anglais', no. 30; *Inventaire sommaire*, 537 – *CDF*, no. 1149. Cf. Round, 'The origin of the Stewarts', *Peerage and Family History* (London, 1901), esp. pp. 115, 120-29: he thought that Sporle was not founded until after the accession of Henry I in 1100, but the dating of these undated documents is by no means easy.

[19] The foundation is noted by the editors of the *Regesta*, I, no. 428 (based only on *CDF* no. 1150) without reference to any MS source. It was regarded as suspect because, although supposedly bearing the date 1100, the grant was witnessed by Ivo Taillebois who was dead by *c*.1098 (cf. *Regesta*, I, nos 408-09). The form in which the St-Florent charters were edited and calendared has obscured the problems relating to this donation which in fact occurs in two separate 'originals' or contemporary documents. (a) The king's grant of Andover is contained within a *pancarta* which includes three distinct notices, separately witnessed. Two of those grants relate to Monmouth and only the third to Andover, Arch. Dép. H.3710, no.4. The *pancarta* was edited by Marchegay as though each grant derived from separate parchments, i.e. (i) two early grants made to Monmouth by *Wihenoecus ...atque Willelmus nepos eius*, 'Les prieurés anglais', no. 12 (cf. *Chartes anciennes* III); and (ii) King William's grant of Andover, 'Les prieurés anglais' no. 31. (b) Thus in Marchegay's edition it appears that the date refers merely to King William's donation of Andover, although it actually applies to the time when all three grants were transcribed (*Hanc cartam dictaverunt Rannulfus atque Gislebertus Sancti Florentii monachi ; hanc etiam descripsit Novis diaconus iiii^{to} idus martias videlicet in festivitate Gregorii papae ab incarnatione Domini anno existente millesimo centesimo, indictione octava, epacta VII habente et concurrentibus VII existentibus*). (c) In any case – and this is not noted in any of the editions – there is a further *pancarta* H.3710 no. 5, in which the king's grant bears no date. Thus there appears to be no good reason for rejecting the donation of Andover as suspect.

years – as has just been seen – the grants in Sussex were given *en bloc* to St-Florent, and were eventually to serve as the endowment for a priory moved out of the castle to Beeding (St Peter of Sele).[20] There can be no doubt that tenurial and jurisdictional complications arising from the creation of the *honor* and castle at Bramber affected the religious arrangements made by William de Briouze and his son Philip, for the grants of land in Sussex which the Briouzes 'gave' to the monks of St-Florent were disputed by the monks of Fécamp whose possessions in the region were alleged to date from the reign of Edward the Confessor. According to those Norman monks, their rights in Sussex had been confirmed even before Duke William crossed the Channel in September 1066; but, although after he became king, William attempted to restore the *status quo*, the dispute was aired in the royal court before eventually being settled by the abbots of the two houses.[21]

[20]   (i) H.3710, no. 2, ed. Marchegay, 'Prieurés anglais', no. 3 = *CDF*, no. 1130 (described as 'quasi-original'). This document specifically mentions a grant made *eiusdem ecclesiae canonicis*, but the notice is similar in form to a number of the other documents preserved in the archives of St-Florent; arguments about its authenticity cannot be rehearsed here. (ii) H.3653 (a), see note 1, above. The 13th-century English cartulary of the house was unfortunately edited only as a calendar, *The Chartulary of the Priory of St Peter at Sele*, ed. L. F. Salzman (Cambridge, 1923), pp. 1-3 (the documents differ considerably in their content from those preserved at Angers). See Mason, 'The rapes of Sussex', pp. 77-78 (and on the dating p.77, n.2); Hudson, 'The origins of Steyning and Bramber', p. 12 – a useful map, although without reference to this 'French' priory.

[21]   For these possessions of Fécamp in England, P. Chaplais, 'Une charte originale de Guillaume le Conquérant pour l'abbaye de Fécamp: la donation de Steyning et de Bury (1085)' in *Essays in Medieval Diplomacy and Administration* (London, 1959, repr. 1981), pp. 93-104 and nn. 355 et seq.; cf. J. Martindale, 'Aimeri of Thouars and the Poitevin connection', *Anglo-Norman Studies*, 7 (1985), 226-27. An agreement from the St-Florent archives between the two abbots over burial rights and tithes *in castellaria Staningensi* survives in an undated notice at Angers, H.3710 no. 3, 'Les prieurés anglais', no. 4 = *CDF* no. 1131 (dated 1080-1108). The Fécamp cartulary, on the other hand, contains the notice of a plea between this house and William de Briouze heard before William I (probably in 1086), *Regesta*, I, no. 220 (ed. in appendix no. XXXII from the *Cartae Antiquae* rolls); Matthew, *Norman Monasteries*, pp. 38-39. In its present form the Fécamp notice appears contaminated, but nevertheless helps to establish an early date for the abbatial agreement. For Steyning's importance in the pre-Conquest period, Hudson, 'The origins of Steyning', pp. 18-19. It is unfortunately impossible to discuss here the details of the endowments made by these founders, but see M. Chibnall, 'Monks and pastoral work: a problem of Anglo-Norman history', *Jnl Ecclesiastical Hist.*, 18 (1967), 165-71; B. Kemp, 'Monastic possession of parish churches in England', *Jnl Ecclesiastical Hist.* 31 (1980), 132-60.

The founder of Monmouth priory does not at first glance seem to have had much in common with the Briouze benefactors of St-Florent; and there is no reason to suppose that the priory was established at Monmouth because of its founder's fears for his fate in battle. *Domesday* shows that by 1086 the monks of St-Florent were already established on the Anglo-Welsh border, since under Monmouth castle the *Terra Regis* entry for Herefordshire reads: '...What the King has in the castle is worth 100s'; while, after a note that William FitzBaderon was custodian of the King's land, it continues: 'The *milites* of this William have seven ploughs. What William holds is worth 30 pounds. St-Florent de Saumur holds the church and all the tithes with two carucates of land'.[22] King William's earlier confirmation of the grant made by *Wethenoc de Monemud* revealed that a man called 'Badoron' was 'Wethenoc's' brother; while it is clear that even before the making of the *Domesday* survey William 'son of Baderon' must have been accepted as the successor to his uncle Wethenoc/Wihenoc.[23] Because of the political upheavals on the Welsh frontier which followed the revolt of 1075, and the break-up of the great complex of lands granted to William FitzOsbern as Earl of Hereford, historians have had a particular interest in the sequence of holders of Monmouth castle; it has been supposed that the initial grant to St-Florent and the replacement of Wihenoc by his nephew must have taken place at some time between c.1075 and 1086, although actually the evidence for this is largely circumstantial.[24] In fact it seems likely that it must have taken place before the year 1083, when Wihenoc is already to be found at

[22] The quotation is preceded by a note about William Fitz Baderon's own holdings as well as those of a number of Welshmen, *DB*, I, 180d; cf. *Domesday Book, A Survey of the Counties of England*, 17, *Herefordshire*, ed. F. and T. Thorn (Chichester, 1983), no.48 (the St-Florent charter confirmed by the king, however, states that the monks were given *terram trium carrucarum*).

[23] The notice of King William's confirmation was witnessed '...*teste Alano comite & Badorono fratre Wethenoci qui donationem fecerat necnon & Radulfo monacho sancti Florentii qui propter hoc regem adierat*' (see Pl. 6).

[24] The assertion was based on the knowledge that tithes at Monmouth (later enjoyed by St-Florent) were at first granted by William FitzOsbern to the abbey of Cormeilles in Normandy, J. H. Round, 'The family of Ballon and the conquest of South Wales', in *Peerage and Family History*, pp.185 n.2 and 184-8 (information derived from a papal bull issued by Alexander III, not naming the original donor); *idem*, 'The origin of the Stewarts', pp.120-21. Round did not discuss the date of Wihenoc's original grant but – if his arguments for the dispossession of FitzOsbern's son are accepted – a date '*ante* 1069 or 1070' is too early for the entry of Wihenoc into Monmouth; see I. J. Sanders, *English Baronies, a Study of Their Origin and Descent, 1086-1327* (Oxford, 1960), p.64 n.7; cf. Graham 'Four alien priories', p.103. The complexities of these changes of 'tenurial geography' have now been convincingly disentangled by C. Lewis, 'The Norman settlement of Herefordshire under William I', *Anglo-Norman Studies*, 7 (1985), 195-217.

Mont St-Michel as one of two monks of St-Florent engaged in the business of his abbey.[25]

The dangers of war may not have prompted Wihenoc of Monmouth to found a priory for St-Florent de Saumur but, as his earliest endowment was soon followed by his own 'conversion' to the monastic life, his motives were perhaps more personally religious in their inspiration than those of many other secular benefactors. His conversion to the monastic life did not involve complete withdrawal from the secular world, since he continued to make numerous appearances in the St-Florent charters relating to Anglo-Norman affairs; while Wihenoc's worldly expertise was apparently of such value to his house that he travelled widely on secular business. In December 1083, before journeying onwards to England, Wihenoc was sent to prevail upon the monks of Mont St-Michel not to dispute St-Florent's possession of Caux in Normandy.[26] Subsequently he was one of the witnesses to King William II's grant of Andover, and – most appropriately in view of his original grant – he was personally present at Monmouth for the dedication of the priory church by the Bishop of Bangor.[27] He was also one of the two monks of St-Florent present at the 'concord' eventually agreed between the two abbots in the chapter of Fécamp over the disputed rights of their two churches in Sussex; and he could have been active as late as 1105 when he brought a complaint before Henry I, which the King ordered to be settled by an inquest of the hundred of Andover.[28]

---

[25] See note 26. For a stimulating discussion of the territorial and political problems confronting this abbey, C. Potts, 'Normandy or Brittany? A conflict of interests at Mont St-Michel (966-1037)', *ibid.*, 12 (1989), 135-56.

[26] *Actum hoc in capitulo S. Michaelis, anno ab Incarnatione Domini MLXXXIIIo, VIIo kalendas januarii, die festivitatis sancti Stephani...* H.3713 (cartulary known as *livre blanc*), f. 85r; Saché, *Inventaire sommaire*, 525 ; 'Chartes normandes', no. 11 = *CDF* no.1117. Cf. Harper-Bill, 'The piety of the Anglo-Norman knightly class', pp. 73-74 for another worldly career being turned to good advantage for his new house after a 'convert' entered the abbey of Marmoutier near Tours.

[27] (i) *'Wihenocus Sancti Florentii monachus & Willelmus monachus'* were witnesses to the grant of Andover with Count Alan and Ivo Taillebois, 'Les prieurés anglais', no.31. (ii) *'Wihenocus monachus'*... was one of many religious present when Bishop Hervey of Bangor dedicated the church during the time that King Henry I's chaplain Bernard *episcopatum Herefordensem custodiebat*, H.3710, no. 5, 'Les prieurés anglais', no. 16 and *Chartes anciennes*, no.VII (dated *c.*1090 by Marchegay) = *CDF*, no.1138 (1101-02). The see of Hereford was vacant between April 1100 (when Gerard was translated to York) and 1102.

[28] (i) For the dispute between Fécamp and St-Florent, above, note 21 : *Ad hanc pacem & concessionem audiendam interfuerunt in capitulo Fiscannensi duo monachi Sancti Florentii Guihenocus de Monemuta & Primaldus qui fuit capellanus Braiosensi & Hugo de Staningis monachus sancti Trinitatis de Fiscanno in capitulo sancti*

The activity of *'Wihenoecus Sancti Florentii monachus'* shows one way in which the ties between a monastic community and its distant dependencies might be maintained; and during the late eleventh and early twelfth centuries many personal links bound benefactors from the new 'Norman Empire' to the monastery of St-Florent on the Loire. In the first place, around the mid eleventh century St-Florent had a great attraction for donors from Brittany: it was a monastic church 'where', in Round's words, 'many Bretons of noble birth were led to take the cowl'.[29] Originally, before being moved to lands dominated by the Counts of Anjou, the abbey church was sited very close to Breton territory near the city of Nantes and the mouth of the River Loire; but in any case by about the year 1070 personal ties appear to have been of greater importance than territorial proximity.[30] Indeed, the abbot elected in 1070 was a man of aristocratic birth from northern Brittany: he was William, elder son of Rivallon lord of Dol, and Dol was at the centre of the region from which both Wihenoc and Baderon originated before they sought their fortunes in England. Moreover, since (as Round showed), Alan FitzFlaald's uncle was the seneschal of the lords of Dol, Sporle – the third of St-Florent's priories in England – was founded by a man whose relatives were even more closely bound in the secular world to Abbot William's family than were the founders of Monmouth priory.[31] In view of these personal connections, it is not surprising that Abbot William travelled as far as Monmouth to attend the consecration of the priory church for, even though Dol was geographically remote from St-Florent (and even remoter from Norfolk or the Anglo-Welsh

Florentii de Salmur. (ii) Wihenoc's complaint over Andover is known only from a late confirmation inserted on the patent rolls (not noted by Marchegay or Round), *Regesta*, II, ed. C. Johnson and H. Cronne, no. 687 (probably Feb. 1105).

[29] Round, 'The origin of the Stewarts', pp. 120-21.

[30] According to a charter of the late 11th century the early site of the abbey church was 24 miles from Nantes (*ab urbe Nannentensium milario XXmo IIII*), *livre blanc*, f. 3-4, Saché, *Inventaire sommaire*, p. 503. It was moved about the mid-10th century; see note 49 for the reference.

[31] Round, 'The origin of the Stewarts', pp. 120-21; cf. Graham, 'Four alien priories', p. 103 (mistakenly citing John as the influential Abbot of St-Florent rather than – as was actually the case – his brother William). The family relationship emerges clearly from King William's undated confirmation of a grant made by John of Dol, *admonitus precibus domni Guillelmi filii Rivallonis de Dolo et eiusdem loci abbatis, et fratris sui Johannis, in eodem loco monachi*, 'Les chartes normandes', no. 10 (from *livre blanc*, f. 96v) = *CDF*, no. 1116, *Regesta* I, no. 158 (before Dec. 1083). Both Alan FitzFlaald and William FitzBaderon witnessed the settlement of the dispute over St-Florent's rights at Andover; ref. above, note 28. The political and family background of the lords of Dol is systematically explored in a paper which was unfortunately not available to me while my own was being completed, K. Keats-Rohan, 'William I and the Breton contingent in the non-Norman Conquest 1060-1087', *Anglo-Norman Studies*, 13 (1990), 157-72, esp. 166-70.

border), the presence of Bretons and of a Breton abbot in Anjou still acted as a focus for the religious aspirations of this group.[32]

Personal associations between the Angevin abbey and the Briouze lords cannot be so easily established. Nevertheless, if William de Briouze's foundation of a priory in Sussex is placed in its wider Anglo-Norman setting, the grant of Bramber to St-Florent becomes a little less puzzling, since this William made provision for another priory to be constructed on the southern frontier of Normandy at his castle of Briouze. This was apparently enacted at exactly the same time that he granted churches and property in England to the monks of St-Florent. In Normandy too the intentions of the lord of Briouze were at first bedevilled by monastic disputes, for his original intention was for monks to come to Briouze from the abbey church at Lonlay; but, because those monks failed to fulfil their benefactor's requirements, William subsequently transferred the endowments to St-Florent – a process which had already taken place by 1080.[33] Then, for whatever reasons, the lord of Briouze eventually decided to endow the same Angevin monastic house with lands and resources on both sides of the Channel; and, although his son Philip was at first reluctant to confirm all his father's grants, he was eventually prevailed upon to do so at the ceremonial dedication of the priory of Briouze. Subsequently Philip made further grants at a journey which he made to the mother-church on the Loire.[34]

A web of even more elaborate personal links among these benefactors of St-Florent had been created before the end of the eleventh century. By the

[32] For the uncertainties over the Breton-Norman border in the Dol region, Potts, 'Normandy or Brittany ?', p. 155. Abbot William's presence at Monmouth is noted twice; but dating problems connected with these notices makes it difficult to know whether one or two journeys were involved, 'Les prieurés anglais', nos. 15-16.

[33] The *pancarta* referred to in note 1 records the grant of both Bramber and Briouze to St-Florent together with William I's confirmation of these donations (which provide the *terminus ante quem* for the transfer of Briouze to St-Florent). The dispute between Lonlay and St-Florent over the church at Briouze twice came before a Norman court. A suit was heard at Caen under William I, *livre blanc*, f. 116 v (a different version is at f. 118), 'Chartes normandes', nos. 16, 15 – CDF nos. 1115, 1114; *Regesta* I, no. 120 (with no explanation of the complications of these judicial notices); cf. D. Bates, *Normandy before 1066*, p. 169. On another occasion a complaint was brought before Duke Robert at Bonneville, 'Chartes normandes', *ibid.* (follows the previous case in the *livre blanc*) – CDF no. 1115; *Regesta* I, no. 342. This was apparently settled soon before the dedication of the church at Briouze on 11 December 1093, *livre blanc*, f. 119, 'Chartes normandes', no. 17 – CDF no. 1118.

[34] 'Chartes normandes', no. 17 (cf. previous note); cf. nos 19 (exists as notice, H.3071 – unnumbered, and f. 119r of *livre blanc*), 20 (only from cartulary) – *Pictavim adeuntem apud cenobium Salmurense hospitari...*

1090s Philip de Briouze was also established in the same region on the Welsh frontier where William FitzBaderon's family and descendants had been settled in the decades after the Conquest. This new thread is revealed through Philip de Briouze's confirmation of all his father's endowments (*elemosynam universam*) 'for the remedy of his mother's and father's soul and of his own'. The ceremonial confirmation was made at Radnor and guaranteed by William FitzBaderon.[35] One figure emerges as a probable agent in the foundation of both the Briouze priories – a man who could have created the vital religious link between the Briouzes as secular founders and the monastic community. This was Primaldus, chaplain of William de Briouze, who drafted the *pancarta* in which the grants of Bramber and Briouze were recorded (*Scriptum hoc dictavit et linavit Primaldus eiusdem Braiocensis Willelmi capellanus*). Like Wihenoc of Monmouth, he must have already been a monk at the monastery on the Loire before the *concordia* was arranged between Fécamp and St-Florent, because on that occasion he was described as ...*Primaldus qui fuit capellanus Braiosensis*... Primaldus could well have been instrumental in persuading his secular patron to give the church and chapel at Briouze castle to St-Florent, and perhaps even encouraging him to found a priory at Bramber.[36]

A 'foreign' priory founded in England by the Conqueror's followers would have one obvious advantage for its patrons. It would be 'staffed' by monks sharing the founder's own speech, who would very probably have been recruited from men familiar with his family, background and achievements. Moreover, the grant of a church or chapel in a castle to a monastic community must in practice also have entailed close association between the lord, his men, and the monks. It is interesting to find that this was an association which the monks of St-Florent were willing to encourage. A sentence inserted into a *pancarta* relating to Monmouth priory states: 'Besides we give notice that we ought to find a chaplain for the lord, who will serve him honestly'.[37] Presumably the monks provided services for the

---

35   *Et hanc concessionem fecit apud Raddenoam* [the castle at Old Radnor?] *Wihenoco & Gisleberto monachis coram Guillelmo filio Baderonis... dicens etiam Willelmo filio Baderonis quod si ipsemet Phylippus vellet se retrahere ab hac concessione idem Guillelmus probaret eum sic concessisse, livre blanc,* f. 119v, 'Chartes normandes', no. 19 (see previous note). On the significance of this territorial expansion and the Briouze lordship, R. R. Davies, *Conquest, Coexistence, and Change, Wales 1063-1415* (Oxford, 1987), pp. 34, 37, 85, 96.

36   Documents cited above, notes 1, 33. In 1097 William's son, Philip de Briouze, had a seneschal called Princaldus who was both *miles* and *frater societatis Sancti Florentii* – a name which suggests some kind of family relationship to Primaldus and continuity of service within the same family, *livre blanc,* f. 120, 'Chartes normandes', no. 21 (not calendared by Round).

37   *Preterea notificamus quia capellanum debemus invenire domino qui honeste sibi* (?)

inhabitants of other castles too; but, although Primaldus apparently ceased to serve William de Briouze as his chaplain once he became a monk, a priory-church might also be entrusted with control of the local clergy.[38] At Briouze for instance, an agreement was eventually made by the monks of the priory with 'Oliver the clerk, son of Herbert the priest' that he should live chastely, and faithfully serve one of the 'literate' monks.[39]

Personal ties between individual members of a monastic community and the families of secular benefactors must have been of great importance in strengthening links between communities settled at places which were geographically remote from each other; but it still sometimes remains difficult to account for the original creation of those links.[40] Moreover, the political divisions of the Capetian kingdom in the mid-eleventh century would not have been particularly favourable for the establishment of connections between the abbey of St-Florent and the 'Norman empire', since at that time the town and castle of Saumur were controlled by the Counts of Anjou – who were normally determined political opponents of the Norman ruler.[41] Presumably the spiritual reputation of the abbot and community of St-Florent must have been considerable and exercised a great influence on prospective secular benefactors.

serviat, 'Les prieurés anglais', no. 12. Cf. Chibnall, 'Monks and pastoral work' pp. 168-69, on the prevalence of this type of practice and the difficulty of interpreting the evidence (e.g. did monks themselves provide the services, and were they charged with any parochial duties?).

[38] When he was witness to the *concordia* between Fécamp and St-Florent, Primaldus was no longer called chaplain, see note 28.

[39] *Livre blanc*, f. 120, 'Chartes normandes', no. 21. At the priory of Pons in the Saintonge, the monks of St-Florent noted the shortcomings of the local clergy, and secured the eviction of two priests for their failings, *livre blanc*, ff. 101v-102v. These men had refused to say mass for a woman recently delivered of a child. In England there are no such early examples of the monks of St-Florent acting as the moral guardians of clerical standards. On the actual and legal position regarding monastic presentation to parish churches in England, Kemp, 'Monastic possession of parish churches', pp. 147-54.

[40] The church of St-Florent de Saumur was over 100 miles from Briouze and the southern frontier of Normandy: it was obviously even further from Monmouth or Sporle – or even from Bramber which was at least sited within a few miles of the Sussex coast. None of the communities was ever large, consisting of between two monks (Sporle and Andover), eight *cum priore* (Sele), twelve *unacum priore* (Monmouth) in the 13th century, 'Les prieurés anglais', p. 165.

[41] As was emphasized by Duke William's biographer, William of Poitiers, *Histoire de Guillaume le Conquérant*, ed. and trans. R. Foreville (*Classiques de l'histoire de France au moyen âge*, Paris, 1952), pp. 37, 75-87; on the political situation at Saumur during the mid-11th century, Martindale, 'Aimeri of Thouars', pp. 237-39.

By the mid-eleventh century the monastery of St-Florent had certainly undergone a period of expansion which put it in the forefront of regional religious houses; and that is reflected in the pride shown by its anonymous historian when (with an obvious reference to the benefactions made by King William's followers) he wrote of a contemporary abbot, 'the fame of our father winged its way, not only to lesser, but also to greater Britain... across the sea.'[42] About the time that Duke William invaded England the reputation of the abbots of St-Florent in fact stood high in a number of fields. After the long abbacy of Frederick (1020-55), Sigo (1055-70) was renowned as a learned monk who allegedly knew both Greek and Hebrew, and who was responsible for the correction *ad unguem* of the abbey's sacred texts. Sigo was praised for the quality of his spiritual advice, as well as for his meditations on the Scriptures; in general his reputation is conveyed by the statement that Hugh of Cluny treated him as his own 'master' or 'superior'. He may also have been responsible for creating the ecclesiastical link between St-Florent and northern Brittany through the restoration of St-Melaine de Rennes, and the eventual promotion of its abbot as Archbishop of Dol.[43] By contrast William, adult convert and Sigo's 'noble' successor, is not depicted in terms of his intellectual or spiritual qualities: apart from bringing considerable property to St-Florent at the time of his 'conversion', Abbot William (1070-1118), 'acquired many things and lost few' (*Multa adquisivit et pauca perdidit*).[44]

Around the mid-eleventh century, then, the abbey of St-Florent de Saumur had considerable attractions for secular benefactors who wished to secure commemoration for themselves and their relatives through the foundation of a religious community. During these years close contacts between lay founders and the mother-house were apparently encouraged (perhaps personally via a brother or some other close relative who had chosen to renounce the world).[45] Surviving documents show, too, that the

---

[42] *Chroniques des églises d'Anjou*, ed. P. Marchegay and E. Mabille (Paris, 1869), *Historia Sancti Florentii Salmurensis*, p. 303: *Nec solum in Minori Britannia sed etiam in Majore* (thus), *ad transmarinas partes, fama patris nostri convolavit, ubi Monemutam et quicquid habemus in Anglia merito suae religionis adquisivit.* (The author also mentions that the *illustris dux Apuliae G.* sent ornaments and precious gifts to this monastery.) These statements are clearly self-interested, but they are borne out by the numerous contemporary grants made to St-Florent preserved in the abbey's charters.

[43] *Historia Sancti Florentii*, pp. 296-97, 300.

[44] *Ibid.*, p.304. The generally high reputation of St-Florent at this time can also be judged by the promotion of monks of this house to the headships of other abbeys – and one, *en route* from Jerusalem, to the bishopric of Catania.

[45] Wihenoc, for instance, seems to have been preceded into the monastery by another brother. He is called *'Rado'* in a confirmation charter of Bishop Roger of

abbot – like many of the greatest aristocratic churchmen of his day – was an active traveller in the interests of his community. As has already been seen monks of St-Florent were also allowed to travel far afield if the abbey's affairs required it: granted these assumptions it would only have been commonsense to employ men who were acquainted with local conditions, and with the individuals whose patronage and protection would be most valuable for a small group of religious, whether in Normandy, England or elsewhere.[46] A further point of significance is that the community of monks established at Saumur undoubtedly had a long experience of living under the most disturbed political conditions: their abbey-church and monastic buildings had suffered extensive damage, and they inhabited fortified sites as a matter of course. It could even be argued that in the mid-eleventh century the monks of St-Florent might have been valued as specialists qualified to establish religious communities in conditions which would eventually be condemned by advocates of a more austere monastic life.[47] The abbey of St-Florent may also have been chosen because it was prepared to accept foundations of relatively modest size.[48]

Furthermore, even though the monastic writer commented that 'habitation of a castle was extremely burdensome... and dangerous and damnable for the brothers' souls', that sentiment had not apparently discouraged the abbots of the house from accepting land and churches situated close to such dangerous sites.[49] Between c.1060 and the late 1080s on

Hereford dated 1144 (*Rado monacus fr. supradicti Guienoci*), H.3710, no.7. The indication *fr[ater]* was omitted from Marchegay's editions of this charter, 'Les prieurés anglais', no. 21 and *Chartes anciennes*, no. XVIII; while it seems clear that Round must have used Marchegay's edition rather than the original, since he printed the translation 'Rado a monk of the said Guihenoc'(?), *CDF* no. 1142. An entry in the cartulary suggests that his name was in fact the rather commoner *Radulfus, livre blanc,* f. 83r-v – charter of the Count of Brittany, dated 1086, Saché, *Inventaire sommaire,* 524. However, there may be room for some doubt over this identification, which has not been made by Keats-Rohan, 'The Breton contingent', pp. 168-69.

46 A comparison may be made with perhaps the best-known monastic 'statesman' of the day, Abbot Hugh of Cluny, H. Diener, 'Das Itinerar des Abtes Hugo von Cluny', in *Neue Forschungen über Cluny und die Cluniacenser,* ed. G. Tellenbach, (Freiburg, 1959), pp. 355-426.

47 *Historia Sancti Florentii,* pp. 267, 269, 272, 295 (but the earlier parts of this narrative embody a considerable amount of legendary matter).

48 Throughout the 12th century Premonstratensians and Augustinians 'recommended themselves as [an] order[s] which did not make too great a demand on one's possessions', H. M. Colvin, *The White Canons in England* (Oxford, 1951), pp. 33-36. Perhaps the abbey of St-Florent de Saumur fulfilled a similar role during the earlier 'Benedictine' centuries.

49 *Ibid.,* 272: *Habitatio castelli erat valde ei* [i.e. to members of the monastic order]

numerous occasions the abbots of St-Florent accepted land to found priories within castles, or to establish a monastic church immediately outside the precincts of a castle – as was eventually the position at both Bramber and Monmouth. During these years castle-priories were scattered throughout Brittany, Normandy, and Aquitaine. Indeed, the grants made by Abbot William and the members of his own family to St-Florent envisaged the foundation of a priory in Dol with land *prope castellum*.[50] In the year 1067 the Viscount of Aunay gave the monks of St-Florent the 'chapel above the gate' which he held in the castle of Pons; while in 1083 his lord the Duke of Aquitaine also transferred to them the 'chapel of the castle'; the same Viscount made a grant for a priory to be established in his castle of Aunay.[51] Further donations were made by the lord of Rochefoucault in the Angoumois; the monks of St-Florent also secured a church and priory in a new castle built by the Viscount of Thouars in northern Poitou (see Fig. 1).[52] St-Florent also held land and churches close to the castles which studded the region of the Loire.[53]

The two earliest and richest of the religious houses created for St-Florent de Saumur in England were originally located either in castles or on lands regarded as being *'in castellaria'*. The church of St Nicholas is described as belonging to 'my castle of Bramber' (*ecclesiam S. Nicholai de meo castello de Brem(b)re*) which was singled out for particular attention in the *Domesday* list of Briouze possessions in Sussex.[54] From the first, the St-Florent church and

---

[50] *onerosa et animabus fratrum periculosa atque dampnosa; sed liberati sunt inde ordinatione divina.* Their priory of St-Gondon in the diocese of Bourges was once placed in an especially perilous position: in the later 12th century during the course of a local conflict the monks found the portal of their church walled up *quod erat in murum castri*, H.3302, Saché, *Inventaire sommaire*, 326.

[50] *Livre blanc*, ff. 75r-85r, Saché, *ibid.*, pp. 521-27. Grants to St-Florent at Dinan were also made *in castellaria*, H.3357, and *livre blanc*, ff. 91-92, Saché, *ibid.*, pp. 346 and 527-8.

[51] H.3618, Saché, *Inventaire sommaire*, pp. 440-41; cf. *ibid.*, pp. 489-91, 529-33 (entries from the cartularies of St-Florent).

[52] The map accompanying the text is not however intended to show all the priories of St-Florent. The donations relating to La Rochefoucault are *livre blanc*, ff. 110v-113v (with a reference to *monach(i) qui in castro Rupis morabantur*), Saché, pp. 532-33. For Chaize-le-Vicomte and the foundation of that castle-priory, Martindale, 'Aimeri of Thouars', pp. 233-34.

[53] E.g. at Trèves, Loudun, Montsoreau, Thouarcé, and at Saumur itself, there were conflicts over rights and revenues claimed both by other religious communities and by laymen (details cannot be given here).

[54] 'The castle of Bramber sits' is the record's uncompromising statement: it had been erected on one of the 59 hides of land formerly held here by Harold Godwineson's brother, Earl Gyrth, *DB* I, 28.

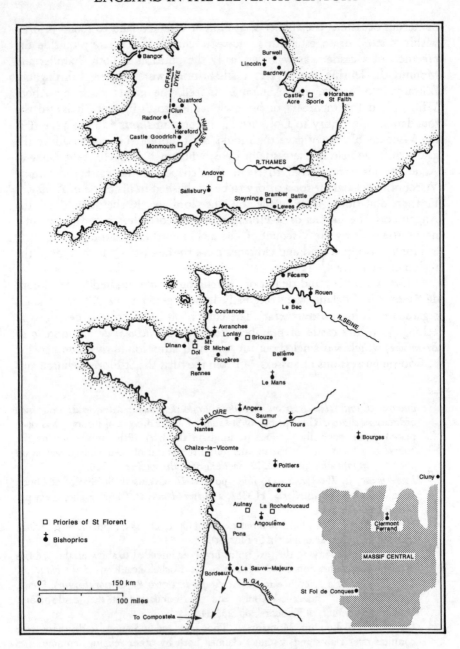

Figure 1: Map to illustrate Priories of St-Florent de Saumur in England
(principal places mentioned in the text).

revenues at Monmouth were centred on the the castle held by the secular founder and his relatives. The general significance of this type of association between monks and castellans is proved by additional grants made to St-Florent, for by the early twelfth century Monmouth priory had attracted further grants of castle-chapels, and churches closely associated with the castles built along the Anglo-Welsh border. These included St Giles of Castle Goodrich, and the chapel of the castle of Clun.[55] Any foreign religious community in England during the generation immediately after the 'great battle' might have thought it prudent to have shelter near at hand; but, because the monks of St-Florent had already been obliged to come to terms with living in castles or close to fortified sites, their castle-priories in England did not represent a novelty, nor would they have been built solely as a response to the conquerors' need for protection. The *pancarta* recording the early endowments made by William de Briouze suggests that in principle the monks of St-Florent saw little difference between accepting a site for a priory at the castle of Briouze in Normandy, or at Bramber in England. Still there is a need to make a distinction between English and continental possessions since some of the castle sites in the French kingdom would have been of considerable antiquity, unlike those in England.[56]

In general, during the late tenth and eleventh centuries, castles performed a crucial function in the transformation of secular 'structures of authority' within the French kingdom. None of the Conqueror's followers would have been surprised to find their religious (or social) arrangements centred on a castle (or castles), even if many clerics would have been well aware of the disadvantages of those arrangements. It seems likely that the close associations between lay lords, their chaplains and clergy created anxiety in reforming circles of the Church; but, as is proved by a prohibition enacted at the Council of Clermont, that was a European-wide problem, not one restricted to the 'Norman empire'.[57] Altogether, the early history of the priories founded for St-Florent in England follows the pattern of settlement

---

[55] For the grant of a meadow *sub castello suo* to Monmouth, together with seven *burgenses* freed from the payment of toll and 'custom' by Wihenoc and William Fitz Baderon, 'Les prieurés anglais', no. 12 (from a *pancarta*); cf. nos 15, 21 (for Castle Goodrich), no. 24 (Clun).

[56] See note 58. As far as I have been able to discover none of the St-Florent sites has ever been the subject of serious excavation.

[57] A decree against a 'prince' or layman taking as his chaplain any priest or clerk without permission of the bishop or archdeacon is preserved in two slightly differing versions of Pope Urban II's Council, *Acta conciliorum et epistolae decretales...*, ed. P. Labbe and P. Cossart, 12 vols. (Paris, 1715) VI (ii), cols. 1719, 1739. Although this does not make a specific reference to 'castle-priories', it would cover the provisions envisaged in n. 37, above; cf. Chibnall, 'Monks and pastoral work', p. 170.

which has been described as the 'complex' of 'castle-bourg-monastery', and judged to be an important 'instrument of colonisation' in England after the victory of 1066. At the same time it would be a mistake to suppose that this was an 'instrument' consciously designed for that purpose alone. What was an appalling novelty to the authors of the *Anglo-Saxon Chronicle* was certainly no novelty to clerks and monks educated on the other side of the Channel. They may not even have regarded the appearance of castles as deplorable.[58]

In his evaluation of the post-Conquest Benedictine houses endowed on behalf of foreign abbeys Dom David Knowles saw few exceptions to 'the loosely knit aggregation of mediocre and half-alien houses' introduced into England in the wake of the Norman Duke's military and political successes. It seems likely that – had Knowles discussed them – he would have dismissed the priories of St-Florent as 'a source of weakness rather than of strength to the monastic body'. Perhaps with Professor Barlow he might have included them among those thirty foundations where foreign 'outposts' became unpopular with monks who 'feared boredom in exile'.[59] Judged by the highest standards of religious observance or by the ideals of the reformed monastic orders of the twelfth century, there may not be much to say in favour of St-Florent and its castle-priories. But those were not the standards of the half century after the Norman Conquest, and it seems historically inappropriate to apply such standards to the religious foundations made by a newly dominant military aristocracy in England. The 'conjunction' of castle and religious community which served as 'one of the chief instruments of Norman colonisation' has to be taken seriously on its own terms, even though eventually this 'conjunction' will be regarded unfavourably by comparison with more austere monastic communities or with the 'best establishments' of the Old English régime. But neither its significance, nor the reasons for its eventual disappearance as a religious phenomenon, can be appreciated unless this 'conjunction' is placed against the Continental background from which it came.

---

[58] 'What is most needed now is to move the debate on from the origins to the uses of castles in the Norman period', R. Eales, 'Royal power and castles in Norman England', *The Ideals and Practice of Medieval Knighthood*, ed. C. Harper-Bill and R. Harvey 3 (1990), pp. 54, 49-58 (my thanks to Richard Eales for sending me this important paper before publication); Le Patourel, *Norman Empire*, pp. 317-18. Space has not permitted detailed discussion of the stages by which *bourgs* came to be associated with this development.

[59] Knowles, *Monastic Order*, p. 153 refers specifically to the Cluniac dependencies, but cf. also pp. 135-36; Barlow, *The English Church*, p.182.

The Waltham Abbey Relic-list
NICHOLAS ROGERS

Some years ago, while browsing for the first time through the unpublished manuscript collection of the recusant hagiologist Nicholas Roscarrock, I came across 'a Note of such Relickes as are mentioned in the Booke of Waltham'.[1] Fascinated, like Roscarrock, by the wealth and variety of the relics which were at Waltham Abbey, I made a transcript of that list. Subsequently I discovered that 'the Booke of Waltham', unlike many of Roscarrock's sources, survived for the most part, though now divided into two manuscripts, British Library, Harley MSS 3766 and 3776. Eric Millar published brief extracts from this list in an article in the *British Museum Quarterly* for 1933, chiefly devoted to reconstructing the original order of the book.[2] He expressed some surprise that it had not yet been printed in full. Strangely enough there has been until now no published edition of the text,[3] although Rosalind Ransford provided a summary description in her edition of the early charters of Waltham,[4] and there is a discussion and transcript of this list in a thesis by I. G. Thomas.[5]

What is the list's particular relevance for eleventh-century studies? Internal evidence indicates that the Book of Waltham was written in the mid 1340s,[6] and this is confirmed by the style of the penwork decoration, which has been characterized as 'sub-sub-Queen Mary'.[7] However, many of the items in this miscellany derive from much older archetypes. That amazing romance the *Vita Haroldi* seems to have been written in the first decade of the thirteenth century, embodying traces of contemporary documents.[8] The tract *De inventione Sancte Crucis de Waltham*, written by one of the last

1   Cambridge, University Library, Add. MS 3041, ff. 45r-49v.

2   E. G. M.[illar], 'A Manuscript from Waltham Abbey in the Harleian collection', *British Museum Quarterly*, 7 (1933), 112-18.

3   For the text see the Appendix to this paper, pp. 170-81.

4   *The Early Charters of the Augustinian Canons of Waltham Abbey, Essex, 1062-1230*, ed. R. Ransford (Woodbridge, 1989), no. 637.

5   I. G. Thomas, 'The Cult of Saints' Relics in Medieval England' (unpublished Ph.D. dissertation, London University, 1974), pp. 256-72, Appendix III.

6   Millar, 'Manuscript from Waltham Abbey', pp. 115-16. The latest of the miracle accounts in Harley 3776, in the same hand as the relic-list, is dated 19 Edward III (1345-46).

7   I am grateful to Dr Lynda Dennison for this stylistic assessment.

8   *Vita Haroldi. The Romance of the Life of Harold, King of England*, ed. and trans. W. de G. Birch (London, 1885); *Three Lives of the Last Englishmen*, ed. and trans. M. Swanton (New York, 1984), pp. xxvi-xxvii, 1-40.

secular canons in the last quarter of the twelfth century, incorporates portions of a lost late eleventh-century history.[9] The relic-list is no exception. It would appear to have been compiled during the rule of Abbot Richard (d.1230), shortly after a verification of the relics on 6 July 1204. It begins in hexameters, with a tally of the relics given by Harold, 'quas tulit ignotis a partibus atque remotis', followed by an account of the examination of 1204. Then there is a change to a straightforward listing of relics, beginning with those acquired by the secular canons before 1177. The donors of these are not identified, and it is clear that by 1204 there were several items 'sine indicio'. The relics acquired by the Augustinian canons are, on the other hand, carefully catalogued under their donors.

In this paper I shall not attempt to look at all 462 names on this relic-list, but shall concentrate on three aspects: the evidence for the appearance of the *raison d'être* of the foundation at Waltham, the miraculous cross found at Montacute in the reign of Cnut; the nature of Harold's donation and the light it sheds on his Continental contacts; and the later donations of relics of English and Celtic saints. However, it is difficult to resist some mention of other acquisitions, such as the 'Quatuor folia parvi libri qui fuit Sancti Jeronimi', given by a Londoner called Maurice late in the twelfth century.

The circumstances of the finding of the holy rood are most clearly recounted in *De inventione Sancte Crucis*, of which Stubbs published an edition in 1861.[10] It was found buried in the hill at Montacute in Somerset, supposedly at a depth of forty cubits (surely an exaggeration), following a vision vouchsafed to the local smith some time during the reign of Cnut. Lying with it under a protective stone were a smaller crucifix, a bell, and the *Liber Niger*, described as a scarcely legible gospel book. Of the great rood at this stage we learn that it was made of black 'silex' and that it was 'miro fabrili et inaudito opere composita'. It was evidently life-size, for Tofig the Proud, on whose estate the crucifix had been found, reputedly girt the image with the sword with which he had first been 'accinctus miles'.[11] A clue as to the nature of the material of which the rood was made is provided by one of the first miracles. Not only is it stated that blood exuded from the right arm when an attempt was made to drive a nail into it (for which there is no

9   Ransford, *Waltham*, p. xxiii n. 2.

10 *The Foundation of Waltham Abbey. The Tract "De inventione Sanctae Crucis nostrae in Monte Acuto et de ductione ejusdem apud Waltham,"* now first printed from the manuscript in the British Museum, ed. W. Stubbs (Oxford, 1861). Dr Marjorie Chibnall and Leslie Watkiss are preparing a new edition of this tract.

11 *De inventione Sanctae Crucis*, p. 12. Cf. Hereward's visit to Abbot Brand of Peterborough, 'ut eum militari gladio et baltheo Anglico more praecingeret' ('Gesta Herwardi incliti exulis et militis', in Geffrei Gaimar, *Lestorie des Engles*, ed. Sir T.D. Harris, C.T. Martin, RS (London, 1888), I, p. 368).

obvious rational explanation), but also that nails could nowhere be hammered into the cross.[12] There is a stone which is black, with a flint-like sheen, and has a hard central core which renders anything more than low-relief carving very difficult: Tournai marble.[13] But is it conceivable that there could be a Tournai marble crucifix in eleventh-century Somerset? A letter from Charlemagne to Offa reveals that 'black stones' were being sent to Mercia c.796, and there may have been later unrecorded imports of this material.[14]

Professor Dodwell, looking at the evidence of De inventione Sancte Crucis from an art-historical viewpoint, has also invoked Tournai marble in this context.[15] His most interesting comments relate to the adornment of the crucifix by Tofig and his wife Githa (or Glitha) after it had been housed in a church on Tofig's hunting ground at Waltham. It was covered in silver plates, and the crucifixus given a gold crown adorned with precious stones, a golden band round Christ's thighs, again set with gems, made from one of Githa's head-bands, and a gold foot-rest made of her necklaces and bracelets.[16] Dodwell links this with the gold- and silver-plated Crucifixion group provided for Durham by Tostig and Judith, and the 'magna crux' at Peterborough, from which a Danish force removed the gold crown and foot-rest in 1070. He then posits a basic relationship between such ornamented images and the gold-bedecked figure of Thor destroyed by St Olaf. The Danes Tofig and Githa were thus enriching the rood in the same way that their ancestors would have treated pagan idols.[17]

De inventione Sancte Crucis relates that when Harold, visiting Waltham after Stamford Bridge, prostrated himself before the rood, the figure of Christ, which had hitherto been upright, miraculously bowed its head, as if in sadness.[18] The Vita Haroldi elaborates on this: 'Although human art could not pierce the thin palm of the divine statue, the statue itself was seen to bend its neck... Because the stone inside was hidden by silver plating on the outside, a double wonder was performed and displayed... Where I understand the jaw of the image originally jutted out, now... we see it dropping downwards resting on the breast'.[19] This could be rationalized as a reference

[12] De inventione Sanctae Crucis, p. 10.

[13] I am grateful to Freda Anderson for her comments on this subject.

[14] C. R. Dodwell, Anglo-Saxon Art: A New Perspective (Manchester, 1982), p. 35.

[15] Ibid.

[16] De inventione Sanctae Crucis, p. 12.

[17] Dodwell, Anglo-Saxon Art, pp. 119-21. Cf. B. C. Raw, Anglo-Saxon Crucifixion Iconography and the Art of the Monastic Revival (Cambridge, 1990), p. 41.

[18] De inventione Sanctae Crucis, p. 26. Cf. Raw, Anglo-Saxon Crucifixion Iconography, pp. 18, 62, 143.

[19] Vita Haroldi, pp. 58-59; Three Lives, ed. Swanton, pp. 22-23. There is a similar

to a mid-eleventh-century refashioning of the crucifixus to make it accord more with the naturalism of contemporary Ottonian and Anglo-Saxon images such as the Gero crucifix[20] or the Langford south porch rood.[21] The rood certainly required maintenance. Among the miracles recorded in *De Inventione Sancte Crucis* is the temporary blinding of Robert, the goldsmith of St Alban's, and others, while engaged in cleaning and burnishing the metal plates.[22] The relic-list usefully records that in 1192 Jordan the goldsmith of Barking replaced the silver plating, using fifty marks of pure silver in the process, but left the crown, the bands (*circuli*) round the loin-cloth, and the foot-rest intact. A fourteenth-century miracle story in Harley 3776 adds a little further detail. It recounts how a resident chaplain called Robert Saleman put up a ladder in order to nail fast the diadem, which was loose, but desisted when his hammer became covered in blood.[23]

Is there any visual evidence for the appearance of the Rood of Waltham? The copy of *De Inventione Sancte Crucis* in Harley 3766 opens on f. 49 with an initial C depicting a man kneeling before a crucifix. The initial is very badly rubbed, but Christ's head is shown as inclined. There is nothing, however, to indicate that this is anything other than a conventional image. The seals of Waltham are interesting, but curiously unrevealing. Both that of Harold's foundation, which survives in a unique impression, and those of the Augustinian abbey show two angels supporting a cross rather than a crucifix, Greek in one case, Latin in the other.[24] Both types show expanded arms with stepped ends, and a similar form of cross occurs on the only pilgrim souvenir linked so far with Waltham, a twelfth-century mould for ampullae.[25] This type, which can also be compared with the Brussels Cross,[26] *may* reflect the

---

legend of St Irmgardis and the Gero crucifix at Cologne (P. Thoby, *Le Crucifix des Origines au Concile de Trente. Supplément* (Nantes, 1963), p. 15).

20 *Ornamenta Ecclesiae: Kunst und Künstler der Romanik in Köln*, ed. A. Legner (Koln, 1985), II, E17.

21 E. Coatsworth, 'Late Pre-Conquest Sculptures with the Crucifixion South of the Humber', in *Bishop Æthelwold: His Career and Influence*, ed. B. Yorke (Woodbridge, 1988), pp. 173-75, pl. IIIa.

22 *De inventione Sanctae Crucis*, p. 44.

23 He became vicar of Caterham, Surrey in 1334-35 (BL Harley MS 3776, f. 37v).

24 C. H. Hunter Blair, 'Seal of Harold's College at Waltham Holy Cross', *Trans. Essex Archaeol. Soc.*, 16 (1922), 131-32; Sir W. St J. Hope, 'Seals of the Abbey of Waltham Holy Cross', *ibid.*, 14 (1917), 303-10.

25 B. W. Spencer, 'Medieval Pilgrim Badges: Some General Observations illustrated mainly from English Sources', in *Rotterdam Papers, a Contribution to Medieval Archaeology*, ed. J. G. N. Renaud (Rotterdam, 1968), pp. 137-53, at 141, pl. IV,4.

26 *The Golden Age of Anglo-Saxon Art*, ed. J. Backhouse, D. H. Turner, L. Webster (London, 1984), no. 75, pl. XXIII.

appearance of the rood at Waltham. Nor does the Dissolution inventory of the abbey afford any clues.[27] The Rood does not appear therein, having presumably been removed earlier 'for the king's use'.

One item which almost certainly does feature in the Dissolution inventory is the *Liber Niger*. The relic-list notes that it got its name on account of its extremely old and vile writing and parchment. We are also informed that at some time prior to 1192 Jordan of Barking was commissioned by Peter the sacrist to provide a jewelled silver-gilt covering with an image of the 'maiestas domini'. This, I suspect, is none other than the 'Gospler, plated with sylver gylte, havynge in the myddes the Ymage of Cryste with the iiij Evangelysts'.[28] The only slight complication is that the extracts from the *Liber Niger* copied in Harley 3766 are from a legendary. Perhaps we are dealing with a composite volume. In passing, it is worth mentioning two other items in the Dissolution inventory which must have dated back to the eleventh century: 'a Gospler of the Saxon Tongue, havynge thone syde plated with sylver parcell gilte, with ye ymage of Cryst' and 'another Gospler of the Saxon Tonge, with the Crucifixe and Mary and John havyng a naked man holdyng up his hands of sylver gilte'.[29]

The third item found at Montacute features in the relic-list as 'tintinnabulum humile ex antiquo opere'. Being of base metal, it escaped inclusion in the Dissolution inventory. *De inventione Sancte Crucis* describes it as looking like the bell hung round an animal's neck.[30] All in all, it sounds as though this was a Celtic hand-bell. The West Country find-spot supports this interpretation. It should be noted, however, that hand-bells do occur in later Anglo-Saxon contexts: for example, they are shown on the Bayeux Tapestry being rung at the burial of Edward the Confessor.[31] The fourth item, the smaller crucifix, was left at Montacute, and nothing more is heard of it.

The Montacute finds had been buried with care under a large, heavy stone. It would seem that they were the treasured possessions of some religious foundation which had taken this step to preserve them from base uses, perhaps during a Danish incursion. A comparison can be made with the deliberate burial of a wooden cross on the site of the church of St Bertelin at

27 'Inventory of Waltham Holy Cross', ed. M. E. C. Walcott, *Trans. Essex Archaeol. Soc.*, 5 (1873), 257-64.

28 *Ibid.*, p. 261.

29 *Ibid.*, p. 261. The 'naked man holdyng up his hands' can be identified as Adam. Cf. Adam beneath the Crucifixion on the portable altar of Mauritius of *c*.1160 at Siegburg (*Ornamenta Ecclesiae*, II, F46).

30 *De inventione Sanctae Crucis*, p. 5.

31 D. M. Wilson, *The Bayeux Tapestry* (London, 1985), pl. 29.

Stafford, some time before 1000.[32] The estate known as Logworesbeorh, which formed the nucleus of the settlement at Montacute, was given to Glastonbury in the late seventh century, and was later known as Bishopston, perhaps in connection with Tunbeorht, abbot of Glastonbury and bishop of Winchester.[33] This seems to me the most likely origin of the rood, the *Liber Niger* and the bell.

According to the *Vita Haroldi*, Harold's devotion to 'the health-giving Cross' stemmed from his miraculous recovery from gout. He had been attended by a doctor called Ailard, sent by the Emperor Henry III.[34] This man, called Adelard in earlier sources, was a native of Liège, who had studied at Utrecht, presumably under Bishop Bernulf. He was to hold the position of 'Magister scholarum' at Waltham, which was refounded by Harold as a collegiate church for an apostolic dozen canons under a dean, Wulwin by name.[35] The inspiration for this establishment, as for the reforms of Leofric at Exeter, Giso at Wells and Ealdred at Beverley, was clearly the canonical revival that had taken place in the Rhein-Maas region.[36] Work on a new, richly ornamented stone church advanced sufficiently for it to be dedicated on the feast of the Invention of the Cross 1060. Two years later Edward the Confessor issued a confirmatory charter which, perhaps because of the sanctity of the king as much as because of its economic value, was by 1204 kept with the other relics, together with a chasuble made from a blue cloak of Edward's. The relic-list describes the charter as prefaced by a chrismon and written in gold in several places.[37] At the dedication Harold gave an abundance of relics, with a further donation after Stamford Bridge. *De inventione Sancte Crucis* records that Adelard felt it appropriate to write a memorial for posterity recording each item in the donation.[38] Ransford has speculated that the first part of the metrical list was written in this period,[39] and there is one piece of evidence which strongly supports this theory. Of the eighty-five relics donated in the pre-Conquest period, according to the poem, at least twenty-five seem to be duplicated in the first (pre-1177) part of the prose list. It may be that some of Harold's gifts had fallen into obscurity, among the 'multa et alia ossa. ligna. capillos dentes. lapides. pannos. sine

32 *The Church of St Bertelin at Stafford and its Cross*, ed. A. Oswald (Birmingham, 1955), p. 17. I am grateful to my father, R. L. Rogers, for this reference.

33 *VCH, Somerset*, III, ed. R. W. Dunning (Oxford, 1974), pp. 212-13.

34 *Vita Haroldi*, pp. 16-21; *Three Lives*, ed. Swanton, pp. 5-7.

35 *De inventione Sanctae Crucis*, p. x; Ransford, *Waltham*, p. xxiii.

36 Cf. F. Barlow, *The English Church 1000-1066*, 2nd edn (London, 1979), p. 90.

37 Ransford, *Waltham*, no. 1. *De inventione Sanctae Crucis*, p. 21 also refers to it as 'litteris aureis scripta'.

38 *De inventione Sanctae Crucis*, p. 21.

39 Ransford, *Waltham*, p. 435.

aliquo indicio'. But it is also likely that many of them were no longer at Waltham in 1204. A particular cause of grievance was the spoliation carried out by William I, who removed 'seven shrines, of which three were gold and four silver-gilt, full of relics and precious jewels; four codices ornamented with gold, silver and jewels; four large gold and silver censers...', and so on, including 'four altars with relics, of which one was gold and the remainder silver-gilt' and 'ten reliquaries, one of which was made from two marks of gold and jewels, the remainder from gold and silver'.[40]

Fifty-nine of the eighty-five relics were acquired by Harold himself, the remainder by Archbishop Ealdred, who gave them as a token of friendship. One's eye goes first of all to the insular names among Harold's donations. Ely was the ultimate source of two relics: some of the hair of St Sexburga, and unspecified 'atheldrithe sacra'.[41] There is, not surprisingly, a group from the West Country: Edward from Shaftesbury,[42] Edwold from Cerne,[43] 'Morenna', presumably the patroness of Morwenstow,[44] and Piran from Perranzabulo.[45] One or two names present problems. I have no idea who 'ermenwarus' is. 'Eswinus' stems from a fourteenth-century mis-reading of a 'g' or an uncial 'd'; Egwin is perhaps more likely, especially since there had been a recent translation of his relics.[46] There was a relic of St Swithun, and Winchester may also have been the immediate source of a relic of St Cecilia.[47] Waltham, like Winchester, claimed to have a portion of the tomb

---

[40] *Vita Haroldi*, pp. 24-25; *Three Lives*, ed. Swanton, p. 8. None of the more distinctive lost items, such as the relics of SS Maternus, Burchard and Leocadia, can be recognized in the late-11th-century relic-list of La Trinité, Caen (*Les actes de Guillaume le Conquérant et de la reine Mathilde pour les abbayes Caennaises*, ed. L. Musset, *Mém. Soc. Ant. Normandie*, 37 (Caen, 1967), no. 29). I am grateful to Dr David Bates for this reference.

[41] Presumably secondary relics similar to those given by Bishop Eustace's chaplain (Appendix, p. 180). Cf. Bede, *Ecclesiastical History of the English People*, ed. B. Colgrave, R. A. B. Mynors (Oxford, 1969), p. 396.

[42] He was translated to Shaftesbury in 980. On the early history of the cult of St Edward see C. E. Fell, *Edward, King and Martyr* (Leeds, 1971), pp. xx-xxv.

[43] D. H. Farmer, *The Oxford Dictionary of Saints*, 2nd edn (Oxford, 1987), p. 137.

[44] *Ibid.*, pp. 310-11.

[45] Drifting sands forced a translation of St Piran's body to a new site in the 11th century (G. H. Doble, *The History of the Relics of Saint Piran at Perranzabulo*, Supplement to 'Cornish Saints', no. 29 (St Ives, Cornwall, 1942), p. 5).

[46] Farmer, *Dictionary*, pp. 137-38.

[47] *Liber Vitae: Register and Martyrology of New Minster and Hyde Abbey, Winchester*, ed. W. de G. Birch, Hampshire Record Society (London & Winchester, 1892), p. 152. On relics of a St Cecilia at the Old Minster see CUL, Add. MS 3041, f. 113r.

of Lazarus,[48] but, like the relic of St Cecilia, this may have come by quite a different way into Harold's hands. With equal caution, a Canterbury origin can be posited for the relic of St Salvius, the Valenciennes martyr whose name occurs in the calendar of the Bosworth Psalter,[49] and for the bone of St Blaise, of whom there was a pre-Conquest relic-cult at Christ Church.[50]

The *Vita Haroldi* gives a colourful account of the earl's visit to Rome, 'an act of natural devotion', which also had the object of bringing back holy relics from the city of Christ's most exalted Apostles. It tells how 'with payment of vows, prayers, and money' he secured the bones of SS Chrysanthus and Daria, but was forced to relinquish them by the populace.[51] Freeman dates this visit to 1058, and links it with Stigand's unsatisfactory acquisition of the pallium.[52] Barlow dates it to about 1056, but notes that the story is weakened by obvious confusion with Tostig's adventures.[53] Certainly the avidity with which late Anglo-Saxon rulers collected relics gave rise to what is virtually a *topos* in hagiographical literature: the Englishman prepared to secure relics by questionable means.[54] Whatever the true circumstances of Harold's visit, the Waltham Abbey relic-list contains several items for which a Roman, indeed a papal, origin is most likely. At the head of the list are several dominical relics, including 'de veste' and 'panibus ex quinis: qui milia quinque replerunt'. Gregory Martin's *Roma Sancta*, compiled in 1581, noted that under the altar of St John Lateran 'there is of Christ's Cote without seame, his purple garment, parte of the five barley loaves'.[55] Another item which may have come from the Sancta Sanctorum at St John Lateran were the bones of St Pancras. One is reminded of the earlier present of bones of St Pancras by Pope Vitalian to King Oswiu of Northumbria.[56] Perhaps the most likely souvenirs of Rome were the fragments of St Peter's beard and chains. It would be interesting to know how these items, which were lost by 1204, were displayed. Was the fragment

[48] *Liber Vitae*, p. lxiv.

[49] A. Gasquet, E. Bishop, *The Bosworth Psalter* (London, 1908) pp. 35-37.

[50] *Ibid.*, p. 58.

[51] *Vita Haroldi*, pp. 43-45; *Three Lives*, ed. Swanton, pp. 17-18.

[52] E. A. Freeman, *The History of the Norman Conquest of England, its causes and its results*, II (Oxford, 1868), p. 636.

[53] Barlow, *English Church*, pp. 59, 291. Harold was at St Omer in November 1056, when he witnessed a charter (*Vita Ædwardi Regis*, ed. and trans. F. Barlow (London, 1962), p. 33 n. 5).

[54] P. J. Geary, *Furta Sacra: Theft of Relics in the Central Middle Ages* (Princeton, 1978), pp. 60, 62.

[55] Gregory Martin, *Roma Sancta (1581)*, ed. G. B. Parks (Rome, 1969), p. 35.

[56] For a full list of relics of St Pancras see *Acta Sanctorum Maii*, III, ed. G. Henschenius, D. Papebrochius (Antwerp, 1680), pp. 18-20.

of chain contained in a symbolic key, like that given by Gregory II to St Hubert, and now at Sainte-Croix, Liège,[57] or the tenth-century reliquary at Maastricht?[58] Other possible Roman relics at Waltham were those of St Sebastian and of St Anastasius, whose body lay at St Paul's outside the Wall.[59] In some cases it is not possible to establish just whose relics were believed to be at Waltham. Which St Justinus did they have, or, for that matter, which St James?

Fortunately it is possible to be precise about the identity of most of the relics which serve to document Harold's contacts with Flanders, Germany and France. The *Vita Ædwardi* tells us that at one stage (perhaps on his way to Rome) he went on a journey through various parts of Gaul, carefully examining the condition of the country and the policy of its rulers.[60] Likely acquisitions from that journey were the 'vestis remigii pars' from Rheims,[61] part of the shoe of St Eligius, presumably from Noyon,[62] the finger of St Vigor of Bayeux, from St-Riquier,[63] and, from Metz in Lotharingia, relics of SS Arnulph and Waldrada.[64] Either St-Amand or Ghent could have provided the relic of St Amand,[65] while St-Ghislain near Mons yielded not only a tooth of its patron but also a tooth and rib-bone of the Toledan martyr Leocadia, whose remains were there from, it seems, the eighth century until Philip II reclaimed them for Spain in 1587.[66] Waltham, like Aachen, claimed a portion of the most important part of St Simeon's anatomy, his arms.[67] To nearby Cologne can be traced not only 'de virginibus agrippinensibus pars', but also the relic of St Severinus.[68] Perhaps the most intriguing items are two relics of St Nicholas, one unspecified, the other described as 'Pars... sancta de

57 A. Delhaes, *L'Église Sainte-Croix à Liège* (Liège, 1963), pp. 20-21, with pl.; *Ornamenta Ecclesiae*, III, H60 (here dated 11th-12th century).

58 J. J. M. Timmers, *St-Servatius' Noodkist en de Heiligdomsvaart* (Maastricht, 1962), Afb. 31.

59 Martin, *Roma Sancta*, p. 30.

60 *Vita Ædwardi Regis*, p. 33.

61 The relics of St Remigius had been elevated in 1049 (F. G. Holweck, *A Biographical Dictionary of the Saints* (St Louis, Mo., 1924), p. 852.

62 Holweck, *Dictionary*, p. 313.

63 On the translation of the body of St Vigor to St Riquier see *Acta Sanctorum Novembris*, I (Paris, 1887), pp. 290-93. A new shrine was made during the time of Abbot Gervinus I (1045-71).

64 Holweck, *Dictionary*, pp. 106, 1030.

65 *Ibid.*, pp. 56, 57.

66 *Ibid.*, p. 601.

67 On the Cologne relic, acquired by Charlemagne, see *Acta Sanctorum Octobris*, IV (Brussels, 1780), pp. 18-19.

68 Holweck, *Dictionary*, p. 905.

veste... quo corpus sancti fuit ambitum nicholai'. Where had these come from before the 1087 translation to Bari? The cult had been introduced to Lotharingia by the Empress Theophano in the late tenth century. At least one *ex ossibus* relic had made its way west; in 1058 Bishop Arnold of Worms installed a finger relic of St Nicholas in a chapel in that city.[69] But the textile fragment at Waltham prompts speculation about a more exotic origin. Following an Arab raid in 1034 John Orphanotrophus, the brother of Michael IV, had restored the church and defences at Myra, and it is possible that the Waltham relics stem from an opening of the tomb of St Nicholas on that occasion.[70]

Whereas the evidence for Harold's travels is in large part circumstantial, Ealdred's Continental visits are better documented. In 1054 he led a legation to Germany, where he was splendidly received by the Emperor and Archbishop Hermann of Cologne. Four years later he went on pilgrimage to Jerusalem by way of Hungary and the Adriatic. And in both 1050 and 1061 he went to Rome, on the latter occasion to collect his pallium.[71] His most significant acquisition was part of the body of St Burchard of Wurzburg, one of the English followers of St Boniface.[72] Presumably this was acquired in 1054, together with relics of SS Marcellinus and Peter from Seligenstadt,[73] and of SS Nabor and Nazarius from either Sankt-Avold or Lorsch.[74] The head of St Maternus, which like the relics of St Burchard was lost by Waltham, probably came from either Cologne or Trier.[75] Likely souvenirs of Ealdred's visits to Rome were part of the rod of Moses, from the Sancta Sanctorum, and bones of St Laurence.[76]

There are certain correspondences between Harold and Ealdred's gifts and the relics at St Donatian's, Bruges *c*.1300. Bruges, like Waltham, had fragments of the five loaves (and also of the baskets!), of the beard of St Peter, the cross of St Andrew, and bones of SS Christopher, Denis and his companions, Pancras, Lambert, Hippolytus, Nicholas and Ambrose, and some of the hair of Martha and Mary.[77] All this may be just coincidence, but

---

[69] C. W. Jones, *Saint Nicholas of Myra, Bari, and Manhattan: Biography of a Legend* (Chicago, 1978), pp. 73, 141.

[70] N. P. Ševčenko, *The Life of Saint Nicholas in Byzantine Art* (Turin, 1983), p. 23.

[71] Barlow, *English Church*, pp. 87-88.

[72] Holweck, *Dictionary*, p. 175.

[73] *Ibid.*, p. 649.

[74] *Ibid.*, p. 137.

[75] *Ibid.*, p. 682.

[76] Martin, *Roma Sancta*, pp. 35, 38.

[77] [W. H. J. Weale], 'Catalogue des reliques conservées à l'église de Saint Donatien à Bruges au treizième siècle', *Le Beffroi*, 4 (1872-73), 199-202.

it is known that Harold's sister Gunhild, in exile in Flanders, gave a collection of relics to St Donatian's, most notably the mantle of St Brigid.[78] It is conceivable that she participated in her brother's relic-gathering.

After the Conquest William I granted Waltham to Walcher, bishop of Durham. Although the canons regained their independence in the reign of William Rufus, links between the two houses were maintained. The best-known evidence of this connection is the architecture of the surviving nave at Waltham.[79] However, the connection was reinforced by gifts of relics. The fragment of the cloth in which St Cuthbert was wrapped sounds like something recovered at the 1104 Translation. Reginald of Durham relates that before the body was revested, three of the wrappings were removed and replaced by others 'more elegant and costly'.[80] As a result of Ælfred Westou's relic-collecting in the mid-eleventh century, Durham was in a position to furnish the 'bone of St Bede doctor of the English'.[81] The bones of Aidan and Ceolfrid, despite their Northern origin, probably came from Glastonbury.[82] In the list they are sandwiched between St Patrick and St Hyldracus, martyr, probably a garbled version of St Indract.[83] The most likely donor is Henry of Blois, who was dean of Waltham c.1141 x 1143, and was notorious there for having attempted to purchase the chief jewel adorning the rood for use in Winchester.[84] Perhaps he, too, was the donor of fragments of the tombs of SS Swithun, Birnstan, Ælwin and Edburga, for the most part Winchester saints.[85]

In 1177 the penitent Henry II refounded Waltham on a larger scale for Augustinian canons regular, the first canons being drawn from Cirencester, Osney and St Osyth.[86] The relic-list now gives precise details about donors, enabling a chronology of acquisition to be established, and also is more informative about the precise nature of relics and the vessels in which they were housed. The offerings from other Augustinian and Arrouaisian houses form a notable feature. As among the Benedictines, relics served as bonds of

[78] J. Penninck, *De St-Salvatorskatedraal te Brugge* (Sint-Andries, Brugge, 1982), p. 77.

[79] E. C. Fernie, 'The Romanesque Church of Waltham Abbey', *JBAA*, 138 (1985), 48-78.

[80] C. F. Battiscombe, *The Relics of Saint Cuthbert* (Oxford, 1956), p. 63.

[81] D. Rollason, *Saints and Relics in Anglo-Saxon England* (Oxford, 1989), p. 212.

[82] *Ibid.*, p. 152.

[83] On St Indract and Glastonbury see M. Lapidge, 'The cult of St Indract at Glastonbury', in *Ireland in Early Mediaeval Europe: Studies in memory of Kathleen Hughes*, ed. D. Whitelock, R. McKitterick, D. Dumville (Cambridge, 1982), pp. 179-212.

[84] *De inventione Sanctae Crucis*, p. 12.

[85] Farmer, *Dictionary*, pp. 15, 48, 129, 150, 395.

[86] Ransford, *Waltham*, pp. xxiv-xxv.

charity between the various houses of the order. Walter of Ghent, who later became the first abbot, in 1184, brought a rib-bone of St Petroc from Bodmin, which was served by Austin canons.[87] William Ver, one of the first canons, who became bishop of Hereford in 1186, gave a portion of one of the arm bones of St Osyth.[88] Peter, the first sacrist, brought a bone of St Frideswide from Oxford.[89] A canon called Brian contributed a relic of the tenth-century St Bernard of Menthon, presumably acquired from the Augustinian foundation at the Great St Bernard pass.[90] A particularly fine donation of forty-six relics was made by Nicholas, the prior of St Gregory's, Canterbury. Included were two of the bones of St Mildred with which Lanfranc had endowed the priory,[91] portions of the chasubles of SS Ælphege and Dunstan, and a strip of the belt St Thomas was wearing when he was martyred. The abbots of Osney and Lesnes provided even richer supplies of relics of St Thomas, to whom the infirmary chapel was dedicated by Walter Ver in 1188.[92]

By the late twelfth century there was a marked increase in the proportion of 'modern' saints represented. Their relics were more easily verifiable, and were often obtained at the translation of remains following canonization. In that way Waltham obtained a rib-bone of St Wulfstan from Silvester, bishop of Worcester.[93] In at least one case the relic was obtained before the saint was formally canonized. Adam of Eynsham, the chaplain and biographer of St Hugh of Lincoln, gave a portion of his stole before 1214, at least six years before Honorius III pronounced him to be a saint. Many of these 'modern' relics were secondary ones, portions of clothing or possessions of the saints, such as St Thomas's comb, which Canon Gilbert gave. Of course, as we have already seen, not only recent saints could generate secondary relics. Ralph the first prior gave a fragment of the shirt of St Edmund, which is documented as having been removed from his body by Abbot Leofstan in 1050.[94] Much more uncertain in its pedigree is the portion

---

[87] D. Knowles, R. N. Hadcock, *Medieval Religious Houses, England and Wales* (London, 1971), p. 148.

[88] He had been a canon at St Osyth from c.1163 (Ransford, *Waltham*, p. 186).

[89] The relics of St Frideswide were translated in 1180 (Farmer, *Dictionary*, p. 171).

[90] Holweck, *Dictionary*, p. 153.

[91] Farmer, *Dictionary*, p. 302.

[92] Ransford, *Waltham*, no. 277.

[93] Silvester was bishop of Worcester from 1216 to 16 July 1218. It is recorded that at the translation of St Wulfstan's relics on 6 June 1218 'ipse propria manu securi secuit, et per loca multa divisit, ac de hoc facto semetipsum laudavit' (*Annales Monastici*, II, ed. H. R. Luard, RS (London, 1865), p. 289).

[94] Hermannus the Archdeacon, 'De miraculis Sancti Edmundi', in *Memorials of St Edmund's Abbey*, I, RS (London, 1890), p. 53. The pillow is also mentioned in this

of the veil of St Mary Magdalene given by Eleanor of Aquitaine.[95] The relic of the garment of St Mary the Egyptian sounds suspiciously like a practical joke played on Robert the chaplain of Windsor, to anyone who knows the legend of that saint:[96] when her clothes wore out during her life of penance in the desert east of the Jordan, their place was taken by her long hair. Perhaps the most delightful of these secondary relics was another of Robert's possessions, a portion of the 'langellus beati Guthlaci', which I venture to translate as 'St Guthlac's woolly vest'. Even more dubious were the Holy Land souvenirs given by Maurice, the Londoner who also had four leaves of one of St Jerome's books. These comprised portions of Christ's crib, the tomb of the Blessed Virgin, the rock on which St Elizabeth was standing when the child leapt in her womb, the rock on which the Lord fasted and a cross made from wood which grew in the field Acheldema. In fact, many of these sites had respectable pedigrees. The stump of the fig-tree in Acheldema is mentioned by the Piacenza Pilgrim of c.570, and the place of the Visitation was already identified in the sixth century.[97] Maurice's gifts are sober tokens of actual contact with the traditional sites of Christ's life, which is more than can be said for one of Adam of Eynsham's offerings: 'De ramis palmarum et vestibus prostratis in via domini'.

Such an entry prompts one to wonder just how the canons viewed their collection. There were bounds to their credibility, since one or two items were marked 'ut creditur'. The more improbable items, given in good faith, were perhaps viewed as substitute relics, analogous to the *brandea* of early Roman practice. At the end of the relic-list the compiler says of the relics 'per quarum merita fiunt miracula multa'. This accords with the Augustinian doctrine that justifies the cult of relics on the ground of the miracles God works through their instrumentality.[98] Harold probably had a more instinctive appreciation of the power of relics. On one level Bryan Houghton's telling sentence is true enough: 'In those days princes collected relics as today boys do postage stamps'; but these were *pignora sanctorum*, sensible reminders of powerful intercessors at God's throne, heavenly reinforcements in time of war and, as Harold's most famous encounter with

---

account of the verification of the body.

[95] Perhaps between 1189 and 1194, at the time when she confirmed the institution of canons regular at Waltham (Ransford, *Waltham*, no. 287).

[96] Cf. *Acta Sanctorum Aprilis*, ed. G. Henschenius, D. Papebrochius, I (Antwerp, 1675), pp. 81, 88.

[97] J. Wilkinson, *Jerusalem Pilgrims before the Crusades* (Warminster, 1977), pp. 83, 156.

[98] For an excellent summary of the doctrine of relics see H. Thurston, 'Relics', in *The Catholic Encyclopedia*, XII (London, 1911), pp. 734-38.

relics reminds us, witnesses to the sanctity of oaths.[99]

How important the relics were at Waltham is a moot point. Only for the rood do we have miracle stories, from the eleventh to the fourteenth century. Unfortunately there seem to be no surviving liturgical manuscripts from Waltham which might indicate what role the relics played in the worship there. It is possible that the original metrical list was designed to be read out when the relics were displayed.[100] We do however have a record of the dedications of some of the altars at Waltham. In the 1190s Simon, bishop of Clonard, consecrated altars to SS John the Baptist and Laurence, the latter probably in the nave, and about the same time Reiner, bishop of St Asaph, consecrated the altars of Our Lady and SS Stephen, Vincent, Catherine and Cecilia.[101] The names are common enough, but it is worth noting that relics of Laurence, Stephen, Vincent and Cecilia were all in the Harold/Ealdred donation, and that before 1177 Waltham had acquired some of the oil of St Catherine, in a small glass vessel. But in the long run the relics, like these side-altars, were secondary to the 'honoris huius loci principalis causa', their gift an acknowledgement by kings, magnates and other good men of the importance of the Holy Rood of Waltham.

Appendix

British Library, Harley MS 3776, ff. 31r-35v.[102]

f. 31r a.

Hoc sacru*m* po*ndus sibi conser*uau*it* harold*us*
Sci*licet* istar*um* thesaur*um* reliq*uiarum*
Quas tulit ignotis a p*artibus* at*que* remotis
Unde crucis *sancte* se premuniret in ede.
De do*mini* ligno: de uesteq*ue* deq*ue* sepulchro.
Panib*us* ex quinis: qui milia quinq*ue* replerunt.
Sancta maria tui: pars illic una sepulchri.
De barba petri pars. eius deniq*ue* cathena.
Uestis remigii pars illic est iacobiq*ue*.
De seuerino. martino de nicholao.
Ex anastasio. stephano prothom*art*yre saluo.
Sic ex ambrosio. swithuno de Cyriaco.

[99] B. Houghton, *Saint Edmund: King and Martyr* (Lavenham, 1970), p. 55. On the role of relics in lay society see D. W. Rollason, 'Relic-cults as an instrument of royal policy *c*.900-*c*.1050', *ASE*, 15 (1986), 91-103; Rollason, *Saints and Relics*, pp. 164-95.

[100] A similar function has been suggested for the Exeter relic-list (Rollason, 'Relic-cults', pp. 92-93).

[101] Ransford, *Waltham*, nos. 278, 279.

[102] The text is written in one hand, in two columns, with 31 lines to a page. In this transcription all expanded contractions are italicized.

De te uincenti de cosma de damiano.
De te pancrati sic de te sebastiano.
Et de lamberto pyerano *christoforoque.*
Ex agatha margareta de ceciliaque.
Et de ueste sua de te waldradaque virgo.
Et de uirginibus agrippinensibus est pars.
Dens ibi leucadie. pars ipsius est ibi coste.
Reliquie sunt iustini. sunt et benedicti.
Sunt simul arnulphi: quintini presulis illic.

f. 31r b.
Os quoddam blasii. bricii pars est ibi uestis.
Non ermenwari. nec atheldrithe sacra desunt.
Non minus edwardi non eswini nec Amandi.
Lazare parte tui modica non absque sepulchri.
Parsque tue crinis ibi dicitur esse georgi.
Pars de ueste tua clemens eligi quoque calce.
Est ibi pars crucis andree: digitusque uigoris.
Deque coma sexburga tua. sunt ossa morenne.
Sunt simul eadwaldi de te dens unus Amanti.
Dens ibi martini. Gilleni dens symeonis
Cuius portarunt infantem brachia *christum.*
Pars eciam sancta de ueste reponitur illic
Quo corpus sancti fuit ambitum nicholai.
Hec et harolde tibi fuerint data. dignaque scribi.
Summa reliquiarum predictarum lx.[103]
Que dedit aldredus dum uult interfore fedus.
De ligno domini: pars est ibi uestis amandi.
Vestis remigii. Jeronime dens tuus unus.

f. 31v a.
Materni capitis pars. et capitis benedicti.
Corporis est ibi pars bursbardi presulis una.
De uirga moysi pars. martir ypolite de te.
Parsque mathee tue latet ille condita coste.
Parsque capillorum uestrorum martha maria.
Pars eleutherii. Basilidis atque Cyrici.
Naboris cum Nazario. de te dionisi.
Rustice sic de te. sic reliquie nicholai.
Pars marcellini. pars est ibi condita petri.
Atque beatricis. Faustini Simpliciique.
Laurentique tui pars est ibi corporis usti.
Has huic ecclesie rex reliquias tribuisse.
Ceditur haroldus iam sanctis connumeratus.
Sane temporibus elapsis. numinis anno.
Incarnati Millesimo ducentesimoque

---

[103] Added in a mid-14th-century hand.

Quarto. pridie nonar*um* Julii. pariterq*ue*.
Anteriore die. ieiunia p*ost* t*ri*duana:
In sabbato facta post uerbera cotidiana.[104]

f. 31v b.
Post correcta simul *et* dicta deo malefacta:
Electi fratres sunt pre reliquis grauiores.
Abbas p*ost* prim*um* primus set honore Ricardus:
Nulli postremus. Petrus prior. atq*ue* Ricardus:
Precentor cum Nigello. Willelmus. et unus:
Nomine Rogerus. set *et* ille laboribus ortus:
Galfridus Rabani scriptor. cum deinde priore:
Henrico. cuncti contriti corde sac*ri*sq*ue*:
Albis induti proni. timidi. reuerentes:
Accessere. sacrum thesaur*um* uisere uisum:
Discreuere suis p*er* sc*ri*pta rep*er*ta locellis.
Que scripto caruere: simul in parte localis.
Que scriptis expressa suis inuenta fuere.
Hic poterunt prompta breuitate notata patere.
De ligno domini.
De uestimento d*om*ini.
De Sepulchro domini.
De ueste d*om*ine n*ost*re s*an*cte Marie.
Costa S*an*cti Mathei Apostoli.

f. 32r a.
Costa S*an*cti ypoliti.
De spina S*an*cti petroci os magn*um*.
De carne S*an*cti laurencii.
Os S*an*cti steph*an*i prothom*artyr*is.
De S*an*cto thoma m*ar*tyre.
Ossa plura de s*an*cto steph*an*o prothom*artyre*.
De oleo S*an*cte katerine. Ampullula uitrea. uestigia t*am* olei
ostend*ens* no*n* autem oleu*m* hab*ens*.
De brachio S*an*cti Mauricii.
Digitus S*an*cti vigoris.
Os de S*an*cto fortunato.
Os de S*an*cto Pantaleone.
De ossibus s*an*cti Blasii.
De costa S*an*cti Swithuni.
Os de S*an*cto Nectano.[105]
Os de S*an*cto Georgio.

---

[104] 'Id est ebd*om*ad*a*' added in red by the main scribe.

[105] From Hartland, Devon, a pre-Conquest minster which became an Arrouaisian priory in the 1160s (Farmer, *Dictionary*, p. 312; Knowles and Hadcock, *Religious Houses*, p. 158).

Item os de Sancto Blasio.

Os de Sancta Cecilia. *virgo et* martyr.

Item de sepulchro domini marie.

De virga moysi.

Item de veste *domine nostre* Sancte marie.

Vt credit*ur* de spina *sancti* swithuni Episcopi os unum.

De uno lapide quo lapidat*us* est Sanctus Stephanus prothom*art*yr.

De lapide qui iacuit sup*er* dominu*m nostrum* in sepulchro.

Vt credit*ur* de sepulchro *domine* nostre Sancte marie.

De ueste Sancte Eugenie.

f. 32r b.

De ueste Sancte Scolastice.

De ueste *sancti* Sebastiani m*artyris.*

Item de sepulchro domini.

De ossib*us* Sancti Pancracii m*artyris.*

De *sancto* hyllario pictauensi.

Item os de Sancto Blasio.

Item de Sancto Thoma m*artyre.*

Item de sepulch*ro domine nostre.*

De petra m*on*tis synai.

Os de Sancto Barnaba ap*ostolo.*

Os de Sancto Sebastiano m*artyre.*

Dens Sancti Gregorii p*ape et* doctoris *et* de capillis eius.

De reliquiis sociorum *sancti* hirenei.

De panno quo i*n*uolutus fuit Sanctus Cuthbertus.

De primitiuo lapide montis caluarie.

Os de Sancto hyldraco m*artyre.*

Os de Sancto Aidano ep*iscopo confessore.*

Os de Sancto ceolfrido Abb*ate confessore.*

Os de Sancto Patricio ep*iscopo confessore.*

Dens Sancti Amancii m*artyris.*

De coma Sancte sexburge *virginis.*

Os de Sancto wulfranno ep*iscopo confessore.*

Os de Sancto Remigio ep*iscopo confessore.*

Os de Sancto Laurencio m*artyre.*

De ossib*us* Sancti Jacobi apostoli.

De ossib*us* Sancti *christ*ofori m*artyris.*

Os de Sancto Stephano prothom*artyre.*

f. 32v a.

De *sancti*s m*artyribus* Cosma *et* damiano ossa duo.

Os de Sancto wiltano fr*atre* Sancti fursei.[106]

Os de Sancto Gildardo doctore *et* sacerdote Regis Arturi.[107]

---

[106] St Ultan's relics were at Fosse in Brabant (Holweck, *Dictionary*, pp. 996-97).

Os de *Sancta* Cecilia m*artyre*.

Os de *Sancto* Georgio m*artyre*.

Os de *Sancto* Cyriaco m*artyre*.

De sepulchris s*anctorum* Swithuni ep*iscopi*. Aelphegi ep*iscopi* m*artyris*.

Birstani ep*iscopi confessoris*. Aelwine s*ancte*. Aedburge v*irginis*.

De Capillis S*ancte* Barbare v*irginis*.

De digito *Sancti* Swithuni ep*iscopi confessoris*.

Os de Capite *Sancti* oswaldi archiep*iscopi confessoris*.

De *Sancta* Agatha ossa *quatu*or *et* alia pl*ura* minuta.

De pane q*ui* iacuit s*uper* mensam domini.

Os de *Sancto* Albane prothom*artyre* anglor*um*.

De patella capitis S*ancti* laurencii m*artyris*.

De cruce S*ancti* Andree apostoli.

De ueste S*ancti* Johannis apostoli *et* eu*angeliste*.

De uestib*us* s*anctorum* innocenci*um*.

De reliquiis S*ancti* Pancracii.

Reliquie de *Sancto* damiano.

Reliquie S*ancti* Bartholomei apostoli *et sancti* martini ep*iscopi*.

confessoris. et S*ancti* Nicholai *et item* S*ancti* martini *et* S*ancti*

Remigii *et* s*anctorum* m*artyrorum* Marcellini *et* petri.

f. 32v b.

De sudario ut credit*ur* Sancti nicholai.

Corporalia sacrame*nto* altaris perfusa.

Os de *Sancto* Petroco.

Reliq*uie* de *Sancto* Winwaleo *et* de *Sancto* Courentino.[108]

De veste *Sancti* laur*entii*.

Os unum q*uod* solum contineb*atur* in uno scrinio magno.

Os de *Sancto* Beda doctore anglor*um*.

Multa *et* alia ossa. ligna. capillos dentes, lapides. pa*nn*os sine aliquo indicio quor*um* essent inuenim*us*. *et* ideo huc usq*ue* nos latent.

quem tu*m* simul p*er* se posita sunt: sicut ignota. Illas vero reliquias quas aperte p*er* scripta notatas in*uenim*us: meli*us et* honesti*us* in bursis sericis. pixidib*us* eburneis siue ligneis.

philacteriis argenteis *et* lapideis seruandas reposuim*us*. Has autem reliquias nobiliter locatas *et* a primo die reposicionis ear*um* in loco suo: intactas in*uenim*us.

De alba ueste saluatoris.

De ligno domini.

[107] Cf. S. Baring-Gould, J. Fisher, *The Lives of the British Saints*, III (London, 1911), pp. 111-12.

[108] Montreuil-sur-Mer claimed relics of SS Winwaloe and Corentine (J. M. H. Smith, 'Oral and Written: Saints, Miracles, and Relics in Brittany, *c.*850-1250', *Speculum*, 65 (1990), 309-43, esp. 321, 327). I am grateful to Dr Caroline Brett for this reference.

Vnum os de Sancto nicholao.
De baculo Sancti petri.
Unum os de Sancto Tyburcio.
Ossa et ligna sine indiculo.

f. 33r a.
Item dentes et uestes preciose et nitide inuente sub sigillo lefwi ducis
minisi absque aliquo indicio quorum essent.
Eciam quod primo et maxime ponendum et notandum fuit. Crux
uidelicet magna et sancta post domini aduocata nostra tocius nostre
religionis et honoris huius loci principalis causa. Que in diebus
nostris. Anno domini. Millesimo. Centesimo. nonagesimo secundo
sub waltero Abbate et iordano sacrista. per manum iordani
aurifabri. de Berkingia de nouo cooperta. In qua expendebantur
quinquaginta marce puri argenti largiter. nam aurum purum quod
in ea est ex antiquo opere fuit. et remansit intactum. scilicet corona
et subpeditaneum et circuli circa precinctorium. quorum pondus est
quinque marcarum argenti et dimidie. Liber etiam qui inuentus
fuerat cum ipsa cruce. qui et niger dicitur: pro eo quod littera et
parcamenum uilissima sint et antiquissima. ab predicto aurifabro
sed precedenti tempore per sacristam petrum argento deaurato et
gemmis cum ymagine maiestatis domini coopertus et ornatus.
Tintinnabulum eciam humile ex antiquo

f. 33r b.
opere cum eadem cruce inuentum. Set et casula ex pallio beati regis
et confessoris aedwardi facta. preciosior cunctis aliis quas adhuc
habemus. que et indici coloris est. Carta quoque eiusdem regis huic
ecclesie facta de confirmacione et etiam adieccione quorundam
possessionum antiquorum. aureis litteris in pluribus locis scripta. et
precipue in principio per hanc figuram ℞ que crismon dicitur que
sola ex uoluntate uniuscuiusque ad aliquid uotandum ponitur.
Que sint Reliquie que tempore religiosi Conuentus sacris prescriptis
sint sociate. Lectorem poterit breuitas
subscripta docere.
In tempore Radulphi prioris primi canonicorum regularium huius
sancte walthamensis ecclesie.[109]
Costa sancti petroci per walterum de Gant. postea Abbatem
predicte ecclesie.
De camisia. puluinari. Sarcofago Sancti edmundi regis. per prefatum
priorem radulphum.
De brachio Sancte osythe virginis et martyris per willelmum ver.
postea episcopum herfordie.

[109] Ralph de Bonelee, a canon of Cirencester, was appointed prior 11 June 1177, and
is last mentioned in 1182 (Ransford, *Waltham*, p. xi).

Os de sancta fritheswida. per petrum primum sacristam
canonicorum regularium.
In diebus domini walteri Abbatis primi huius ecclesie:[110] per
eundem walterum a fundatore nostro rege henrico secundo.
Porcio una de ligno domini nobis transmissa. in capsula parua
argentea. cum scrinio maiori ligneo mire fabricato. Hec porcio
nigra est. et posita in medio crucis quam idem abbas postea fecit
fieri ex argento et lapidibus preciosis. cum aliis particulis eiusdem
ligni: sed non eiusdem coloris. Hec crux quatuor suas extremitates
habet rotundas. ligno domini insignitas.
De ligno domini in parua cruce aurea et de uase in quo lauit
dominus pedes discipulorum. per quendam clericum regis ricardi.
nomine Ricardum de Cliniui.
De sepulchro domini per regem iohannem ex adquisicione Regis
Ricardi.
De uelo Sancte marie magdalene per reginam alienor aduocatam
nostram.
De oleo ymaginis domine nostre sancte marie de Sardelai. per
fratrem Rogerum elemosinarium.[111]
De ossibus sanctemonialium que incense fuerant a paganis in
ecclesia

f. 33v b.
Berkingensi. et de interiori parte sepulchri Sancte athelburge ibidem
quiescentis.[112]
De oleo Sancti Nicholai in uasculo cristallino. Per petrum priorem.
Os unum de Sancto Pierano episcopo et confessore. Per danielem
suppriorem nostrum.
De Reliquiis Sancti Augustini Anglorum apostoli. per monachum
quendam ecclesie eius.
Reliquie willelmi presbyteri de Guthlande. nacione Anglici quas
nobis dedit.
Os unum de sancto Bartholomeo apostolo.
Os de sancta sabina virgine.
Os de Sancta pinnosa maiore.[113]
Ossa de .xi. milium virginum.
Os de Sancto pancracio martyre.
De ueste Sancti Johannis euangeliste.

---

[110] Walter de Gant, a former canon of Osney, appointed July 1184, died 2 May 1201
(*ibid.* p. xi).

[111] On the icon of Our Lady of Saidenaya, near Damascus, see *Mandeville's Travels*,
ed. M. C. Seymour (Oxford, 1967), pp. 90, 243.

[112] Cf. *VCH, Essex*, II (London, 1907), p. 116.

[113] One of the Ursuline martyrs of Cologne, first mentioned in the 8th century
(Holweck, *Dictionary*, pp. 817-18).

De sanguine *Sancti* laur*entii* m*artyris* puro *et* de panno sanguine
eius intincto.
De *sancta* perpetua.
De pane d*omi*ni. Et alia ignota.
De dono brienni cuiusdam canonici n*ost*ri.
De S*an*cto Amphibalo m*artyre. et* de quod*am* socio ei*us.*[114]
De S*an*cto Bernardo de monte iouis.
De ossib*us et* sepulchr*is* s*an*ctorum ignotis.
Sub d*omi*no Ricardo Abb*at*e sec*un*do hui*us* ecclesie.[115]
Os unu*m* de brachio s*an*cti Dunstani. p*er* ipsu*m et* brienu*m*

f. 34r a.
concan*onicum* n*ost*ru*m* adquisitu*m.*
V*n*us ex capillis d*omi*ne n*ost*re S*an*cte marie in botione[116] aureo ex
dono magis*tri* Oton*is* Canonici S*an*cti Pauli londoniar*um.*
De ueste d*omi*ni n*ost*ri per unu*m* co*n*uersum n*ost*ru*m.*
De ligno ut credim*us* d*omi*ni sub sacrista iordane i*n*uento cu*m*
paruula cruce. nescio q*u*o ligno in medio eius posito.
Reliquie de S*an*cto nectano.
De pellicio s*an*cte ut credim*us* Gedewise.
Pili duo p*er* predictum abb*at*em Ric*ardum.* quod ex hericiis fuit.
cui eciam ipsa adhuc uiuens contulit. De cilicio quo usus est S*anctus*
Hugo ep*iscopus* lincolnie *in* obitu suo. p*er* petru*m* priore*m*
n*ost*ru*m.*[117]
Os unu*m* de s*an*cta Barnaba ap*osto*lo. p*er* que*n*dam abb*at*em de
furneis.
De Capucio S*an*cti Godrici heremite *con*fessoris. p*er* alanu*m* de
mu*m*bi milite*m et* amicum n*ost*ru*m.*[118]
De ossib*us* s*an*ctarum virginu*m et* m*artyru*m Colonie videl*icet*
odilie *et* segilie. p*er* herma*n*nu*m* mercatore*m.*
De Grabato S*an*cti Gregorii p*ap*e per osmu*n*du*m* presbyteru*m* de
londoniis.
De cappa S*an*cti will*elm*i archiep*iscop*i de punteise. p*er* nichol*aum*
mon*ach*um de s*an*cto Albano.[119]
Os unu*m* de S*an*cto Rufo huc usq*ue* ex adquisicione pe*tr*i prioris.

[114] The relics of St Amphibalus were invented in 1178 (Farmer, *Dictionary*, p. 17).
[115] Richard, consecrated in 1201 or 1202, died by 18 March 1230 (Ransford, *Waltham*, p. xi).
[116] 'Botan' added in red by the main scribe.
[117] On this hair-shirt see H. Thurston, *The life of Saint Hugh of Lincoln* (London, 1898), pp. 521, 529.
[118] Alan of Mumby, son of Eudo of Mumby, came of age in 1199-1200 and died before 1216 (Ransford, *Waltham*, p. 291).
[119] Possibly St William, an English priest at Pontoise, who died in 1193 (Holweck, *Dictionary*, p. 1036).

f. 34r b.

Item. De ligno domini ut credimus. per Gilebertum conuersum nostrum morientem.

De cilicio et coopertorio beati Thome martyris ut credimus.

Ex dono cuiusdam uiri londoniensis nomine Maurici.

Quator folia parui libri qui fuit Sancti Jeronimi.

De ueste Sancti Thome martyris

De presepi in quo reclinatus est dominus.

De sepulchre beate marie.

De rupe in qua stetit Sancta Elisabeth quando exultauit infans in utero eius.

De ligno per preces achasti Regis hispanie elongato.[120]

De puluere cumpassi.

De rupe in qua sedit iacobus apostolus.

De altari in quo sanctus petrus apostolus celebrauit.

De rupe in qua dominus ieiunauit.[121]

Crux quedam facta de ligno quod creuit in agro acheldemach. qui comparatus est precio domini.

De dono domini Nicholai prioris Sancti Gregorii cantuarie.

De ligno domini. et de lancea eius et de oleo Sancte katerine.

De costa Sancte marie egipciace.

De sanguine sancti Thome martyris.

f. 34v a.

De corpore Sancti Alphegi et de casula eius.

De tunica Sancte marie magdalene.

Duo ossula de sancto egidio confessore.

De costa Sancti Gregorii pape.

Os de Sancto Gileberto de semplingham.[122]

Os de Sancto Andrea apostolo.

Os de Sancto Hereberto confessore.

Item de Sancto Egidio.

De sotulari Sancti Willebrordi confessoris.

De Sancto Cuthberto et de sociis Sancti Mauricii martyris.

De Sancto luciano martyre.

De zona Sancti Bartholomei apostoli.

Os de Sancto leonardo.

De zona Sancte margarete virginis.

De Sanctis Confessoribus Martino. Nicholao Gregorio Benedicto.

---

[120] Perhaps Alfonso II el Casto, King of the Asturias and Leon (d. 842), in whose time the tomb of St James was discovered (*Acta Sanctorum Julii*, VI (Antwerp, 1729), pp. 15-19).

[121] Cf. the relic 'de monte in quo Christus jejunavit quadraginta diebus et quadraginta noctibus', recorded at St-Jans Hospitaal, Brugge (Brugge, St-Jans Hospitaal, ch. 1333).

[122] St Gilbert of Sempringham was canonized in 1202 (Farmer, *Dictionary*, p. 183).

De uestimento Sancte dei genitricis.
Os de Sancto leodegario.
De capillis Sancte Agathe virginis.
Osula de Sancto Siluino Thosolano episcopo.
De capillis uestimento cruce sancti petri Apostoli.
Duo ossa de Sancta mildreda.
De Grabato Sancti Gregorii pape.
De presepe domini de monte caluario et loco Ascensionis.
De Casula Sancti dunstani confessoris

f. 34v b.
Os de sancta Eufemia.
De uestimento et craticula sancti laurencii martyris.
Item de sancto leodegario.
De sepulcro domini.
De zona Sancti Thome martyris. in qua occubuit. corrigia longa.
Summa numeri harum reliquiarum xlvi.
Has Reliquias dominus Adam Capellanus Sancti hugonis Episcopi
lincolniensis postea Abbas de Eignesham nobis dedit.[123]
De ueste domini et de cunabulo eius.
Scedula infecta de lacte matris.[124]
De brachio Sancti luce euuangeliste.
De maxilla precursoris domini.
De corona vel barba beati petri apostoli.
De brachio Sancti senis symeonis.
De Capite Sancti Cosme martyris.
De ossibus sociorum Sancti dionisii.
De puluere uestium carnis et sanguinis Sancti luciani martyris.
De panno quo inuolutum est caput Sancte Anne matris domine
nostre.[125]
De ramis palmarum et uestibus prostratis in uia domini.
Ossa duo de duobus innocentibus.
De maxilla Sancti Sebastiani martyris.
De cera que fuit circa clauum domini.
De stola Sancti hugonis episcopi lincolniensis.
De Sancto Pantaleone martyre. os unum.
De Sancto dionisio os unum.

---

[123] Adam of Eynsham became Abbot of Eynsham by 1 July 1214, and was deposed
in 1228 (D. Knowles, C. N. L. Brooke, V. C. M. London, *The Heads of Religious
Houses, England and Wales, 940-1216* (Cambridge, 1972), p. 49).

[124] On relics of the milk of Our Lady see E. Waterton, *Pietas Mariana Britannica*
(London, 1879), pp. 195-205.

[125] On relics of the head of St Anne see *Acta Sanctorum Julii*, VI (Antwerp, 1729),
pp.255-57. The cloth was most probably associated with the relic which came to
Chartres in 1205.

f. 35r a.

De sepulchro domini *et* alie *sancte* Reliquie.

Ex dono Thome monachi eliensis capellani d*omini* Eustachii ep*iscopi.*[126]

De s*anct*o symeone iusto.

De S*ancto* nicholao.

De Sepulchro S*ancti* Joh*annis* Baptiste.

De duab*us* costis s*anctorum* Cosme *et* damiani.

Os unu*m* de humero S*ancti* Nathanaelis *christ*i discip*uli.*

De S*ancta* Anastasia *virgine.*

De S*ancto* Epafra qui fuit unus de lxx ap*ostoli*s.[127]

De camisia *et* cista lignea in quib*us* sancta Ætheld*r*eda uirgo *et* regina iacuit xvi annis sepulta *et* incorrupta.

Has itaq*ue* reliquias misit p*re*fatus monach*us* Abb*ati* Ric*ard*o *et* co*n*uentu n*ost*ro: in pixide eburnea q*ue* fuit Eustach*ii* u*e*n*er*abilis Ep*iscopi* in q*u*a anulus consecracion*is* sue. *et* celebracionis seruab*atur.*

Per Henric*um* priorem: pars parua vni*us* ossis. *et* semiscincia dalmatice seu tunice S*ancti* Patricii apostoli hyb*er*nie.

De zona b*eate* Brigide *virginis.* pars parua.

Item pars vni*us* ossis pred*ict*i S*ancti* patricii.

De uno osse S*ancti* Blasii.

De casula S*ancti* Cuthberti.

De S*ancto* Ceolfrido Abb*ate.* os *unum.*

De sepulchro d*omini.*

De lecto s*ancti* Gregorii.

De cappa S*ancti* Will*el*mi Gallie.

f. 35r b.

Os de S*ancto* Martino.

Quiddam ignotu*m.*

De cappa S*ancti* petri ep*iscopi* confessoris de Tarenteise.[128]

De bancario sup*er* q*uod* d*omin*us sedit in cena cu*m* suis apostolis.

Per quenda*m* sacerdotem: de oleo S*ancti* Nicholai.

Reliq*ui*e q*u*as roger*us* de Werchent co*n*uersus n*oste*r adquisiuit.

De ligno d*omi*ni. De presepe d*omi*ni.

De sepulchro d*omini.*

De apostolis philippo *et* jacobo. ossula *et* puluis.

Ossula de S*anctis* abraham *et* ysaac *et* lazaro.

Os de S*ancto* Stephano.

---

[126] Eustace was consecrated bishop of Ely on 8 March 1198 and died on 3 February 1215.

[127] St Epaphras of Colossae (Holweck, *Dictionary*, p. 323).

[128] On Peter II, archbishop of Tarantaise, died 14 September 1174, canonized 10 May 1191, see *Bibliotheca Sanctorum*, X (Rome, 1968), pp. 782-87. The cult of Peter I of Tarantaise only dates from 1636 (*ibid.*, p. 774).

Os de Sancto christoforo.
Os de Sancto Machario.
Lapillus de monte synai.
Ex dono nobis clerici de bassingeburne.
De ligno domini.
De ueste beate uirginis.
Os de Sancto paulo apostolo.
Os de Sancto Andrea Apostolo.
Pecten Sancti Thome qui nobis adquisiuit Gilebertus canonicus
noster.
De dono Henrici monachi de Cogeshale.
De carne beati Thome martyris. resoluta cum quadam parte
dalmatice in qua sepultus fuit.
De baculo suo. De sandaliis suis.

f. 35v a.
De particula panni cui adheret puluis carnis sue resolute.
Ex dono dompni abbatis de osenei.
De panno intincto in sanguine beati Thome martyris.
De baculo pastorali eius inuento in tumba eius.
De carne que adhesit cuidam panno in quo inuolutum erat corpus
eius dum iacuit in sepulchro.
Ex dono domini Abbatis de lesnes.
De femorali cilicio beati Thome martyris.
De casula intincta in sanguine eius. cum qua etiam abstersum fuit
cerebrum eius.
Ex inuentis apud Robertum Capellanum de windeshor.
De vestimento Sancte marie egypciace.
De langello beati Guthlaci.
Ex dono siluestri Wigorniensis episcopi.
De costa Sancti wulstani.
Item Reliquie Sancti wulstani quas dedit nobis wobode.
Ex dono domini Ricardi de templo.
Os sancti Seueri confessoris.
Item Os sancte Candide virginis.
Item De hanca Sancti martini confessoris.
Ex dono domini iohannis del wich canonici nostri.

f. 35v b.
Dens sancti wulstani.
Item dens sancti Aidani episcopi.
Omnes iste reliquie superius nominata perquisite fuerunt per Reges
et magnates et alios bonos uiros in diuersis Regionibus: et date huic
monasterio Sancte Crucis de Waltham. Per quarum merita fiunt
miracula multa. Anime eorum et omnium bona hunc ecclesie
faciencium vel conferencium per misericordiam ihesu christi in pace
requiescant sine fine. Amen.

Symeon of Durham and the Community of Durham in the Eleventh Century

DAVID ROLLASON

Symeon of Durham's *History of the Church of Durham*, or more properly *Libellus de exordio atque procursu...Dunhelmensis ecclesie*, was written at Durham between the years 1104 and 1107.[1] It describes the foundation of the monastery of Lindisfarne and its early history, particularly as regards its principal saint, Cuthbert, the Viking attacks on Lindisfarne, and the eventual departure in 875 of the community bearing the undecayed body of St Cuthbert. It then tells how the community was transformed from a monastic body to one of secular clerks, how it settled in 883 in Chester-le-Street a few miles to the north of Durham, and how in 995 it moved finally to Durham. Symeon follows the history of the community at Durham in the eleventh century, but what was for him the climax of his story came in 1083, when the second Norman bishop of Durham, William of St Calais, replaced the secular clerks of this community with monks and established the cathedral of Durham as the Benedictine monastery which it was to remain until the Dissolution. Symeon's *Libellus* ends with William of St Calais beginning work on the great Norman cathedral, followed by his death in 1096.

The need to justify the introduction of monks to Durham in 1083 was arguably Symeon's chief purpose in writing his *Libellus* and that is also the principal subject of this paper. Let us look in more detail at Symeon's account of how monks came to Durham. It begins at the monastery of Winchcombe in Gloucestershire. There a monk called Aldwin had 'learned from the *History of the English* [presumably Bede's *Ecclesiastical History of the English People*] that the province of the Northumbrians had once been full of

[1] For the text, *Symeonis monachi Opera omnia*, ed. T. Arnold, 2 vols, RS (London, 1882-85), I, pp. 3-135. I am preparing an edition and translation for Oxford Medieval Texts. The attribution of the work to Symeon, which seems likely and is accepted in this paper, is admittedly not entirely certain. For a sceptical view of this as well as a discussion of the general character of the work, see A. Gransden, *Historical Writing in England c.550 to c.1307* (London, 1974), pp. 114-21. The date of the composition can be fixed because in its original version the work referred to the translation of St Cuthbert in 1104 (*Symeonis Opera*, I, p. 34) and to Turgot as still fulfilling the office of prior (*ibid.*, p. 111 n. a). Turgot ceased to be prior when he was nominated Bishop of St Andrews in 1107 (*Symeonis Opera* II, p. 204 and, for the date of Turgot's predecessor's death, p. 213). Cf. H. S. Offler, *Medieval Historians of Durham* (Durham, 1958), pp. 6-8. My debt to the late Professor Offler will be clear from the footnotes which follow. I should like also to acknowledge the many suggestions made to me by participants at the 1990 Harlaxton Symposium.

choirs of monks and many armies of saints'.[2] He accordingly went to Evesham where, having recruited a deacon called Ælfwig and an unlettered man called Reinfred, he and his two companions set off for the north in 1073-74. They settled first at Monkchester (that is, Newcastle) but the first Norman bishop of Durham, Walcher (1071-80), transferred them to the then ruined monastery of Jarrow which they re-established and there lived in poverty. Symeon tells us that Walcher, although himself a secular clerk, in fact wished to become a monk and to establish monks at Durham, but he was murdered in 1080 and the latter task was left to his successor William of St Calais (1080-96).[3] In Symeon's words,

> he asked the senior and wiser men of the whole bishopric how things had happened with St Cuthbert in the beginning, and they replied that his episcopal see had been on the island of Lindisfarne and that during his life and when in his grave he had been served there reverently by monks. Their assertion was in agreement with the little book about his life [presumably Bede's prose *Life of St Cuthbert*] and with the *Ecclesiastical History of the English People*.[4]

Spurred on by these historical observations, St Calais consulted William I, Queen Matilda and, for good measure, Pope Gregory VII; duly encouraged by them, he proceeded to expel the secular clerks from Durham, replacing them with the monks whom Walcher had established at Jarrow, and made their leader, Aldwin of Winchcombe, prior of the new cathedral monastery.[5]

This attractive and often-repeated story imbues the establishment of the monastic regime at Durham with an aura of piety and sanctity, and links the episode directly to the northern monastic reformation which, stemming from Aldwin's mission, is supposed to have led to the revival not only of Jarrow but also of Tynemouth, Wearmouth and Whitby and to have had a major impact on the Cistercian movement of the twelfth century.[6] Our problem is to consider whether Symeon told the whole truth about the introduction of monks to Durham, particularly as regards the motives and purposes of the two Norman bishops, Walcher and St Calais. Can we accept Symeon's picture of the influence on them of the piety of Aldwin and his companions

---

2 *Symeonis Opera*, I, p.108 (III.21).

3 *Ibid.*, pp.108-13 (III.21-22).

4 *Ibid.*, p.120 (IV.2).

5 *Ibid.*, pp.121-24 (IV.2-3).

6 *Ibid.*, p.111 (III.22) and p.124 (IV.4). See also *Symeonis Opera* II, pp.201-13, and *Cartularium Abbathiae de Whitby*, ed. R. J. Atkinson, Surtees Soc. 69 (Durham, 1879), pp.1-8. For modern discussions, see for example D. Knowles, *The Monastic Order in England* (Cambridge, 1966), pp.159-71, and L. G. D. Baker, 'The Desert in the North', *Northern History*, 5 (1971), 1-11.

and of the writings of Bede? Is there reason to suspect that there were in fact political considerations?

It is important first of all to emphasise that Symeon's *Libellus* is anything but an historical account. On the one hand, it has a strongly hagiographical character, being replete with miracle stories such as the account of how, on the community's wanderings, the bishop of Lindisfarne wished to take the saint's body to Ireland but was discouraged when waves washed into the boat and turned to blood.[7] Symeon's famous story of the foundation of Durham in 995, in which the site was chosen because Cuthbert's body became too heavy to move at a place near the peninsula of Durham and the saint's wishes regarding the choice of the site for his church were then made known by means of a vision, is of course simply another miracle story of a type found elsewhere in hagiographical literature.[8] On the other hand, Symeon's *Libellus* seems starkly propagandist. We know from other sources that his hero William of St Calais joined Odo of Bayeux's revolt in 1088, 'doing as Judas did to our Lord' as the *Anglo-Saxon Chronicle* puts it,[9] but Symeon glosses over this treachery and contrives to make St Calais appear as an injured party: 'Dissension arose between bishop and king as a result of the machinations of others.'[10] The exile which the Council of Salisbury consequently imposed on the bishop is treated as a fruitful visit to Normandy: 'The bishop was expelled from his bishopric and went overseas, where the Duke of the Normans received him not as an exile but as a father, and held him in great honour during the three years that he stayed with him.'[11]

This propagandist tendency is equally apparent in Symeon's treatment of the history of the Lindisfarne community. His aim seems to be to present the introduction of monks to Durham in 1083 as a natural consequence of that history, to which end he makes the implausible and surely propagandist claim that until the accession of Walcher, with the sole exception of the brief and unhappy episcopate of Eadred in 1040, the bishops of the community whether at Lindisfarne, Chester-le-Street or Durham had always been monks,

7   *Symeonis Opera* I, p. 64 (II.11).

8   *Ibid.*, pp. 78-80 (III.1); cf., for example, *Symeonis Opera* II, p.10, and J. Raine, *The Priory of Hexham*, I, Surtees Soc. 44 (Durham, 1864), pp. 209-10.

9   *Two of the Saxon Chronicles Parallel*, ed. C. Plummer and J. Earle, 2 vols (Oxford, 1892), I, p.222 (s.a. 1087, *recte* 1088). For other sources, see E. A. Freeman, *The Reign of William Rufus* (Oxford, 1882), II, pp. 469-74, who concludes 'we can have little doubt in accepting the fact of the Bishop's treason.'

10   *Symeonis Opera* I, p .128 (IV.81).

11   H. S. Offler, 'William of St. Calais, First Norman Bishop of Durham', *Trans. Architect. Archaeol. Soc. Durham Northumberland*, 10 (1946-53), 258-79 at pp.271-72.

even though after 875 the community itself consisted of secular clerks.[12] Not only is this improbable, but the fact, known from the text called the *Siege of Durham*, that the founder of Durham, Bishop Ealdhun, was a father casts doubt on his alleged monastic status.[13]

The propagandist elements in Symeon's *Libellus* should be seen against a background of historical forgery and distortion in twelfth-century Durham. This concerned particularly the events of William of St Calais's episcopate, for the episcopal charters and papal bulls relating to the events of 1083 are palpable forgeries. Although most of these spurious documents were apparently compiled in the time of Bishop Hugh du Puiset (1153-95), the earliest, which draws extensively on Symeon's narrative, is copied into the *Liber Vitae* of Durham and may date from the period immediately after the composition of the *Libellus*, perhaps before 1123.[14] Moreover, if we accept H. S. Offler's unanswered case, the first half of the twelfth century saw the compilation at Durham of the *De Iniusta Vexacione Willelmi Episcopi Primi*, a tractate designed to exonerate William of St Calais from the charge of treachery by presenting a fictitious account of his trial at Salisbury in 1088, representing him as the defender of ecclesiastical privileges rather than the traitor to the English king which he obviously was.[15] In view of all this, we cannot adopt Symeon's account of the introduction of monks to Durham uncritically, and we shall now turn to a detailed consideration, beginning with the problem of the condition of the clerical community in the years before 1083.

---

12 *Symeonis Opera* I, pp. 57-58 (II.6), p. 86 (III.6) and p. 91 (III.9).

13 Printed in *Symeonis Opera* II, pp. 215-20.

14 The discussion in *Feodarium Prioratus Dunelmensis*, ed. W. Greenwell, Surtees Soc. 58 (Durham, 1871), pp.xxvii-lxxxi, has been superseded by G. V. Scammell, *Hugh du Puiset, Bishop of Durham* (Cambridge, 1956), pp. 300-07. A definitive edition of the purported charters of St Calais and minor revisions of Scammell's datings are to be found in *Durham Episcopal Charters 1071-1152*, ed. H. S. Offler, Surtees Soc. 179 (Gateshead, 1968), nos 3-7. The *Liber Vitae* charter is no. 3, printed and discussed pp.6-15. For a facsimile, see *Liber Vitae Ecclesiae Dunelmensis*, ed. A. H. Thompson, Surtees Soc. 136 (Durham, 1923), ff. 49r-50r.

15 H. S. Offler, 'The tractate *De Iniusta Vexacione Willelmi Episcopi Primi*', *EHR*, 66 (1951), 321-41. The numerous attacks on this study (e.g. R. W. Southern, *Saint Anselm and his Biographer* (Cambridge, 1963), p. 148 and n.1, Gransden, *Historical Writing*, p. 122 and n.113, and M. Gibson, *Lanfranc of Bec* (Oxford, 1978), pp. 220-21) do not seem to weaken the main thrust of Offler's case and are effectively rebutted in *De iniusta vexacione Willelmi episcopi primi per Willelmum regem fil<l>lium Willelmi Magni Regis*, ed. H. S. Offler (unpublished typescript). I am very grateful to the late Professor Offler for giving me a copy of this edition.

Symeon's description makes it clear that he regarded the state of the clerical community as a major justification for its dissolution. Regarding the expulsion of the clerks, he wrote:

> The bishop ordered that those who had previously dwelt in the church, and who had had the name only of canons since they in no way followed the rule of canons, should henceforth lead their lives with the monks and as monks if they wished to reside in the church.

With one exception they did refuse and the community was duly dispersed.[16] Doubt is cast on this picture, however, by other statements in the *Libellus*. There would appear to be some contradiction between the passage quoted above and that in which Symeon says that in the years after 1070 Bishop Walcher 'when he found clerics there [at Durham], taught them to observe the customs of clerics in the day and night office'.[17] It is possible that Walcher's work had been undone before 1083, but it seems unlikely. Moreover, Symeon's incidental references to the pre-Conquest community of Durham suggest that he knew very well that it was by no means the disreputable body whose allegedly lax condition he wished to use as a justification for the events of 1083. Although in connection with the election of Bishop Edmund in c.1020 he says damningly that 'it was hard for any of them to give up the joys of the world, to relinquish the charms of life, to eschew pleasures' (i.e. to take on the duties of a bishop),[18] elsewhere he praises ' the innocence and pious simplicity of the men of that time' (that is, the earlier eleventh century);[19] and it is notable that the witnesses he cites to pre-1083 miracle stories involving the Durham community are often members of that community who are clearly still held in high esteem, as in the case of 'certain devout priests who ... are now advanced in age and entirely crippled'.[20] Moreover the member of the pre-1083 community about whom Symeon knew most was the sacristan Alfred son of Westou. His zeal for the collection and translation of relics placed Durham on a par with the enthusiasm for this type of pious activity pursued by the reformed monasteries of the south, and so also did his concern for education.[21] In Symeon's words, 'He was very assiduous in the education of the boys who

16   *Symeonis Opera* I, pp. 122-3 (IV.3).

17   *Ibid.*, p. 106 (III.18).

18   *Ibid.*, p. 85 (III.6).

19   *Ibid.*, pp. 89-90 (III.7).

20   *Ibid.*, p. 82 (III.3); cf. p. 86 (III.6), p. 94 (III.10), p. 101 (III.15), and p. 102 (III.16).

21   *Ibid.*, pp. 87-90 (III.7). On southern relic-translations, see D. W. Rollason, 'The Shrines of Saints in Later Anglo-Saxon England: Distribution and Significance', in *The Anglo-Saxon Church: Papers on History, Architecture and Archaeology in Honour of Dr H. M. Taylor*, ed. L. A. S. Butler and R. Morris (London, 1986), pp. 32-43.

were being trained for the service of God, and every day he would attend to teaching them singing and reading and to informing them about the offices of the church.' It appears that one of his pupils was living in Symeon's day and had become a monk.

The impression given by all this is that, regardless of what Symeon wished to represent in connection with the clerical community's expulsion, its standards were not in fact so debased. This impression is confirmed by independent evidence. Edmund Craster's reconstruction of a chronicle which was preserved in the *Liber Magni Altaris* at Durham and was written between 1072 and 1083 shows that the clerical community of Walcher's time was scholarly and literate and had historical interests which were by no means dissimilar to Symeon's.[22] Earlier on, in 970, the community had acquired the so-called *Rituale Dunelmensis ecclesie*, a collectar written in southern England, to which they added various materials including collects for St Cuthbert, hymns which are amongst the earliest examples of the introduction of the New Hymnal into England in the early eleventh century, and miscellaneous pieces such as a list of the resting-places of the apostles and an account of the 'octo pondera de quibus factus est Adam' which suggest a certain amount of learning and of scholarly activity. A similar impression is given by the handwriting which, while not good by southern standards, shows a progressive modernisation of script through the early eleventh century.[23]

Further evidence of the religious devotion of the secular clerks is furnished by a carved cross-head (Pl.7), one of a group of four recovered from the foundations of the Norman chapter house at Durham and dated to the early eleventh century.[24] One of these shows on one side a lamb and on the other a scene generally interpreted as a baptism. According to the following interpretation, the former would seem to be a representation of Revelation 4. The lamb has its foot on a rectangle which represents the book with seven seals and the arms of the cross have four winged figures which are the creatures surrounding the throne in John's vision. The human heads in relief on the upper arm, one full-face and one profile, however, represent the sun and moon of Crucifixion iconography; including the cross and the raised circle in front of the lamb which may represent the host, the iconographic

---

[22] H. H. E. Craster, 'The Red Book of Durham', *EHR*, 40 (1925), 504-32, at pp.523-32.

[23] *The Durham Ritual: A Southern English Collectar of the Tenth Century with Northumbrian Additions: Durham Cathedral Library A.IV.19*, ed. T. J. Brown, Early English Manuscripts in Facsimile 16 (Copenhagen, 1969), and, on the hymns, H. Gneuss, *Hymnar und Hymnen im englischen Mittelalter* (Tübingen, 1968), pp.101-02.

[24] R. Cramp, *Corpus of Anglo-Saxon Stone Sculpture, Volume I. County Durham and Northumberland*, 2 vols (Oxford, 1984), Durham nos 5-8 (pp.68-72 and pls 43-47).

programme of this face may be intended to link Revelation 4 with John 1.29 and thus with the eucharistic liturgy, particularly the *Dona nobis pacem* chant introduced in the early eleventh century. Such an association would suggest a link with the opposite face which shows an eagle, representing John, and a baptism scene (note the ladle for the baptismal oil) which relates to John's 'Lamb of God which taketh away the sins of the world'.[25]

In addition to this cross and its companions, there also survive from the early eleventh century a coped grave cover from the Durham chapter house and a cross which, although found in the fabric of the church of St Oswald just across the river Wear from Durham cathedral, is presumed to have been produced by or for the cathedral clerks.[26] These objects indicate a fairly high level of craftsmanship in the Durham community, and are notable for their use of earlier Northumbrian styles of interlace; they suggest that the clerical community had just the same interest in establishing the continuity of their history with the pre-Viking past which is such a dominant theme of Symeon's *Libellus*.

One accusation could nevertheless have been levelled at the clerks of Durham: they were married. Alfred son of Westou had a wife from the family of the priests of Hexham,[27] and the clerks who were supposed to have carried St Cuthbert's body on its wanderings were the founders of clerical families.[28] It might be argued that, in the context of the late eleventh-century

25   *Ibid.*, no. 5 (pp. 68-69 and pls 43-44). The iconography is discussed by E. Coatsworth, 'Four Cross-Heads from the Chapter House, Durham', in *Anglo-Saxon and Viking Age Sculpture and its Context: Papers from the Collingwood Symposium on Insular Sculpture from 800 to 1066*, ed. J. Lang, BAR, British Series 49 (Oxford, 1978), pp. 85-96, citing in connection with 'Dona Nobis Pacem' M. Dolley, 'The Nummular Brooch from Sulgrave', in *England before the Conquest*, ed. P. Clemoes and K. Hughes (Cambridge, 1971), pp. 333-49, especially pp.342-45. Cf. B. Raw, 'The Archer, the Eagle and the Lamb', *Jnl Warb. Court. Insts* 30 (1967), 391-94.

26   The grave cover is described in Cramp, *Corpus: Durham and Northumberland*, as Durham 11 (pp.49-50) and the St Oswald's cross as Durham 1 (pp. 66-67 and pls. 37-38). On these see also R. Cramp, 'A Cross from St Oswald's Church, Durham, and its Stylistic Relationships', *Durham Univ. Jnl*, 57 (1966), 119-24, and R. Cramp, 'The Pre-Conquest Tradition in Durham', in *Medieval Art and Architecture in Durham Cathedral*, ed. N. Coldstream and P. Draper (London, 1980), pp 1-10. Other sculptures from the Durham chapter house and St Oswald's Church dated to the late 10th or early 11th century are Cramp, *Corpus: Durham and Northumberland*, Durham nos 2-4, 9-10 and 12.

27   *Priory of Hexham*, ed. Raine, pp. lv-lxii and lxvii-lxviii; and Walter Daniel, *The Life of Ailred of Rievaulx*, ed. F. M. Powicke (London, 1950), pp.xxxiv-xxxv.

28   *Symeonis Opera* I, pp. 79-80 (III.1), on which see D. J. Hall, *The Community of St Cuthbert: Its Properties, Rights and Claims from the Ninth Century to the Twelfth* (unpublished D.Phil. thesis, University of Oxford, 1984), pp.109-19. I am very

Gregorian reforms with their emphasis on clerical celibacy, this was what Symeon really had against them and this was why, whatever their achievements and standards, they had to be replaced.[29] No doubt this consideration played a part in the events of 1083, but if so it might have been anticipated that William of St Calais would simply have regularized the clerical community as, according to Symeon, Bishop Walcher had already begun to do.[30] However, it can be doubted whether the issue of clerical celibacy was a prime consideration at that time, for Gregorian ideas of celibacy may not have made much progress in northern England by the late eleventh century.[31] Ranulf Flambard, bishop of Durham (1099-1128), was himself married;[32] and Archbishop Thomas of York did not find it a straightforward matter to replace the clerks of Hexham with regular canons in c.1112, although there is no doubt that they too were married. F. M. Powicke commented that these clerks, the last of whom was the father of Ailred of Rievaulx, were 'learned, respectable, conscientious' and further that 'if there were many such families in Northumbria, it is easy to understand why the movement for a celibate clergy made such slow progress in the eleventh and twelfth centuries'.[33] Such considerations may also explain Symeon's otherwise puzzling reluctance to use the married status of the clerks as ammunition against them. It is true that he was the first to introduce the notion that St Cuthbert himself avoided women, but it is not clear that this quite fallacious picture of the saint as misogynist was really a veiled attack on the married clerks, as Victoria Tudor has suggested.[34] One of Symeon's stories concerning the earlier eleventh century is of a woman who was struck down and died after putting a foot inside the churchyard of the cathedral, because she had thus offended the saint with her female

---

grateful to Dr Hall for permission to use this work.

[29] A. Fliche, *La Réforme grégorienne et la Reconquête chrétienne (1057-1123)* (Paris, 1946), pp. 30-32 and passim.

[30] *Symeonis Opera* I, p. 106 (III.18).

[31] C. Brooke 'Gregorian Reform in Action: Clerical Marriage in England, 1050-1200', in his *Medieval Church and Society: Collected Essays* (London, 1971), pp. 69-99, esp. pp. 82-83.

[32] Brooke, *Medieval Church*, p. 87 and H. S. Offler, 'Rannulf Flambard as Bishop of Durham (1099-1128)', *Durham Univ. Jnl*, 64 (1971), 14-28, esp. pp. 22-23.

[33] J. Raine, *The Priory of Hexham*, 1, Surtees Soc. 44 (Durham, 1864), l-lxviii, and Walter Daniel, *Life of Ailred*, ed. F. M. Powicke (London, 1950), pp. xxxiv-xxv.

[34] *Symeonis Opera* I, pp. 58-60 (III.7). See A. J. Piper, 'The First Generations of Durham Monks and the Cult of St Cuthbert', in *St Cuthbert, his Cult and his Community to AD 1200*, ed. G. Bonner, D. Rollason and C. Stancliffe (Woodbridge, 1989), pp. 437-46, at p. 443, criticizing V. Tudor, 'The Misogyny of St Cuthbert', *Archaeologia Aeliana*, 5th series, 12 (1984), 157-67.

presence. This story could easily have been arranged to feature one of the wives of the clerks, but in fact it names the woman in question as a servant of Tostig's wife Judith who was anxious to test the truth of stories concerning the saint's antipathy to the female sex.[35] Another miracle story concerns the priest for whom the host tasted insufferably bitter when he celebrated mass the day after sleeping with his concubine. Here too the story could have been turned against the clerks of Durham but in fact it was not – it appears that the priest in question was a parish priest.[36]

In any case the later history of the Durham clerks suggests that *pace* Symeon, their influence and respectability were such that they could not be simply dispersed without provision being made for them. In the earliest manuscript of Symeon's *Libellus*, the early twelfth-century Durham, University Library, Cosins MS V.ii.6, some fourteen lines were erased at a point in the narrative where we might have expected an account of the fate of the canons (ff.80v-81r). This erasure was evidently made soon after the *Libellus*'s composition, for there is no trace of the original text in another copy of the *Libellus* made very soon afterwards (BL, Cotton MS Faustina A.v). In the early fourteenth-century copy in York, Minster Library, MS XVI.I.12, however, there is at the point of the narrative where there occurs the erasure in Cosins V.ii.6 an account of how the sustenance of the displaced canons was provided for by the establishment of prebends at Auckland (presumably St Andrew Auckland at South Church), Norton (near Stockton), Darlington and Easington (both in County Durham).[37] To judge from the

<hr/>

35   *Symeonis Opera* I, pp. 94-95 (III.11).

36   *Ibid.*, pp. 93-94 (III.10). In a vision experienced by a knight called Boso (*ibid.*, pp.130-33 (IV.9)), married priests are represented as awaiting the fires of hell, but they are not specifically associated with the clerks of Durham and they are only one of several classes for whom an evil fate was prepared.

37   This version of the *Libellus* in York XVI.I.12 seems to have been copied into Oxford, Bodleian Library, MS Fairfax 6, but the scribe mis-read *Esington* as *Ekington* (f.239v). The account of Auckland, Norton, Darlington and Easington is found also in the version of the *Libellus* in Oxford, Bodleian Library, MS Laud misc. 700, which may be a copy of Fairfax 6 but where *Ekington* appears as *Egington* (f.61v). Both these manuscripts are of mid- to late-14th-century date. An early modern archaicizing hand has inserted the account (with the form *Ekington*) over part of the erasure in Cosins V.ii.6; and another version omitting the name of Easington altogether has been added in the lower margin at the appropriate place in another copy of the *Libellus* in the early 14th-century manuscript BL Cotton MS Titus A.ii. There is no evidence that the account is earlier than York XVI.I.12 and it must be admitted as a possibility that it is an early-14th-century invention (Mr Martin Snape, pers. comm.). Cf. A. Hamilton Thompson, 'The Collegiate Churches of the Bishopric of Durham', *Durham Univ. Jnl*, n.s. 5 (1944), 33-42; J. Blair, 'Secular Minster Churches in Domesday Book', in *Domesday Book: A Reassessment*, ed. P. Sawyer (London, 1985), p.132 n.135; and

fine eleventh-century cruciform church at Norton and from the grand later medieval churches at St Andrew Auckland and Darlington, these places were not places of ignominious exile, but respectable bases for clerks lacking neither abilities nor pretensions.[38]

In short, Symeon's claim that the establishment of monks at Durham in 1083 was explicable in terms of the state of the clerical community will not pass muster. The expulsion of the clerks was by no means a self-evident necessity for the Norman bishops – indeed a document of 1136 shows that even by that date the monks were still in a position of having to justify their take-over of the church of Durham to the papal court on the grounds (which we now see to be spurious) of the 'depraved and incorrigible behaviour of the secular clerks'.[39] Moreover, we should emphasise that there was nothing inevitable about a Norman bishop, even a monk like St Calais, wishing to have a cathedral served by monks. In many respects a clerical community would surely have been more attractive, notably because of the patronage which it placed in the bishop's hands and the control to which it could be subjected, and indeed we find that from the time of du Puiset, if not before, the bishops seem to have thought better of it and were striving to introduce into their diocese secular communities to counterbalance the power of the Durham monks.[40]

With this in mind, we must turn to consider Symeon's account of Bishop Walcher's motives and actions and in particular his statement that Walcher wished to become a monk himself and to establish monks at his cathedral.[41] There is no corroboration of this and, despite Walcher's alleged contacts with the monks of Jarrow, it seems inherently improbable.[42] Walcher was a

Hall, 'Community of St Cuthbert', p. 118. For a full account of this problem, see my forthcoming edition.

[38] N. Pevsner, *The Buildings of England: County Durham*, 2nd edn, revised E. Williamson (Harmondsworth, 1983), pp. 140-3 and 411-13 and, on Norton, H. M. and J. Taylor, *Anglo-Saxon Architecture*, I (Cambridge, 1965), pp. 465-70. Note Hamilton Thompson's suggestion that St Calais established the clerks in three places so that 'by distributing them here or there he could keep them in check' ('Collegiate Churches', p. 33).

[39] Donald Nicholl, *Thurstan, Archbishop of York (1114-1140)* (York, 1964), p. 91, citing MS Eccl. Dun. Cartuarium Vetus, f.13r.

[40] Hamilton Thompson, 'Collegiate Churches', pp. 33-34. See also Scammell, *Hugh du Puiset*, pp. 109-10.

[41] *Symeonis Opera* I, p. 113 (III.22).

[42] *Ibid.*, pp. 110-13 (III.22). The purported charter of Earl Waltheof granting Tynemouth to the monks of Jarrow in 1074-75 refers to Walcher's plans to transfer the monks to Durham (printed Offler, *Episcopal Charters*, no.5a, pp.45-46) and is accepted as corroboration of Symeon's account by F. M. Stenton, *Anglo-Saxon England*, 3rd edn (Oxford, 1971), p. 678 n.2. The charter seems,

secular priest of the church of Liège and is hardly likely to have thought naturally in terms of a monastic cathedral.[43] Moreover, his reform of the clerical community as described by Symeon suggests that what he really had in mind was a revamped secular church rather than a cathedral monastery. This impression is strengthened by the fact that he had William I grant him the church of Waltham, a house of regular canons with Lotharingian connections like his own – a house in fact, as David Hall has pointed out, which would have provided an ideal source of manpower and inspiration for the reform of the Durham community as a house of regular canons.[44]

If Symeon's account of Walcher is thus highly dubious, what of his treatment of William St Calais himself and his alleged consultation of the men of the diocese about the past monastic associations of the see?[45] This is somewhat more plausible. It is true that one of the books given to the Durham monks by this bishop was a copy of Bede's *Ecclesiastical History*.[46] It is also true that, although in origin a secular clerk of the church of Bayeux, William early on in his career became a monk of the monastery of St Calais near Le Mans from which he took his surname; and in 1078 he was made abbot of the monastery of St Vincent at Le Mans.[47] Despite this early career in monastic foundations, it is by no means clear that St Calais's credentials as an enthusiastic patron of monks were really as strong as Symeon maintained. As H. S. Offler has pointed out, the best evidence that Symeon was able to adduce to show St Calais's enthusiasm for monastic life at Durham was the text of a letter which the bishop sent to the monks from his exile in Normandy after his participation in the 1088 revolt and even in Symeon's pages there are hints that St Calais's endowments of the new cathedral monastery fell short of what was needed and expected.[48] Moreover, Symeon

however, to be a forgery based on a later modification of Symeon's *History* which in its original form attributed the gift of Tynemouth to Walcher himself (*Symeonis Opera* I, p. 124 and note 1). The modification of the History and the forgery of this and other charters were part of a long-running battle between Durham and St Albans over possession of Tynemouth (Offler, *Episcopal Charters*, p. 42 and pp. 3-6).

[43] *Dictionary of National Biography*, ed. L. Stephen and S. Lee (Oxford, 1917-), 20, pp. 466-67.

[44] *Symeonis Opera* I, p. 106 (III.18) and pp. 113-14 (III.23); and Hall, 'Community of St Cuthbert', pp. 115-18.

[45] *Symeonis Opera* I, pp. 120-21 (IV.2).

[46] Durham, Cathedral Library MS B.ii.35, on which see R. A. B. Mynors, *Durham Cathedral Manuscripts to the End of the Twelfth Century* (Oxford, 1937), no. 47.

[47] L. Guilloreau, 'Guillaume de Saint-Calais, Évêque de Durham', *Revue historique et archéologique du Maine*, 74 (1913), 209-12 and Offler, 'William of St Calais', pp.260-63.

[48] Offler, 'William of St Calais', p. 270 and *Symeonis Opera* I, p. 124 (IV.3).

included in his work an account of a vision of the other world experienced by a knight of the bishop's household called Boso. The bishop himself featured in this vision in a rather alarming way. In Boso's words:

> Then in a place of vast and foul solitude I saw a house of great height entirely made out of iron, whose door was very often open, very often closed, and suddenly Bishop William put his head out and asked of me where the monk Gosfrid [his procurator] was. 'He should be with me here at the trial,' he said.

When Boso related this vision to him together with the information that it foreshadowed his imminent demise, St Calais 'was much afraid and began thenceforth to take greater care of the health of his soul, making more generous alms, longer and more intent prayers, not allowing any business to put off the demands of his daily private prayer'.[49] No doubt we may charitably attribute his lack of attention to religious life to the demands of his political career, to his work as a Domesday commissioner, to his intolvement in the 1088 revolt, to his dealings with William Rufus and Robert Curthose, and to his leadership of the attacks on Anselm at the Council of Rockingham. As Offler has remarked, 'St Calais was a very political prelate, and in politics his conduct was not pretty'.[50] In short it is hard to accept Symeon's picture of a saintly bishop influenced above all by love of monasticism and respect for the traditions of Lindisfarne as relayed by Bede.

In place of Symeon's clearly propagandist picture, we need to see the introduction of monks to Durham in the wider context of the ecclesio-political situation of early Norman England and particularly of Northumbria, which was in a state of chronic instability in the decades following the Conquest. Robert Cumin, the first Norman earl of Northumbria, never got farther than Durham. As he was staying in that city on his way to the north, Northumbrian insurgents burst in through the city gates, massacred his followers and burned him alive in the house in which he was staying. Native earls such as Waltheof proved rebellious, and the Conqueror's ploy of appointing Bishop Walcher as earl ended when that prelate was mercilessly struck down at Gateshead under circumstances which we must examine a little later.[51]

In such a context, the bishops could not help but be deeply involved in politics and neither could the clerks of Durham. From the time of its

---

[49] *Symeonis Opera* I, 130-32 (IV.9)

[50] Offler, 'William of St Calais', pp. 271-79, and P. Chaplais, 'William of Saint-Calais and the Domesday Survey', in *Domesday Studies*, ed. J. C. Holt (Woodbridge, 1987), pp. 65-77.

[51] W. E. Kapelle, *The Norman Conquest of the North: The Region and its Transformation 1000-1135* (Chapel Hill, 1979), pp. 120-57 and, for an account of Cumin's death, *Symeonis Opera* I, pp. 98-99 (III.15).

foundation, their church, which occupied a defensive site of immense strategic significance, controlling a major route from York northwards to the Tyne and beyond, had been intimately linked with the Northumbrian earls of the house of Bamburgh. Symeon tells us that it was Earl Uhtred of Bamburgh who assisted in clearing the site on the peninsula for Bishop Ealdhun and the community to settle there, and further that the bishop leased lands to the earls when they were in need.[52] The text on the *Siege of Durham* adds that Ealdhun's daughter Ecgfritha was married to Uhtred himself and, if William Kapelle's arguments are correct, the alliance which this union embodied continued even after Ecgfritha's divorce, for her subsequent marriage was part and parcel of a combined campaign by Uhtred and Ealdhun to extend their power into Yorkshire.[53]

Is it possible that a continuing association between the house of Bamburgh and the clerks of Durham played a part in the introduction of monks to Durham in 1083? Although it appears that Bishop Walcher was closely allied with Earl Waltheof of Northumbria, a scion of this house through his mother, Waltheof's revolt in 1075 presumably broke this relationship. Walcher remained loyal to the king and we find Lanfranc instructing him late in 1075 to fortify and provision his castle against the Danes who were to have helped Waltheof.[54] Walcher himself then became earl as well as bishop, only to be murdered by a member of the house of Bamburgh in 1080. Symeon's *Libellus* briefly glosses over the story of this event but 'Florence of Worcester' provides a detailed account.[55] It seems that, presumably to placate the house of Bamburgh, Walcher took as his adviser a man called Ligulf. Although this man was only linked to the house of Bamburgh by marriage, being the husband of Ælfgith, another daughter of Earl Ealdred,[56] 'Florence', who was presumably drawing on some northern source, emphasizes his devotion to St Cuthbert, suggesting that like Uhtred and the line of Bamburgh he was closely associated with the clerks of Durham. Ligulf's position, 'Florence' tells us, aroused the jealousy of Walcher's chaplain Leobwine, who accordingly incited the bishop's kinsman Gilbert to kill Ligulf. Gilbert, to whom Walcher had delegated the administration of the earldom, promptly went at night to the place where Ligulf was staying and massacred him and his whole *familia*. Walcher failed

[52] *Symeonis Opera* I, pp. 80-81 and 83-84 (III.2 and III.4).

[53] *Ibid.*, p. 215, and Kapelle, *Norman Conquest*, p. 16.

[54] *Symeonis Opera* II, p. 200; *The Letters of Lanfranc Archbishop of Canterbury*, ed. H. Clover and M. Gibson (Oxford, 1979), no.36 (pp. 126-27); and Kapelle, *Norman Conquest*, pp. 136-37.

[55] *Symeonis Opera* I, pp.116-18 (III.24), and *Florentii Wigorniensis monachi Chronicon ex chronicis*, ed. B. Thorpe, 2 vols (London, 1848), II, pp. 13-16.

[56] *Symeonis Opera* II, p. 209.

administration of the earldom, promptly went at night to the place where Ligulf was staying and massacred him and his whole *familia*. Walcher failed to dissociate himself from this killing, for he neglected even to remove Gilbert from his entourage and the wrath of the Northumbrians and the house of Bamburgh was not assuaged. Eventually the bishop met them for negotiations at Gateshead but their aim was clearly not peace. As soon as the bishop had gone into the church they proceeded to massacre his companions and then set fire to the church to smoke Gilbert and Leobwine out. Walcher persuaded Gilbert to go out and meet his death but, when Leobwine would not do so, the bishop went to the door of the church and pleaded for his own life. When it was clear that his enemies were implacable, he covered his face with his cloak, left the church and was cut down. The church was then set on fire, Leobwine ran out half-burned and he too was cut down. The bishop's body was taken by the monks of Jarrow and brought to Durham for burial. According to Symeon the 'author' of the murder was a certain Waltheof, probably the son of the exiled Earl Cospatric of the house of Bamburgh, while the *History of the Kings* states that the man who killed Walcher with his own hand was Eadwulf Rus, another scion of the house of Bamburgh.[57]

Table: The House of Bamburgh

Eadulf of Bamburgh (d. 912)
|
Aldred
|
Earl Osulf
|
Earl Waltheof

Earl Uhtred — (1) Ecgfritha	— (2) Sigen	— (3) Ælfgifu
(1006-16)		
Earl Aldred	Earl Eadulf	Gospatric
Ælfleda — Earl Siward	Ælgitha — Ligulf	Uhtred
(1042-55)		
Earl Waltheof		Eadulf Rus
(d. 1075)		

57 *Ibid.*, I, p. 115 (III.23), and II, pp. 197-98 (cf. *ibid.*, II, p. 383, where a slightly different and possibly erroneous version of Eadwulf Rus's parentage is given). See my genealogical table which is extracted from W. Page, 'Some Remarks on the Northumbrian Palatinates and Regalities', *Archaeologia*, 51 (1888), 143-55, at p.155. On the identity of the killers, see Kapelle, *Norman Conquest*, p. 140 and p.271, n. 75, and Hall, 'Community of St Cuthbert', pp. 162-63.

We have seen that on his side Walcher was associated with the monks of Jarrow. In view of their past history, it is hard not to see the clerks of Durham connected in their turn with Ligulf, Eadwulf Rus and the house of Bamburgh. If that is so, we have here a reason why St Calais had to replace them, namely that they were deeply implicated in the house of Bamburgh's treason and thus at least indirectly in the killing of Walcher. That at least, as Offler noted, would seem to be the implication of a passage in a bull of Pope Gregory VII which, although certainly not authentic, may nevertheless embody genuine Durham traditions. The bull refers to the punishment of Walcher's murderers by means of Odo of Bayeux's ravaging of Northumbria, and then notes that the king requested the elimination of the evil-acting clerks of the church of Durham, 'who also arose from the execrable line of those sacrilegious men'.[58] We have here a clear hint that the expulsion of the clerks of Durham was connected with their close links with the house of Bamburgh and with the consequent presumption of some association between them and the death of Walcher.

The introduction of monks to Durham, however, cannot be regarded simply as a reaction to that murder. It must be seen as part of a policy of Norman control of the north. For, even in Symeon's own terms, it is hard to visualize the transformation of the Durham community as deriving from purely local circumstances. Symeon's report that St Calais consulted Lanfranc is significant, for it was Lanfranc who was responsible for the introduction of monks at Canterbury and Rochester and it was Lanfranc's *Monastic Constitutions* which came into the library of the monks of Durham and provided the basis of their observance.[59] In view of St Calais's deficiencies as a monk, we may well suppose that the idea of introducing monks to Durham was as much his as St Calais's, indeed perhaps wholly his. Nor is it clear that Aldwin's mission, without in any way casting doubt on its piety, was really the causative factor in the foundation of the monastery of Durham. As Anne Dawtry has shown, that monastery's learning and culture owed little to English traditions, apart perhaps from a self-conscious desire to establish a spurious continuity with the community of Lindisfarne, and looked rather to the learning of the continent. Neither Durham nor the other northern houses were the 'last bulwark of Anglo-Saxon monasticism'.[60] Rather Durham represented the replacement of a clerical community of very strong and very political local connections with a monastic community which through its celibate nature had at least in origin none of the close connections with local

58 Offler, 'William of St Calais', p. 267 and n.29 and p. 269 n.36, citing W. Holtzmann, *Papsturkunden in England* (Berlin, 1935), 2.2, p. 134.

59 Offler, 'William of St Calais', pp. 268-69.

60 A. Dawtry, 'The Benedictine Revival in the North: The Last Bulwark of Anglo-Saxon Monasticism?', *Studies in Church History*, 18 (1982), 87-98.

society which the clerks may be presumed to have had. The Jarrow monks were ideal for this purpose for by Symeon's account few of them were even Northumbrians; most came from the south.[61]

So the replacement of the secular community of Durham by a monastery may have been as much a part of the advancement of Norman control in the north as of a process of ecclesiastical reform. It may not have been the first attempt by kings of England to use such means of increasing their control over Durham, for it is possible that such an aim lay behind the appointment of Æthelric (1041-56) and Æthelwine (1056-72), two Peterborough monks, as successive bishops of Durham. Certainly it was deeply resented by the clerks of Durham.[62] The history of eleventh-century Durham thus assumes importance in the whole question of the relationship between monastic reform and political control in the eleventh century. The same question should be asked of the other northern reformed monasteries of the period, not least those deriving from Aldwin's mission: Durham was not alone in having close links with the Norman political settlement in the north.[63] When Aldwin sought to re-establish the abbey of Melrose the king of Scotland had no doubt that there were political overtones, for he showed himself anxious to obtain the oaths of allegiance of the monks.[64] The picture resulting from such an interpretation may not be as pretty as the charming scenes from Symeon's Libellus with which we began but it is perhaps closer to the reality of life in northern England in the late eleventh century.

[61] Symeonis Opera I, pp. 109-10 (III.21).

[62] Symeonis Opera I, pp. 86-87 (III.6), pp. 91-92 (III.9), and p. 94 (III.11). Cf. Hall, 'Community of St Cuthbert', pp. 101-02, Kapelle, Norman Conquest, pp. 32-33, and B. Meehan, 'Outsiders, Insiders and Property in Durham around 1100', Studies in Church History, 12 (1975), 45-58, esp. pp. 47-53.

[63] Dawtry, 'Benedictine Revival', pp. 93-94.

[64] Symeonis Opera I, pp. 111-12 (III.22), but cf. the interpretation of R. H. C. Davis, 'Bede after Bede', Studies in Medieval History Presented to R. Allen Brown, ed. C. Harper-Bill, C. J. Holdsworth, J. L. Nelson (Woodbridge, 1989), pp. 103-16, at p.109.

The Dissemination of Wulfstan's Homilies: the Wulfstan Tradition in Eleventh-Century Vernacular Preaching
JONATHAN WILCOX

Archbishop Wulfstan describes the responsibilities of bishops in the *Institutes of Polity*:

> Bisceopas syndon bydelas and Godes lage lareowas, and hi sculan riht bodian and unriht forbeodan... And gif bisceopas forgymað, þæt hi synna ne styrað ne unriht forbeodað ne Godes riht ne cyþað, ac clumiað mid ceaflum, þæt hi sceoldan clypian, wa heom þære swigean![1]

> Bishops are heralds and teachers of God's law, and they must preach right and forbid wrong... And if bishops neglect to punish sins or forbid injustice or make known God's law, but mumble with their jaws, where they ought to call out, woe to them for that silence![2]

He speaks in similar terms of the duties of the priest: 'Ægðer hi sculan, ge wel bodian ge wel bysnian oðrum mannum'.[3] Wulfstan's contribution to 'preaching well' is a collection of sermons dealing with the fundamentals of the faith and with the need for moral reform, composed in a striking and memorable rhetorical style. The significance of Wulfstan's preaching in England in the eleventh century and beyond can be seen: (1) from the manuscript distribution of his sermons; and (2) from the use of his works by later sermon writers. In this paper I will attempt to measure Wulfstan's impact on preaching in eleventh-century England by assembling both forms of evidence.

Wulfstan and Ælfric were the two most significant literary figures produced by the tenth-century monastic reform in England and their work is often compared.[4] Wulfstan's career differed considerably from Ælfric's, as does the corpus of his works. Bishop of London 996-1002, Bishop of Worcester and Archbishop of York 1002-16, and Archbishop of York until

---

1   II Polity, §§42-43, ed. K. Jost, *Die 'Institutes of Polity, Civil and Ecclesiastical'*, Swiss Studies in English, 47 (Berne, 1959), pp. 62-63.

2   All translations are my own unless otherwise noted.

3   II Polity, §103; ed. Jost, pp. 84-85: 'They must both preach well and set a good example to other men.'

4   See, for example, P. A. M. Clemoes, 'Late Old English Literature', *Tenth-Century Studies: Essays in Commemoration of the Millennium of the Council of Winchester and 'Regularis Concordia'*, ed. D. Parsons (London, 1975), pp. 103-14 and 230-33; or, for a more political account, P. A. Stafford, 'Church and Society in the Age of Ælfric', in *The Old English Homily and Its Backgrounds*, ed. P. E. Szarmach and B. F. Huppé (Albany, NY, 1978), pp. 11-42.

his death in 1023,[5] Wulfstan led a more active public life than Ælfric, monk and mass-priest and subsequently abbot. Wulfstan also produced a considerably smaller body of writing than did Ælfric.

There is plentiful evidence for establishing the corpus of Wulfstan's works. The *nom de plume*, 'Lupus', demonstrates Wulfstan's authorship of five sermons and three penitential letters, while two other works were circulated under his real name.[6] He wrote in a distinctive style, both in terms of lexical and syntactic choice and in terms of rhythm, which has made it possible to identify further works written by him.[7] The task of identification is made easier in that certain manuscripts are closely associated with his works: copies survive of a 'commonplace book' which comprised works of interest to him as potential sources and ten manuscripts survive which contain annotations by him.[8] From these sources of evidence the Wulfstan canon has been established by Jost, Bethurum, and Whitelock.[9]

The corpus of Wulfstan's homiletic works comprises the homilies edited by Bethurum and additional undeveloped homiletic pieces.[10] My list of such additional pieces comprises those edited by Napier[11] as his homilies I (in MSS CL),[12] XXIII, XXIV, XXV, XXVII, XXXV, XXXVI (?), XXXVIII (?),

5　He probably gave up Worcester to a suffragan in 1016. For summary accounts of Wulfstan's life and career, see D. Bethurum, *The Homilies of Wulfstan* (Oxford, 1957), pp. 54-68 and D. Whitelock, *Sermo Lupi ad Anglos*, 3rd edn (London, 1963), pp. 7-17.

6　'Lupus' is used in three penitential letters dating from his London episcopate and printed by Bethurum, *Homilies*, appendix 2; in the rubric 'Incipiunt Sermones Lupi Episcopi' preceding the sequence Bethurum VI and Bethurum VII in three manuscripts; in the rubric to the famous *Sermo Lupi ad Anglos* (Bethurum XX) in three of its five manuscripts; in the rubric to Bethurum XXI in one of its four manuscripts; and in the rubric to Napier LIX in its unique manuscript. Explicit attribution to Wulfstan is made in the opening of one version of Bethurum XIII and in the Latin version of the law-code V/VI Æthelred.

7　See, respectively, K. Jost, *Wulfstanstudien*, Swiss Studies in English, 23 (Berne, 1950) and A. McIntosh, 'Wulfstan's Prose', *Proc. Brit. Acad.*, 35 (1949), 109-42.

8　See D. Bethurum, 'Archbishop Wulfstan's Commonplace Book', *PMLA*, 57 (1942), 916-29 and N. Ker, 'The Handwriting of Archbishop Wulfstan', in *England Before the Conquest: Studies in Primary Sources Presented to Dorothy Whitelock*, ed. P. Clemoes and K. Hughes (Cambridge, 1971), pp. 315-31.

9　For considered statements, see Jost, *Wulfstanstudien*, *passim*, Bethurum, *Homilies*, pp. 24-49, and Whitelock, *Sermo Lupi*, 3rd edn, pp. 17-28.

10　See Bethurum's principles of exclusion, *Homilies*, pp. 36-41.

11　A. Napier, *Wulfstan: Sammlung der ihm zugeschriebenen Homilien* (1883; repr. with a bibliographical appendix by K. Ostheeren, Zürich, 1967).

12　See below, pp. 204-05.

L, LI, LII, LIII, LIX, LX, LXI, along with the Copenhagen fragment,[13] the traces in BL, Add. MS 38651, ff. 57-58,[14] and a number of the pieces edited by Jost in the appendices to his edition of *Polity*, namely appendices a, b, c, e, k (?).[15]

Wulfstan's homiletic works are rarely expositions of a pericope; generally they expound straightforward catechetical instruction or centre on eschatological themes, especially in relation to a perception of current moral and political decline. His other writings share similar preoccupations. Instruction is pursued in the pastoral letters, while the degeneration of society is addressed by the law-codes and, in a more general way, by the *Institutes of Polity*. There is a substantial overlap between Wulfstan's sermons and his legal writings. He uses both to teach 'God's law... preach right and forbid wrong'. Such overlap is particularly obvious in pieces like Napier LIX-LXI, where homiletic injunctions are created from a collection of legal statements. Nevertheless, Wulfstan's legal writings have a different status from his homiletic writings: the law-codes reflect the outcome of legislative meetings of the king and his counsellors.[16] The dissemination of the law-codes and of the pastoral letters have been discussed by other scholars;[17] I shall confine my consideration to the homiletic texts.

The dissemination of Ælfric's homilies provides a useful point of comparison. The surviving manuscripts demonstrate the considerable popularity of Ælfric's writings: there are twenty-four surviving major manuscripts drawing on the *Catholic Homilies*, nine fragments 'probably from large collections' and six manuscripts with just one or two homilies.[18] These manuscripts provide evidence for the circulation of Ælfric's homilies to Canterbury, Rochester, Winchester, Worcester, the West Midlands, Exeter,

---

[13] Copenhagen, Kongelike Bibliotek, Gl. Kgl. Sam. 1595, f. 66v, printed Ker, 'Handwriting', p. 320.

[14] See Ker, *Catalogue*, pp. 162-63.

[15] See D. Whitelock, review of Jost, *Die 'Institutes of Polity, Civil and Ecclesiastical'*, in *Rev. English Stud*, n.s., 12 (1961), 61-66. Napier XXXIX is by Wulfstan but is excluded from the list as it is simply a version of the law-code VII Atr.; *Polity*, apps. f, g, i, and l are by Wulfstan but are not homiletic.

[16] See, especially, P. Wormald, 'Æthelred the Lawmaker', in *Ethelred the Unready: Papers from the Millenary Conference*, ed. D. Hill, BAR, British Series, 59 (Oxford, 1979), pp. 47-80. See also P. Stafford, 'The Laws of Cnut and the History of Anglo-Saxon Royal Promises', *ASE*, 10 (1982), 173-90.

[17] On the law codes, see Wormald, 'Æthelred the Lawmaker'; on the pastoral letters, see J. Hill in this volume.

[18] M. Godden, 'Ælfric and the Vernacular Prose Tradition' in *The Old English Homily*, ed. Szarmach and Huppé, pp. 99-117 at p. 110. See further N. R. Ker, *Catalogue of Manuscripts Containing Anglo-Saxon* (Oxford, 1957), esp. pp. 511-15.

East Anglia, and Durham, from the evidence of those manuscripts which can be localized.[19] The impression of considerable popularity is borne out to a lesser degree by the use of passages drawn from Ælfric's homilies in later works.[20]

One might expect a similarly wide distribution of Wulfstan's homiletic works. While Wulfstan wrote less than Ælfric, his sermons are of general applicability and, as we have seen, he was insistent that priests and bishops had a responsibility to transmit their content. Some evidence for such a popularity is suggested by a letter addressed to Wulfstan while still bishop of London, which refers to the 'very sweet wisdom of your eloquence and the richness of your composition fittingly organised'.[21]

The Manuscript Evidence

The manuscript evidence for the transmission of Wulfstan's homilies is by no means as extensive as that for Ælfric's. A significant series (i.e. five or more homilies of those homilies edited by Bethurum) circulated in five manuscript collections:

London, British Library, Cotton MS Nero A. i, ff. 70-177 (I; s. xi^{in}, Worcester or York), contains Wulfstan's commonplace book and his annotations.

Cambridge, Corpus Christi College MSS 419 and 421 (B and A; s. xi^1, south eastern?), a related pair which travelled to Exeter after their writing;

Cambridge, Corpus Christi College MS 201, pp. 1-178 (C; s. xi^{med}, Winchester);

Oxford, Bodleian Library, Hatton MSS 113 and 114 (E and F; s. $xi^{3/4}$, Worcester), a single homiliary;

Oxford, Bodleian Library, Bodley MS 343 (H; s. xii^2, West Midlands?).[22]

A range of other manuscripts contain a small number of Wulfstan's homiletic pieces:

[19] P. Clemoes, *Catholic Homilies I*, introduction (forthcoming) and Godden, 'Vernacular Prose Tradition', p. 110.

[20] *Ibid.*, p. 110 and his 'Old English Composite Homilies From Winchester', *ASE*, 4 (1975), 57-65.

[21] Printed by Bethurum, *Homilies*, pp. 376-77 and translated by Bethurum, 'Wulfstan', in *Continuations and Beginnings*, ed. E. G. Stanley (London, 1966), pp. 210-46, at p. 211.

[22] For details of the manuscripts, see Ker, *Catalogue*; on their Wulfstanian contents, see Bethurum, *Homilies*, pp. 1-8. Sigla throughout are those of Napier, *Wulfstan*, and Bethurum, *Homilies*. Subsequent references to the manuscripts in this and the next list are by sigla or abbreviated call mark.

London, British Library, Add. MS 38651, ff. 57-58 (s. xi^{in}, Worcester or York?), possibly in Wulfstan's hand;

Copenhagen, Kongelike Bibliotek, Gl. Kgl. Sam. 1595 (s. xi^1, Worcester or York), a copy of Wulfstan's commonplace book, includes his annotations;

York, Minster Library, MS Add. 1, the York Gospels (Y, relevant homilies added s. xi^1, York), corrections by Wulfstan;

London, British Library, Cotton MS Tiberius A. xiii (L, s.xi^1, Worcester), corrections by Wulfstan;

London, British Library, Cotton MS Otho B. x (M; s. xi^1, unknown), mostly destroyed by the fire of 1731 in the Cotton Library;

London, British Library, Cotton MS Tiberius A. iii, ff. 2-173 (K; s. xi^{med}, Christ Church, Canterbury);

Cambridge, Corpus Christi College MS 190 (W; s. xi^{med}, Worcester origin, donated to Exeter in s. xi), the best witness of Wulfstan's commonplace book;

Cambridge, Corpus Christi College MS 265, ff. 1-268 (s. xi^{med}, Worcester), a copy of Wulfstan's commonplace book;

Oxford, Bodleian Library, Junius MS 121 (G; s. xi$^{3/4}$, Worcester), a copy of Wulfstan's commonplace book;

London, British Library, Cotton MS Cleopatra B. xiii, ff. 1-58 (N; s. xi$^{3/4}$, Exeter);

Oxford, Bodleian Library, Hatton MS 115 (R, a sentence on an inserted leaf, s. xi^{ex}, Worcester?);[23]

Cambridge, Corpus Christi College MS 302 (D; s. xi/xii, unknown);

London, British Library, Cotton MS Vespasian D. ii (s. xi/xii, unknown);

Oxford, Bodleian Library, Barlow MS 37 (s. xii^{ex}, unknown).

Of the total of nineteen manuscript collections, at least nine were written at Wulfstan's dioceses of York or Worcester. Many of the remainder are of unknown place of origin and provenance. Those which can be localized provide evidence that Wulfstan's homilies were copied at Winchester (C) and Canterbury (K) and were taken to Exeter in two collections (A/B and W), where three homilies not available in those two collections were also copied (A and N). There is further evidence from Exeter in the record of an incipit of a lost Wulfstan work from a lost manuscript

---

[23] Ker's item 19; it is also present in CCCC 201 (ed. Napier XLI, 191/20-23). R as a whole was written elsewhere but travelled to Worcester sometime before s. xiii^1.

from there.[24] Wulfstan's homilies were also available in the as-yet-unlocalized library in the south-east where A/B was copied and in the West Midlands where H was copied. The bulk of the copying was going on in the eleventh century, but one major and one minor manuscript of the homilies was written in the second half of the twelfth century (H, Barlow 37).

Use by Later Sermon Writers

There is a further range of evidence for the spread of Wulfstan's preaching and the effectiveness of his mission which has never been systematically considered for this purpose. Wulfstan's works were often plundered by later sermon writers and passages from them taken over into other sermons. His generalized statements of moral concern and preoccupation with the fundamentals of the faith lent themselves to this kind of use in a way that the more cohesive works of Ælfric did not. A consideration of such re-use of Wulfstan's homiletic work will provide additional evidence for their dissemination. It will also reveal attitudes towards his works in the eleventh century.

There are two complications to be resolved before assembling the evidence. One is Wulfstan's tendency to borrow from his own work. For example, the three short homiletic pieces about the role of various orders of society, Napier LIX-LXI, are clearly assembled from writings by Wulfstan.[25] These pieces do not provide evidence for the popularity of the sources for later writers as they were written by Wulfstan himself – confirmed by the presence of his own annotations. The abbreviation of the *Sermo Lupi ad Anglos* printed as Napier XXVII presents a similar case. Here the evidence for Wulfstan's authorship is his use of this piece in his later composition, Napier L. Such homiletic works give an insight into Wulfstan's process of composition and his own attitude towards his works rather than into their dissemination to later writers.[26]

A second complication is the need to distinguish later borrowings of Wulfstan's works from Wulfstan's own borrowing and rewriting of earlier work. The problem is well illustrated by Napier I. This homily exists in two different versions, one in MSS CL, the other in E, differing primarily in their endings. The common material at the heart of both versions is a description of mankind's remoteness from Paradise drawn from Gregory's *Dialogues*, book 4, chapter 1. This was not written by Wulfstan.[27] The ending of the

---

[24] See Ker, *Catalogue*, no. 407, pp. 471-72.

[25] See S. Keynes, 'The Additions in Old English' in *The York Gospels*, ed. N. Barker (London, 1986), pp. 92-95.

[26] I plan to gather such borrowings by Wulfstan himself and consider them as a group in a subsequent article.

[27] It contains numerous usages alien to the archbishop; see Jost, *Wulfstanstudien*,

homily in CL tells how good people will have an appropriate final reward. This ending is in Wulfstan's style and yet is not drawn from his surviving works. Like the body of the homily, it includes a translation from book 4 of Gregory's *Dialogues*.[28] These facts suggest, as Jost first speculated, that Napier I in CL comprises an anonymous translation of Gregory which has subsequently been adopted by Wulfstan, who returned to the source to continue the homily and added a homiletic ending.[29] Such speculation receives confirmation from Wulfstan's corrections to the text in L. He makes only two slight corrections to the body of the text but nine revisions to the conclusion. The revisions emphasize Wulfstan's characteristic style by adding clarifying phrases (e.g. 'þa hwile, þe hy libbað' 4/7) or favourite tags ('for oft' 4/10). C and L, then, contain a homily created by Wulfstan, with L preserving evidence of the process of creation.

In E, on the other hand, the common material has a different ending, comprising exhortation to remember what Christ did for us and the need to give account on the day of Judgement. Most of the passage is taken almost verbatim from another work by Wulfstan, Napier XXV. It is only generally relevant as a homiletic conclusion to Napier I and by no means as relevant as the conclusion in CL. There is nothing to indicate that Wulfstan himself substituted this ending, which will be considered among the re-uses of Wulfstan's homilies charted below.

In the remainder of this paper, I will gather together all Old English homilies which draw on Wulfstan's works. For reasons of economy of space, I will present the evidence of each borrowing in tabular form. In each case, I will identify the composite homily,[30] the manuscripts which contain it, the extent and source of the borrowing, and the date and place that the borrowing occurred.[31] Any significant additional evidence will be discussed in full. I will deal with the relevant composite homilies in chronological

---

pp.184-87. On the borrowing from Gregory, see P. Szarmach, 'Another Old English Translation of Gregory the Great's *Dialogues?*', *English Stud.*, 62 (1981), 97-109, at pp. 107-09.

[28] In this case, from chap. 6. See Jost, *Wulfstanstudien*, pp. 185-87.

[29] *Ibid.*, p. 187.

[30] Homilies will be identified by their number in an edited collection, their title in the manuscripts, and the reference number assigned them by A. Cameron, 'A List of Old English Texts' in *A Plan for the Dictionary of Old English*, ed. R. Frank and A. Cameron (Toronto, 1973), pp. 25-306.

[31] The date of borrowing is usually delimited by the date of Wulfstan's composition (s. x/xi) and the date of the earliest manuscript containing the composite text. The suggested place of borrowing will require further discussion.

order of the manuscripts containing them.[32]

Napier XL, 'In die iudicii' (B. 3.4.32), MSS B, C, F, N.

182/2-6 in FN	< Wulfstanian commonplaces;[33]
188/11-189/2 in CFN	< Bethurum VII, 165-69 and Bethurum XIII, 98-100, somewhat rearranged;
189/3-5 in CFN	< Bethurum XIII, 12-14;
189/5-7 in CFN	< Bethurum XX (EI), 7-9;
189/11-15 in CFN	< Bethurum II, 65-68.
188/15n in B	< a tract on the vices and virtues in MS C;[34]
Ending in B	< Bethurum IX, 107-50 (where B's text is collated);
Ending in B	< Bethurum III, 74-80 (printed Bethurum IX, 150n).

Borrowing: s. xi[1], Winchester?[35]

This homily on the day of Judgement, drawn in large part from an earlier anonymous homily (Vercelli II), exists in different versions in different manuscripts. One introduction and two conclusions are compiled from the works of Wulfstan. The ending in CFN – general homiletic exhortation about the day of Judgement – comprises short, rather obvious, and somewhat approximate borrowings from Wulfstan's homilies. Such short and slightly-adapted borrowings suggest the probability of transmission by memory. In B, on the other hand, a substantial and appropriate ending has been created through access to three homiletic pieces by Wulfstan.

---

32 My task has been made easier by the 19th-century editor of Wulfstan's homilies, Napier, who included in his edition all those homilies attributed to Wulfstan. Napier promised a second part, which was to sort out the authentic texts from those merely borrowing from Wulfstan's works or mistakenly identified with him, but the second part was never published. The sorting task was subsequently achieved by Jost, *Wulfstanstudien*, on whose work I will draw extensively. Ker, *Catalogue*, provides a useful analysis of those homilies not edited by Napier.

33 The longest parallel is for three clauses (182/2-3) shared with Bethurum XIII, 53-54.

34 Printed by J. Wilcox, 'Napier's "Wulfstan" Homilies XL and XLII: Two Anonymous Works from Winchester?' *Jnl English and Germanic Philology*, 90 (1991), 1-23. The passage is like Bethurum Xc, 62-71.

35 See Wilcox, 'Napier XL and XLII', where there is a full account of the composition of this homily. The evidence for localizing the composition is the significant textual link with C.

Napier XLII, 'De temporibus Anticristi' (B. 3.4.34), MSS B, F.

191/25-192/3	<	Bethurum IV, 3-6;
192/3-8	<	Bethurum III, 56-60;
192/8-10	<	Bethurum IV, 6-8;
192/11-13	<	Bethurum IV, 71-73.
202/4-6	<	Bethurum VI, 207-09;
202/6-15	<	Bethurum IV, 74-77, 79-83;
202/19-203/24	<	Bethurum VII, 104-13, 115-31;
203/25-204/1	<	Napier LVII, 298/19-21;
204/1-23	<	Bethurum VII, 132-51.

Borrowing: s. xi[1], Winchester?[36]

A principal source, Adso's *De ortu et tempore Antichristi*, has been put into an eschatological context of a beginning and ending drawn from Wulfstan's homilies. The Wulfstan passages are taken over virtually verbatim except that the compiler occasionally adds minor phrases, presumably for stylistic effect. The account of Judgement Day in Bethurum VII includes the details: 'Eall middaneard bið þonne on dæg byrnende, 7 eall mancyn sceall þænne of deaðe arisan' (lines 111-13); which becomes in Napier XLII: 'Eall middaneard bið þonne on dæg byrnende, and ælc man sceal þonne *on dæg* of deaðe arísan, *þe æfre on life wæs*' (203/1-3). The repetition of 'on dæg' balances the earlier verb followed by 'þonne on dæg' and alliterates with 'of deaðe', a phrase which is balanced by the additional 'þe æfre on life wæs'. Such concern with balance and rhythmical effect suggests a compiler who has taken over Wulfstan's stylistic concerns along with his text.

Napier XLIII, 'Sunnandæges spell' (B. 3.4.35), MS B.

208/1-209/9	<	Napier XXIII, 116/1-119/11;
209/9-25	<	Bethurum XIII, 80-92.[37]

Borrowing: s. xi[1], unknown.

The Wulfstan passage – defining tithes and the times when they must be paid, commanding men to give to the poor, and exhorting them to avoid hell – is a digression in this Sunday Letter homily.[38] The reason for its inclusion is

---

[36] See Wilcox, 'Napier XL and XLII', where there is a full account of the composition of this homily. Again there is a significant textual link with C.

[37] Napier XXIII and XXIV are closely associated with Bethurum XIII in manuscripts and in content: 'they make particular the general admonitions to virtue in that homily', as Bethurum observes, *Homilies*, p. 36.

[38] There is nothing corresponding to this passage in the otherwise-related Sunday Letter homily, Napier XLIV.

probably that the injunctions in Napier XXIII include a requirement to honour Sundays (117/3-5).

Napier XLVII, 'Larspel and scriftboc' (B. 3.4.38), MS A.

    242/23-243/21   < Wulfstan's own condensing and re-writing of the moral point of the *Sermo Lupi ad Anglos*, analogous with Napier XXVII.[39]

Borrowing: s.xi[1], Ramsey?[40]

Napier LVIII, title lost (B. 3.4,47), MS M.

299/27-300/3	<	Napier XXIV, 119/15-120/1;
300/3-6, 9-15	<	Episcopus (ed. Liebermann, *Gesetze*, I, 477-79), §§13-15;
300/6-9	<	Bethurum VIIIb, 59-63;
300/16-301/5	<	Napier XXIV, 120/8-121/5;
301/5-302/10	<	Bethurum VIIIc, 116-155;
303/20-24	<	Bethurum VIIIb, 3-5;
303/24-304/14	<	Bethurum VI, 5-20;
304/16-305/6, 305/17-26	<	II Polity, §§187-97;
305/7-17		may derive from a revised lost Wulfstan source;[41]
306/8-13	<	Napier XXIV, 122/4-9;
306/17-30	<	Bethurum VI, 22-31.

Borrowing: s. xi[1], unknown.[42]

Napier LVIII is a homily in a sorry state: the beginning and ending are missing due to the burnt condition of M.[43] What survives is a homily on various fundamentals of the faith which draws on a broad range of vernacular

---

[39] See J. Wilcox, 'The Compilation of Old English Homilies in MSS Cambridge, Corpus Christi College, 419 and 421' (Unpublished Ph. D. dissertation, Cambridge, 1987), pp. 129-36.

[40] The second part of this homily derives from Byrhtferth's *Enchiridion* or *Manual*, which was written at Ramsey. Ramsey is also a possible place of origin for MS A; see Wilcox, 'Compilation'.

[41] Suggested by Jost, *Wulfstanstudien*, pp. 264-65.

[42] A version of Wulfstan's texts like the adaptations in M was known to the creator of Pope XXVII (place of adaptation unknown) and to the compiler of Bazire and Cross 7 (written at Winchester).

[43] If, as Ker suggests, this is the 'Sermo Bone Prædicatio' described in Wanley's catalogue, the incipit is from an unknown source and the sermon already ended imperfectly in Wanley's time.

sources, mostly by Wulfstan but also by other writers. Some adaptations of the text are uncharacteristic of Wulfstan, indicating that he was not responsible for the compilation.[44]

The passages drawn from Wulfstan are often adapted here in a more substantial manner than in most of the composite homilies, as can be illustrated by the borrowings from Bethurum VI. Some changes are stylistic, as in the expansive alteration of '*scortlice* hit eow sum *asecgan*' (Bethurum VI, 24) to 'hit sum *asecgan and areccan mid feawum wordum*' (Napier LVIII, 306/19-20), or of 'ece God' (Bethurum VI, 24) to '*éce ælmihtig* god' 306/21. Other changes are presumably made for clarity. In Bethurum VI, Lucifer considered that he might be the equal of him who created him (lines 29-30); in Napier LVIII, his challenge is made explicit through an addition: 'and wolde dælan rice wið god ælmihtigne' (306/26-27: 'and he intended to share the kingdom with God almighty').

Pope XXVII, addition to Ælfric's 'Dominica XVI post pentecosten', *Catholic Homilies* II, XXXI (B. 1.4.28), MS BL, Cotton Vitellius C. v.[45]

      Lines 1-6   <   Bethurum XIII, 80-84;

      lines 6-11   <   Bethurum XIII, 103-06.

Borrowing: s. xi[1], unknown.

A reviser of Ælfric's homily has expanded it by adding to the end exempla on the going forth of a bad and a good man's soul written by Ælfric for another context. These additions are embedded in material not by Ælfric, including an introduction drawn from Wulfstan's sermon. The Wulfstan text appears to be heavily revised but, in fact, is close to the version contained in M.[46] Pope suggests that the additional Ælfric exemplars and their surrounding non-Ælfric context were probably available to the reviser already combined.

Bazire and Cross 7, 'Feria tertia in letania maiore' (B. 3.2.41),[47] MS Cambridge, University Library, Ii. 4. 6.

      Lines 16-66   <   Napier XXX, 149/14-152/6;

      lines 63-66   <   Napier XXX, 152/2-5 augmented by Bethurum XIII, 53-55;

---

[44]   See Jost, *Wulfstanstudien*, pp. 262-66.

[45]   Ed. J. C. Pope, *Homilies of Ælfric*, 2 vols., EETS o.s. 259 and 260 (Oxford, 1967-68), II, 775-79. See Pope's discussion, I, 770-74.

[46]   The version in M (Ker's item 17) is now lost, but the incipit and explicit were recorded by Wanley and consequently the second borrowing is still available from M, where the affinity is obvious.

[47]   Ed. J. Bazire and J. E. Cross, *Eleven Old English Rogationtide Homilies* (Toronto, 1982), pp. 90-100.

lines 66-67 < Napier LVIII, 306/15-16.
Borrowing: s. xi[med], Winchester.[48]

Wulfstan's works mostly influence this rogationtide homily by way of other composite homilies, Napier XXX and LVIII. The concluding general exhortation of Napier XXX is augmented by the insertion of a sentence of exhortation (commanding that we be mindful of our need, cease sins, and turn to right) drawn from Bethurum XIII. The addition is so short and the subject-matter so commonplace, that this seems to be a likely case of the remembrance of a relevant passage.[49]

Napier I, 'De initio creature' (B. 3.4.21), MS E (other versions in C and L).[50]
4/4n in E < Napier XXV, 123/16-124/7;
4/4n in E < Bethurum XX (EI), 192-4 rearranged.
Borrowing: by s. xi[3/4], Worcester?[51]

The brevity of the correspondence with Bethurum XX and the rearrangement of the relevant phrases suggests that this borrowing was made from memory.

Napier XXX, 'Be rihtan cristendome' (B. 3.4.27), MS E.
143/7-144/28 < II Polity, §§203-34 (augmented with Wulfstanian commonplaces);[52]
150/3-9 < Polity, appendix b (§8);
150/9-12 < Bethurum XIII, 103-06;
150/12-15 < Bethurum XIII, 67-68;[53]
150/15-23 < II Polity, §§167-69;
150/23-151/14 < Napier XXIV, 121/6-122/9;

[48] The place and date of composition are demonstrated by Godden, 'Composite Homilies From Winchester'.

[49] Memorial transmission is suggested by Bazire and Cross, p. 90

[50] For a discussion of the version in CL, see above. The title is in E only, where this piece begins the homiliary.

[51] It may be significant that this ending is only present in E, a manuscript written at Worcester. D. Yerkes, 'The Place of Composition of the Opening of Napier Homily I', *Neophilologus*, 60 (1976), 452-54, assembles evidence which suggests that the CL version of Napier I was not composed in Worcester, but his evidence does not apply to the E version.

[52] See D. G. Scragg, 'Napier's "Wulfstan" Homily XXX: Its Sources, Its Relationship to the Vercelli Book and Its Style', *ASE*, 6 (1977), 197-211, at p. 206, n. 3 for the commonplaces and parallels from Wulfstan's homilies, perhaps drawn from Bethurum VIIIc, 95-96 and 112-14, although both ideas recur elsewhere in Wulfstan's writing.

[53] The parallels are brief and approximate.

151/27-152/6 < Bethurum VI, 193-201, 214-17.

Borrowing: s. xi$^{2/4}$, origin: unknown.[54]

The borrowings from Wulfstan are of both substantial passages and of short commonplaces or echoes probably transmitted by memory. Scragg's analysis of the *modus operandi* of the compiler is of interest here: he adds 'intensifying pairs and empty phrases which add to the rhetorical effect'; 'he even "Wulfstanizes" Wulfstan's authentic work', for example, by adding the phrases 'wordes ne weorces' and 'Godes lagum fyligean' to the passage drawn from *Polity*.[55]

Napier LV, untitled (B. 3.4.44), MS F.

282/22-283/18 < Bethurum VI, 3-24;

284/28-285/14 < Bazire and Cross 8, 18-28.

Borrowing: by s. xi$^{3/4}$, Worcester?[56]

Bazire and Cross 8, 'De letania maiore' (B. 3.2.30), MS F.

Lines 2-71 < a lost Wulfstan homily on Rogationtide
(see discussion below);

lines 131-43 < Bethurum III, 65-80.

Borrowing: by s. xi$^{3/4}$, Worcester?[57]

The first section of this homily on fasting (lines 2-17) is based on Ælfric's 'In letania maiore' (CH I, XVIII), but with revisions which bear the hall-mark of Wulfstan's authorship; a subsequent section (lines 29-41) draws on another Ælfric rogationtide sermon ('Feria secunda: letania maiore', CH II, XIX) also adapted in Wulfstan's style; and two further sections (lines 42-71), which deal with the concerns of the day (i.e. the pericope Luke 11:5-13) and with the end of the world, include brief passages which can be paralleled from elsewhere in Wulfstan's writing. This has led to the convincing speculation that the opening is drawn from a lost homily on rogationtide by Wulfstan.[58] Wulfstan did not usually write homilies for specific occasions, but there is a specific appropriateness in his having written a rogationtide homily: VII

54 Scragg, 'Napier XXX', discusses the homily in full and suggests the possible claims for origin of the south-east, Winchester, or Worcester (p. 211).

55 *Ibid.*, pp. 208-09.

56 F is a Worcester manuscript and the other sources of the homily were (probably) available there: Ælfric's CH I, XVIII in CCCC 178, Belfour X in the south-western H, Bazire and Cross 8 elsewhere in F.

57 Again the tentative assignment to Worcester is based upon the place of origin of the manuscript and the likely presence there of most of the identified sources.

58 First made by Whitelock, *Sermo Lupi*, 3rd edn, pp. 22-23, and worked out further by Bazire and Cross, pp. 104-06.

Æthelred, composed by him, institutes a call for national prayer to avert the disaster of external attack, which was the traditional foundation of the rogationtide observance; see, for example, the account at the opening of this homily, lines 2-17.

Unedited, 'Item alia' (On the dedication of a church, B. 2.3.6),[59] MS F, ff. 242v-46v.

> Ending   <   Bethurum XVIII, 124-149 (where it is collated by Bethurum).
> Borrowing: by s. xi$^{3/4}$, unknown.

Napier LVII, 'Sermo ad populum dominicis diebus' (B. 3.4.46), MS Z.

> 298/12-22   <   a list of sinners by Wulfstan (see discussion below).
> Borrowing: by s. xi$^{3/4}$, unknown.

In the course of a warning in this Sunday Letter homily that no man can serve two masters, the Almighty and the devil, the homilist interrupts his principal source to expand upon those who serve the devil with a list of sinners clearly drawn from Wulfstan's works. Such alliterating and balanced lists of sinners are common in the works of Wulfstan.[60] The version here starts out like the list in Napier L, but augments this with additional material. The augmented version was probably taken over whole from a now-lost source rather than combined together for the first time here since part of the additional material was used in the list of sinners drawn upon in Napier XLII.

Unedited, untitled (variant of B. 1.1.21), MS Z, ff. 31r-38r.

> ff. 36v15-37r1   <   Bethurum VIIIc, 148-53;[61]
> f. 37r1-10   <   Bethurum XIII, 8-12;[62]
> f. 37r10-16   <   Napier XL, 189/3-7;
> ff. 37r17-37v1   <   Napier XXIV, 122/4-9.

---

[59] This Cameron number is that for Wulfstan's Dedication of a Church homily in Cleopatra B. xiii; the Hatton 114 Dedication of a Church homily is a separate anonymous piece which makes use of Wulfstan's homily and should have a separate Cameron number, as Scragg has pointed out, 'Corpus', p. 255, n. 2.

[60] They occur in the homilies at Bethurum VII, 128-34, Bethurum XIII, 92-96, Bethurum XX (EI), 161-66, Napier L, 266/25-29, Napier LX, 309/27-310/6. On Wulfstan's development of the list, see Bethurum, *Homilies*, p. 310, note to VII, 128-34.

[61] The compiler first picks up an idea and some phrasing from line 138.

[62] With an initial reminiscence from line 7.

Borrowing: by s. xi3/4, Exeter?[63]

A version of Ælfric's homily on the Lord's Prayer for Tuesday in Rogationtide (CH I, XIX) has been adapted by some omissions and the substitution of three passages drawn from other homilies.[64] Two of the augmentations are from other homilies by Ælfric, but the ending of the sermon is made up from a catena of passages, including excerpts from Wulfstan's homilies.[65] The excerpts are intelligently interleaved and adapted with an eye to their context. For example, the passage from Bethurum VIIIc has one added phrase, 'æt his endedæge' (inserted at Bethurum VIIIc, 151) which gives additional emphasis on learning the Pater Noster before death, the subject of the next extract. The next excerpt has an addition which neatly anticipates the following section: the original Bethurum XIII passage contains the sequence that humans were created 'of eorðan' and will return 'to eorðan' (lines 8-10), the version here provides an eschatological extension in balanced phrasing like Wulfstan's own: '7 of eorðan we sceolon ealle arisan on domesdæg.'

Warner XLII, 'Of Seinte Neote' (B. 3.3.28),[66] MS BL, Cotton Vespasian D. xiv.

133/26-37 < the account of the deterioration of the world from the opening of *Sermo Lupi ad Anglos* (phrases from Bethurum XX (EI), 8-68 adapted and modernized)

Borrowing: s. xii¹, St Albans?[67]

An English translation of the first Latin *Vita* of St Neot has been subject to frequent homiletic adaptations, including an ending adapted from Wulfstan's *Sermo Lupi ad Anglos*.

---

[63] Exeter is the place of writing of the manuscript. One of the sources, Napier LVII, 299/16-26, only survives elsewhere in this manuscript, suggesting the homily may have been compiled from sources available where the manuscript was written.

[64] Described by Ker, *Catalogue*, p. 344.

[65] The remainder of the augmentation comprises excerpts from the preceding homily, Napier LVII, and from Ælfric's Christmas homily, CH II, I.

[66] Ed. R. D.-N. Warner, *Early English Homilies From the Twelfth Century MS Vesp. D. XIV*, EETS o.s. 152 (London, 1917), pp. 129-34.

[67] The piece is discussed by M. P. Richards, 'The Medieval Hagiography of St Neot', *Analecta Bollandiana*, 99 (1981), 259-78, at 262-67, who suggests, on slight evidence, Crowland as place of composition; and by M. Lapidge, 'Vita Prima Sancti Neoti et Translatio: Introduction' in *The Annals of St. Neots with Vita Prima Sancti Neoti*, ed. D. Dumville and M. Lapidge, *The Anglo-Saxon Chronicle: a Collaborative Edition*, 17 (Cambridge, 1985), pp. cxvi-vii and p. cxxiii, n. 135, who points to its connections with a manuscript of the main source written at St Albans.

Conclusions

Fifteen sermons contained in nine manuscript collections have been identified here as drawing on Wulfstan's homiletic works. The pattern of dissemination they reveal confirms and augments that suggested by the manuscript evidence. The place of copying of the manuscripts and the place of composition of the homilies (where this can be speculated at) demonstrate the following spread of Wulfstan's works:

–**Worcester** had access to many composite homilies preserved in EF, namely, copies of Napier I, XXX, XL, XLII, LV, Bazire and Cross 8, and the church dedication homily. Napier LV, Bazire and Cross 8, and this version of Napier I may have been composed there.

–**Winchester** saw the copying of C, containing Napier XL, and Ii. 4. 6, containing Bazire and Cross 7. It is likely that Napier XL, XLII, and Bazire and Cross 7 were composed there.

–**Exeter** saw the copying of N, containing Napier XL, and Z, containing Napier LVII and the adapted form of CH I, XIX. The latter may have been compiled there.

–the unknown south-eastern place of origin of A/B saw the copying of the composite homilies Napier XL, XLII, XLIII, XLVII;

–the unknown place of origin of M and of Vitellius C. v (possibly the same place) saw the copying of Napier LVIII and of Pope XXVII.

–**Ramsey** possibly saw the composition of Napier XLVII.

–**Canterbury** or **Rochester** saw the copying of Vespasian D. xiv, containing Warner XLII, perhaps composed at St Albans.

The vast majority of the composite homilies using Wulfstan were copied in the eleventh century; one example dates from the first half of the twelfth.

Caution must be used in interpreting this evidence: the recurrence of Exeter in the copying of relevant homilies, for example, may be simply a reflection of the survival of a group of Anglo-Saxon manuscripts clearly identifiable with this centre. Certain patterns are apparent from the evidence of both the manuscripts and the re-use of Wulfstan's homilies. Wulfstan's diocese of Worcester was clearly vital to the transmission of his homiletic works as, probably, was York.[68] Winchester was also important as, at a later

---

68 See D. Whitelock, 'Wulfstan at York', in *Franciplegius: Medieval and Linguistic Studies in Honor of Francis Peabody Magoun, Jr.*, ed. J. B. Bessinger and R. P. Creed (New York, 1965), pp. 214-31 for speculation that many of the unattributed manuscripts may have been written at York.

date, was Exeter. Canterbury, on the other hand, played a strikingly minor role. The only copying known to have occurred there are two sermons contained in K and the echoes of *Sermo Lupi ad Anglos* in Vespasian D. xiv, copied in Canterbury or Rochester. This lack may reflect a preference for Ælfric's homilies in the ecclesiastical capital in view of the extensive evidence for the copying of his works there.[69] There is also no surviving evidence for Wulfstan's homilies in London or from the north of England apart from York. It is perilous to press such negative evidence too far, however: the lack of Wulfstan's works from certain centres may reflect simply the chance loss of manuscripts.

The passages drawn upon by eleventh-century sermon writers provide clues as to the nature of the popularity of Wulfstan's writings. The later compilers tend to borrow passages of basic catechetical-style instruction, such as the oft-repeated injunction to learn the Pater Noster and Creed: 'forðam he ne bið wel cristen þe þæt geleornian nele...' (Bethurum VIIIc, 148-49; Napier LVIII, 302/3-4; and adaptation of CH I, XIX in Z), or heightened passages of eschatological warning, like this account of hell:

> Wa þam þonne þe ær geearnode helle wite. Ðær is ece bryne grimme gemencged, 7 ðær is ece gryre; þær is granung 7 wanung 7 aa singal heof; þær is ealra yrmða gehwylc 7 ealra deofla geþring. (Bethurum III, 65-68; Bazire and Cross 8, 131-34)

The most popular sermon by Wulfstan for later compilers proves to be the one based on his pastoral letter, Bethurum XIII, drawn upon in six subsequent compilations. Other popular sermons, providing the source for substantial passages in three or more later compilations, are Bethurum III, an eschatological homily, Bethurum VI, Wulfstan's sermon on Christian history, and Napier XXIV, injunctions related to Bethurum XIII. Surprisingly rare are borrowings from the *Sermo Lupi ad Anglos*. Brief reminiscences from it are used in Napier I in E and in Napier XL in CFN and heavily revised reminiscences are present in the twelfth-century homily, Warner XLII. Otherwise, it is only used in Wulfstan's adapted form in Napier XLVII.

The composite homilies also provide evidence for the existence of homilies by Wulfstan which are now lost. The most interesting such example is of a lost Wulfstan homily for Rogationtide used in Bazire and Cross 8. Other passages are suggestive of only brief extracts from lost homilies. The opening of Napier XL in FN contains a short Wulfstanian passage on the

---

[69] From the 11th century: Bodley 340 and 342 (Canterbury or Rochester), CCCC 162 (Canterbury or Rochester), Cotton Tiberius A. iii (Canterbury), Junius 85 and 86 (Canterbury or Rochester), Trinity, Cambridge, B. 15. 34 (Canterbury); from the 12th century: CCCC 303 (Canterbury or Rochester), Cotton Vespasian D. xiv (Canterbury or Rochester).

transitoriness of life. The augmented list of sinners from Napier LVII (partly used again in Napier XLII) probably derive from a lost version of such a list by Wulfstan. A short passage on lechery in Napier LVIII may derive from another lost source by Wulfstan.

The composite homilies are an interesting phenomenon in their own right. Most survive in only one copy, suggesting that they may have had only limited circulation. Those which are preserved in multiple copies often appear in different versions in different manuscripts, suggesting an unstable tradition in which copyists or users felt free to modify the texts. In most composite homilies, the substantial borrowings from Wulfstan are taken over virtually verbatim.[70] Other vernacular sources are also borrowed and treated in the same way, although the preponderance of works by Wulfstan is striking.

It is likely that substantial verbatim borrowings were created by a compiler simply marking a passage in an existing manuscript for copying by a scribe directly into his new compilation. Slight revisions could be made at this stage.[71] The numerous examples of the borrowing of only a few short clauses are different in kind. These were probably adopted from memory. They provide evidence for a different kind of popularity of Wulfstan's texts. They suggest that the audience to Wulfstan's preaching included some (priests?) who internalized what they heard sufficiently to reproduce it when an appropriate opportunity arose in the course of composing a sermon of their own. The tendency to borrow such passages suggests either that particular kudos attached to echoing the wording of Archbishop Wulfstan or that subsequent compilers recognized the stylistic power of Wulfstan's work.

Sensitivity to Wulfstan's stylistic power is suggested also in some of the substantial borrowings. More than one compiler has been seen to Wulfstanize the style of Wulfstan's own texts through the addition of redundant words or phrases, especially intensifiers, for the sake of style or rhythm. There are numerous examples of this in Napier XLII and Napier XXX and, to a lesser extent, in Napier LVII and Napier LVIII.

The essential thrusts of Wulfstan's work – catechetical instruction and eschatological urgency – are reflected in many of the later compilations which draw on that work. Wulfstan would probably have been happy to know that subsequent writers took over both his style and his message in order to convey the point, expressed in the passage most-borrowed from his writings:

Utan andettan ure synna þa hwile þe we magan 7 motan, 7 betan 7 a
geswican 7 don to gode swa mycel swa we mæst magan. Þonne beorge we us

70 Napier LVIII is a significant exception.

71 See Wulfstan's revisions to the L-text of Napier I for the potential for minor revisions while using this method.

sylfum wið ece wite, 7 geearniað us heofona rice. (Bethurum XIII, 103-06; Napier XXX, 150/9-12; Pope XXVII, 6-11; adaptation of CH I, XIX in Z)

Let us confess our sins while we may and are able, and atone and ever cease and do for good as much as we may. Then we may save ourselves from eternal torment, and merit for ourselves the kingdom of heaven.

The use of Wulfstan's homiletic works by later compilers augments the evidence of their manuscript distribution to reveal that Wulfstan was a significant and influential voice for preaching in England throughout the eleventh century.

Prayers for King Cnut:
The Liturgical Commemoration of a Conqueror
JAN GERCHOW

'Cnut's is the neglected conquest of eleventh-century England, yet no less important, because it proved less permanent than 1066' (P. Stafford).[1] This neglect is confirmed by the fact that since Larson's study of 1912 about the Danish conqueror and king of England (1016-35) no major work has appeared.[2] The same could hardly be said of William the Conqueror. Cnut's modern historical *memoria* faded in comparison with that of his 'overmighty' follower on the English throne, William the Bastard. I shall concentrate on another, perhaps a more medieval, form of *memoria:* Cnut's liturgical commemoration.

Cnut's father Svein Forkbeard, king of Denmark (986-1014), together with other mighty Viking leaders, had since the 980s renewed the tradition of Viking attacks on the British Isles. Svein eventually succeeded in expelling the English king, Æthelred 'the Unready'. In January 1014, Æthelred fled to his Norman brother-in-law, Duke Richard II, at whose court his wife Emma-Ælfgifu and their sons Alfred and Edward had already taken refuge. Svein's army acclaimed him king of England and the English are said to have acknowledged him as their lord – but the Dane died unexpectedly on 3 February 1014. This was Cnut's hour: the younger, it seems, of Svein's sons was proclaimed his father's successor in the English kingdom at the age of about eighteen. His elder brother Harold succeeded to the Danish throne. But at this point the Anglo-Saxons recalled King Æthelred from Normandy. The subsequent story of campaigns, defeats and victories, of treaties and treachery, is too well known to be recalled here: Cnut could consider himself to be king of all England only after Edmund Ironside's death on 30 November 1016.

1   P. Stafford, *Unification and Conquest. A Political and Social History of England in the Tenth and Eleventh Centuries* (London, 1989), p. 69. I want to thank above all Peter Cramer for many discussions on the subject and for generous assistance in translating this paper into English, as well as Michelle Brown, Cecily Clark, Signe Horn Fuglesang, Patrick Geary, Sandy Heslop, Andrea von Hülsen, Bernhard Jussen, Simon Keynes, Ken Lawson and Otto Gerhard Oexle for their help, advice and encouragement.

2   L. M. Larson, *Canute the Great 995-1035 and the Rise of Danish Imperialism during the Viking Age* (New York, 1912). Larson did not however supersede the masterly account of J. Steenstrup in his *Normannere III* (Copenhagen, 1882), pp. 273-412, esp. 333ff.

219

What matters most in this context is that Cnut as conqueror and king of England was in a different position from his father or brother: he had to secure his rule in a foreign kingdom without having a firm base in Scandinavia. He needed more than regular tributes and hostages. But, as a consequence of Cnut's success, England remained the basis of his power, even when in 1019 Cnut succeeded his brother Harold as king of Denmark, and even after he had subjected Norway to his direct rule in 1028. It was from England that Cnut built up his Norse empire of three *regna;* it was in England that Cnut died in 1035 and was buried in the Old Minster of Winchester.

Cnut's relation to Christianity before he came to England with his father is not entirely clear: Svein had certainly accepted Christianity as his religion – but Cnut seems to have been baptised as an adolescent, not as an infant. He was a convert in the proper sense.[3] In England, his own and his father's troops had, in previous years, pillaged monasteries, villages and boroughs, and were regarded by the Anglo-Saxons as descendants of the heathen armies of the ninth century.[4] At the same time, Cnut came from a young church. The Danish church was undeveloped compared with the Anglo-Saxon or German churches and still lacked a firm diocesan organisation.[5] This made him still more of a newcomer on the Anglo-Saxon and European stage. He had to prove himself a Christian king in England, a legitimate king in all his *regna* and a king equal in rank to others on the Continent. Against this background, I want to draw attention to a neglected aspect of Cnut's kingship.

Attention has usually been given to the secular means employed by Cnut to secure his power in England. Cnut destroyed some of his Anglo-Saxon political enemies by exile or murder, nor did he spare his Danish rivals.[6]

---

3   See below, p. 236.

4   A good selection of sources for the notoriety of the Vikings as 'heathens' or 'barbarians' in the 11th century in England and on the Continent, especially in connection with destroyed or pillaged churches, can be found in *Diplomatarium Danicum* I. Raekke 1. Bind: Regester 789-1052 ed. C. A. Christensen and H. Nielsen (Copenhagen, 1975) passim.

5   P. Sawyer, 'The Process of Scandinavian Christianization in the Tenth and Eleventh Centuries', *The Christianization of Scandinavia.* Ed. B. Sawyer, P. Sawyer, I. Wood (Alingsås, 1987), pp. 68-87. See also E. Roesdahl, *Viking-Age Denmark* (London, 1982), ch. 9, p. 176ff. Stone carvings, inscriptions and pectoral crosses are discussed by S. H. Fuglesang, 'Ikonographie der skandinavischen Runensteine der jüngeren Wikingerzeit', *Zum Problem der Deutung frühmittelalterlicher Bildinhalte,* ed. H. Roth (Sigmaringen, 1986), pp. 183-210, and eadem, 'Viking and medieval amulets in Scandinavia', *Fornvännen,* 84 (1989), 15-27.

6   K. Bund, *Thronsturz und Herrscherabsetzung im Frühmittelalter* (Bonn, 1979), pp.

With the four great earldoms he introduced a new political structure. What was more important in persuading the English to acknowledge him as their king was his confirmation of Edgar's laws, that is, the tradition of English law and kingship.[7] Cnut's two marriages also helped to establish his position as English king, his first marriage *more danico* with Ælfgifu of Northampton and his second, higher ranked marriage of July 1017 with Emma-Ælfgifu, the widow of King Æthelred.[8] Cnut's dealings with the English church are usually given rather short shrift. Frank Barlow wrote in his history of the English church in the eleventh century 'Cnut and Emma had not forced the pace in ecclesiastical affairs... their extravagances had been private and had not disturbed vested interests'. He concludes that Ælfric and Wulfstan were responsible for the rather unadventurous well-being of the English church under Cnut.[9]

This was not the opinion of Anglo-Saxon contemporaries nor of Anglo-Norman historians. William of Malmesbury, for instance, praises Cnut for his zeal in restoring and founding churches: 'Thus anxious to atone for the offences of himself and of his predecessors, perhaps he wiped away the foul stain of his former crimes in the sight of God – certainly he did so with man'.[10] Cnut's fame as donor of precious relics as well as manuscripts, church ornaments and land is mentioned by nearly all important post-Conquest chronicles and cartularies of Anglo-Saxon monasteries or monastic cathedrals.[11] Clearly, there was no contradiction, to Cnut's contemporaries, in the notion that in doing all this the king also promoted the salvation of his soul.

724-25.

[7] H. Loyn, *The Governance of Anglo-Saxon England 500-1087* (London, 1984), passim.

[8] M. W. Campbell, 'Queen Emma and Ælfgifu of Northampton: Canute the Great's Women', *Medieval Scandinavia*, 4 (1971), 66-79.

[9] F. Barlow, *The English Church 1000-1066* (London 1966), pp. 40-41. After drafting this paper, I read M. K. Lawson's chapter on the church from his forthcoming book about Cnut which he kindly sent me. He and T. A. Heslop (see note 11) deal with Cnut's relations with the church more thoroughly than I can do here.

[10] *Willelmi Malmesbiriensis Monachi De Gestis Regum Anglorum*, ed. W. Stubbs, RS I (London, 1887), pp. 219-20: *Monasteria per Angliam suis et patris excursionibus partim foedata, partim eruta, reparavit; loca omnia in quibus pugnaverat, et praecipue Assandunam, ecclesiis insignivit (...). Ita omnia, quae ipse et antecessores sui deliquerant, corrigere satagens, prioris injustitiae naevum apud Deum fortassis, apud homines certe abstersit;* p. 226: *Ejusdem etiam archipresulis monitu, rex ad transmarinas ecclesias pecunias mittens, ...*

[11] T. A. Heslop, 'The Production of *de luxe* Manuscripts and the Patronage of King Cnut and Queen Emma', *ASE*, 19 (1990), 151-195: I would like to thank him very much for letting me read the proofs of this article.

221

Barlow's 'private extravagances' should be put in a new context, that of commemorative documents.[12] The question is whether there could be any 'private extravagances' for an early medieval king, or whether the royal munificence to the church and royal commemoration did not necessarily have a 'public character'? Were they not an aspect of royal rule and legitimacy?

The first part of this paper examines the famous frontispiece of the New Minster *liber vitae* which shows Cnut and Emma placing a golden cross on the altar of the New Minster. The second part deals with the manuscript as a whole as the main example of Cnut's liturgical *memoria* in England. In the third part I shall show briefly Cnut's role in other Anglo-Saxon commemorative documents.

I. The frontispiece of the New Minster 'liber vitae'

The best known part of BL Stowe MS 944 is its frontispiece (Pl. 8).[13] The partly coloured line-drawing is dated together with the manuscript 1031/32. It represents King Cnut and his Queen Ælfgifu (Emma) as benefactors, together offering a large cross, which Cnut places on the altar with his right arm. Both figures are named. The two royal donors are placed in the middle of three zones in the picture. The zone above shows the patrons of the New Minster in Winchester, St Mary and St Peter. They flank Christ in Majesty in a mandorla. Two angels connect the upper and middle zone, descending from Christ to the two benefactors. They bring Christ's heavenly reward for the donation: Cnut receives a crown, Emma a veil. The altar belongs to a monastery, to the New Minster. Its monks are depicted as witnesses in the lower zone of the picture, under the arcades of their monastic church, which also forms a kind of globe, on which Cnut and Emma stand.

The miniature is extraordinary, not only from the artistic point of view: in England there are hardly any comparable pictures.[14] The only image

---

12 See below, p. 231ff.

13 An edition of the texts and names by W. de Gray Birch (ed.), *Register and Martyrology of New Minster and Hyde Abbey Winchester*, Hampshire Record Society (London-Winchester, 1892); a full description and bibliography in J. Gerchow, *Die Gedenküberlieferung der Angelsachsen. Mit einem Katalog der libri vitae und Necrologien*, Arbeiten zur Frühmittelalterforschung, XX (Berlin-New York, 1988), pp. 155-85 (hereafter, Gerchow). For the line-drawings see E. Temple, *Anglo-Saxon Manuscripts 900-1066* (London, 1976), no. 78.

14 Kings appear again in other illuminations: in the well-known portraits of King Æthelstan as donor of a manuscript to St Cuthbert (Cambridge, Corpus Christi College MS 183, f. 1v), and of King Edgar in synod with Æthelwold and Dunstan (BL Cotton MS, Tiberius A. iii, f. 2v); and Queen Emma receives a copy of her *vita* by the monk of Saint Bertin in BL, Add. MS 33241, f. 1v. Only the Æthelstan picture, however, represents the king as donor and he stands before a

closely related to Cnut's and Emma's donor-portrait is the so-called New Minster Charter of King Edgar, dated 966 but probably written between that year and 984 (Pl. 9).[15] The similarities are not accidental: both pictures were produced for, and presumably in, the same monastery. Edgar's charter, the only Anglo-Saxon charter in the form of a book, was written in commemoration of the introduction of monks in 964 and was presumably preserved and shown on the altar of the New Minster on special occasions, perhaps the prescribed lections of the text in the (lost) last chapter. King Edgar holds up his charter for the reformed monastery in his left hand, presenting it to Christ in Majesty. Four angels hold the mandorla, while the Virgin and St Peter flank the donor-king. Edgar's is the only royal portrait from Anglo-Saxon England, other than Cnut's and Emma's, to show the king in direct relationship with Christ. I want to look at the meanings and messages which the pictures contain, and at the models they followed.

The Cnut/Emma frontispiece is clearly related to the Edgar picture. This is evident from comparisons of style but also from the scene itself, the iconographical elements and the arrangement of the persons. 'They form, as it were, a pair' according to Francis Wormald.[16] Certainly the artist of the New Minster *liber vitae* had seen the Edgar Charter and used it as a model. But there are differences too. These differences, I believe, are deliberate attempts to catch the eye, and thus to convey certain messages. After all it is probable that both manuscripts were presented on the same altar, opened at their frontispieces.

I will concentrate on two distinctions: in the frontispiece not just the king, but Cnut *and* Emma are depicted, and they are not only shown as givers but also as receivers, of the heavenly rewards, the crown and the veil. In the charter Edgar receives nothing. So the personnel are changed and the interaction of gift and reward has been added. The drawing of Cnut and Emma has obviously more layers of meaning than Edgar's picture. There are reasons for this.

My theory concentrates on two important, because precarious, aspects of Cnut's kingship and his legitimacy as English king: his marriage with Emma and his coronation as king of the English. The marriage of Cnut and Emma

---

saint, not before Christ. The ultimate source of royal power and heavenly reward is not depicted in this picture.

[15] BL, Cotton MS, Vespasian A. viii, f. 2v. No. 745 of P. H. Sawyer, *Anglo-Saxon Charters. An Annotated List and Bibliography* (London, 1968). Temple, *Anglo-Saxon Manuscripts* no. 16. Good colour illustration in D. Wilson, *Anglo-Saxon Art* (London, 1984) pl. 261. The date is according to F. Wormald, 'Late Anglo-Saxon Art. Some Questions and Suggestions', *Studies in Western Art. Acts of the 20th Congress of the History of Art*, ed. M. Meiss (Princeton, 1963), I, pp. 19-26.

[16] *Ibid.* p. 26.

had considerable diplomatic repercussions. For example it secured the alliance of Duke Richard II of Normandy, host to Emma's children by Æthelred. Emma also offered Cnut a genealogical connection, however weak, with the Anglo-Saxon kings, and consequently played a part in his representation as English king. Furthermore, Emma had been in England from 1002 to 1013 as well as 1016 and consequently, apart from her maturity and vigorous character, played an important role in Cnut's effort to establish himself as Anglo-Saxon king. Emma's special attachment to Winchester after Cnut's death and her connections to the reform monastery of Peterborough have recently led to the view of her as driving force behind the royal couple's enormous display of munificence to churches and monasteries.[17] Emma's prominent position in the *liber vitae* frontispiece on the right hand side of the cross (seen from the cross), a position otherwise often reserved for the principal donor, supports this view.[18] Emma's extraordinary position as queen is clearly reflected by her position on the picture. On the other hand this should not be exaggerated: it is Cnut who holds the cross in his right hand and places it on the altar, Emma only points to it. It is Cnut under whom Winchester becomes the most prominent of all royal residences, a kind of English capital.[19] His own and his son Harthacnut's affection for the place can be seen from their graves in the Old Minster.[20] Cnut's attachment to the place and Emma's role in his *memoria* led perhaps to Emma's special position in the city *after* Cnut's death. And, as will be seen later, the depiction of a royal couple instead of the king alone may have followed Continental models and should perhaps therefore be interpreted in this context.

The heavenly gifts to Cnut and Emma also attract attention: Edgar in his New Minster Charter wears the lily-crown, which identifies him as king.[21] Cnut receives a crown but, unlike Edgar, he also carries a sword. Emma

[17] Heslop, 'Manuscripts and Patronage' p. 180.

[18] *Ibid.* p. 157 n. 16; portraits of queens are, however, not so rare: see the examples of Ottonian ruler-couple portraits cited below, pp. 225ff., and references given there. But in these portraits the queen normally stands or kneels to the left of Christ.

[19] M. Biddle, in *The Vikings in England and their Danish Homeland*, Exhibition Catalogue (Copenhagen, 1981-82), pp. 165ff.

[20] *Handbook of British Chronology* ed. E. B. Fryde and others (London, 1986), pp. 28-29.

[21] The second English coronation-*ordo* of either Edward or Edgar (see D. H. Turner, ed. *The Claudius Pontificals*, Henry Bradshaw Society, XCVII (Chichester 1971), pp. xxxi ff., and Janet Nelson, *Politics and Ritual in Early Medieval Europe* (London, 1986) nos. 15 and 16, for the first time mentions a crown instead of a helmet). The New Minster Charter is the first picture of an Anglo-Saxon king wearing the crown with trefoils or lilies. For coins see below, p. 227.

wears a circlet under her veil, which together signify her as royal – or at least noble – as well as a married woman.[22] But curiously she is being handed by the angel another veil in addition to the first. This second veil has been interpreted recently by the German art historian Renate Kroos as *stola secunda* – that is, one of the garments of the blessed body at the Last Judgement, worn to distinguish it from the naked body of the damned.[23] I agree with this interpretation: the veil certainly signifies the salvation of the donor's soul as heavenly reward for the donation. But it could also mean the *stola prima*, that is the clothing of the rescued soul immediately after death. I know of no parallel for this duplication of the veil.[24] The unusual iconography lays a particular stress on the veil, both as a sign of marriage and as eschatological sign.

The detail of the veils or *stolae* is also striking in the continental miniatures showing Ottonian and Salian ruler-couples receiving heavenly reward, for instance in the evangeliary *(Perikopenbuch)* of the Emperor Henry II (1002-24).[25] Here both the emperor and his queen, Kunigunde, receive the 'crown of heavenly life' (Pl. 17). On the ivory plaque in the Musée de Cluny of Paris, the Emperor Otto II (967-83) and his Byzantine wife Theophanu (972-91) are both shown with crowns, blessed by Christ,[26] and in the *codex aureus* of Speyer, showing the Emperor Conrad II (1024-39) and Empress Gisela, the empress wears a veil. In each case, the couples wear or receive crowns.[27] What does it mean, that Cnut and Emma receive two different symbols in the New Minster frontispiece? With the two different symbols

22 Ch. Frugoni, 'L'Iconografia del matrimonio e della coppia nel medioevo', *Il Matrimonio nella società altomedievale*, Settimane di Studio del Centro Italiano di Studi sull'Alto Medioevo 24 (Spoleto, 1977), II, pp. 901-964, esp. 953ff.

23 R. Kroos, *Der Schrein des hl. Servatius in Maastricht und die vier zugehörigen Reliquiare in Brüssel* (München, 1985), p. 176.

24 *Ibid.* pp. 172ff. for the *stola prima.*

25 München, Staatsbibliothek, cod. lat. 4452, f. 2r. Cf. P.E. Schramm, *Die deutschen Kaiser und Könige in Bildern ihrer Zeit 751-1190*, new ed. by F. Mütherich (München, 1983), cat. no. 122.

26 Paris, Musée de Cluny, no. 1035. Cf. Schramm, *ibid.* cat. no. 91, with full-page illustration.

27 Madrid, Escorial cod. Vitrinas 17, f. 2v. Cf. Schramm, *ibid.* cat. no. 143, with full-page illustration. For the codicological contexts of these ruler-couple portraits, in liturgical MSS, see J. Wollasch, 'Kaiser und Könige als Brüder der Mönche. Zum Herrscherbild in liturgischen Handschriften des 9. bis 11. Jahrhunderts', *Deutsches Archiv für Erforschung des Mittelalters* 40 (1984), 1-20; H. Keller, 'Herrscherbild und Herrscherlegitimation. Zur Deutung der ottonischen Denkmäler', *Frühmittelalterliche Studien*, 19 (1985), 290-311, and H. Hoffmann, *Buchkunst und Königtum im ottonischen und frühsalischen Reich*, Schriften der Monumenta Germaniae Historica, XXX (Stuttgart, 1986).

the picture stresses two stories: Cnut's and Emma's marriage and Cnut's coronation.

In this context, it is significant that we know almost nothing about Cnut's coronation as king of England: no contemporary or reliable later source even mentions this event.[28] The *Anglo-Saxon Chronicle* refers to his election and acclamation, but not to his unction or coronation, as described explicitly not only for Edgar and Æthelred but also for Edward the Confessor and of course William the Conqueror.[29] This is strange, because the precarious legitimacy of Cnut 'the Conqueror' should have led to a special emphasis on the legitimizing acts and symbols of kingship. Now, I cannot solve here (or indeed at all) the riddle of Cnut's English coronation, but I can try to interpret the meaning of the crown in the *liber vitae* of New Minster. In the first place the crown is the eternal reward in return for the royal act of donation. But the crown has a detail, which is not in the New Minster Charter of Edgar: both are lily-crowns, but only Cnut's is arched at the top. It is not enough to explain this detail by saying that the angel in Cnut's picture needs a handle by which to hold the crown. Instead, the arch seems to be an echo of the same feature in the Ottonian imperial crown (Pl. 15).[30] Cnut was the first English King who had the chance to see the imperial coronation and insignia with his own eyes. He attended the imperial coronation of the German Emperor Conrad II in Rome at Easter 1027 and, together with Duke Rudolf of Burgundy, led the emperor back to his chambers afterwards.[31] Conrad had added something to the crown of his

---

[28]   *Handbook of British Chronology*, p. 28. P. Stafford, 'The Laws of King Cnut and the History of Anglo-Saxon Royal Promises', *ASE*, 10 (1982), 173-90, believes that Cnut's second law code ch. 69-83 refers to a coronation-charter of 1016-17. This seems possible, but there remains the striking fact that neither the *Anglo-Saxon Chronicle* nor any other reliable source says anything about a coronation of Cnut.

[29]   Cf. the references in K.-U. Jäschke, *Willhelm der Eroberer. Sein doppelter Herrschaftsantritt im Jahre 1066*, Vorträge und Forschungen, Sonderband XXIV (Sigmaringen, 1977), pp. 93-97.

[30]   H. Decker-Hauff and P. E. Schramm, 'Die "Reichskrone", angefertigt für Kaiser Otto I.', *Herrschaftszeichen und Staatssymbolik. Beiträge zu ihrer Geschichte vom dritten bis zum sechzehnten Jahrhundert*, von P. E. Schramm, Schriften der Monumenta Germaniae Historica, VIII, 2 (Stuttgart, 1955), pp. 560-637. But see J. Deér, 'Kaiser Otto der Große und die Reichskrone', *Beiträge zur Kunstgeschichte und Archäologie des Frühmittelalters* (1961), pp. 261-277: Deér argues for a much later date for the imperial crown: the crown was presumably produced for Emperor Henry II (1002-24). M. Schulze-Dörlamm, *Die Kaiserkrone Konrads II. (1024-1039)* (Sigmaringen, 1991), appeared too late to be taken into account.

[31]   For Cnut's journey to Rome cf. H. Bresslau, *Jahrbücher des Deutschen Reiches unter Konrad II.*, I (Leipzig, 1879), pp. 139 ff., *Die Regesten des Kaiserreiches unter Konrad II., 1024-39*, ed. H. Appelt, Regesta Imperii III (Graz, 1951), no. 73c, and

Ottonian predecessors, perhaps to make his appropriation of the crown visible. He replaced the old arch of the Ottonian crown with a new one which carried his name and title written in pearls.[32]

Perhaps Cnut's coins can add something to this interpretation. His penny of 1018-24 shows the English king for the first time with the lily-crown (Pl. 12).[33] Here we have an example of Cnut's stress on his insignia. But the crown has no arch. Cnut saw the imperial crown in or after 1027 and the *liber vitae* was produced in 1031/32. I regard the form of the heavenly crown in the *liber vitae* as a deliberate citation of the imperial crown. In the case of William the Conqueror, the *Carmen de Hastingae Proelio* describes the new crown, which was made for William's coronation in 1066, as a crown with an arch and twelve jewels, and this has been interpreted by Schramm and others as the effect of imperial aspirations.[34] In another Ottonian ruler-portrait, that of Emperor Henry II in his Bamberg sacramentary of 1002-14 (Pl. 16),[35] Christ himself is shown crowning the emperor, holding the crown at its arch. Given that Cnut's coronation in the New Minster *liber vitae* alludes to the imperial crown, we can only suppose that this reflects the idea he had of his own kingship as an imperial kingship over three *regna*. A further question would lead us into speculation: are we

Diplomatarium Danicum, no. 422, with full references.

32   *CHUONRADUS DEIGRATIA ROMANORU(M) IMPERATOR AUG(USTUS).* Cf. P.E. Schramm and F. Mütherich, *Denkmale der deutschen Könige und Kaiser. Ein Beitrag zur Herrschergeschichte von Karl dem Großen bis Friedrich II. 768-1250,* (München, 1962), cat. no. 146. The arch is dated here 'um 1030'; it could certainly also have been produced on the occasion of the imperial coronation.

     Although it is not entirely clear which crown the Salian king wore at his coronation in Rome – a Cluniac source claims that Conrad gave his insignia *quae Rome gestavit in regni adeptione* to Cluny – Cnut's close relations to the German empire before and after the event (see below p. 230) suggest that he had personal knowledge of Conrad and his efforts to enhance his imperial representation. If the Ottonian imperial crown was not used in 1027 in Rome, the one which was used and later given away to Cluny would have closely resembled the original. The Cluniac source is *Vita Hugonis abb. Cluniacensis,* ed. *Acta Sanctorum* III, 19 April, p. 655; cf. P. E. Schramm, 'Herrschaftszeichen: gestiftet, verschenkt, verkauft, verpfändet', *Nachrichten der Akad. d. Wiss. in Göttingen,* Phil.-Hist. Klasse 1957, 161-226, at p. 178.

33   Cf. *The Golden Age of Anglo-Saxon Art, 966-1066,* ed. J. Backhouse, D. H. Turner, L. Webster (London, 1984), no. 213. Thereafter Cnut's moneyers returned to the older helmet or diadem types. Only Edward in the later years of his reign takes up the crown again as insignia on coins (*ibid.* p. 187).

34   P. E. Schramm, 'Die Kronen des frühen Mittelalters', id. *Herrschaftszeichen* II pp. 377-417 (p. 393).

35   München, Staatsbibliothek, cod. lat. 4456, f. 11r. Cf. Schramm, *Die deutschen Kaiser,* cat. no. 124.

seeing in this imperial element in the crown Cnut's attempt to rise above the problem of not having been properly crowned as king of the Anglo-Saxons?

This is not the only hint of deliberate copying of foreign models of ruler-representation: Cnut gave a crown to Christ Church Canterbury in 1023.[36] There is no other example of an English king before him doing this. But on the continent, especially in the German empire, it was common practice. Emperor Henry II's gift of crown and insignia to Cluny is only one of many examples.[37]

In addition, Cnut's golden cross for the New Minster can be interpreted as a reference to the German emperors who had given many sumptuous crosses to their churches.[38] I reproduce only one of them, the so-called Lothar cross, given about 1000 by Otto III to Aachen, whose form, especially the ends of the cross-arms, resembles Cnut's cross (Pl. 14).[39] Another cross, the so-called imperial cross, could itself have been a model for Cnut's cross: this was the reliquary cross which belonged to the imperial insignia and was in its present form ordered by Conrad II.[40] The donation of gold crosses to churches by Anglo-Saxon kings is also recorded: Æthelstan gave a cross to Chester-le-Street in 934,[41] and Edgar gave to Ely a cross which also contained relics.[42] But only one Anglo-Saxon cross, the Drahmal cross at Brussels, has survived.[43] However, the form of Cnut's cross, as depicted in the *liber vitae*, resembles strongly the continental crosses of the Lothar type,[44] and it was in

---

[36] Sawyer, *Anglo-Saxon Charters*, no. 959. See N. Brooks, *The Early History of the Church of Canterbury from 597 to 1066*. Studies in the Early History of Britain (Leicester, 1984), pp. 292-94.

[37] J. Wollasch, 'Kaiser Heinrich II. in Cluny', *Frühmittelalterliche Studien*, 3 (1969), 327-342 at p. 327. Schramm, *Herrschafszeichen*, lists many more examples, but not Cnut's donation to Canterbury.

[38] One has only to look at the sumptuous crosses in the 'Münsterschatz' of Essen: H. Köhn, *Der Essener Münsterschatz* (Essen, 1950); Schramm and Mütherich, *Denkmale*, cat. nos 106 ('Lothar-cross'), 119, 139, 143.

[39] J. Deér, 'Das Kaiserbild im Kreuz', *Schweizer Beiträge zur allgemeinen Geschichte*, 13 (1955), 48-110. For the cult of the cross around the year 1000, in England and on the continent, see J. Fried, 'Endzeiterwartung um die Jahrtausendwende', *Deutsches Archiv für Erforschung des Mittelalters*, 45 (1989), 381-473, pp. 449ff.

[40] Schramm and Mütherich, *Denkmale*, cat. no. 145.

[41] *Historia de Sancto Cuthberto*, ed. T. Arnold, *Symeonis Monachi Opera Omnia*, RS (London, 1882), I, pp. 211.

[42] *Liber Eliensis*, ed. E. O. Blake, Camden 3rd. Ser. XCII (London, 1962), ch. II, 4, p. 76.

[43] *Golden Age of Anglo-Saxon Art*, no. 75, pl. XXIII.

[44] Florence of Worcester describes it as *crux magna, crux sancta, iussu regis Canuti dudum fabricata, et ab eodem auro et argento, gemmis et lapidibus pretiosis decentissime adornata. Florentii Wigorniensis monachi, chronicon ex chronicis*, ed. B.

the Ottonian empire that the tradition of cross-donations was so well established.

Did the Ottonians derive the main features of their ruler-representation from Byzantium? Otto II's wife Theophanu was the main source of Byzantine influence on the Ottonian court. She lived after her consort's death (983) until 991 with a Byzantine 'court' in the monastery of St. Pantaleon at Cologne.[45] But we also have some evidence of direct contacts between England and Byzantium in the late Anglo-Saxon period.[46] Cnut's Danish connections across the Baltic Sea no doubt reinforced these links with the East.[47] But the whole issue of Byzantine influence on late Anglo-Saxon England cannot really be discussed here. Apart from direct contacts it can however be agreed that the Ottonian empire and especially the Ottonian court played an important, if not leading, part in transmitting Byzantine 'images of rulership' to western Europe, including Anglo-Saxon England.

Thorpe, 2 vols. (London, 1849), II, p. 133. Cf. Heslop 'Manuscripts and Patronage', p. 187.

[45] For references to Byzantine influences on the Ottonian ruler-representation, see J. Deér, *Byzanz und das aberländische Herrschertum. Ausgewählte Aufsätze*, ed. P. Classen, Vorträge und Forschungen, XXI (Sigmaringen, 1977). There are Byzantine ruler-portraits which closely resemble their Ottonian counterparts and form perhaps their direct models. For example, in the Psalter of Basil II Bulgaroctone (976-1025), Venice, Biblioteca Marciana, MS Gr. Z 17 f. iiir, of 1017, the standing emperor is crowned by the archangel Gabriel, who evidently receives the crown from Christ depicted above the emperor. Archangel Michael hands a spear over to him (colour plate in D. Talbot Rice, ed. *The Dark Ages*, (London 1965)), p. 115; A. v. Hülsen kindly drew my attention to this manuscript. There is a similar picture in the (perhaps earlier) sacramentary of Henry II (above, note 35), where however there are no angels. The angels appear in much the same form in the drawing of Cnut and Emma. The role of angels as intermediaries between Christ and kings is typical of Byzantine ruler-portraits of the 11th and 12th centuries: see I. Spatharakis, *The Portrait in Byzantine Illuminated Manuscripts*, Byzantina Nederlandica, fasc. VI (Leiden, 1976), pp. 20ff., 99ff. (Cod. Sin. Gr. 364). It is not entirely clear who was influenced by whom!

[46] With full references, K. Ciggaar, 'England and Byzantium on the Eve of the Norman Conquest (The Reign of Edward the Confessor)', *Anglo-Norman Studies*, 5 (1982), 78-96. See the *Andreas grecus* in the New Minster list of the *liber vitae* of New Minster, an entry of about 1030. Emma's relic-shrine, which she gave to the New Minster, is described in this codex as *Greccyscan scrine* (*ibid.* ff. 58r-v; cf. Heslop, 'Manuscripts and Patronage' pp. 187-188). Also William the Conqueror's crown was made by a Greek goldsmith: see above, note 34.

[47] Cnut was the son of Gunhild, the Polish first wife of Svein, and sister of Bolizlav Chrobry. For Viking connections with Byzantium see Roesdahl, *Viking Age Denmark*, p. 199ff.

And there is, in addition to Cnut's journey to Rome, plenty of evidence for contacts between Cnut and the courts of the emperors Henry II, Conrad II and Henry III and with German churches.[48] To mention only four: in 1025 Cnut had established an agreement with the archbishop of Hamburg-Bremen, Unwan, about the metropolitan rights of this church in his Danish kingdom. Cnut received the border region Schleswig as compensation from the German king.[49] Cnut gave two *de luxe* manuscripts to the church of Cologne, where Theophanu had once lived, and which were returned later in the century to England.[50] Henry II is said to have been in possession of Anglo-Saxon *de luxe* vessels;[51] finally, in 1036 the future emperor Henry III married Cnut's daughter Gunhild/Kunigunde, a marriage which had been negotiated by Cnut himself.[52] This evidence points rather to direct Ottonian contacts than to Byzantine ones as sources of inspiration for Cnut's royal representation.

The New Minster frontispiece therefore shows at least three iconographic elements which explicitly recall Ottonian models: the picture of the royal couple receiving heavenly reward from Christ, the imperial crown of Cnut, and the donation of a cross. Royal donorship, representation and particularly legitimacy, appear in close association. It is impossible to distinguish between the secular and the sacred elements.

II. *The* liber vitae *of New Minster*

Until now the book and its frontispiece have seldom been considered together, and yet it is impossible to understand one without the other. The frontispiece depicts two books, the heavenly book of life held by Christ in the mandorla, and in the bottom scene, the earthly *liber vitae* held by the monk in the centre, in fact the actual manuscript of which this is the first page. These two books are books of *memoria, memoria* as inscription in the earthly *liber vitae*, and as constant liturgical commemoration in order to be written into the heavenly *liber vitae*. Therefore our frontispiece is also a

---

[48] R. Deshman gives full references: '*Christus rex et magi reges:* Kingship and Christology in Ottonian and Anglo-Saxon Art', *Frühmittelalterliche Studien*, 10 (1976), 367-405, pp. 391ff.

[49] *Die Regesten des Kaiserreiches unter Konrad II., 1024-1039*, ed. H. Appelt, Regesta Imperii III, 1 (Graz, 1951), no. 48b.

[50] William of Malmesbury, *Vita S. Wulfstani*, ed. R.R. Darlington. Camden 3rd Ser., XL (London, 1928), p. 15-16. Cf. Heslop 'Manuscripts and Patronage', pp. 159-60, 180.

[51] References in Deshman, 'Kingship', pp. 390ff. esp. 398.

[52] *Regesten*, ed. Appelt, nos. 225c, 238c. On the occasion of the royal couple's engagement in May 1035 in Bamberg Conrad II and Cnut bound themselves by a *fedus amicitie*.

'Memorialbild', or commemoration picture.[53] This becomes the more evident when one turns the page: the famous Last Judgement on the following pages ff. 6v and 7r of Stowe 944 (Pl. 10) was drawn by the same artist and, with its three registers and its depiction of the walled city of Jerusalem, it echoes the donation picture. The book appears again in the Judgement scene, now in use: in the middle register of the right leaf the angel at Peter's side holds it open, and Peter strikes the devil with his keys. The devil also holds an open book, the book of sins. Those who are inscribed in the book of Heaven come into the heavenly city of Jerusalem in the upper scene, which again shows Christ in the mandorla; those whose names stand in the book of sins come into Hell in the lower scene, shown as Hades' jaws. The group of people in the left upper rank are the saved souls, the choir of the elect: saints, the laity, clerics and monks, who are led by the angels into Heaven. The two figures on the left in the middle register have been interpreted as Bishop Æthelwold of Winchester and Abbot Æthelgarus of the New Minster, whose name also stands, near the left-hand edge of the page *(Ælgarus)*.[54] If this interpretation is correct, we have again the connection with the New Minster – represented in the frontispiece by the choir of monks in the lower zone. This sequence of pictures is of great importance for the history of *memoria*, in fact it is the only known direct pictorial comment on commemoration in a *liber vitae*.

What is *memoria*, what is the nature of these commemorative sources? The manuscript itself gives one answer.[55] A text on ff. 13r-v explains the theology and liturgy of *memoria*:

> In this due order follow the names of the brethren and monks as well as friends and benefactors, that they be inscribed into the pages of the heavenly book by the *temporalem recordationem* of this script: that is the names of those, by whose alms this community in Christ is daily nourished. And all who commend themselves to the prayers and fraternity of this community, are written into this book so that their commemoration be performed daily in holy mass and psalms.

The text proceeds to the liturgy of *memoria:*

> And these names are to be presented *per singulos dies* by the subdeacon in front of the altar at matins and the main mass, and they are to be read –

[53] O. G. Oexle, 'Memoria und Memorialbild', *Memoria. Der geschichtliche Zeugniswert des liturgischen Gedenkens im Mittelalter*, ed. K. Schmid and J. Wollasch, Münstersche Mittelalter-Schriften, XLVIII (München, 1984), pp. 384-440 (pp. 392ff. for references to the *liber vitae*).

[54] Birch, Register, p. vii.

[55] For the answer given by modern research see my report, with bibliography: 'Societas et Fraternitas. A Report on a Research Project at the Universities of Freiburg and Münster', *Nomina*, 12 (1988-89), 153-71.

prout tempus permiserit.[56]

So the pictures and the following texts are connected not only codicologically but also by contents. In the same quire as the pictures follows the well-known history of the New Minster.[57] It commences with a statement about the royal *fundatores* and benefactors: 'their names are written down and are daily recited in the mass in that holy place where· they are buried'.[58] The list of kings since Edward the Elder appears as a list of benefactors of the monastery *regalibus usibus*: King Alfred's remains were transferred into the New Minster by Edward and the founder himself was buried in the appropriate place on the right side of the main altar. The history of this royal abbey is told according to the kings, not its abbots. Edgar and Æthelred the Unready are the kings whose acts are praised in detail. The test ends with Æthelred and was apparently written in Æthelred's lifetime. Cnut is missing.

This is only one of many hints that the manuscript of 1031/32 was compiled from older material, which was not always updated and continued. The codex had at least one predecessor which was possibly begun in the time of Edgar, Æthelwold and Abbot Ælfgar, after the reform of 964. Many entries date also from Æthelred's time, as for instance, that about Bishop Ælfheah as *hodie prae est*, although the bishop left Winchester for Canterbury in 1006 and was killed by the Danes in 1012.[59] The compiler, the writer Ælsinus, did not update the following lists of kings and bishops. In the case of the history of New Minster this was not necessary: the frontispiece *is* the continuation of the foundation history.

This is not the place to explain the structure and contents of the name-lists.[60] It is necessary only to divide them into three main groups of *ordines*: firstly (ff. 14r-17v) the royal succession of Wessex (again only up to Æthelred), the king's sons, the bishops of West Saxon sees, the dukes or

---

[56] Birch, Register, p. 11: *hic ordine condecibili onomata progrediuntur fratrum et monachorum nec non et familiariorum uel benefactorum uiuorum seu defunctorum, ut per temporalem recordationem scripture istius in celestis libri conscribantur pagina. Quorum beneficiis elemosinarum cotidie hec ipsa familia Christo largiente pascitur. Et omnium qui se eius orationibus ac fraternitati commendant, hic generaliter habeantur inscripta. Quatinus cotidie in sacra missarum celebrationibus vel psalmodiarum concentibus eorum commemoratio fiat.*

[57] Gerchow, pp. 158-59 with collation of the manuscript and detailed table of contents.

[58] Birch, *Register*, p. 4: *eorum pariter annotata nomina in sacro eodem loco quo tumulati tenentur dietenus recitentur in diuinis missarum sollempniis.*

[59] The Ælfheah entry is on f. 18r.; for the dating of the different parts of the MS see Gerchow, pp. 163ff., 183ff..

[60] *Ibid.* pp. 164ff.

ealdormen and the *ministri* or thegns. After this come the confraternity lists of the Old Minster, the New Minster itself, the male and female benefactors, the lists of Abingdon, Ely and Romsey as well as the names of lay people (ff. 17v-29r). The last, rather bulky, part (ff. 29v-68v) is an extremely interesting mixture of various texts whose composition still needs explanation. Many parts of it contain royal *memoria*.[61] Cnut's and Emma's names are to be found, as well as in the frontispiece itself, in the *Nomina familiariorum vel benefactorum* (Pl. 13) and in the *Nomina feminarum illustrium* (here *Santslave*, Cnut's otherwise unknown sister, occurs).[62] Cnut's is the last entry in the *Nomina regum* containing the kings of Wessex and England from Ini to Cnut. Two lists of relics apparently can be interpreted as donations of Cnut and Emma: the text on f. 55v, *Iste reliquie sunt in magna cruce*, might thus be a description of the contents of Cnut's and Emma's cross, while the text on ff.58r-v gives the contents of a 'Greek shrine', which *seo hlaefdige* gave to the New Minster. Both texts are written in hands of the later eleventh and twelfth centuries.

The new compilation of a *liber vitae* from old material at the beginning of the 1030s in the New Minster cannot be explained without the context of Cnut's and Emma's donations, especially the donation of the cross. This was probably the occasion for the new compilation, and suggests why the picture had such a prominent position. One need only recall Edgar's portrait in the frontispiece of his charter, or its continental counterparts. The Ottonian and Salian ruler portraits are integral to the liturgical manuscripts, given by these rulers to their churches and monasteries.[63]

But the compilation of a *liber vitae* is not accounted for by a royal donation alone. The monks themselves had to make the effort and reconstruct their commemoration. Research on commemorative documents on the continent has shown, for instance in the case of the Reichenau *liber vitae* in 824, or the Cluniac obituaries in the eleventh century, that they are testimonies of monastic reform, of a reflection on the monastery's aims and its history.[64] I plan to argue in another paper that this *liber vitae* also contains

61 Apart from the frontispiece and the *historia* at the beginning, see *Nomina regum occidentalium Saxonum*, *Nomina regum*, *Nomina familiariorum vel benefactorum*, *Nomina feminarum illustrium*, King Alfred's will, the *Tha halgan* and *Secgean*-texts on Kentish and English royal saints, *Nomina regum*, the Edward charter for Bishop Denewulf of Winchester, Sawyer, *Anglo-Saxon Charters*, no. 1443, the relic-lists of the cross and Emma's Greek shrine. See Gerchow, pp. 160-62.

62 For *Santslave* see Larson, *Canute*, p. 57 and 262, who suggests an otherwise unknown sister of Cnut by their Polish mother Gunhild.

63 Note 30, above.

64 K. Schmid, 'Bermerkungen zur Anlage des Reichenauer Verbrüderungsbuches. Zugleich ein Beitrag zum Verständnis der Visio Wettini', idem, *Gebetsgedenken*

strong evidence of a reform impulse both in the New Minster and elsewhere.[65]

The use of the *liber vitae* as the context for the royal donation picture raises a question which leads back to the initial comparison of Edgar's portrait with that of Cnut and Emma. Edgar's portrait is a partly gilded painting on purple stained ground: it is comparable with Ottonian specimens of ruler-representation in liturgical manuscripts. Cnut's and Emma's portrait is a line-drawing, in which certain features are coloured. The cross, for example, is coloured yellow so as to suggest the gold of the original. Although line-drawing might be regarded as a fashion in this period, the *liber vitae* was not meant to be a *de luxe* manuscript. Artistic content might suggest that the two pictures are not comparable, and that one was an effect of royal munificence while the other was a more austere, monastic, reflection on the implications of benefaction. The subject matter, however (as I have argued), points to a similar inspiration behind both books; also, the New Minster charter was produced in the New or Old Minster and reflected the views of king and monks alike. The same applies to the *liber vitae* frontispiece: the manuscript was not to be given away, donated by the royal couple to a monastery or church, like a charter or other *de luxe* manuscripts. It was produced by the monks as their book for themselves; but the king played such an important part in the liturgical and communal life of the monastery through his patronage and donations that the codex was interwoven with royal commemoration. And just as the king moved into the monastic sphere, so the monks took their part in royal affairs: for example we know that Abbot Lifing of Tavistock was one of Cnut's companions to Rome. On this diplomatic pilgrimage there were certainly other monks, probably of the New or Old Minsters, the main churches in his 'capital'. As such they might have witnessed the coronation scene at Easter 1027 which provided such inspiration to Cnut.[66]

King Cnut appears and was meant to appear in the context of the *liber vitae* as Edgar *redivivus*, and therefore as protagonist of monastic reform. This supports the idea that Cnut's and Emma's dedication picture was an imitation of Egar's New Minster charter. His incorporation into the

---

und adliges Selbstverständnis im Mittelalter. Ausgewählte Beiträge. Festgabe zu seinem sechzigsten Geburtstag (Sigmaringen, 1983), pp. 514-31; J. Wollasch, Mönchtum des Mittelalters zwischen Kirche und Welt, Münstersche Mittelalter-Schriften, VII (München, 1973), pp. 53ff.

65 For the moment Gerchow, p. 180ff.

66 Cnut's grave was in the Old Minster. But the two monasteries, the Old and the New Minster, were closely interconnected, not only as immediate neighbours. Cf. for instance the list of the Old Minster community in the New Minster *liber vitae*; and the writer and artist Ælsinus, who seems to have been an inmate of the Old Minster. See Gerchow, art. B.

succession of English kings in the lists of the *liber vitae*, as well as the role of the royal couple as donor of relics, show that royal *memoria* was inseparably interwoven with monastic *memoria*.

III. Cnut, Emma and the Danes in the Anglo-Saxon commemorative sources
An early obituary of New Minster in the breviary of Abbot Ælfwinus has under 12 November *Obitus Cnud rex* and under 7 March *Imma obiit regina*.[67] Cnut's name was inscribed in six English obituaries up to 1100, more often than Alfred, Edgar, Æthelred and also William the Conqueror, who figure only five times each. Emma has four entries.[68]

In the so-called Leofric Collectar[69] there is an entry of special interest. Under 11 November it records: *Obitus Landberti piissimi regis*. Who is this King Lambert? The editor Frederick Warren suggested he was the 'King of Italy, emperor of the Romans':[70] that is Emperor Lambert who died in 898. But firstly his obit is otherwise kept on 15 October[71] and this would have been in any case a rather far-fetched solution. Secondly Adam of Bremen in his *Gesta episcoporum* of Hamburg and Bremen (+1081) wrote a generation after Cnut's death that Cnut accepted on the occasion of his baptism the Christian name *Lambertus*, and that he together with his wife Emma and his son (Hartha)cnut was inscribed with this name in the Bremen confraternity book.[72] Thirdly the 11, 12 and 13 November are documented by other

---

[67] BL, Cotton MS, Titus D. xxvii., See Gerchow, pp. 233-44, 332-35 (art. 17) for the obit-notes.

[68] *Ibid.* The basis for this argument is the collection of material in my book. On pp.102ff., this date and the selection of obituaries is explained (some are transmitted later than 1100, but contain clearly Anglo-Saxon material); pp. 415-17 contain a survey of obits of dignitaries. Later obits of Cnut and Emma would include those of Abingdon, Durham, Christ Church and St Augustine's Canterbury and St Alban's.

[69] Oxford, Bodleian Library, MS Bodley 579, f. 44r. See note 70 and Gerchow, pp. 253-57.

[70] *The Leofric Missal*, ed. F. E. Warren (Oxford 1883), p. li.

[71] Cf. *Lexikon für Theologie und Kirche* 2nd edn., VI (Freiburg, 1961), col. 759.

[72] Scholia 37 to book II 52 of Adam von Bremen, Bischofsgeschichte der Hamburger Kirche, in: *Quellen des 9. und 11. Jahrhunderts zur Geschichte der Hamburger Kirche und des Reiches*, ed. W. Trillmich, R. Buchner, Ausgewählte Quellen zur deutschen Geschichte des Mittelalters, XI (Darmstadt, 1978), p. 290: *Chnut filius Suein regis abjecto nomine gentilitatis in baptismo Lambertus nomen accepit. Unde scriptum est in libro fraternitatis nostrae: 'Lambrecht rex Danorum et Imma regina et Chnut filius eorum devote se commendaverunt orationibus fratrum Bremensium'.* For the baptism cf. Larson, *Canute*, p. 164f., and G. Thoma, *Namenänderungen in Herrscherfamilien des frühmittelalterlichen Europa* (Kallmünz, 1985), pp. 36-39 on the date of Cnut's baptism. Cnut would not have been

obituaries and chronicles as Cnut's obit.[73] So the Exeter entry certainly belongs to Cnut.

This entry is very interesting, because it throws some light on Cnut's baptism, which he apparently received at a later age, not in his infancy, perhaps on the feast of Lambert, 17 September.[74] Anyhow, Cnut accepted a Christian name, which was used in his commemoration.

Certainly Cnut's status as neophyte, in other words an adult convert, was a strong motive for his donations and benefactions. But it also throws light on the basis of Cnut's rule as conqueror and English king. Cnut could not use the Danish church to support his position, as William the Conqueror had done with the Norman church. He had to establish a relationship with the Anglo-Saxon church; he had to repent, and make good the destruction he and his father had caused, and he totally relied on the Anglo-Saxon church for his spiritual legitimacy as a Christian king. Cnut's foundations, translations and his donations to the Anglo-Saxon church document his efforts to gain the support and backing of the English ecclesiastical establishment. His *memoria* is the most prominent of all Anglo-Saxon kings and reflects the extraordinary strength of these efforts.

Finally I would like to consider an Anglo-Norman *liber vitae*, that of Thorney Abbey, which was begun under Abbot Gunther around 1100.[75] The first list on f. 10r (Pl. 18) after the heading *hec sunt nomina fratrum istius loci*, begins with *Rex Cnut*, followed by his sons Harold and Harthacnut as well as *Imma regina et Ælfgifu*.[76] Again, it is worth pointing to one detail, the list of Danish earls and housecarls, published by Dorothy Whitelock in 1945.[77] The appearance of Cnut's five earls Turkil, Hakon, Eiric, Eglaf and Ulf and the following twenty-nine housecarls show that not only Cnut and his family

---

baptised at the time of Svein's relapse into heathendom after the marriage with Sigrid Storråda (according to Adam of Bremen II, 27, 29-30, 34, 39), but later, when Svein returned to the Christian faith. The Exeter obit is an important new testimony of Cnut's use of this baptismal name, which obliterates Thoma's comments on p. 38.

[73] See note 68 above.

[74] The feast of the martyr saint of Liège is present in nearly all surviving Anglo-Saxon calendars, though not as a major feast; see *English Kalendars before A.D. 1100*, ed. F. Wormald, The Henry Bradshaw Society, LXXII (London, 1934), passim.

[75] BL, Add. MS 40000, f. 10r. Cf. C. Clark, 'British Library Additional MS 40000, ff. 1v-12r', *Anglo-Norman Studies*, 7 (1984), 53-72, and Gerchow, pp. 186-97, 326-28.

[76] For the question whether Emma and/or Ælfgifu of Northampton are represented by this entry cf. Gerchow, pp. 190ff.

[77] D. Whitelock, 'Scandinavian Personal Names in the Liber Vitae of Thorney Abbey', *Saga Book of the Viking Society for Northern Research*, 12 (1945), 127-53.

figure in the commemoration of English monasteries. His Danish followers were also eager to gain the prayers of the monks. Again, in Cnut's Gospel-book at Christ Church Canterbury, where Cnut and his brother Harold are included in a confraternity (Pl. 11), three other Danes are named as brothers of the monks, *Thorth, Kartoca, Thuri*.[78] In the *liber vitae* of New Minster there are several other Danish names.[79] Cnut included his Danish followers in his efforts to gain the prayers of the English church. This was another means by which he attempted to stabilize his rule as king of the English.

IV. Summary

1. The commemoration picture in the New Minster *liber vitae* appears to have three meanings, understood as intentions:

a) It is a donor's portrait. Cnut and Emma give the golden reliquary cross to the altar of the New Minster and receive the reward of the heavenly crown and the *stola prima* or *secunda*.

b) It is a coronation picture. Cnut's 'coronation' in the *liber vitae* is what distinguishes it above all from its direct model, the frontispiece to Edgar's New Minster Charter. Whether it refers to Cnut's coronation as king of the English, not known from elsewhere, or whether Cnut wished to compare his rule with that of the emperors by alluding to the arch of the imperial crown, like William the Conqueror later on, cannot be established.

c) It is a portrait of the royal couple with an iconography of matrimony which recalls that favoured by Ottonian and Salian Germany. Thus the picture stresses Cnut's link to the Anglo-Saxon dynasty of Wessex.

All these readings make deliberate allusion to Ottonian models of ruler-representation, and more distantly to their Byzantine origins.

2. The commemoration picture is part of a *memoria* codex: the *liber vitae* of New Minster. The compilation of 1031/32 uses material from the time of Edgar and Æthelwold onwards and was presumably inspired by the occasion of Cnut's and Emma's donation of the cross. The *memoria* of the kings and queens is incorporated into the monastic *memoria*. Cnut appears as 'new Edgar' in a manuscript which should be taken as a document of monastic reform.

---

[78] BL, Royal MS 1.D.ix., f. 43v. For the text cf. N. Ker, *Catalogue of Manuscripts containing Anglo-Saxon* (Oxford, 1957), no. 247a: + *In nomine domini nostri iesu cristi. Her is awriten. CNUTES. kynges nama the is ure leofa hlaford for worulde, and ure gastlica brothor for gode, and harold thaes kinges brothor. Thorth ure brothor. Kartoca ure brotheror. Thuri ure brother.*

[79] Among many examples, nos. 47-50 of the *Nomina familiariorum vel benefactorum* (Gerchow, p. 325): *Thored danus, Toui danus, Thored danus, Toca danus* (Pl. 13).

3. Cnut is the Anglo-Saxon king with the most entries in English obituaries up to 1100. He also had his Danish earls and housecarls inscribed in the *libri vitae*, notably that of Thorney.

Cnut's *memoria* is part of the legitimization of a Viking conqueror, a neophyte and founder of a northern empire, as king of the English. By his gifts, Cnut expressed repentance for damage done in the course of military campaigning. In return he received the *memoria* of the monks, which was of vital importance for the spiritual legitimization of his kingship. He could not, like William the Conqueror, draw resources from his own Danish church but depended on the Anglo-Saxon church for the administrative and ideological basis of his kingship. Cnut's historical *memoria* fell a long way short of William's; his liturgical commemoration was at least of equal rank.

The Idiosyncrasy of Late Anglo-Saxon Religious Imagery
GEORGE HENDERSON

The loss of many works of art makes it difficult to be sure of the rules which Anglo-Saxon artists followed in their depiction of sacred scenes and persons. The archive of early models also has certainly been much reduced, and consequently it is not easy to know when originality has intervened, over against the reproduction of an impressive late Antique or Carolingian exemplar. Some things that have survived are altogether singular, difficult to 'place'. They warn us of our ignorance about the whole context of other works.

The perplexities of the situation are well illustrated by the former Damme, now the Getty, leaves.[1] It is doubtful quite what we are dealing with, since the one surviving page of text starts like a Gospel Lectionary, 'In illo tempore', yet is marked up like a Gospel Book with the relevant marginal entry from Canon 2; oddly, there are two mistakes out of the three citations![2] As problematic as the function of the original book is its iconography. On the recto of f.2r, overleaf from the painting of the Tribute Money (Matthew 17. 26), is a unique version of the scene of the Transfiguration (Matthew 17. 1-8), if so it be (Pl. 19). There are too many attendant figures for a Transfiguration; it looks more like the Sermon on the Mount, with cascades of water representing the rain that falls upon the just and the unjust (Matthew 5. 45); alternatively, these cascades are like the Rivers of Paradise, though here they flow down into a single sea. Perhaps the most exceptional feature of all is the upside-down foot in the water, just below the right foot of the seated Christ, the first reflexion, as I take it, since Antiquity. That level of pictorial representational coherence is unexpected; it may signify the obedience of Christ in his *humanitas* to the laws of Nature, or it may be a tribute to the objectivity of us the spectators. If the latter, this image would tend to support Meyer Schapiro's speculation that another seemingly original contribution of the Anglo-Saxons to Christian art, the motif of the 'disappearing Christ', arises from a shift of viewpoint, specifically to that of the Apostles, earthbound, below.[3]

1 Malibu, the J. Paul Getty Museum MS 9, for which see A. Boutemy, 'Les feuillets de Damme', *Scriptorium*, 20 (1966), 60-65 and E. Temple, *Anglo-Saxon Manuscripts 900-1066* (London, 1976), pp. 72-73, no. 53.

2 The Mark reference is given as LXVII, not XLVII; the Luke reference is given as LXXXIIII, not LXXXIII. For the relevant passage see *Novum Testamentum Latine Secundum Editionem Sancti Hieronymi*, ed. J. Wordsworth and H. White (Oxford, 1911), xvii and p. 18.

3 M. Schapiro, 'The Image of the Disappearing Christ', in his *Late Antique, Early Christian and Mediaeval Art: Selected Papers* (London, 1980), 267-287, esp. p. 282.

I would not, however, press for the widespread existence of that kind of coherence of vision, because it seems to me that the real idiosyncrasies of Anglo-Saxon art spring from another sort of sensibility, a careful connecting of sacred words and visual images, a first-hand commitment to literal illustration. We can understand the point of Anglo-Saxon images of 'the disappearing Christ' well enough if we concentrate, as I believe the Anglo-Saxons did, on the relevant words of the Scripture, Acts 1. 9, 'Elevatus est: et nubes suscepit eum ab oculis eorum.' That is what is literally illustrated. The words and the image reflect one another exactly. The picture has an intelligent commitment to the text it stands in, or to the texts it naturally brings to mind under thoughtful scrutiny.

In the papers from the 1987 St Cuthbert conference David Rollason has published his fully documented interpretation of Cambridge, Corpus Christi College MS 183 as a book planned for Athelstan's own use in Wessex, not primarily as a gift to the community at Chester-le-Street. He acknowledges the validity of my suggestion that we are not dealing in the famous prefatory miniature with a presentation scene.[4] The fact that the king is looking at the open book, not putting the closed book into the hands of the recipient, makes it reasonable to interpret the picture as a meditation on the saint in a general way. I would add further to Rollason's account the proposition that the picture is a straight illustration of Bede's prologue to his prose *Life of St Cuthbert*. Bede advocates the use of his book, celebrating the pious memory of the holy father Cuthbert, to uplift the reader's heart 'to a more eager desire for the heavenly kingdom'. Athelstan is shown doing exactly that; we can juxtapose text and picture as mirrors and reflections of one another.[5]

If one presses very hard this idea of an intimate bond between the sense of the text and the contents of the illustration, one might find an explanation for an odd difference between an illustration in the Utrecht Psalter and in its Anglo-Saxon copy, BL Harley MS 603. The Harley MS essentially reproduces the Utrecht Psalter's illustration of Psalm 2. At verse 9 of the Psalm we read: 'Thou shalt rule them with a rod of iron and shalt break them in pieces like a potter's vessel.' In Utrecht the vase is duly broken, cracked across by Christ's rod. But in Harley MS 603 it is still intact. In Utrecht the entire text of Psalm 2 stands alongside the illustration, but in the Harley MS we turn the page over after verse 8, so that verse 9, with the reference to the shattering of the

---

[4] D. Rollason, 'St Cuthbert and Wessex: The Evidence of Cambridge, Corpus Christi College MS 183', in *St Cuthbert, His Cult and His Community to AD 1200*, ed. C. Bonner, D. Rollason, C. Stancliffe (Woodbridge, 1989), 413-424, esp. at pp. 421-423.

[5] *Vita Sancti Cuthberti Auctore Beda*, in *Two Lives of Saint Cuthbert*, ed. B. Colgrave (Cambridge, 1940), pp. 144-46: *...sed cum eundem librum relegentes, pia sanctissimi patris memoria vestros animos ad desideria regni coelestis ardentius attollitis...'*

vase, is on the verso.[6] It seems to me just possible that the unshattered vase represents not mere negligence of the dictates of the exemplar, but an experiment with the niceties of text-and-picture juxtaposition.

Be that as it may, there are a number of cases where the adjacent text can be seen positively to colour and explain the choice of a particular illustration. As is well known, Cambridge, University Library MS Ff. 1.23, a *Romanum* Psalter, contains full-page coloured drawings before Psalms 1, 51, 101 and 109. In her survey of Anglo-Saxon manuscripts Eliżbieta Temple describes the third miniature, on f. 171r, thus: it 'shows Christ seated in a mandorla held by four angels; His right hand raised in blessing. His left resting on a book, He is supporting an inscribed scroll laid across His arms, and the whole is enclosed by a frame with acanthus medallions and contains leaf patterns on dark ground'. (Pl. 20). Temple's study is mainly stylistic, and so we are left with no further comment on the meaning or purpose of the illustration placed before Psalm 101.[7] Is it selective and appropriate, or is it merely conventional – some sacred subject or other – that is inserted here?

In the first place it is useful to read the inscription on the scroll supported by Christ: 'Ego sum Deus qui reddet unicuique juxta opus eius.' This text has good antecedents. St Paul, in Romans 2. 5-6, speaks of 'the day of wrath' and of 'the just judgement of God, who will render to every man according to his works (*secundum opera ejus*)'. Proverbs 24. 12 speaks of God 'That seeth into the heart... and he shall render to a man according to his works (*juxta opera sua*).' Our 'juxta' agrees with Proverbs. At the end of Revelation 22. 12, Christ declares that he will 'come quickly... to render to every man according to his works (*reddere unicuique secundum opera sua*)'. The most central source for the inscription, however, seems likely to be Matthew 16. 27, where Christ says to his disciples: 'For the Son of man shall come in the glory of his Father with his angels: and then he will render to every man according to his works (*reddet unicuique secundum opera ejus*).'

Given the biblical context of its inscription there can be no doubt that the drawing on f. 171r of the Cambridge manuscript represents the Last Judgement, even if it takes a form independent of the more familiar picturesque imagery of the wounds, instruments of the Passion, intercessors, the dead rising, etc.[8] But why should the Judgement, as opposed to the Crucifixion or Christ trampling the beasts be here, before Psalm 101? I

---

[6] Utrecht, University Library MS 32, f. 2r for which see E. T. Dewald, *The Illustrations of the Utrecht Psalter* (Princeton, 1933). For London, BL Harley MS 603, f. 2r, see Temple, *Anglo-Saxon Manuscripts*, pl. 200.

[7] *Ibid.*, pp. 97-98, no. 80.

[8] Incidentally it helps us to understand the tympanum of the Prior's doorway at Ely Cathedral as a Last Judgement; see E. Prior and A. Gardiner, *An Account of Medieval Figure-Sculpture in England* (Cambridge, 1912), p. 206, fig. 185.

suggest that it is part of the planning of the book, which placed the text of Psalm 100 on f. 170v and had this miniature visible on the adjacent recto. 'Misericordiam et judicium', starts Psalm 100, 'Mercy and judgement I will sing to thee, O Lord', and after repudiating 'any unjust thing... the perverse heart... the malignant...' the Psalm ends: 'He that speaketh unjust things shall not prosper before my eyes. In the morning' (that is, the day of Judgement) 'I put to death all the wicked of the land: that I might cut off all the workers of iniquity from the city of the Lord (*ut disperderem de civitate domini omnes operantes iniquitatem*).' So it is not enough to call this 'Christ seated in a mandorla'; this is Christ of the Second Coming, who will also 'build up Jerusalem' as the following Psalm 101, 'Domine exaudi', implores him to do. The adjacent text, or the specific words which give rise to a particular visual image, are always worth considering. We cannot simply attach ready-made labels to Anglo-Saxon images, according to some stereotyped system of identification.

Jane Rosenthal has disputed the belief of Wormald, Deshman, and others that the Sherborne Pontifical represents on ff. 5v, 6r, and 6v the three Persons of the Trinity in anthropomorphic form, and argues instead that they each represent 'aspects of Christ'.[9] As a parallel for the first figure, who wears a crown, Rosenthal points to the Benedictional of St Æthelwold as the earliest Anglo-Saxon portrayal of the crowned Christ.[10] The Sherborne Pontifical drawing is not much later, and is recognised by Rosenthal as '*Christus rex*, Christ the King, ruler of Heaven and earth'. To those who regarded the figure as God the Father, she responds that the crown is an attribute of Christ, which could, theoretically, be transferred to another Person of the Trinity. But since Christ's cross-nimbus can, according to Rosenthal, only be transferred to another Person when it is also retained by the Son – it is not passed exclusively to another Person – so likewise the crown of Christ could not become the exclusive property of the Father, when the Son did not wear it. Reverting to the Benedictional, identified by Rosenthal as displaying the earliest crowned Christ, it is worth noting that the crowned enthroned figure inhabits the 'O' of the text 'Omnipotens Trinitas Unus et Verus Deus, Pater et Filius et Spiritus Sanctus', so it is potentially an image with a number of facets.[11] Of course we know that

[9] J. Rosenthal, 'Three Drawings in an Anglo-Saxon Pontifical: Anthropomorphic Trinity or Threefold Christ?', *Art Bull.*, 63 (1981), 549-562: Paris, BN lat MS 943.

[10] London, BL Add. MS 49598, f. 70r.

[11] See F. Wormald, 'The Benedictional of St Ethelwold', in *Collected Writings, I: Studies in Medieval Art from the Sixth to the Twelfth Centuries* (London, 1984), p, 98 and pl. 103. Wormald calls the figure 'Christ in Majesty'. H. Swarzenski, *Monuments of Romanesque Art* (London, 1954), fig. 140, calls the figure 'The Trinity'.

when Philip asks 'shew us the Father', Christ replies 'he that seeth me seeth the Father also' (John 14. 8-9); but does it really follow that when in the Anglo-Saxon period we have a portmanteau image, a single figure for 'Omnipotens Trinitas', its attributes are exclusively or particularly those of the Son? The crown on the head seems to make sense in the context of the words of the *Gloria*, 'Gloria in excelsis Deo', in which God is praised and glorified, on account of His Glory: 'Domine Deus Rex Coelestis, Deus Pater Omnipotens'. Only then is the only-begotten Son, Lamb of God, addressed; so is not the 'Rex Coelestis', crowned, a possible conventional illustration of God the Father? The Nicene Creed rehearses the Persons of the Trinity, and begins: 'Credo in Unum Deum, Patrem Omnipotentem, Factorem Coeli et Terrae, et in Unum Dominum Jesum Christum etc.', so the image of God creating heaven and earth in BL Cotton MS Tiberius C.vi, for example, could or should represent God the Father, 'Pater Omnipotens', and He is crowned.[12] Is He not crowned in His own right?

The Landsdowne Psalter, in the following century, might seem to wish to represent God the Father crowned as King, issuing orders to Gabriel to announce the mystery of the Incarnation to the Virgin Mary.[13] I do not suppose that post-Conquest conventions are Anglo-Saxon ones necessarily, although in view of its cult St Edward's, Shaftesbury, had a good chance of having continuity of outlook. In Anglo-Saxon art the crown could as well be an attribute of God the Father as the cross-nimbus is. Rosenthal denies that the cross-nimbus could become the exclusive property of the Father, but this does happen in the prefatory picture in BL Harley Ms 603. This supremely beautiful drawing shows inventiveness and deep understanding of its theme.[14] It violates Rosenthal's canon of equality expressed by equal sizes for anthropomorphic representations of the Persons of the Trinity. In Harley MS 603 we see nothing routine, but the felicitous result of the search for imagery in the text of scripture. Christ is small, protected. Here the artist literally illustrates Christ's statement in John 14. 28 that 'the Father is greater than I (*Pater major me est*),' and also another passage from John 1. 18: 'The only begotten Son which is in the bosom of the Father (*unigenitus filius qui est in sinu Patris...*)'. The artist interprets in unusual, unique, imagery the mutual love of the Father and Son. The picture in Harley 603 has its own theological and literary sources, and its own validity. It would be quite wrong to suppose that it was 'copied' from a picture of the Virgin and Child.

---

12 See F. Wormald, 'An English Eleventh-Century Psalter with Pictures', in *Collected Writings*, p. 131 and pl. 126.

13 London, BL Landsdowne MS 383, f.12v, for which see C. M. Kauffmann, *Romanesque Manuscripts 1066-1190* (London, 1975), pl. 131.

14 Temple, *Anglo-Saxon Manuscripts*, pl. 210.

Rosenthal disputes the Trinity interpretation of the figures on ff. 5v and 6r of the Sherborne Pontifical, viewable as a pair, and the third figure overleaf on f. 6v on the basis of the Grimbald Gospels, where the three anthropomorphic Persons are united, visible at a single glance.[15] This argument that two plus one cannot represent the equality of the Three Persons perhaps neglects an aspect of the mystery of the Trinity, that the Holy Spirit proceeds from the Father and the Son. They function together to send out the Holy Spirit, as is carefully illustrated in the Carolingian Metz Sacramentary[16] and the twelfth-century Pembroke 'Gospels'.[17] The principal attribute of the third figure in the Sherborne Pontifical is recognised by Rosenthal as a palm frond, symbol of Christ's martyrdom; so the third figure is 'Christ the man'. It is awkward for this argument that the Crucifixion is also illustrated in the Sherborne Pontifical, even if it is, as Rosenthal maintains, by another artist. He is clearly a contemporary; he would read the imagery at least as well, as critically, as we can. So why would he add a redundant image of a suffering Christ? Rosenthal makes the point that the attribute she calls a palm frond had never before been properly identified. J. O. Westwood called it a 'long red feather', or 'a bit of herbage'. Temple calls it 'virga'.[18] The palm branch in an Utrecht Psalter illustration used as an analogy by Rosenthal is quite different, much more bushy.[19] In the Sherborne Pontifical the long slim branch or feather is bent and swaying. It is the sense of its being blown that seems to me diagnostic. The Holy Spirit comes as a wind. Psalm 47, 'Magnus Dominus', at verse 7 uses the words 'In spiritu vehementi, conteres naves Tharsis' for a gale-force wind, and the same wind is heard at Pentecost, Acts 2. 1-2: A sound fills the whole house 'tamquam advenientis spiritus vehementis'. Again in the Psalms, in Psalm 146. 18, God's spirit blows, 'flabit spiritus ejus...' The Anglo-Saxon artist has created, I suggest, a good attribute for his anthropomorphic God the Spirit. This is invention, allegorical imagery of a very sophisticated kind.

I would restore the meaning 'Trinity' to the preface of the Sherborne Pontifical. The last figure is the Holy Spirit entering into the framed zone of God's church on earth, coming to His task as healer and comforter. The

---

15   BL Add. MS 34890, f. 114v, for which see M. Rickert, *Painting in Britain: The Middle Ages*, 2nd edn (Harmondsworth, 1965), pl. 36 (B).

16   Paris, BN MS lat. 9428, f. 78r, for which see J. Hubert, J. Porcher, W. F. Volbach, *Carolingian Art* (London, 1970), p. 161, pl. 148.

17   Cambridge, Pembroke College MS 120, f. 6r, for which see Kauffmann, *Romanesque Manuscripts*, pl. 101.

18   Rosenthal, 'Three Drawings', p. 555, n. 44.

19   The palms held by the martyrs in the illustration to Psalm 5 on f. 3r of BL Harley MS 603 are more like the 'palm' on f. 6v of the Sherborne Pontifical, but are still larger in proportion to the figures.

three drawings show particular attention to attributes of the Three Persons, so as to identify them specifically. God the Father is the crowned first figure. God the Father, after all, does markedly appear in Anglo-Saxon art – one of its idiosyncrasies. Regularly He takes anthropomorphic form, when the Son is the Lamb and the Holy Spirit is the Dove. This occurs in the 'Dixit Dominus' initial in BL Cotton MS Tiberius C.vi and in the initial in the Boethius manuscript in Paris, BN MS Lat. 6401.[20] This imagery is a deeply rooted element in Anglo-Saxon art. It goes back to the man, lamb and dove of the prefatory diagrams in the first quire of the Codex Amiatinus.[21]

There are other clear ways of depicting specifically God the Son, Christ, in late Anglo-Saxon art, again traceable to Early Christian models. Christ in Psalm 90 tramples on the lion and the dragon as a sign of his victory over Death and Hell.[22] This is the triumph of God the Son, without a doubt. God the Son, 'Verbum Dei', is similarly clearly signalled when we find 'King of Kings, Lord of Lords' written on His vesture, as in the Trinity College Homilies[23] and more precisely in the Benedictional of St Æthelwold,[24] following Revelation 19. 16: 'Et habet in vestimento, et in femore suo scriptum: Rex regum, et Dominus dominantium.'

God the Son, as we have seen, is frequently symbolised in later Anglo-Saxon art as the Lamb, Agnus Dei. In earlier Insular art the Agnus Dei appears in the arms of St John the Baptist on the Ruthwell Cross, in remembrance of St John the Baptist's acknowledgement of Christ as Saviour in John 1. 36.[25] In Early Christian art Christ as Lamb is accompanied by the four beast symbols of the Evangelists, for example in the great ivory diptych in Milan Cathedral treasury,[26] a primitive zoomorphic approach to Christ and his four Evangelists perhaps also used in early Insular art, in the lost picture formerly opposite the gold and silver inscription on f. 1v of BL Royal MS I.E.vi, 'the glorious team of the four Evangelists declare the goodness of

[20] See Wormald, *Collected Writings*, pls. 153, 84.

[21] Florence, Laurentian Library, Amiatinus MS 1, ff. VIr, VIIr, 8r, for which see R. L. S. Bruce-Mitford, 'The Art of the Codex Amiatinus', *JBAA*, 32 (1969), pls. IX, XI.

[22] See for example the Crowland Psalter, Oxford, Bodleian Library Douce MS 296, f. 40r, in Temple, *Anglo-Saxon Manuscripts*, pl. 259. For the antecedents of this image see F. Saxl, 'The Ruthwell Cross', *Jnl Warb. Court. Insts.*, 6 (1943), 1-19, esp. pp. 10-12.

[23] Cambridge, Trinity College MS B. 15.34, f. 1r, in Temple, *Anglo-Saxon Manuscripts*, pl. 241.

[24] Wormald, *Collected Writings*, pl. 101.

[25] G. Henderson, 'The John the Baptist Panel on the Ruthwell Cross', *Gesta*, 24/1 (1985), 3-12 and fig. 1.

[26] See W. F. Volbach, *Early Christian Art* (London, 1961), pls. 100-01.

God with one voice through the mouth of the Lamb'.[27]

The representation of Christ the Lamb, accompanied by the four Evangelist symbols, is required by the text of Revelation 5, when a Lamb, 'as it were slain', takes its place at God's throne and is hailed as worthy to receive honour and glory for ever and ever. 'Et quattuor animalia dicebant: Amen' (Revelation 5.14). The Apocalypse origin of the New Testament preface in the Carolingian Bamberg Bible is made clear by the lance and chalice which are the attributes of the Lamb at the centre of the page – this is 'Agnus qui occisus est'.[28] The Lamb appears literally 'occisus', slain, at the centre of the cross on the early Insular Wirksworth slab, accompanied by the four beasts,[29] and this imagery survived the Viking invasions and appears again on the Anglo-Saxon Brussels Cross[30] and on a walrus ivory reliquary cross in the Victoria and Albert Museum (Pl. 21); again the Lamb is accompanied by the Evangelist symbols. The four Evangelist symbols continue to accompany Christ when he appears on the Cross, not symbolically as 'Agnus Dei' but in His own shape as the incarnate Saviour, in the Victoria and Albert Museum's enamel and gold reliquary cross (Pl. 22), and in an ivory plaque on loan to the British Museum.[31]

This particular juxtaposition of Christ the Lamb, or Christ Crucified, with the four Evangelist symbols, brings me to another idiosyncrasy of late Anglo-Saxon art. In the early Insular period, when the riches of Early Christian art were showered on Bede's Northumbria, the great basic image of the 'Majestas Domini', the Lord enthroned, accompanied by four beasts, was employed, copied presumably from a sixth-century Cassiodoran exemplar, as the picture preface to the New Testament in the *Codex Amiatinus*.[32] The same image is familiar in the same position in the Carolingian bibles, and is found in the ninth century in other media such as the ivory plaque, with later gilding, in the Fitzwilliam Museum.[33] The enthroned figure accompanied by the four beasts continued to hold a central place in Christian art on the

---

27 P. McGurk, 'An Anglo-Saxon Bible Fragment of the Late Eighth Century', *Jnl Warb. Court. Insts.*, 25 (1962), 18-34, esp. at p. 23 and pl. 4a.

28 Bamberg, Staatliche Bibliothek, misc. class. Bibl. I, f. 339v, for which see Hubert, Porcher, Volbach, *Carolingian Art*, p. 133, pl. 121.

29 See D. M. Wilson, *Anglo-Saxon Art* (London, 1984), p. 84, pl. 95.

30 Brussels, Cathedral of S. Michel, for which see the catalogue of the exhibition, *The Golden Age of Anglo-Saxon Art 966-1066*, ed. J. Backhouse, D. H. Turner, L. Webster (London, 1984), pp. 90-91, no. 75, and pl. XXIII.

31 *Ibid.*, pp. 117-18, no. 118 and pl. XXVI, and pp. 124-25, no. 127.

32 Codex Amiatinus, f. 796v; see Bruce-Mitford, 'The Art of the Codex Amiatinus', pl. XIII.

33 Cambridge, Fitzwilliam Museum M. 14, 1904.

Continent, in Ottonian art,[34] and on through the eleventh and twelfth centuries. We see it on a monumental scale at Moissac, and at Chartres.[35] It is the standard last picture, after Pentecost, in the prefatory bible cycles in English twelfth-century psalters, for example the Winchester Psalter.[36] It becomes much less common as a generalized image of God's power after the twelfth century, although it occurs memorably in the mid-thirteenth-century Cambridge *La estoire de Seint Aedward le Rei*, where St John the Evangelist and St Peter introduce King Edward the Confessor, after his death, to the enthroned Deity, in a mandorla, surrounded by four beasts. The text says that Edward is brought 'Devant la Majesté'.[37]

This image of the 'Majestas Domini' occurs commonly in the English thirteenth-century Apocalypses, in the proper literary context from which it sprang, namely chapter four of the Book of Revelation. The worship by the four beasts of 'one seated upon the throne' in Revelation 4 precedes the worship of the Lamb by the same four beasts in Revelation 5. That there is ambiguity about the precise significance of the 'one seated upon the throne' can be gauged from the influential commentary on the Apocalypse by Berengaudus.[38] We can follow Berengaudus's subject matter conveniently with pictures in the mid-thirteenth-century Trinity College Apocalypse.[39] In 'De visione secunda' we read: 'He who was seated on the throne had the appearance of a jasper and a sardine stone. The colour of jasper is green and sard is red. By the green of jasper is meant the *divinitas* of our Saviour, by the red of sard is indicated his *humanitas*. Thus Christ is present in the image.' However, the text of 'De visione tertia' takes perforce another line. He who was seated on the throne had a sealed book in His hand, and in Revelation 5. 7, the Lamb came and took the book out of the right hand of Him who sat 'super thronum'. 'Above we have said', writes Berengaudus, 'that by him sitting on the throne Christ is signified, but because He himself said, I am in

[34] See for example the golden altar frontal in the Palace Chapel at Aachen, and the book-cover of the Gospels of Bishop Notger of Liège, in P. Lasko, *Ars Sacra 800-1200* (Harmondsworth, 1972), pls. 131, 170.

[35] P. Kidson, *Sculpture at Chartres* (London, 1958), pls. 25, 117.

[36] BL Cotton MS Nero C. iv, f. 28r, for which see F. Wormald, *The Winchester Psalter* (London, 1973), pl. 31.

[37] Cambridge, University Library MS Ee.3.59, p. 53. For the picture, see M. R. James, *La estoire de Seint Aedward le Rei*, Roxburghe Club (Oxford, 1920). For the text see *Lives of Edward the Confessor*, ed. H. R. Luard, RS (London, 1858), p. 136.

[38] Berengaudus, *In Apocalypsin Expositio*, printed among works of St Ambrose by J. P. Migne, *Patrologia Latina*, 17 (Paris, 1845), cols. 765-970, esp. 794, 809.

[39] Cambridge, Trinity College MS R.16.2, ff. 4v, 5r, for which see P. Brieger, *The Trinity College Apocalypse* (London, 1967).

the Father, and the Father in me, and who sees me, sees the Father, in this place, the one seated upon the throne signifies the Father (*sed quia ipse dixit, Ego in patre et pater in me est, et qui videt me, videt et patrem, in hoc loco, sedens in throno patrem designat*).' Berengaudus probably wrote these words in the twelfth century,[40] but in the Carolingian period also, in art, we see the possibility, indeed the inevitability, of the splitting of this central Apocalypse image into the two persona, the Redeemer, the Lamb, and the Father to whom He offers His death for the redemption of mankind. The one seated on the throne appears certainly not as Christ, but probably as God the Father, the Ancient of Days, in the Moûtier-Grandval Bible.[41]

In late Anglo-Saxon art the image of the 'Majestas Domini', the enthroned figure accompanied by the four Evangelist symbols, seldom if ever appears.[42] Its absence is disguised in the literature by the loose use of the term 'Christ in Majesty' for other quite discrete images, anything from the Creator dividing light from darkness at the beginning of Ælfric's Hexateuch to the golden-robed crowned figure placed after the canon tables in the Trinity College Gospels.[43] In the Catalogue of *The Golden Age of Anglo-Saxon Art* the enthroned figure on the obverse of the Metropolitan Museum's walrus ivory pectoral cross is called 'Christ in Majesty'.[44] But we have only to turn to the reverse to see that, as in the unfolding imagery of the later Trinity College Apocalypse, we move from the omnipotent Father on the obverse to the revelation of His nature in the person of his Son on the reverse

40 For the date of Berengaudus's Commentary, see B. Nolan, *The Gothic Visionary Perspective* (Princeton, 1977), pp. 9-13, and n. 16.

41 BL Add. MS 10546, f. 449r; see G. Henderson, *From Durrow to Kells* (London, 1987), p. 120 and pl. 176.

42 I know only one example, and it may be the exception which proves the rule. This is the pierced ivory plaque in New York, Pierpont Morgan Library M 319. Swarzenski, *Monuments to Romanesque Art*, p. 47 and fig. 122, attributes it to Lorraine at the end of the 10th century. J. Beckwith, *Ivory Carving in Early Medieval England* (London, 1972), p. 129, no. 49, tentatively suggests that it is Anglo-Saxon and dates it to the late 11th century. In *Golden Age of Anglo-Saxon Art*, p. 39, no. 21, Webster argues for a very early date, in the second quarter of the 10th century, and speculates that it might have been sent abroad by King Athelstan as a gift. Contemporary analogies for the foliage appear plausible, but the figure and drapery style and the animated movement of the Evangelist symbols point to a rather later period, as Beckwith sensed. The plaque is exceptional in a number of ways apart from its subject matter: in the foliate context of God and the symbols, in the material used (elephant ivory) and in its Continental provenance.

43 BL Cotton MS Claudius B.iv, f 2r and Cambridge, Trinity College MS B.10.4, f. 16v. For illustrations see Temple, *Anglo-Saxon Manuscripts*, pls. 265, 212.

44 *Golden Age of Anglo-Saxon Art*, pp. 121-22, no. 124.

(Pls. 23, 24). The enthroned crowned figure on the obverse of the Metropolitan ivory should be God the Father. We would truly confront the 'Majestas' image only if the enthroned Deity was accompanied by the four Evangelist symbols. Idiosyncratically, this formula, despite its popularity before and after, does not appear to have been favoured by Anglo-Saxon artists. Its comparative neglect may be a symptom of the imaginative and spiritually charged experiments we see in this period in developing differentiating visual attributes and roles for the three Persons of the Trinity. Given its textual ambiguities, the 'Majestas' image was perhaps simply not sharply enough focused to serve the artists' purpose. It is the chief idiosyncrasy of late Anglo-Saxon religious imagery that it is uniquely specific and exact.

The Borders of the Bayeux Tapestry
CAROLA HICKS

The Bayeux Tapestry is a work of art, an historical document and a familiar icon. This study concentrates on one aspect of it which has not perhaps received the attention which it deserves, the ornament of the borders above and below the central narrative strip. This ornament is composed extensively of birds and animals, the study of whose type and style contributes to our knowledge of the sources of Romanesque art.

Approximately 530 creatures are depicted in the borders. They are generally placed in separate compartments marked by pairs of diagonal lines which enclose foliage ornament alternating with the animals. Each compartment normally contains one creature but can sometimes hold a pair or a group. The animals often impinge on the dividing lines as if stepping out of their frame, with wing, tail or paw touching the margin and with some of the birds biting at the foliage in the next panel.

The Tapestry is made out of eight strips of linen whose joins are so skilfully sewn as to be virtually imperceptible. The first two pieces are each approximately 13.7m long, the third 8.35m, the fourth 7.75m, the fifth, sixth and seventh between 6.6 and 7.15m, the eighth incomplete at 5.25m.[1] The consistency of the first two measurements might imply a potential calculation of the amount of time to be spent on the whole: if it takes one needlewoman x days to embroider 1m and there are to be eight pieces of set lengths, then the necessary skilled workforce can be accurately recruited. It may also be possible to reconstruct the sequence of work. The unity of style in the central portion suggests that the strips were embroidered by the same hand/small group consecutively. However there are certain aspects of the borders which might suggest an alternative scheme of different groups working concurrently to a master design for the central portion but with some discretion as to the border details. This is clearly visible in the treatment of the diagonal dividing lines and foliage, which show some differences in the eight strips, both through the angles of the framing lines and the changes in the type and position of the foliage.[2] It is harder to trace

---

[1] S. Bertrand, *La Tapisserie de Bayeux* (La Pierre-qui-Vire, 1966), pp. 24-25.

[2] In the first strip, the diagonal frames tend to alternate direction, forming an overall chevron pattern and enclosing small foliage sprigs of which every other is suspended upside down from the upper margin. There is no foliage. The second strip has very rudimentary cruciform-shaped foliage. The third strip's foliage has fleshy lobate scrolls and a few examples of a more delicate linear type. The frames begin to be parallel. The fourth has candelabra-like foliage. The fifth returns to the chevron diagonals containing delicate scrolls. The sixth has two parallel diagonals with some examples of the rudimentary foliage of the second piece. The

equivalent changes in the border animals, which are consistent in style and selection throughout, with the marked exception of the long group of fable scenes in the lower border of the first strip. The join between this strip and the second is the most clumsy, because the upper borders are not the same depth: that on the right is several millimetres narrower than the one on the left, with no space left for the dividing lines and foliage; there is also an uncharacteristic blank space in the central portion (Pl.25). The subsequent joins show that these mistakes were not repeated for the first two strips were then followed by shorter ones with the joins fairly successfully concealed under embroidery. A hypothetical sequence for the work might be as follows: the first two equally long strips were embroidered concurrently; as the subsequent join was clumsy and the great length found either difficult to handle or too much for a single worker, they were followed by shorter strips either made consecutively or concurrently but with the subsequent joins being better disguised.

The border animals can be divided into two main groups, ornamental and narrative. The former are arranged almost invariably in pairs, symmetrically confronted or addorsed; occasionally two pairs can be alternated or, very rarely, one animal of the standard repertoire appears without a partner. The general impression is that of a series of mirror images, imitating the loom-repeated patterns of woven fabrics, although the hand-sewing here makes such a design unnecessary. These pairs form the greatest proportion of the ornament with a total of around 450 animals. Interspersed with them are motifs of a different type, groups of narrative scenes, some of which can be firmly identified as illustrating the fables of Aesop while others are genre scenes familiar from other media. Although an apparent unity of style has been imposed by the laid and couched embroidery technique, the animals derive from two quite separate sources. This duality of origin can be recognized both from the types of animal selected, the pairs including many exotic creatures while the narrative groups are of familiar or domestic beasts, and from the positions they are shown in, since the pairs have a set range of stylized postures not seen at all in those of the groups.

The borders are for the greater part of the Tapestry quite clearly separate from the central portion in both style and content. However, there are a few examples where they are occupied by the main text, both when there is not enough space in the centre, as when Harold's ship and, later, those of the Norman fleet cross the Channel; and during the battle, when the fate of ordinary soldiers in the lower border forms an ironic counterpoint to the inscribed historical events above. There is also an evocative panel where the newly crowned Harold is told of the ill omen of Halley's comet, shown in

---

seventh and eighth continue the parallel diagonals with elaborate linear scrolls, with some fruit-bearing examples in the latter.

the border above, while a ghost navy appears below. This suggests that the designer intended in these cases to use the border area as a part of the main narrative; and it also raises a question about the role of the borders in general, whether the animals should be seen as pure decoration, reflecting the contemporary ornamental repertoire, or whether those who have interpreted them as relating, however obscurely, to the main text are right.

I: The Narrative Scenes
The animals in these scenes belong to a manuscript tradition which comes via proto-bestiaries, books of fables and monster lore, and calendar and natural history illustrations from late antique art. A number of the scenes illustrate the fables of Aesop, but estimates of the precise number vary from a modest eight to an improbable forty-two.[3] The reason for this confusion is that while some of the incidents are immediately recognizable and are in one place grouped together, others cannot be satisfactorily attributed to any known fable, although in style and subject clearly of more than ornamental significance. Attempts to link the fables to a specific manuscript tend to fail because it is necessary both to define the number, sequence and content of the scenes shown and to make the assumption that the designer was in fact copying all his illustrations from the same source. But there is more than one version of the fable of the Fox, Crow and Cheese, which is shown in different places in three different forms, suggesting either that more than one source was being used or that the designer was creating his own formula (Pls.26, 27). Three others, the Wolf and Crane, Wolf and Ass, and Bitch and Puppies, are shown twice. This repetition, together with the random distribution of fables throughout the borders, implies that it was not intended to follow one consecutive scheme. Nor did the designer have to be copying directly from an illustrated manuscript; the fables were sufficiently well known by the eleventh century to appear on their own without accompanying text in various media including wall paintings, decorated initials and stone carving.[4]

3   F. Wormald recognises eight fables, in 'Style and Design', *The Bayeux Tapestry*, ed. F. Stenton (London, 1965), pp.26-37. H. Chefneux identifies nine, 'Les fables dans la Tapisserie de Bayeux', *Romania*, 40 (1934), 153-94, A. Goldschmidt twelve, *An Early MS of the Aesop fables of Avianus* (Princeton, 1947), and L. Herrman forty-two, *Les Fables Antiques de la Broderie de Bayeux*, Collection Latomus, 69 (1964), based on his preconceived notion that the designer was copying directly from an entire illustrated Phaedrus collection of fables.

4   For example, on the 9th-century Flabellum of Tournus, L. E. Eitner, *The Flabellum of Tournus*, Art Bulletin Supplement, 1 (1944); wall paintings at St-Savin sur Gartempe in the form of friezes with the fable scenes separated by foliage, G. Gaillard, *Les Fresques de St-Savin: 1, La Nef* (Paris, 1944), pls.V and VII; the refectory walls of St Benoit sur Loire abbey of *c*.1030, P. Deschamps and M.

The fables of Aesop were only one example of a range of texts transmitting animal lore of classical origin into the art of the Middle Ages. Greek and Latin observations on animal appearance and behaviour, including the works of Aristotle, Pliny and Solinus, were brought together by the Naturalist, or Physiologus, an Alexandrian Greek who compiled a text which was translated into Latin and widely diffused by the fifth century. The seventh-century version in the Etymologies of Isidore of Seville became a major source for compilers of medieval bestiaries. The various manuscripts of the Marvels of the East show the transmission of another text with animal illustrations from the fourth down to the twelfth century.[5] This is the sort of background for those border scenes which are not obviously fables. Others are taken from calendar illustrations, such as the adjacent scenes of ploughing, sowing, harrowing and bird-scaring; and astrological manuscripts provide a source for the Pisces motif of the pair of fish, which is shown twice. The opposed posture of both and the linked mouths of one pair originate in late antique art, but more immediate connections can be seen in the manuscripts of the Canterbury school, which have many other features in common with the motifs of the Tapestry.[6] Another group which has been interpreted as illustrating the constellations is the sequence of a shoal of eels, man with sword, wolf, bird, another wolf and centaur, each one gripping his neighbour (Pl. 28). This scene does however relate to the events in the central portion of the Tapestry immediately above it, where Harold rescues two Norman soldiers from quicksands during William's crossing of the river Couesnon. The pair of fish and the group of eels are appropriate references to the water scene above, as is the tugging sequence to Harold's brave deeds.

This is a rare example of an enclosed border scene paralleling the main text. The only other occurs in the inscribed scene of Ælfgyva and the clerk where in the border a naked man crouches, his arms in the exact position of those of the man above. These are the only clear examples of border designs visually relating to the central narrative.

Thibout, *La Peinture Murale en France* (Paris, 1951), p.21; for the post-Conquest period, carved capitals from Westminster Hall, completed 1099, *English Romanesque Art 1066-1200* ed. G. Zarnecki (London, 1984), fig. p.155; decorated initials, C. Dodwell, *The Canterbury School of Illumination* (Cambridge, 1954) pl.43a. Later examples of French Romanesque sculpture cited by E. Mâle, *L'Art religieux du 12ème siècle en France* (Paris, 1953) p.337 and figs.196-97.

5   M. R. James, *Marvels of the East* (Oxford, 1929); J. B. Friedman, 'The Marvels of the East: Tradition in Anglo-Saxon Art', in P. E. Szarmach, ed., *Sources of Anglo-Saxon Culture*, Studies in Medieval Culture, 20 (Kalamazoo, 1986), pp. 319-44.

6   Dodwell, *Canterbury School*, pls. 38 d,e, for two early-12th-century examples, one showing two fish linked by a wingless dragon to form the initial Z in the Pseudo-Isidore MS Claudius E. v, and the other from a calendar.

The many interpretations which have been placed on them must remain speculation. The reasons for this are the relative rarity and sporadic placing of the narrative scenes in contrast to the main ornament of confronted pairs. If the assumption can be made that the latter are in this context purely decorative because of their symmetrical design and deliberately varied nature, then it would appear that the purpose of the whole border is decorative; the narrative scenes should therefore also be regarded as a subordinate part of this structure. A significant factor is the recognition that they do not occur in relationship to the key scenes in the main text, in particular those of Harold swearing his oath on the sacred relics, his coronation and his death, which would all appear to be highly appropriate moments for a moral to be drawn, if this had ever been the designer's view of the border's function.

The casual nature of the distribution can be demonstrated. A continuous sequence of nine groups depicting Aesop's fables is used soon after the beginning of the Tapestry in the lower border under the scene of Harold's arrival in France and capture by Count Guy; then there are three conventional pairs and then a group of farming and hunting scenes, then a naked couple. The varied nature of these scenes has no ostensible connection with the events above, for there is not just one allegedly meaningful fable but two distinct sets of scenes, the first a coherent sequence illustrating a group of fables from one source, the second a series of five self-contained but related narrative incidents: the fact is that they relate each other rather than to the central portion of the Tapestry. The lower border then resumes the more standard arrangement of confronted pairs. This might suggest that the border design for the first of the eight strips was experimental but that there was felt to be too much narrative content, since the subsequent strips have a much higher proportion of confronted pairs. The later fable scenes appear singly above or below contexts which it is very hard to interpret as being of more significance than those bordered by the pairs.[7] One function for the fable

---

[7] The second use of the Bitch and Puppies fable (the first having appeared in the sequence of fables under Harold's departure for France) is under two Norman knights advancing into the battle of Hastings. The first Fox, Crow and Cheese starts that sequence but illustrates the middle phase of the tale, with the cheese in mid air; the second example, below two Normans in the Brittany campaign, shows the final phase, with the cheese in the fox's mouth; the third, above Harold's return to England, illustrates the beginning, with the cheese in the bird's mouth. If the cheese is to be interpreted as the English crown or kingdom (T. A. Heslop, pers. comm.) with Harold as crow, it would surely be more appropriate to show the successful fox towards the end of the narrative. Adjacent to this third phase is a second version of the Wolf and Crane, whose positions are reversed from the first example, which, Heslop has suggested, may point the safe return of Harold from France above, symbolized by the move of the crane from left to right.

255

scene does appear to be as an occasional space filler when the confronted pairs have got out of rhythm.

Another interpretation which has been placed on some of the border scenes is their role as chronological indicators. It has been suggested that the pair of fish in the form of the Pisces symbol below the crossing of the Couesnon means that this event took place in February or March; the second pair of fish, which appears below the news being taken to William of Harold's coronation on 6 January 1066 has similarly been used to suggest that this also took place in February or March of the following year.[8] But Halley's comet, which was visible from February until May 1066, is shown vividly in the upper border before the fish; it is more likely that the latter were simply being used as an appropriate space filler between the ghost invasion fleet which immediately precedes them in the lower border and the next sequence of confronted pairs, in order to avoid a single animal without a partner. A chronological meaning has also been placed on the agricultural scenes below William's messengers with Turold, to indicate that Harold's arrival in France was in the autumn; but the sequence from ploughing through to scaring birds from the young shoots takes place over a more extended period and is probably drawn from manuscript versions of the labours of the months and other rural activities.[9]

It has also been argued, particularly by David Bernstein, that the moral aspects of the border fables are intended to refer to the deeds and motivation of the main actors in the events leading up to the battle of Hastings.[10] This view is hard to sustain not only because of the random placing of such scenes already discussed but also because the interpretation of the fables in connection with the historical events is so ambiguous. Although the themes of the identifiable fables are those of treachery, ingratitude or folly, these are in fact the themes of most fables. If a moral judgement was being made, was it William or Harold who was being criticised? If the Tapestry was intended to put the Norman case for the Conquest then it was presumably Harold who was symbolized by the lying fox, the ungrateful wolf, the usurping bitch. But if, as Bernstein claims, the Anglo-Saxon makers of the Tapestry

---

[8] A. Levé, *La Tapisserie de la Reine Mathilde* (Paris, 1919), p.122; J. Verrier, *La Broderie de Bayeux* (Paris, 1946), p.7.

[9] As shown in the early-11th-century calendars BL Cotton MSS Julius A. vi and Tiberius B. v, M. Rickert, *Painting in Britain in the Middle Ages* (Harmondsworth, 1965) pl. 34; and Ælfric's Pentateuch, Claudius B. iv, Wormald, 'Style and Design', fig. 16.

[10] *The Mystery of the Bayeux Tapestry* (London, 1986) passim and esp. pp.128-34; see also C. R. Dodwell, 'The Bayeux Tapestry and the French Secular Epic', *Burlington Magazine*, 108 (1966), 549-60 and R. Wissolik, 'The Saxon Statement: Code in the Bayeux Tapestry', *Annuale medievale*, 19 (1979), 69-97.

were trying to put in a secret and subversive sub-text, then William must be seen as the villain of the same fables. The inconclusive nature of such arguments can of course itself be taken as evidence for the subtlety of the Anglo-Saxon designer. And there are certainly essential contradictions in the Tapestry: it was made by the vanquished for the victors, designed by the cleric and read by the layman, sewn by craftspeople for use by the nobility. Bernstein uses the border fables as part of his case that the Tapestry does not just give the Norman version of the Conquest but uses the deliberate ambiguities of Anglo-Saxon art to provide one version for a Norman audience and an alternative reading providing the Canterbury attitude to the Conquest. Fables have traditionally been used as instruments of dissent and Bernstein claims that their placing in the border is meant to draw less attention to these transgressive comments; this is hard to defend artistically, since the border scenes are just as prominent a part of the structure as the central zone and should therefore not detract from the overall design in having a secondary meaning comprehensible to Anglo-Saxon but not to Norman spectators. Also, if the work was made for a Norman patron such as Bishop Odo of Bayeux, it was likely that a mainly Norman audience was intended from the first rather than the Anglo-Saxon clerics who would be the only people capable of appreciating the work on all its alleged levels.

II: The Ornamental Pairs

Even harder to interpret as contributing to this hypothetical sub-text are the symmetrically confronted and addorsed pairs of animals which form the greatest proportion of the border ornament. The range of birds and beasts has some very close links with the marginal and decorative creatures of English eleventh-century manuscript drawing; some of the subject matter also suggests the influence of woven silks from Sassanian Iran, Byzantium and the Islamic world which were to affect so much of Romanesque art. This influence was however not necessarily direct but already diffused through the medium of manuscript illumination, since the borrowing of motifs from such textiles can be demonstrated from the later Carolingian period onwards, with constant reinforcements.

The most frequent creature is the bird. Apart from an identifiable pair of cockerels and two pairs of peacocks, there are 170 examples which are not of any immediately recognizable species but which can be divided into three main types. The first, with the general proportions of a goose, has a relatively large body, longish neck and legs; it is often shown ornamentally twisted, biting at its foot, wing tip or tail, with the head frequently backward-turning (Pl.25, on the right). The second type is smaller, proportioned like a pigeon with short neck and slender legs; it is frequently shown standing upright with both wings extended, the front wing sometimes touching that of its mirror image. It may have a leaf or sprig of foliage in its beak. The third type has longer thinner legs and neck than the first and resembles a crane; the neck can be looped and the head backward-turning. Features common to all birds are the treatment of the wing and tail plumage, indicated by broad parallel lines, and the exaggeratedly large claws.

Extremely close parallels can be found in later tenth- and eleventh-century Anglo-Saxon manuscripts with a range of birds which must have been borrowed directly by the Tapestry designer[11] but then restructured into the symmetrical pairs which are not particularly appropriate to manuscript drawing but which originate as textile borders. These non-specific birds appear in association with more recognisable types including cockerel and peacock, as well as other creatures also common in the Tapestry borders, such as lion and dragon, in the canon table spandrels of the group of late tenth- and eleventh-century Ottonian manuscripts with full pages directly imitating Byzantine and Sassanian silks, demonstrating the new phase of Byzantine influence on the west which developed as a result of direct contact with Constantinople.[12]

The lion, with 140 examples, is the second most recurrent border animal. Around half have a clearly depicted mane; those without mane show an otherwise identical range of features and may therefore be regarded as lionesses. Distinctive attributes can include a tail which curves down between the hind legs and passes up across the body, a backward-turning head often biting at the tail, and a prominently protruding tongue. Some examples have the head turned to face the front with the curls of the mane indicated beneath the chin (Pl.29); when in profile the mane is treated as a row of lobate curls. The direct sources for all these features lie in the same range of Anglo-Saxon manuscripts as those which inspired the birds.[13] But one of the main reasons for the selection of the lion as a recurrent ornamental motif on the Tapestry is its presence in the repertoire of animals decorating eastern silks which were copied on those Ottonian manuscript pages imitating textiles; there are rows of confronted and addorsed lions with features which were then

[11] For example, in the margins of the frontispiece to Bede's Lives of Cuthbert of c.934 AD, the late 10th-century Trinity Arator from Christ Church, Canterbury, the Monte Cassino Gospels of c.1050, in E. Temple, *Anglo-Saxon Manuscripts 900-1066* (London, 1976), pls.29, 125, 287.

[12] For manuscript birds showing the direct influence of textile ornament, see A. Boeckler, *Das Goldene Evangelienbuch Heinrichs III* (Berlin, 1933), pls.36, 37, for rows of Sassanian-type birds with ribbons round their necks and bells in their mouths, mid-11th-century, as well as those on its canon table spandrels.

[13] For example, the lion crouching beneath the feet of Christ in the Douce Psalter of c.1020, the confronted pair at the opening of the Gospel of St Luke in the Monte Cassino Gospels, Temple, *Anglo-Saxon Manuscripts* figs. 259, 288; those in the margins of the Trinity Gospels, Dodwell, *Canterbury School*, pl.7a.

adopted in metalwork and sculpture.[14] Actual textiles decorated with such lions survive in the west, including a group of tenth-century Imperial Byzantine silks characterised by pairs of lions with head facing the front, front paw raised, and tail curling down between the legs and up over the back.[15] The delicacy of the Anglo-Saxon scribe has transformed these solemn heraldic creatures into the lively sinuous border animals, but the postures are those established by Sassanian art, in particular the distinctive treatment of the tail, which becomes characteristic of Romanesque lions; Achaemenid examples may have a tail which curves down between the legs, but from the Sassanian period it is extended up and over the back, a device which is then adopted on the Byzantine silks.

The next most frequent creature is the griffin, of which there are forty-three (twenty-one pairs and a single example). There are two main types, eagle-griffin (Pl.30) and lion-griffin (Pl.31); both are winged, the former has the head and beak of a bird, front legs usually ending in talons and hind legs in paws, while the latter has the head of a lion and four paws. But there is also some overlapping of these types. The wings are treated exactly like those of the birds and some of the griffins are shown biting at a wing tip. The griffin is relatively rare in Anglo-Saxon manuscripts (although it does appear on Anglo-Saxon coins and on pre-Conquest carving) but is entirely characteristic of imported silks from the late eighth century onwards, and is included among the rows of other Byzantine/Sassanian creatures in Ottonian manuscripts.[16]

---

[14] Rows of confronted lions in the Codex Aureus Epternacensis (Nuremberg), c.1040, P. Metz, *Das Goldene Evangelienbuch von Echternach* (Munich, 1956), pls. 65-66; the Codex Aureus (Gotha) of c.990, A. Goldschmidt, *German Illumination II, Ottonian* (Florence, 1928), pl.48; the Abbess Uota's Gospel Book, c.1020, *ibid.* pl.76; the Codex Aureus of Henry III in the Escorial, Boeckler, *Evangelienbuch*, pls. 4,5. I am grateful to Dr R. McKitterick for help with these references. An example in metalwork is the gold lion plaque on the Trier Reliquary of c.977-93, forward-facing, with lobed mane and tail down between the legs and up over the back, J. Beckwith, *Early Medieval Art: Carolingian, Ottonian, Romanesque* (London, 1964), pl. 121.

[15] P. Ackerman, 'A Goldwoven Byzantine silk of the tenth century', *Revue des Arts Asiatiques*, 10 (1936), 86-91, citing examples in the treasuries of Maastricht, Siegburg and Chinon.

[16] Griffins are shown in the Gotha Codex Aureus, Goldschmidt, *Evangelienbuch*, pl. 48, and Uota's Gospel Book, *ibid.* pl. 76. For textile examples, O. Von Falke, *Decorative Silks* (London, 1936) p. 25, an 8th-century silk in Cologne, and Dodwell, *Canterbury School* p. 77 and fig. 46 for Byzantine silk griffins compared to Canterbury manuscript examples. For its proto-bestiary role in the Marvels of the East, James, *Marvels*, Tiberius f.86b, no.34.

Another exotic is the winged dragon, of which there are seven pairs and one single example. The head can resemble that of a quadruped or a bird. It has two legs and a long tail, generally knotted and ending in a trilobate tip; but four terminate in the head of a snake, two of which bite the dragon's own paw. The occasionally protruding tongues are longer and more elaborate than those of the lions. Two dragons have internal body decoration of scalloped lines to represent scales. Very similar creatures inhabit pre-Conquest manuscripts, decorating initials and as a symbolic foe. They are also present in the Ottonian group, both in the carpet pages of fully Sassanian/Byzantine animals and among the canon table decoration.[17] This dragon survives in the bestiaries of the twelfth and thirteenth centuries to represent *draco*, *serpens* and particularly *amphisbaena*, a two-legged serpent with a body looped round in a circle whose tail terminates in another head;[18] one Tapestry pair depicts an already fully developed form of this (Pl.32).

A related but less frequent fantasy beast, only two pairs of which are shown in the borders, has the head, body and wings of a conventional bird but the paws of a quadruped and a curious rounded tail. This appears to be the designer's interpretation of the senmurv or dog-bird, a hybrid of a dog and a peacock, achieving a specific form in Sassanian art where it was a favourite motif for silks, metalwork, stucco and stone-carving, being subsequently adopted by Byzantine and Islamic craftsmen; it reached the west on the imported silks, its presence being reinforced by its popularity in Mozarabic art, where it was adopted in manuscripts, and on the Cordoban ivory caskets which drew heavily on textiles for their animal repertoire.[19]

[17] See the dragon being trampled by Christ in the Douce Psalter, Temple, *Anglo-Saxon Manuscripts*, fig. 259; and fig. 126 for that in the late-10th-century BL Harley 5431 from St Augustine's, Canterbury. Anglo-Saxon manuscript dragons are discussed generally by F. Wormald, 'Decorated initials in English manuscripts from AD 900 to 1100', *Archaeologia*, 91 (1945), 107-35. Ottonian examples with knotted tails in the canon-table spandrels of the Escorial Codex Aureus, Boeckler *Evangelienbuch*, pls.22, 23; and in the textile-imitating pages of the earlier Gotha Codex Aureus, Goldschmidt, *German Illumination*, pl. 48.

[18] G. C. Druce 'The Amphisbaena and its connections in ecclesiastical art and architecture', *Archaeological Jnl*, 67 (1910), 285-317; G. Zarnecki, *English Romanesque Sculpture 1066-1140* (London, 1951) for a late 11th-century example of the headed tail in sculpture on a lintel from Newton in Cleveland, Yorks. For later examples, D. N. Johnson, 'An unusual amphisbaena in Galway City', *Figures from the Past* ed. E. Rynne (Dun Laoghaire, 1987), pp. 232-41.

[19] History and symbolism of the senmurv discussed by C. Trever, *The Dog-bird Senmurv-paskudj* (Paris, 1938); R. Ghirshman shows many examples in Iran: *Parthians and Sassanians* (London, 1962); J. Beckwith, *Caskets from Cordoba* (London, 1960) fig. 25 for a Mozarabic manuscript example. For examples in western art, D. Talbot Rice, 'Some Byzantine motifs in Romanesque Sculpture',

There are two pairs of centaurs. One pair is shown with head and upper body facing the front, with extended arms and large hands in the *orans* posture, and the rear in profile (Pl.34). Females may be intended since the hair is long. The figures are not confronted since each faces to the right, although they are identical in other respects. As this does not happen in the case of any other pair, this may be an error by the embroiderer. The second pair, in a heavily restored section of the Tapestry, is conventionally confronted; the heads appear to show a male in profile with wings instead of arms and a strand of drapery passes across the front of the body. A single centaur is included in the group of tugging creatures below Harold's brave deeds in the quicksands; it is male, with the upper part of the body facing the front but with the head backward-turning; it has a belt around the waist and the animal half of the body is that of a feline rather than a horse (Pl.28). The centaur is mainly used in Romanesque art to represent the figure of Sagittarius, holding a bow and turning backwards to shoot, a position derived from the Sassanian metalwork or textile scenes of the royal hunt; however there is another version which carries a branch, the classical attribute of the healing centaur Chiron. Both types exist in the range of manuscripts drawn on by the Tapestry designer, and are included amongst the monster lore in the Anglo-Saxon versions of the Marvels of the East; they also appear in pre-Conquest sculpture.[20] The long hair and raised arms of the one Tapestry pair are more commonly attributes of the mermaid, a figure which reached Christian art through the Physiologus, where it was always described in the same section as the centaur; the features were perhaps regarded as interchangeable.

Another winged creature shown only once is a pair of grazing horses (Pl.35). Although winged horses and grazing horses appear on Byzantine silks, I cannot yet cite an example with both features. They do however combine on Sassanian silver, which has many motifs in common with textile subjects; the source lies in Roman art and the posture is appropriate both for drinking from a fountain and for grazing on grass.[21] The winged horse

---

Byzantion, 39 (1969), 170-79.

20 It is shown with a branch in the early 11th-century Canterbury Apuleius Herbarium, associated with a group of varied animals and snakes of a similar range to those in the tugging frieze, Temple, *Anglo-Saxon Manuscripts*, pl. 188, and in the Tiberius B. v Marvels of the East, on the same page as a pair of entwined snakes, *The Golden Age of Anglo-Saxon Art*, ed. J. Backhouse, D. H. Turner, L. Webster (London, 1984), pl. 31, and with a bow in the canon table spandrels of the Echternach Codex Aureus, Metz, *Goldene Evangelienbuch*, pl.22. Another example in the Marvels of the East, the Vitellius A. xv of c.1000 AD, has the upper part of the body turned to the front with the arms in the *orans* position, James, *Marvels*, Vitellius f.102b.

21 *Wealth of the Roman World*, eds. J. P. C. Kent and K. S. Painter (London, 1977),

reached western manuscripts with the rest of the Byzantine/Sassanian repertoire and can again be seen in the Ottonian manuscript group. The Tapestry pair therefore seems to represent the designer's adaptation of such a manuscript motif.

Another exotic creature, again represented by only one pair, is the camel (Pl.36); it is drawn quite realistically, as if the designer was working from a model which was close to nature. The camel is illustrated in a fairly unrecognisable manner in various western manuscripts, including the Utrecht Psalter, the Marvels of the East and later bestiaries, but is not seen at all in Anglo-Norman stone carving. It is however depicted in a more convincing way as a confronted pair or in a border frieze on the imported textiles, which would again appear to be the most likely source for the Tapestry examples.[22]

The infrequent appearance of these non-native or fantastic forms – centaur, senmurv, winged horse and camel – in the Tapestry borders and the various manuscript sources must be contrasted with the recurrent birds and lions, which were themselves already well established in Anglo-Saxon manuscripts from the late tenth century.

There are also a few examples of animals treated as ornamentally confronted pairs whose origins seem however to lie in the narrative tradition and whose closest parallels are in the central portion of the Tapestry or in the Aesop fables and genre scenes in the borders. Among the more recognisable are three pairs of sheep with curved horns and heavy body, one pair of deer with spiky antlers, three pairs of ponies, a pair of ferrets and some rather indeterminate quadrupeds.

A few animals do not fall neatly into either the narrative and genre or the heraldically confronted groups. These include predatory scenes of an

---

no. 311, p. 148, for a Sassanian 4th- or early 5th-century example in silver; I am grateful to Dr Anna Muthesius for this reference. For a grazing horse without wings in silk, see von Falke, *Decorative Silks*, fig. 28 and p. 26 for discussion of pegasi; for winged horse textiles in the west, W. F. Volbach, *Early Decorative Textiles* (Feltham, 1969), pp. 112-13 and fig. 27.

22   For example, D. Talbot Rice, *Islamic Art* (London, 1965), fig. 49, for camels on the Josse-sur-Mer silk, Sassanian style but with Kufic inscriptions. Camels were known in Europe and were said to be used as pack animals in Spain and Gaul after the migration period, H. Pirenne, *Mohammed and Charlemagne* (London, 1939), p. 93. The 'elephants' in the Vitellius Marvels of the East look more like camels than the camels in the manuscript do; these both have only one hump, but those in the Tiberius version have two, as do those in the Tapestry, James, *Marvels*, Vitellius f. 101a, nos. 9,10, f. 101b, Tiberius f. 80, no. 10. Another two-humped version is drawn in the early 11th-century Cotton Claudius B. iv from St Augustine's, Canterbury, F. Wormald, *English Drawings of the Tenth and Eleventh Centuries* (London, 1952), pl. 19b.

eagle swooping on a rabbit, a hound catching a very small quadruped, a fox carrying off a cockerel and a spotted feline with a goose (Pl.38). The theme of bird of prey with victim is widely used in early medieval art; the most immediate source is in the Ottonian manuscript group, where an eagle catching fish or hare is a recurrent motif in the spandrels of the canon tables.[23] Harold is of course shown taking a bird of prey as a gift for William, so the border may here be illustrating the popular pastime of falconry. Although there are examples of hounds chasing hares in Roman art, I can cite no interim examples of this motif. The scene of the fox and cock is common in medieval art as part of the Reynard epic, but the fox which catches a bird through trickery originates in much earlier bestiary and fable sources, with examples in contemporary stone carving.[24] The same theme is repeated in the adjacent panel, where the spotted feline with goose could be the designer's attempt at a domestic cat; a cat was one of Reynard's main enemies and rivals in the epic. However, cats with bird or mice victims already appear in Insular art, for example in the Book of Kells and on the Monasterboice South Cross. Other predatory scenes are those of another spotted feline creeping up on a grazing donkey and a wolf watching another donkey.

One obscure group, above the landing of the Norman fleet, is a procession of animals, all advancing to the right and in separate compartments; there are two small birds, two wolf-like creatures of different size, a stag and a lion; the row is concluded by a bird which faces the left. Another group of varied animals is being led by a monkey towards a crouching lion (Pl. 39). This may represent another part of the Reynard epic[25] but such groups and processions of different animals, together with some individual motifs such as the man fighting a bear, can be found in the illustrations to zoological manuscripts of Byzantine origin, copying Greek originals.[26] The existence of such a manuscript at Canterbury, amongst the known classical selection there, could account for these obscurer aspects of the Tapestry borders.

---

[23] Boeckler, *Evangelienbuch*, pl. 31, Escorial Codex Aureus; pl. 166, Ste Chapelle Gospel Book; pl. 179, Gotha Codex Aureus; pl. 197, fragment from Luxeuil. For further discussion of earlier and related examples, C. Hicks, 'The Birds on the Sutton Hoo Purse', *ASE*, 15 (1987), 153-65.

[24] K. Varty, *Reynard the Fox* (Leicester, 1967), for full discussion and illustrations, especially pls. 9, 10, 61-64 for Romanesque examples.

[25] *Ibid.*, chs. 3 and 5.

[26] Z. Kadar, *Survivals of Greek Zoological Illuminations in Byzantine Manuscripts* (Budapest, 1978), pl.138.

III: The Purpose of the Borders

The Tapestry as a whole has been the subject of exhaustive studies examining most aspects of its style, meaning, historical background and so on. The borders however have been literally regarded as marginal and generally only discussed as a very minor part of the whole. They have been considered in detail only by Yapp[27] and Bernstein.[28] One of Yapp's main concerns is to show that medieval artists drew from nature or from their own memories rather than only using the established formats or copy books which are generally regarded as the source for animals in medieval art. Applying this theory to the Tapestry animals, and particularly those in the borders, he does concede existing illustrated sources for the representation in the borders of evangelist symbols and a range of bestiary creatures. Like the other more ornamental animals, these are necessarily disguised in the form of confronted pairs. His evangelist symbols are difficult to accept, since the alleged 'winged lions' of St Mark are in fact griffins of the more lion-like variety, there are many birds but none specifically resembling eagles and there are no winged calves or men. Evangelist symbols can only safely be claimed when two or more of the above are shown in definite association or if one appears singly holding a book. Given the determinedly secular nature of the Tapestry in an age of otherwise almost exclusively religious art, random evangelist symbols would appear inappropriate here. His hypothetical bestiary source for some of the animals is of interest and accounts for some of the rarer types; he makes several possible identifications, including phoenix, amphisbaena and centaur, to which should be added the wolf licking its paws so as to creep up more quietly on its prey (representing the evil man who proceeds by stealth) (Pl.37). The only problem with this theory is that it presupposes the existence of an illustrated bestiary of early-eleventh-century date containing the particular range of types claimed, although no such early bestiary survives. Relevant manuscripts of suitable date such as the Physiologus or Marvels of the East do not contain all the appropriate beasts, which are not otherwise associated until the twelfth and thirteenth centuries. However, the bestiary theory is an attractive one and the presence of such illustrated volumes in a great monastic library seems perfectly feasible.

Bernstein's interpretation of the border fables as part of an Anglo-Saxon sub-text has been discussed above (p. 256). His main theory about the Tapestry is that the hidden message is based on the Hebrew scriptures: the Babylonian conquest of Judah is a paradigm for contemporary events, with the pagan Babylonians as God's instrument to chastize the Jews paralleled by

[27] W. Brundsdon Yapp, 'Animals in medieval art: the Bayeux Tapestry as an example', *Jnl Medieval History*, 13 (1987), 15-73.

[28] Bernstein, *Bayeux Tapestry.*

the Norman invaders imposing suffering on the defeated Anglo-Saxons; William therefore represents Nebuchadnezzar with Harold as the Hebrew king Zedekiah. While it is not the purpose of this article to discuss this overall interpretation, it is relevant to consider how Bernstein uses the borders as an important part of the evidence for this claim. He says that the winged lion, described in the Book of Daniel as representing the kingdom of Babylon, appears repeatedly in the borders in particular association with William, to symbolise the parallel being drawn with the duchy of Normandy. However, this winged lion is simply one of the versions of the griffin, which can be shown with various permutations of lion- and bird-like features. There are twenty-one pairs of griffins in the borders, of which ten pairs have the lion head; of these, seven pairs do appear above, below or near William and his entourage. However, as the Normans occupy about 75% of the central portion, this seems statistically unremarkable. Three pairs of lion-griffins are not associated with the Normans and one pair actually appears above the funeral procession of Edward the Confessor. Therefore Bernstein's claim that the 'winged lion of Babylon' has a specialised relationship with William cannot be sustained on the basis of either type or distribution. The griffin is simply the third most popular border animal and as such appears above and below Normans and Anglo-Saxons alike; like all the other border animals, its role here is purely ornamental.

It has been the intention of this article to suggest that the borders are decorative and that it is not part of their function to contribute to the message of the central text. But pure ornament does not imply ornament without meaning. The range of sources behind the borders – late antique texts, eastern silks and Anglo-Saxon manuscripts – provides a complex range of symbols selected by the designer and his workshop as a dazzling demonstration of contemporary design. Their individual meanings are not significant here but in association they demonstrate the constant process of assimilation which animal ornament always represents. In the case of the Tapestry borders, much adaptation has already taken place in Ottonian and Anglo-Saxon manuscript illustration from the end of the tenth century; it is certainly manuscript drawing which is the immediate source of the great majority of the animals. However, behind many of these drawings lie at second and third hand the animals of the east, the lions, griffins, senmurvs and winged horses present in Sassanian and Byzantine art, constantly being brought to the west on the imported silks which must be seen as a main inspiration for the animal ornament of Romanesque art. The integral role of animals on such textiles contributes to their selection as appropriate border ornament on such a prestigious piece of work as the Bayeux Tapestry.

Eadui Basan: Scriptorum Princeps?
RICHARD W. PFAFF

In the last twenty years or so there has emerged a monk of Christ Church, Canterbury, who now seems a discernible, perhaps a major, figure in the cultural history of eleventh-century England.[1] That there was a monastic scribe called Eadui Basan whose autograph appears at the end of an eleventh-century English Gospel book in Hanover has been known since at least the beginning of the present century.[2] A local habitation for this scribe was provided in 1935, when it was recognized that a fragmentary flyleaf in a Lambeth Palace manuscript (430) belonged to the widely-known Christ Church obituary in BL Cotton MS Nero C.ix, so that there was now placed in a plausible context 'Eadwius sacerdos et monachus'.[3]

But the emergence of Eadui as a figure of some magnitude is owed almost entirely to the discerning eye of T. A. M. Bishop, who in his *English Caroline Minuscule* (1971) provided a list of eleven specimens of that scribe's hand.[4] He described it as 'round, upright, deliberate, and artificial but not mannered, with characteristic g, &, ct, ra, question mark, and various forms of cedilla'. This 'deliberate hand' he spoke of in his preface as marking 'the beginning at Christ Church, Canterbury, of the "formalism" seen in other English manuscripts of the period' (p. xxiii). It was, as he had put it a few years earlier, 'a clear, carefully formed, slightly denatured script... well calculated

---

[1] I am indebted for assistance and advice to Janet Backhouse, Michelle Brown, Richard Gameson, Elizabeth Teviotdale, and especially to T. A. Heslop, who generously sent me proofs of his *Anglo-Saxon England* article. Abbreviations used in the notes are as follows: Bishop, *ECM* = T. A. M. Bishop, *English Caroline Minuscule* (Oxford, 1971); Bishop, 'Notes' = 'Notes on Cambridge Manuscripts', *Trans. Cambridge Bibliographical Soc.* 1953-63 (7 parts); Brooks = Nicholas Brooks, *The Early History of the Church at Canterbury* (Leicester, 1984); Heslop = T. A. Heslop, 'The Production of *de luxe* Manuscripts and the Patronage of King Cnut and Queen Emma', *ASE*, 19 (1990), 151-95; Ker, *Catalogue* = N. R. Ker, *Catalogue of Manuscripts containing Anglo-Saxon* (Oxford, 1957); Temple = Elzbieta Temple, *Anglo-Saxon Manuscripts, 900-1066* (London, 1976).

[2] S. Beissel, *Geschichte der Evangelienbücher* (Freiburg, 1906), p. 137, citing C. Graeven, 'Die drei ältesten Handschriften des Michaelisklosters', *Zeitschrift des historische Vereins für Niedersachsen* for 1901, 284-85. Beissel surmised that this scribe might have come from Winchester.

[3] A. Boutemy, 'Two Obituaries of Christ Church, Canterbury', *EHR*, 50 (1935), 292-99, at p. 295. The date of this Eadwius's death is said to be 22 September, but there is of course no indication of year.

[4] Bishop, *ECM*, p. 22.

to set off the elaborate ornament of manuscripts':[5] an acute assessment, as we shall see, though in what sense it is 'slightly denatured' is not clear to me.

The current foundation of our knowledge of Eadui then is Bishop's list; but it would of course be naive to suppose that the eleven items on it represent anything like Eadui's *oeuvre* as a scribe. This is simply what has both survived and been identified by one distinguished scholar. Grateful as we are for the list, it may perhaps be added to in the future. I do not think it possible to establish a chronology of the surviving specimens of his writing purely on palaeographical grounds. Bishop speaks of one piece as seeming 'to be the late and degenerate work' of Eadui,[6] and Janet Backhouse, finding the script in another 'uneven and sometimes almost quavering', thinks it 'perhaps not too imaginative to see it as the work of an elderly or infirm man';[7] but it would be a perilous set of judgements which tried to go beyond that.

Instead, I propose to notice the surviving specimens of his work according to the kind of text they represent. We have from his hand the following: three Gospel books or lectionaries of which he seems to be the sole scribe, and a fourth in which he wrote a single page; one complete psalter (i.e. written completely by him, though it has since been altered considerably), part of another, and a third, much earlier one, for which he supplied a missing quire; finally a few charters.[8] These items may not seem like a great deal on which to base even an assessment, let alone a claim; but they represent a considerable amount to have been identified as the work of one named scribe of the eleventh century. Brief consideration of each of them may set us some way towards being able to surmise something about Eadui's stature.

As has been mentioned, we are able to assign a name to this distinctive hand because of the autograph that survives at the end of the Hanover Gospels (Pl. 40): 'Pro scriptore precem ne tempnas fundere pater. Librum istum monachus scripsit EADUUIUS cognomento BASAN. Sit illi longa salus. Vale seruus dei .N. & memor esto mei.'[9] It is so exciting to have his signature in this helpful way that it is easy to ignore the wording of this closing formula; but it does tell us quite plainly that the book has been

5   *Idem*, 'Notes on MSS in Cambridge, part vii', *Trans. Cambridge Bibliographical Soc.*, III (1963), 413-22, at p. 420.

6   See below, note 32.

7   See below, note 18.

8   There is a further item in Bishop's list, identified as Cambridge, Gonville and Caius College MS 732/734, 'leaf from a service book'. But nothing in the library of that college seems to correspond to this (I am grateful to the entire staff for an exhaustive but fruitless search), and further enquiry has not yielded any result.

9   Hanover, Kestner-Museum Hs. W.M. XII^a, 36 (f. 183v). Temple, no. 67.

written for a specific 'pater .N.' – and also provides the basic fact that this scribe is himself a monk. The 'servus dei .N.' can be interpreted in two ways. T. A. Heslop maintains that this 'suggests that Eadui was working for an intermediate patron. The book's ultimate recipient was unknown to him by name, indeed perhaps he had not yet been chosen.' But this seems to be not very flattering to that ultimate recipient, especially if, as the same scholar also supposes, such a book as this may have been used as a present by Cnut in the course of his trip to Rome in 1027.[10] An alternative possibility which seems to me preferable is that Eadui is writing this book for a recipient yet to be elected – a bishop or abbot to be chosen to fill a vacancy. Such a person could plausibly be thought to be grateful for the book personalized in this way rather than 'depersonalized' in the setting Heslop suggests, and indeed likelier to pray for the scribe who so carefully names himself. The book was in Germany already in the later eleventh century;[11] how it got there is not known.

How the Gospel lectionary now in Florence[12] got to its first home outside England is also a mystery, though again, since Bishop has noted added matter in an eleventh-century Continental hand, it presumably did so quite early. It has only one illustration, a drawing of Christ enthroned and flanked by Peter and Paul. Though the text of the book proper is unquestionably in Eadui's hand, Heslop finds this drawing very similar in style to the Matthew portrait in the Pembroke Gospels (Cambridge, Pembroke College, MS 301), and suggests that 'while the monumental capitals beneath the drawing in Florence are by Eadwig, the uncials and rustic capitals on the same folio are also entirely within the tradition of scribes B and C' (p. 173), these being the now customary designations for those who wrote, among other books, the sacramentary of Robert of Jumièges (Rouen, Bibl. mun. MS Y.6) and the Kederminster Gospels (BL Loan MS 11). I do not find this notion very realistic, supposing as it does that Eadui wrote the third line while a second scribe wrote lines 1, 5, and 8 and another wrote 2, 4, 6, and 7. The weak link here seems to be the supposition that the three words 'In illo tempore' are written by Eadui; they are not much to go on in the assigning of scripts, and it would seem preferable to suppose that Eadui was supplied with the title page complete and began his work on f. 1v.

10 Heslop, pp. 176, 180.

11 *The Golden Age of Anglo-Saxon Art, 966-1066*, ed. J. Backhouse, D. H. Turner, L. Webster (London, 1984), no. 56. Cf. Temple, no. 67: 'German additions (ff. i, 183v, 194) of 11th and 12th centuries indicate that the volume left England at an early date.'

12 Florence, Bibliotheca Medicea-Laurenziana MS Plut. XVII.20. Temple, no. 69.

The third of Eadui's books of this kind, that called the Grimbald Gospels (BL Add. MS 34890), is a very grand book indeed.[13] It has come by its nickname because of a letter supposedly from Archbishop Fulk of Reims recommending Grimbald of St Bertin's to Alfred the Great. The hand which added the letter is apparently slightly later than Eadui's, and, as Temple has pointed out, may indicate no more than that this book was made for the New Minster, Winchester (to which Ker assigns it, with a query).[14] As, however, this localization is made on the basis of the letter about Grimbald, who was a great New Minster figure, the argument is a rather circular one.

Still, it is relevant to consider whether the Grimbald Gospels (there is no reason to discard the conventional name) represents Eadui writing on commission, so to speak, for another great monastic house, or whether the book should be seen as one of a series of Gospel texts, to which an interesting addition happens to have been made but which was not written to order. Though there can be no certainty, signs of incompleteness in this otherwise sumptuous book rather suggest that it was being made against some pressure of time. In the evangelist portraits, their 'books' are blank – perhaps incomplete, perhaps awaiting the evangelistic pens; but the scrolls carried by the human symbol of Matthew and bovine symbol of Luke are likewise devoid of writing, and there is a puzzling blank green surface to the right of the evangelist John. Furthermore, though the book is written almost flawlessly to the end of the Fourth Gospel, in the Gospel list which follows (f. 145v-57) every other initial is omitted (they have subsequently been pencilled in, with a good attempt at imitation of the original letter forms). It is reasonable to wonder whether the book was not sent off – as it were, to meet a deadline – before these last, not very time-consuming, details could be finished.

It is, therefore, possible to suggest that Eadui was asked to write a Gospel book for a rich and proud house, one which cannot be thought to have lacked scribes of its own. If this should be the correct understanding of the Grimbald Gospels, it would help us also to understand one of the major puzzles surrounding Eadui's career: his writing of a single, oddly isolated, leaf in the York Gospels.[15] What happened can be stated simply, but explanation is both complicated and controverted. The verso (23v) of the first, display page of Mattthew's Gospel (which faces the Evangelist portrait on 22v) was originally left blank; and the missing words, from 'Esrom' through 'qui uocatur Christus' in the Matthean genealogy, were subsequently supplied by

13 Temple, no. 68.

14 N. R. Ker, ed. *Medieval Libraries of Great Britain*, 2nd edn, (London, 1964), p. 103; see under Hyde.

15 York Minster, MS Add. 1. A facsimile edition, edited by Nicolas Barker with four substantial introductory essays, was published for the Roxburghe Club in 1986.

Eadui. The questions raised by this curious manner of proceeding begin with why the page was left blank in the first place and how long the interval was between when f. 23 (and, apparently, the rest of the codex) was written and when Eadui filled in the blank space. Michelle Brown has dealt with these problems admirably in a recent review of the facsimile.[16] The salient point for our purposes is her questioning of the long-held assumption that the York Gospels (which seem quite clearly to have reached York by c.1020-23) was written – save for f. 23v – in the late tenth century and that a gap of some twenty years or more supervened before Eadui wrote his page. Brown sees 'fewer obstacles to viewing Eadui's work as part of the original campaign, with his contribution forming the final stage in the work' (p. 554) - though this does not explain why the filling in of the blank page should have constituted the final stage. On balance she favours moving the dating of the volume to the early eleventh century, thus casting Eadui's role as part of 'a continuous working sequence'. Even so, we are left with the question with which we started: roughly, is it Eadui's eminence or his 'juniority' which was responsible for his being chosen to fill in the blank?

Heslop agrees that the idea that this book should have been in production for twenty to thirty years is inherently implausible, but does not speak in terms of filling a blank space. He reminds us that Bishop once suggested that Eadui had actually, as the writer of the first page of Gospel text proper, 'established the mise-en-page merely, the rest of the Gospels being written in a clear but non-calligraphic hand,' though later Bishop seemed to change his mind. As a new way out of the dilemma, Heslop suggests ingeniously that 'scribes of different ages were working side by side'[17] – a suggestion which incidentally reinforces the one made just above about the little signs of haste in the Grimbald Gospels.

A similar question about Eadui's involvement in a collaborative work confronts us with an even more famous codex, the Harley Psalter.[18] This extraordinarily complicated book is not only incomplete but unfinished, despite (or perhaps because of) the efforts of at least three scribes and some eight artists.[19] As the book has come down to us it has seventy-three folios;

[16] M. P. Brown in *The Book Collector*, 38 (1989), 551-55.

[17] Heslop, p. 169. The reference to Bishop is from part ii of the 'Notes', 1955, p.186.

[18] BL Harley MS 603. Temple, no. 64. See most recently J. Backhouse, 'The Making of the Harley Psalter', *British Library Jnl*, 10 (1984), 97-113; also of interest are R. Hasler, 'Zu zwei Darstellungen aus der ältesten Kopie des Utrecht-Psalters,' *Zeitschrift für Kunstgeschichte*, 44 (1981), 317-39, and an unpublished doctoral thesis by Judith Duffey, *The Inventive Group of Illustrations in the Harley Psalter* (Univ. of California, Berkeley, 1977). Further light is expected to be shed in the forthcoming thesis of William Noel.

[19] The numbering of the artists is that of Francis Wormald, *English Drawings of the*

there is no prefatory matter, and it stops in the middle of Psalm 143, at the end of a gathering. One scribe wrote ff. 1-27 and from the middle of 54v to 73; another wrote a brief section, ff. 50-54v; and Eadui wrote four gatherings in the middle, ff. 28-49. Though some leaves are now missing, his section seems to begin at Psalm 49 and to end at Psalm 97.[20] The following section (Psalms 100 to 105.25), that begun by the third scribe, provides one of the major enigmas of the Psalter, for it is in the Gallicanum version whereas the other parts of the text – both the initial scribe's section and Eadui's – are basically in the Romanum.[21] Indeed, it looks as though the third scribe was replaced summarily by the original one when it was realized that he was writing the 'wrong' version.

But some uncertainty about versions is also apparent in Eadui's section. In several places he has written a Gallicanum reading – for example, in Psalm 95.2 the Gallicanum 'benedicite nomini' rather than the Romanum 'benedicite nomen', in 51.11 a 'quia' instead of 'quem', in 52.6 a 'quoniam' in place of a probable Romanum 'quia'. These tiny instances suggest that Eadui may have in some way been 'thinking Gallicanum', as the third scribe definitely was. This is intrinsically not very surprising, since the Utrecht Psalter, on which the illustrations are clearly based, is itself Gallicanum.

The major curiosity about Eadui's section is in any case not his slight textual wavering but the fact that it was in his time virtually not illustrated. A few faint initials are all that seem to have been accomplished in his part in the early eleventh century, though some decades later an artist did illustrate the first of the folios he wrote (28) and in the twelfth century, probably around the middle, ff. 29-35 were elaborately illustrated (but again not completely, there being only faint sketchwork on ff. 34-35). The last fourteen of Eadui's folios have no illustration whatever.

From such indications as these we can hazard the following guess about Eadui's role in the making of this book. Clearly he is neither the starting nor the principal figure. Another scribe begins the psalms; it is this scribe rather than Eadui who takes over when the third has to be replaced. And whatever part Eadui may have had in the decoration of some of the books he wrote, he does not have such a part here. It seems reasonable to suppose that he is a somewhat junior figure in the scriptorium when he works on the Harley Psalter, and the date most often assigned to it, the first ten or so years of the eleventh century, seems consonant with this – though again the danger of circular reasoning must be kept in mind: is this book to be dated then partly

---

Tenth and Eleventh Centuries (London, 1952), no. 34.

[20] These are quires V to VIII, of six, eight, six, and two leaves (as they now stand) respectively.

[21] Brooks, p. 381 n. 28, says that the Gallicanum text of pss. 100-105.25 was supplied at the end of the 11th century, but this is simply wrong.

because Eadui seems to work on it in a subsidiary capacity or do we regard his part as secondary because we have otherwise assigned an early date?[22]

Janet Backhouse advances a different line of argument.[23] She points out that Eadui's section is written on inferior vellum, that the pages are not laid out like those in the earlier part of the book, and that there is no illustration by the artist who busily filled gaps in parts one, three, and four but not in (Eadui's) part two. In short, she feels, his section has 'every appearance of being a later substitute for a lost or damaged portion of the original work'. She tends to prefer a rather late date for the inception of the book, toying intriguingly with a time as late as c.1020, which would put Eadui's section quite far along in his career as a scribe, and cast him in the light not of a relatively junior member of the scriptorium but as a senior, even elderly, figure. Indeeed, this is where Backhouse maintains that his hand is 'uneven and sometimes almost quavering', and concludes that 'it is perhaps not too imaginative to see it as the work of an elderly or infirm man', whose part of the book could have been written as late as the 1040s. I find this rather difficult to accept, simply because there is not a shred of evidence which otherwise places any of Eadui's work later than 1023: which of course is not to say that he stopped writing then. And if the arguments rehearsed earlier about the York Gospels hold water, his *floruit* is even more firmly established in the second decade of the century. In this as in other respects the key document in interpreting his importance is probably the Arundel Psalter.

Here no questions about collaborative involvement arise. The Arundel Psalter (BL Arundel 155) is almost certainly datable to the period 1012-23, and was written solely (in its original state) by Eadui.[24] The dating framework comes from the presence as an original entry in the calendar of 'Passio sancti Ælfheahi archiepiscopi' (martyred 19 April 1012) and from the absence of his translation on 8 June 1023.[25] Such a clear framework helps to make the Harley Psalter seem earlier, though there is in theory no absolute reason why it has to be. Whatever may be the relationships of time or causation between the two books, it is clear that Arundel is not only a one-man but a very individual production. Indeed, it should more fittingly be

22 This discussion assumes that the Harley Psalter was made at Christ Church and not at St Augustine's. Again the danger of circular argument exists, but Eadui's role does seem one of the deciding factors for Christ Church. Backhouse also favours this location (note 18).

23 Backhouse, 'Harley Psalter', p. 106. The article makes several stimulating suggestions about the book as a whole.

24 Temple, no. 66.

25 The calendar is printed in F. Wormald, ed. *English Kalendars before A.D. 1100* (Henry Bradshaw Society 72, 1933), pp. 169-81.

called the Eadui Psalter, for it bears his stamp in three distinctive ways beyond his merely having written it: textual, liturgical, and iconographic.

The first aspect relates again to the textual question that arose with the Harley Psalter. Though, as we saw, Eadui seems to have had some Gallicanum readings in his head while he was writing his section of Harley, the Arundel Psalter is once more of the Romanum – that is, old-fashioned – version. Much remains to be done before the fortunes of these versions in eleventh-century England can be straightened out. Preliminarily (or perhaps superficially), it seems to be the case that the Gallicanum version gets an English foothold in the late tenth century, the Salisbury Psalter (Salisbury Cathedral, MS 150) being apparently the first psalter made in England to contain it; and that it has taken over at Winchester by the middle of the eleventh, in such books as BL Stowe 2, Cotton Tiberius C.vi, Cotton Vitellius E.xviii, and Arundel 60, all probably having some connection with one or another of the scriptoria at Winchester.[26] What is not clear is whether there was at Canterbury a corresponding conservatism about abandoning the older version, for the relevant pieces of evidence are really only two: the Bosworth Psalter (BL Add. MS 37517), virtually contemporary with the path-breaking Salisbury Psalter, and Harley 603, with its suggestions that the Gallicanum is about to break in.

The question is heightened rather than resolved by the text of the Arundel Psalter; for though Eadui wrote it in the Romanum version, he subsequently made extensive corrections to try to bring it into conformity with the Gallicanum. (The full extent of this is a bit hard to see because even more widespread corrections were made in the twelfth century, not at all to our purpose.) Eadui's changes are often over careful and complete erasures: for example, a 'conteruisti' changed to 'contriuisti' (ps. 3.8), 'iniusticia' to 'iniquitate' (ps. 51.3), 'bene nunciate' to 'annunciate' (ps. 95.2), 'potentatibus' to 'virtutibus' (ps. 150.2). The result is far from being a complete Gallicanum text, but the overall effect is of a version that will now, as it were, stand muster in the wider world. Did Eadui try to produce a revised text of this kind because he was asked to do so or because it fell to him, at least in part, to make that kind of decision for the community?

The second respect in which the Arundel Psalter may bear witness to Eadui's stature is in the contents of the calendar which stands at the head of the book. Again, his potential contribution has to be approached cautiously, because there is very little in the way of comparative calendarial material for Christ Church from before or during his time, and because the numerous and complex subsequent additions make it hard to ascertain exactly what the document looked like when it left Eadui's hands. These cautions stated, it does appear possible that the calendar of this psalter represents a stage of

[26] See, e.g., the discussion in Brooks, pp. 261-65.

'normalizing' the saints honoured at Christ Church. If this is the case, the intelligence behind such 'normalizing' would almost certainly be that of someone of both perceived stature and future influence.

The primary point of comparison here has to be with the calendar of the Bosworth Psalter, extensively studied by Edmund Bishop and Aidan Gasquet in 1908.[27] It would be too much to claim that Bosworth's calendar was anything like an official Christ Church document of the beginning of the eleventh century,[28] any more than that Arundel's had that character perhaps twenty years later. This is not the place to discuss in detail the comparative tables Bishop provides, but a brief juxtaposition with Bosworth's calendar may tell us something useful about the nature of Eadui's. There are three strong contrasts. First, Bosworth contains many more saints than Arundel – approximately fifty-five more. Secondly, to a striking extent the saints present in Bosworth's calendar but missing from Eadui's are not just obscure persons from Continental martyrologies but English (and British) figures of considerable familiarity: such names as abbot Hadrian, Guthlac, Aldhelm, Botulf, Eadburga (15 June), Aethelburga, Aidan, Paulinus, and Wilfrid, plus a whole group of (arch)bishops of Canterbury – Mellitus, Deusdedit, Honorius, Nothelm, Justus. The relative spareness of Arundel's calendar, especially at the expense of all these figures from the Anglo-Saxon past (between fifteen and twenty in all), is so striking that it misled as great a scholar as Edmund Bishop into regarding the Psalter as post-Conquest and its calendar as a document of the so-called Lanfrancian purge.[29]

Eadui's calendar is in a sense purged, though not by supposed archiepiscopal action; but the contrast with Bosworth's is not solely in the direction of sloughing off excess saints. For the Arundel calendar also includes some thirty names lacking in Bosworth. Only three of these are primarily English, all with Winchester affinities – the translations of Cuthbert and Birinus 4 September, Birinus alone 3 December, and perhaps Judoc on 13 December – together with Ælfheah. The great majority of these additional names are Continental. A few can be connected with relics at Christ Church (for example, Blaise), but the majority imply Continental sacramentary traditions of some complexity: Emerentiana and Macharius (23

27 F. A. Gasquet and E. Bishop, *The Bosworth Psalter* (London, 1908).

28 Two difficulties in so doing would be 1) that Bosworth's calendar has some clear Glastonbury affinities, e.g. its entries at 23 Aug. 'Patricii senioris in Glaestonia' and 25 Sept. 'Ceolfrithi abbatis in Glaestonia'; and 2) that its calendar seems to be somewhat later than the rest of the book, though exactly how much later is not clear. For further complications see M. Korhammer, 'The Origin of the Bosworth Psalter', *ASE*, 2 (1973), 173-87.

29 Gasquet and Bishop, pp. 30-32.

January), Vitus and Modestus (15 July), Pantaleon as well as Sampson (28 July), Symphorian as well as Timothy (22 August).

These details permit us to understand Arundel's calendar. First, there is a general if quite selective awareness of the English past: Alban, Augustine, Oswald, Cuthbert, Boniface, Erkenwald. Secondly, particular attention is paid to observances connected equally with both great Winchester houses.[30] Thirdly, limited but striking awareness is shown of Continental saints, both of early Christian antiquity and of Frankish origin: figures like Vedast and Amand (6 February, with Vedast again, joining Remigius and Germanus, on 1 October), Leodegar (Leger, 2 October), Lambert (17 September). None of these is included in Bosworth's calendar (and none primarily connected with areas where Cnut had his major dealings). The determining intelligence is at once historically and liturgically sophisticated; is it also Eadui's? It may of course belong to someone else entirely, but until a better candidate can be suggested, he would seem to hold the field. At the least, the suggestion is not implausible, nor inconsistent with the other evidence considered.

The very substantial, perhaps pre-eminent, position which the Arundel Psalter suggests that Eadui held by about 1020 may help to explain the nature of his involvement in the third psalter associated with him. This is the Vespasian Psalter, mostly written in the eighth century (in the Romanum version), and with continuous interlinear Old English gloss added in the ninth.[31] It was kept at St Augustine's in the fifteenth century, and there is no reason to think that it was not there in the eleventh. The book is not only splendid but also quite complete. As it stands, it contains the full psalter (plus the extranumeral psalm, added in the ninth century at f. 141), nine canticles, and three hymns. Then comes a new quire, ff. 155-60, containing Te Deum, Quicunque vult, and various prayers, and written by Eadui. This is the work of his which T. A. M. Bishop refers to as 'late and degenerate; mainly deliberate, but in places negligently formed'.[32]

---

[30] Brooks's discussion of these matters on p. 265 is interesting but a bit simplistic in two respects. It is not enough merely to say that 'By the time of the Arundel Psalter, Christ Church had changed to a calendar of Winchester origin', because the 'Winchester' saints reflect both those of the Old Minster (Swithun, Birinus) and the New (Grimbald, Judoc): this is no more a single calendarial tradition than would a mix of Christ Church and St Augustine's be a 'Canterbury' tradition. Nor is it quite accurate to characterize the removal of English saints from Arundel's calendar as 'an apparent attempt in the early 11th century to remove the feasts of saints whose cult has developed in other Kentish houses'; because too many of the 'purged' saints do not fall into that category – Gildas, Maerwynna, Guthlac, Botulf, Aidan, Aldhelm, Rumwold – for that to be the whole story.

[31] BL Cotton Vespasian A. i; facsimile edn, D. H. Wright, *The Vespasian Psalter* (Early English Manuscripts in Facsimile 14, Copenhagen 1967).

[32] Bishop, *ECM*, p. 22; he notes 'Two forms of the ct-ligature; the frequent hooked e

Three unanswerable questions that arise here begin with one perhaps irrelevant to Eadui: what had happened to the final quire of the original psalter? The second is the most obvious one: why was Eadui asked to supply the gap? And the third is: to what extent is he responsible for the choice of the prayers that follow the Quicunque – especially the first, the 'Oratio Eugenii Toletani episcopi' ('Rex Deus inmense qui constat machina mundi')? We might also ask why the Te Deum and Athanasian Creed have Old English glosses, apparently also in Eadui's hand,[33] whereas the prayers, equally in Latin, do not.

If we simply suppose that Eadui was asked to complete what was clearly regarded as a prize possession because he was known to be an eminent scribe, we still need to consider the issues implied by this. To take one obvious aspect, was he paid for his work? Far-fetched as that possibility may sound, there is some reason to entertain it. Heslop cites the mention in Ælfric Bata's *Colloquia* of the scribes who 'write books and sell them and thence gain for themselves lots of money'.[34] If payment seems unlikely – it is, after all, only six folios – can we rather imagine a friendly exchange of scribes between the two great Canterbury houses, not themselves always on such friendly terms? To prove such an idea we would need to find a Christ Church book similarly supplied by a known St Augustine's scribe, but without proof this must remain hypothetical.

It is more likely that the monks of St Augustine's turned to Eadui because he was known to be an expert on the contents of psalters. If it is true, as Bishop has suggested, that this is a late, let alone degenerate specimen of Eadui's hand, it is more probable that he would be asked to take on this work as one whose knowledge about such matters was worth having rather than because of the beauty of his writing.

There is, however, one further possibility which should be mentioned. This is that the Vespasian psalter was for some reason loaned to Christ Church and that while it was there something – spillage, rats, a small fire – ruined the final gathering: whereupon the monks not of St Augustine's but of Christ Church naturally turned to their eminent master-scribe Eadui Basan to supply the damaged material. This is far-fetched, perhaps, but it does fit the facts of the existing situation.

---

occurs, less frequently, in the scribe's portion of Harl. MS 603.'

[33] Ker, *Catalogue*, no. 203, describes the hand as 'a very fine upright hand of s. xi med, apparently an early version of the St Augustine's hand found in Cambridge Corpus Christi College, MS 270 and in other manuscripts: in OE *s* is regularly long and *y* is straight-limbed and dotted: hyphens are on a level with the base-line'.

[34] Heslop, p. 177, citing the text in *Early Scholastic Colloquies*, ed. W. H. Stevenson (Oxford, 1929) p. 50.

The kind of eminence here presupposed also explains Eadui's work on Christ Church charters, work which in turn makes his stature much clearer. The most important of these documents is the celebrated confirmation of privileges of Christ Church by Cnut within the period 1017-20, most likely in 1018: an Old English document of thirteen lines written by Eadui on the top half of a blank leaf in an early eleventh-century Gospel book, BL Royal MS 1. D.ix (f. 44v).[35] This is a book whose special donation (because it was believed to have been given by Cnut) and beautiful execution (because it was written largely by the scribe who wrote the Trinity Gospels and the Robert of Jumièges Sacramentary)[36] made it a highly suitable location for the insertion of a document which clinched the resecuring of the *freols* of the monastery – a process begun by a ceremony in which Cnut had himself laid certain charters granted by earlier kings on the high altar at Canterbury. It is the description of this solemn public act which Eadui recorded in the Gospel book: 'Then I myself took the charters of freedom and laid them on Christ's own altar, with the cognizance of the archbishop and of earl Thurkill and of many good men who were with me...'.[37] Thus, as Nicholas Brooks has put it, 'the skill of the outstanding writer at Christ Church reinforced the authority of the royal act by associating it with the holy gospels that were kept upon the most sacred altar in England'.[38]

Equally striking is Eadui's involvement in preserving a bilingual charter linked with Æthelred II and the year 1006, similarly written on blank leaves between the gospels of Luke and John in an even more venerable Gospel book, the late ninth- or early tenth-century continental codex given to Christ Church by King Athelstan before his death in 939.[39] This is a very extensive and important privilege, securing for the cathedral establishment its distinctive status as a monastic community. It is therefore an appropriate text

[35] Temple, no. 70; f. 44v is printed and translated in F. E. Harmer, *Anglo-Saxon Writs* (Manchester, 1952; reprint Stamford, 1989), no. 26. Here Ker, *Cat.*, no. 247, notes that 'long and low s are initially used indifferently and round s initially: high e occurs once in the combination *æ*'. The blank leaves are the last two of a quire of eight, and come between the Markan prologue and title page; presumably they were left blank so that his portrait could be placed at the head of a new gathering.

[36] Respectively, Cambridge Trinity College MS. B.10.4 and Rouen, Bibl. mun. Y.6. Both were written by the scribe generally known as B in the identification by Bishop, *ECM*. A colleague, Bishop's C, also worked on the Royal Gospels.

[37] As translated by Harmer, *Writs*, p. 182.

[38] Brooks, p. 288.

[39] BL Cotton Tiberius A.ii, from which were detached before 1621 seven leaves which now make up Cotton Claudius A. iii (and four more now in Cotton Faustina B. vi): N. R. Ker, 'Membra Disiecta', *British Museum Quarterly*, 12 (1937-38), 130-31.

to be written by a prominent scribe and preserved in a book of solemn importance, especially since, again in Brooks's words, this 'monastic refoundation charter is in fact a forgery, and it is very possible that it was Eadui Basan himself who both doctored the gospel book to receive it and concocted the text of the charter'.[40]

We know of at least two other charters written by Eadui, and may assume that he wrote more. One is a charter for Cnut dated 1018, the contents of which also concern Christ Church, or at least the archiepiscopal estates, and which was probably granted at the same time as Cnut visited the cathedral to take part in the ceremony of confirming its previous privileges just described.[41] The other is a copy of the confirmation at the Synod of Cloveshoe in 716 of a charter of liberties granted to the religious establishments of Kent by King Wihtred twenty-five years before. This is by far the earliest manuscript of this charter to have survived, probably with a major interpolation in a kind of postscript which threatens dire penalties to anyone who 'tyrannica potestate inflatus ex habitu secularium seu ecclesiasticarum infringere minuere temptauerit auctoritatem archiepiscopi et Christi ecclesie uel libertatem coenobiarum'.[42]

The overall import of Eadui's activity with the Christ Church charters may be summed up by referring once more to Brooks's assessment of the 1018 episode. He finds it likely '1) that prior to Cnut's visit Eadui re-examined the charters of his house and recopied them where necessary; 2) that the Christ Church monks stage-managed the king's elaborate ceremony at the altar of Christ; and 3) that Eadui prepared the text of the royal writ to be sent to the shire-court'.[43] Such an assessment puts us in a position to consider Eadui's impact on his community as a whole.

Three further pieces of evidence are crucial in any attempt to evaluate Eadui's overall importance. The first is the famous illustration on f. 133 of Eadui's own Arundel Psalter (Pl.41).[44] The kneeling monk crouching at the

[40] Brooks, p. 257. As to a precise date, he notes that 'the script of the refoundation charter compares rather with the late and somewhat less carefully written work of this scribe, and we have no information about how long he lived. The forgery had certainly been entered into the gospels before another scribe added another series of notes of subsequent bequests to Christ Church apparently early in Edward the Confessor's reign.' He therefore suggests a date in the early part of the second quarter of the century.

[41] BL Stowe Charters 38, printed in B. Sanders, ed., *Facsimiles of Anglo-Saxon Manuscripts*, 3 vols (Ordnance Survey, 1878-84), III.39. Cf. Brooks, pp. 277 and 288.

[42] BL Stowe Charters 2, printed in Sanders, *Facsimiles*, III.2.

[43] Brooks, p. 290.

[44] BL Arundel MS 155, f. 133, illustrated in colour in *Golden Age of Anglo-Saxon Art*,

foot of St Benedict and holding a book in his left hand is generally taken to be Eadui, a portrait of the scribe, so to speak – indeed, if Eadui is also the illustrator of this manuscript (a possibility we shall consider presently), a self-portrait. The book he holds is presumably this psalter (the letters 'Lib ps' are evident to the left of where his hand is holding the book); the prostrate monk is in physical contact with the saint (whose footstool he is and whose foot he is kissing); the girdle around his waist is lettered 'zona humilitatis'. His whole figure is coloured, like Benedict's; since the other monks are virtually monochrome, he is clearly the second most important figure in the picture. Is this a piece of mere self-advertisement or a fair reflection of his status in the community? So prominently is he depicted that one would almost prefer that the figure be meant as someone else, but the carrying of the book in his hand makes this all but impossible.

Related to the impression conveyed by this (self-) portrait is a further puzzling question: the meaning of 'cognomento Basan'. Do we best infer from the Hanover Gospels colophon that Basan is a surname in an age when surnames as such were very little known; or that it is what we would more accurately call a nickname; or – the least desirable alternative – that it is a now incomprehensible sign of demarcation in a community where there may have been a number of people with names like Eadui? A search through modern works on personal names in this period has so far drawn a total blank. The only, admittedly far-fetched, possibility I can think of is a corrupt form of the colour adjective *basu*, purple, perhaps related to the Gothic word for berry.[45] This hypothetical question is made chiefly because in the Arundel Psalter illustration just discussed, the face in profile of the kneeling monk whom we have assumed to be Eadui is not only shaded (as is Benedict's) but curiously mottled by nine or so little double marks, like double inverted commas. Can these be meant to represent some sort of disfigurement, like a widespread birthmark? If this should indeed be a self-portrait, it is Eadui who chooses to emphasize this aspect; which would in turn be congruous with the display-letter prominence of 'cognomento BASAN' in the Hanover Gospels colophon, itself the only source we have for this puzzling name.

The second indication of Eadui's overall status in Christ Church is again admittedly conjectural but cannot be ignored. This is a marginal note in a Christ Church manuscript of first importance to the community in the mid-eleventh century – the period, we would suppose, around the time of or just after Eadui's death: BL Cotton Tiberius A. iii, which contains a (the?) Christ Church copy of the *Rule* of Benedict and various supplements, the

---

pl. xviii.

45 J. Bosworth and T. N. Toller, *An Anglo-Saxon Dictionary* (Oxford, 1882-98), p. 68. I am grateful to Bernard O'Donoghue for discussing this point with me.

Regularis Concordia, the *Colloquy* of Ælfric, and further miscellaneous contents. Most of the items are supplied with interlinear Old English gloss.[46] After Benedict's *Rule* (ff. 118-63v as the manuscript is now constituted) comes a seven-line injunction to observe it (beginning 'Dicebat uero sanctus Fulgentius') and what is here called an 'Epitome of the Rule' but is in fact part ii of Benedict of Aniane's *Memoriale* (ff. 164-68v). As the latter document begins there are in the margin of fol. 164 in a late-eleventh-century hand the words 'Eadwi m[...] me ah' (as read by Ker; we may conjecture *-unuc*, giving 'munuc', in the illegible space). The presumption is that the writer of these words thought that an 'Eadwi' either possessed the book or had obtained the book, or was the author ('owner') of the Benedict of Aniane treatise on the Rule or even the maker of the collection of largely monastic documents that comprise the codex.

Before we turn to the third and most speculative suggestion as to Eadui Basan's stature at Christ Church, we need to notice the possibility of his having been what we would call an artist as well as a scribe. Probably neither of two extreme positions is correct: that all decoration in every book he wrote is by another hand than his, or that he is responsible for most of the illustrative material in the books he wrote – indeed, if the latter were the case Eadui would immediately become the major named artist of his time. A middle-ground position must take seriously the possibility that at the least he did a good deal of the decoration of 'his' psalter, including the somewhat self-advertising depiction at Benedict's feet. The two most recent students of the manuscript both suggest that Eadui had a major hand in the decoration of this book. Brooks says that Eadui 'produced a superbly written and decorated psalter'; while Heslop notes that Arundel 155 and the Hanover Gospels 'are fairly clearly painted by the same hand, and in both books minuscule and capital letters very like Eadui's form an integral part of the visual imagery', and remarks that 'the case for these being Eadui's own paintings and drawings is strong if not yet conclusive'.[47]

The third possible indication of Eadui's importance at Christ Church is connected with the question of how his memory was chiefly preserved there. Was it as a scribe, or as an artist, or as one whose sagacity was vital in preserving (or improving) the house's privileges? There can be little doubt that the primary category was that of scribe, an understood, even dignified position which might extend on one side to the decoration of manuscripts and on the other to controlling the wording of the charters he wrote. And it is as scribe that this final possible clue presents itself as to how lasting his impact may have been.

46 BL Cotton Tiberius A. iii is analysed at length in Ker, *Cat.*, no. 186. Temple, no. 100.

47 Brooks, p. 264; Heslop, p. 176.

This has to do with the Leonine hexameter verses around the famous portrait of the monk-scribe on f. 283v of the Eadwine Psalter (Cambridge, Trinity College MS R.17.1/987; pl. 42):

SCRIPTORUM PRINCEPS EGO. NEC OBITURA DEINCEPS
LAUS MEA NEC FAMA. QUIS SIM MEA LITTERA CLAMA.
TE TUA SCRIPTURA QUEM SIGNAT PICTA FIGURA
PREDICAT EADWINUM FAMA PER SECULA VIVUM.
INGENIUM CUIUS LIBRI DECUS INDICAT HUIUS
QUEM TIBI SEQUE DATUM MUNUS DEUS ACCIPE GRATUM.

The curious thing about these often-quoted verses is that the distinguishing characteristic of the verse form as fully developed – the bisyllabic internal rhyme – breaks down at what seems to be the crucial place, the name of the person being honoured. Since as these words stand the whole point of the inscription seems vitiated by the defective rhyme 'Eadwinum/vivum', it is tempting to wonder whether the verses – and, just conceivably, the portrait itself – were not originally meant to refer to someone other than the figure we think of as Eadwine, ostensibly a Canterbury monk-scribe of the twelfth century. And one cannot help noting that 'Eaduiuum' makes a true, if not elegant, rhyme with ('secu)la uiuum'. Of course, Eadui Basan signs himself, in the rustic capitals of the Hanover Gospels colophon, EADUUIUS, not EADUIUUS. But such a name in minuscule script could, by a misreading of the seven vertical strokes which form UUIU as UIUU, be rendered as EADUIUUS: in the accusative case, therefore, not 'Eaduuium' but 'Eaduiuum', which creates the true rhyme for '-la uiuum'.[48]

Clearly this suggestion hovers between plausibility and absurdity, but this may not be an inappropriate posture in which to end this preliminary enquiry. In descending order of likelihood, the following points should be considered. 1) It is highly probable that if Eadui Basan 'signed' one of his books (and that one intended for a recipient whose name he does not seem to have known) he signed others as well. 2) It is certainly possible that one or more such 'signatures' existed in minuscules, giving rise to the possibility of misunderstanding just noticed. 3) It may well be the case that the import of the 'portrait' in the Arundel Psalter was understood for some decades after his death; without question, the book was used in the mid-twelfth century (extensive additions to its calendar, further prayers, numerous hymns, and a concerted effort to make the text conform to the Gallicanum) and also

[48] I have broached this question at somewhat greater length in chapter III of M. Gibson, T. A. Heslop, R. W. Pfaff, ed., *The Eadwine Psalter. Text, Image, and Monastic Culture in Twelfth-Century Canterbury* (London and University Park, PA, 1992).

thereafter (further additions to the calendar, even into the fifteenth century). 4) It is conceivable that the memory of Eadui's role in securing Christ Church privileges at the time of a new, foreign dynasty (Cnut's) survived, and was viewed gratefully, in the time of another new and foreign dynasty, that of William. 5) It is not inconceivable that this memory is somehow perpetuated in the Leonine verses of the Eadwine Psalter which (whatever their relevance to Eadui) clearly do not seem to have been composed originally in honour of someone named Eadwine.

As we look over this chain of probabilities, possibilities, and guesses, it seems unwise to discard entirely the figure of Eadui Basan. There can be little doubt that on the basis of what we now know about him he qualifies amply for the sobriquet 'scriptorum princeps'. Whether he was so known at Christ Church either during his lifetime or after his death, and whether the appellation is in some distant way preserved in the Eadwine Psalter inscription with its false rhyme, we can probably never establish with certainty. But there can be no doubt about the importance of his role in English eleventh-century studies.

What do we Mean by the Source of a Picture?
BARBARA RAW

As is well known, many of the pictures in late Anglo-Saxon manuscripts were based very closely on earlier models. The numerous early medieval copies of Prudentius's *Psychomachia* contain cycles of illustrations whose composition is virtually identical, even though they differ stylistically.[1] Artists working at Canterbury in the eleventh century based many of their psalter illustrations on the miniatures in an early ninth-century continental manuscript, the Utrecht Psalter.[2] Many of the Genesis illustrations in the early eleventh-century MS Junius 11 in the Bodleian Library, Oxford, can be shown to derive from an early Christian cycle of pictures similar to that in the sixth-century Cotton Genesis.[3] When we say that the pictures in these manuscripts were based on earlier models, we are talking about the surface layout of the pictures, about the picture as a material object. But a picture consists of more than its surface layout: it has a meaning and a context. In talking of sources, therefore, one cannot confine oneself to considerations of style and layout: one must also consider the meaning of the picture and how the meaning gets into the picture.

In the psalters and the Prudentius manuscripts, text and pictures were transmitted together; the context of the pictures remained the same and so, therefore, did their meaning. The same is true of the Genesis illustrations in MS Junius 11, for the vernacular paraphrase which they illustrate differs very little from the biblical Genesis.[4] In other manuscripts the position is not so simple. A composition designed for one text may be transferred to another; motifs from several sources may be combined to create new compositions; a

1   Three of these Prudentius manuscripts were produced in England in the late 10th century: Cambridge, Corpus Christi College, MS 23; BL Cotton MS Cleopatra C. viii; BL Add. MS 24199. For reproductions see R. Stettiner, *Die illustrierten Prudentius-Handschriften* (Berlin, 1905).

2   BL Harley MS 603 and Utrecht, Universiteitsbibliothek, MS 32. F. Wormald, *English Drawings of the Tenth and Eleventh Centuries* (London, 1952), pp. 69-70 and J. Backhouse, 'The Making of the Harley Psalter', *British Library Jnl*, 10 (1984), 97-113.

3   BL Cotton MS Otho B. vi; for the parallels with Junius 11 see B. C. Raw, 'The Probable Derivation of Most of the Illustrations in Junius 11 from an Illustrated Old Saxon *Genesis*', *ASE*, 5 (1976), 133-48, and G. Henderson, 'Late-Antique Influences in some English Medieval Illustrations of Genesis', *Jnl Warb. Court. Insts.*, 25 (1962), 172-98.

4   This is not, of course, true of the drawings of the rebellion and fall of Satan and the temptation of Adam and Eve by an angel, which are unbiblical and do not derive from the Cotton cycle.

picture devised originally as a textual illustration may be separated from the text and used independently, perhaps as the frontispiece to a manuscript; in some cases, new iconographies are developed with little or no dependence on artistic sources.[5] An artist who transferred an illustration from one text to another presumably did so because he thought the meaning of the illustration appropriate to the new text: for example, pictures of gospel scenes were often included in psalters because the psalms were traditionally interpreted as prophecies of the life of Christ. The layout of these pictures may be based on an artistic source but their meaning derives from the exegetical link between psalter and gospels. When motifs are brought together from several different artistic sources to create a new composition, the source of the picture is not simply the artistic models for the separate motifs but the overall idea in the artist's mind, whether this derived from a specific text or, more generally, from ideas current at the time. The meaning of the frontispiece to a text or manuscript has to be considered in relation to its function as well as to any textual and artistic parallels.

The present article deals with three pictures which illustrate different aspects of the problem of sources: two drawings from the Ælfwine Prayerbook[6] and a painting from the Weingarten Gospels.[7]

The drawing of the crucifixion on f. 65v of the Ælfwine Prayerbook, written and decorated at New Minster, Winchester, between 1023 and 1035, shows Christ with open eyes, crowned with a jewelled circlet, standing before the cross; above his head are the *dextera dei* and the *titulus* inscribed with the words 'Hic Ihesus Nazarenus rex Iudeorum' (Pl. 43). Above the arms of the cross are two torch-bearing figures, labelled 'sol' and 'luna'. Mary and John are shown standing below the cross; Mary is represented as an orant figure and John writes in a book; both are labelled with their names, 'Sancta Maria' and 'Sanctus Iohannes'. Across the top of the picture is the inscription:

Hec crux consignet Ælfwinum corpore mente
In qua suspendens traxit deus omnia secum.[8]

This drawing is the earliest of a group of four crucifixion pictures which are distinguished from other late Anglo-Saxon representations of the crucifixion by the combination of a crowned figure of Christ, an orant figure

---

5   See, for example, M. Schapiro, 'The Image of the Disappearing Christ', in his *Late Antique, Early Christian and Mediaeval Art: Selected Papers* (London, 1980), 267-87.

6   BL Cotton MS Titus D. xxvii.

7   New York, Pierpont Morgan Library MS 709.

8   The emphasis on Christ's divinity is seen again in the drawing of Mary with the Trinity on f. 75v of the manuscript; see below, pp. 294-96 and B. C. Raw, *Anglo-Saxon Crucifixion Iconography and the Art of the Monastic Revival* (Cambridge, 1990), 173-75.

of Mary and inscriptions identifying the figures. The other pictures in the group are those in the Winchcombe Psalter, the Arundel Psalter and a collection of homilies now at Corpus Christi College, Cambridge.[9] The link between the four pictures is not simply a thematic one; parallels in layout and motifs show that they share artistic sources. They are not straightforward copies from a single archetype, however, for there are striking differences among them. The drawing in the Ælfwine Prayerbook is the only one of the four to include the *titulus* above Christ's head, to represent Christ as alive on the cross, and to show the sun and moon as classical, torch-bearing figures. Only two of the four pictures (those in the Ælfwine Prayerbook and the Winchcombe Psalter) include the motif of St John writing in a book. The drawing in the Cambridge homilies manuscript omits the symbols of the sun and moon and adds a dragon beneath Christ's feet. In the Winchcombe Psalter the cross is inscribed with the words *lignum vite*, and in the Arundel Psalter it takes the form of two roughly lopped tree trunks, symbolizing Christ's tree of life.[10]

Discussion of the sources of these four pictures will be limited in the present article to those of the earliest of the four, that in the Ælfwine Prayerbook. No parallels to the overall iconography of this drawing can be found in earlier Anglo-Saxon manuscripts or carvings, or in Carolingian, Ottonian or Byzantine art. Parallels do exist to individual motifs, however. The torch-bearing symbols of the sun and moon are a commonplace of Carolingian crucifixion scenes.[11] Crowned crucifixes are rare before the eleventh century but there is one early parallel to the jewelled fillet in the Ælfwine manuscript: the pearl-studded band which encircles Christ's head in the crucifixion painting at the *Te igitur* in the ninth-century Metz Coronation Sacramentary.[12] The plants which spring from the ground at the feet of Mary and John are similar to those in the evangelist pictures in three Carolingian manuscripts: the Godescalc Gospels, the Gospels of Saint-Médard of Soissons and the Ebbo Gospels.[13]

---

[9] Cambridge, University Library MS Ff. 1. 23, f. 88r; BL Arundel MS 60, f. 12v; CCCC, MS 421, p. 1. See Raw, *Crucifixion Iconography*, pp. 129-46, pls. VIII-XI.

[10] *Ibid.*, p. 150; J. O'Reilly, 'The Rough-Hewn Cross in Anglo-Saxon Art', in *Ireland and Insular Art AD 500-1200*, ed. M. Ryan (Dublin, 1987), 153-58.

[11] G. Schiller, *Iconography of Christian Art*, 2 vols., trans. J. Seligmann (London, 1971-72), II, p. 109, pls. 360, 361, 374, 382 and 390.

[12] Paris, Bibliothèque Nationale, MS lat. 1141, f. 6v, reprod. *Sakramentar von Metz Fragment, MS lat. 1141, Bibl. Nat. Paris. Vollständige Faksimile-Ausgabe*, ed. F. Mütherich (Graz, 1972); Raw, *Crucifixion Iconography*, p. 135.

[13] J. Hubert, J. Porcher, W. F. Volbach, *Carolingian Art* (London, 1970), pls. 64-65, 76 and 93.

Whereas these details point to a possible Carolingian model for the Ælfwine picture, the figures of Mary and John suggest influence from an English source. No manuscript before the Ælfwine Prayerbook depicts Mary as an orant beneath the cross, though orant figures of Mary are common in ascension scenes from the sixth century onwards.[14] A painting of the ascension added to the Athelstan Psalter in about 925 (Pl. 44)[15] offers a particularly close parallel to the portrayal of Mary in the Prayerbook, and the possibility of direct influence from the Psalter is strengthened by the presence in both pictures of very similar plants and by the inscriptions identifying the figures. Writing figures of St John are found in crucifixion pictures in four late Anglo-Saxon manuscripts: the Ælfwine Prayerbook, the Ramsey Psalter,[16] the Winchcombe Psalter and the Weingarten Gospels.[17] The earliest of these manuscripts is the Ramsey Psalter, written and decorated at Winchester in about 990, and it is generally thought that the motif of St John writing beneath the cross was invented by the artist of this book. The artist of the Ælfwine Prayerbook, working at Winchester some thirty years later than the artist of the Psalter, could have been influenced by this figure though it is unlikely that he was actually copying from it. Jennifer O'Reilly, who has recently studied the motif of the writing St John in some detail, has pointed out that the artists of the Ramsey Psalter, the Winchcombe Psalter and the Weingarten Gospels show St John standing with one knee bent and one foot higher than the other, whereas the artist of the Ælfwine Prayerbook shows him standing with feet side by side. She argues convincingly that the writing figures of St John in crucifixion pictures were based on seated evangelist figures, where the asymmetrical position of the feet would be normal; the figure in the Ælfwine Prayerbook, on the other hand, is simply a normal standing evangelist figure with the addition of a pen.[18]

The parallels noted above rule out the possibility that the artist of the Prayerbook invented his crucifixion picture without reference to artistic sources, but they leave open two other possibilities: that he brought together motifs from a number of different sources to create a new iconography or

14 For early examples of orant figures of Mary in ascension scenes see R. Deshman, 'Anglo-Saxon Art after Alfred', *Art Bulletin*, 56 (1974), 176-200, at 186-90.

15 BL Cotton MS Galba A. xviii, f. 120v.

16 BL Harley MS 2904, f. 3v.

17 Raw, *Crucifixion Iconography*, pls. XIV, X and XVI.

18 J. O'Reilly, 'St John as a Figure of the Contemplative Life: Text and Image in the Art of the Anglo-Saxon Benedictine Reform', in *St Dunstan: His Life, Times and Cult*, ed. N. Ramsay, M. Sparks and T. Tatton-Brown (Woodbridge, 1992), pp. 174, 178-79. I am grateful for being allowed to read this article in typescript before its publication.

that he made a more or less exact copy of a single picture which has since been lost. The resemblances between the Ælfwine crucifixion picture and the ascension picture in the Athelstan Psalter have led some scholars to suggest that this hypothetical model was a painting of the crucifixion which once stood before Psalm 51 in the Psalter.[19] The suggestion cannot be disproved: a picture has certainly been lost from the Psalter at this point because there are traces of paint on f. 80r of the manuscript, and a representation of the crucifixion would fit neatly between those of the nativity at Psalm 1[20] and the ascension at Psalm 101. But even if the Ælfwine crucifixion picture were an exact copy of the one missing from the Psalter (and the writing figure of St John suggests that this was not the case) it would simply push the problem of sources back a century. One would still need to explain why the motifs of the orant Virgin and the writing St John were added to a traditional crucifixion iconography and why a crown was placed on Christ's head.

The drawing of the crucifixion in the Prayerbook is followed by a series of prayers to be recited in front of the feet, hands, mouth, breast and ears of the crucifix (ff.66r-67v); these prayers are followed by the elaborate *Kyrie* sung at the office of Tenebrae during Holy Week (ff. 67v-68r), and a series of prayers and antiphons to the cross interspersed with seven recitations of the *Pater noster* (ff. 68r-70r). The inscription across the top of the drawing echoes a phrase from the *Kyrie*, 'Qui expansis in cruce manibus traxisti omnia ad te secula', and this raises the possibility that the drawing was devised in order to illustrate the themes of the prayers.[21] There are some references to Christ's kingship and to Mary's intercession in the prayers[22] but the parallels are not close enough to support the view that the drawing was based on the texts, though it is clearly appropriate to them.

Parallels to individual motifs can also be found in the literature of the period. The central meaning of the drawing in the Prayerbook is the kingship

---

[19] M. Wood, 'The Making of King Athelstan's Empire: an English Charlemagne?', in *Ideal and Reality in Frankish and Anglo-Saxon Society*, ed. P. Wormald, D. Bullough, R. Collins (Oxford, 1983), pp. 250-72, at 268, n. 84; *The Golden Age of Anglo-Saxon Art 966-1066*, ed. J. Backhouse, D. H. Turner, L. Webster (London, 1984), p. 20.

[20] Now Oxford, Bodleian Library MS Rawlinson B. 484, f. 85r.

[21] f. 67v; for the full text of the *Kyrie* see *Corpus antiphonalium officii*, ed. R.-J. Hesbert, 6 vols., Rerum ecclesiasticarum documenta, Series maior, Fontes 7-12 (Rome, 1963-79), II, 320, no. 74c, Hartker Antiphoner. The parallel between the inscription and the phrase in the prayers is also noted by O'Reilly, who connects it with the passage from John 12.32 and texts associated with it, rather than with the Holy Week liturgy.

[22] See below, p. 290.

of Christ, symbolized by the fillet on his head.[23] The church had always celebrated Christ's kingship, but the theme received a new impetus in monastic circles in England and Germany during the tenth century, possibly as a result of the links between church and state associated with the monastic reform.[24] The subject was clearly of particular interest in Winchester, with its close links between palace and minster. Ælfric discussed the nature of Christ's kingship and its relationship to the rule of earthly kings in several of his homilies[25] and two of the prayers in the Ælfwine Prayerbook itself recall Christ's kingship on the cross. The prayers to be said in front of a crucifix, which follow the drawing of the crucifixion, include one which begins, 'Ave rex noster, fili David, redemptor mundi' (f. 66r) and the Office of the Cross later in the manuscript includes the responsory, 'O crux benedicta que sola fuisti digna portare regem celorum et dominum' (f. 80r). The orant figure of Mary embodies two ideas: her steadfast faith at Christ's death and her prayer for the church.[26] Religious writers had stressed Mary's faith in her son's divine nature long before the eleventh century. Ambrose described Mary standing below the cross and looking forward to the salvation of the world, and Bede emphasised her firm belief in her son, even while she watched him die.[27] The theme of Mary's intercession for the church was also well-established from an early period, but it was only in the tenth century that it came to be linked with her presence beneath the cross.[28] A prayer to Mary found in the Ælfwine Prayerbook and in another Winchester manuscript, the Arundel Psalter, recalls Christ's words from the cross to Mary and John (John 19.26-27) and calls on her to help the suppliant.[29] This

---

[23] Raw, *Crucifixion Iconography*, pp. 133-35.

[24] R. Deshman, '*Christus rex et magi reges*: Kingship and Christology in Ottonian and Anglo-Saxon Art', *Frühmittelalterliche Studien*, 10 (1976), 367-405, and '*Benedictus Monarcha et Monachus*: Early Medieval Ruler Theology and the Anglo-Saxon Reform', *ibid.*, 22 (1988), 204-40.

[25] E.g. Catholic Homilies, I.v and x, in *The Homilies of the Anglo-Saxon Church*, ed. B. Thorpe, 2 vols. (London, 1844-46), I, 82 and 162; *Ælfric's Lives of the Saints*, ed. W. W. Skeat, EETS o.s. 76, 82, 94 and 114, repr. as 2 vols. (1966), nos xxvii and xxxii, II, 148-50 and 320-22; Raw, *Crucifixion Iconography*, pp. 141-43.

[26] Ambrose, *Expositio evangelii secundum Lucam*, x.132, ed. M. Adriaen, CCSL 14 (1957), 383; Bede, *Homiliae evangelii*, i.18, ed. D. Hurst, CCSL 122 (1955), 132. See Raw, *Crucifixion Iconography*, pp. 100-02.

[27] Ambrose, *In Luc.* x.132, CCSL 14, 383; Bede, *Hom.* i.18, CCSL 122, 132; Raw, *Crucifixion Iconography*, p. 100.

[28] Raw, *Crucifixion Iconography*, pp. 101-03.

[29] 'O virgo virginum', BL Cotton MS Titus D. xxvii, ff. 84r-85r; BL Arundel 60, f. 142r-v; pr. H. Barré, *Prières anciennes de l'occident à la Mère du Sauveur des origines à Saint Anselme* (Paris, 1963), pp. 137-38.

particular passage does not occur in the only other known example of the prayer, that in the eleventh-century Nonantola Psalter, and it is possible that it represents a Winchester development.[30] The writing figure of St John, which derives ultimately from two passages in St John's Gospel (John 19.34-35, 21.24-25), is closely paralleled by a passage in Ælfric's homily on the assumption which describes how John made a written record of his presence, with Mary, beneath the cross.[31] The homily is based on the *Epistola ad Paulam et Eustochium*, attributed in the Middle Ages to St Jerome but probably by Paschasius Radbertus, but the reference to John's written record does not occur in the Latin text and seems to represent a Winchester addition to it. The artist of the Ælfwine Prayerbook was therefore working in a milieu where these ideas were known, even though there seems to be no textual source where they are combined.

So far I have talked of the meaning of the picture from the point of view of the artist and the artistic and textual sources at his disposal. But it is also important to consider the viewer's sources, including the function of the picture as well as its textual and artistic context. The Prayerbook contains a collection of devotional material for private use and the pictures in it were presumably intended as a focus for prayer and meditation. The way in which the crucifixion picture was understood by someone praying in front of it would depend on his or her background and experience, something which need not necessarily include the artistic or textual sources which inspired the artist. Knowledge of St John's account of the crucifixion, read on Good Friday, would have allowed the viewer to identify the scene with the incident just before Christ's death, when he entrusted his mother and his disciple to each other (John 19.26-27). Understanding of the nuances of the picture, however, would require knowledge from other sources. Some details would be intelligible from common experience. One does not need to have read Ælfric to understand that St John is writing or to infer that he is recording the details of Christ's death. Mary's orant position would be familiar both from the position of the priest when saying mass and from the more general habit of praying in this position. Ælfric describes King Oswald as praying with the palms of his hands raised towards the sky:[32] the passage suggests that the orant position was the normal position of prayer in the late tenth century, for Ælfric has changed Bede's description of Oswald praying in a seated position, with his hands resting, palm upwards, on his knees.[33]

30   Raw, *Crucifixion Iconography*, p. 102.

31   Ælfric, Catholic Homilies I.xxx, *Homilies*, ed. Thorpe, I, p. 438; Raw, *Crucifixion Iconography*, p. 97.

32   *Lives of the Saints* xxvi, ed. Skeat, II, 132.

33   *Historia ecclesiastica gentis Anglorum: Bede's Ecclesiastical History of the English People*, ed. B. Colgrave, R. A. B. Mynors (Oxford, 1969), III.xii, p. 250.

The jewelled fillet on Christ's head would almost certainly have been identified as a royal symbol and might well have been linked to the crown placed by Cnut on the head of the crucifix at the Old Minster, a gift intended to demonstrate the difference between Christ's kingship and that of earthly kings.[34] But the significance of these motifs for the viewer would derive from the situation in which he confronted the picture. For someone praying before a crucifix two things were necessary: a firm belief in Christ's redemptive death and confidence that one's prayer would be heard. The first was provided by the writing figure of St John, the authoritative witness whose testimony was known to be true (John 19.35 and 21.24-25). The second was provided by the figure of Mary praying beneath the cross as a sign of her constant intercession for men.[35] The source of these ideas, of the meaning of the picture for the viewer, is the relationship between picture and viewer, and the needs of someone praying in front of a crucifix, not a written text.

My second example is a drawing known as the Quinity of Winchester (Pl. 45); like the drawing of the crucifixion discussed already, it comes from the Ælfwine Prayerbook (f. 75v) and is associated with a collection of private prayers. Kantorowicz showed many years ago that the three figures at the top of the picture were based either directly or indirectly on two drawings in the Utrecht Psalter, Rheims work of about 820.[36] The figure of Mary holding the Christ Child, and with the dove of the Holy Spirit perched on her head, derives from a detail of the illustration to the *Gloria* (f. 89v); the two figures seated next to Mary are adapted from the illustration to Psalm 109 (f. 64v). The opening verse of this psalm, 'Yahweh's oracle to you, my Lord, Sit at my right hand and I will make your enemies a footstool for you', was interpreted from the time of the New Testament as a prophecy of the resurrection and ascension of Christ.[37] The two seated figures in the Psalter illustration must therefore represent Christ taking his seat at his Father's side, and the two figures under Christ's feet, the enemies over whom Christ triumphed.[38] As

---

[34] Henry of Huntingdon, *Historia Anglorum*, ed. T. Arnold, RS 74 (London, 1879), vi.17, 189; Raw, *Crucifixion Iconography*, p. 144.

[35] Cf. the painting in a sacramentary fragment stitched into a gospel-book from Reichenau, Leipzig, Stadtbibliothek, MS cxc, f. 1v; Raw, *Crucifixion Iconography*, pp. 81-82.

[36] E. H. Kantorowicz, 'The Quinity of Winchester', *Art Bulletin*, 29 (1947), 73-85. For a reproduction see *Utrecht-Psalter: Vollständige Faksimile-Ausgabe im Originalformat der Handschrift 32 aus dem Besitz der Bibliotheek der Rijksuniversiteit te Utrecht*, ed. K. van der Horst and J. H. A. Engelbregt, 2 vols. (Graz, 1984).

[37] Acts 2.29-36; cf. Rom. 8.34, Heb. 10.12 and I Pet., 3.22.

[38] The seated figures cannot represent the *Logos* welcoming the incarnate Christ, as Kantorowicz claimed ('Quinity', 76), because Christ is specifically said in both the

St Paul said, 'When he ascended to the height, he captured prisoners, he gave gifts to men' (Ephes. 4.8). In contrast to this triumphal view of the ascension, the illustration to the *Gloria* stresses the forgiveness brought by Christ to man and the honour paid to his humanity, now raised to the divine throne.[39] To God's left is the lamb who takes away the sins of the world; to his right, the figure of Mary holding her son.

The drawing in the Ælfwine Prayerbook brings together these contrasting views of Christ's return to his Father and develops their implications. The enemies beneath Christ's feet in the Psalter illustration are replaced by a figure of the devil, chained in the jaws of hell, and by representations of Arius and Judas. Whereas St Augustine identified the enemies of Psalm 109 as pagans, Jews and heretics,[40] the artist of the Ælfwine Prayerbook is more specific. The bound devil reminds the viewer of Christ's prophecy of his death: 'Now sentence is being passed on this world; now the prince of this world is to be overthrown. And when I am lifted up from the earth, I shall draw all men to myself' (John 12.31-32).[41] The belief that Christ triumphed over the devil when he rose from the dead was central to early medieval redemption theology,[42] and the binding of Satan during Christ's descent to hell is referred to many times in Anglo-Saxon literature and art. The artist of the Tiberius Psalter, Winchester work of about 1050, placed a manacled figure of the devil beneath Christ's feet in his drawing of the harrowing of hell.[43] The author of the Blickling Easter homily describes how Christ 'onsende his þone wuldorfæstan gast to helle grunde, and þær þone ealdor ealra þeostra and þæs ecean deaþes geband and gehynde'.[44] The poet Cynewulf adds a reference to the binding of Satan to a passage borrowed from the sermons of Pope Gregory the Great:

> Wæs se fifta hlyp
> þa he hellwarena   heap forbygde
> in cwicsusle,   cyning inne gebond,

Gloria and the Nicene Creed to be seated at the right hand of the Father.

[39] Cf. Cassiodorus, *Expositio psalmorum*, ed. M. Adriaen, CCSL 97-98 (1958), 1006-08.

[40] *Enarrationes in psalmos*, ed. E. Dekkers and J. Fraipont, 3 vols, CCSL 38-40 (1956), 1610.

[41] The second verse of this quotation forms the basis for the inscription across the top of the crucifixion picture; see above, p. 286.

[42] Raw, *Crucifixion Iconography*, pp. 137, 148-49 and 167-70.

[43] BL Cotton MS Tiberius C. vi, f. 14r, reprod. F. Wormald, *Collected Writings, I: Studies in Medieval Art from the Sixth to the Twelfth Centuries*, ed. J. J. G. Alexander, T. J. Brown, J. Gibbs (Oxford, 1984), pl. 139.

[44] *The Blickling Homilies*, ed. R. Morris, EETS o.s. 58, 63 and 73, repr. as one vol. (1967), p. 85.

feonda foresprecan,   fyrnum teagum,
gromhydigne,   þær he gen ligeð
in carcerne   clommum gefæstnad,
synnum gesæled.[45]   *Christ II* 730-36

The artist of the Ælfwine Prayerbook transferred the motif of the bound devil from the iconography of the harrowing of hell to that of Christ's enthronement at his Father's side. In doing so, he made clear the identity of the central figure in the Prayerbook drawing. This is not the *Logos*, as Kantorowicz believed,[46] but the risen and glorified Christ, the victor over death and hell.

The second enemy depicted by the Prayerbook artist is the heretic, Arius. Arius, a priest of Alexandria, denied Christ's equality with the Father, claiming that he did not exist before his birth from Mary: the point is recalled in a painting in the early eleventh-century Eadwig Gospels, which shows Arius crouched beneath the feet of St John, grasping a scroll bearing the words, 'Erat tempus quando non erat'.[47] The views of Arius were condemned at the Council of Nicaea in 325, when Christ was defined as being of the same substance as the Father, and, again, at the Council of Constantinople in 381. There was an important development of this definition at the Council of Ephesus in 431, when Mary was accorded the title of *Theotokos*, Mother of God, to demonstrate that her son was both God and man. This link between Marian doctrine and Christology is apparent in the Ælfwine Prayerbook drawing, where the figure of Arius is placed below that of Mary with her child.

Kantorowicz considered that the artist of the Prayerbook added the figure of Arius to those borrowed from the Utrecht Psalter because verse 3 of Psalm 109, 'Royal dignity was yours from the day you were born, on the holy mountains, royal from the womb, from the dawn of your earliest days', was frequently used against the Arians to prove that Christ was co-eternal with the Father.[48] Judith Kidd prefers to associate the drawing with ideas current in Winchester during the early eleventh century, relating it to an antiphon which praises Mary as the destroyer of all heresies:

> Gaude Maria Virgo, cunctas haereses sola interemisti quae Gabrielis archangeli dictis credidisti; dum Virgo Deum et hominem genuisti, et post

---

[45] The passage from Gregory, Homily 29, is translated in D. G. Calder and M. J. B. Allen, *Sources and Analogues of Old English Poetry* (Cambridge, 1976), p. 80.

[46] Kantorowicz, 'Quinity', p. 79.

[47] Hanover, Kestner Museum, MS WM XXIa 36, f. 147v, noted by O'Reilly, 'St John', p. 182.

[48] Kantorowicz, 'Quinity', p. 80. See also J. A. Kidd, 'The *Quinity of Winchester* Reconsidered', *Studies in Iconography*, 7-8 (1981-82), 21-33, at p. 26. The point is clearer in the Latin: 'ex utero ante luciferum genui te'.

partum virgo inviolata permansisti. Gabrielem archangelum credimus divinitus tibi esse affatum. Uterum tuum de Spiritu Sancto credimus impregnatum. Erubescat Judaeus infelix, qui dicit Christum ex Joseph semine esse natum.[49]

Both Kidd and Kantorowicz interpret the Prayerbook drawing as a representation of the two natures of Christ, 'the divine Son beside the Father and the human child with Mary'.[50] This cannot be correct. Although the drawing is clearly concerned with the doctrine of the divine and human natures of Christ, it does not represent them as two separate figures. To do so would, in fact, be heretical. The child in Mary's arms is God as well as man and the artist emphasises the point by his representation of the dove of the Holy Spirit through whom Mary conceived (Luke 1.35).[51] The seated figure is not the *Logos* but the risen Christ, again, both God and man. The two figures together illustrate Christ's dual origin, not his dual nature. Christ is shown, first, in the arms of his mother and, secondly, at the side of his Father, in order to demonstrate that he is the eternal son of God and also the descendant, through his mother, of King David. The point is important because the Messiah was known to be descended from David, as Christ pointed out when he questioned the pharisees about the prophecy in Psalm 109:

'What is your opinion about the Christ? Whose son is he?' 'David's' they told him. 'Then how is it' he said 'that David, moved by the Spirit, calls him Lord, where he says: The Lord said to my Lord: Sit at my right hand and I will put your enemies under your feet? If David can call him Lord, then how can he be his son?' (Matt. 22.42-45)[52]

The relevance of Arius to the figures in the upper part of the Prayerbook drawing has to be considered in relation to the other two enemies of Christ: Satan and Judas. The figure of Arius is appropriately placed below the feet of Mary because his heresy lay in claiming that Christ did not exist before his birth from Mary. The artist denies this claim by depicting Mary overshadowed by the Holy Spirit, through whom she

---

49   Kidd, 'Quinity', pp. 21 and 23-24.

50   Kidd ('Quinity', pp. 21, 22 and 27) and Kantorowicz ('Quinity', p. 79) sometimes seem to imply that the child in Mary's arms in the Prayerbook drawing represents only Christ's human nature, an interpretation which would, of course, be heretical.

51   The theme of the picture is very similar to that of the Old English poem, *Christ I*; see the discussion of this poem in B. C. Raw, 'Biblical Literature: the New Testament', in *The Cambridge Companion to Old English Literature*, ed. M. Godden and M. Lapidge (Cambridge, 1991), pp. 227-42, at 233-35.

52   The passage is discussed at some length by Augustine in his commentary on Psalm 109: *Enarrationes in psalmos*, CCSL 40, 1603-07.

conceived the Christ. Satan, like Arius, failed to grasp that Christ was both God and man, but he did so in relation to Christ's death, not his birth. In the *Gospel of Nicodemus* he says to Hell, 'Prepare yourself to receive Jesus who boasts He is the Son of God; but He is a man who fears death'.[53] Hell replies, 'Who is He so mighty, if He is a man afraid of death? . . . If He is so mighty in His humanity, I tell you truly He is omnipotent in His divinity and none can resist His power.'[54] Satan's power was destroyed because he laid claim to Christ as though he was a man, subject to death.[55] The artist of the Prayerbook represents this by showing the risen Christ throned above the devil. Judas, who betrayed his lord, was a symbol of treachery and also, because of his suicide, a symbol of despair (Matt. 27.5). Kantorowicz suggested that he was included with Arius because they were thought to have died in the same way.[56] Judith Kidd links him with the reference to the unhappy Jew in the final line of the antiphon, *Gaude Maria Virgo*.[57] A better explanation of his presence is found in Ælfric's homilies on the creation and on the creed.[58] In the first of these sermons, Ælfric links Judas's betrayal of Christ to the overthrow of the devil: the devil forfeits his power because he seduces Judas into betraying Christ, an act which leads inevitably to Christ's death and descent to hell, where he defeats the devil.[59] In the second sermon, on the Catholic faith, Ælfric completes his long discussion of the nature of the Trinity by describing the heresy of Arius; he then goes on to talk of the way in which the devil destroyed himself when he incited the Jews to kill Christ.[60] Ælfric does not mention Judas by name, as he does in the sermon on the creation, but he is clearly making the same point in both.

There are parallels, then, in both literature and art to some of the elements of the Prayerbook picture, but there is no artistic or literary 'source' for the picture as a whole. In so far as there was a source, it was the mind of the artist, meditating on groups of inter-related ideas familiar at the time at which he was working. The person viewing the picture, on the other hand, would not necessarily need to be familiar with exegetical works like the commentaries on Psalm 109 which seem to have influenced the artist. The context within which he confronted the picture was one of prayer. There are some echoes of the themes of the picture in the prayers to the

53 Calder and Allen, *Sources*, p. 179.
54 Calder and Allen, *Sources*, pp. 179-80.
55 Raw, *Crucifixion Iconography*, p. 170.
56 Kantorowicz, 'Quinity', p. 80.
57 Kidd, 'Quinity', p. 30.
58 Catholic Homilies I.i and xx, *Homilies*, ed. Thorpe, I, 8-28 and 274-94.
59 Catholic Homilies I.i, *Homilies*, ed. Thorpe, I, 26.
60 *Homilies*, ed. Thorpe, I, 290-92.

Trinity which follow it in the manuscript. As might be expected, Christ is constantly addressed as the one who is coeternal with the Father.[61] Mary is the mother of her creator,[62] queen of heaven and earth through her son, who lives with his Father and the Holy Spirit in heaven.[63] The parallels are very slight, however, and there is nothing in the prayers to explain the overall conception of the picture; in particular, there are no parallels to the devil bound in the jaws of hell, or to the figures of Arius and Judas. The main source of the meaning for the viewer is the spatial arrangement of the scene. Mary and her child are placed within the glory which surrounds the figures of God the Father and God the Son, while Judas and Arius are visibly crushed beneath it. The simple meaning which comes over is that Mary has been assumed into heaven, and reigns there with the Trinity, while traitors and heretics are condemned to hell with the devil. The diagrammatic way in which meaning is conveyed in this drawing is very different from the method used in the crucifixion picture discussed earlier in this article. The drawing of Mary with the Trinity is self-contained: the participants do not interact with the viewer. In the crucifixion picture, on the other hand, the figures of Mary and John mediate between the picture and the viewer. John vouches for the reality of the event portrayed, while Mary obtains for the viewer the effects of that event. But, in different ways, both pictures succeed in exploiting a visual medium to organise their ideas in a way which is impossible in a text.

So far, I have tried to distinguish between the picture as a material object and as a set of ideas, and between the artistic and textual sources used by the artist and the more varied influences on the way in which pictures were understood by someone looking at them. Finally, I should like to look briefly at the way in which the quest for artistic sources tends to inhibit appreciation of the developments in religious thought which were taking place in the late Anglo-Saxon period.

The painting of the crucifixion which forms the frontispiece to a gospel-book owned by Judith of Flanders (Pl. 46) has no known artistic or textual source, though there are parallels to some of the motifs in it in other Anglo-Saxon manuscripts. The figures of the sun and moon hiding their

---

61 'tu misericors deus filius dei, conditor et redemptor noster, qui es coeternus et coequalis patri cum sancto spiritu' (f. 78r); also (f. 86r), 'Domine sancte pater, omnipotens et misericors deus, qui coequalem coeternum et consubstantialem tibi ante omnia secula filium ineffabiliter genuisti, cum quo atque cum spiritu sancto ex te eodemque filio procedente, celum et terram mare et quecumque in eis existunt visibilia atque invisibilia creasti, te laudo'.

62 'Beata es Maria que omnium portasti creatorem deum genuisti qui te fecit' (f. 81v).

63 'Te mitissima mundi polique regina interveniente et christo filio tuo annuente qui cum coeterno patre et almo pneumate vivit et gloriatur' (f. 83r); see also the description of her as queen of angels (f. 84r).

faces, who symbolize the darkness at Christ's death and the grief of the created world, appear again in the crucifixion picture in the Winchcombe Psalter.[64] The tree cross, which symbolizes the tree of life, can be paralleled in three other eleventh-century crucifixion pictures.[65] The writing figure of John goes back to the St John of the Ramsey Psalter.[66] The motif of Mary wiping the blood from Christ's side and the figure embracing the foot of the cross, on the other hand, are quite new.

Gertrud Schiller identifies the figure at the foot of the cross as Mary Magdalen.[67] Elżbieta Temple, on the other hand, believes that the figure represents the owner of the manuscript, since most representations of Mary Magdalen at the foot of the cross date from much later than the eleventh century.[68] Donor figures are frequently included in crucifixion pictures: Charles the Bald was represented in his prayerbook, kneeling in front of a crucifix, and there are similar kneeling figures in the crucifixion pictures in the Psalter of Louis the German and the Gundold Gospels.[69] These figures are really very different from the woman in the Weingarten Gospels, however: they merely kneel in prayer before the cross whereas she participates in the event in a way which implies more than the role of a donor. Yet her contemporary dress, and the fact that she has no halo, suggests that she is the owner of the manuscript, Judith of Flanders.

The figure of Mary is sometimes said to be based on representations of *Ecclesia*, who is often shown holding a chalice to Christ's side to catch the blood from his wounds.[70] At first sight, the suggestion seems plausible. English artists must have been familiar with representations of *Ecclesia* beneath the cross, for the motif appears on the Brunswick Casket and, as is well known, this casket or something virtually identical to it was used as a model by Winchester artists in the late tenth and early eleventh centuries.[71]

---

64 CUL, MS Ff. 1. 23, f. 88r.

65 O'Reilly, 'Rough-Hewn Cross', pp. 153-58; see above, p. 287, n. 10.

66 BL Harley MS 2904, f. 3v; see p. 288, above.

67 Schiller, *Iconography*, II, p. 117.

68 Temple, *Anglo-Saxon Manuscripts*, p. 109.

69 Munich, Schatzkammer der Residenz, Prayerbook of Charles the Bald, ff.38v-39r, reprod. P. E. Schramm and F. Mütherich, *Denkmale der deutschen Könige und Kaiser. Ein Beitrag zur Herrschergeschichte von Karl dem Grossen bis Friedrich II* (Munich, 1962), pl. 43; Berlin, Staatsbibliothek, MS Theol. lat. fol. 58, f. 120r (Psalter of Louis the German), reprod. A. Goldschmidt, *German Illumination*, 2 vols. (Florence, 1928), I, pl. 63; Stuttgart, Wurttembergische Landesbibliothek, Cod. Bibl. 402, f. 9v (Gundold Gospels), reprod. *ibid.*, II, pl. 88.

70 See Schiller, *Iconography*, II, pls. 364, 365, 367, 371, 372, 373.

71 *Ibid.*, pl. 372. For discussion see O. Homburger, *Die Anfänge der Malschule von Winchester im X. Jahrhundert* (Leipzig, 1912) and 'L'art carolingien de Metz et

On a superficial level, Mary's gesture resembles that of *Ecclesia*, yet it seems highly unlikely that it carries the same meaning. *Ecclesia's* gesture with the chalice is meant to stress the precious nature of Christ's blood, and the identity of that blood with the wine of the eucharist. The painting in the Weingarten Gospels, on the other hand, has no obvious eucharistic significance and Mary makes no attempt to catch Christ's blood: her gesture seems rather to be one of compassion.

In seeking to understand this picture it is better to study its context and probable function than to look for sources which might have influenced the artist. Like the two drawings in the Ælfwine Prayerbook discussed earlier in this article, the Weingarten painting has a meditative function, though its relationship to the text it accompanies is very different. The meaning of the drawings in the Prayerbook was broadly related to that of the collections of prayers with which they were associated, and it seems likely that they formed an adjunct to the recitation of those prayers. The frontispiece to the Weingarten Gospels may have served as a reminder that the gospels, the word of God, are also the Word of God, namely Christ.[72] The painting is not an aid to the reading of the gospels, however, nor are the ideas expressed in it based on the gospels. They come from the devotional life of the period. The picture expresses the desire of the woman at the foot of the cross to share the experience of those present at Christ's death. But whereas the figures in the three continental manuscripts mentioned above simply observe the scene,[73] the woman in the Weingarten painting takes part in it. The practice of imagining oneself present at biblical events is often thought of as a late medieval phenomenon, but it is clear that it existed very much earlier. Edith of Wilton portrayed herself in the role of the penitent Mary Magdalen on an embroidered alb she made[74] and Odilo of Cluny imagined himself sharing in the grief of Christ's mother at his death.[75] Mary Magdalen's love for Christ and her presence beneath the cross played a part in Cluniac devotion as early as the first half of the tenth century,[76] and there seems no reason why Judith should not have had herself portrayed in the role of Mary Magdalen at the

---

l'école de Winchester', in *Essais en l'honneur de Jean Porcher: Etudes sur les manuscrits à peintures*, ed. O. Pächt (Paris, 1963), pp. 35-46.

[72] Raw, *Crucifixion Iconography*, pp. 27, 106 and 138.

[73] p. 298.

[74] *De Sancta Editha*, I.iv.16, in A. Wilmart, 'La légende de Ste Edith en prose et vers par le moine Goscelin', *Analecta Bollandiana*, 56 (1938), 5-101 and 265-307, at p.79. Raw, *Crucifixion Iconography*, p. 24.

[75] *De vita et virtutibus S. Odilonis abbatis*, I.xiv, *Patrologia latina* 142, 910; Raw, *Crucifixion Iconography*, pp. 157-58.

[76] Odo of Cluny, *Sermo ii*, *Patrologia latina* 133, 713-21, espec. 714 and 718. Raw, *Crucifixion Iconography*, p. 160.

foot of the cross. Repentance for one's sins played a major part in meditative prayer, and the woman who loved much because her sins, which were many, had been forgiven seems an ideal model for imitation. The painting in the Weingarten Gospels is an important testimony to beliefs and practices of which barely a hint survives in other works of art from the eleventh century.

The Making of the Cotton Troper
E. C. TEVIOTDALE

The Cotton Troper is a fragment of an illustrated English troper. It forms the first portion (ff. 1-36) of British Library, Cotton MS Caligula A.xiv.[1] It is a codex of modest dimensions (220 x 132mm), and the writing space is tall and narrow (161-63 x 71-74mm; 15 long lines), as is common among tropers. The manuscript is fragmentary in two respects. Not only does it end *in medias res*, but there are several lacunae within the preserved portion of the manuscript.[2] The codex contains tropes to the proper chants of the mass arranged in an annual cycle (with combined *temporale* and *sanctorale*) extending from Advent to the feast of St Andrew (ff. 1r-9v, 35r-v, 10r-31r) followed by a fairly extensive *commune sanctorum* (ff. 31v-34v, 36r-v) (see Appendix I). The *sanctorale* includes only figures of widespread veneration, and the feast of the dedication of a church is not included in the annual cycle but is placed at the end of the commons. There is no scholarly consensus as to its date or specific place of origin, although the text script and the musical notation leave little doubt that it was written in England in the eleventh century. The major decoration consists of one painted initial, which introduces the third mass for Christmas day (f. 2r), and eleven paintings of Christological and hagiographical subject matter introducing ten feasts and surrounded by Latin verse inscriptions (see Appendix II).

The Cotton manuscript is a troper of the anthology type. Rather than containing enough tropes to accommodate a single complete troped performance of each of the proper chants for a given feast day, it is a collection of tropes from which pieces could be chosen to be sung on a given feast day each year. Whoever decided what tropes should be included in the Cotton manuscript, therefore, was more a compiler than an editor. In this respect, his activity was essentially different from that of the medieval editors of the famous Winchester tropers (which are the only other trope manuscripts surviving from Anglo-Saxon England), for both Winchester manuscripts are prescriptive liturgical books (although they differ from one another in the genres of chant included).[3]

The Cotton fragment contains the overwhelming majority of the proper tropes represented in the Winchester manuscripts, including a series of

---

[1] J. Planta, *A Catalogue of Manuscripts in the Cottonian Library deposited in the British Museum* (London, 1802), p. 45; E. Temple, *Anglo-Saxon Manuscripts: 900-1066* (London, 1976), no. 97.

[2] See Appendix I.

[3] Cambridge, Corpus Christi College, MS 473 and Oxford, Bodleian Library, MS Bodley 775 (SC 2558).

hexameter tropes for the Annunciation very probably composed by Wulfstan of Winchester.[4] It also contains a substantial number of unique tropes, but these are extremely varied in style and language: it is unlikely that they are new compositions. The compiler of the Cotton codex most probably had available to him the corpus of tropes that lies behind the Winchester manuscripts (including some local compositions) but was less selective in drawing from that repertoire than were his Winchester counterparts.[5] There are indications that he was, in fact, essentially non-selective in his approach, for the manuscript includes one hopelessly garbled piece and a number of tropes cued to proper chants that may not have been sung in Anglo-Saxon England.[6]

The written model(s) for the troper, therefore, would have reflected the repertoire that was available to the editors of the Winchester manuscripts. It is very difficult to speculate what form the model(s) might have taken, whether a codex or codices or *libelli* of just a few leaves, or the extent to which oral transmission may have played a role. In any event, it is extremely unlikely that an illustrated trope manuscript served as a model. Only four tropers with picture cycles survive from the eleventh century.[7] They are from fairly widely dispersed centres, and their picture cycles seem to have been developed independently. Not only tropers, but also graduals, were very rarely illustrated in the early middle ages. The decision to provide the Cotton Troper with paintings, therefore, marked a significant departure from early medieval conventions for producing music manuscripts for the mass. It would be prudent to remember, however, that both Winchester tropers are extremely handsome manuscripts by comparison with their often scruffy continental counterparts. Within Anglo-Saxon England, therefore, the production of an attractive trope manuscript was perhaps not so unusual as we might at first suppose.

The Cotton Troper was clearly always intended to be a handsome book; the parchment is well prepared, the *mise en page* is spacious, and the text and music scripts are of high calligraphic quality. A single scribe seems to have

4   A. Planchart, *The Repertory of Tropes at Winchester*, 2 vols (Princeton, 1977), I, pp. 147-48 and II, pp. 155-56, 196-97 and 224.

5   R. Jacobsson, 'Unica in the Cotton Caligula Troper', forthcoming in a volume commemorating the centenary of the Plainsong and Mediaeval Music Society. I am grateful to Dr Jacobsson for having allowed me to read her essay in typescript.

6   The version of *Agmine credendum* (f. 5r) in the Cotton manuscript betrays serious confusion at some point in its written transmission. The most conspicuous group of tropes cued to unusual proper chants is that for the feast of St Andrew (ff.30v-31r).

7   Besides the Cotton manuscript: Bamberg, Staatsbibliothek, MS Lit. 5; Paris, Bibliothèque de l'Arsenal, MS 1169; Paris, Bibliothèque Nationale, MS lat. 9448.

been responsible for all of the text and musical notation in the manuscript, the sole exception being the inscriptions in artists' colours in two of the paintings.[8] Throughout the manuscript the scribe was reluctant to make corrections. This was not simply the result of heedless copying, for there are many instances of the scribe having transformed one letter (or the initial strokes of a letter) into another, and the text is not altogether devoid of erasures. The scribe attended, therefore, to the accuracy of his text, but he was probably more concerned not to spoil the manuscript's appearance through extensive scraping and rewriting.

Although apparently the work of a single scribe, the manuscript is not the work of a single uninterrupted scribal campaign. Folio 6 seems to have been written by the principal scribe but not in succession after folio 5 and before folio 7. The scribe has used a broader nib on this leaf than on the surrounding pages, and some of the usual mannerisms of his writing are not in evidence.[9] This folio, which is anomalous in several respects, is and always was a singleton.[10] The scribe would have copied the text on this leaf under some special circumstances after the adjacent pages had been written. This may point to a process of revision to the text of the manuscript, with this leaf as a replacement. There is no obvious crowding or spacing out of the text, however, which suggests that it is a line for line copy of its predecessor. Perhaps the original leaf contained an error and the text was rewritten

[8]   The main text, the notation, the writing on the scrolls on f. 22r, and the hexameter inscriptions surrounding the paintings were all written in ink of the same composition, as evidenced by their identical appearance under light of different frequencies and through a variety of filters when viewed with the aid of a video spectral comparitor. Furthermore, the writing on the scrolls and of the picture inscriptions shares a number of features with the writing of the main body of the codex. Finally, a base chant cue at the bottom of f. 12v is written entirely in brownish-red (capital, minuscule, and neumes). The minuscule is recognizable as the work of the main text scribe and the notation as the work of the main music scribe. This points unequivocally to a single scribe having been responsible for text and music (and the coloured capitals) throughout the codex. A. E. Parker (Manuscripts Conservation Section, British Library) carried out the examination with the video spectral comparitor and instructed me in interpreting its results.

[9]   The openings ff. 5v-6r and 6v-7r are reproduced in R. Jonsson, *Tropes du Propre de la Messe 1: Cycle de Noël*, Corpus Troporum, 1, Studia Latina Stockholmiensia, 21 (Stockholm, 1975), Pls. X and XI.

[10]   The leaf is of thicker membrane than that of the bulk of the manuscript. It was ruled in drypoint for another purpose and then was ruled with lead on the recto and brown pigment on the verso according to the usual scheme for this codex. The drypoint ruling was for a larger book than the present codex, and the leaf would have been made from parchment either left over from an earlier project or cut out of another manuscript.

because it was considered undesirable to disfigure the manuscript by making a correction.

The main text (in English Caroline minuscule with incipits in display scripts) and the music (in Anglo-Saxon notation) were written first. Then the coloured capitals were executed, almost certainly by the scribe responsible for the main text and music.[11] These are of three grades: small coloured capitals that introduce each trope element and each base chant cue, enlarged monochrome capitals (sometimes modestly flourished) that introduce each trope, and enlarged capitals in gold leaf that initiate most feast days.

A system for the minor decoration of the book was only arrived at as the work was accomplished. In its developed form, the system was to supply an enlarged capital in purple, green, orange, or brownish-red for each trope, except for the first capital of each feast day, which was to be of gold leaf. The smaller coloured capitals within tropes were to alternate between orange and brownish-red. Green makes its first appearance on folio 4, and purple was not introduced until folio 7 (the first leaf of the second quire). The beginning of the manuscript, therefore, shows less variety in the colours of the enlarged capitals and correspondingly more chromatic homogeneity among the smaller and larger capitals. The more colourful system, developed during the course of work on the first quire, was established by the initiation of the second quire and was fairly rigorously adhered to thereafter. The replacement leaf, the present folio 6, would already have been a part of the manuscript before the capitals were executed, for its capitals reflect the formative stages in the development of the system.

Thanks to the unusual juxtaposition of some coloured capitals, we can infer something of the temporal sequence of work on them. On folio 12r the enlarged V of *VIRGINIS* (line 14) was written before the enlarged A of *AD* (line 13) (Pl. 47). This is attested by the unusual shape of the A, with the left shoulder deformed so that it would not collide with the V below. This indicates that the enlarged capitals were not written strictly in the order in which they appear on the page. On folio 17r the enlarged Q of *QUOS* (line 1) must have been written before the smaller V of *Venite* (line 3), the latter being separated from the rest of the word to which it belongs by the descender of the Q (Pl. 48). This establishes that the small coloured capitals either were written as a part of the same phase of activity as the enlarged capitals or were done after them. These are not mutually exclusive possibilities, and it seems most probable that the writing of all of the capitals (except perhaps those in gold) was accomplished in one phase of work but that the green and purple capitals were done first, and then the orange and brownish-red capitals (both small and large) were done. The occasional

---

[11] See note 8. Coloured capitals overlap the notation on ff. 4r, 6r, 15r, 28r, 29r, 30r, 31r, 34r and 34v.

flourish on a small capital shows that the distinction between the two grades was not strictly respected. This would have resulted from slips in concentration, a situation we can better imagine if both grades were being executed as a part of a single phase of activity.

At some time after the coloured capitals were finished, the rubrics were added. Most of the rubrics are in display script, but some are in rustic capitals, and four are in rustics initiated by a letter borrowed from the vocabulary of display script letter forms. The rubrics in rustic capitals are confined to folios 1-3 and 7: it is possible that the scribe considered them visually weak and so came to abandon them. The rubrics in display script certainly provide a more forceful counterbalance to the display script incipits of the tropes. Whatever the reason for the change to display script rubrics, it was effected during the copying of the first several leaves of the manuscript, much as the formulation of the system for the minor decoration was achieved during the copying of the first several leaves.

We would expect all of this work (the writing of the main text, the music, the coloured capitals, and the rubrics) to have been completed in a given portion of the codex before the illustrations in that section were executed. It is manifest that the pictures were painted after the main text (with its notation) was written,[12] but the temporal sequence between the writing of the capitals and the painting of the pictures was not strictly consistent throughout the book. On folio 26r the wing of the angel in the Annunciation to Joachim has been painted around the purple I of the last line of text (Pl. 49). On folio 22r, on the other hand, the C of the communion trope for the Nativity of John the Baptist (*Corda patrum*) was certainly written after the outlines of the painting had been established (Pl. 50). Furthermore, it was most probably executed after the verses had been inscribed around the painting, for the scribe has not added a T to introduce the base chant cue (*Tu puer propheta*) on line 2, probably because the end of the inscription already occupied the space he would have used. This page is remarkable by virtue of the incorporation of a trope into the painting, and the sequence of work on this page may have been unusual due to these special circumstances.[13] This suggests that as a rule the paintings were executed after the coloured capitals.

Although arguments have been made to the contrary, the paintings are, I think, the work of a single artist.[14] The characteristic style of the paintings,

---

[12] Paintings overlap the text or the notation on ff. 22r, 26r, 29r, 30v, 36r.

[13] This page is unique in another respect. The frame of the painting covered some of the notation for *Corda patrum*. When neumes were subsequently added on top of the painting, the melody was changed.

[14] D. T. Rice, *English Art 871-1100* (Oxford, 1952), p. 212; J. Marquardt-Cherry, 'Ascension Sundays in Tropers: The Innovative Scenes in the Prüm and

which is most comprehensively represented in the early part of the codex, is modified in some of the paintings.[15] The first modification is the abandonment of gold as a material. Gold is employed only in the first five surviving paintings in the book; the remaining six include no gold at all. A further modification involves the use of reserve (i.e., unpainted) parchment in the last four surviving paintings, but these pictures do not form a separate, stylistically homogeneous group. Moreover, all of the illustrations that include passages of unpainted parchment share some features of the prevailing style of the codex, and each passage executed in black outline with touches of colour shares some characteristic with a fully-painted passage. These changes in materials and techniques represent a gradual stylistic modification, attributable more probably to constraints placed on a single artist than to a change in personnel, to be further discussed below (pp. 309-10).

The eleven surviving paintings in the troper present considerable variety in terms of subject matter and format. They include both narrative illustrations and portraits. The narrative paintings may be single scenes or may contain more than one scene, and both individual and group portraits are included among the non-narrative paintings. There are three full-page paintings and eight smaller ones, and there is great variety in the treatment of frames. In short, there is very little sense of this assemblage of illustrations as a proper picture cycle.

The iconography of the individual paintings is often innovative. The Ascension (f. 18r), for example, is distinguished by the unprecedented inclusion of an arcade (most probably meant to evoke the architecture of the pilgrimage church of the Ascension) and an inscription labelling the site.[16] The subject of one of the narrative paintings, the Temptation of St Martin (f. 29r), is otherwise entirely unknown in early medieval art (Pl. 51). The specific iconography of at least one of the paintings, St Peter's Release from Prison (f. 22r), was inspired by the sung liturgy for the feast day illustrated.[17] In one instance, the Community of the Apostles (f. 31r), an established visual formula has been adapted to a new subject (Pl. 53).[18] The iconography of the

---

Canterbury Tropers and Their Relationship to the Accompanying Texts', *Essays in Medieval Studies: Proceedings of the Illinois Medieval Association*, 6 (1989) 68-78 at p. 68.

[15] See Appendix II.

[16] Reprod. F. Wormald, *Collected Writings, I: Studies in Medieval Art from the Sixth to the Twelfth Centuries*, ed. J. J. G. Alexander, T. J. Brown, J. Gibbs (London, 1984), ill. 120.

[17] Reproduced in *The Golden Age of Anglo-Saxon Art 966-1066*, ed. J. Backhouse, D. H. Turner, L. Webster (London, 1984), colour pl. XXI. The configuration of the picture would have resulted from a desire to incorporate the scene of the angel's departure at the city gate, the moment specifically evoked by the introit for the feast of St Peter.

paintings in the troper points to a situation in which the artist was constantly improvising, at times creating entirely new imagery, at times modifying existing iconographic types, at times adapting well established pictorial conventions to new subjects.

The second half of the fragment is much more densely illustrated (and correspondingly sparsely rubricated) than the first half. Indeed, it can be suggested that the decision to illustrate this book was taken after a portion of it had already been written. There is a conspicuous absence of the pictures which we would expect toward the beginning of the manuscript. The texts of all three masses for Christmas day have been preserved, but there is no illustration for Christmas. Similarly, the feasts of the Holy Innocents and Palm Sunday, generally illustrated in liturgical books with picture cycles, are presented here without paintings. Furthermore, the feast of St John the Evangelist, which has two masses and therefore presumably was of special importance, is not illustrated.

The presence of the portrait of St Stephen (f. 3v) has apparently affected the surrounding text.[19] The introit tropes for the feast of St Stephen begin in the middle of a word on the top of folio 4r. The space now occupied by the picture at the bottom of folio 3v may once have been taken up with the usual English *versus ante officium* for St Stephen and the missing portion of the introit trope.[20] Although physical evidence for a text having been effaced in this place is lacking, the impasto and generally dark colouring of the painting may well have obliterated either the text itself or evidence of its having been scraped away. Folio 3v, therefore, may once have appeared as follows: four lines of tropes concluding the third mass for Christmas (still present), one line left blank for a rubric, nine lines occupied by the *versus ante officium* and one line by the beginning of the introit trope. No space was left by the scribe for a picture because it had not yet been decided that the codex should be illustrated. The decision to introduce a painting here must have been made before the rubrics were written in this part of the manuscript, for no text has been effaced from line 5.

I would like to suggest that it was decided to provide this codex with pictures only after a significant portion of its text had already been written and that the portrait of St Stephen was inserted in an effort to bring the previously unillustrated first portion into harmony with the revised plan for the bulk of the manuscript.[21] The first illustration painted on parchment

18 The picture is modelled on established Pentecost iconography.
19 The opening ff. 3v-4r is reproduced in Jonsson, *Tropes*, pl. IX.
20 Planchart, *Repertory of Tropes*, I, p. 49.
21 There is an offset of some oxidized pigment on f. 9v that betrays the former presence of a painting on the facing page, almost certainly the Adoration of the Magi for Epiphany. This picture too probably would have been inserted in the

reserved for the purpose would have been either an Easter picture (if there was one) or the Ascension (f. 18r). The decision to supply the troper with a picture cycle, therefore, would have been made after the main text of the first two quires (ff. 1-12) had been written.

Once it had been decided that the manuscript should be illustrated, the scribe would have reserved spaces for paintings. He may not have intended, however, the codex to be as densely illustrated as it now is. The feast of the Nativity of the Virgin is illustrated by two paintings: (1) the Annunciation to Joachim at the bottom of folio 26r and (2) Joachim and Anne with the infant Virgin at the top of folio 26v.[22] This is the only example of a pair of paintings illustrating a single feast day. The Annunciation to Joachim does not fit very well into the five lines it occupies. The painting extends almost up to the ruling line for the text immediately above it, and there is no crowning element to the frame. This painting is one of the shortest in the book, and one wonders, considering the presence of a picture at the top of folio 26v, whether the space at the bottom of folio 26r was originally intended for a picture at all. The five lines at the bottom of the recto may well have been left blank in order that the texts for the feast of the Nativity of the Virgin might begin on the verso, following an illustration.

Close analogies for such a situation can be found on folios 20 and 30 (fig. 2). On folio 20 the texts for Trinity Sunday end on line 11 of the recto. Four lines are blank at the bottom of the page. The verso carries at the top the painting for the feast of the Nativity of John the Baptist. Then follow the main rubric for the feast and the tropes. Similarly on folio 30 three lines have been left blank at the bottom of the recto in order to set up the beginning of the new feast day (St Andrew) with an illustration at the top of the verso. It seems very likely that at the time the text was written only one illustration for the Nativity of the Virgin was envisaged and it was to occupy the top eight lines of folio 26v.

The Annunciation to Joachim is not the only illustration that may occupy a space not originally intended for a painting. The Temptation of St Martin at the bottom of folio 29r and the Community of the Apostles at the bottom of folio 31r would seem also not to have been a part of the scribe's original design. The Temptation of St Martin, while taller than the Annunciation to Joachim (six to seven lines as opposed to five lines), fits rather badly into its space. Furthermore, the painting has virtually no frame; only a fine line defines the left side of the picture. The portrait of the

---

manner of the portrait of St Stephen.

22 Reproduced in Temple, *Anglo-Saxon Manuscripts*, pl. 294 and T. H. Ohlgren, ed., *Insular and Anglo-Saxon Illuminated Manuscripts: An Iconographic Catalogue c. AD 625 to 1100*, Garland Reference Library of the Humanities, 631 (New York, 1986), ill. 40.

Apostles (f. 31r), like the Annunciation to Joachim, occupies only five text lines. It does so rather less awkwardly, although its frame, like those for the Annunciation to Joachim and the Temptation of St Martin, lacks a horizontal member at the top.

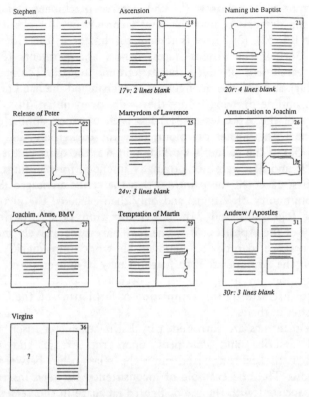

Figure 2: Drawing of the disposition of the paintings in London, British Library, Cotton MS, Caligula A. xiv.

The hypothesis that the paintings on folios 26r, 29r and 31r did not belong to the design of the book at the time the text was written is supported by stylistic features of the paintings. It has already been remarked that these paintings have less substantial frames than is common in this book. More revealing, but also more puzzling, are the style and technique of the Temptation of St Martin and the Community of the Apostles. These two paintings can be seen to reflect many features of the characteristic style of the paintings in this manuscript, but they include more reserve parchment than any other paintings in the book. There is reason to believe that they may have been the last to be painted and that perhaps the painter was working to a deadline.

The Temptation of St Martin and the Community of the Apostles are contained in the last surviving quire of the codex (which was, most probably, the last quire to contain illustrations).[23] Among the paintings of this quire, increasing use has been made of reserve parchment by degrees as follows: (1) In the portrait of St Andrew (f. 30v), reserve parchment stands for one surface of the drapery behind the saint's throne and for elements of the architecture (Pl. 52). (2) There is reserve parchment in the Community of Virgins (f. 36r) at the virgins' faces, hands, and garments (Pl. 54). (3) Unpainted parchment provided the background for the Temptation of St Martin (f. 29r), and perhaps the figure of St Martin and the hand of God were executed in outline drawing before they were overpainted (Pl. 51). (4) The Community of the Apostles (f. 31r) has been executed almost entirely in black outline with touches of colour; only the background has been fully painted (Pl. 53). If the painter's working unit was the quire and if the spaces on folios 29r and 31r were not originally intended for paintings, the artist may have first executed the paintings that the scribe envisaged (St Andrew and the Community of Virgins) and only then executed the pictures at the bottoms of folios 29r and 31r (the Temptation of St Martin and the Community of the Apostles). If so, he may have progressively modified his technique, perhaps in order to complete his work more quickly. It is also possible that the Annunciation to Joachim may have been painted after the other illustrations in its quire, for it occupies a position in its opening analogous to that held by the Temptation of St Martin and the Community of the Apostles in theirs.

All the paintings are surrounded by Latin hexameter inscriptions. The hexameters describe and comment upon the events and personages represented in the paintings, and often the relationship between text and image is close. The one example of inconsistency between inscription and picture is associated with the use of figured language in the verses. Thus the hexameters were almost certainly composed for their present context. It is manifest that the inscriptions were copied into the manuscript after the outlines of the illustrations had been established, for the texts follow the frequently irregular contours of the pictures. The verses seem to be the work of the scribe responsible for the main text and would have been written as an integral part of the principal campaign of production of the codex.[24] The

---

[23] W. H. Frere's suggestion that f. 36 was once the first leaf of a quire now otherwise entirely lost was based on the assumption that the manuscript was originally composed of regular quaternions, which is unlikely to have been the case (W.H. Frere, *The Winchester Troper: From Manuscripts of the Xth and XIth Centuries*, Henry Bradshaw Society, 8 (London, 1894), p. xxx, n. 1).

[24] See note 8.

copying of the inscriptions, therefore, represents the final phase of work on the manuscript (unless the rubrics were inserted even later).

If the arguments I have presented here can be accepted, we can isolate phases of activity and identify changes in plan in the creation of the Cotton Troper. A handsome manuscript was to be made that would contain an anthology of the available trope repertoire. A single scribe set to work on this project, either interrupting his work or returning at the end to write a replacement leaf. After the main text with its notation had been written, the coloured capitals were added. These capitals (except perhaps the gold letters that introduce the feast days) were executed as a part of a single campaign, although they are of more than one grade. The conventions for their colouration were developed during the course of work on the early part of the manuscript, the fully-developed system being in place by the time the second quire received its minor decoration. Similarly, the script for the rubrics was altered (from rustic capitals to display script) during the course of the rubrication of the first quire.

The first two quires were copied before the decision was taken to provide the book with pictures. Once it was decided to include paintings, the portrait of St Stephen was inserted on folio 3v in a place previously occupied by text. Faced with the task of providing illustrations, the painter was extremely resourceful in fashioning his pictures, drawing inspiration from pictorial tradition, from textual sources, and from the liturgy. Three illustrations (the Annunciation to Joachim, the Temptation of St Martin, and the Community of the Apostles) may not have been a part of the scribe's design for the book, and this would be the indirect cause of their unusual appearance. The style of the paintings was modified during the course of work on the manuscript, precious metals no longer being employed after f. 25 and reserve parchment being used towards the end of the fragment. The illustrations may not have been painted in the order of their appearance in the manuscript. Within a quire the paintings on parchment reserved for the purpose may have been executed before those for which the scribe had not planned. The stylistic modifications give us reason to suspect that the painter was over-ambitious and that he found himself working under both material and temporal constraints toward the end of the project.

Only two people, one scribe and one painter, participated in the physical production of the Cotton Troper, the painter not becoming directly involved in the project until after the first two quires had been written. Perhaps the decision to supply the manuscript with paintings was made upon the artist's arrival at the centre where the codex was made. Once the painter joined the project, he would have worked in fairly close collaboration with the scribe. This did not prevent him, however, from altering his colleague's plan for the manuscript by including paintings where they were not originally intended.

It was undoubtedly extraordinary to embark upon the production of an illustrated troper, particularly after a portion of the text had already been written. Although it is unlikely that the scribe and painter who made the Cotton Troper would have seen an illustrated trope manuscript before making this one, the painter should have been familiar with other sorts of liturgical books with picture cycles. The creators of this manuscript, however, do not seem to have adapted an established formula for the production of illustrated liturgical books. It appears instead that a concentrated series of *ad hoc* decisions guided the making of the manuscript.

Appendix I

Outline of the Contents of the Cotton Troper (Cotton MS Caligula A.xiv, ff. 1-36)

Quire	Fol	Main rubric and contents	Painting
A	1r	(First Sunday in Advent)	
		introit tropes	
		offertory trope	
		communion trope	
		TROPI DE NATALE DOMINI IN GALLICANTU (25 Dec)	
		introit tropes	
	1v	TROPI IN NATALI DOMINI IN PRIMA MANE (25 Dec)	
		introit trope	
	2r	HI TROPI CHRISTI SUNT NATIVITATE CANENDI (25 Dec)	
		versus ante officium	
		introit tropes	
	3r	offertory trope	
		communion tropes	
	3v	(St Stephen) (26 Dec)	*St Stephen*
	4r	introit tropes (incomplete)	
	4v	offertory tropes	
	5v	communion tropes	
		TROPI IN VIGILIA IOHANNIS	
		introit trope	
		IN NATALE EIUSDEM APOSTOLI ET EVANGELISTAE (27 Dec)	
		versus ante officium	
	6v	introit tropes	
B	7v	offertory trope	
		communion trope	
		TROPI IN NATALE SANCTORUM INFANTUM (28 Dec)	
		versus ante officium	
	8v	introit tropes	
	9r	offertory tropes	
		communion tropes	
	9v	IN DIE CIRCUMCISIONIS DOMINI (1 Jan)	
		introit tropes (incomplete)	

(lacuna)

(Epiphany) (6 Jan)
35r	introit tropes (incomplete)
35v	offertory trope
	communion tropes (incomplete)

(lacuna)

10r	**TROPI IN PURIFICATIONE SANCTAE MARIAE** (2 Feb)
	introit tropes
11r	offertory tropes
11v	communion tropes
	TROPI IN ADNUNCIATIONE SANCTAE MARIAE (25 Mar)
	introit tropes
12r	offertory trope (incipit only)
	communion trope
12v	**TROPI IN DOMINICA DIE PALMARUM**
	introit tropes (incomplete)

(lacuna)

(Easter)
C	13r	introit tropes (incomplete)
	14r	alleluia prosula
		offertory tropes
	14v	communion tropes
	15r	fraction antiphon
		FERIA SECUNDA
		introit tropes
	15v	offertory trope
	16r	communion trope
		FERIA III
		introit tropes
	16v	offertory tropes
		communion tropes
		FERIA IIII
		introit tropes
	17r	offertory trope
		communion trope
		TROPI DE INVENTIONE SANCTAE CRUCIS (3 May)
		introit tropes
	18r	*Ascension of Christ*
	18v	versus ante officium (for Ascension)
		IN DIE ASCENSIONIS DOMINI
		introit trope (incomplete)

(lacuna)

(Pentecost)

D   19r   introit tropes (incomplete)

19v   offertory trope

communion trope

TROPI DE SANCTA TRINITATE

introit tropes

20v   *Naming of John the Baptist*

IN NATIVITATE SANCTI IOHANNIS BAPTISTAE (24 Jun)

introit tropes

21v   offertory trope

22r   communion trope

                                    St Peter's Release from Prison

22v   (St Peter) (29 June)

introit tropes

23v   offertory trope

communion tropes

(lacuna)

(Translation of St Benedict) (11 July)

E   24r   introit tropes (incomplete)

24v   offertory trope

communion trope

25r   *Martyrdom of St Lawrence*

25v   (St Lawrence) (10 Aug)

introit tropes

offertory trope (incomplete)

(lacuna)

(Assumption of the Virgin) (15 Aug)

26r   introit tropes (incomplete)

offertory trope

communion trope

                                     Annunciation to Joachim

26v   *Joachim and Anne with the infant Virgin*

(Nativity of the Virgin) (8 Sept)

introit tropes (incomplete)

(lacuna)

(St Michael) (29 Sept)

28r   introit tropes (incomplete)

28v   offertory tropes

communion trope (incomplete)

(lacuna)

(All Saints) (1 Nov)

F   29r   introit trope (incomplete)
            offertory trope
            communion trope

Temptation of St Martin

(St Martin) (11 Nov)
    29v   introit tropes
    30r   communion trope (incipit only)
    30v

St Andrew

(St Andrew) (30 Nov)
            introit tropes
    31r   offertory trope
            communion tropes

Community of the Apostles

    31v   (Common of Apostles)
            introit tropes (incomplete)

(lacuna)

(Common of Martyrs)
    32r   introit tropes (incomplete)
            offertory tropes
    32v   communion trope
            introit trope
            DE UNO MARTYRE
    33r   introit tropes
    33v   offertory trope
            communion tropes

(Common of Confessors)
            introit tropes
    34r   offertory trope (incipit only)
            communion trope (incipit only)
            TROPI IN NATALE UNIUS CONFESSORIS
            introit tropes (incomplete)

(lacuna)

Community of Virgins

    36r
            (Common of Virgins and a single virgin)
            introit tropes
    36v   offertory tropes
            TROPI IN DEDICATIONE AECCLESIAE

315

Appendix II

The Paintings in the Cotton Troper

quire	fol	painting	height	G	S	P
A	3v	Stephen	116mm	x		
C	18r	Ascension	161mm	x		
D	20v	Naming the Baptist	91mm	x		
	22r	Release of Peter	181mm	x	x	
E	25r	Martyrdom of Lawrence	162mm	x	x	
	26r	Annunciation to Joachim	71mm			
	26v	Joachim, Anne, Virgin	102mm			
F	29r	Temptation of Martin	80mm			x
	30v	Andrew	108mm			x
	31r	Apostles	61mm			x
	36r	Virgins	114mm			x

G – gold
S – silver
P – passages of reserve parchment (other than on scrolls)

Domesday Book - a Great Red-herring:
Thoughts on some Late-Eleventh-Century Orthographies
CECILY CLARK

Some dozen years ago an eminent English toponymist declared of Domesday Book that it enabled us 'to study the effects of Norman French pronunciation on English place-names'. Only two or three years ago a distinguished medieval historian expressed to me in conversation his surprise at discovering, in an English monastic obituary compiled about a century later than Domesday Book,[1] numerous spellings, of personal names and of place-names, markedly more traditional than those of the older document. For all the eminence of the scholars concerned, neither viewpoint is, I contend, a true one; if so, then the acceptance of both among scholars of distinction lends urgency to the task of their redressing.

I: Defining the Domesday texts
Before anatomizing either misapprehension, we must first define, in linguistic terms, the corpus of Domesday texts and its place among source-materials bearing upon late-eleventh-century English socio-linguistic conditions.

It is unfortunate that it should be Domesday Book which happens to provide not only the earliest extant records of perhaps 40% of English place-names[2] but also the most extensive as well as the best-known corpus of eleventh-century English personal names; and doubly so that this mischance should, for personal names, have been compounded by Olof von Feilitzen's magisterial treatment of those recorded in the pre-1066 stratum of that document.[3] For it is to von Feilitzen's monograph that everyone concerned with eleventh-century English personal-naming inevitably – and rightly so – turns, only to absorb from it, along with the author's scholarship, an impression (often, it seems, a dangerously subliminal one) that the orthographical styles characteristic of the Domesday manuscripts were typical of that time. To deplore this is neither to impugn the information laid up in Domesday Book nor to decry the young von Feilitzen's remarkable and lasting achievement – all the less, since (as we shall shortly see) he himself

---

1   The obituary in question is published as No. 24 in *Die Gedenküberlieferung der Angelsachsen, mit einem Katalog der* libri vitæ *und Necrologien*, ed. J. Gerchow (Berlin, 1988), pp. 280-89 and 343-50. (References to the two misapprehensions cited are withheld.)

2   See, e.g., P. H. Sawyer, 'The Place-names of the Domesday Manuscripts', *Bull. John Rylands Library*, 38 (1955-56), 483-505, esp. p. 483.

3   Olof von Feilitzen, *The Pre-Conquest Personal Names of Domesday Book*, Nomina Germanica 3 (Uppsala, 1937) (hereafter *PNDB*).

was careful not to present Domesday orthography as typical of late-eleventh-century English usages. The present concern is solely with the matter – which some might perhaps regard as marginal – of spelling traditions; but to philologists orthography, far from being marginal, is the foundation of all their study, and it may further be considered a crucial, albeit subtle, indicator of cultural patterns, and even of cultural health.[4]

What is the charge now brought against Domesday Book and its orthography? Why ought not spellings from these records to be accepted as central source-material for the history of the English language and, in particular, for mainstream developments of English place-names? Simply because, from a linguistic point of view, the Domesday texts are not 'English' ones at all.

That assertion may not seem new. The young von Feilitzen, for instance, in his *Pre-Conquest Personal Names*, described the Domesday texts as 'the oldest extant A[nglo-]N[orman] record',[5] a definition on which he elaborated, making clear his adherence to the lines of orthographical interpretation laid down by his supervisor, R. E. Zachrisson:

> From the point of view of phonology D[omesday] B[ook] is essentially an A[nglo-]N[orman] record, and in attempting to elucidate the manifold phonetic and orthographic problems ... one of our principal tasks will consequently be to ascertain the significance and the range of the A[nglo-]N[orman] influence.[6]

That point of view was questioned by Peter Sawyer thirty-five years ago;[7] nor has it since found many active defenders. To stress that is by no means to dismiss it as wholly false; for, as might *a priori* be expected, there are Anglo-Norman strains clearly represented in the Domesday complex, and the late John Dodgson, for one, several times made great play with the clashes between the English and the French orthographies manifest in the rendering of certain name-items.[8]

---

4   See, e.g., C. Clark, 'L'Angleterre anglo-normande et ses ambivalences socio-culturelles: un coup d'oeil de philologue', in *Les Mutations socio-culturelles au tournant des XIe-XIIe siècles*, ed. R. Foreville, Spicilegium Beccense, 2 (Paris, 1984), pp. 99-110.

5   *PNDB*, pp. 40-41, esp. 41, n.1.; cf. pp. 3, 8, 34.

6   *PNDB*, p. 41. See R. E. Zachrisson, *A Contribution to the Study of Anglo-Norman Influence on English Place-names*, Lunds Universitets Årsskrift I, iv, 3 (Lund, 1909) (hereafter *ANI*); also *idem*, 'The French Element', in *Introduction to the Survey of English Place-Names*, ed. A. Mawer and F. M. Stenton, English Place-Name Society 1, i (Cambridge, 1924), pp. 93-114.

7   Sawyer, 'Place-names', pp. 497-98, also 495, 505-06.

8   John McNeal Dodgson, 'Some Domesday Personal Names, mainly post-Conquest', *Nomina*, 9 (1985), 41-51; 'Domesday Book: Place-names and

Such Anglo-Norman strains are not, however, the ruling element there, and so ought not to be made the methodological basis for a comprehensive analysis. Von Feilitzen himself, handicapped though he was by having as his mentor the main proponent of pervasive phonological as well as orthographical 'Anglo-Norman influence', had already acknowledged something of the true complexity of the situation:

> O[ld] E[nglish] documents were sometimes used in the compilation of the original D[omesday] B[ook] returns, and it is even possible that native scribes were occasionally employed on the clerical staff of the ... commissioners and perhaps in the Anglo-Norman chancery.[9]

How accurate that suggestion was half a century of research has underlined, making it ever clearer how much allowance must be made for influence from lost sources, exemplars and drafts as well as for the varying palaeographical and orthographical practices visible in the extant texts, and at the same time bringing out the extent and the range of the native elements present. Sawyer, pointing to the correction in the principal Domesday texts of many place-name forms garbled or over-Gallicized in extant exemplars, confirmed von Feilitzen's suggestion that some at least of 'its scribes were familiar with O[ld] E[nglish] orthography and probably included Englishmen'.[10] More telling still, in so far as obviating risk of arguing from orthography to orthography, are the palaeographical findings. Several hands employed on the Domesday complex, including that of the principal scribe of Great Domesday Book, are reckoned by recent scholarship, as exemplified in several papers published over the last five years by Alexander Rumble and independently by Pierre Chaplais, to show English, perhaps pre-Conquest English, traits.[11] That is not, of course, true of all the hands contributing to the extant corpus (some texts, including *Liber Exoniensis*, have in any case not yet been fully analysed). In the main, however, recent work has pretty unanimously been discrediting old assumptions about the overridingly 'Anglo-Norman' character of the record.

Personal Names', in *Domesday Studies*, ed. J. C. Holt (Woodbridge, 1987), pp.79-99; 'Notes on some Bynames in Domesday Book', in *Le Nom propre au carrefour des sciences humaines et des sciences sociales: Actes du XVIe Congrès international des sciences onomastiques*, ed. J.-C. Boulanger (Quebec, 1990), pp.221-28.

9 *PNDB*, p. 41, cf. pp. 6-8.

10 Sawyer, 'Place-Names', p. 495.

11 A. R. Rumble, 'The Palaeography of the Domesday Manuscripts', in *Domesday Book: A Reassessment*, ed. P. Sawyer (London, 1985), pp. 28-49, esp. 41-49, and 'The Domesday Manuscripts: Scribes and Scriptoria', in *Domesday Studies*, ed. Holt, pp. 79-99, esp. 84, 97; P. Chaplais, 'William of Saint-Calais and the Domesday Survey', in *ibid.* pp. 65-77, esp. 69-70, 72-74; cf. *Regesta regum Anglo-Normannorum*, I, ed. H. W. C. Davis (Oxford, 1913), p. xvi.

Yet this exposition began with a denial that the Domesday corpus of records was an 'English' one: has there then been a volte-face? By no means. For all their weight, the palaeographical findings are not, for the present purpose, the nub of the matter. Nor yet are the 'nationalities' (if so anachronistic a term be permitted) of the individual scribes; nor even their backgrounds or training. The assertion that these are not 'English' documents is meant in the simplest sense: all were drawn up in Latin, not in English; and the Latin usages represented were, besides, not in the main those of pre-Conquest Anglo-Latin records but normally the Continental ones favoured by the Anglo-Norman administration.[12] The specifically Insular letters of the alphabet were eschewed, so making impossible traditional spelling of many names, whether of places or of people.[13] That must not be deemed a shortcoming, for (as will appear) there were principles involved that set other considerations above traditional, let alone 'phonetic', spelling of vernacular elements. Nor did traditional Old English spelling just go by default, for (as will even sooner appear) the England of the 1080s, and even that of over a generation later, was amply supplied with men who could readily, if but asked, have furnished impeccably Late-West-Saxon spellings. The aim of those responsible for the Domesday texts was not to observe vernacular traditions of any sort, English or Norman, but to Latinize as thoroughly as possible every item that could be Latinized; witness the frankly Latin forms used for specifying certain well-known places, e.g., *IN CIVITATE CANTVARIA, IN EBORACO CIVITATE*, and so on.[14] How thoroughly Latinate the ambience of the scriptorium might be is suggested by certain marginalia in *Liber Exoniensis*.[15]

If it is, then, tenable to interpret the name-spellings found in Domesday Book and its satellites, not as consciously representing current pronunciations used either by scribes or by informants, but rather as aimed at bringing vernacular intrusions into harmony with the orthographical as well as the

[12] The orthographical affinities of Domesday Book may be appreciated by comparing the treatment there of names of all kinds, first, with that in Late Old English documents like those published as *Charters of Rochester*, ed. A. Campbell, *Anglo-Saxon Charters* I (London 1973), nos 29 and 30, and as *Charters of Burton Abbey*, ed. P. H. Sawyer (London, 1979), nos 23, 27 and 32 (all those cited being preserved in contemporary single-sheet form), and, secondly, making due allowance for the difference in underlying vernacular, with that in Norman documents such as those published in *Recueil des actes des ducs de Normandie (911 - 1066)*, ed. M. Fauroux, Mém. Soc. Ant. Normandie, 36 (Caen, 1961).

[13] For the GDB alphabet, see Rumble, 'Scribes', pp. 82-91, esp. 84 ('not thorn, eth or wynn'). Cf. Clark, 'Ambivalences', pp. 101-03.

[14] *Domesday Book: Kent*, ed. P. Morgan (Chichester, 1983), C1; *Domesday Book: Yorkshire*, ed. M. L. Faull and M. Stinson (Chichester, 1986), 1a.

[15] See Chaplais, 'William of Saint-Calais', pp. 66-67.

grammatical norms of medieval Latin, then as a guide to the state of vernacular English orthography in the late 1080s these documents have little standing. That anyone should, even momentarily, have thought otherwise results from the compartmentalization that dominates academic life, discouraging linguists from getting to grips with administrative records and, conversely, historians from mastering philology.

II: Post-Conquest English spelling
Assertions that the Domesday texts were, whether deliberately or not, distanced from vernacular usages and that they therefore carry, on a linguistic level, less weight than some other records from this period are not new. Twenty years ago Gillian Fellows-Jensen scrutinized the Lindsey Survey datable 1115 x 1118 – a good generation, that is, later than Domesday Book – and found it, not surprisingly perhaps, to be in some ways more traditional and truer to local usages than the corresponding sections of the central, governmental record.[16] From the point of view of English historical linguistics, those scholars stressing the 'Norman' affinities of the Domesday corpus might, even though arguing from what I consider a false premiss, be thought to have made an analogous point. The present aim is not, however, so much to elucidate Domesday Book for its own sake as to marginalize its linguistic testimony. For, once we glance up from this particular corpus of records and allow our gaze to rove across other survivors from early post-Conquest England, we cannot but perceive that it was Domesday Book that was anomalous, that was – evidently by design – out of step with the England all around.

There is a wealth of contemporary vernacular material extant, far more than sometimes seems realized. What is extant probably, moreover, represents a mere fraction of the vernacular writing produced. David Pelteret's new *Catalogue* of administrative records happening to survive in English versions apparently (though not always unambiguously) dating from the first century after the Conquest runs to some 140 items, about a third of them consisting of royal writs and charters;[17] and these documents illustrate a variety of vernacular orthographies. That the English language was readily, and so much more widely than is sometimes appreciated, used as a post-Conquest medium of administrative record and communication is in itself important for socio-linguistic history; but, because so many of the items

---

[16] G. Fellows-Jensen, 'The Scribe of the Lindsey Survey', *Namn och Bygd*, 57 (1969), 58-74; cf. *eadem*, 'The Domesday Account of the Bruce Fief', *Jnl English Place-Name Soc.*, 2 (1969-70), 8-17.

[17] D. A. E. Pelteret, *Catalogue of English post-Conquest Vernacular Documents* (Woodbridge, 1990).

preserved are not only brief but fairly idiosyncratic, only limited use will be made of them here.

Recourse to miscellanea is indeed unnecessary, in so far as there is available at least one substantial piece of testimony as to the state of the English language, orthography included, from the time of the Conquest on into the 1120s – during, that is, the first half-century or, to put it more pertinently, the first two generations after Hastings: the only period when foreign-born scribes, or others, can have been at all thick on English ground. The text in question runs to some forty pages of modern print, being the Laud version of the *Anglo-Saxon Chronicle*, especially its annals up to and including that for 1121.[18] This is the section which it is not – except as shorthand, or code – accurate to call a 'Peterborough' chronicle. Its provenance remains obscure: certainly, the extant text was recopied, with local interpolations, at Peterborough Abbey in 1121 x 1122, probably to replace a chronicle lost in the fire of 1116; but whence the abbey had obtained the exemplar is nowhere stated, nor (so far as I am aware) has modern scholarship had much to say on the matter, beyond recognizing that the range of reference implies a house, or series of houses, somewhere in the south-east.[19] Exact provenance may, luckily, be beside the point, because for the present purpose the importance of this text lies in the proof that by itself it gives that somewhere in south-east England there was at least one scriptorium, perhaps more than one, where the capacity as well as the will to write good Late West Saxon persisted through at least two generations following 1066. It is chiefly because the West Saxon used did remain so conventional that the exemplar's provenance is difficult to determine.[20]

It is not, however, the vernacular orthography that is most telling for the present argument. So far were the authors and scribes (the plurals are used because in over half a century changes of personnel surely occurred) of the late *Chronicle* from losing their grasp of native conventions that they uncompromisingly rendered in Insular terms all French personal names and place-names figuring in the narrative, freely deploying the Old English characters æ, þ, ð, and *wynn*. At first sight, this might seem a mirror-image of the sorts of sporadic Anglo-Normanism that John Dodgson and others have identified in the Domesday texts;[21] but upon scrutiny the chroniclers' Anglicism proves to be more systematic, more competent as well as more confident, than the occasional Gallicisms of some Exchequer clerks. The chroniclers' procedure was, besides, for their particular purpose the only one

[18] *The Peterborough Chronicle 1070 – 1154*, ed. C. Clark, 2nd edn (Oxford, 1970), (hereafter *PC*), pp. 1-40.

[19] *PC*, pp. xxi-xxiii.

[20] *PC*, pp. xli-xlv.

[21] See note 8 above.

appropriate: in any vernacular record, let alone an English one, the conventionalized Latin forms in which Norman names were set down in Norman records[22] would have been incongruous; and, as for French vernacular spellings, these were in the early twelfth century, and for some time to come, so far from being standardized as scarcely to afford any model at all.[23] Authentic French spellings would, in any case, have clashed with the English alphabetical values underpinning the text as a whole: a general principle to which we shall return.

Because the Peterborough hand of c.1121 in which this part of the *Chronicle* survives is in the main a traditional Insular one,[24] there is no call to enumerate all the many times when Insular forms of <r> and of <s> figure in foreign names. Certain usages are, however, noteworthy (because the Peterborough scribe was an accurate copyist,[25] these may be presumed, even though not proved, to have been imitated from the lost exemplar, especially as the local usages of the 1120s partly differ from them):[26]

(i) Where in Latin, and usually also in French vernacular spelling, an <e> would have been used, there sometimes appears an <æ> or a digraph <ea>, these various graphs being by this date partly interchangeable in

---

22 See, e.g., Fauroux, *Recueil*.

23 For a general view, see, e.g., C. T. Gossen, 'Graphème et phonème: le problème central des langues écrites du Moyen Âge', *Revue de linguistique romane*, 32 (1968), 1-16; for the areas in question, see, e.g., *The Anglo-Norman Voyage of St Brendan by Benedeit*, ed. E. G. R. Waters (Oxford, 1928), pp. 143-74, and *La Vie de Saint Alexis*, ed. C. Storey (Geneva, 1968), pp. 32-51 ('ses graphies sont, pour la plupart, celles des textes anglo-normands de la bonne époque').

24 See *The Peterborough Chronicle (The Bodleian Manuscript Laud Misc. 636)*, ed. D. Whitelock, Early English Manuscripts in Facsimile, 4 (Copenhagen, 1954), p. 15. For the degree to which Insular styles of writing generally prevailed in early 12th-century England, see N. R. Ker, *English Manuscripts in the Century after the Norman Conquest* (Oxford, 1960), pp. 32-34.

25 See *PC*, pp. xli-xliii.

26 Cf. Clark, 'Ambivalences', pp. 103-04. Space allows here no more than token illustration: the sample Normanno-Latin forms are taken mainly from Fauroux, *Recueil*, and from *The Ecclesiastical History of Orderic Vitalis*, ed. M. Chibnall, 6 vols (Oxford, 1969-80). Citation of reference works is likewise kept to a minimum: for personal names, M.-Th. Morlet, *Les Noms de personne sur le territoire de l'ancienne Gaule du VIe au XIIe siècle*, 2 vols (Paris, 1968-72) (hereafter *NP*) and C. Marynissen, *Hypokoristische Suffixen in oudnederlandse Persoonsnamen* (Ghent, 1986) (*HS*); for place-names, the articles published by J. Adigard des Gautries in *Annales de Normandie* I (1951) – IX (1959) (*AN*), and also C. de Beaurepaire, *Dictionnaire topographique du département de Seine-Maritime*, 2 pts (Paris, 1982-84) (*SM*).

English, both for long and for short vowels:[27] e.g., *Bæc* 'Bec' 1093 (< ON *bekkr*, *AN* IV, 49; Lat *Beccum*); *Bælesme*, *Bælæsme* 'Bellême' 1102-08 (Lat *Bellisma*, *Bellismum*); *Bærneȝe* 'Bernay' 1076 (*AN* IV, 50; Lat *Bernaicum*, *Berniacum*); *Ræins* 'Rheims' 1119 (Lat abl. pl. *Remis*, OFr *Reins*); *Ansealm* 1095-1115 (CG *ans/helm*, *NP* I, 39a; Lat *Anselmus*); *Heanriȝ(e)*, *Heanric*, *Heanri* 1087-1120 beside *Henri* from 1106 on (CG *haim/rik*, *NP* I, 122a; Lat *Henricus*); *Herbearde* 1094 (CG *here/berht*, *NP* I, 125a; Lat *Herbertus*); *Moræl* 1093, *Moreal* 1095 (Lat *Maurellus*, *Morellus*, *NP* II, 77a); *Rodbeard*, *Rotbeard* up to 1095 beside *Rotbert* from 1095 on (CG *hrod/berht*, *NP* I, 136a; Lat *Ro(d)bertus*); *Waltear* 1095 (CG *wald/here*, *NP* I, 213a-b; Lat *Walter(i)us*). Although use of <æ> instead of <e> might by itself be attributed to the interchangeability of those two graphs in medieval Latin, here the variation between <æ> and <ea> points rather to the contemporary English near-equivalence of these two graphs, as seen in the surrounding *Chronicle* text. In so far as any phonological deduction might be legitimate, we might surmise that to an English ear the vowels in question sounded noticeably open, that is, as [ɛ] rather than [e]: a surmise proving compatible with what Romance linguists believe about realizations at this time of OFr /e/ before /l/ and before /r/ as well as before nasals.[28]

(ii) The French medial and final dentals destined for early effacement[29] were often represented here by <Þ> or by <þ>: *Caþum* 'Caen' 1087, 1105 (*AN* II, 222; Lat *Cadomum*, *Cadon*); *Maðante* 'Mantes' 1087 (Lat *Metanta*, acc. *Metantem*); *Natiuiteð* 1102-16; *Aðelis* 1121 (CG *adal/haid*, *NP* I, 16b; 12th-c. OFr *Aelis* or *Aaliz*, Lat *Adelaidis*, *Adelicia*, etc.); *Gosfrið* 1088 (CG *gaut/frid*, *NP* I, 165a; 12th-c. OFr *Gefreid* or *Gefrei*, Lat *Gosfridus*); *Loðepis* 1108, 1116 (CG *hlud/wig*, *NP* I, 133b; 12th-c. OFr *Loewis*, Lat *Ludouicus*).

(iii) Because Caroline <g> was rare in this text,[30] the only significant cases of Insular <ȝ> are ones not corresponding to <g> in conventional Latin (or French) orthography, as in the *Bærneȝe* already cited. Most noteworthy are several names ending in stressed [iː] or [iːə]: *Cluniȝ* 'Cluny' 1119 (Lat *Cluniacum*; cf. *Clunni* 1127-31); *Lumbardiȝe* 'Lombardy' 1117 (12th-c. OFr *Lumbardie*; Lat *Lombardia*); *Normandiȝ(e)* 'Normandy' passim (12th-c. OFr *Normendie*; Lat *Normannia*); also *Maniȝe* beside *Mannie* 'Maine'; *He(a)nriȝ*, etc., sporadically to 1120 beside *He(a)nri*

---

27 See, e.g., *PC*, pp. xliii-xliv (NB: I no longer support blanket ascription of these spellings to 'Latin and French influence'), cf. pp. xlvi-xlvii, xlix-li.

28 See, e.g., M. K. Pope, *From Latin to Modern French*, 2nd edn (Manchester, 1952), §§. 447, 492, 493, 1089, 1098.

29 *Ibid.*, §§. 346, 347, 1097, 1113, 1175-1177.

30 See Whitelock, *MS Laud Misc. 636.*, p. 15.

from 1104 on, possibly by analogy with the traditional spellings of native names in *-si e* and *-wi* .

(iv) The Caroline form for < w > appears only for the capital,[31] the small letter being regularly represented by *wynn*. Capricious initial capitalization means that often this letter appears as initial of a foreign name: *sce paleri* 'Saint-Valery' 1090 (*AN* IX, 161-62, *SM* 939; Lat *Sanctum Walaricum*); *palcelin* 1098 (CG *walh* + dimin., *HS*, 231-32; Lat *Walc(h)elinus*); *palchere* 1080 (CG *walh/here*, *NP* I, 214b-215a; Lat *Walcherus*); and *pillelm* passim alongside forms in < W- >. (On the other hand, < W- > sometimes appears in native names like *Walþeof* 1075 and *Wlstan* 1088.) Medial and final occurrences of *wynn* appear in: *Anʒeop* 1110-19 (12th-c. OFr *Anjou*, cf. Lat acc. *Andegauem*); *Punti* 'Ponthieu' 1120 (cf. Lat *Pontiuum*); *Baldepine* 1070-1119 (CG *bald/wini*, *NP* I, 50b; Lat *Balduinus*), probably assimilated to native names in *-wine*; and *Loðepis* 1108-16 (see above).

Interpretation of such spellings as systematic Anglicization seems confirmed by some frank replacements, not only here but also in other records from this time, of Continental personal names by English (or Anglo-Scandinavian) ones of similar form, sometimes but not necessarily cognate: e.g. occasional renderings of the name of Odo of Bayeux (CG *aud-*, *HS*, 196-200) as OE *Oda*, obl. *Odan*, 1082, 1088 3x, and, even more strikingly, the attribution to a notorious Norman abbot of Glastonbury, a former monk of Caen, of the Anglo-Scandinavian name *Þurstane*, dat. 1083, not only spelt with small initial < þ > but also having as second element *-stan*, instead of Normanno-Scandinavian *-stein* or *-stin*.[32] Second elements of foreign place-names too seem sometimes to have been identified with native generics of similar form: e.g., the *Bærneʒe* already cited looks as though remodelled on native place-names in *-eg*,[33] such as *Anʒleseʒe* 'Anglesey' 1098, *Ceortesæʒe/eʒe* 'Chertsey' 1084, 1110, and *Rumeseʒe* 'Romsey' 1086. Later in the Middle English period, similar adaptation of French place-names transferred to English soil was to be common enough.

On its own, therefore, this section of the *Chronicle* testifies to the tenacity of native orthographical traditions during the first two generations after the Conquest; but its testimony does not – and this must be emphasized – in fact stand alone. Related sorts of Anglicization are, to begin with,

---

31 *Ibid.*, pp. 16-17.

32 J. Adigard des Gautries, *Les Noms de personnes scandinaves en Normandie de 911 à 1066*, Nomina Germanica, 11 (Lund, 1954), pp. 167-69, also 253, 326-40. For some instances on English soil, see, e.g., O. von Feilitzen, 'The Personal Names and Bynames of the Winton Domesday', in *Winchester in the Early Middle Ages*, ed. M. Biddle (Oxford, 1976), pp. 143-229, esp. 175. Cf. note 36 below.

33 See, e.g., M. Gelling, *Place-Names in the Landscape* (London, 1984), pp. 34-40.

frequent in the first series of Peterborough Continuations: that is, the annals from 1122 to 1131, written up in six stints.[34] Despite being less accomplished in Late West Saxon (here an alien dialect), the scribe(s) of these annals continued confidently to Anglicize spellings of foreign names: <æ> appears in, e.g., *Sæis* 'Sées' 1130 (cf. Lat dat. pl. *Sagiis*), *Æðelic* 1127 (here probably assimilated to native names in *Æðel-*), *Martæl* 1127 (cf. Lat *Martellus*); in *Henri* the digraph <ea> varies with <e> and may even have been preferred, in so far as the annals for 1129 and 1130 show *Henri* fairly consistently corrected to *He'a'nri*; <ð> or <þ> figures in *Æðelic*, *Godefreið* 1123 (CG *god/frid*, *NP* I, 112a; Lat *Godefridus*), *Gosfreið* 1125, 1127, *Loðepıs* (as before, spelt also with *wynn*), *Pecceþ* (Lat *Peccatum*) 1123, and *Roðem* 'Rouen' 1124 (*AN* IX, 153-54, *SM* 859; Lat *Rotomagus*, *Rodomum*). Apparent assimilation of a foreign place-name to native patterns appears in *Mun(d)ford*, as if with the native generic *-ford*,[35] for French *Montfort* (*AN* IV, 254-55). Again, too, *Þurstan* varies with *Turstein*, this time for the name of the Norman archbishop of York.[36]

In the later *Chronicle*, admittedly, such usages might be taken as imitation by the Peterborough scribe(s) of ones from the preceding copied text; might be so taken, were it not that, fortunately for the present argument, they can be paralleled from independent materials. Thus, the H-Fragment giving annals for 1113-14 shows two instances of *Caðum* 'Caen', one of *Goisfriðe*, one of *Henriȝ*, and one of *Turstane* for the name of the archbishop of York.[37] Analogous spellings appear in the *Liber Vitae* of Thorney Abbey, begun during the first decade of the twelfth century: <Æ> appears as initial capital in *Æmma* (CG *erm-*, *irm-*, *HS*, 108-10; Lat *Emma*), *Ærmentruða* (CG *ermin/trudis*, *NP* I, 83a; Lat *Ermentrudis*), *Ærnis* (CG *arn/gis*, cf. *NP* I, 41b; Lat *Ernisius*), *Ærnoldus* (CG *arn/wald*, cf. *NP* I, 41a; Lat *Arnoldus*, *Ernaldus*), *Ærnulfus* (CG *arn/wulf*, *NP* I, 41a; Lat *Arnulfus*, *Ernulfus*), *Æscelinus* (CG *ad(al)*+dimin., *HS*, 53-4; Lat *Azzelinus*), *Æþeliza*,

---

34   See Whitelock, *MS Laud Misc. 636*, p. 14, and Clark, *PC*, pp. xvi-xvii (both quoting Neil Ker).

35   See, e.g., Gelling, *Landscape*, pp. 67-72.

36   Note that *Hugh the Chanter: The History of the Church of York 1066-1127*, ed. and trans. C. Johnson, rev. M. Brett *et alii*, Oxford Medieval Texts (Oxford, 1990), regularly names the archbishop, who was of Norman parentage (*ibid.*, pp. xxvii-xxviii and references there given) as *Turstinus*, which the translator renders as *Thurstan*. Cf. note 32 above.

37   The text used is that in *Two of the Saxon Chronicles Parallel*, I, ed. C. Plummer and J. Earle (Oxford, 1892), pp. 243-45; cf. J. Zupitza, 'Fragment einer englischen Chronik aus den Jahren 1113 und 1114', *Anglia*, I (1878), 195-97. For the predominantly Insular hand involved, see N. R. Ker, *Catalogue of Manuscripts containing Anglo-Saxon* (Oxford, 1957), p. 188.

Æpelina (CG *adal*+dimin., *HS*, 51; Lat *Adelina*) – as alternative, that is, sometimes to <A>, sometimes to <E> – and <æ> appears medially in *Bæta* (CG *berht*, *HS*, 74-77; Lat *Berta*), *Dræp.e* (Lat *Drogo*, *HS*, 102-03; later OFr *Dreu*), *Roæis* (CG *hrod/haid*, *NP* I, 137a), and so on; <Þ> and <ð> appear, more or less interchangeably, in *Albreþa/Albreðe* (CG *alb/rada*, *NP* I, 29b; Lat *Alberada*), *Ærmentruða*, *Æðelic/Æpeliza*, *Frepesenda* (CG *frid/sindis*, *NP* I, 93b), *Gosfriþ*, *Haðeuuis/Hapeuuis* (CG *had/widis*, *NP* I, 119b); <ʒ> appears in *Aʒnes*, *Ʒrantamaʒni* 'Grandmesnil' (*AN* III, 26; Lat *Grentemaisnilium*) where the second example renders a French preconsonantal <s>, *Huʒo* (CG *hug*, *NP* I, 140a, *HS*, 156-63), *Liʒarda / Liʒard* (CG *leud/gardis*, *NP* I, 159b; Lat *Ligardis*), *Roʒer* (CG *hrod/gair*, *NP* I, 136b) *le byʒod*, and so on; and <p> in *Baldepinus*, *Dræp.e*, *Happ.is*, *palter*.[38] A few more such spellings can be gleaned from the documents calendared by Pelteret: *Hæimonem* (CG *haim*, *HS* 146-47), *Hugæn* (with OE obl. case), *Rodbært*, *Wælcælin*, *Willælm*, *Aðelicc*, *Josfreʒð* and *Viðel* (Lat *Vitalis*, OFr *Viel*), also *Eorlawine* for *Herluin* (CG *erl/wini*, *NP* I, 81b-82a).[39] If an 'iceberg' principle of calculation be admissible, then from these stray sightings of Anglicized names it might be deduced that, for at least the first half-century after the Conquest, English cultural and linguistic attitudes had been marked by a robust self-assurance that unhesitatingly subjugated foreign items to native structures and usages – and that despite the ubiquity of immigrant abbots and bishops as well as of alien administrators.

Domesday Book spellings of English place-names and personal names are thus by no means to be taken as typical of current native usages. Vernacular spelling traditions not only remained in force for the English language itself but retained vigour and authority enough to subjugate any foreign items falling within their ambit. Nor ought English monastic houses and their scriptoria to be supposed as in the main either culturally or linguistically swamped by the Continental, mainly Norman-French, usages associated with the foreign prelates presiding over them.

---

38 British Library Add. MS 40,000, ff. 1v-12r. See Clark, 'Ambivalences', pp. 104-05, also 'British Library Additional MS 40,000 ff. 1v-12r', *Anglo-Norman Studies*, 7 (1984), 50-65, esp. p. 52, and 'A Witness to post-Conquest English Cultural Patterns: the *Liber Vitae* of Thorney Abbey', in *Studies in Honour of René Derolez*, ed. A. M. Simon-Vandenbergen (Ghent, 1987), pp. 73-85, esp. pp. 80-82.

39 Pelteret, *Catalogue*, nos 8, 25, 31, 32, 33, 62, 96, 105; for the form *Josfreʒð*, see *Facsimiles of English Royal Writs to A.D. 1100 presented to Vivian Hunter Galbraith*, ed. T. A. M. Bishop and P. Chaplais (Oxford, 1957), pl. XIV ('the work of a scribe thoroughly practised in the OE minuscule').

III: Questions of phonetic implication

To return, now that the onomastic orthography of Domesday Book has been set in a wider and – it is to be hoped – truer perspective, to the first proposition cited: the one asserting that the spellings in question enable us to 'study the effects of Norman French pronunciation on English place-names'. This rests on a many-layered complex of assumptions.

On one level, it assumes 'Norman French' pronunciation to have had upon a fair number of English place-names effects permanent enough to merit more than passing attention. Over the past eighty years this Zachrissonian notion has become so entrenched as to pass in some quarters for 'fact' rather than hypothesis.[40] It has been urged elsewhere how shaky its foundations are.[41] Points telling against it include, first, the unlikelihood of a supposed snobbish affectation that, although widespread socially, confined itself linguistically to place-names, leaving personal names and common vocabulary untouched; and, even more, the existence of an alternative possibility, probability rather, that most of the modifications imputed to 'Anglo-Norman influence' could well have arisen spontaneously in rapid and casual speech. Such matters of long-term development are, however, tangential to the present theme.

A second, and more fundamental, set of assumptions is, first, that Domesday Book spellings of vernacular items were essentially intended to transcribe actual pronunciations, perhaps the scribe's own, perhaps an informant's; and, further, that such 'phonetic transcription' was precise and explicit enough to be accurately interpretable nine centuries later. Spelling must not, however, be confused with phonetic transcription: a point that should be self-evident to anyone conversant either with Modern English or with Modern French, let alone (as most medievalists are) with both. Spelling – at least as long understood in Western Europe – involves a system of conventionalized representation to which any alien elements must in some measure be adjusted (in modern usage, for instance, by italicization). In discussing eleventh-century English renderings of foreign proper names, emphasis has been given to the regular imposition upon these of specifically English spelling conventions and to occasional further assimilations towards native structure. Now, if English vernacular conventions were thus capable of subjugating alien intruders, then so *a fortiori* must have been those of Latin, at this date not only more prestigious but also more systematized than English ones, never mind such French vernacular ones as existed. When any vernacular item was adopted into Latin, some adjustment was inescapable,

---

[40] For Zachrisson's work in this field, see note 6 above.

[41] See Clark, 'Towards a Reassessment of "Anglo-Norman Influence on English Place-Names"', in *Language Contact in the British Isles*, ed. G. Broderick and S. F. Ureland (Tübingen, 1991), pp. 275-93.

because Latin syntax relied upon inflections and so required any adopted item to be tricked out with a set of these. At alphabetical level, degrees of adjustment varied, with pre-Conquest Anglo-Latin charters and chronicles sometimes showing native names spelt with the appropriate Insular characters but Norman records, composed as they were with small background of vernacular literacy, showing more thoroughgoing Latinization.[42] That the latter tradition was the one governing the drafting of Domesday Book can be deduced not just from *a priori* notions about 'Anglo-Norman' administration but, more cogently, from the avoidance in its text of the Insular characters needed for traditional and precise representation of English material.

With this in mind, a fresh eye may be cast over the Domesday texts. One widely accepted line of interpretation begins by postulating a 'Norman inability to pronounce /þ/ and /ð/', goes on to suppose those sounds to have been replaced in speech by /t/ and /d/, and then invokes this supposed oral substitution in explanation of the <t> and <d> spellings found in Anglo-Latin documents for names containing the spirantal sounds.[43] We have, however, observed – as indeed did von Feilitzen – that the sorts of Old French with which late-eleventh-century writers of English and of Anglo-Latin were coming into contact did contain sounds that English-speakers identified with their own dental spirants;[44] and, if we look at French and Franco-Latin materials of this date, we find those Old French sounds regularly spelt with <t> and with <d>.[45] It is thus unwise to dogmatize about phonetic implications of spellings in <t> or <d> found in Domesday Book or, for that matter, elsewhere in medieval materials. Given that the Latin alphabet afforded no means of distinguishing between dental stops and dental spirants, orthographic approximation or compromise was inevitable. Given too what has lately been put forward as to the Englishness of several hands responsible for the Domesday record,[46] it makes better sense to take approximate spellings as conventional rather than as

---

42 See references in note 12 above.

43 *ANI*, pp. 39-49, 82-116. This tradition of interpretation was reviewed in my paper, 'The Myth of "the Anglo-Norman Scribe"', *Proceedings of the Sixth International Conference on English Historical Linguistics, Helsinki 1990* (forthcoming, Berlin, 1992), a principal contention being that its underlying socio-linguistic premisses (e.g. *ANI*, p. 11) are gravely flawed.

44 See Pope, *From Latin to Modern French*, §§. 1175-77 (pronunciation), 1210, 1215 (spelling). Cf. *PNDB*, pp. 100-02, where it is recognized that [θ] and [ð] did occur in Anglo-Norman speech.

45 Cf. Waters, *Brendan*, pp. clviii-clxii, and Storey, *Alexis*, pp. 47-48 (but this includes an unintelligible reference to 'la graphie anglo-saxonne *th*').

46 See note 11 above.

reflecting faulty pronunciation. So too with another frequent line of interpretation: the one assuming <c>, when found in names like *Cicestre* 'Chichester' or *Glouuecestre* 'Gloucester', to signify, not the [tʃ] expected as reflex of Old English palatalized <c>, but, instead, a Gallicized replacement of this by [ts] (soon to be simplified to [s]).[47] This assertion is, if anything, odder than the previous one, in so far as the traditional English spelling here always had been <c> and remained so well into the twelfth century[48] and in so far as [tʃ] would seem not to have been alien to eleventh-century Norman French.[49] What alternative graph the commentators in question envisage as available for [tʃ] is unclear, for at this time <ch> most often denoted [k].[50] To argue the case more closely would demand confident knowledge, such as few can now possess, of just how Exchequer clerks of the 1080s and English monastic scribes of the early twelfth century pronounced their Latin.

If, then, the name-spellings found in Domesday Book reflect in general a Procrustean attempt to accommodate English materials within an alien and, for this purpose, inadequate set of alphabetical conventions, it must follow that what these spellings reveal about anyone's pronunciation, whether a scribe's or an informant's, must be limited. As a present-day partial analogue, I propose the sort of 'imitated pronunciation', which 'should be read as if it were English', that is offered in the otherwise admirable Berlitz phrase-books. That the analogy is imperfect must be stressed; for the Berlitz versions are aimed at representing pronunciation, whereas the Domesday Book ones (it is argued) were precisely not so aimed; but for the discrepancy to go that way only makes the comparison more telling. The Berlitz procedure – intended, one supposes, to spare learners the trauma of encountering anything as logical and clear as the International Phonetic Alphabet – consists of transcribing foreign phrases into a sort of code based upon English alphabetical values:

---

[47] *ANI*, pp. 18-32; *PNDB*, p. 110, likewise assumes partial substitution of [ts] for OE [tʃ].

[48] See, e.g., A. Campbell, *Old English Grammar* (Oxford, 1959), §§. 431-34, and cf. *Ciceastre, Cæstre, PC*, s.aa. 1130, 1140. R. Jordan, *Handbuch der mittelenglischen Grammatik*, i: *Lautlehre* (Heidelberg, 1934), §§. 177, 179, dates the appearance of ME <ch> spellings for [tʃ] to the second half of the 12th century; D. G. Scragg, *A History of English Spelling* (Manchester, 1974), pp. 44-45, cf. p. 28 n.2, dates it 'about 1200'.

[49] For [tʃ] in Norman-French, see Pope, *From Latin to Modern French*, §§. 1092, 1181.

[50] For <ch> representing [k], *ibid.*, §. 1029; Waters, *Brendan*, pp. 44-45, 172, cf. 173, and Storey, *Alexis*, p. 46 ('l'occlusive gutturale est donc représentée par *k, ch, qu* et *q*'); also *PNDB*, pp. 107-09.

Zher ner kawngprahng pah. Pooreeay voo pahrlay plew lahngtermahng?
Pooreeay voo raypaytay, seel voo pleh? Mawngtray mwah lah frahz dahng
ler leeyr – ang nangstang, zher vay vwahr see zher lah troov dang ser
leevr.[51]

The crucial question is this: can any transcription so approximate tell us
anything about anyone's pronunciation of French? Nothing, surely, about
that of the compilers, whom one would assume to be, if not native speakers,
at all events accomplished linguists. And, if these transcriptions, aimed as
they are at 'imitating' pronunciation, reveal so little, how much could
anyone hope to discover from Domesday Book spellings, intended as these
evidently were to cast a Latinate veil over the rugosities of the vernacular?

The end of the trail is, however, no dead end. Details have been added to
the picture compositely painted over the last few decades of a post-Conquest
England that was for the most part sturdily Anglophone. More than that:
there now opens up before us a potential new field of study, in which
orthographical analysis, palaeography and textual history would combine to
complement and cross-fertilize each other. One might, for instance, ask how
far (if at all) particular orthographical usages, especially perhaps ones found in
Little Domesday Book and in *Liber Exoniensis*, might prove to correlate with
individual hands identifiable there. Or one might consider how far
orthographical styles correlate with textual history; with, for instance,
apparent shifts between documentary and oral inputs, or with links between
the Domesday texts themselves and their satellites. In considering this
complex of records, we must always bear in mind that the nickname by
which its central monument has been known from the late twelfth century
on is an unimpeachably English one, which 'Anglo-Norman' administrators
seem nevertheless soon to have made their own.[52]

---

[51] *French for your Trip*, Éditions Berlitz (Lausanne, 1979), pp. 17-18 (the phrases
excerpted having been minimally repunctuated), also p. 12.

[52] *Dialogus de Scaccario*, ed. C. Johnson (Edinburgh, 1950), p. 64. Cf. M. T.
Clanchy, *From Memory to Written Record: England 1066-1307* (London, 1979), pp.
18, 110.

The English Language in the Eleventh Century: The Evidence from Inscriptions
ELISABETH OKASHA

The title of this paper raises an immediate question: what is it about inscriptions that is so unusual or so useful as to merit a whole paper on inscriptional evidence? One answer is that inscriptional texts are on the whole less well-known than are manuscript texts. This is understandable: the amount of evidence to be gleaned from an inscription is small in comparison with the effort involved in locating it, deciphering it and interpreting it. Another answer is that there are some advantages that inscriptions have when compared to manuscript texts. Inscriptions, for example, were not copied and recopied in the way that some manuscripts were; an inscription contains an original text in a sense that is only rarely true of a manuscript. Then again, texts inscribed on large pieces of stone are unlikely to have been moved far from their place of manufacture: the inscriptions I shall discuss from Breamore (Pl. 55), Great Edstone and Kirkdale have probably remained part of the fabric of their churches from the eleventh century until today. This gives us an historical context for certain inscriptions which is not always available for manuscripts. Of course inscriptions on smaller inscribed objects are portable in the same way that manuscripts are portable: the censer-cover from Pershore, the Sutton brooch and the tiny piece of carved stone from Barton St David (measuring c. 7 x 2 x 1 cm) are examples of such small objects.

Inscriptional texts in Old English share with manuscript texts the problems that not all dialect areas are as well represented as others and that carvers, just as readily as scribes, could work in a part of the country whose dialect differed from their own. In one respect inscriptions are at a disadvantage when compared with manuscripts: they are often less easy to date. Some of the inscriptions that I am going to discuss as eleventh-century may in fact date from the end of the tenth century or the beginning of the twelfth but the evidence does not allow us to date them more precisely.

The eleventh-century inscriptions discussed in this paper are those with texts in Old English which employ roman script and which are reasonably legible. Some forty eleventh-century texts are excluded from discussion either because they are in Latin (even if they contain an Old English personal name), or because they are fragmentary or scarcely legible, or because they consist only of an alphabet, or because they are in runic script. Such texts are excluded both when they occur alone on an object and also when they occur alongside an Old English text. There remain twenty-one texts which provide direct evidence about the English language in the eleventh century; these texts are listed in the Appendix. The vocabulary of the texts is discussed first, followed by the syntax, the morphology and finally the spelling.

Vocabulary

The inscriptions furnish us with three Old English words not elsewhere recorded as well as with four instances of Old English words used with unusual meanings. In view of the brevity of some of these texts, this may seem a surprisingly large number. The three otherwise unrecorded words are GECWYDRÆDNES in Breamore I (Pl. 56), SOLMERCA in Kirkdale, text (i) (Pl. 55) and [S]YB[STEL] in Lanteglos.

The meaning of GECWYDRÆDNES in Breamore I is suggested by the existence of the related Old English word *gecwedraeden, gecwydraeden* meaning 'agreement'. The Breamore text is inscribed on an inside archway of the church. A meaning 'agreement' could have legal significance, perhaps referring to the ownership of the church or of its possessions. Alternatively, and perhaps more likely in view of the location of the text, an 'agreement' could have a religious significance, possibly closer to the meaning 'covenant'.

The meaning of SOLMERCA in Kirkdale, text (i) is not in dispute: from the context the meaning is clearly 'sun-marker' or 'sun-dial', since text (i) is placed inside the carved sun-dial. SOLMERCA could have been coined from Old English *sōl* 'sun' and the rare *mearca* 'space marked out'. The latter occurs, for example, in Gregory's *Dialogues, he ... wæs belocen binnan þam mearce þæs hringes*, 'he ... was enclosed within the space marked out by the ring'.[1] Alternatively, and more probably, Kirkdale's SOLMERCA was coined from the Old Norse words *sól* 'sun' and *merki* 'sign, mark', both of which are considerably more common than their Old English cognates. I do not know of an Old Norse compound *sólmerki* meaning 'sun-dial', although if it existed the Kirkdale word could have been borrowed as it stands. The Old Norse compound *sólmerki* is recorded in the twelfth century but with the meaning 'sign of the zodiac'.[2]

The word [S]YB[STEL] in Lanteglos is now rather damaged but earlier epigraphists confirm the reading. The context suggests that the [S]YB[STEL] is the piece of inscribed stone. Its meaning is therefore 'memorial-stone' or something similar. The stone itself is not *in situ*, nor is there a reliable find-report, and so we do not know whether or not the stone was originally associated with a burial. The first part of the word is probably Old English *sib-* meaning 'family' or 'peace'; both meanings are recorded in compounds,

---

[1] H. Hecht ed., *Bischof Wærferths von Worcester Übersetzung der Dialoge Gregors des Grossen* (Leipzig, 1900), p. 197, lines 3-4. The reading is from Cambridge Corpus Christi College MS 322; BL Cotton MS, Otho C. i has *mearcan*.

[2] R. Cleasby and G. Vigfusson, *An Icelandic-English Dictionary*, 2nd edn (Oxford 1957).

for example *sibgedryht* meaning 'related band' and 'peaceful host'. The second part of the word is probably Old English *-steall* 'place' as in compounds like *weardsteall* 'guard-place, watch-tower'. The literal meaning of [S]YB[STEL] would then be 'family-place' or 'place of peace'. Either meaning would be appropriate for a memorial-stone, whether or not it marked a grave.

The four words used in the inscriptions with unusual meanings are MACAN and ILCVM in Kirkdale (Pl. 55), [OF]ER and STAN in London I (Pl. 57).

MACAN in Kirkdale, text (iii) is Old English *macian* 'to do'. From early Middle English this word comes to have the additional meaning of 'to construct'. This meaning occurs as early as the twelfth-century *Peterborough Chronicle s.a.* 1097: ... *he be þam gemæron castelas let gemakian*, '... he caused forts to be constructed alongside the boundaries'.[3] The Kirkdale text is earlier, being dated to the decade 1055 to 1065, and is the earliest example known to me of *macian* meaning 'to construct'.

ILCVM occurs in Kirkdale, text (i). The context shows that, despite the spelling, Old English *ælc* 'each' is intended here, not Old English *ilca* 'same'. In Middle English, confusion between these words is common and occurs as early as the twelfth-century *Peterborough Chronicle s.a.* 852: *he scolde gife ilca gear in to þe minstre sixtiga foðra wuda...*, 'each year he must give to the monastery sixty waggon loads of wood...'.[4] The charter which this Chronicle entry summarizes makes it quite certain that Old English *ælc* 'each' is the word intended, despite the spelling *ilca*.[5] The Kirkdale text shows that the beginnings of this confusion are found in Old English. In this connection the ninth-century *Vespasian Psalter* gloss is interesting. There the words are kept distinct but their spellings are rather similar: *ilca* glosses *ipse* and *ylc* (once *oelc*) glosses *omnis*. Such similarity in spelling could have aided the later confusion in meaning.

[OF]ER in London I is the Old English preposition *ofer* which has various meanings such as 'beyond', 'above', 'across', 'during' and others. As far as I know, however, it is not recorded elsewhere in Old English or Middle English meaning 'in memory of', as it means in London I. The usual Old English preposition used for setting up a stone in memory of someone is *aefter*. In Scandinavian runic inscriptions the usual word used is Old Norse *eptir* but there are some instances of Old Norse *yfir*, including UBIR for *yfir* on a tenth- or eleventh-century Scandinavian runic stone on Iona.[6] Old

---

3   C. Clark ed., *The Peterborough Chronicle 1070-1154*, 2nd edn (Oxford, 1970), p.26.

4   C. Plummer ed., *Two of the Saxon Chronicles Parallel...* I (Oxford, 1892), p. 65.

5   This charter is preserved in a 12th-century cartulary of the Abbey of Peterborough; A. J. Robertson ed., *Anglo-Saxon Charters* (Cambridge, 1939), no. VII, pp. 12-13. The charter spells the word *elce*.

6   *The Royal Commission on the Ancient and Historical Monuments of Scotland: Argyll*

English *ofer* may have been used on the London stone with an extension of the literal meaning 'above', possibly influenced by Old Norse epigraphic usage.

The fourth word is STAN in the same text, London I. The context suggests that the stone referred to is a grave-stone or a memorial-stone. The actual stone, the top part of a wheel-headed cross, is not unsuitable for a grave-marker. However, as with the Lanteglos stone, this stone is not *in situ* and there is no find-report: once again, we cannot tell whether or not it was originally associated with a burial. Old English *stān* is not elsewhere recorded with the meaning 'grave-stone' or 'memorial-stone'. In place-names and in charters, the meaning 'standing-stone' is quite common. STAN on London I is probably best taken as having an extension of the meaning 'standing-stone', perhaps 'standing-stone set up over a grave' or 'standing-stone set up as a memorial'.

Syntax

For two reasons there is less to be said about the syntax than about the vocabulary of the eleventh-century inscriptions. Firstly, several of the texts are very short: not much syntactical evidence can be gleaned from, for example, the text DRAHMAL ME WORHTE (Brussels I, text (i)). Secondly, the majority of the syntax is entirely regular. We may note, for example, that LET in Kirkdale, text (iii), [HE]T in Aldbrough and HET in Brussels I, text (iii) are all followed by infinitives,[7] and that the four instances of the present subjunctive in Sutton are entirely regular: AGE and AWERIE express a wish or a desire, ÆTFERIE is in an adjectival clause dependent on a clause of wishing or desiring, and SELLE is the verb of a conditional clause introduced by BVTON meaning 'unless'.[8]

The texts do, however, furnish four structures of particular syntactical interest. The first is in Lanteglos, a text easy neither to read nor to interpret but with only one unusual syntactic feature. This is the lack of concord between the plural subject ÆLSEL[Ð] 7 GENE[REÐ] and the singular verb [W]O[H]TE which follows it. Such apparent lack of concord occurs regularly in Old English when a verb precedes a subject consisting of two or more singular nouns joined by 'and'. An example of this occurs in Brussels I, text (iii), ÞAS RODE HET ÆÞLMÆR WYRICAN 7 AÐELWOLD HYS BEROÞO[R]..., 'Aeþlmaer, and Aðelwold his brother, ordered *[singular]* this cross to be made ...'. The Lanteglos example may be explained as having a singular verb because the two people forming the subject were perceived as a unit. Mitchell gives some similar instances from Ælfric, for example: *Se*

Vol. 4, *Iona*, HMSO (1982), p. 190 and figs.

[7] B. Mitchell, *Old English Syntax* (Oxford, 1985), §§679-80, 955.

[8] Mitchell, *OE Syntax* respectively §§898, 1675; §2391; §§3634-40.

frumsceapena man and eall his ofspring wearð adræfed..., 'The first-created man and all his posterity was driven...'.[9] This syntactical structure in Lanteglos is thus not unknown in Old English although it is unusual.

The second point of syntactical interest is from the text of Breamore I (Pl. 56) and concerns the words ÐE and SWVTELAÐ. ÐE could be either the second person singular pronoun in the dative, meaning 'to you', or the indeclinable relative pronoun 'which'. The verb SWVTELAÐ has an expressed subject, SEO GECWYDRÆDNES, 'the agreement'. The Old English verb *sweotolian* can be used personally ('reveals') or impersonally ('it reveals') but clearly it cannot be used impersonally in this text since the subject is expressed.[10] SWVTELAÐ must therefore mean 'reveals' and the sentence must be incomplete. The text is unlikely to have continued with a direct object, 'Here the agreement reveals x ...', since the word-order would be unusual if ÐE meant 'to you' and impossible if ÐE meant 'which'. It is therefore likely that the text originally continued with a clause, 'Here the agreement reveals to you [that ...]' or 'Here the agreement which ..., reveals ...'. The latter is the more probable, with ÐE meaning 'which'. ÐE 'to you' would imply that the text was addressed to only one person, but its location in a public building suggests that it was addressed to people in the plural. Two other fragments of inscribed stone have been found at Breamore, confirming the existence of further text now lost. Unfortunately they are too fragmentary to aid interpretation of the text: one contains the letters -DES- and the other has only the letter -G-.

The third point of syntactic interest concerns the use of the word ÐONNE in Kirkdale, text (iii) (Pl. 55). Mitchell states that Old English *ðonne* 'when' is sometimes used with the preterite indicative (as here) to refer to frequentative acts in the past or to a continuous state; he goes on to suggest that in the Kirkdale text the reference is to a continuous state.[11] A 'continuous state' would presumably imply that, when Orm bought the MINSTER, it had been 'completely ruined and collapsed' for a long time and still was so. This may have been what the author of the text intended. Alternatively, and perhaps more likely, he was implying nothing so subtle as the length of time in which the MINSTER had been in such a state of disrepair but was simply using ÐONNE as equivalent to Old English *þā*. These two conjunctions, *þonne* and *þā*, finally fell together in usage and sporadic instances can be found in Old English texts of various dates, as

---

9   Mitchell, *OE Syntax* §§ 29-31. The Ælfric quotation is taken from B. Thorpe ed., *The Homilies of the Anglo-Saxon Church* I (London, 1844), p. 118, lines 23-24.

10   The dictionaries suggest that a passive meaning, 'is revealed', is also recorded but I can find no instance in Old English where a passive, as opposed to an impersonal, meaning is necessitated.

11   Mitchell, *OE Syntax* §§ 2562-72; Kirkdale is mentioned in § 2568.

Mitchell demonstrates.[12]

Kirkdale text (iii) also contains the fourth point of syntactic interest which concerns the word NEWAN. This word could be an adjective, a verb or an adverb. It could, firstly, be the Old English adjective $nīwe$, $nīewe$.[13] There are however both morphological and syntactical objections to this. An adjective agreeing with the neuter noun MINSTER, whose gender is confirmed by the neuter pronoun HIT, should have no inflexional ending in the accusative singular. Moreover NEWAN, if an adjective, would be a weak form; yet, with no demonstrative or possessive expressed, the strong form of the adjective would be expected. Exceptions to this rule concerning weak and strong forms of the adjective do occur, but rarely.[14] Secondly, NEWAN could be a form of the verb $nēwian$ 'to renew'; the loss of -i- would be exactly paralleled in the spelling MACAN for $macian$. However, the lack of a co-ordinating conjunction 'and' suggests that NEWAN is unlikely to be a verb. Thirdly, and most likely, NEWAN is the Old English adverb $nīwan$, $nēowan$. In Old English this adverb almost invariably means 'recently', not 'anew', a meaning confirmed by Middle English $neuen$. In only a handful of instances, out of over sixty listed in the *Microfiche Concordance to Old English*, could $nīwan$ mean 'anew', and in each case the meaning 'recently' is equally possible.[15]

Morphology

The Old English inflexional system is largely preserved in the language of the inscriptions. This conclusion may be surprising. By the eleventh century we might have expected a greater loss of inflexional endings, and a greater confusion of the unstressed vowels in those endings, than does actually occur.

The verbal inflexions are almost entirely regular. The infinitive, the preterite indicative (both weak and strong), the present indicative, the present subjunctive and the weak past participle all appear with the regular endings. There are two examples of confusion in the strong past participle, both in Kirkdale, text (iii): TOFALAN and TOBROCAN both have -*an* for -*en*. There is one possible example of a late loss of verbal inflexion, WVORHT in

---

12   *Ibid.*, § 2572.

13   This interpretation is accepted by R. I. Page, 'Dating Old English Inscriptions: the Limits of Inference', in *Papers from the 5th International Conference on English Historical Linguistics*, ed. S. Adamson *et al.*, *Current Issues in Linguistic Theory*, 65 (1990), pp. 357-77. Kirkdale is discussed on pp. 361-62.

14   Mitchell, *OE Syntax* §§ 128-41.

15   See, for example, the instances quoted under Boethius *Metres* 28, 70, Ælfric *Lives of Saints (Sebastian)* 323 and Ælfric *Letter to Sigeward (Sigeward Z)* 925 in A. Di P. Healey and R. L. Venezky, *A Microfiche Concordance to Old English* (Toronto, 1980).

Pershore, for Old English *worhte*. However, this is more probably the metal-worker's error. Although he had run out of space after inscribing the letter H, he managed to find an odd corner for the T, on the side of the adjacent animal's head. The verb form was then recognizable, although erroneous, being the form of the past participle not the past indicative; the metal-worker seems therefore to have abandoned the attempt to find a space for the E.[16]

The same sort of conservatism in inflexion is apparent in the common nouns. The majority of the nouns, like almost all the verbs, have perfectly regular endings in all cases of the singular, both in the weak and in the strong declensions. There are only two occurrences of nouns in the plural, both DAGVM, the regular dative plural, in Kirkdale, text (iii).

There are four instances of nouns showing a loss of inflexion: DRACA in Ipswich I and CYRICE in Aldbrough lack the usual *-an* ending of masculine and feminine weak nouns in the accusative singular, while in the strong nouns EORL appears in Kirkdale, text (iii) for genitive singular *eorles* and S[O]UL in Lanteglos for dative singular *sāule*. There are also two nouns with a confused ending: SUNA in Kirkdale, text (iii) has *-a* for *-u* in the nominative singular and SAVLA in Aldbrough has *-a* for *-e* in the dative singular. The genitive singular phrase AGENES WILLES in Sutton might be thought to show confusion between strong and weak nouns and between strong and weak forms of the adjective. It can be explained, however, by the fact that when Old English *willa* is used adverbially the apparently strong form *willes* is recorded. Ælfric has, for example: *...þæt he nolde his willes heora geferrædene forlætan*, '... that he did not intend against his will to abandon their companionship'.[17] The adjective *agen*, as Mitchell demonstrates, is usually declined strong not weak after a possessive.[18]

The systems of personal and demonstrative pronouns, in so far as they are recorded, are preserved intact. The only odd form is H[A]NVM in Aldbrough, perhaps to be explained as a borrowing of Old Norse *honum*, possibly to indicate a reflexive 'for himself', although the Old Norse reflexive form would correctly be *sér*. The indefinite pronoun *ælc* when used adjectivally should agree with the following noun: ILCVM in Kirkdale, text (i) is, as indicated above, rather confused but seems to be a form of *ælc* used adjectivally. It contains a masculine dative singular inflexion, either in error for the feminine *-re*, or because Old English *tīd* was here assumed to be masculine/neuter, as it sometimes is elsewhere; cf. *Durham Ritual ðæm*

16 See the discussion in Page, 'Dating OE Inscriptions', pp. 360-61.

17 B. Thorpe ed., *The Homilies of the Anglo-Saxon Church* II (London, 1846), p. 334, line 25.

18 Mitchell, *OE Syntax* § 501.

tide.[19]

These few instances of loss of inflexion and confusion of inflexion have to be seen in the context of the majority of the Old English verbs, common nouns and pronouns which occur in perfectly regular form in the inscriptions. The position with the proper nouns, that is, with the vernacular personal names, is however rather different.

This can be illustrated from the seven personal names appearing in the genitive singular. Two of these have a regular ending, ÆLFRICES in Brussels I, text (iii) and EORLES in Winchester I. Two of them have a confused ending, ÆLWYNEYS in Lanteglos with *-eys* for *-es*, and GVN[WARA] in Aldbrough where the final *-a* is probably for *-e*. The remaining three names have no ending at all: GAMAL, EADWARD and TOSTI, all in Kirkdale, text (iii). In the case of anglicised Old Norse names it could be argued that there might be difficulty in deciding what ending would be appropriate in the genitive singular. This argument might explain GAMAL, TOSTI and perhaps GVN[WARA] but it is inapplicable in the case of EADWARD and ÆLWYNEYS. It may be relevant to note that TOSTI is in apposition to EORL, which is the only example of a common noun lacking a genitive singular inflexion. Taken as a group, the personal names demonstrate a breakdown in the morphological system which is not found in the common nouns, pronouns or verbs of the inscriptions.

Spelling

The spelling of the ordinary Old English words in the inscriptions is considerably more conservative than that of the personal names. This difference in spelling between the two groups is parallel to the difference in morphology noted above.

Some spellings found in the inscriptions, although not regular Old English forms, occur from time to time in various dialects and are not of particular significance to the eleventh century. Examples include SWVTELAÐ for *sweotolað* in Breamore I, ÐANE for *ðone* in Ipswich I, WES for *wæs* in Kirkdale, text (iii) and the various spellings of *sāwol* 'soul' in Aldbrough, Lanteglos and Brussels I, text (iii). Some non-West-Saxon spellings also occur in the texts but, again, these are not specific to the eleventh century. Such are the stem vowels of BESTEMED in Brussels I, text (ii) and of AWERIE in Sutton, both of which show *ēa* subject to *i-* mutation appearing as *e*, and TOFALAN in Kirkdale, text (iii), showing retraction, not fracture, of *ae* before *l* and a consonant. The form AROERAN in Aldbrough is perhaps to be explained as an example of the rare, but recorded, instances of *ā* subject to *i*-mutation appearing as *oe*, as in the *Vespasian Psalter's*

[19]   U. Lindelöf ed., *Rituale Ecclesiae Dunelmensis*, Surtees Society 140 (Durham, London, 1927), p. 162, line 17.

oeghwelc.[20]

There are however certain sorts of spelling which are typical of late Old English texts. Firstly, there is the confusion, or falling-together, of *i* and *y* in stressed syllables.[21] Examples are CYRICE in Aldbrough, WYRICAN in Brussels I, text (iii), MINSTER in Kirkdale, text (iii) and DRIHTEN in Sutton. A similar falling-together is apparent in syllables with lower stress as in HYS in Brussels I, text (iii) and in HYO for *hēo* in Sutton.

Secondly, there is the introduction of a parasite vowel in WYRICAN in Brussels I, text (iii) and in the two examples of BEROÞOR in the same text.[22] Thirdly, the falling-together of medial *-i-* and *-ig-* can be seen in L[I]Đ in Winchester I and perhaps in the ending of BYFIGYNDE in Brussels I, text (ii)[23]: this ending may be explained as an amalgamation of the late forms *-ynde* (from earlier *-iende*) and *-igende.*

Fourthly, the spellings of consonants include several late forms. Examples are: both the simplification of the geminate in ÆL and TOFALAN in Kirkdale, text (iii) and also the doubling of the single consonant in WORRD in London II;[24] the spelling *v* for *f*, which became common in Middle English, in LOVE in Stow (but note the retention of *f* in the same word in Brussels I, text (iii) and in Lincoln I); the loss of *r* in [W]O[H]TE in Lanteglos,[25] with which can be compared WROHTE in Kirkdale, text (ii) and in Great Edstone, where in both cases the *r* is retained but metathesised.[26]

The Old English spelling system as found in the ordinary words of the inscriptions thus contains some late features but is still comparatively conservative, especially in the retention of diphthongs and of the vowel *æ*. Similar spellings occur in the proper nouns. The four late features mentioned above are all evidenced in the personal names also. Examples include, firstly, WINSIE in Barton St David, text (i) where the first element is probably Old English *wyn*; secondly, a parasitic vowel is probably present between the elements of GENE[REÐ] in Lanteglos; thirdly, the falling-together of *-i-* and *-ig-* occurs in the second element of WINSIE in Barton St David, text (i); fourthly, there are various late spellings of consonants: *v* for *f* occurs in

20   *Vespasian Psalter* 64, 3 and 142, 2: H. Sweet ed., *The Oldest English Texts*, EETS 83 (Oxford, 1885), pp. 273 and 392. See A. Campbell, *Old English Grammar* (Oxford, 1959), §§ 132n, 233n. Cf. *Vespasian Psalter* 63, 10 *oghwelc*, Sweet, *OET* p.273.

21   Campbell, *OE Grammar* §§ 317-18.

22   Campbell, *OE Grammar* §§ 360-67.

23   Campbell, *OE Grammar* §§ 267, 757.

24   Campbell, *OE Grammar* § 457.

25   Campbell, *OE Grammar* §§ 475-76.

26   Campbell, *OE Grammar* § 459.3.

AELVBRH in London IV (twice), although the *f* is retained in ÆLFRICES in Brussels I, text (iii), and consonant loss is found in the second element of WELV[A]R in London I, which is probably from Old English *-weard*.

There are other late spelling features that occur only in the personal names, not in the other Old English words. Old English short *æ*, for example, can appear as *ae*, in the first element of ÆÞLMÆR in Brussels I, text (iii); it can also occur as *e*, in WELV[A]R in London I, and as *a* in AÐELWOLD in Brussels I, text (iii). The late monophthongisation of diphthongs is found, although not consistently: Old English *ēa* in the element *ēad-* remains in EADWARD in Kirkdale, text (iii) and in EADRI[C] in Bishopstone; it is however spelt *ae* in ÆDVWEN in Sutton and seems to appear as *i* in IDHILD, Barton St David, text (ii). Similarly, the Old English element *ēan-* is likely to be the origin of the first element of GENE[REÐ] in Lanteglos, in which case it has been monophthongised and has an added *g*, a spelling which can be paralleled in *Domesday Book*.[27]

The Old English names in the inscriptions seem then to be spelt in a less conventional way than the Old English words are. We may associate this with the rather less strict observance of the Old English system of nominal inflexion in the personal names as compared with the Old English common nouns. It might be that conventions of spelling and morphology were felt to be less applicable, or less obligatory, when inscribing personal names and that in these names we see the beginning of changes that were not to appear in the written language as such until the early twelfth century.

Conclusions

If we leave aside the personal names, the language of the eleventh-century inscriptions appears to be rather conservative. There are late spellings, but the spelling system is still clearly Old English. We can observe occasional changes in morphology, but it is still the Old English inflexional system. The Old English syntactical system remains intact. The vocabulary shows the introduction of no French words at all. A comparison with the first continuation of the *Peterborough Chronicle*, dated *c.*1130, is instructive. In vocabulary, in syntax, in morphology and in spelling the language of the eleventh-century inscriptions can be described as Old English in a way that the language of this part of the Chronicle cannot.

It is in the field of vocabulary that the inscriptions seem to have most to offer linguists. Not only are there no French borrowings, in itself interesting, but as noted above a significant proportion of the words used in the inscriptions are either unrecorded elsewhere or are used with an unrecorded or rare meaning. This contribution to eleventh-century lexical studies is small

[27] O. v. Feilitzen, *The Pre-Conquest Personal Names of Domesday Book* (Uppsala, 1937), § 136, p. 118.

but not insignificant. We may enquire why it is that such a proportion of the inscriptional vocabulary should be unusual.

I would suggest that the answer to this question is also the answer to the question posed at the beginning of this paper. What it is that is unusual or useful about inscriptional evidence is that inscriptions provide us with a different sort of vocabulary from that encountered in many manuscript texts. Inscriptional texts are not precisely literary, nor legal, nor historical, nor religious texts, although they may bear resemblance to some or all of these. Inscriptions, like coins, stand apart from these neat categories. The importance of inscriptions, I would suggest, lies in their furnishing us with a rather different context from that to which we are accustomed for the study of the Old English language in the eleventh century.

Appendix

Texts of the Eleventh-century Inscriptions in Old English

The running numbers are taken from my Hand-list and Supplements, where the texts are fully discussed and illustrated.[28] The texts are divided into words but word-division symbols are omitted. Uncertain letters are placed in square brackets and loss of text indicated by a dash. The Old English letters Þ, Ð and Æ appear as in the texts but p is printed as W and ligatures are ignored.

1   *Aldbrough* + VLF [HE]T AROERAN CYRICE FOR H[A]NVM 7 FOR GVN[WARA] SAVLA, 'Ulf ordered the church to be erected for himself and for Gunwaru's soul'.

12 *Bishopstone* +EADRI[C], 'Eadric'.

15 *Breamore I* (Pl. 56) HER SWVTELAÐ SEO GECWYDRÆDNES ÐE -, 'Here the agreement which [-] reveals -'.

17 *Brussels I* (i) + DRAHMAL ME WORHTE, 'Drahmal made me'.
(ii) + ROD IS MIN NAMA GEO IC RICNE CYNING BÆR BYFIGYNDE BLODE BESTEMED, 'Cross is my name. Once, trembling and drenched with blood, I bore the mighty king'.
(iii) ÞAS RODE HET ÆÞLMÆR WYRICAN 7 AÐELWOLD HYS BEROÞO[R] CRISTE TO LOFE FOR ÆLFRICES SAVLE HYRA BEROÞOR, 'Aeþlmaer, and Aðelwold his brother, ordered this cross to be made to the glory of Christ (and) for the soul of Ælfric their brother'.

41 *Great Edstone* + LOÐAN ME WROHTE A-, 'Loðan made me-'.

58 *Ipswich I* HER SCE [M]IHA[E]L FEHT WIÐ ÐANE DRACA, 'Here St Michael ?fights (or ?fought) against the dragon'.

64 *Kirkdale* (Pl. 55) (i) + ÞIS IS DÆGES SOLMERCA + ÆT ILCVM TIDE +, 'This is the day's sun-marker at each hour'.
(ii) + 7 HAWARÐ ME WROHTE 7 BRAND PRS, 'And Hawarð made me and Brand the priest'.
(iii) + ORM GAMAL SVNA BOHTE SCS GREGORIVS MINSTER ÐONNE HIT WES ÆL TOBROCAN 7 TOFALAN 7 HE HIT LET MACAN NEWAN FROM GRVNDE XPE 7 SCS GREGORIVS IN EADWARD DAGVM CNG 7 N TOSTI DAGVM EORL +, 'Orm son of Gamal bought St Gregory's church when it was completely ruined and collapsed and he had it constructed recently from the ground to Christ and St Gregory in the days of King Eadward and in the days of Earl Tosti'.

---

28 E. Okasha, *Hand-list of Anglo-Saxon Non-runic Inscriptions* (Cambridge, 1971), texts 1 to 158 inclusive; *eadem*, 'A supplement to *Hand-list of Anglo-Saxon Non-Runic Inscriptions*', *ASE*, 11 (1983), 83-118, texts 159 to 184 inclusive; *eadem*, 'A second supplement to *Hand-list of Anglo-Saxon Non-Runic Inscriptions*', (*ASE*, forthcoming), texts 185 to 211 inclusive.

69   *Lanteglos* + ÆLSEL[Ð] 7 GENE[REÐ] [W]O[H]TE ÞYS[N]E [S]YB[STEL] FOR ÆLWYNEYS S[O]UL 7 [F]OR HEY[SEL], 'Aelselð and Genereð made this ?family-place for the soul of Aelwine and for ?Heysel'.

73   *Lincoln I* - [C]RISTE TO [L]O[F]E [7] SC͞E M[AR]IE, '-to the glory of Christ and St Mary'.

87   *London I* (Pl. 57) - STAN WELV[A]R LET SE[TTAN] [OF]ER HERE-, '-Welvar had (this) stone set up in memory of Here-'.

88   *London II* - ERH[E-] WORRD, '- word'.

100 *Pershore* + GODRIC ME WVORHT, 'Godric made me'.

114 *Sutton* + ÆDVWEN ME AG AGE HYO DRIHTEN DRIHTEN HINE AWERIE ÐE ME HIRE ÆTFERIE BVTON HYO ME SELLE HIRE AGENES WILLES, 'Aedvwen owns me; may the Lord own her. May the Lord curse him who takes me from her unless she gives me voluntarily'.

118 *Wallingford II* (i) + EADBVRH MEC AH-, 'Eadburh owns me -'.
     (ii) + EADBVRH [M]EC AH [AH]-, 'Eadburh owns me-'.

138 *Winchester I* + HER L[I]Ð G[VN]N[I] EORLES FEOLAGA, 'Here lies Gunni, Eorl's companion'.

146 *York 1* - M[I]NSTER SET[TON] [-]ARD 7 GRIM 7 ÆSE O[N] [NA]MAN DRIHTNES HÆ[LGES] CRISTES [7] SC͞A MA[RIE] [7] [SC]E MARTINI 7 SC͞E C[-]TI OMNIVM SC͞OR[VM] [CONS]ECRATA EST AN[-] IN VITA ET-, '-(this) minister [-]ard and Grim and Aese set up in the name of the ?holy Lord Christ and of (*or* to) St Mary and St (?Cuthbert) and All Saints. It was consecrated -'.

174 *Putney* OSMUND, 'Osmund'.

186 *Barton St David* (i) + WINSIE ÞISNE ÆA-, 'Winsie (?made) this -'.
     (ii) + IDHILD ME, 'Idhild me'.

198 *London IV* (i) AELVBRH, 'Aelvb(u)rh'.
     (ii) AELVBRH, 'Aelvb(u)rh'.

205 *Stow* -ST TO LOVE 7 S-, '-to the glory of -'.

206 *Thornton-le-Moors* + GOD HELPE -, ' May God help -'.

Spelling Variations in Eleventh-Century English
D. G. SCRAGG

N. R. Ker's *Catalogue of Manuscripts Containing Anglo-Saxon*[1] has a total of 189 manuscripts described in detail of which more than two-thirds are firmly dated in the eleventh century. If we add to these the single page documents that Ker excluded from his survey, and also the wide variety of less substantial writings in Old English, such as the marginalia in earlier manuscripts and short entries, glosses and bounds in Latin documents, we have a larger corpus of English vernacular dating from the eleventh century than from any comparable period of English until the fourteenth. The potential that this gives us for analysing the language of the eleventh century is theoretically great. Yet grammarians of Early English have in general neglected this evidence for their survey of what we know as Old English, preferring to concentrate on those few manuscripts dated before the year 1000 (twenty-nine in Ker's *Catalogue*). Their reasons for doing so are clear enough: because of the stabilization of spelling in late West Saxon, eleventh-century written English gives little evidence of developments in the spoken language. Campbell's *Grammar*,[2] the standard linguistic survey of Old English in English, falls broadly into two halves which may be called 'Phonology' and 'Accidence'. The one chapter in the work which deals with written forms *per se* is called 'Writing, Orthography, *and Pronunciation*' (my italics). His preface is contemptuous of an approach that considers symbols before sounds: 'Most other books have traces of a merely alphabetic arrangement, treating first *a*, and then *e*, &c., and finally reverting to the sound-changes' (p. v), and the conclusion to his chapters on stressed vowels sums up his attitude to the eleventh century neatly: 'The eleventh century was a period of great change in the accented vowels, but these changes did not generally receive expression in the by then fairly stable Old English spelling, and they are to be traced mainly through Middle English evidence' (p. 135). Concentration on the development of sounds has led to the virtual rejection of the substantial eleventh-century evidence because all that it offers is occasional variations of spelling.

Campbell, following in the footsteps of Karl Luick,[3] was drawn into the great intellectual cul-de-sac of the twentieth century, structural linguistics, whose architect, Ferdinand de Saussure, maintained that in linguistic matters, speech is primary and writing secondary.[4] Campbell's dismissal of an

1   N. R. Ker, *Catalogue of Manuscripts Containing Anglo-Saxon* (Oxford, 1957).
2   A. Campbell, *Old English Grammar* (Oxford, 1959) (hereafter 'Campbell').
3   Karl Luick, *Historische Grammatik der Englischen Sprache* (Stuttgart, 1914-40).
4   De Saussure's lectures were published posthumously by his students as *Cours de*

alphabetic arrangement – which is surely aimed at Sievers-Brunner[5] whose more detailed account of late Old English has a fuller survey of eleventh-century forms – is written from the assumption that sound-changes (diachronic phonology) are more important than mere orthography. Now there is nothing wrong with studying phonological development. It is necessary that we should have as firm a grasp as possible of the pronunciation of Old English, and phonological studies help us to that. Likewise, the sequence of Old English changes – and also those of the transition to Middle English – is a vital link in the great chain of the history of the English language. But it is important that students of Old English should not be blinded by the prescriptions of linguists who are principally concerned with living languages. However poorly spelling variation charts developments in eleventh-century phonology, it gives ample evidence of scribal habits, manuscript relations, scriptorium practices and the development of a formal written language. As far as the study of Old English is concerned, the written language in which it is recorded for us is primary, and any deductions we may make about sounds are secondary. Since Campbell's *Grammar* was published in 1959, significant advances have been made in the study of Old English prose, particularly in the work of the great prose writers of the Benedictine Reform period, both named – Æthelwold, Ælfric, Wulfstan and Byrhtferth – and the unnamed writers and translators of the large body of religious and secular literature of the last decades of the Anglo-Saxon state.[6] So many prose texts survive in multiple copies – unlike those on which Campbell bases most of his evidence – that some forms of scribal alteration of the language of the copy-text have now been more thoroughly investigated.[7] The publication of the Toronto Microfiche Concordance in 1980 has given a considerable fillip to lexical studies, and recently we have

---

Linguistique générale in 1916. An English translation is available by W. Baskin, *Course in General Linguistics* (New York, 1959).

5   Karl Brunner, *Altenglische Grammatik nach der Angelsächsischen Grammatik von Eduard Sievers*, 3rd edn (Tübingen, 1965).

6   Advances in the study of prose are considered in Milton McC. Gatch, 'Beginnings continued: a decade of studies of Old English prose', *ASE*, 5 (1976), 225-43, and more recently in the reviews in each Spring issue of *Old English Newsletter*.

7   A good example of the sort of results that can be achieved here may be found in studies detailing linguistic changes in late copies of Alfredian prose such as David Yerkes, *The Two Versions of Wærferth's Translation of Gregory's 'Dialogues': An Old English Thesaurus* (Toronto, 1979), Dorothy M. Horgan, 'The lexical and syntactic variants shared by two of the later manuscripts of King Alfred's translation of Gregory's *Cura Pastoralis*', *ASE*, 9 (1981), 213-21, and Raymond J. S. Grant, *The B Text of the Old English Bede: A Linguistic Commentary* (Amsterdam, 1989).

had major progress in the study of syntax.[8] It seems to me that the time is now ripe for a new initiative in spelling, and my object here is to suggest a few possible lines of enquiry.

Although the study of late Old English dialects has been much inhibited by the existence of the late West Saxon scribal tradition,[9] it has long been recognized that there is considerable variation within that scribal tradition – the problem is that it has not been seriously documented. John Pope's introduction to his edition of Ælfric's homilies,[10] for example, has an illuminating sentence towards the end of his discussion of Cambridge, Corpus Christi College MS 178: 'A few of [the] spellings... are unlike those that prevail in the other manuscripts of the first half of the eleventh century, but there is nothing, so far as I am aware, that can be regarded as a deviation from West Saxon', and he gives as examples the forms *þar* and *hwar*.[11] Pope is of course writing with very considerable knowledge of Ælfric, and of the spellings regularly used by Ælfric scribes, and his awareness that something odd is at work in CCC 178 should be taken seriously. The spellings *þar* and *hwar* that he cites are used quite widely by eleventh-century scribes, but their pattern of occurrence has yet to be investigated. There has certainly never been any attempt to localize them in geographic or scriptorium terms. To do so would require subtle investigation. To take the single instance of CCC 178 as an example: it is a copy 'substantially unchanged'[12] of an Ælfric collection

8   *A Microfiche Concordance to Old English*, compiled by Antonette diPaolo Healey and Richard L. Venezky (Toronto, 1980) (hereafter 'Toronto Microfiche Concordance'); Bruce Mitchell, *Old English Syntax* (Oxford, 1985).

9   The standard view is best expressed by Kenneth Sisam, *Studies in the History of Old English Literature* (Oxford, 1953), p. 153: 'the early 11th century was the period in which West Saxon was recognized all over England as the official and literary language. The York surveys of about 1030 supply a good instance in local documents from the North. The prayers to St Dunstan and St Ælfheah in MS Arundel 155 give an equally striking example from Kent, for though they were certainly copied at Christ Church, Canterbury, into an official service-book, and were presumably composed and Englished at Canterbury, yet they are normal West Saxon. Dialect does break through, the more frequently as the eleventh century advances; but good West Saxon may be written anywhere in its first half.'

10 *Homilies of Ælfric: A Supplementary Collection*, ed. John C. Pope, EETS (London, 1967-68), pp. 259-60.

11 *Ibid.*, p. 67. On p. 178 he adds specific examples: '[the manuscript] tends to prefer *þar*, *hwar* to *þær*, *hwær*, and to substitute *a* for *o* in the verbal endings *-on* and *-ode*'. As other examples of idiosyncratic spellings in this manuscript I would add the doubling of final consonants in common words, e.g. *þiss*, *þuss*, *inn(to)* (contrast *þyses*, *þysum*), and the erratic use of vowel spellings in unstressed positions (*oðor*, *þeahða*).

12 Pope, *Homilies of Ælfric*, p. 62.

but one which was not put together under Ælfric's supervision. It reached Worcester during the eleventh century but may not have been written there. To establish from where the unusual spellings *þar*, *hwar* were introduced, we should need to consider whether they were first used by the scribe of that manuscript, or copied by him in a mechanical way from his archetype. And we can never establish from this manuscript alone whether or not they are spellings which were particularly favoured in Worcester.

The fullest account of spelling variation in the eleventh and twelfth centuries is Willy Schlemilch's short study published in 1914.[13] While this continues to be a useful survey – particularly in the absence of anything else – it does have drawbacks now. Since 1914 we have reached new conclusions about dating many of the manuscripts and their contents. Schlemilch's list of early eleventh-century manuscripts can be extended considerably, and some of his items, e.g. the Martyrology, deleted. There are problems about the way in which the evidence is presented, particularly in the search for its phonological significance. Thus although the arrangement is what Campbell described as alphabetical, with each paragraph devoted to an individual graph (*a*, *a* + nasal, *æ*, *e*, etc.), it is at the same time largely concerned with the sounds which the symbols are supposed to represent and the sound-changes that produced them. An instance of this is that examples of *þar* and *hwar* are excluded from the survey because the phonological significance of the variation is not clear.[14] And there are other ways in which the study is outdated. Much of the material on consonants is grouped around Skeat's list of Anglo-Norman scribal features,[15] even though Schlemilch himself recognized the limitations of Skeat's study. The appearance of the Anglo-Norman scribe produces a lot of unnecessary confusion; for example under the heading of the Skeat feature 'Final *th þ*, especially in an unaccented syllable, is turned into *d* or *t*',[16] Schlemilch has instances which are merely graphic, *d* written for *ð*, for example, where all that is involved is presence or absence of a cross-stroke through the ascender, alongside those that have more important ramifications, including phonological ones, such as examples of the confusion of *t* and *þ/ð*. Schlemilch rightly points out that *t* for *þ/ð* cannot be an Anglo-Norman trait because examples occur before the Conquest, and indeed they occur much earlier than the period he covers, many in the second half of the tenth century, with occasional instances as early as the eighth-century glosses.[17] Nevertheless there is undoubtedly an

13 W. Schlemilch, *Beiträge zur Sprache und Orthographie spätaltengl. Sprachdenkmäler der Übergangszeit (1000-1150)* (Halle, 1914).

14 Schlemilch, p. 19, Anm. 1.

15 Walter W. Skeat, *Notes on English Etymology* (Oxford, 1901).

16 Schlemilch p. 56.

17 See Campbell, §57.7.

increase in instances in the eleventh century, and although Schlemilch gives sporadic examples from a range of manuscripts in his period, a fuller survey is obviously desirable. In it, we need to distinguish between confusion of the graphs in verb inflections – where it may be influenced by Latin, as the reverse spelling of þ/ð for t occurs occasionally in Latin copied by English scribes[18] – and its occurrence elsewhere. All Schlemilch's examples of t for þ/ð in word-final position are in verb inflections (e.g. det, secgat, cwæt, restet), and we need to know if the phenomenon is largely confined to this context or if it is found in others. The converse, ð for t, is found in many twelfth-century manuscripts (where it is presumably a sign of the demise of the ð graph), but it is also found in a few eleventh-century ones; for example Schlemilch's list shows that it occurs occasionally after an s in a version of the West Saxon Gospels: to be precise (as Schlemilch on this point is not), nysðon, þyrsþendne, wesðen occur in CCC 140, a manuscript which was at Bath late in the eleventh century but may not have been written there. The same feature of ð for t before s occurs sporadically in the language of the scribe of a series of items added in the middle of the eleventh century in blank spaces and in the margins of the copy of the Old English Bede in CCC 41 (a manuscript not in Schlemilch's survey).[19] This is one of the manuscripts which were presented to Exeter by Bishop Leofric, and it has sometimes been assumed that the marginal items were added either there or somewhere nearby. But some of the material has definite associations with the south-east, and any possibility of locating the writing of the texts through idiosyncratic features of their language needs to be investigated. Only a detailed survey of all examples of this graphological feature of late West Saxon can take the point any further. We should forget for the moment any underlying phonological significance. Complete cataloguing of the written phenomenon should be our first objective.

Such cataloguing needs to be done with precision. It is not enough to note the range of manuscripts in which a particular graphological feature occurs. We need to know which items they are found in, and in which hands, so that deductions can be made about the manuscript sources used by the scribe(s): for instance, if a manuscript in more than one hand exhibits minor spelling variation between the hands, this points to idiosyncratic spellings being the work of the latest scribes, whereas a manuscript in a single hand which shows minor spelling variation between its items suggests that its scribe has drawn items from several exemplars with different spelling practices. The cataloguing must be concerned with unusual spellings of

[18] See, for example, *Vercelli Homilies IX-XXIII*, ed. Paul E. Szarmach (Toronto, 1981), homily XVI, line 10: *prohibebað*.

[19] See MS D in D. G. Scragg, 'The corpus of vernacular homilies and prose saints' lives before Ælfric', *ASE*, 8 (1979), 223-77, at p. 237.

specific words as well as with the more general tendencies that Schlemilch investigated. For example, the Toronto Microfiche Concordance reveals that the word *godcund* 'divine' appears as *codcund* in two eleventh-century manuscripts, Oxford, Bodleian Library, MS Junius 85/86, and BL Cotton Tiberius MS A.vii. This might easily be dismissed as a mechanical error (scribes failing to add the tail of *g* to the bow, and so leaving what looks like a *c*) were it not that the spelling occurs no fewer than five times in the Tanner manuscript of the Old English Bede (Bodleian Library MS Tanner 10). Likewise, the spelling *leornigcniht* 'disciple' in the Vercelli Book and again in BL Cotton Tiberius MS A.iii might be seen as having lost its *n* through scribes' overlooking of a mark of abbreviation, were it not that five examples occur in the CCC 140 copy of the West Saxon Gospels. Occasional variation in the spelling of common words needs to be carefully listed in case the examples throw up distinctive patterns. Such variant spellings as *eam* 'am', *heom, hiom* 'them' and *þyssere* 'this' (feminine genitive and dative singular) are widespread in eleventh-century texts, but they may well have originated in a particular written dialect or school. Until occasional spellings are properly catalogued, editors will continue to relegate isolated examples to their apparatus, where they will remain isolated because grammarians fail to pick them up.[20]

Careful cataloguing will give us a great deal more information about the manuscript distribution of occasional forms, but because almost all eleventh-century Old English is a copy of earlier written material, we can never be sure that the forms are those of the latest scribes. Given the rarity of autograph writing in Old English, can we ever hope to be any nearer to isolating the schools or individuals who first used the variant forms? For this we need to concentrate on a particular and limited source of evidence: marginalia and late alterations to the texts. A great many annotators were at work in the eleventh century, and although a small number can be shown to be copying their annotations from one manuscript to another, the majority must be assumed to be writing free from the constraints of the spelling forms of a copy-text. We are even able to identify some of these annotators, from Ælfric and Wulfstan at the beginning of the century, to Coleman working at

---

[20] In Campbell there is so little recognition of forms found in 11th-century texts that *eam* is recorded as occurring only in non-West Saxon §768 (*d*), and *hiom* is not listed anywhere. David Yerkes, in his admirable edition of *The Old English Life of Machutus* (Toronto, 1984), emends the single form *are* to *anre* 'one' (feminine dative singular), reasonably because – as far as I know – no grammar of Old English lists it as a permissible variant. Yet the Toronto Microfiche Concordance lists it in a wide variety of 11th-century texts, and the form is comparable with the equally widespread *mire* and *þire* for *minre, þinre*.

Worcester at the end. I want to look more closely at the work of just one of them. He wrote in what Kenneth Sisam called a 'large rough hand'[21] about the middle of the century in the two-volume homiliary which itself was written about the year 1000, the largely Ælfric manuscript, Bodley 340/342. This double volume was very heavily used during the next hundred years or so, as we can see from the frequent accent marks entered evidently to help those reading the material aloud with their pronunciation.[22] The importance of the books in the present context is that we know precisely where they were in the early Middle Ages. The mid-eleventh-century annotator went through the homiliary most carefully and made frequent minor alterations to the text, but he also added a short piece in a blank space at the end of the second volume, a brief résumé of the career of Paulinus, that he went to preach to the Northumbrians but retired to Kent on the death of King Edwin and was given the see of Rochester. Most of the material is drawn from Bede, but rather than saying directly that Paulinus was given Rochester, the writer actually says 'Þa wæs þes stede biscopleas, and he ða Sanctus Paulinus... undorfeng þisne biscopstol, and her þa þurhwunode oð his liues ende, wearð þa her bebyrged' ('Then this place was without a bishop, and St Paulinus was given this bishopric, and he remained here until the end of his life and was buried here'). The use of 'this' and 'here' show that the piece was written in Rochester for Rochester consumption. The text lacks a couple of lines cut off by a binder, but it is probable that restoration of these would complete it, and that it was actually composed for the space that it occupies so neatly rather than being copied into it. The problems of determining who is responsible for the precise spellings of material which has passed through many scribal hands in the course of transmission, and those of locating scribes in particular centres, are here simplified. In this manuscript we have a text composed in Rochester by a Rochester scribe.

Of course, even if we assume that the Paulinus piece was first written in Rochester for its present position, we can never be completely sure that its author was not influenced by the spellings of any written sources that he may have been using – and after all he is ultimately dependent on a written source, Bede, whether or not he drew on a Latin Bede or an Old English one. So I shall ignore here the Paulinus piece and concentrate on the other work of this Rochester scribe, his alterations to the rest of the manuscript. What is most illuminating in them are his changes not to Ælfric, which are relatively few, but those to the pre-Ælfrician texts that are found interspersed with Ælfric. These almost invariably represent linguistic changes rather than changes of substance.[23] In them we find, as indeed we might expect, that early or

[21] *Studies*, p. 151.

[22] *Ibid.*, p. 186.

[23] Details may be found in N. R. Ker, *A Study of the Additions and Alterations in*

non-West Saxon forms are amended, e.g. expanded verb forms are contracted, *ie* is changed to *i* or *y* in pronouns and the substantive verb, the grammar is updated, e.g. instrumental phrases become dative after a preposition, and he altered the occasional archaic word such as *symle* to *æfre*. But some of his choices are less predictable: he disliked the weak form of the noun for 'love' (cf. Ælfric who generally uses the strong form but admits the weak one occasionally – our man was so concerned to exclude the weak form that he went to the trouble of erasing and substituting), and he was obsessive about the prefix *ge-* in verbs, not just in the past participle but in finite forms as well: the adding of this prefix is one of the commonest features of his language. Such changes are so pervasive and yet to our eyes so insignificant that we ought to note them. He clearly believed that good late West Saxon demanded them. And his idiosyncratic changes then become all the more significant: e.g. he was so unsure about the etymology of words with an initial *h* that he sometimes added an unhistoric one superscript, even in common words like *eow* 'your', he spelled the word for 'thing' with *nc*, the feminine genitive and dative singular of 'this' when it occurred as *þysse* was changed to *þyssere*, and *him* (dative plural) to *hiom*. Presumably *þyssere* and *hiom* were – for him – standard forms.

What is the significance of all this? After all, there is nothing here that, in Pope's words, 'can be regarded as a deviation from West Saxon'. What we can say, however, is that these are the variant spellings that at least one Rochester scribe preferred. I doubt if this is the beginning of the compilation of a linguistic atlas of eleventh-century England comparable with that now available for the later Middle English period. But in these days of sophisticated mechanical aids to manuscript collation, such as that now being devised by Peter Robinson at the Oxford University Computing Service, it may be – and should be – the beginning of a much fuller analysis of late West Saxon than we have at the moment. Nearly twenty years ago I wrote a book which I insisted on calling *A History of English Spelling*,[24] although the general editor of the series that published it would have preferred a title beginning *The*. The definitive history of English spelling has yet to be written – and it is to our discredit as historical linguists that that is so. But until spelling variation in the eleventh century has been more thoroughly investigated, the first chapters of a work which may justly be called *The History of English Spelling* are beyond our reach.

MSS Bodley 340 and 342 (unpublished Oxford dissertation, 1933).

[24] D. G. Scragg, *A History of English Spelling* (Manchester, 1974).

The Harlaxton Symposium on Medieval England:
A Bibliographical Note
SHAUN TYAS

The first symposium was held at Harlaxton College near Grantham in Lincolnshire, in July, 1984. The College is the British Campus of the University of Evansville, Indiana. Since then a new symposium has been held each year. The regular aim has been to provide a multi-disciplinary approach to medieval studies, bring together scholars in a diversity of disciplines from all over the world. Since its inception the symposium's *Proceedings* have been published by three different publishers: first by Harlaxton College itself, then by Boydell and Brewer of Woodbridge, Suffolk and most recently by Paul Watkins of Stamford. The latter publisher has relaunched the *Proceedings* as a new series, although there is some continuity of style and content with the old series, and each volume is a separate book in its own right. This checklist is provided as a guide for librarians and academics, and includes mention of the two forthcoming volumes. The few remaining copies of the Old Series volumes were purchased by Paul Watkins from Boydell and Brewer in 1991 and can be ordered from their Stamford address.

Old Series

(1*a*) ORMROD, W. M. (ed.), *England in the Thirteenth Century: Proceedings of the 1984 Harlaxton Symposium* (Harlaxton, Harlaxton College, 1985). ISBN 0 9510358 00. The volume contains 17 essays.

(1*b*) *Remaining copies of this volume were rebound in 1986 by Boydell and Brewer in hardback and with a new title-page. ISBN 0 85115 445 X*

(2) ORMROD, W. M. (ed.), *England in the Fourteenth Century: Proceedings of the 1985 Harlaxton Symposium* (Woodbridge, Boydell Press, 1986). ISBN 0 85115 448 4. The volume contains 22 essays.

(3) WILLIAMS, Daniel (ed.), *England in the Fifteenth Century: Proceedings of the 1986 Harlaxton Symposium* (Woodbridge, Boydell Press, 1987). ISBN 0 85115 475 1. The volume contains 23 essays.

(4) WILLIAMS, Daniel (ed.), *Early Tudor England: Proceedings of the 1987 Harlaxton Symposium* (Woodbridge, Boydell Press, 1989). ISBN 0 85115 511 1. The volume contains 15 essays.

(5) WILLIAMS, Daniel (ed.), *England in the Twelfth Century: Proceedings of the 1988 Harlaxton Symposium* (Woodbridge, Boydell Press, 1990). ISBN 0 85115 531 6. The volume contains 16 essays.

New Series
(6) ORMROD, W. M. (ed.), *Harlaxton Medieval Studies, I: England in the Thirteenth Century: Proceedings of the 1989 Harlaxton Symposium* (Stamford, Paul Watkins [Paul Watkins Medieval Studies, 9], 1991). ISBN 1 871615 30 5. The volume contains 13 essays.

(7) HICKS, Carola (ed.), *Harlaxton Medieval Studies, II: England in the Eleventh Century: Proceedings of the 1990 Harlaxton Symposium* (Stamford, Paul Watkins [Paul Watkins Medieval Studies, 12], 1992). ISBN 1 871615 50 X. The volume contains 20 essays.

Forthcoming
(8) ROGERS, Nicholas (ed.), *Harlaxton Medieval Studies III: England in the Fourteenth Century: Proceedings of the 1991 Harlaxton Symposium.*

(9) The 1992 Symposium will be held on *England in the Fifteenth Century.*

1. (Potts) St Ouen, ADSM 14H 915A, ed. Fauroux no. 13

2. (Potts) St Ouen, ADSM 14H 570, ed. Fauroux no. 37

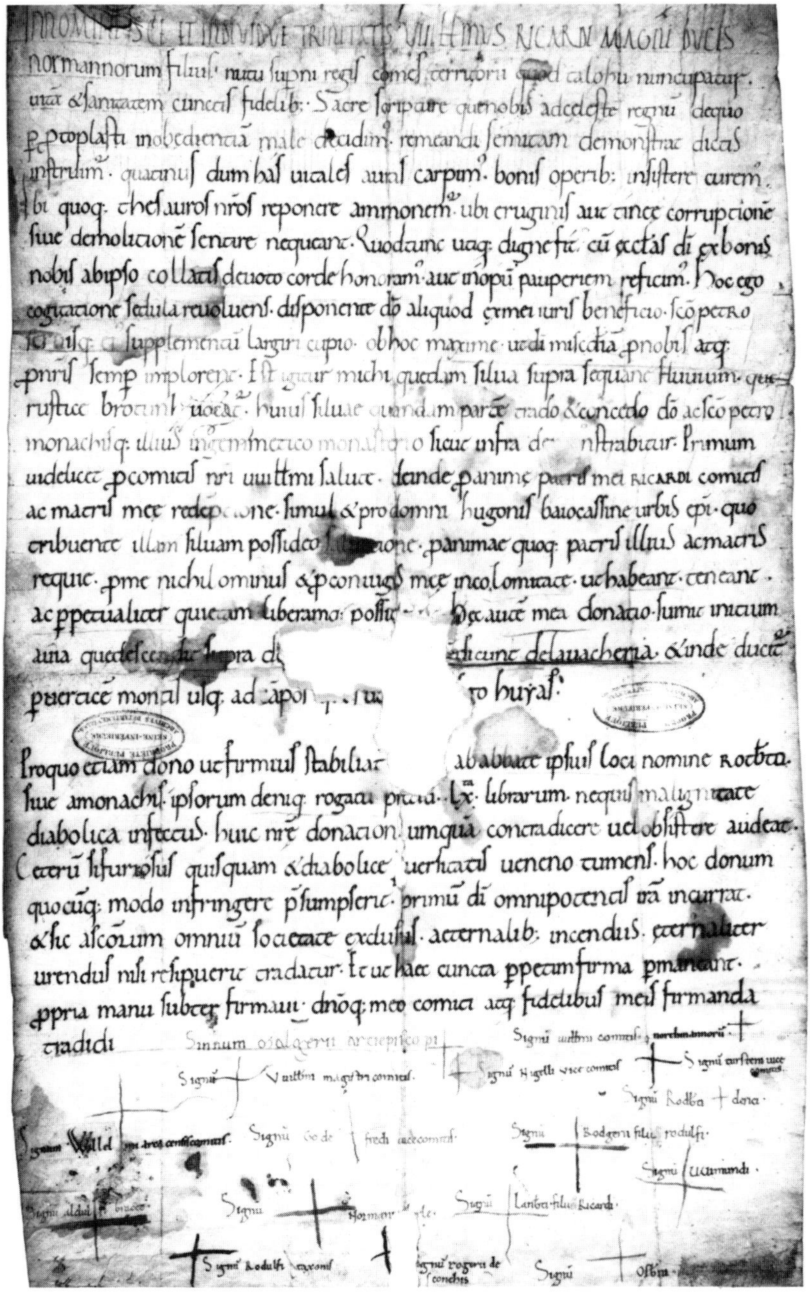

3. (Potts) Jumièges, ADSM 9H 30, ed. Fauroux no. 100

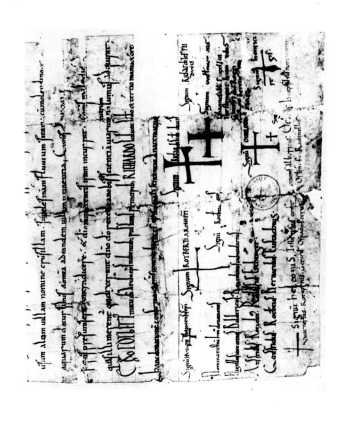

4. (Potts) St Wandrille, Bib. Nat. MS. lat. 16738, plate 3, ed. Fauroux no. 55

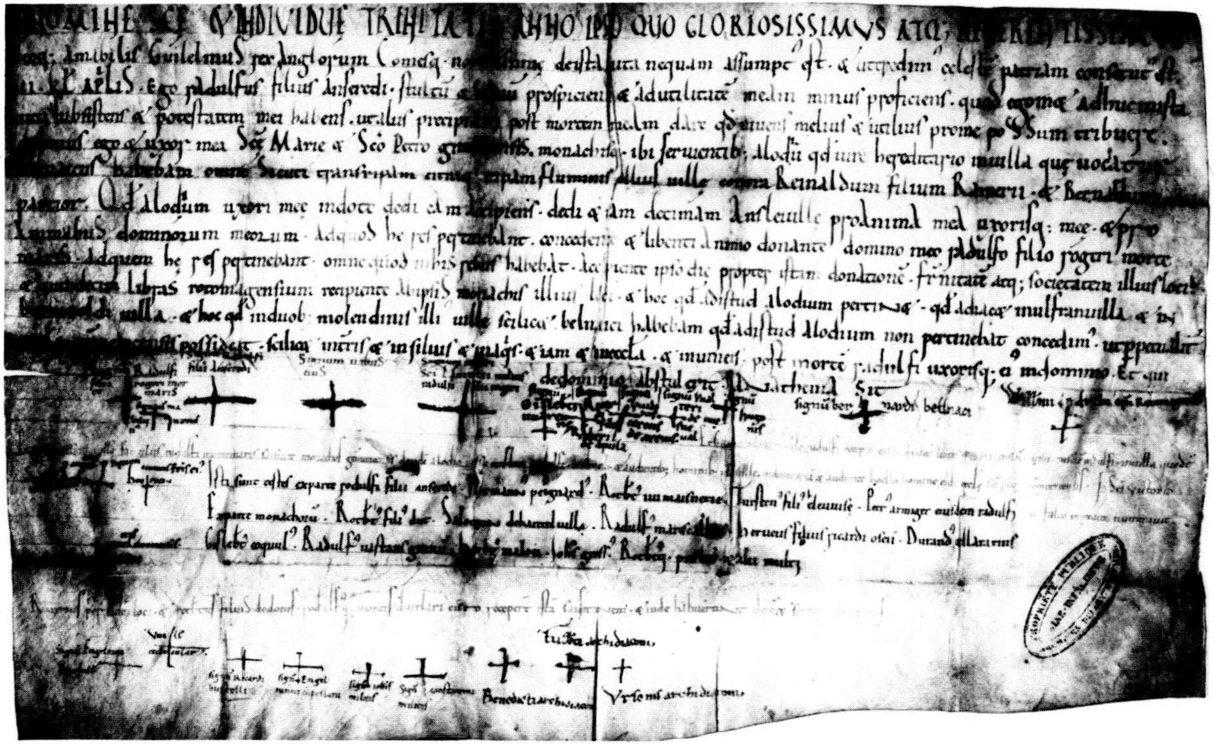

5. (Potts) Jumièges, ADSM 9H 1739, ed. Vernier no. 37

6a/6b. (Martindale) King William I confirms grants to St-Florent.
Archives Départementales de Maine-et-Loire, H. 3710 no. 1 (irregular parchment 250 x 150mm with margin of 10mm)

7. (Rollason) Part of a Cross Head, Monks' Dormitory, Durham Cathedral

8. (Gerchow) *liber vitæ* of New Minster, BL Stowe MS 944, f. 6r,
frontispiece with King Cnut and Queen Emma

9. (Gerchow) New Minster Charter of King Edgar,
BL Cotton MS Vespasian A. viii, f. 2v

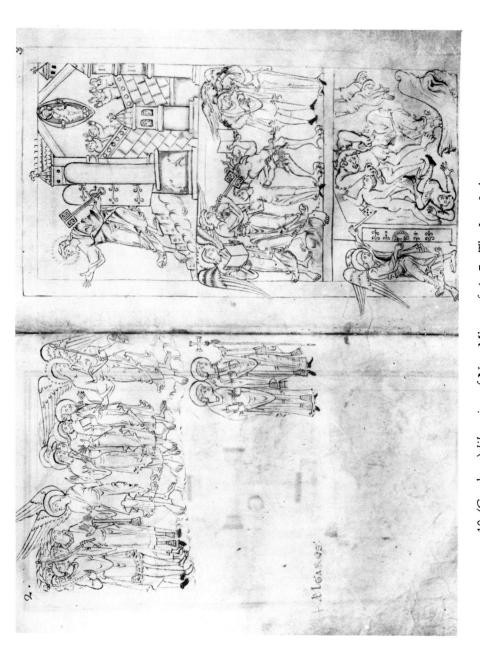

10. (Gerchow) *liber vitae* of New Minster f. 6v-7r, The Last Judgement

11. (Gerchow) BL Royal MS I.D.ix, f. 43v, note of confraternity

12. (Gerchow) Penny of Cnut, 1018-24

13. (Gerchow) *liber vitae* of New Minster, f. 25r, list of benefactors

14. (Gerchow) 'Lothar-Cross', Aachen, Münsterschatz

15. (Gerchow) 'Reichskrone' (Ottonian imperial crown), Vienna, Schatzkammer

17. (Gerchow) 'Perikopenbuch' (evangeliary) of Emperor
Henry II, clm 4452, f. 2r, Henry II and Kunigunde

16. (Gerchow) Sacramentary of Emperor Henry II,
clm 4456, f. 11r

18. (Gerchow) *liber vitæ* of Thorney Abbey, f. 10r

19. (Henderson), Malibu, The J. Paul Getty Museum, MS 9, f. 2r, detail

20. (Henderson) Cambridge, CUL MS Ff. 1.23, f. 171r

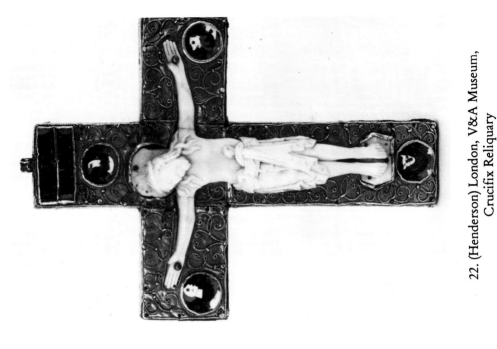

22. (Henderson) London, V&A Museum,
Crucifix Reliquary

21. (Henderson), London, V&A Museum, Reliquary Cross

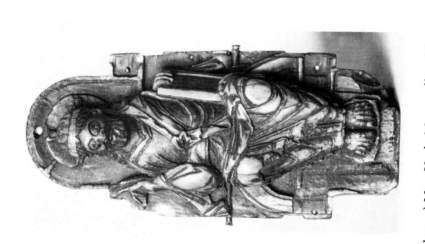

23. (Henderson) New York, Metropolitan Museum of Art, obverse of Pectoral Cross

24. (Henderson) New York, Metropolitan Museum of Art, reverse of Pectoral Cross

25. (Hicks) Bayeux Tapestry; junction of strips 1 and 2

26. (Hicks) Bayeux Tapestry; Fox, Crow and Cheese, first version

27. (Hicks) Bayeux Tapestry; Fox, Crow and Cheese, second version

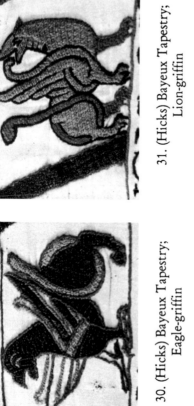

30. (Hicks) Bayeux Tapestry; Eagle-griffin

29. (Hicks) Bayeux Tapestry; Lion

31. (Hicks) Bayeux Tapestry; Lion-griffin

28. (Hicks) Bayeux Tapestry; the tugging sequence

32. (Hicks) Bayeux Tapestry; Amphisbaena

33. (Hicks) Bayeux Tapestry; Senmurv

34. (Hicks) Bayeux Tapestry; Centaur

35. (Hicks) Bayeux Tapestry; Winged horse

36. (Hicks) Bayeux Tapestry; Camel

37. (Hicks) Bayeux Tapestry; Wolf

38. (Hicks) Bayeux Tapestry; predators

39. (Hicks) Bayeux Tapestry; group with monkey

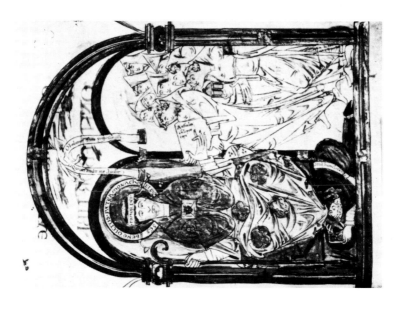

SCDM IOHANNEM

discipulus ille non moritur · et non dixit ei ihc non moritur: sed si eum uolo manere donec ueniam quid ad te: hic est discipulus ille qui testimonium phibet dehis · et scripsit haec · et scimus quia uerum est testimonium eius.

Sunt autem et alia multa quae fecit ihc quae scribantur psingula. nec ipsum arbitror mundum capere eos qui scribendi sunt libros · Amen:

Pro saeptaore precamini eternpnas fundere pacer. Librum istum monachus scripsit Eaduuigus cogno minte Basan · Sit illi longa salus: Uale seruus dni · N · & memor esto mei ·

40. (Pfaff) Hanover Gospels, Eadui Basan's autograph

41. (Pfaff) Arundel Psalter, St Benedict and Eadui Basan

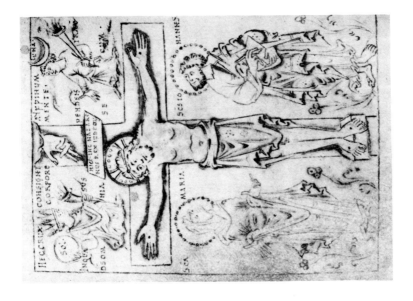

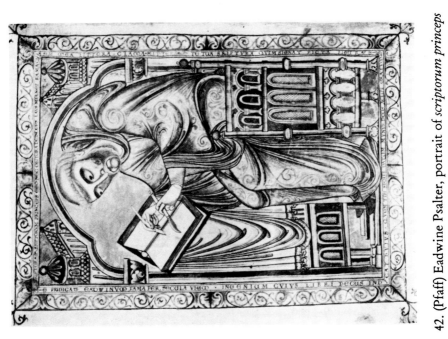

43. (Raw) BL Cotton MS Titus D.xxvii, f. 65v

42. (Pfaff) Eadwine Psalter, portrait of *scriptorum princeps*

44. (Raw) BL Cotton MS Galba A.xviii, f. 120v

45. (Raw) BL Cotton MS Titus D.xxvii, f. 75v

46. (Raw) Pierpont Morgan Library, MS 709, f. 1v

47. (Teviotdale) BL Cotton MS
Caligula A.xiv, f. 12r

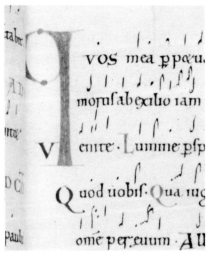

48. (Teviotdale) BL Cotton MS
Caligula A.xiv, f. 17r

49. (Teviotdale) BL Cotton MS
Caligula A.xiv, f. 26r

50. (Teviotdale) BL Cotton MS
Caligula A.xiv

51. (Teviotdale) BL Cotton MS Caligula A. xiv, f. 29r

52. (Teviotdale) BL Cotton MS Caligula A. xiv, f. 30v

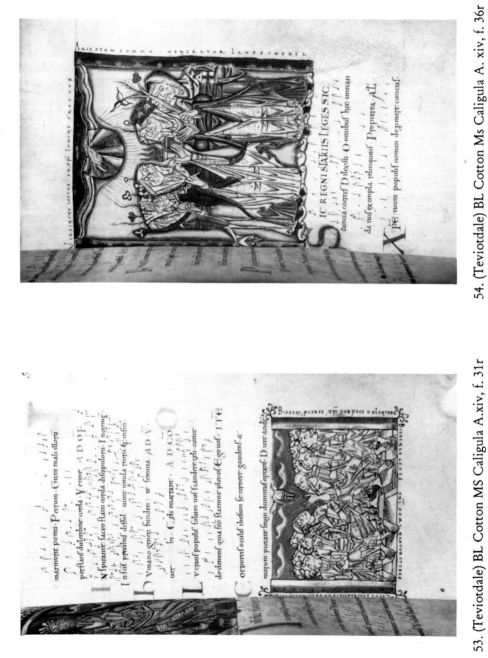

53. (Teviotdale) BL Cotton MS Caligula A.xiv, f. 31r

54. (Teviotdale) BL Cotton Ms Caligula A. xiv, f. 36r

55. (Okasha) 64 Kirkdale

57. (Okasha) 87 London I

56. (Okasha) 15 Breamore I